ABRAHAM
KUYPER

Collected Works in Public Theology

GENERAL EDITORS

JORDAN J. BALLOR

MELVIN FLIKKEMA

AbrahamKuyper.com

Weil, Roman, 438, 439
Weinberger, Alfred, 441
Weiss, Lawrence A., 148, 205, 207
When-issued securities, 93
Whirlpool Corporation, 188
Whole-loan CMOs, 287
Wholly owned subsidiary, 318
Wilson, Richard W., 147, 183
Wolff, Eric D., 202
World Bank (International Bank for Reconstruction and Development), 1, 340, 344
World War II, 156
WPPSS. See Washington Public Power Supply System
Wruck, Karen Hooper, 206
Wyss, David, 202

Y

Yield, 8, 61. See also Bank discount basis; Benchmark; Bond-equivalent yield; Cash flows; CD-equivalent yield; Coupon-equivalent yield; Current yield; Municipal bonds; Premium above yield; Tax-exempt yield; Treasury securities; Treasury yield
bid, 91
calculations, 94–98. See also Treasury bills; Treasury coupon security yield calculations
contrast. See U.S. bond yields
Eurodollar bond yields, contrast. See U.S. bonds
key points, 85–87
maintenance charges, 308, 309
ratio, 138
spread, 115–116, 295–297. See also Treasury securities
relationships. See Municipal market structure, 281–282
traditional measures, 63–71
Treasuries, comparison, 241–242
usage, 176–178, 238–242, 321–322
Yield curve, 98. See also Inverted yield curve; Negatively sloped yield curve; Normal yield curve; Positively sloped yield curve; Treasury yield
environment, 76
flattening, 99
humpedness, change, 99
nonparallel shift, 99
parallel shift, 51
shift, 99
assumption. See Parallel yield curve shift assumption
slope, 140
twist, 99
steepening, 99
steepness/slope, 99
strategies, 422, 425–429
trading strategies, 422

Yield spread measures, 61, 75–79
key points, 85–87
Yield to call, 65–67
measures, limitations, 67
Yield to first call, 65
Yield to first par call, 65
Yield to maturity, 63–65, 67, 71, 409
Yield to next call, 65
Yield to put, 67
Yield to refunding, 65
Yield to worst, 67–68
Youngstown Sheet and Tube Company, 152

Z

Z-bonds, 272
Zero-coupon bonds, 3–4, 13, 37, 65, 185, 205
call schedule, 11
package, 38, 39
price sensitivity, 16
similarity, 259
valuation, 34
Zero-coupon convertible bonds, 188
Zero-coupon instruments, 62, 72, 101, 195
Zero-coupon rate, 71
curve. See Benchmark
Zero-coupon Treasury receipts. See Trademark zero-coupon Treasury receipts
Zero-coupon Treasury securities, 71–73, 83
Zero-volatility OAS, 78–79
Zero-volatility spread (Z-spread), 75–79, 238, 246–249, 281. See also Benchmark
Z-spread. See Zero-volatility spread

tranches; Nonaccelerating senior; Planned amortization class; Sequential-pay tranches
TRANs, 125
TransAmerica Finance Corporation, 169
Transportation revenue bonds, 126, 127
Transportations, 147
Treasuries. See Spread over Treasuries comparison. See Yield
Treasury benchmark, 239
Treasury bills, 82, 89–90. See also Fixed-rate Treasury bills
yield calculations, 94–97
Treasury Bond Receipts (TBRs), 102
Treasury bonds, 90. See also Callable Treasury bonds
Treasury Constant Maturity (CMT), 110
Treasury coupon security yield calculations, 97–98
Treasury Income Growth Receipts (TIGRs), 100
Treasury inflation indexed securities (TIIS), 93
Treasury inflation protection securities (TIPS), 93, 94
Treasury method, 97
Treasury notes, 101. See also Fixed-rate Treasury notes
Treasury rate, 69
Treasury Receipts (TRs), 102–103. See also Trademark zero-coupon Treasury receipts
Treasury sector, 404
Treasury securities, 115. See also Comparable-maturity Treasury security; Coupon-bearing Treasury securities; Stripped Treasury securities; U.S. Treasury securities; Zero-coupon Treasury securities
maturity value, 100
yield, 98–99
spreads, 104
Treasury spot rates, usage. See Valuation
Treasury strip, 103
Treasury yield, 50
curve, 83, 201
Treasury-indexed ARM pools, 227
Triggers. See Early amortization triggers
Tri-party repo, 363
Triple-A Guaranteed Secondary Securities (TAGSS), 160
TRs. See Treasury Receipts
Trust Indenture Act of 1939, 162
Trustees, 164–165
bonds, 13
Tullett & Tokyo Liberty, 92
Tunnel sinking fund, 170
TVA. See Tennessee Valley Authority

U

UBS Warburg, 238
Undated issue, 343
Underlying mortgage loans, characteristics, 237
Underwriting
process, 344
standards, 225. See also Loan originations
Union Pacific Railroad Company, 154
Unit Priced Demand Adjustable Tax-Exempt Securities (UPDATES), 126
United Illuminating Company, 149
Unleveraged strategy, 356, 357
Unrestricted subsidiaries, 168
Unsecured creditors, 208
Unsecured debt, 157–162
UPDATES. See Unit Priced Demand Adjustable Tax-Exempt Securities
Upgrade, 19
Upper medium grade, 172
Upside potential. See Convertible bonds
Urban Development Corporation (New York), 133
U.S. bonds
market indexes. See Broad-based U.S. bond market indexes; Specialized U.S. bond market indexes
yields, Eurodollar bond yields (contrast), 343–344
U.S. City Average All Items Consumer Price Index for All Urban Consumers (CPI-U), 93
U.S. Department of the Treasury, 46
U.S. dollar cash flows, 20
U.S. Treasury coupon securities, 244
U.S. Treasury securities, 37, 89, 132
key points, 105–107
types, 89–94
US West Capital Funding, Inc., 159
User-charge covenants, 136
U.S.-pay foreign bonds, 340
Utilities, 147
Utility revenue bonds, 126, 127

V

VA. See Veterans Administration
VADM. See Very accurately determined maturity
Valuation. See Coupon payments; Fixed-income securities; Non-Treasury securities; Semiannual cash flows; Zero-coupon bonds approach. See Arbitrage-free valuation approach
discount rate, usage, 33
models, 28, 41–44, 77. See Binomial valuation model; Monte Carlo
principles, 27–37

traditional approach, 37–38
Treasury spot rates, usage, 40
Value
date, 8, 348
interest rate volatility assumption (impact), 43–44
Value-added strategies, 422–433
Vanguard Group, 418
Variable periodic payments, 13
Variable-rate demand obligations (VRDOs), 126
hybrid. See Commercial paper/VRDO hybrid
Variable-rate HELs, 305
Variable-rate SBA loans, 313
Variable-rate securities, 4
Vasicek, Oldrich A., 439
Venture capital situations, 184
Very accurately determined maturity (VADM) bonds, 272–277
Veterans Administration (VA), 127, 215, 225, 306
VIPS, 110
Visa, 314
Volatility. See Bonds; Interest rate; Short-term interest rates assumption, impact. See Value spread. See Zero-volatility spread
Volpert, Kenneth E., 418, 421
Voluntary advancing, 288
Voluntary bankruptcy, 148. See also Involuntary bankruptcy
Voting capital stock, 160
Voting rights, 200
VRDOs. See Variable-rate demand obligations

W

WAC. See Weighted average coupon
Walt Disney Co., 2, 10
Walt Disney Corporation, 193
WAM. See Weighted average maturity
Wang, Paul C., 220
Warrants. See Currency; Debt; Equity; Gold warrants inclusion. See Bonds; Convertible bonds
Wash sales, 392
provisions, 379
Washington Metropolitan Area Transit Authority, 109
Washington Public Power Supply System (WPPSS), 133
Weighted average coupon (WAC), 243, 315. See also Gross WAC; Net WAC
rate, 222, 255, 264
Weighted average loss, 317
Weighted average maturity (WAM), 232, 302
rate, 222, 255, 264
Weighted average rating, 332

Stock dividends, payment, 168
Stop yield, 91
Stop-out yield, 91
Story bond, 184
Strahan, Philip E., 197
Straight value, 189–191
Strategic strategies, 422
Street method, 35, 97
Strip obligations. See Municipal strip obligations
Stripped coupon/principal obligations, 384
Stripped MBS, 215, 245–250
   trading/settlement procedures, 249–250
Stripped Treasury securities, 88–103
Stripping. See Coupon; Securities
STRIPS. See Separate Trading of Registered Interest and Principal of Securities
Structural call protection, 308–310
Structural protection. See Commercial MBS
Structural risks, 317–318
Structure trades, 433
Structured IO tranche, 277
Structured MTNs, 194–195
Structured notes, 112
Structured portfolio strategies, 437–442
Student loan asset-backed securities (SLABS), 311, 312
Student Loan Marketing Association (SLMA), 111, 114
Student loan-backed securities, 311–313
Subcustodian, 363
Subordinate interest, 293
Subordinate notes, 33
Subordinated Benchmark Notes, 112
Subordinated bonds, 205
Subordinated debt, 184
Subordinated Debt Securities, 113
Subordinated lenders, 198
Subordinated structure. See Senior-subordinated structure
Subordinated tranche, 204, 292–293
Subordinate/equity tranche, 327–332
Subordination, level, 293
Subperiod returns, 399
   annualizing, 402
Subprime borrowers, 286
Subsidiaries. See Restricted subsidiaries; Unrestricted subsidiaries
Substitute payment, 371
Sudo, Toshihide, 148, 205–207, 209
Sumitomo Bank, 160
Super sinkers, 132
Supplemental indentures/covenants, 166
Supplemental Loans to Students (SLS), 312

Supply/demand, temporary imbalances, 140–141
Support bonds, 263, 268, 278–280
   classes. See Accrual support bond classes; Floater support bond classes; Inverse floater support bond classes; Sequential-pay support bond classes
Surety bond, 196
Surplus fund, 135
Swap counterparty, 329
Swap PCs, 226, 227
Syndicated bank loans, 198

T

TAC. See Targeted amortization class
TAGSS. See Triple-A Guaranteed Secondary Securities
Takeovers, 19
TANs. See Tax anticipation notes
Tap method, 345, 346
Target portfolio duration, 424
Targeted amortization class (TAC) bonds, 271–272. See also Reverse TAC bonds
Tax anticipation notes (TANs), 125
Tax authorities, 345
Tax basis, 378. See also Capital asset; Capital gain; Capital loss
Tax considerations. See Collateralized mortgage obligations
Tax debt. See Limited ad valorem tax debt
Tax effect. See Total dollar contributions
Tax provisions, impact. See Municipal securities
Tax Reform Act of 1986, 280
Tax revenue bonds, 127
Tax risk, 137
Tax treatment. See Interest income; Local level; State level
Taxable bonds, 385
   treatment. See Callable taxable bond
Taxable income, 377
Taxable municipal securities, 119–120
Tax-backed debt, 122–126, 134–135
   obligations, 122
Tax-backed obligations. See Dedicated tax-backed obligations
Tax-deductible expense, 388
Tax-exempt bonds, 388. See also Original-issue discount
   tax treatment, 387
Tax-exempt commercial paper, 126
Tax-exempt income, 131
Tax-exempt issues, 387
Tax-exempt municipal bonds, usage. See Collateralized borrowing
Tax-exempt municipal issuance, 125–126

Tax-exempt municipal securities, 119–120, 137, 396
Tax-exempt securities, 373, 387
Tax-exempt yield, 139
Taxpayers, classification, 379
TBA. See To be announced
TBRs. See Treasury Bond Receipts
Telerate, 238
Tender Offer Bond (TOB), 131. See also Plain-vanilla TOBs
Tennessee Valley Authority (TVA), 2, 6, 10, 109–110
Term loans, 198
Term maturity structure, 132
Term repo, 359
Term structure. See Interest rate; Spot rates
Term to maturity, 2, 96, 140
Termination. See Early termination
Texas Utilities Electric Company, 151
Theoretical spot rates, 71–75, 81
Third-party credit enhancements, 159
Third-party entity, 318
Third-party providers, 318–319
Thomas, Lee, 435
Thomson Financial, 139
Thrifts, calculated cost of funds, 217
TIGRs. See Treasury Income Growth Receipts
TIIS. See Treasury inflation indexed securities
Time horizon, 436
Time tranching, 304
Time-weighted rate of return. See Return
TINT, 104
TIPS. See Treasury inflation protection securities
Title insurance, 236
To be announced (TBA) trade, 243
TOB. See Tender Offer Bond
Tobacco settlement payment, 124
Torous, Walter N., 148, 205
Total dollar
   contributions, taxes (effect), 410–411
   return, 407
Total return, 407–408. See also Maturity; Option-adjusted spread; Portfolio
   framework, 406–413
Trade date, 8
Trademark products, 100–102
Trademark zero-coupon Treasury receipts, 102
Tradeweb system. See Dealer-to-customer Tradeweb system
Trading blocs, 339
Trading procedures. See Agency passthroughs; Stripped MBS
Tranches, 130, 253–263. See also Accrual tranches; Collateralized mortgage obligations; Floating-rate tranches; Mezzanine

ON THE CHURCH

ABRAHAM KUYPER

Edited by John Halsey Wood Jr. and Andrew M. McGinnis

Introduction by Ad de Bruijne

LEXHAM PRESS

ACTON INSTITUTE
FOR THE STUDY OF RELIGION AND LIBERTY

On the Church

Abraham Kuyper Collected Works in Public Theology

Copyright 2016 Acton Institute for the Study of Religion & Liberty

Lexham Press, 1313 Commercial St., Bellingham, WA 98225
LexhamPress.com

Print ISBN 9781577996750
Digital ISBN 9781577997603

Translators: Harry Van Dyke, Nelson D. Kloosterman, Todd M. Rester,
    Arjen Vreugdenhil
Lexham Editorial: Brannon Ellis, Joel Wilcox
Cover Design: Christine Gerhart
Back Cover Design: Brittany Schrock
Typesetting: ProjectLuz.com

CONTENTS

General Editors' Introduction vii

Editor's Introduction xi

Volume Introduction xxv

Abbreviations xxxviii

Commentatio 1

Rooted and Grounded 41

Tract on the Reformation of the Churches 75

Twofold Fatherland 281

Lord's Day 21 315

State and Church 373

Address on Missions 439

Bibliography 458

Appendix: Detailed Table of Contents 465

About Abraham Kuyper (1837–1920) 469

About the Contributors 471

Subject/Author Index 472

Scripture Index 490

GENERAL EDITORS' INTRODUCTION

In times of great upheaval and uncertainty, it is necessary to look to the past for resources to help us recognize and address our own contemporary challenges. While Scripture is foremost among these foundations, the thoughts and reflections of Christians throughout history also provide us with important guidance. Because of his unique gifts, experiences, and writings, Abraham Kuyper is an exemplary guide in these endeavors.

Kuyper (1837–1920) is a significant figure both in the history of the Netherlands and modern Protestant theology. A prolific intellectual, Kuyper founded a political party and a university, led the formation of a Reformed denomination and the movement to create Reformed elementary schools, and served as the prime minister of the Netherlands from 1901 to 1905. In connection with his work as a builder of institutions, Kuyper was also a prolific author. He wrote theological treatises, biblical and confessional studies, historical works, social and political commentary, and devotional materials.

Believing that Kuyper's work is a significant and underappreciated resource for Christian public witness, in 2011 a group of scholars interested in Kuyper's life and work formed the Abraham Kuyper Translation Society. The shared conviction of the society, along with the Acton Institute, Kuyper College, and other Abraham Kuyper scholars, is that Kuyper's works hold great potential to build intellectual capacity within the church in North America, Europe, and around the world. It is our hope that translation of his works into English will make his insights accessible to those seeking to grow and revitalize communities in the developed world as well as to those in the global south and east who are facing unique challenges and opportunities.

The church today—both locally and globally—needs the tools to construct a compelling and responsible public theology. The aim of this translation project is to provide those tools—we believe that Kuyper's unique insights can catalyze the development of a winsome and constructive Christian social witness and cultural engagement the world over.

In consultation and collaboration with these institutions and individual scholars, the Abraham Kuyper Translation Society developed this 12-volume translation project, the Abraham Kuyper Collected Works in Public Theology. This multivolume series collects in English translation Kuyper's writings and speeches from a variety of genres and contexts in his work as a theologian and statesman. In almost all cases, this set contains original works that have never before been translated into English. The series contains multivolume works as well as other volumes, including thematic anthologies.

The series includes a translation of Kuyper's *Our Program* (*Ons Program*), which sets forth Kuyper's attempt to frame a Christian political vision distinguished from the programs of the nineteenth-century Modernists who took their cues from the French Revolution. It was this document that launched Kuyper's career as a pastor, theologian, and educator. As James Bratt writes, "This comprehensive Program, which Kuyper crafted in the process of forming the Netherlands' first mass political party, brought the theology, the political theory, and the organization vision together brilliantly in a coherent set of policies that spoke directly to the needs of his day. For us it sets out the challenge of envisioning what might be an equivalent witness in our own day."

Also included is Kuyper's seminal three-volume work *De gemeene gratie*, or *Common Grace*, which presents a constructive public theology of cultural engagement rooted in the humanity Christians share with the rest of the world. Kuyper's presentation of common grace addresses a gap he recognized in the development of Reformed teaching on divine grace. After addressing particular grace and covenant grace in other writings, Kuyper here develops his articulation of a Reformed understanding of God's gifts that are common to all people after the fall into sin.

The series also contains Kuyper's three-volume work on the lordship of Christ, *Pro Rege*. These three volumes apply Kuyper's principles in *Common Grace*, providing guidance for how to live in a fallen world under Christ the King. Here the focus is on developing cultural institutions in a way that is consistent with the ordinances of creation that have been maintained and preserved, even if imperfectly so, through common grace.

The remaining volumes are thematic anthologies of Kuyper's writings and speeches gathered from the course of his long career.

The anthology *On Charity and Justice* includes a fresh and complete translation of Kuyper's "The Problem of Poverty," the landmark speech Kuyper gave at the opening of the First Christian Social Congress in Amsterdam in 1891. This important work was first translated into English in 1950 by Dirk Jellema; in 1991, a new edition by James Skillen was issued. This volume also contains other writings and speeches on subjects including charity, justice, wealth, and poverty.

The anthology *On Islam* contains English translations of significant pieces that Abraham Kuyper wrote about Islam, gathered from his reflections on a lengthy tour of the Mediterranean world. Kuyper's insights illustrate an instructive model for observing another faith and its cultural ramifications from an informed Christian perspective.

The anthology *On the Church* includes selections from Kuyper's doctrinal dissertation on the theologies of Reformation theologians John Calvin and John à Lasco. It also includes various treatises and sermons, such as "Rooted and Grounded," "Twofold Fatherland," and "Address on Missions."

The anthology *On Business and Economics* contains various meditations Kuyper wrote about the evils of the love of money as well as pieces that provide Kuyper's thoughts on stewardship, human trafficking, free trade, tariffs, child labor, work on the Sabbath, and business.

Finally, the anthology *On Education* includes Kuyper's important essay "Bound to the Word," which discusses what it means to be ruled by the Word of God in the entire world of human thought. Numerous other pieces are also included, resulting in a substantial English volume of Kuyper's thoughts on Christian education.

Collectively, this 12-volume series will, as Richard Mouw puts it, "give us a much-needed opportunity to absorb the insights of Abraham Kuyper about God's marvelous designs for human cultural life."

The Abraham Kuyper Translation Society along with the Acton Institute and Kuyper College gratefully acknowledge the Andreas Center for Reformed Scholarship and Service at Dordt College; Calvin College; Calvin Theological Seminary; Fuller Theological Seminary; Mid-America Reformed Seminary; Redeemer University College; Princeton Theological Seminary; and Southeastern Baptist Theological Seminary. Their financial support and partnership helped facilitate these translations. The society is also grateful for the generous financial support of Dr. Rimmer and Ruth DeVries and the J. C. Huizenga family, which has enabled the translation and publication of these volumes.

This series is dedicated to Dr. Rimmer DeVries in recognition of his life's pursuits and enduring legacy as a cultural leader, economist, visionary, and faithful follower of Christ who reflects well the Kuyperian vision of Christ's lordship over all spheres of society.

Jordan J. Ballor
Melvin Flikkema

Grand Rapids, MI
August 2015

EDITOR'S INTRODUCTION

The church problem is "none other than the problem of Christianity itself," concluded Abraham Kuyper.[1] Although Kuyper is celebrated for his achievements in the academy, politics, and culture, concern for the church predated and permeated all of these other concerns. Kuyper's student days were marked by a master's thesis and then a doctoral dissertation on the history and theology of the church. He then served in several pastoral positions in the Dutch Reformed Church (*Nederlandse Hervormde Kerk*, or NHK), the broad national church of the Netherlands. Parallel to the founding of the Free University of Amsterdam and the Antirevolutionary political party, Kuyper instigated a secession from the national church, and in addition to his roles as politician, journalist, and educator, Kuyper remained an active teacher, preacher, and churchman. One of his last writings was a series of articles on ecclesiology, which remained unfinished because of his death.

In the nineteenth century, higher criticism and modern historical science challenged the doctrine of Scripture. Enlightenment rationalism continued to challenge Christian epistemology.[2] In addition, a changing social landscape, as much as the changing intellectual one, also posed a

---

1. Abraham Kuyper, "Conservatism and Orthodoxy: False and True Preservation," in *AKCR*, 69. See also, "De Sleutelen," in *Uit het Woord. stichtelijke Bijbelstudiën* (Amsterdam: J. A. Wormser, 1896), 41–42.
2. See, for example, Claude Welch, *Protestant Thought in the Nineteenth Century*, 2 vols. (New Haven: Yale University Press, 1972–85), 1:30–51, 2:213.

challenge to theology and the church. In Kuyper's estimate "a time like ours" was a time "when especially the church question dominates every other issue."[3] Therefore Kuyper devoted himself to the doctrine of the church, and he developed his distinctive ecclesiological answer, the church as organism and as institution, in response to the social challenges of his day.

TWO ECCLESIOLOGICAL QUESTIONS

Ecclesiology concerns the social nature of humanity's relation to God. The social disintegration that characterizes the modern world has made two ecclesiological questions especially important. First, how do people become members of the church? The rising importance of the individual and new forms of political association, such as the social contract, brought this question to the fore. Are people born into the church, or do they join voluntarily? This question concerns the very nature of the church. Does the church make Christians, or do Christians make the church?

Second, ecclesiology asks how the church, the Christian society, relates to the broader society within which it finds itself.[4] What is the church's relation to the world outside its walls? This question became more pressing as the church became increasingly separate from other social entities like state and school, as religious pluralism increased, and as Christianity lost its taken-for-granted status in the West. There is usually a relationship between the way a church addresses its nature and the way it relates to society, as Ernst Troeltsch showed. Membership in "churches" tends to be automatic, by birth. Consequently churches tend to maintain close relationships with society around them. "Sects," on the other hand, tend to be voluntary and more distant from society. Beyond those two general paradigms, however, the possibilities are countless. Peculiar to modernity is the situation in which the voluntary, sect system became taken-for-granted and automatic.[5] Abraham Kuyper found himself on the cusp of that unexpected development, and his ecclesiology addressed these questions of the church's nature and its place in this emerging society.

---

3. "Rooted and Grounded," in *On the Church*, 62.

4. These two questions are suggested by Ernst Troeltsch's method. See Ernst Troeltsch, *The Social Teaching of the Christian Churches*, trans. Olive Wyon, 2 vols. (Louisville: Westminster John Knox, 1960), 1:34.

5. Peter Berger puts this paradoxical situation well when he describes it as a "heretical imperative." See Peter Berger, *The Heretical Imperative: Contemporary Possibilities of Religious Affirmation* (Garden City, NY: Anchor, 1979).

HISTORICAL CONTEXT

DISESTABLISHMENT

Several broad trends defined the new social landscape and raised new questions for the churches in the nineteenth century. Disestablishment, the separation of church and state in its various forms and stages, disrupted the social position of churches, especially that of socially dominant churches like the Dutch Reformed Church into which Kuyper was born. Disestablishment in the Netherlands was not as simple or as clean as a mere constitutional fiat. Since the Reformation, the Reformed church had enjoyed a privileged status in the Netherlands. In 1796, with the establishment of the Batavian Republic, the separation of church and state was constitutionally enshrined and reforms were implemented. For example, government approval was no longer needed for calling ministers. With the rise of Napoleon, revolutionary measures were moderated. The church was recognized as an institution of public good in the new constitution of 1801, and again it came under the sponsorship of the government. Ministers would again be approved by the state. Further Napoleonic reforms established the Kingdom of Holland in 1806 with Louis Napoleon as king and as head of the church. Then, with the end of the French period in 1815, William I became king of the Netherlands. The era of the Dutch Republic was over. The age of the centralized nation-state had begun, and the church had to conform. Freedom of worship was granted to all religions, and all denominations received state funding as well as state oversight; however, the Reformed Church was first among equals and the church of the king. In 1816 William established a new church polity, the *Algemeen Reglement*, and a new church, the Dutch Reformed Church, with himself at the head of the church bureaucracy. So important was religion for civil order that it was enforced by the state. When Isaac da Costa (leader of the Dutch *Réveil*, and whom Kuyper regularly invoked) challenged the consensus enlightened Protestantism of the educated classes with a more orthodox version, his house was placed under police observation.[6] Protestantism in the Netherlands was not necessarily orthodox, but it was strict.

---

6. See James W. Skillen, "Introduction," in Abraham Kuyper, *The Problem of Poverty* (Sioux Center: Dordt College Press, 2011), 11–13; G. J. Schutte, "De ere Gods en de moderne staat. Het antwoord van de Anti-Revolutionaire Partij op de secularisatie

In 1848 a new, liberal constitution disestablished the church again. The national synod remained, but the church once again could call ministers without the approval of the state. The synod would not, however, involve itself in doctrinal matters. In fact, even under the king, the responsibility of the synod was not doctrinal but organizational and for the "cultivation of love for the King and Fatherland." That did not change under the new constitution or the new church order that followed.[7] Kuyper found himself in a disestablished church that retained a concern for the fatherland and was directed by a central synod, but which did not provide theological guidance.

PLURALIZATION

Although one of the chief aims of the NHK was unity within the church and society, the nineteenth century was an age of religious pluralization. Religious options multiplied within the church and outside of it. Modernist theologians like Kuyper's professor J. H. Scholten at Leiden University made the most radical reconstructions, rejecting supernaturalism, divine revelation, and miracles like the virgin birth that did not accord with modern science. The Ethical theology movement represented a mediating approach to modernity that stressed inner religious experience and piety over outward forms like doctrinal confessions. Various orthodox theologians defended the old supernaturalism and traditional Protestant confessions like the Canons of Dort and the Belgic Confession.[8] The *Afscheiding* of 1834, a conservative secession church from the NHK, exemplified how pluralization meant new churches as well as new theologies. Further, new religious movements arose, including non-Christian and quasi-Christian ones, such as the theosophy of Madame Blavatsky,

---

en de democratisering van Nederland: antithese, soevereiniteit in eigen kring en gemene gratie," in *Het Calvinistisch Nederland: Mythe en Werkelijkheid* (Hilversum: Verloren, 2000), 126.

7. See *Algemeen Reglement voor de Hervormde Kerk van het Koningrijk der Nederlanden* (The Hague: H. C. Susan, C.Hz., 1852), art. 11.

8. George Harinck and Lodewijk Winkeler, "De Negentiende Eeuw," in *Handboek Nederlandse Kerkgeschiedenis*, ed. Herman J. Selderhuis (Kampen: Kok, 2006), 656–60; ET: George Harinck and Lodewijk Winkeler, "The Nineteenth Century," in *Handbook of Dutch Church History*, ed. Herman J. Selderhuis (Gottingen: Vandenhoeck & Ruprecht, 2015), 474–76.

the Christian Science of Mary Baker Eddy, and the animal magnetism of Franz Mesmer.[9]

MOBILIZATION

One important consequence of the emancipated, enlightened Christian and the increasing number of religious options, was the growth of voluntary religion and the rise of charismatic figures who could mobilize the masses to exercise their new power in a variety of different ways, whether in churches, schools, political organizations, or social welfare causes. Due to an economic downturn, disappointing agricultural produce, and widespread epidemics, the 1880s—when Kuyper led a group of churches in secession out of the NHK—were particularly ripe for organizing. Ferdinand Domela Nieuwenhuis left his Lutheran pastorate and faith in Christianity altogether to agitate for workers as writer for the Netherlands General Workers Union and as leader of the socialist Social Democratic Party. Catholic priest Herman Schaepman established the Catholic opinion journal *The Guardian* and developed Catholic social policy as a member of parliament. Nevertheless, in the era of community organizing, "without exception the most skillful organizer was Abraham Kuyper," and the church was one of the key sites of Kuyper's organizing efforts.[10]

KUYPER'S ECCLESIOLOGY

Modern ecclesiology answered these changes with a more dynamic account of the church. Rather than a single unitary society, modern ecclesiology distinguished between different forms and aspects of the church.

---

9. Joris van Eijnatten and Fred van Lieburg, *Nederlandse Religiegeschiedenis* (Hilversum: Verloren, 2005), 275; Jasper Vree, "More Pierson and Mesmer, and Less Pietje Baltus: Kuyper's Ideas on Church, State, and Culture During the First Years of His Ministry (1863-1866)," in *Kuyper Reconsidered: Aspects of His Life and Work*, ed. Cornelis van der Kooi and Jan de Bruijn (Amsterdam: VU Uitgeverij, 1999), 299-309. On pluralization, see Hugh McLeod, *Secularization in Western Europe, 1848-1914* (New York: St. Martin's, 2000); Peter Berger, "Secularization Falsified," *First Things*, February 2008, 23-27.

10. Van Eijnatten and van Lieburg, *Nederlandse Religiegeschiedenis*, 283. On Kuyper and mobilization, see also James D. Bratt, *Abraham Kuyper: Modern Calvinist, Christian Democrat* (Grand Rapids: Eerdmans, 2013), 156-58; Jan de Bruijn, "Abraham Kuyper as a Romantic," in *Kuyper Reconsidered*, 42-52; Charles Taylor, *A Secular Age* (Cambridge, MA: Harvard University Press, 2007), 423-72; G. J. Schutte, "Abraham Kuyper—vormer van een volksdeel," in *Het Calvinistisch Nederland: Mythe en Werkelijkheid*, 146-65.

Theologians distinguished the outer, formal, and institutional structures from the inner, spiritual, subjective, and intersubjective forms of the church. Thus the organism (inner) was distinguished from the organization (outer), and the community (inner) from the institution (outer). This distinction is not generally found in older Protestant ecclesiologies, as elaborated in the Westminster Confession or Faith or the Belgic Confession, for example. But this distinction addressed questions that arose from modernity's attention to individual and subjective experience, from modernity's emancipation of the individual from traditional social attachments, and also from the abiding recognition that humans are, nevertheless, social beings. Friedrich Schleiermacher and Johan Möhler, two representative modern ecclesiologists, made this distinction, as did Abraham Kuyper.[11]

HISTORICAL AND INTELLECTUAL BACKGROUND

Kuyper's distinction between the church as organism and the church as institution is his most well-known contribution to ecclesiology. Broadly speaking, romanticism provided the intellectual soil for this distinction. Romanticism prized feeling, freedom, and spontaneity over rigid, predetermined forms. Kuyper's elevation of "our instinctive life" reflects just such a preference.[12] Romanticism was not necessarily individualistic, however, since besides freedom it also valued unity. The idea of the *volk*, the nation, as an integrated community with a distinctive history and identity but that could be distinguished from the artificial apparatus of the state—was another characteristically romantic ideal.[13] Kuyper's defense of historic Dutch cultural "multiformity" over against the steamroller of industrial and imperial "uniformity" was equally romantic in character: "Hence the slogan of false unity today has become: through uniformity to unification, by centralization toward Caesarism. Should that

---

11. On this distinction in Möhler and Schleiermacher, see Roger Haight, *Christian Community in History: Historical Ecclesiology*, 3 vols. (New York: Continuum, 2004), 1:357–62.

12. Consider the line: "Among tribes that still live in the state of nature this instinctive life is much more vigorous than among the more developed nations" (Abraham Kuyper, "Our Instinctive Life," in *AKCR*, 259).

13. Romanticism took various forms in Western culture and is notoriously hard to define. For an overview with special concern for the relation between nationalism and romanticism, see George L. Mosse, *The Culture of Western Europe: The Nineteenth and Twentieth Centuries*, 3rd ed. (Boulder: Westview Press, 1988), esp. 56–64.

effort succeed, the victory of that false unity will be celebrated on the ruins of what land and folk, race and nation, had that was peculiarly their own."[14] The distinction between nation and state offers a rough parallel to Kuyper's ecclesiological organism-institution distinction. It is noteworthy that in his 1870 address "Uniformity" Kuyper applied this logic to both the nation and the church.

CONVERTED TO THE CHURCH

The distinction between church as organism and as institution did not spring forth fully grown for Kuyper. Rather, it was the fruit of his own intellectual development and historical circumstances. The visible, organic church, one of the key developments in Kuyper's ecclesiology, first appeared in his prize-winning essay and doctoral dissertation on the ecclesiologies of John à Lasco and John Calvin. In an earlier thesis on Pope Nicolas I, Kuyper praised Nicolas for his concern for the poor, but Kuyper also admitted that the church belonged to an earlier stage of human development that was now destined to pass away.[15] The *Commentatio* on Calvin and à Lasco exhibited a revived appreciation for the church for Kuyper, albeit in a new form. It was written for a prize competition sponsored by the University of Groningen, whose faculty of theology blended a Schleiermacher-style mediating theology with national fervor. Kuyper's essay appealed precisely to these ideals. He chose à Lasco's more heartfelt religion as a forerunner of Schleiermacher, over Calvin's rigid churchly spirituality with its sacraments and dogma. The church, Kuyper said, was a society, an organism bound by feeling and moral life, not an institution, though it was a visible organism (he rejected Augustine's and Calvin's invisible church). Further à Lasco, who had pastored a church of Dutch exiles in London, was more authentically Dutch. Calvin, on the other hand, had poisoned the Dutch church, and following Calvin instead of à

---

14. Abraham Kuyper, "Uniformity: The Curse of Modern Life," in *AKCR*, 24. On Kuyper's romantic ecclesiology, see also Bratt, *Abraham Kuyper*, 183–84.

15. Jasper Vree and Johan Zwaan, "Historical Introduction," in *Abraham Kuyper's Commentatio (1860): The Young Kuyper about Calvin, à Lasco, and the Church*, 2 vols. (Leiden: Brill, 2005), 1:7–66; Johan Zwaan, "Sociale bewogenheid in een jeugdwerk van Abraham Kuyper," in *Een vrije universiteitsbibliotheek: studies over verleden, bezit en heden van de Bibliotheek der Vrije Universiteit*, ed. Johannes Stellingwerf (Assen: Van Gorcum, 1980), 203–19.

Lasco, the Synod of Dort "imposed upon our national church that foreign way of thinking in its horrid decree."[16]

Kuyper's construal of the church as a spontaneous, "from-below" social body remained a permanent feature of his ecclesiology and marks his ecclesiology as distinctively modern. Yet Kuyper did not remain hostile to Calvin for long, and his turn to Calvin marked an ecclesiological conversion to the church as an institution. Several things precipitated this conversion. In 1863 his fiancée, Jo Schaay, sent him the novel *The Heir of Redclyffe*, by Charlotte Yonge, who was an adherent of the high church Oxford movement. Kuyper saw himself reflected and condemned in the novel's ambitious and vain Philip de Morville, but he was not moved to a vague moral renovation; he was moved to the church. As Kuyper described his feelings, "At that moment the predilection for prescribed ritual, the high estimation of the Sacrament, the appreciation for the Liturgy became rooted in me for all time. ... I remembered what Calvin had so beautifully stated in the fourth book of his *Institutes* about God as our Father and 'the church as our Mother.'"[17] Calvin, as well as the old Dutch puritans of the "further reformation" (*nadere reformatie*), also confronted Kuyper at his first parish in Beesd in the form of some obstinate conventiclers—especially one, Pietje Baltus, who would not have anything to do with the new, reputedly Modernist pastor. Kuyper found that these malcontents, despite their apparent backwardness and their irascibility, had an abiding and deep piety rooted in the old writers. He was touched. At about the same time, Allard Pierson, a prominent Modernist pastor, came to the conclusion that the church as an institution (though not religion in general) had come to the end of its useful life. The modern state would now assume the role that formerly belonged to the church.[18] Good as his word, Pierson resigned his ecclesiastical position. Kuyper was forced to answer this challenge, and that meant a renewed concentration on the validity of Christianity and the church. Finally, Kuyper was also studying the polity and worship of the early Dutch church, and these studies evidence an emerging appreciation for the institutional church and Calvin's ideas about the separation of church and state. It is difficult to pinpoint an exact moment or cause, but the confluence of these forces in the late 1860s led the young pastor to a

---

16. "Commentatio," in *On the Church*, 8.
17. Abraham Kuyper, "Confidentially," in *AKCR*, 54–55, 60.
18. J. Trapman, "Allard Pierson en zijn afscheid van de kerk," *Documentatieblad voor de Nederlandse Kerkgeschiedenis na 1800* 19 (1996): 15–27.

new appreciation of John Calvin—his consistent predestinarianism and his more churchly spirituality.

At the same Kuyper, whose ideas always developed alongside his practice, became engaged in various disputes within the Dutch Reformed Church. Many of his efforts for church reform in the late 1860s and 70s exemplify the high view of the institution to which he had come. The *volkskerk* accommodated pluralism within its ranks by lowering doctrinal and liturgical hurdles. While Kuyper was pastor in Utrecht, the synod decided to permit a variety of baptismal formulas alongside the traditional Trinitarian one so that members were now baptized "into the name of the Father," "into the name of the congregation," "into faith, hope, and love," or "for the initiation into Christendom."[19] Kuyper summed up the result: "in order to maintain doctrinal freedom the synod abandons Christian baptism." And so he defended the traditional formula.[20] The synod also allowed greater doctrinal variety by not enforcing the church's confessional statements, though it continued to visit the congregations with questionnaires inquiring into the doctrine and life of the consistory members. Kuyper and the Utrecht consistory simply refused to answer such questions from a body that they regarded as delinquent in its doctrinal responsibilities.[21] Yet Kuyper was also frustrated both by conservatives who rested too much in institutional inertia and by the Ethical wing of the church who, inspired by Schleiermacher, neglected institutional forms.[22]

Kuyper made several attempts to make theological sense of the inner and the outer, the organic and institutional nature the church. On one occasion he appealed to the language of incarnation to explain the church's form and essence, but this construal had pantheistic tones and was deemed too speculative.[23] At his inauguration as a pastor in Amsterdam

---

19. David Bos, *In dienst van het koninkrijk: beroepsontwikkeling van hervormde predikanten in negentiende-eeuws Nederland* (Amsterdam: Bakker, 1999), 61–62.

20. Abraham Kuyper, "De Doopskwestie," *De Heraut*, October 7, 1870.

21. Jasper Vree, *Kuyper in de kiem: de precalvinistische periode van Abraham Kuyper, 1848–1874* (Hilversum: Verloren, 2006), 163–324; Bratt, *Abraham Kuyper*, 52–56.

22. Abraham Kuyper, "Conservatism and Orthodoxy: False and True Preservation," in *AKCR*, 65–85; C. H. W. van den Berg, "Kuyper en de kerk," in *Abraham Kuyper: zijn volksdeel, zijn invloed*, ed. Cornelius Augustijn, J. H. Prins, and H. E. S. Woldring (Delft: Meinema, 1987), 154.

23. Abraham Kuyper, "De menschwording Gods: het levensbeginsel der kerk (1867)," in *Predicatiën, in de jaren 1867 tot 1873, tijdens zijn predikantschap in het Nederlandsch Hervormde Kerkgenootschap, gehouden te Beesd, te Utrecht, en te Amsterdam* (Kampen: Kok, 1913).

in 1870, Kuyper offered another biblical metaphor, "rooted and grounded" (Eph 3:17). That seemed more fruitful. Insofar as it was rooted, the church had an inner organic life that flowed directly from the Spirit of God. This was indicated by the various biological metaphors used in Scripture, especially the church as a body. This also explained the familial character of the church. Whatever disestablishment meant, the church was not a mere club, but instead made claims even on those born to its bosom apart from any deliberate choice of their own. Nevertheless, the life of the church was not to be taken for granted, as perhaps a national church was prone to do. It must be deliberately built. The church was not only a body but also a house founded and built by human hands. This building had a solid outward form that shaped and protected the inner organism. Through various metaphors Kuyper explained the inseparability of the organism and the institution: the church as a mother who gives birth and who nurtures, the church as a free-flowing river whose power is directed by its banks, and the church as "a multitude of priests, legitimated through birth but consecrated only through anointing."[24] Kuyper set this organic-institutional church over against Hegelian liberals like Pierson who envisioned the state absorbing the church, and against Roman Catholic institutionalism, exemplified by the First Vatican Council being held that same year.

During the 1860s and 70s Kuyper aimed to reform the national church. The institution was his foremost concern. Kuyper gave his account of his spiritual journey in *Confidentially* (1873). In fact, Kuyper's personal testimony was part of a larger *apologia pro vita sua*, wherein he explained the origin of his concern for the church and the principles of a true Reformed church. He insisted again on the inseparability of the church's essence and form, an expression synonymous with organism and institution, and he attributed both a soteriological and social-ethical significance to the church as institution. The church was the mother apart from which no one can have God as Father, and it stood as a rampart against the overwhelming state. Such a church should be Reformed in its confessions; democratic rather than patrician; free instead of coerced; independent of the state; and all this in its doctrine, worship, and work of mercy.[25]

---

24. "Rooted and Grounded," in *On the Church*, 50.

25. See Abraham Kuyper, *Confidentie: schrijven aan den weled. Heer J. H. van der Linden* (Amsterdam: Höveker & Zoon, 1873); ET (selections): "Confidentially," in *AKCR*, 45–61.

Reforming the Church

Theological modernism continued to make inroads into the Dutch Reformed Church through the 1870s and 80s. The church's doctrinal commitments were progressively diluted, especially its commitment to traditional institutional forms, namely, the confessions. In 1875 the church decided that it no longer bore the responsibility of maintaining doctrine. In 1878 it was decided that membership could not be denied on the basis of religious convictions. Those coming for confirmation in the church were required only to accept the "spirit and the essentials" of the church's confessions. In 1882 a change was made to the requirements for ministerial candidates so that adherence to the forms of unity (Belgic Confession, Heidelberg Catechism, and Canons of Dort) was replaced with commitment to "interests of the Kingdom." Conservatives were in uproar.[26]

Meanwhile Kuyper was building a confessional Reformed (*Gereformeerd*) constituency in the church and in the sphere of education, especially through various voluntary societies. Kuyper and his Reformed party opposed Modernism, but by the 1880s it was not their main opponent in the church fight; the Ethical-Irenical group was. This group was sympathetic to many of the traditional Protestant concerns, but they were also willing to accommodate Modernism. They only assented to the essentials of doctrine rather than to the full confessional statements, and many of them embraced forms of mediating theology. At one time Kuyper made common cause with the Ethical-Irenicals, but by the late 1870s, especially when they did not support his Free University, Kuyper parted ways with them. They were not willing to take radical action, especially if it might compromise the integrity of the Dutch Reformed Church. Ironically Kuyper had more respect for Modernists, who took principled positions, than for the Ethicals, who would not.[27]

Besides Modernism, Kuyper also opposed the synodical hierarchy of the NHK, which he regarded as an illegitimate imposition on the Dutch Reformed tradition. The synod, he said, was evidence of conformity to the world and its power structures,[28] and in fact it did look a lot like the

---

26. C. H. W. van den Berg, "De ontstaangeschiedenis van de Doleantie te Amsterdam," in *De Doleantie van 1886 en haar geschiedenis*, ed. W. Bakker, et al. (Kampen: Kok, 1986), 93–96.

27. See van den Berg, "De ontstaangeschiedenis van de Doleantie te Amsterdam"; Bratt, *Abraham Kuyper*, 149–71.

28. For example, Abraham Kuyper, "It Shall Not Be So among You," in *AKCR*, 125–42.

centralized, bureaucratic state. Kuyper and the people of his party generally came from lower social ranks than those who populated the ecclesiastical boards, and consequently the democratic election of ministers, which Kuyper helped push through in 1867, empowered his orthodox party. In the place of the synod and its courts, the classis, and the provincial boards, Kuyper advocated for free churches—autonomous local congregations with democratically elected ministers—bound to each other only by voluntary confederation. Thus modern democratic means supported orthodox ends.

Kuyper drew up his blueprint for a free church, and a plan for how to get there, in his 1883 *Tract on the Reformation of the Churches*. The *Tract* is mainly about the reformation of the institutional church and takes an innovative and dialectical account of the course of the church's life—its formation, deformation, and reformation. However, the organism, the gathering of believers apart from the institution, gains priority in this account. The organism forms the institution. It is the historical manifestation of the invisible church, which is formed directly by God in his counsel of election, and Kuyper always argues on the premise that this organism is behind and before the organization of the church.[29] This explains how believers may circumvent normal ecclesiastical channels if necessary, an important point if one is dealing with a corrupt institution.

REFORMING SOCIETY

If the *Tract* provided a rationale for the internal working of the church, "Twofold Fatherland" provided an account of the church's relation to society at large. Kuyper gave this address in 1887 at a gathering of the Free University. The university was entering its seventh year, and Kuyper's secession church (the *Doleantie*, meaning "aggrieved") was newly born. In the address, Kuyper encouraged the faithful by offering a vision for how this group of outsider Calvinists might remain culturally relevant and even a salutary force in their beloved homeland. Withdrawal from the national church and from national schools did not mean withdrawal from the nation or society. As with the *Tract*, the priority in this address belonged to the organic church. The organic church, not the institution, would be the locus of Christian action in the world. As Kuyper described the situation, the Dutch church had long benefited from its place in a

---

29. Kuyper does not often use the language of "organism," but the concept is clearly present and plays an important part. See especially *Tract*, in *On the Church*, 111–17, 223–36.

predominantly Christian nation, and the nation had benefited from it. But the nation's Christian identity could no longer be taken for granted. The church found itself in an increasingly hostile environment. It was a tricky task to explain how the nation could be a genuinely good thing and yet no longer a true home for the church. In "Twofold Fatherland" Kuyper makes his first appeal to the doctrine of common grace, and it was prompted precisely by this ecclesiological predicament.

While the organic church may come to mind first when considering Kuyper's social ethics, the institutional church was equally important, and it was the main concern of Kuyper's reflections in "State and Church," part of his *Antirevolutionary Politics*. As in "Twofold Fatherland," so also in this work the emphasis fell on the antithesis between Christianity and modern society, specifically, between the modern state and the church. The church, Kuyper said, was a colony of heaven on earth.[30] The church existed as an entirely separate institution from the state, and contrary to Hegelians like Allard Pierson, the church was the eternal institution. The state would wither away. Many familiar themes appear, and the NHK is always a more or less explicit target. The church is local and catholic but never a national church, not a *volkskerk*, and it is entirely separate from the state. It was precisely the separation of the institutional church and the state that made the introduction of a new social ethic necessary—a more dynamic ethic that addressed the complexity of the pluralist society that resulted from disestablishment.[31]

CONCLUSION

The pieces included in this anthology open a variety of new questions about Kuyper's theology and about ecclesiology in general. Is the distinction between organism and institution justified? Can the church ever be considered apart from the work of the Spirit in the institution and its means of grace, as Kuyper's understanding of the organism appears to do? How does Kuyper's ecclesiology compare to Schleiermacher's, and does he rescue Schleiermacher's church from imprisonment in the immanent frame? Does Kuyper's ecclesiology provide an adequate account of Christian experience? In particular, do Christians become Christians by experience of a mystical organism first and only arrive at the institution

---

30. See "State and Church," in *On the Church*, 377–81.
31. See John Halsey Wood Jr., *Going Dutch in the Modern Age: Abraham Kuyper's Struggle for a Free Church in the Nineteenth-Century Netherlands* (New York: Oxford University Press, 2013).

later? There are also apparent tensions in Kuyper's ecclesiology. In some places Kuyper imagines a robust and enduring church, one even able to outlast the ominous state, while elsewhere the church appears to be a rather weak voluntary institution.[32]

Kuyper's ecclesiology remains timely because the church continues to face many of the same challenges that it faced in Kuyper's time. Christians are often told to be "spiritual but not religious"—a formula that exalts inner experience and belittles outward ritual. Harvey Cox and Diana Butler Bass, liberal and evangelical Protestants respectively, both expect the supplanting of the church by a more individualistic and freely formed religion.[33] They hope for a recovery of the "lost Christianities" of the second-century Gnostics. Others, like Ross Douthat (a Roman Catholic), lament the loss of an identifiable center for Christianity.[34] It seems that some form of Jesus-mysticism is ascendant in the West. Yet everywhere one hears the call for community.

Abraham Kuyper knew firsthand the mystical side of Christianity. He had multiple conversion experiences. The organic, or "rooted" nature of the church accounted for the unaccountable work of the Spirit, but Kuyper also saw the excesses to which unrestrained mysticism could lead, namely, "the draining away of our lifeblood as a result of spiritualism."[35] If Cox, Bass, and Douthat are right, one might wonder whether the church as an institution has any remaining relevance. The "grounded" institutional church needs shoring up and must be related to the mystical experience of the Spirit. Kuyper's ecclesiology found biblical warrant for both the mystical and the institutional nature of the Christian church, and he made a case that the institution is inseparable from the organism. If successful, Kuyper may offer a starting point for addressing the contemporary ecclesiastical malaise.

John Halsey Wood Jr.

---

32. For example, Kuyper says that Calvinism allowed people to serve God according to the dictates of their own heart. See Kuyper, "Calvinism: Source and Stronghold of Our Constitutional Liberties," in *AKCR*, 292; "Uniformity: The Curse of Modern Life," in *AKCR*, 38–39.

33. Harvey Cox, *The Future of Faith* (New York: HarperOne, 2009); Diana Butler Bass, *Christianity after Religion: The End of the Church and the Birth of a New Spiritual Awakening* (New York: HarperOne, 2012).

34. Ross Douthat, *Bad Religion: How We Became a Nation of Heretics* (New York: Free Press, 2012).

35. "Rooted and Grounded," in *On the Church*, 49.

VOLUME INTRODUCTION

OVERVIEW

This volume is a collection and translation of some of Abraham Kuyper's most significant writings on the church. Such a volume has historical value because Kuyper was certainly one of the greatest theologians and Christian thinkers since the Enlightenment.[1] As with other important historical figures, it is not surprising that themes from Kuyper's writings continue to be investigated. And in a globalized world, it is fitting that his works be translated into English. Yet what meaning could Abraham Kuyper's ecclesiology have for the church today? Kuyper's historical significance does not necessarily imply that his thoughts about the church are still relevant. Although the lasting importance of his public theology is self-evident, given the ongoing and even increasing attention that both Western and non-Western Christians have paid to it,[2] the modern value of other themes from his body of work—such as his doctrine of the church—is not as clear.

---

1. Richard F. Lovelace even calls him "the greatest evangelical theologian after Edwards." See Lovelace, *Dynamics of Spiritual Life: An Evangelical Theology of Renewal* (Downers Grove, IL: InterVarsity Press, 1979), 374.
2. See, e.g., James D. Bratt, *Abraham Kuyper: Modern Calvinist, Christian Democrat* (Grand Rapids: Eerdmans, 2013); James W. Skillen and Rockne M. McCarthy, *Political Order and the Plural Structure of Society* (Atlanta: Scholars Press, 1991).

Today's emerging manifestations of the church are characterized as post-institutional. These forms leave conventional, fixed church structures behind and present themselves as fluid and flexible.[3] An alternative vision regarding the church's public calling is gaining ground among younger generations of evangelicals. These young Christians envision the church as neither withdrawing into the private sphere nor seeking public influence and power, whether directly or mediated through faith-based initiatives. The church ought to form a contrasting community that confronts the existing political societies of this world with the way of life of the world to come, thereby presenting a challenging public alternative.[4] These views culminate in the argument that Christendom—the Constantinian world in which the church was the dominant public reality—is gone forever.[5]

Kuyper presents a different perspective, as the champion of the re-Christianization of Dutch society.[6] He was convinced of the institutional dimension of the church and even created new Christian organizations that were meant to fight a visible battle in all spheres of life. Those who sympathize with contemporary ecclesiological trends would probably depict him as Constantinian; later in the twentieth century his own Dutch neo-Calvinist heirs explicitly distanced themselves from his doctrine of the church. In particular, the theologian Klaas Schilder expressed fierce criticisms of two aspects of Kuyper's approach. Kuyper's distinction between the organic and institutional aspects of the church, Schilder believed, was a nineteenth-century philosophical construct rather than a suitable way to do justice to the biblical passages dealing with the church, and this doctrine of the church's pluriformity contradicted the biblical

---

3. Neil Cole, *Organic Church: Growing Faith where Life Happens* (San Francisco: Jossey-Bass, 2005); Eddy Gibbs and Ryan K. Bolger, *Emerging Churches: Creating Christian Community in Postmodern Cultures* (Grand Rapids: Baker Academic, 2005); Ryan K. Bolger, ed., *The Gospel after Christendom: New Voices, New Cultures, New Expressions* (Grand Rapids: Baker Academic, 2012).

4. Jonathan R. Wilson, *Living Faithfully in a Fragmented World: From* After Virtue *to a New Monasticism* (Eugene, OR: Cascade, 2010).

5. Stuart Murray, *Post-Christendom* (Carlisle: Paternoster, 2004); Peter J. Leithart, *Defending Constantine: The Twilight of an Empire and the Dawn of Christendom* (Downers Grove, IL: IVP Academic, 2010); John D. Roth, ed., *Constantine Revisited: Leithart, Yoder, and the Constantinian Debate* (Eugene, OR: Pickwick, 2013).

6. A. A. van der Schans, *Kuyper en Kersten: ijveraars voor herkerstening van onze samenleving* (Leiden: J. J. Groen, 1992).

emphasis on visible unity and the communion of all believers.[7] Kuyper's ecclesiology also seems at odds with modern ecumenical movements.

This volume demonstrates, on the contrary, that Kuyper's ecclesiology has far more than mere historical value. Kuyper himself consciously distinguished between the basic concepts of his doctrine and their applied forms in his proposals for his own day. He was aware that contexts other than his own would require different applications and even gives hints of these possibilities in ways that are suprisingly close to contemporary forms of the church. The selections presented in this volume thus offer a very relevant contribution to our debates.[8]

A TWOFOLD FATHERLAND

The relevance of Kuyper's ecclesiology is demonstrated in his lecture to the Free University in Amsterdam titled "Twofold Fatherland," which is contained in the present volume. Kuyper here characterizes the church as "a colony of heaven."[9] For Kuyper, this characterization was no accidental metaphor; he drew it from Philippians 3:20 and 2 Corinthians 5:6. His systematic exposition of the church in "Lord's Day 21" of *E Voto Dordraceno* contains exactly the same phrase, which can be translated literally as "a colony of the heavenly country."[10]

According to Kuyper a Christian is a citizen of two homelands. In both homelands the Christian lives under a divine calling. The earthly homeland originates in God's common grace, by which the Lord confronts evil after the fall. At the same time common grace facilitates the growth of creation with all its potential, even under the conditions of sin. From the beginning God's plan included the outgrowth of a global society over which he would be king in an unmediated manner. Under his government this united worldwide community would at the same time contain

---

7. Klass Schilder, *De Kerk*, 2 vols. (Goes: Oosterbaan & Le Cointre, 1960–1962), 1:303–445. See also C. Trimp, "De kerk bij A. Kuyper en K. Schilder," in *De Kerk: Wezen, weg en werk van de kerk naar reformatorische opvatting*, ed. W. van 't Spijker, et al. (Kampen: De Groot Goudriaan, 1990).
8. A recent study by John Halsey Wood Jr. shows how Kuyper's ecclesiology can contribute to today's discussions: *Going Dutch in the Modern Age: Abraham Kuyper's Struggle for a Free Church in the Nineteenth-Century Netherlands* (New York: Oxford University Press, 2013).
9. "Twofold Fatherland," in *On the Church*, 307.
10. "Lord's Day 21," in *On the Church*, 323.

an infinite diversity and plurality. This would reflect God's endlessly rich Trinitarian life, in which humanity was allowed to participate.

With the fall, however, humanity rejected God's authority and handed over creation to the devil. Since that moment, a unified world would pose a threat to God's purposes, since in it evil would also be unified, thereby making the originally intended variety impossible. Kuyper calls this "the curse of uniformity."[11] God broke this false unity and for the rest of history has divided the earth into separate nations and states, each with their own governments. Only in the eschatological future, when sin will be destroyed, will the situation change. Earthly nations and governments will disappear. God himself will once more become the only authority, and he will reign over a fully developed and infinitely varied creation. The earthly homeland, therefore, is certainly indispensable, but only as an interim establishment for the present age.[12]

Parallel to this common grace, God also grants his particular grace to the world in order to save humanity and creation. In his Son, Jesus Christ, he establishes atonement and a source of new life. A new humanity, destined to be cititzens of his coming kingdom, will grow from that life. In addition to their first births from earthly fathers, God's elect receive a second birth from their heavenly Father. Kuyper characterizes this regeneration as "the invisible commencement of a heavenly country." This heavenly homeland has been established with Christ's ascension. It already exists in heaven, and one day it will replace the existing earthly homelands. Then Christ will return the kingdom to his Father, so that in the end God's original intentions for creation and humanity will be realized.

In the meantime, however, this heavenly fatherland already influences our earthly reality. The new life in Christ wages war against the old life of sin—a spiritual war fought across the whole range of the created spheres of life. The church is the product of this heavenly influence. It consists of people who have been born again, partake in the heavenly life, and therefore have become citizens of the heavenly homeland. Yet at the same time they live on earth, where they participate in their earthly homelands. These earthly countries also stem from God's work—from his common grace, and thus, members of the heavenly fatherland should

---

11. "Twofold Fatherland," in *On the Church*, 288. Compare Abraham Kuyper, "Uniformity: The Curse of Modern Life," in *AKCR*, 19–44.

12. "State and Church," in *On the Church*, 377–437; Abraham Kuyper, *De overheid: Locus de Magistratu* (Kampen: Kok, 1901), 65–66.

fully acknowledge their citizenship in their earthly ones. This leaves them with two homelands, one of which is fundamental.

Thus, Kuyper's characterization of the church as an "earthly colony of the heavenly homeland" is clear. Precisely because it is a colony, the church should join Christ in his spiritual battle on earth. The church should not avoid its formidable task here on earth.[13] It will be the means by which Christ's new life will penetrate to the marrow of creation. This requires church members to found Christian organizations for public action in all spheres of life, thus developing these spheres in the direction of God's creational purposes. Kuyper's university was one of those Christian organizations, and his lecture "Twofold Fatherland" was an effort to mobilize widespread support for it among his fellow church members.[14]

KUYPER IN NEW CONTEXTS

Kuyper's lecture leaves no doubt that he was fully aware of the context in which he spoke. He even acknowledges that other contexts would provoke different conclusions. The two parties of opponents that posed a threat to his public endeavors—the Anabaptists and Moderates—are quite similar to contemporary positions like the Neo-Anabaptists and the propagators of Christianity as a civil religion.[15] Kuyper's vision is once again more relevant than it initially appears because he agrees with these parties in some ways.

Anabaptists, he wrote, rightly considered the heavenly country to be the real fatherland. They would affirm Kuyper's characterization of the church as a colony; both they and Kuyper saw Christians as sojourners who are homesick for their true fatherland and are always calling out, "Come quickly, Lord." Anabaptists, however, incorrectly held a dualistic view of creation and kingdom—they ignored God's intent to bring about a re-creation rather than a totally new creation. They also ignore God's common grace forming the backdrop to the earthly homeland. In their confusion, they cease being colonists and abstain from responsibilities

---

13. "Lord's Day 21," in *On the Church*, 335–342; PR 2.I.1.4.
14. "Twofold Fatherland," in *On the Church*, 284–314.
15. Compare Stuart Murray, *The Naked Anabaptist: The Bare Essentials of a Radical Faith* (Scottdale, PA: Herald Press, 2010); James Davison Hunter, *To Change the World: The Irony, Tragedy, and Possibility of Christianity in the Late Modern World* (New York: Oxford University Press, 2010), 154–65; Mary C. Segers and Ted G. Jelen, *A Wall of Separation? Debating the Public Role of Religion* (Lanham, MD: Rowman & Littlefield, 1998).

in the homeland below. Kuyper frequently detected traces of Anabaptist views among his Reformed compatriots.[16] His public endeavors, however, depended on his Reformed fellows. This made it urgent to critically address their views, albeit in a friendly tone. In doing so, he hoped to mobilize them for the church's public calling.

However, Moderates made an even worse mistake. They proclaimed that the Netherlands' history as a Christian nation was a permanent standard. They believed that the church did not need any separate organization apart from the institutions of the nation itself. For them, the earthly homeland *was* the kingdom of Christ. According to this viewpoint, the government has authority within the church, thus diluting the genuine doctrinal and moral character of the Christian church. Though some Moderates would regret this result, they believed such weaknesses should not be countered by reformation of the church leading to secession; they wanted to counter it "medically" by gradual correction and improvement.

Thus, these Moderates fiercely opposed the contextual consequences of Kuyper's ecclesiology—both the reformation of the church as institute and the formation of separate Christian organizations for public and societal action. Kuyper criticized them for losing the decisive rootedness of Christians in the homeland of heaven, even though he shared their conviction that the church should bear public responsibility in their earthly country. Kuyper's characterization of the church as colony indicates his closer alignment with the Anabaptists on this point, at least in his own context—it is incompatible with the Moderates' view. This becomes even clearer in Kuyper's repeated criticisms of the changes in the relationship of church and society that Constantine introduced.[17] In rejecting Constantine he looks very similar to modern anti-Constantinians like John Howard Yoder and Stanley Hauerwas.[18]

It is quite remarkable, then, that Kuyper could see possibilities in other contexts for both Anabaptist and Moderate models of public responsibility. He foresaw times and circumstances in which either model could be

---

16. Kuyper, *De overheid*, 240.
17. Kuyper, *Bekeert U, want het Koninkrijk Gods is nabij!: leerrede op den laatsten dag van 1871 gehouden* (Amsterdam: De Hoogh, 1872), 12; "Lord's Day 21," in *On the Church*, 336; PR 1.II.15.2, 4.
18. John Howard Yoder, *The Politics of Jesus: Vicit Agnus Noster*, 2nd ed. (Grand Rapids: Eerdmans, 1994); Stanley Hauerwas, *After Christendom? How the Church Is to Behave if Freedom, Justice, and a Christian Nation Are Bad Ideas* (Nashville: Abingdon, 1991).

at least partly adequate. In this he ignored neither his earlier criticisms of the Anabaptists' dualism nor the Moderates' identification of an earthly nation with the kingdom of Christ. Yet he saw that in some contexts, their practical applications could come close to what he himself would desire.

When, for example, an entire nation belongs to the heavenly homeland because its population in general consists of believers, the earthly and the heavenly homelands coincide. Their earthly citizenship still originates in common grace, while their heavenly birthrights arise from particular grace. But the church then does not need separate organizations, since it would be possible to instill new life in all created spheres just by participating in the institutions of the nation itself. For Kuyper, this was more than a thought experiment. He discerned this exact social situation in the Dutch nation of the sixteenth and seventeenth centuries, as well as in the independent American colonies.[19]

Conversely, Kuyper expected times when the devil, as the ruler of this world, would exercise such influence on the nations and their leaders that the church would be persecuted and have no ability to develop new life in the realm of creation. Even public pressure to adapt to society is tantamount to that state of affairs. In such times, the church must take up its cross, accept suffering, and withdraw from the public life of its earthly homeland. This is no mere theoretical possibility either. Biblical eschatology prompted Kuyper to expect such troubled days to be the outcome of world history. Already in his own times he sensed this imminent release of the demons.[20]

It follows that Kuyper did not mean for his vision of forming Christian organizations in all spheres of life to be the universal standard for all times and situations. His specific application in his own context—and his refutation of both Moderates and Anabaptists—depended on careful observations and interpretations of that context in light of the gospel. He characterized his nineteenth-century Dutch surroundings as "no longer Christian" or, more correctly, "no longer *purely* Christian."[21] According to Kuyper, Calvinism was crossing the ocean to flourish again and reach its peak in North America. He predicted that thereafter, the final eschatological battle would start—begun by confrontation between Christian

---

19. "Twofold Fatherland," in *On the Church*, 308.
20. "Twofold Fatherland," in *On the Church*, 299; *Bekeert*, 7; *PR* 1.I.4.2; 1.II.16.2; 3.V.11.4.
21. "Twofold Fatherland," in *On the Church*, 309.

America on the one hand and the Islamic and Asian peoples of the East on the other. He foresaw the Christian character of the Dutch nation fading away in this penultimate period of world history. Yet Kuyper defined his own time as transitional as well. His earthly homeland, he said, had not yet become unchristian, but was no longer purely Christian. Since the world-historical role of Calvinism was not yet complete, Kuyper still dared to expect some hope for the Calvinist Netherlands. Under the wings of Calvinist America, Dutch Calvinism would once more flourish.[22]

This analysis and foresight guided Kuyper's public commitment and explains why he viewed an Anabaptist-like retreat as premature. Yet for him, the Moderates' Constantinian model completely failed to acknowledge the changing tide of history and the growing divide in Dutch society. Kuyper's commitment to both the reformation of the church and the formation of Christian organizations was deliberately tailored to his specific context. All people who wish to apply even the basics of his ecclesiology to other contexts would be well-advised to develop a similarly careful analysis of their surroundings.

KUYPER'S UNIQUE ECCLESIOLOGY

Kuyper's concept of the church as a colony of heaven and his careful contextualization shed new light on well-known emphases in his ecclesiology. Particularly notable are his distinction between the church as institute and as organism, as well as his doctrine of the pluriformity of the church.

INSTITUTE AND ORGANISM

Many interpreters of Kuyper's ecclesiology consider his emphasis on the church as organism as the core of his contribution to the doctrine of the church. He went beyond the conventional vision of the church as merely an institution and further depicted the church as forming Christian communities in all spheres of life. Through this doctrine, he was able to both meet the liberal demand for the church's withdrawal into the private sphere and also regain public impact for the church in the post-Enlightenment world. However, these Kuyper readers see his deepest sympathies tied to the church as organism—as if, for him, the institution of the church was only mechanical and pragmatic for his public ambitions.

---

22. See Abraham Kuyper, *Lectures on Calvinism: Six Lectures Delivered at Princeton University Under Auspices of the L. P. Stone Foundation* (Grand Rapids: Eerdmans, 1931); PR 2.I.5; 3.IV.22.4; 3.V.8.2; 3.V.11.4.

However, we have already called this interpretation into question. As we have seen, Kuyper's emphasis on Christian organizations in all areas of life was a deliberate contextual choice because of the transition he saw in Dutch society. Looking both to the past and future, he could see times when this specific application of the church as organism would be inadequate. In these times, the organic church would be conflated either with the nation or with a marginalized institute. We must also mention a second oft-repeated and equally inadequate evaluation of Kuyper's ecclesiology—namely, viewing the organic church as substantially different than the institutional church. For Kuyper, the institute was the primary structure from which the church as organism emerged.

It seems strange at first glance that after distinguishing between organism and institute in "Rooted and Grounded," Kuyper did not revisit those concepts for many years. Even in his *Tract*, which is his most elaborate treatment of the doctrine of the church, one can search for it in vain. The *Tract*, however, aims at the reformation of the institute; when considered carefully, this necessitates the presence of the organic church. For example, Kuyper used the undeniably organic image of the church as a mother who gives birth to new life in Christ.[23] At the same time, the institutional church becomes the first earthly form of this new creation.

One could agree with later critics like Schilder on semantic grounds. Yet this should not obscure how Kuyper, no less than his critics, remained true to the New Testament vision of the church as the re-created community, formed and organized around the gospel. Kuyper, however, saw that the new creation desires to grow into the whole of creation. When that happens, the organic church can be found outside the institute as much as within it. The specific forms of this expansion remain secondary and contextually determined. And if, one day, this expansion is no longer possible, then the church as organism and the church as institute will fully coincide again—but only temporarily.

Kuyper's personal history also serves to correct the traditional interpretation of his distinction between organism and institute. In modern terms, his attention to the church as organism seems the more unusual aspect, because we are used to seeing churches as institutions. But Kuyper began his theological career as a believer in German idealism. He may have been the first Dutch theologian who adopted the German idealist concept of the

---

23. *Tract*, in *On the Church*, 133; see also "Rooted and Grounded," in *On the Church*, 56.

organic—even while he was still young. This German philosophy called for dissolving the church as a separate institution in the modern state. Kuyper's *Commentatio* testifies that he began his thought process in that tradition. He sided with Schleiermacher and also with the more organic reformer à Lasco in opposing Calvin's institutional approach.[24] Only later in his career, when he converted to the classical Reformed position, did he start to appreciate Calvin. Following this he started to emphasize the necessity of the church as institute, which subsequently stimulated his commitment to reform the institution of the church. At the same time, his affinity for the organic aspect remained strong as ever—this is clear in his continual use of the terminology of "life" in all his works. And Kuyper's early concept of the institutional church's gradual dissolution into society remained in his thought. He simply came to believe it would happen at the parousia rather than during history.

Kuyper's concept of the institute also, not surprisingly, contains overtones specific to nineteenth-century thought. At that time, the existent category of the institutional became the central category for the many structures that were perceived within the newly defined conception of society.[25] In Hegelian thought especially, society was developed as a third entity lying between individual and state. It was not understood as part of the private sphere, but rather as an extended version of the public sphere. By adopting the terminology of institutionality, Kuyper guaranteed a new public place for the church that was suited to nineteenth-century circumstances—even after the separation of church and state. Dissociated from the public framework of the state, the church could now be conceived of as a public reality of its own kind within society. Note that this does not refer to the organic church, but to the church as institute. However, this also implied that society could potentially deny the church such a position in these new contexts, thus once again necessitating a new model.

PLURIFORMITY

Kuyper's doctrine of pluriformity is also a well-known concept within his ecclesiology. This doctrine can similarly be understood through his

---

24. "Commentatio," in *On the Church*, 14–16, 28–29, 34–37; Jasper Vree and Johan Zwaan, *Abraham Kuyper's* Commentatio *(1860): The Young Kuyper about Calvin, a Lasco, and the Church*, 2 vols. (Leiden: Brill, 2005), 1:2, 4, 14, 39, 49–51, 56–57, 61.
25. Anthony Giddens, *The Constitution of Society: Outline of the Theory of Structuration* (Cambridge: Polity Press, 1984).

characterization of the church as a colony of heaven. Kuyper often draws a notable parallel between earthly states and the institutional church. He regards both as unnatural, mechanical entities which God created after the fall, to guarantee the continued existence and growth of organic life under the reality of sin. The state serves the organic life of creation, while the institutional church does the same with the life of God's re-creation. Kuyper warns more than once against the Anabaptist error of separating the two. The new life in Christ is not separate from creation, but is only the redeemed and restored life of creation.[26] During history, however, this new life will not become perfect and remains trapped in a fallen world. The church as institute, therefore, cannot establish a pure and perfect hiding place to escape the realities of this world. It must reckon with the existence of states, as these are fruits of God's common grace. Therefore, while in fact international in character, the church has to respect state borders.[27]

We must remember here that Kuyper considered humanity's division into separate states as a necessary but unnatural plurality that would not have developed in a sinless world. By means of this dividedness, Kuyper says, God protects his fallen creation against a possible unification in evil that would spoil the intended diversity of creation. With this in mind, one can see a comparable phenomenon within the church as institute. Re-created life must display God's Trinitarian diversity. But there is opportunity for the church to face the same failing as the state, because of the necessary earthly placement of the church as institution. As with states, institutional unity opposes the development and growth of the new creation in all its diversity. If all believers were to unite in the Reformed tradition and adopt that historical identity, all the important dimensions of the new creation that exist in other ecclesial traditions would be missing. In order to protect the diversity of the re-created world against this threat of uniformity—which inescapably affects earthly life after the fall—forms of unnatural plurality are as essential within the church as they are in the state.

Kuyper's doctrine of pluriformity simultaneously contains these two aspects of unnatural (even sinful) yet inevitable dividedness along with creational diversity. Moreover, he deliberately limits the acceptable range

---

26. For example, see Kuyper, *De overheid*, 238.
27. *Tract*, in *On the Church*, 114–117.

of ecclesial division. While uniting confessional traditions is undesirable, churches that share the same confession should overcome their barriers and allow pluriformity within a unified institute. Yet all of this is often overlooked. But Kuyper dares far more than his opponents do to suppose that there is a divine plan behind the historical reality of ecclesial plurality.[28] One could say that with his theory of pluriformity, Kuyper allows for a trace of common grace within the ecclesial reality, though the church itself is part of particular grace.

KUYPER AND CONTEMPORARY ECCLESIOLOGY

It is clear that Kuyper's foundational concept of the church as a colony of heaven was meant to adjust to changing circumstances in his own time and even in his own works. This deliberate contextuality makes Kuyper's view a challenging voice in ecclesiological debates in today's post-Constantinian age. His emphasis on the coexistent organic and the institutional dimensions of the church challenges both sides in current discussions. New, experimental church forms and new proposals for the relation between church and society are often met with suspicion or are even simply rejected. Because of their habituation to already-existing institutional forms, conservatives equate their institutions with the core reality of the church itself; they are unable to imagine the possibility that the church's true nature could be expressed in other forms. Conversely, proponents of new shapes for the church are too quick to equate post-Constantinian with post-institutional.

Kuyper, however, would admonish both sides to use caution. As long as this world lasts, institutionality will be necessary; it can be acknowledged even by someone who—like Kuyper himself—explicitly opts for a post-Constantinian stance and predicts an even more marginalized church. The post-Constantinian era should not be treated as the end of history and thereby seduce us into a romantic farewell to institutionality. At the same time, as in Kuyper's day, the church as institution may have to put on new creative forms that reflect the direction of society's movement. This possibility should not be cut off by default, out of mistaken conservatism. Even as Kuyper's later neo-Calvinist critics propose establishing a stronger tie between Christian public organizations and the institutional

---

28. "Lord's Day 21," in *On the Church*, 357–363.

church, they do not contradict Kuyper's foundational ideas.[29] Kuyper's basic model was specifically meant for his partially secularized context. In a different situation, the model could be changed again.

Kuyper's sustained emphasis on the priority of organic, communal life in Christ also contains a double message for today. Those who oppose post-institutional claims and newly created church constructs should freely appreciate the organic reality of the shared new life that such forms display. This organic reality signals the essence of the church—no matter what points of debate are appropriate. Supporters of experimental church life, who seem to secure their identity by continually criticizing traditional forms and habits, should realize that even these have contained—and still contain—this same new life.

Finally, Kuyper's parallel between state and church is still important today. Several analysts foresee humanity's imminent departure from the centuries-old model of the nation-state.[30] They predict alternative ways of building community; these will have local, global, and technological characterisitics. Kuyper's parallel, then, would lead to challenging ecclesiological debates. Our time would become a time of transition comparable to the changes of the sixteenth, seventeenth, and nineteenth centuries—the times when most Protestant ecclesial theories, forms, and habits originated, and within which they are deeply interwoven.

Kuyper proposes an inescapable, defining reality for any new institutional church form. In his view, the function of the church is to bring new, heavenly life into God's fallen creation. The regular proclamation of God's Word, which is the seed of that life, must be central to any new church form. This proclamation itself always comes embedded in what the Bible names "calling upon the name of the Lord," that is, liturgy.[31] New forms of Christian community life must always have this institutional aspect, no matter how organic they may strive to be.

Ad de Bruijne

---

29. Richard J. Mouw points in the same direction in *Abraham Kuyper: A Short and Personal Introduction* (Grand Rapids: Eerdmans, 2011), 99–104.

30. Philip L. White, "Globalization and the Mythology of the 'Nation State,'" in *Global History: Interactions Between the Universal and the Local*, ed. A. G. Hopkins (New York: Palgrave Macmillan, 2006), 257–84.

31. See James K. A. Smith, *Desiring the Kingdom: Worship, Worldview, and Cultural Formation* (Grand Rapids: Baker Academic, 2009).

ABBREVIATIONS

GENERAL AND BIBLIOGRAPHIC

AKCR   *Abraham Kuyper: A Centennial Reader*. Edited by James D. Bratt. Grand Rapids: Eerdmans, 1998.

CG   Kuyper, Abraham. *Common Grace*. Translated by Nelson D. Kloosterman and Ed M. van der Maas. Edited by Jordan J. Ballor and Stephen J. Grabill. 3 vols. Bellingham, WA: Lexham Press, 2016–.

ESV   English Standard Version

Inst.   Calvin, John. *Institutes of the Christian Religion* (1559). Edited by John T. McNeill. Translated by Ford Lewis Battles. 2 vols. Philadelphia: Westminster, 1960.

KJV   King James Version

LEB   Lexham English Bible

On the Church   Kuyper, Abraham. *On the Church*. Edited by John Halsey Wood Jr. and Andrew M. McGinnis. Bellingham, WA: Lexham Press, 2016.

PR   Kuyper, Abraham. *Pro Rege: Living under Christ's Kingship*. Edited by John Kok with Nelson D. Kloosterman. Translated by Albert Gootjes. 3 vols. Bellingham, WA: Lexham Press, 2016–.

SV   *Statenvertaling* ("States Translation" of the Dutch Bible, 1637)

OLD TESTAMENT

Gen	Genesis	Song	Song of Songs
Exod	Exodus	Isa	Isaiah
Lev	Leviticus	Jer	Jeremiah
Num	Numbers	Lam	Lamentations
Deut	Deuteronomy	Ezek	Ezekiel
Josh	Joshua	Dan	Daniel
Judg	Judges	Hos	Hosea
Ruth	Ruth	Joel	Joel
1–2 Sam	1–2 Samuel	Amos	Amos
1–2 Kgs	1–2 Kings	Obad	Obadiah
1–2 Chr	1–2 Chronicles	Jonah	Jonah
Ezra	Ezra	Mic	Micah
Neh	Nehemiah	Nah	Nahum
Esth	Esther	Hab	Habakkuk
Job	Job	Zeph	Zephaniah
Psa (Pss)	Psalm(s)	Hag	Haggai
Prov	Proverbs	Zech	Zechariah
Eccl	Ecclesiastes	Mal	Malachi

NEW TESTAMENT

Matt	Matthew	1–2 Thess	1–2 Thessalonians
Mark	Mark	1–2 Tim	1–2 Timothy
Luke	Luke	Titus	Titus
John	John	Phlm	Philemon
Acts	Acts	Heb	Hebrews
Rom	Romans	Jas	James
1–2 Cor	1–2 Corinthians	1–2 Pet	1–2 Peter
Gal	Galatians	1–3 John	1–3 John
Eph	Ephesians	Jude	Jude
Phil	Philippians	Rev	Revelation
Col	Colossians		

COMMENTATIO

TEXT INTRODUCTION

Abraham Kuyper's doctoral dissertation and prize-winning essay exemplifies several lifelong concerns, as well as his early attempt to address them. Like many of his contemporaries, Kuyper lamented the decrepit state of the Dutch church, and he sought a remedy inspired by Friedrich Schleiermacher. In 1860 the theological faculty of the University of Groningen sponsored an essay competition on the subject of the church for the purpose of bringing more attention to it. The fact that the university chose the subject of the church and that Kuyper's essay was the only submission (though no less outstanding and deserving of first prize) perhaps illustrates both the concern for and simultaneous neglect of this subject in the Netherlands.

Kuyper's own conception of the church is a spiritual and moral society united in Christ. Its essence lies not in its outward forms or institutions but in a mystical, spiritual bond. It is a particular society that nonetheless lays claim to the entire world. Kuyper's concern for social ethics also emerges in his early wrestling with the nature of the church. The Dutch church, he believed, had a special bond with the Dutch nation. Kuyper opposed Calvin and championed John à Lasco. He believed that Calvin had misconstrued divine predestination and that Calvin's view had been codified in the Synod of Dort, introducing a foreign idea that diminished the freedom characteristic of the Dutch spirit. John à Lasco, who led the sixteenth-century Dutch exile church in London, better exemplified the Dutch spirit also in evidence in Thomas à Kempis and Erasmus.

This translation is a selection of elements drawn mostly from the third part (which itself has three parts) of the larger work, originally composed in Latin. A horizontal bar represents omitted sections. The original section numbers have been retained so that the corresponding sections in the original may be more easily consulted. These sections capture Kuyper's early views of the doctrine of the church, which would prove significant for the later development of his ideas.

Source: Vree, Jasper, and Johan Zwaan, eds. *Abraham Kuyper's* Commentatio *(1860): The Young Kuyper about Calvin, a Lasco, and the Church*. Vol. 2. Leiden: Brill, 2005. Translated by Todd M. Rester.

COMMENTATIO

A study on a question posed by the order of theologians in a contest of letters.
Publicly appointed for April 15 in the year of our Lord 1859.
Lemma: Do not let Moses speak to me . . . but You speak, O Lord.

The author of this study was A. Kuyper, who finished it within eight months. K.[1]

OVERVIEW

Truly, O most illustrious men, your venerable order could not pose a more suitable or fitting question to students for a contest of letters than what would turn our minds at this very moment to Johannes à Lasco. Our Emden neighbors have just now wreathed him with gladsome leaf on the 300th anniversary [of his death],[2] for which reason they piously honored the memory of this excellent man. Now I offer to you my study on this question. I freely leave to your judgment—which I value most—whether or not

---

1. Kuyper's own annotation at the bottom of the title page.
2. John à Lasco (Jan Łaski, 1499–1560) was a Polish reformer who pastored churches at Emden (east Frisia, the northern border between the Netherlands and Germany) and then, at the invitation of Thomas Cranmer, pastored a church of Dutch refugees in London. Kuyper's 1866 edition of à Lasco's works continues to be a valuable scholarly resource.

the matter might be too hastily treated than is appropriate for the task, but I did not forget that golden Horatian command:

> Take up the timber of a topic, Writers, equal to your strength,
> consider it a long time, doing so at length:
> what thy shoulders would decline to carry
> and what they would bear powerfully.[3]

Even if this little by-product of burning the midnight oil may be lacking such that it does not win the prize, and in your opinion should be cast into eternal oblivion, it still has been sweet and pleasant in my opinion. For nearly a year it yoked me to the remarkable man continuously and familiarly, and our good and great God sustained me with his comfort in the meantime. To him I—being incited to some sense of his kindness that he bestowed upon me in seeing this work through to completion—defer all praise, glory, and honor.

The thought of John Calvin and Johannes à Lasco on the church are compared. It is explained how these may have originated from the history and character of both Reformers as well as how their views both cohere with the rest of their teaching, respectively, and how they should be judged according to the norm of the gospel.

§ 1   Introduction

There is light only in Christ alone.

— I. à Lasco, *On the Sacraments*, fol. 101

On this point all equally agree: The church as it is displayed to us today is feebly wasting away and decrepit, surviving only to become more miserably slothful. And this is no wonder, because the magnificent edifice of orthodox doctrine—on which the church rests as a foundation—collapses half-ruined and day by day proceeds to more ruin. On the other hand, the feeling of Christians regarding the church has been characterized, however gradually, by the opinion that the church must not be abolished; on the contrary, and much more, it must be placed in a position more honored than the older dogmaticians had granted it. The church of the Christian religion is not like some appendage that we might easily lack without great loss. On the contrary, it is the whole of religion—more correctly, it is the ultimate consummation of the highest counsel of God.

---

3. Horace, *Ars Poetica*, lines 38–40.

These two things, even if they are quite different in themselves, must nevertheless equally drive a Christian theologian and powerfully motivate him: (1) that he would desire to investigate the true and genuine notion of the church better and more blessedly; and (2) once [it has been] investigated, that he would desire to bear it out it in his life. Certainly even some theologians, especially the German ones, have thoroughly understood that this is their duty and office; in recent times there have not been so many and such great battles over any other point of the whole Christian religion as there have been over the church. They have not disputed among themselves as harshly as possible and have not generally waged deadly war. So I will remain silent about Löhe, Delitzsch, Klieforth, Rückert, Andersen, Münchmeyer, Hansen, Müller, Flörke, Höfling, Brömel, Harless, and Evers (persons to whom Schenkel has recently attached himself). All these have been disgusted with the contemporary condition of the church, and each has desired to offer his own remedy for the declining church.

For this reason they principally divide into three parties: Namely, some fall into the opinion that the church has already lost its life—an opinion that in our way of thinking, of course, is inadequate. Others suppose that the most ancient condition of the church, such as the one flourishing in the age of the Reformation, must be restored again in its entirety. These have more astutely argued against the new change that the church is undergoing, striving with all their might that at last such a church may escape—a church of such a kind that ought to exist according to God's and Christ's intention. In such a great uproar of nearly the whole of Christianity, it is truly remarkable that for such a long time the majority of the theologians of our fatherland, having been lulled to sleep by an incomprehensible lethargy, have scarcely—and not even scarcely—cared about the matter of the church. The majority of the idle persons who praise the conduct of the age lament the ruin of the church; even worse, in other churches that are entirely unconcerned about salvation, the church wastes away and is not even discussed. Indeed, if you exclude the one study of Kist,[4] I do not see anywhere that Dutch theologians have provided for the church except in the University of Groningen, which strenuously and by all means has sustained this divinely entrusted part of theology over the course of many years. Therefore, for this reason the argument

---

4. Nicolaas Christiaan Kist (1793–1859) was a Reformed pastor and church historian at Leiden University.

of our study, which likewise calls attention back to the church, is already greatly commended.

But if someone asks whether there is a certain path and method by which we must make progress toward the desired end of that controversy concerning the church, who does not see that we must resort especially to history? Only history will teach us what was vicious and depraved in the old system of the church; only history reveals to us as well the clear source of the gospel from which the healthier and purer doctrine of the church ought to be imbibed; finally, only history will lead us by the hand back to the more felicitous times of the church, so that our ancestors may teach us a better opinion of the church. The matter itself tells us to turn to Calvin so that in the very first beginnings and traces, as it were, we may discover the vices under which the national church so miserably labors. Although the whole aim of Calvin's plan in theological matters was supported by the public authorities and reigned supreme in the Reformed church of the Netherlands for nearly two centuries, the poison in the deadly system of Calvin himself in fact cannot escape notice—that poison which has been poured into the church and by which the church gradually lost its power to live. Therefore, a more meticulous study of Calvin's thought on the church will indicate the chief causes of this most serious disease. We should also inspect anyone who allegedly possesses a cure. Now, indeed, those most joyful times of the national church immediately come to mind, when in the dullness of nearly the whole of Europe, the vigor of Christian life splendidly boiled up in our Netherlands; when idle people were not peacefully following the opinions of others in divine things, but they themselves were advancing onto the stage, and they were elevating others because they were imitating their example; when in the course of one century we were enriched by three—not to mention many more—of our most precious lights, namely, Kempis, Wessel, and Erasmus; and, indeed, when the Synod of Dort had not yet imposed upon our national church that foreign way of thinking in its horrid decree and, with its advance, suffocated and extinguished the entire life of the church.[5] After the political upheaval of things, our church, which began at the beginning of this

---

5. Thomas à Kempis, Wessel Gansfort, and Erasmus were fifteenth- and six-teenth-century Dutch church reformers who advocated a more heartfelt piety and whose approach was favored by the nineteenth-century Groningen movement over overly rigid doctrinal formulas like that of the Synod of Dort. Moreover, the Groningen movement did not cherish these reformers for their Protestantism

century,[6] has been purged and revived such that it drinks of life fully and assumes a strength and vigor that must bring it back to the very source of life. Then it would tirelessly continue and advance what our forefathers had begun so auspiciously. Moreover, in addition, at the forefront of the rest of the gems of the national church, Johannes à Lasco—whom we should diligently hear—commends himself to us. No one has produced a greater treatise on the church than him, and he lived at the time when Calvin's gloomy theology had already begun to be disseminated more and more widely. Yet so that we may not be induced by love of country to fall from one error into another, we must rightly take care that we never set down any touchstone and fixed rule other than what the gospel supplies to us. Whatever controversies may arise regarding the church, these must be adjudicated and directed according to the divine plan of the gospel.

If we have rightly explained these things, then our study, which displays the right way to this threefold goal, will by no means be of minor importance. We have, of course, compared the opinions of Calvin and à Lasco concerning the church so that we might bring into the brightest light how much the mode of thinking imported from elsewhere differs from the Dutch mode of thinking. We have also immediately inquired as accurately as possible into its life and character so that we might detect the source both of those things that incur censure and those that seem worthy of praise. Finally, we have endeavored to be taught by the mind of Christ, so that it would not be far from the genuine notion of the church, and so we might follow his footsteps more closely. But if now at long last with our study in some measure complete, we are asked what sort of opinion history would give, it seems that it must be suggested that the sooner we would drive out with all our might whatever reeks of Calvinism, striving with all our strength and power for the example of our forefathers, the sooner such a church would arise among us from the renewed font of the gospel—one that would provoke our neighbors to envy. But also let us add reasons why it seems that this must be done. In the correction of holy things, in every way Calvin surpassed the most experienced theologian in celebrating the supreme majesty of God, such that he miserably crushed

---

(none of them were Protestants) but for their Dutch heritage. In contrast, Calvin, with his supposedly decretal theology, was thought to have introduced into the Netherlands a foreign way of thinking.

6. The Dutch Reformed Church, the so-called national church (*volkskerk*), was established by William I in 1815.

the character and rights of man. He rejected whatever the Roman church had imported from paganism—namely, whatever exalted creatures beyond their very own creator. He strenuously refrained from traces of Judaism, although he also cultivated it the most. Whoever—not controlled by human nature's reason—only has regard for God, necessarily becomes a Jew. Fortunately, Johannes à Lasco sailed between Scylla and Charybdis and brought into the Christian church neither paganism, which diminishes the honor and majesty of God, nor Judaism, which diminishes the right and advantage of man; rather, being uniquely devoted to Christ as both God and man, he carefully kept his method to the form of the gospel. Moreover, Thomas à Kempis, who prophetically divined the danger which Calvinism posed to the national church, excellently testified that the character of the Dutch people is inclined toward and prone to the gospel and away from Judaism. He declared to his contemporaries, "Do not let Moses speak to me . . . but You speak, O Lord," which words are from book 3, chapter 2 of *The Imitation of Christ*.

§ 2   THE PLAN OF THE ARGUMENT

The very question which we are approaching has been conceived of so simply and clearly that it will freely show us the way that this study may safely progress. The thought of John Calvin and Johannes à Lasco on the church ought to be compared, must be explained historically, and finally the norm of the gospel will judge between them. Then, because a threefold question is set before us, the solution will also be divided into three parts.[7]

THE VIEWS OF JOHN CALVIN AND JOHANNES À LASCO JUDGED ACCORDING TO THE NORM OF THE GOSPEL

§ 164   INTRODUCTION

The matter now comes to the third and last part of the study. The opinions of John Calvin and Johannes à Lasco on the church, having been

---

7. The three parts of Kuyper's work are an exposition of Calvin's (Part 1), and then à Lasco's (Part 2) ecclesiologies, followed by Kuyper's analysis and critique (Part 3). What follows from this point comes from Part 3. Part 3 is further divided into three smaller parts, which have their own section and chapter divisions.

investigated properly from their writings and their method of treatment, compared carefully and genetically from their life and character, and illustrated from their doctrinal connection, now at last will be entrusted to the gospel's judgment. This part of the inquiry is a sweeter pleasure to us because we dwell upon the gospel and most excellently substitute the clear and serene font of the perennial gospel for the frequently sordid and quite filthily polluted source that the writings of the Reformers offer. Yet, so that we might not immediately hasten to criticism (reason, which persuades us, forbids this), we must set forth a few things concerning the grounds of our judgment.

First, therefore, it will not seem wrong to inquire regarding the extent to which our Reformers received or in fact rejected the judgment of the gospel. In this regard, indeed, it must be frankly confessed that à Lasco, who everywhere customarily derives his points from the source of the gospel, would not be judged disobedient if anyone should desire to judge and examine his opinions according to the rule of the gospel. A very different method is found in Calvin, who indeed would also most freely accept the judgment of the gospel provided that he might adjoin to it the Old Testament, to which he is accustomed to appeal constantly, since he received the custom and practice of that ancient church under the Israelites in an entirely intact and holy veneration. Therefore, the judgment of the gospel admits à Lasco, and in part also reasonably admits even Calvin.

But what concept of the gospel do they have in mind? The term *gospel* is especially understood as the New Testament, whereby it is chiefly juxtaposed with the Old Testament. Thus, if our Reformers appeal to the gospel, they especially have the teaching of Christ and the apostles in view—or, if you prefer, they customarily cite this or that obvious verse in the New Testament in the likeness of a classical witness, which would always bind the church of whatever time or place. The question of whether in this way they may have incorrectly pursued the right method of investigating the truth is certainly in need of an extensive demonstration in our time. For this reason it is sufficient to briefly set forth what method we are pursuing in our judgment. Moreover, to us the gospel means that joyful message of God's fullest revelation in Christ, the kind that is known historically from the account of Christ's life, and of the apostles' thoughts concerning that sublime act of God. The gospel neither decreed rules nor did it sanction certain laws that, being reduced into a system, might be forever imposed on the Christian church. On the contrary, the gospel is the beginning and soul of life; it displays certain inviolable first principles and foundations to which that inward essence of the Christian church must always and everywhere be brought back—or rather, on the very question beautifully and most truly posed, it supplies the norm.

Accordingly, from an assiduous study in consideration of those things that Christ and the apostles confessed or cherished, we are attempting to elicit the entire counsel of God and Christ concerning the church. We desire to be instructed in the first principles and outlines of this church and, supported by them, in those truest marks of the church of Christ. Those marks would remain if you were to remove and take away whatever has been said or done according to a certain time or place.

We must inquire by these principles, when duly constituted: (1) whether in the opinions of Calvin and à Lasco these principles are found intact; (2) whether these opinions that they have formulated concerning the church properly correspond to these principles, or in fact are more or less compatible with them. Furthermore, in judging this, as much as possible we will pursue a procedure so that in the aforementioned exposition of these figures we may consider what is from the true mind of Christ and the apostles; and so that we may earnestly inquire what the gospel approves of in both, what it condemns in both, and finally what it either approves of or condemns in one or the other.

---

§ 166   ON THE NOTION OF THE CHURCH ACCORDING TO THE MIND OF THE GOSPEL, OR, ON THE BASIS FOR JUDGMENT

Since by far there is no ubiquitous agreement or unanimous voice heard in establishing what sort of church Christ wanted and expected, it is necessarily required in the introduction of the judgment to consider very briefly what sort of opinion we have concerning the church according to the mind of Christ. Yet let no one marvel that we do not cite anything in the margin as proof. We have decided to refrain from these kinds of hodgepodge methods, because below in the judgment itself they will be supported expressly by testimonies of the gospel, which we have endeavored to set forth here in a manner neatly fastened together and joined with glue.[8]

Moreover, the Christian church, according to the thought of the gospel, is a spiritual brotherhood of the children of God—or rather, a religious and moral society founded by Christ according to God's eternal counsel and good pleasure. Without any particular visible external form, it appears only under the form of a friendly association and, therefore, has no external marks or characteristics but is recognized by a new principle and method of perception, thought, and will; by eagerness for pursuing truth and virtue; and, at the very least, by the way that they mutually embrace each other with the love of a friend. God founded this fellowship through Christ to this end: that more and more the darkness might be dispersed and splendidly the clearest light of truth might brilliantly begin to dawn through the scattered fog. Thus, discord, wrath, hatred, and whatever else has customarily divided mortals might pass away, and on the contrary, the essence of God, which consists of love, might all the more rain down on the human race today drop by drop. Then at last the image of God in humankind might begin to shine forth gradually with greater force not only in those who are members of this fellowship, but also the multitude of human beings throughout the whole earth might press toward and arrive at true holiness and might achieve the greatest perfection until "you all are sons of our Father and should be perfect as our Father in heaven is perfect" [see Matt 5:48].

Christ, whom God sent in the fullness of time, is actually the living bond of this union. He unites mortals in intimate friendship both with himself and through himself with God; and by a new principle of living and acting, which he introduced, he joins friends together with each other by the most delightful knot of love. God is personally in charge of this fellowship through Jesus Christ, whom he established as the king of this eternal kingdom, and Christ advances it today more and more by his own divine Spirit, so that the end is attained. There is a duty incumbent upon these fellow companions that, by an assiduous preaching of the truth that is in Christ, they may both inwardly perceive as well as experience for themselves that very same truth and may disseminate and propagate it

---

8. *Note by the author*: We have consulted A. Diemont, *De ecclesia Christianae Christi mente disquisitio* (Groningen, 1844); the most brilliant Pareau, *De leer van Paulus omtrent den aard van Jezus kerk* in WIL [*Waarheid in liefde*] 1842, 711–750 and N.C. Kist, *De christelijke kerk op aarde*, editionem laudatam.

far and wide. Moreover, these fellow companions of this church have this commandment chiefly so that by an indefatigable and nearly perfect imitation of Christ himself, in the vigorous pursuit of virtue, and also by rendering mutual charity and love, they might all the more bewilder others with their reproach of evil, draw them to themselves, and finally instill in them a love of Christ himself. According to their own strength and the talents of mind granted to them by God, each one ought to strive with all strength and might so that one may advance the common salvation of all. In summary, as they rejoice in and enjoy the liberty of fellow companions, no domination is endured, but all consider themselves as equals and as having the same position, taking heed of this one thing especially: that they would not inflict a loss of dignity and order. Those who manifest a pious wisdom lead the troop; the weaker ones follow. Initiation into the communion of this fellowship occurs in baptism, and in memory of Christ they celebrate a fraternal meal.

§ 167   THE PATH THROUGH THE COURSE OF AGES THAT THE DOGMA
CONCERNING THE CHURCH HAS TRAVELED

From this very opinion of the gospel concerning the church, which has been poorly understood and greatly deformed, all manner of opinions about the church have sprung up—as many as the Christian church has produced through the course of ages. The opinions of Calvin and à Lasco call us back from the furthest point to this very source. Yet, because their opinions only sprung from the font of the gospel through various streams, it is clear that it would be advantageous to note the various opinions in the passage of time that grew up in the Christian church. However, the Leeuwarden minister Diemont excellently supplies us with a survey of this sort in his learned commentary *De Ecclesia Christiana e Christi mente*, which we therefore follow to the letter as a compendium, with little changed.[9]

Thus, "By the Christian church, the apostles understood a moral and religious society in which all participants are animated by the divine spirit, united to God and Christ, as well as with each other."[10] The apostolic fathers referred to the Christian church as a visible society with an

---

9. Kuyper refers here to the dissertation of Abrahamus Diemont, *Disquisitionem de Ecclesia Christiana e Christi Mente* (Groningen: J. B. Wolters, 1844).

10. *Note by the author*: Compare Diemont, *De ecclesia*, 26; Kist, *De chr. kerk*, 97–99; Pareau and Hofstede de Groot, *Compendium dogmatices et apologetices*, 209.

external guidance, erected by Christ, outside of which there is no salvation, whose members, distinguished by their purity of faith and holiness of morals, had been united to Christ by the fraternal bond of love.[11]
"The Greek church presented itself as a philosophical school resting upon
a certain system of doctrine whose members were glued together by the
unity of faith" (the Orthodox Church).[12] "The Latin church presented itself

---

11. *Note by the author*: Compare Kist, *De christelijke kerk*, 199ff.; Hagenbach, *De ontwik-
    kelingsgesch.*, 170; Diemont wrote, "as the kingdom of Christ, in whom all have been
    joined with God and Christ as well as with each other, in the common observance
    of the commands of God in the unity of love" (*De ecclesia*, 26); this opinion by no
    means differs in the least from ours, which therefore we will attempt to present
    briefly. We have said that they had commended the church as a fellowship "visi-
    ble by an external direction": which we prove from the words of Ignatius (*To the
    Trallians* 3): "Let everyone respect the deacons ... the bishop ... and the presbyters
    ... Without these no group can be called a church" (compare 1 *Clement* 38; Ignatius,
    To the Ephesians 3-4); "established by Christ" (1 *Clement* 42; *Shepherd of Hermas*,
    Similitudes 9.12; and 1 *Clement* 58). Outside the church there is no salvation: "For
    it is better for you to be found small but included in the flock of Christ ... yet be
    excluded from his hope ... I therefore will laugh at your destruction" (1 *Clement* 57);
    "If anyone follows a schismatic, he will not inherit the kingdom of God" (Ignatius,
    To the Philadelphians 3; *To the Trallians* 7); whose members are notable by the purity
    of their faith: "Now if those who do such things physically are put to death, how
    much more if by evil teaching someone corrupts faith in God" (Ignatius, *To the
    Ephesians* 16; compare *To the Philadelphians* 3; *Shepherd of Hermas*, Visions 3.7);
    and by the holiness of their morals: "to the holy church" (*Martyrdom of Polycarp*
    391); "whose God is their belly, who desire earthly things ... who have a form of
    godliness ... who are enemies of the savior, children of destruction" (Ignatius, *To
    the Magnesians* 9; compare *Epistle of Barnabas* 19; *Shepherd of Hermas*, Visions 3.8;
    2 *Clement* 4; 7); joined by the most tender bond of love: "Therefore as children of the
    light of truth flee from division. ... Where the shepherd is, there follow like sheep"
    (Ignatius, *To the Philadelphians* 2); "that all things might be harmonious in unity"
    (Ignatius, *To the Ephesians* 5); "in Jesus Christ love one another always" (Ignatius,
    To the Magnesians 6; compare *Shepherd of Hermas*, Visions 3.2; Similitudes 8.10;
    9.13; 9.16). Moreover, in fact the same was considered the universal church, as is
    evident from the adjective "catholic," which is attributed to the church (Ignatius,
    To the Smyrneans 8; *Martyrdom of Polycarp* 8; 19); furthermore, it is evident from
    the metaphor of the tower, under which the church is set forth in *Shepherd of
    Hermas* [Visions, 3]. [Ed. note: Here, where available, quotes from the Apostolic
    Fathers have been provided from *The Apostolic Fathers: English Translations*, ed.
    J. B. Lightfoot and J. R. Harmer, rev. Michael W. Holmes, 2nd ed. (Grand Rapids:
    Baker, 1999).]
12. *Note by the author*: Hofstede de Groot, *Over de namen der drie christelijke hoofdkerken*
    in WIL 1852 II, 417ff.; Kist, *De christelijke kerk*, 211ff.; Pareau and Hofstede de Groot,
    Compendium dogmatices et apologetices, 210.

as the city of God, in which the true worshipers of God are united by external bonds, outside of which there is no salvation" (the Catholic Church).[13] "The Reformed presented itself as a spiritual assembly of Christians, or as a congregation of saints, in which the gospel is correctly taught and the sacraments are rightly administered, ... in which all who adhere to the gospel live, although they are less united to each other than to God and Christ" (the Evangelical Church).[14] At last, Schleiermacher has brought to light the truest notion of the church from the dark gloom, and has uncovered the innate strength of the church in Christians' mutual union and closest cohesion in Christ.[15] From this point in time, the dawn of a better, more blessed, and more prosperous condition of the church has gradually and little by little dawned and begun to shine.

But if Calvin and à Lasco must be given their own place in our survey, without a doubt both must be located in the line of the Reformers, yet in such a way that Calvin should be more accurately judged as having departed from the dogma of the Latins concerning the church, even more than the others who with him tried to correct holy things. Conversely, à Lasco must be said to have in a certain way foretold and entered upon a better notion of the church, which at long last has begun to gain strength and vigor in our age, for which reason you may rightly say that he was Schleiermacher's forerunner.

---

13. *Note by the author:* Hagenbach, *De ontwikkelingsgesch.*, 318, 488; Kist, *De chr. Kerk*, 217ff.; Pareau and Hofstede de Groot, *Compendium dogmatices et apologetices*, 210.

14. *Note by the author:* Hagenbach, *De ontwikkelingsgesch.*, 662; Kist, *De christelijke kerk*, 223ff.; Diemont, *De ecclesia*, 26; Hofstede de Groot, *Geschiedkundige opmerkingen over de bijzondere eigenaardigheid der christelijke kerk* in *WIL* 1838 I, 95ff.

15. *Note by the author:* Compare his renowned oration: *Ueber das gesellige in der Religion oder über Kirche und Priesterthum* in *Ueber Religion* (Berlin: 1843), 174–243; and *Der christliche Glaube* (Berlin: 1835), 1:6–120; especially see p. 33: "Fellowship, then, is demanded by every person's indwelling consciousness of their kind, which finds its satisfaction only in the emergence from the confines of their own personality, and takes up the facts of other personalities into their own"!

PART I - WHICH IS PREPARATORY. ON THE DOGMAS RELATING TO THE CHURCH, AND ON THE ORIGIN OF THE CHURCH

CHAPTER 1 - DOGMAS CONCERNING THE CHURCH

THE DOGMA CONCERNING THE INVISIBLE AND VISIBLE CHURCH[16] § 169

The dogma concerning the twofold church—one visible and the other, in fact, invisible—closely coheres with the preceding section. Indeed, empirically the church is neither one, nor holy, nor catholic. Therefore, those who believe that such a church exists, yet do not see it with their eyes, necessarily propose an invisible church. After the example of Augustine, Calvin stands as the primary patron of this dogma that was entirely ignored by à Lasco. Thus, let us see what the gospel estimates of this trite distinction. In the opinion of the gospel, from what I see, neither Christ nor the apostles ever actually thought about such a twofold church. In fact, the true opinion of Christ is exceedingly averse to it. First, we will defend our assertion, then we will try to rebut the objections of our adversaries.

The church that is adorned with invisibility by all the patrons of this dogma is celebrated as the mystical body of Christ. Yet even if we attend to this similitude in which Christ compares himself to a vine and his followers to branches (John 15:1-6), we see some branches bearing fruit and others not bearing fruit, which are nevertheless "in me" (John 15:6), that is, in Christ. This proves that the body of Christ embraces the wicked as much as the good. With the same sense, Paul teaches: "For as many of you as were baptized into Christ have put on Christ" [Gal 3:27], because the evil and the good are equally initiated by baptism. Furthermore, the kingdom of heaven, if you would distinguish between both churches, will necessarily be the invisible church. However, nearly all Christ's parables

---

16. *Note by the author*: Compare Julius Müller, *Die unsichtbare Kirche* in *Deutsche Zeitschrift für christliche Wissenschaft und christliches Leben* 1850 no. 2–5, 11–15; 27–30, who upholds the contrary opinion; *Zeitschrift für die historische Theologie* 1840, 1st ed., 32; Krehl, *Luthers Begriff von der Kirche*; Schleiermacher, *Der chr. Glaube* II inp., 246ff., 440ff.; A. Ritschl, *Die Begriffe sichtbare und unsichtbare Kirche* in *Theologische Studien und Kritiken* 1859, 2nd ed., 189ff.; Münchmeyer, *Das Dogma von der sichtbaren und unsichtbaren Kirche* (Göttingen, 1854), see Theil II. Zustimmende, 102–44 and especially §18 (133–44); *Hansen*, 5,72–85; and Kist, *De christelijke kerk*, 213ff.

concerning this kingdom abundantly teach that true believers dwell in this kingdom intermingled with hypocrites. If one listens to John the Baptist, in the winnowing fork there is grain and also chaff (Matt 3:12). Likewise, in the field both wheat and tares sprout (Matt 13:30); in the nets dropped into the sea one gathers bad fish together with good (Matt 13:47); and the parables of the wedding (Matt 22:2–14), ten virgins (Matt 25:1–13), and the good shepherd (John 10:1–16; compare Luke 15:2–7; Matt 25:31–46) plainly teach the same thing. What are we to think then? In the body of Christ, in the kingdom of heaven, and in Christ's opinion, the good and the wicked dwell intermingled. However, the invisible church does not include any except the good, from which it follows that a church of this sort is nothing but a fantasy, contrary to Christ's counsel on the matter.

But let us listen also to the other side. Our adversaries especially refer to Ephesians 2:20–22; 4:4–6; 5:25–27; 1 Peter 2:4–5; Hebrews 12:23 (taken with Luke 10:20 and Philippians 4:3); and Luke 17:20. These words that we read from Ephesians 2:22, "You also are being built together into a dwelling place for God and the Spirit,"[17] are about the visible church, and it is obvious that what has been said in the context burns with this. Of course, the letter was given to the visible Ephesian church. Who would contend that it was given to the invisible one? Therefore, those Paul speaks to when he says "you" are none other than the members of the visible church. Moreover, what precedes this in verse 19? "So then you are no longer strangers and aliens, but you are fellow citizens with the saints and members of the household of God" [Eph 2:19] and then immediately the phrase "being built" follows, which therefore is in apposition to the pronoun "you." What they object—that the church plainly is not yet and in no way can be called holy—falls apart with the phrase "a holy temple in the Lord," if we observe that this is not about the individual members of the church but the whole church, as this was said in a certain way with respect to the church in its entirety.

Ephesians 4:4, "One body and one Spirit," does not favor their distinction either. No one could easily contend that there was, in fact, such great harmony in the Ephesian church, and this is not what the words of Paul mean. He does not write, "You are one body," but, in fact, "I urge you to walk in a manner worthy of the calling" (Eph 4:1). Therefore, he describes

---

17. Kuyper's rendering is provided here; most modern translations render the last words of the verse as "by the Spirit" or "in the Spirit."

to them the perfect condition of the church so that, in admiration of it, they would avoid being so carried away from it in the future. The "one baptism" (Eph 4:5) is like a finger pointing out the visible church to us.

The same thing is entirely applicable in Ephesians 5:25–27. It is not said that the church is now currently "without spot, blemish, or wrinkle," but only this: that "Christ loved the church and gave himself up for her so that he might present the church to himself," and thus the counsel of God and Christ explains what sort of church she will be at some point in the future.

Among those things which are read in 1 Peter 2:5, these words especially are customarily pressed and urged: "You yourselves like living stones are being built up as a spiritual house, to be a holy priesthood." Indeed, these words considered in themselves give such an appearance, but if, on the contrary, they are explained from the context, they have another sense entirely. For with these words he begins his exhortation: "So put away all malice and all deceit … long for the pure spiritual milk … if indeed you have tasted that the Lord is good you come to him … like living stones being built up as a spiritual house." Thus, he describes the same persons as "living stones" and as having evil and deceit (which of course ought to be abolished). Therefore, the saying is paraenetic or exhortatory, which explains in what way these things ought to be ascribed to the church. With respect to Hebrews 12:23, our adversaries believe that the phrase "the assembly of the firstborn who are enrolled in heaven" defends the doctrine of the invisible church. Who then are called "the firstborn"? Only in this passage does this term refer to human beings, and it allows a double signification, because these are understood either as those who are the first of all that have been led to Christ (see Eph 1:12) or those who of course have been acknowledged as brothers of Christ and occupy the first place among the rest of the creatures (see Col 1:15; Jas 1:18). Therefore, the term "firstborn" is not a matter that is settled in the least since it can refer to both parts. But what of those whose names are enrolled in heaven (see Luke 10:20; Phil 4:3)? I do not see why all those who have been baptized would not have their names written in heaven, unless we have considered them as those whose names have not been written in the book of life. The book of Revelation teaches us that none but the most disgraceful sinners have been deprived of this privilege, the sort who worship the devil (Rev 13:8), who were "thrown into the lake of fire" (Rev 20:15). Moreover, we can easily conceive in our minds that the apostolic church has not yet been purged of these sorts of blemishes.

But I truly admit that I have been firmly persuaded that in this verse there is not even one trace regarding the church properly speaking. Heavenly glory and blessedness, where everything palpable passes away and the highest divinity is worshiped with the mind and spirit, is especially opposed to the sensual and to local religion, as well as the ceremonial worship of the Jews. "You have come to Mount Zion and to the city of the living God, the heavenly Jerusalem, and to innumerable angels," says the author [Heb 12:22]. No reasonable person will deny that all these things must refer to heavenly things above. Why? The Palestinian Jerusalem is juxtaposed with the heavenly city, and in the same way the congregation of the Israelites is plainly juxtaposed with the other heavenly congregation of the firstborn, whose names have been recorded in the book of life, which, if our interpretation is valid, must not be translated as "church" (*kerk*) or "congregation" (*gemeente*), but as "public assembly" (*volksvergadering*), and thus no mention is made of either a visible or invisible church.

But for our adversaries an impregnable fortress yet remains: "The kingdom of God is not coming in ways that can be observed, nor will they say, 'Look, here it is!' or 'There!'" [Luke 17:20-21]. Although they argue eloquently and reasonably, this passage cannot vindicate the invisible church. Surely one may see for oneself how this passage refutes those who cannot see any other church than that exclusive form of the church which they call, in the vernacular, a denomination. However, whoever holds that the church is a spiritual society not bound to any particular form will have the best response. And so the gospel condemns in Calvin that wild and crippled distinction of a twofold church; and on the other hand, with exceptional praises it adorns à Lasco—who stated that there is nothing except one undivided and unbroken church of Christians.

PART II - THE CHURCH CONSIDERED IN ITSELF

SECTION 1 - ON THE NOTION OF THE CHURCH

§ 172   THE CHARACTER OF THE CHURCH
In the brief compendium in which we desired to treat in a straightforward manner in §166 the intention of the gospel, the church's own and proper character was revealed in this: it is certainly a fraternal fellowship. That this was the mind of Christ and the apostles is aptly demonstrated in the

following way. A fellowship necessarily arises and appears from many people being united into one certain thing, from which, with a common practice in a united force, they aim at one and the same thing. Moreover, for those who have been clothed with Christ, it is necessary that they should be a certain common entity, who are described by Paul completely in a beautiful way as "one and the same Spirit" (1 Cor 12:11; compare 12:13, 4, 9; 2 Cor 4:13; 12:18; 1 Cor 6:17; Eph 2:18; 4:4; Phil 1:27; John 17:6, 9–10, 12, 14, 22; Matt 12:49)—that new principle of feeling and thinking that was in Christ and the power innate to him that he transfers to the human race. They all love "the same Lord" in common (1 Cor 12:5; John 10:16; Eph 4:5; 1 Tim 2:5), adore the same God (1 Cor 12:6; Matt 23:9; 12:29; John 8:41; 14:1; 1 Cor 8:4; Gal 3:20), "are being transformed into the same image" (2 Cor 3:18; compare Rom 1:23), and are "engaged in the same conflict" (Phil 1:30). "You also should be glad" (Phil 2:18), and "you suffered the same things," (1 Thess 2:14; Acts 14:15; Jas 5:17; 1 Cor 12:26), agreeing in the Lord (Phil 4:2), having "unity of mind [and] sympathy," (1 Pet 3:8; Phil 2:2), who all commonly "reign in life through the one man Jesus Christ" (Rom 5:17), partaking of one bread (1 Cor 10:17), being initiated in the same baptism (1 Cor 12:13; Eph 4:5), "therefore all have died" (2 Cor 5:14), by which there is one faith (Eph 4:5; John 14:1), "one heart and one soul" (Acts 4:32), and finally "you are called to ... one hope" (Eph 4:4; [compare] John 14:3; 16:33).

Surely among human beings who have so much and such great things in common, there cannot help but arise the most intimate union, a fellowship in the truest sense, which both Christ and his apostles perceived quite clearly. Even if they never employed the term "fellowship" (*societas*) in explaining the innate character of the church (except that John said that "we have fellowship with one another"; 1 John 1:7; compare 1:3; Heb 13:16; 2 Cor 9:13; Acts 11:42), nevertheless, those who are in the church are not each considered individually; rather, as Christ himself entreated the Father, they are one "just as we are one" [John 17:22]. Thus, he calls those who believe in him the friends of the one bridegroom (Matt 9:15), the crowd of friends (John 15:14), or even depicts those who believe in him under the imagery of a vine (Matt 20:1–16) or a flock of sheep (John 21:15–17; 10:2, 11, 14, 16; Luke 12:32; Matt 18:12; Luke 15:4). Paul considered the mark of this fellowship when he calls the church God's field (1 Cor 3:9), God's house (1 Cor 3:16; Eph 2:21; 1 Tim 3:15), the body of Christ (Eph 1:23), members of the household of God (Eph 2:19), citizens of one city, "in one body" (Rom 12:4–8; 1 Cor 12:12), or the wife of one husband [1 Tim 5:9];

and Peter also employs the image of royal priests and a beloved people (1 Pet 2:9). Finally, what can be eloquently and evidently thought other than what Paul said, "You are all one in Christ" (Gal 3:28), so that you would offer your heart to God and glorify God with one voice (Rom 15:6)?

Nevertheless, to the fellowship that must be spoken of in the universal church, we therefore have added the adjective "fraternal," because its omission would do no slight harm. In fact, Christ and the apostles customarily set forth such a great and beautiful economy of God so that of course the kingdom of heaven is a vast family, whose *paterfamilias* is God himself. He decreed through Christ our older brother to closely unite Christ's younger brethren to himself. At this point it is applicable that Christ is especially accustomed to call those who believe in him by the name of brother (Matt 5:22–24, 47; 7:3–5; 10:21; 12:50; 18:15, 21, 35; 25:40; 28:10; Mark 3:35; 13:12; Luke 6:41–42; 7:21; 15:27, 35; 17:3; 22:32; John 20:17; 21:23)—those whom he willed to be united by the most vigorous bond of love.[18] The apostles Paul,[19] James,[20] and John,[21] but especially Peter,[22] deliberately followed the example of their master. Happily, Peter even employed the word "brotherhood" in completely defining the character of the church (1 Pet 2:17; 5:9), and together with Paul chiefly impressed "brotherly love" upon Christians (1 Pet 3:8, 1:22; twice in 2 Pet 1:7; Rom 12:10; 1 Thess 4:9).

With these things duly examined, surely no one will deny that according to Christ's intention the church must deservedly be called a fraternal fellowship [*fraterna societas*]. But if we might wish to judge the thought of Calvin and à Lasco, one evidently detects on all counts enough to condemn Calvin according to the gospel, who rather reforged the orthodox school of the Greeks in the church for us, and who wretchedly overlooked the character of the church and entirely misunderstood it. Moreover, on the contrary, à Lasco is to be praised; he admirably understood the intention of the gospel on this point as he depicted the fellowship in the church

---

18. *Note by the author*: "You are all brothers," Matt 23:8.

19. *Note by the author*: Acts 13:26, 38; 20:32; 21:17; 22:1; 28:17; Rom 1:13; 7:1; 8:12; 9:3; 10:1; 11:25; 12:1; 14:10, 13, 15, 21; 15:14, 30; 16:17; and 94 times in the rest of the epistles. Pay special attention to 1 Cor 6:8: "But you yourselves wrong and defraud even your own brothers!"

20. *Note by the author*: Jas 1:2, 9, 16, 19; 2:1, 5, 14; 3:1, 10, 12; three times in 4:11; 5:7, 9, 10, 12, 19.

21. *Note by the author*: 1 John 2:7, 9–11; 3:10, 12–17; 4:20–21; 5:16; 3 John 3, 5, 10; Rev 1:9; 6:11; 12:10.

22. *Note by the author*: 1 Pet 5:12; 2 Pet 1:10; 3:15; Acts 1:16; 2:29, 37; 3:17; 6:3; 7:26; 15:7.

according to its true meaning and thoroughly understood and realized this and fixed the mark of brotherhood close to the nature of the church.[23]

THE BOND OF THE CHURCH   § 173

So that various things may be collected into one thing, a bond is required. Or if you prefer the image of a building, unless it is built upon a solid foundation, it would fall down quickly. Thus also, no one will readily call into question that the members of the church have been joined by a certain and fixed bond. Therefore, we must discuss this very bond from the intent of the gospel so that the idea of the church may be understood better and perceived more clearly. Moreover, this bond (if I am permitted to use the clearest words of Hofstede de Groot) "is not the corpus of holy dogmas, depending upon the advances of philosophy; it is not philosophy, with its gradually greater worship of the human race, that must always explain it further. It is something greater, more sublime, and more efficacious. It is a stimulus and principle of understanding, feeling, and living; it is the most fertile fodder of conducting life in the new heavens and new earth; it is the air and breath from heaven to earth; ... it is power that has proceeded from God destined for each one to acquire salvation," that living principle, by which all are animated and driven, and which truly must be considered the bond of true ecclesiastic unity.[24] Or even—if you were to pay attention to the gospel—Jesus Christ himself can be established as the binding agent of the fellowship of the church. He in fact must be the lively center of the whole organism of the church; he is like the hub of the wheel, by whose rotations and circular motions the entire effort of the church receives its impulse and is moved. He is that splendid sun, whose shining radiance glitteringly illuminates the whole church body, by whose glowing heat the heart of the whole church is warmed and inflamed.

---

23. *Note by the author*: See J.F. van Oordt I.G. filius, *Disputatio theologica de religion christiana ad coniunctionis et societatis studia alenda et promovenda, cum aptissima tum efficacissima* (Trajectiad Rhenum, 1821); Pareau and Hofstede de Groot, *Compendium dogmatices et apologetices* §90, 213; Pareau, *Een woord over evangelische opbouwing der kerk* in WIL 1851 IV, 792ff.; most famously Hofstede de Groot, *Institutiones theologiae naturalis* §37, 231ff.; Coolhaas van der Woude, *De kerk de moeder der geloovigen* in WIL 1857 III, 415ff.

24. Petrus Hofstede de Groot (1802-86) was one of the early leaders of the Groningen movement and professor at the University of Groningen, which sponsored the contest for which Kuyper's essay was written. Against rationalism, Hofstede de Groot championed a romantic religion of the heart.

Now, in this well-founded illustration the thing itself is proclaimed. The bond of domestic society has been born from the blood of the same father. When the head of that family dies, the fellowship is immediately broken and collapses. The bond of a philosophical school is some excellent person, whose wisdom far excels that of his contemporaries, who commends his own teaching to his followers. Depending on whether his teaching stands or falls, either the school will flourish, or it will topple headlong into destruction as soon as it is revealed and rejected as false. The domestic life is ruptured and ruined, because the father, who was the bond, departs from among the living. The school that loses its vim and vigor, because of the common bond of the spirit in another certain and more outstanding way of life, dies. But, therefore, if we see that the church has been founded by Christ and animated by his spirit, Christ himself, who also lives and will live eternally, is on display and is the primary bond of ecclesiastical fellowship, and the one by whom it is preserved. Christ himself also remarkably supports our assertion. He shows this everywhere by his own example, which the disciples deliberately imitated (John 13:15, 34–35; 15:12, 17; 5:24; 12:48; 14:23; 15:10, 20; Matt 12:30; 11:29–30; 20:22, 28; Mark 10:38; Luke 9:28). He called himself the good shepherd, whose voice his sheep should hear (John 10:11, 14; 18:37). They should change Christ into life and blood, they should eat his flesh and drink his blood (John 6:51, 54; 10:27), because he had presented himself as the bread of eternal life (John 6:35, 41, 48, 51; 10:10; 11:25; 14:19). He showed himself as the light of life (John 8:12; 12:46; 14:6), the door of the house (John 10:7, 9), the way that must be entered, and finally as truth itself (John 14:6). He had declared that he was the steward of the "spring of water welling up to eternal life" (John 4:14), who at last could in fact declare, "Whoever believes in me ... out of his heart will flow rivers of living water" (John 7:38). Likewise, in the image of the vine he portrayed himself as the very medium joining the disciples (John 15:1, 5; compare 17:23; 6:56; 14:20; 15:4; 17:24; 12:50). Each of the faithful should love and esteem the rest of the followers of Christ as Christ himself (Luke 10:16; 9:48; Matt 25:40, 45; 10:40; 18:5; Mark 9:37). In his name nothing must be undertaken (Matt 10:22; 24:5, 9; Mark 9:37, 39; 13:6, 13; Luke 21:8, 12, 17; John 14:13–15; 15:16) except whatever would increase his cause (Matt 10:18, 39; 16:25; Mark 8:35; 10:29; 13:9; Luke 9:24). In common, they should all love the one Christ (John 16:27; 14:21, 28), they should place their faith in him (John 6:35, 47; 12:44, 46; 14:12; 21:15), who would rule all of them by his own Spirit (Luke 21:15, 27; Matt 18:20), without whom it is evident that no one approaches the Father (John 14:6; 15:5, 9), in whose communion all enjoy tranquil peace (John 16:33; 14:27), who finally called himself the chief cornerstone by whom the entire edifice of the church is sustained (Matt 21:42). What, I ask, is the bond of the flock except the shepherd? What is the union of the branches except the vine? Moreover, who is the tie except Christ—or, if you prefer, his remarkable and illustrious excellence, his divine nature, or what we call in the vernacular his "personality."

It is not difficult to demonstrate that the apostles entirely adopted the same thought. So let us begin with Paul, who expressly declared that in Jesus Christ we have been united in one body (Rom 12:5). He declared the same sole foundation (1 Cor 3:11; Eph 2:20) of the church and also expressly declared, "You all are one in Christ" (Gal 3:28). All members of the church are co-participants of the same gospel, that is, of Christ (1 Cor 9:23). God "made us alive together" in the same Christ (Eph 2:5; Col 2:13). We have "been baptized into Christ" (Rom 6:3), with whom we grow together like one plant. It is certainly more difficult to find the end of the examples than it is to find a single example, because the apostle overflows with them. Being made into the same image (Rom 8:29; Phil 3:21), being joined together in the one Christ (Eph 4:16; 1 Cor 2:2, 16), reigning together with him (2 Tim 2:12), all nations in Christ "are fellow heirs, members of the same body, and partakers of ... the gospel" (Eph 3:6; 5:7), and there are very many other examples that are too many to enumerate (e.g., 1 Cor 12:27; Eph 3:6; Heb 2:9; Rom 8:17; 15:17; Phil 4:3; Eph 2:21; 4:16; Col 3:1; 1 Cor 15:22; 2 Cor 6:15). If someone would object that in other passages either "love" (Col 3:14), "grace" (Phil 1:7), "peace" (Eph 4:3), or "the Spirit"[25] is presented by Paul as the social force of the church, he would certainly plead the appearance of truth. Yet if you would investigate the matter a little more carefully and deeply, it will be evident, I believe, that the peace is the peace of Christ, that the love is the love in Christ, and that the grace has been communicated to us by Jesus.

Peter likewise eloquently exhorts us that we should all vigorously imitate Christ alone, and in Christ alone we would cherish the most intimate concord (1 Pet 2:21; 3:8; compare 3:7; 1:3), and John also admonishes

---

25. *Note by the author*: 1 Cor 12:11 and elsewhere; compare C. Ph. Hofstede de Groot, *Pauli conversio, praecipuus theologiae Paulinae fons* (Groningae, 1855), 150ff; WIL 1840 II, 221ff. Swiers: *Paulus voorstelling van de vereeniging enz.* and WIL 1842 IV, 715ff: Pareau, *De leer van Paulus.*

us that we should properly preserve "the anointing" that we all received from the same Christ (1 John 2:27; compare 2:6), by necessarily attesting to the mutual "fellowship" that has arisen among us "if we walk in the light" (1 John 1:7). What they were so firmly convinced of, they bore out by their own example. Wherever they are engaged in the apostolic office, they are all in Christ, and they do not declare anything additional (Acts 1:14; 2:15-41; 9:22; 18:5, 28; 19:4; Rom 15:20; 2:16; 15:19; 1 Cor 9:14; 2 Cor 10:14; Gal 1:11; Eph 6:19; Phil 1:27; 1 Thess 2:9; 3:2; 1 John 3:23-24). In his name they chastised evildoers (1 Cor 1:10 and elsewhere) and lavished blessings (Rom 1:7; 1 Cor 1:3; 2 Cor 1:2; Gal 1:3; Eph 1:2; 1 Pet 5:14). They joyfully receive all Christians equally, and address each other as brethren, because of course they are followers of Christ (e.g., Rom 15:30; 1 Cor 10:16; James 1:2; 1 John 3:13; 2 Pet 1:10).

And certainly these things concerning the bond of the church thus have been explained from the intention of the gospel, according to which the thought of Calvin and à Lasco must be judged. These men also occasionally declare Christ the Lord as the foundation of the church, yet in such a way that here also a great distinction exists between Calvin and à Lasco. Namely, Calvin wrongly understood this dogma that has been handed down from the ancients and soon substituted in the place of Christ himself or his Spirit the orthodox *doctrine* of Christ, or, what is even worse, he praised this as the very bond of the church: that all should embrace with a silent faith whatever the church teaches. So Christ entirely disappeared, and in place of a living Christ, a blind faith in the church's doctrine of Christ was substituted. In these things, however, he strayed from the true intention of the gospel, which is not something that needs extensive demonstration. On the contrary, I cannot deny—more correctly, it must be willingly conceded—that in these things indeed à Lasco approached much more closely to the intention of the gospel to the extent that he was much less attentive to the consensus of church doctrine, everywhere returned to the gospel itself, and declared Christ himself to the people more than the received doctrine of Christ. This extraordinary man saw rightly that the church would not be one because in dogmatic matters all agreed to the letter, but because they loved each other in a holy way, burning with the love of Christ, imbued with his divine Spirit, and animated with mutual fraternal love. The funeral pyre of Servetus sadly bears witness to how much Calvin is inferior to à Lasco in these matters.[26]

SECTION 2 – ON THE MEANS OF THE CHURCH

CHAPTER 1 – ON THOSE MEANS THAT THE CHURCH USES

ECCLESIASTICAL PROPERTY   § 182

Although the Christian church may truly be a spiritual society, yet it requires goods and resources: (1) So that it may pay wages to those who especially live for the salvation of the church without regard for their own affairs; Christ himself said, "The worker is deserving of his provisions" (Matt 10:10 [LEB]), and Paul testifies that whoever preaches the gospel ought to have the means to live from the gospel (1 Cor 9:14). (2) So that it may succor the poor. In fact, what kind of Christian love—which seeks others, not itself—could abound in wealth while a brother lacks bread? (3) So that by fleshly kindnesses it may break the hardness of a hardened heart and thus at last the rich are led to better things. This you may also safely deduce as most true from the mind of Christ because both he and the apostles—endowed with divine power—were healing diseases, bringing medicine to the infirm, and offering food to the famished.

These three things cannot be permitted to be cared for by individual members, but must be done in common. The very name of *church* demands this of this fellowship. So also in the fellowship of the apostles (as is evident from the twice repeated comments of John; see John 12:6; 13:29) there was a common purse, committed to the care of Judas, in which

---

26. *Note by the author:* Hofstede de Groot, *Jezus Christus, de grond van de eenheid der christelijke kerk; woorden van vrede envereeniging voor alle christenen* (Groningen, 1846) and Pareau, *Beantwoording,* etc. in *WIL* 1838 IV, 701; Van Oordt, *Recensie* of W.R. van Hoëvell responding to A. Stieren regarding Irenaeus in *WIL* 1839 I, 159; Metzlar, *Paulus blik in de toekomst* etc. in *WIL* 1840 IV, 765ff.; Hofstede de Groot, *Waarom niet door begrippen* etc. in *WIL* 1845 II, 338; Pareau, *Hoe er bij christenen* etc. in *WIL* 1850 III, 417ff.[Ed. note: Michael Servetus (1509/11–1553) was famously executed as a heretic in Geneva during Calvin's time.]

all eleven commonly brought together the money collected into one. Even if Calvin and à Lasco touch upon this matter lightly, it is still enough that they accommodated themselves to the gospel, and I do not see a difference between the two on these points.

SECTION 3 – THE ORGANISM OF THE CHURCH

CHAPTER 1 – THE BELIEVERS OR MEMBERS OF THE CHURCH THEMSELVES

§ 188

WHO AND WHAT SORT THEY ARE

Our inquiry has arrived at the organism of the church. Now, indeed, so that the order of the disputation may also approach as closely as possible to the mind of the gospel, in the first place we will speak about the members of this church themselves. Well then, let us see who and what sort of members they are. To a certain extent, however, this question has already been explained and investigated in what has been said above. We have attempted to show, namely, that by nature the church of Christ is universal; thus there is nothing of race from which you would deduce its origin, or of place by which you may derive a distinction to exclude yourself from its fellowship, much less also anything to hinder you by the phantasm of reprobation. But on the contrary, God equally summons and invites all to himself without exception. But it is also evident that this church is spiritual, from which it follows that none can enjoy the communion of this society unless they will have more or less renounced whatever things are vile and vicious, and there is in them some certain indicator of spiritual life. Thus, according to the mind of the gospel no one will be kept away from the church other than those who exclude themselves. Neither John the Baptist nor Jesus opened wide the entrance into the kingdom of heaven unless a person first manifested repentance, and Jesus sharply rebuked the Jews: "Unless your righteousness exceeds that of the scribes and Pharisees, you will never enter the kingdom of heaven" (Matt 5:20). "Not everyone who says to me, 'Lord, Lord,' will enter the kingdom of heaven, but the one who does the will of my Father" (Matt 7:21). Those who are humble like children (Matt 19:14; Mark 10:15) and poor in spirit, theirs is the kingdom of heaven (Matt 5:3), in which no one is granted the right of citizenship except the one who has been born again of the Spirit

(John 3:3, 5). Nevertheless, those who are contrite in heart and weary will not seek comfort and help in vain (Matt 11:28).

For this reason it seems that it can be safely concluded that, according to the mind of Christ, entrance into the kingdom of heaven is not possible unless the Spirit has certainly kindled some sort of new spark. With respect to this, the rationale of the Christian religion also teaches the same thing. The bond by which members of the church are conjoined is neither baptism nor the confession of a certain doctrine, but truly is the uniquely divine Spirit of Christ. Therefore, how can someone be related to this fellowship when he is entirely devoid of this Spirit and not united to the rest by this bond? Moreover, the entry rites of the new life are not sufficient to supply the genuine holiness about which Paul abundantly teaches us when he compares the church to a great house in which there are not only gold and silver vessels, but also wooden and earthen vessels (2 Tim 2:20). Jesus also taught about the wheat and tares in his parables (Matt 13:24-30). Thus, the gospel is by no means lightly impeded and hindered by the following diminished opinion: namely, Calvin and à Lasco equally attributed more weight to baptism and the confession of faith; however, they also deserve praise because they endeavored to introduce a correction to the Roman error, which taught that baptism alone was sufficient. Furthermore, the same distinction that we have everywhere observed between Calvin and à Lasco is also entirely applicable here. To a certain extent à Lasco was a participant in Calvin's error, yet he approaches closer to the gospel. They both require faith from the members of the church, but Calvin almost uniquely refers the notion of faith to doctrine, whereas à Lasco refers it also to the heart and soul.

Chapter 2 – Ecclesiastical Rule

The Duties of Those Who Lead the Church   § 196

The duties of ecclesiastical rule, as we have seen above, concern the preaching of the gospel, the celebration of worship, the management of property, and the representation of the church. And concerning these things we ought to at least say a few words, since Calvin and à Lasco both have quite abundantly treated this matter. But we will say only a few words, since these things actually pertain to the external form of the church, concerning which almost nothing is stable, and in itself must be rejected. Nevertheless, let us consider each of these things separately.

(1) The preaching of the gospel. The example of the apostles clearly teaches us that the gospel, or rather Christ himself, must be preached. There are these outstanding words of Paul: "If anyone teaches a different doctrine and does not agree with the sound words of our Lord Jesus Christ and the teaching that accords with godliness, he is puffed up with conceit and understands nothing," with a "craving for controversy" (1 Tim 6:3-4). Therefore, it is violently repugnant to the thinking of the gospel if the sound teachings of Christ are replaced by finely spun hallucinations that have absolutely no usefulness (Heb 13:9; 1 Tim 1:4; 6:20; 2 Tim 2:23; Titus 3:9). Christ must be declared to believers, just as he lived for us and even now lives for us. But it is impermissible to impose particular dogmas on others. Neither may a confession of faith be conceived in such a way that something must be believed by others—something prescribed as that which must be thought (1 Pet 5:3; 2 Cor 1:19). Christian liberty opposes that which it condemns as severely as possible, namely, whatever binds the conscience (Jas 2:12; 1 Cor 3:17b; Gal 5:1, 13). Every preaching of the gospel should be done for others, as Paul says, for the sanctification of the saints and edification of the body of Christ.[27] At this point Calvin certainly and undoubtedly fails, since he imposed his own doctrine on the church and bound consciences to received formulas more than he advocated that the living Christ be preached. With Calvin, the confession of faith and catechism take the place of the gospel, which necessarily must vigorously resist the thinking of the gospel. To a certain extent, I freely concede that à Lasco falls into the very same error. But there is the greatest distinction possible between the two! More correctly, à Lasco certainly earned a vast amount of praise because he strenuously vindicated Christian liberty, never imposed his doctrine upon others, and finally kept himself from fantastical dogmatics and singularly preached the gospel almost exclusively.

---

27. *Note by the author*: Eph 4:12; compare the most brilliant Muurling, *Wat ontbreekt er nog aan de Christus-verkondiging* etc. in *WIL* 1849 IV, 748ff.

(2) The celebration of worship. According to the mind of the gospel, nothing could be prescribed as fixed and certain in every time by either Christ or the apostles. Yet they were not so averse to all worship that they would wish to wickedly force upon us anything that goes beyond the rationale of their own conduct. On a certain day they customarily assembled (Acts 20:7; 1 Cor 16:1; Rev 1:10), expounded the gospel (1 Cor 14:1-5; 1 Tim 4:13; 2 Tim 4:2; Col 4:16; 1 Thess 5:27), solemnly sang hymns (1 Cor 14:15; Eph 5:19; Col 3:16), prayed (1 Cor 14:13; 1 Tim 2:1), and dispensed the sacraments (Acts 20:7; 1 Cor 11:17-34; Jude 12). Therefore, as much as is possible and suitable to the place and time, the example of the apostles is deservedly applicable to us. Moreover, those presiding should remember well that God is not a God of "confusion" (1 Cor 14:33), and thus they should take care that all things are done "decently and in order."[28] Nevertheless, this orderliness should not be excessively attributed to worship. Worship should not take hold of the understanding, but should draw the heart to God. As has been mentioned above, now, in a word, we say that sobriety in worship ruled among Calvin and à Lasco to too great an extent. However, it is not easy to say which of the two was more sober than the other. They did not adequately note that in addition to a mind, a human being has been endowed with feeling, and no view is complete unless it regards the whole person. On the one hand, the gospel would readily choose for itself à Lasco as its patron in this regard because he was far more averse to the fixedness of worship; on the other hand, even Calvin would never have approved of the excessive fixedness of the gospel in these matters. Of course, it must be granted to both that they paid attention to order and decency in a remarkable way.

(3) The management of property. There is a twofold purpose of the church's property. The first of these, namely, is discharged in the use of the whole fellowship, so that provisions are made for those who attend and so that worship can be solemnly and decently

---

28. *Note by the author*: 1 Cor 14:40. Furthermore, the church of the apostles already teaches us that nothing in the church that pertains only to form is in itself absolute and fixed. The new office of the deacons is instituted, elders are elected everywhere, and finally there is a transition from Judaism to universalism (Acts 6:1ff.; 15:23); compare Planck, *Geschichte der christlich kirchlichen Gesellschafts-Verfassung*, I, 1; 5; 141ff.

celebrated. In the second place, however, it must assist those who lack. We have already spoken about the first purpose above. Now let us inquire regarding the second. If it is correct that it is the duty and office of one brother to assist and run to help a needy brother, then the innate character of a fraternal fellowship cries out that the rich should help the poor. Christ did not consider such beneficence in the church to be a trivial matter, as he very clearly taught that during the last judgment he expected to generally speak in this way: "'Come, you who are blessed by my Father, inherit the kingdom prepared for you. ... For I was hungry and you gave me food, I was thirsty and you gave me drink, I was a stranger and you welcomed me, I was naked and you clothed me, I was sick and you visited me, I was in prison and you came to me" (Matt 25:34-36). He expressly taught, "Sell your possessions, and give to the needy" (Luke 12:33), and to the rich young ruler who from childhood had kept all the commandments, he said, "You lack one thing: go, sell all that you have and give to the poor" (Mark 10:21; Luke 18:22; Matt 19:21). Finally, I do not know whether such liberality could be more beautifully commended than in the parable of Lazarus and the rich man (Luke 16:19-31), to which parable of Jesus you should aptly add the dictum preserved for us by Paul: "It is more blessed to give than to receive" (Acts 20:35). So also the apostolic church generously and abundantly gave to those in need (Acts 2:45; 4:35), and the apostles are tireless in commending charity. Paul exhorts the Corinthians that on the Lord's Day each person should set aside an offering for alms (1 Cor 16; compare Rom 12:13; 15:26; Gal 2:10; 1 Tim 6:18), and James solemnly would threaten that "judgment is without mercy to one who has shown no mercy" (James 2:13; compare 1 Pet 4:8-9; 1 John 3:17). Thus, it is not only an obligatory duty of the church to give an offering to one who asks, whether to nourish the hungry or to give drink to the thirsty, but also to clothe the naked, to take in strangers, to sustain the sick, and lastly to visit those in prison. I wish to say this: according to the mind of the gospel, those who are cared for in our time by the institutions of beneficence properly and actually belong to the church. Now, if the opinions of Calvin and à Lasco are held to this standard, I have nothing specific or in particular to condemn, although on the whole the gospel condemns this in both of them: that they considered Christian beneficence of lesser import than is proper, for which reason the apostolic church, which they took as their pattern in all things, certainly surpasses them by far.

(4) The representation of the church. The representation of the church is necessary whenever there is a matter between the whole church as a body and a certain one of its members; representation is also necessary when the church must conduct business with some other fellowship (Acts 11:30; 15:2; 20:17; 21:18; Jas 5:14). However, no church board may bear that name with honor unless it is a true representation of that name—that is, it must be elected by the church from the church itself, and may do nothing except by the authority of the church itself (Acts 15:2, 23). À Lasco's system very nearly corresponds with the gospel in every point. He presents the true representation of the church in the assembly of elders, which has also been chosen by the church from the church, and does not busy itself with anything apart from the authority of the church. In theory, Calvin generally held a similar opinion, for which he is more to be lamented than celebrated, in which the church is entirely lacking a true representation—the elders are neither elected by the church nor from the church, and they plainly neglect the authority of the church itself when they busy themselves attending to the service of the magistrate and the pastors instead of the auspices of the members themselves. Calvin publicly favored the aristocracy in the governance of the church; à Lasco was more content with a moderate democracy, for which reason the latter certainly understood the mind of the gospel better. Because in an aristocracy some citizens enjoy conveniences and privileges ahead of others, which the rest lack, that rationale of governance cannot be endured in the church where all ought to be equal. Yet it should be a moderate democracy, as was present in à Lasco's system, so that it does not charge headlong into mob rule.

———————————

PART III - THE CHURCH'S RELATIONSHIP TO OTHER THINGS

SECTION 2 - THE CHURCH'S RELATIONSHIP TO WORLDLY THINGS

§ 205   THE CHURCH'S RELATIONSHIP TO THE STATE

The state, to the extent that it is a political society, strives toward a double goal. It provides for and looks after the common good of the state; that is, it is occupied with making its citizens happy. Moreover, secondly, it aims to make people better. To the extent that it strives to improve and perfect its citizens, it attempts to achieve its most refined purpose by dread of the law, and so it must also be positioned with the economy of the Old Testament in one and the same class of societies. The church seeks the same purpose entirely, but it attempts to achieve it by a vastly different method. This is of course because the church substitutes the persuasion of the truth spoken in love for the fear of the law. Therefore, if there is no other purpose proposed for the state except that it should correct human beings, then the church would destroy the state, and for that reason the church would approach the most perfect ideal, and the state would necessarily decrease, diminish, and be confined within narrower bounds over time, until it would be dissolved (Matt 5:25; 1 Cor 6:6). However, as long as the greatest number of people always remain in whom self-love is the highest law, and who pursue nothing except what is worthless and worldly; and as long as brutes dominate others by force, then the state is undeniably required so that force may be repulsed with force (1 Pet 2:14; Rom 13:4). Furthermore, since the state has set for itself another goal—that doubtless it must pay attention to the external needs of its citizens, which are administered better corporately than by each person individually—it must never die, but will occupy its place alongside the church.

With these things rightly and carefully assessed, we see that the members of the church dwelling in the midst of the state obey its laws no longer out of fear of the law, but with a free will (John 17:15; 8:23; Matt 17:25-27; 22:15-22; Mark 12:17; 1 Pet 2:16; Rom 13:6; Luke 20:25). They bestow the highest reverence on the rule of the state, inasmuch as they rightly discharge their own duty, and they especially strive for what is good and true (1 Pet 2:13; Titus 3:1; Rom 13:3–7). However, as often as it would incur loss to the honor of God, or whenever the obedience offered by them would impede the true prosperity of the citizens, then the members of the church are called—in order to reveal the power of the Holy Spirit in themselves—to endure the cruelest punishments and tortures with a cheerful heart, rather than renounce the divine power.[29] In addition, you may justly deduce nothing from the mind of the gospel regarding the relation between the church and the state. Neither Christ nor the apostles discussed much regarding this matter, and it is deficient to draw conclusions from that time to ours. For certainly there was some exchange between the Jewish state, and the heathen, as with Christ and the apostles, and the Christian state, in which the church dwelled in the time of Calvin and à Lasco.[30]

Now to the judgment: Calvin and à Lasco, each by his own warlike spirit, were eager to join the church and state, and certainly on this account they departed from the right track into erring ones, because they attributed too great a power to the state in the church. This was especially strong in Calvin, if we pay attention to that church that he founded in Geneva. To a certain extent à Lasco surely differs from him. Rather than concede the right in holy matters to the magistrate, à Lasco perhaps granted too much to the liberty of the gospel, but this certainly is a very small matter if you should compare him to his contemporaries. Moreover, those things that they dispute regarding the divine right of kings cannot be discerned from the gospel.

THE CHURCH'S RELATIONSHIP TO THOSE WHO ARE ALONGSIDE IT § 206

There are three kinds of people alongside the members of the church:
   (1) Those to whom the gospel has not yet come;
   (2) Those who separate themselves from the church on account of dogmatic disagreements;
   (3) And finally those who brilliantly demonstrate by the way they order their lives that they pursue the flesh rather than Christ.

---

29. *Note by the author*: I appeal to the example of Christ and the apostles. Did not Christ himself endure the most cruel death rather than place the human will above the divine will? Concerning the apostles, see Acts 4:3; 19; 5:18, 29–41; and elsewhere.

30. *Note by the author*: *Vereeniging van kerkenstaat* in WIL 1839 II, 436ff.; Sonius Swaagman, *Mag de christen zich afscheiden van de wereld?* etc. in WIL 1855 I, 9ff.; Schleiermacher, *Der Christliche Glaube* II, 310ff.; Pareau, *Initia institutionis theologiae moralis* §38.334ff.

In the first place, it is clear from the things we said above regarding the preaching of the gospel that it is a duty incumbent upon each and every one of the members of the church to lovingly have concern for the heathens and support them with all our strength and vigor (Matt 5:37), so that from day to day the church of Christ would be broadly increased among them (Matt 8:5–13; 15:22–28; 24:14). The whole human race is within the realm of the church, for which reason there is nothing so small that it may remain untouched until every knee bows at the name of Jesus (Phil 2:10).

Furthermore, those who still embrace Christ as the only foundation of truth must not be banished from the church on account of any dogmatic dissension. Indeed, those who dissent—being influenced by error—falsely suppose that they must leave the bosom of the church, which they no longer consider the true church; yet the genuine members of the Christian church cherish and concern themselves with a far different opinion (John 20:25; Acts 15:23; 1 Cor 5:12). The genuine members of the church have firmly persuaded themselves that the religion of Christ depends neither on the letter nor on the formulas of faith, but is, on the contrary, an uprightness of the mind and soul. Thus, they seek those who have wandered far off, and with fraternal love they pursue them and strive to convince them of the true character of Christianity (Luke 10:25, 37), until they also realize that Christian love is not destroyed by dogmatic disagreements and join themselves again to the church (John 4:1–19; Acts 18:26).

Lastly, even those who in fact disagree with the genuine members of the church—that is, those who consider sacred and righteous things of hardly any importance, but being especially devoted to their own desires, run after those things which are worthless and disgraceful—I assert that the church must even pursue these people in love. As a matter of fact, since Christ commanded all the members of the whole human race to love one another, he did not exclude anyone. Yet since this is taken for granted, Christ himself rebuked the Pharisees sharply so that brotherly love may not be considered as entirely foreign to a holy anger (Matt 23:13; John 8:44). Sin has dangerously advanced in people, and because it is vile Christ is eager to rip anything shameful out by the roots (John 16:8–11; 1 Cor 6:2; Jas 1:27; 4:4). Nevertheless, he embraced these very people with the most tender love (John 3:4; 17:21, 23; Matt 19:13–14; Mark 10:15; Luke 18:17). Therefore, in this way the members of the church, certain of victory with the highest confidence, wage a devastating war, yet that prophecy of Christ is eminently fulfilled, "I have overcome the world" (John 16:33;

compare Luke 10:18; 1 John 5:4–5; Matt 16:18), and his divine spirit pervades the whole world—or, if you would permit me to use the words of Christ, he will leaven all things with his holy leaven (Matt 13:33; 5:14; John 3:19).

But let us go on to the determination. We have already condemned Calvin and à Lasco previously for having entirely neglected missionary matters and thus also all concern for the salvation of the heathens. With regard to those who leave the church for dogmatic disagreements, Calvin, who persecuted his own brethren even to the point of blood, miserably falls before his judge—the gospel. Conversely, à Lasco deserves praise, because on these matters he especially perceived the mind of the Christ. Finally, both Reformers desired to check corrupt and worthless little men with the severest ecclesiastical discipline, which is partly approved by the gospel, though the gospel partly opposes their intention. The gospel approves because with all strength and effort they struggled to root out moral evil; but indeed, it condemns the reason by which they attempted to achieve their most humane plan, which of course can in no way be consistent with brotherly love.

CONCLUSION OF THE THIRD PART   § 207

Finally, in this way we have brought the third part of this inquiry to its end. However, in order that the things I have explained, having been separated into parts and torn into pieces, should not carry too much weight individually, it would seem that a brief summary of the judgment should be made. Therefore, if we should be asked which of the two Reformers' cases the gospel would approve—without a doubt and without any hesitation we openly confess that on almost all counts Johannes à Lasco retires from the contest as the victor. Nevertheless, you should not understand this in such a way, I beg you, as if the gospel finds nothing in his thought on the church that in some way is truly worthy of censure or is subject to correction. This is far removed from our intention. We wish to say only this: According to the method of his time, it certainly is amazing that he would advance a sound and true opinion regarding the church, that he would have thoroughly inquired into the mind of the gospel, that he would have perceived and esteemed the plan of Christ to a remarkable degree, and finally received in himself the spirit of a divine teacher. He shows us in a singular way the true path by which we may safely advance, and he presents an Ariadnean thread by which, when we hold it, we may happily escape the labyrinth of human inventions.

If these things are now abundantly sufficient so that we would be seized with admiration for that excellent man, nevertheless he would be addressed with an even greater eulogy if his thought were compared proportionally to the system of Calvin. For truly no one can be found who would detract from a great theologian the honor he deserves, which, against the Roman errors, he upheld on that savage page. Now, to be sure, as far away as Calvin was from the papists, à Lasco was about that far from Calvin, and by about that distance our Reformer came closer to the intention of the gospel. Without a doubt the church—the kind we recognize from the gospel—cannot be understood in its entirety unless you closely connect it with the person and service of Christ. À Lasco saw this and by far maintained this perspective much more clearly than Calvin, who connected the church rather with God, and thus he wretchedly overlooks the church's own proper character that is discerned in its connection with Christ. The church, whose acquaintance the gospel supplies to us, calls and invites mortals, one and all, to itself in an exceedingly kind way, and does not drag anyone to itself. À Lasco thoroughly felt this in his heart and set up a universal church, for which reason he clearly embraced the intention of the gospel more than Calvin, who, like a bad omen of things to come, cut it up into the most inauspicious particularism.

The church that Christ founded is a moral and religious fellowship which especially strives to reconcile hearts and souls to himself and is bound by the holiest bond of love. This does not escape Johannes à Lasco, who, being careful of taking too much pride in orthodoxy—especially since he was generally concerned for holiness and a sincere love of Christ, with which he also was ardently inflamed—also strove to pass this on to others. Conversely, Calvin, that unconquerable patron of orthodoxy, was opposed to the direction of the mind of the gospel. He cared for nothing more studiously, and supported nothing with greater concern, than a doctrine of spotless purity, which in fact must be said to have priority over divine love; thus, what is more, he exalted doctrine above even virtue itself.

Furthermore, the gospel portrays the church to us as most intimately connected, and as a fellowship most tightly bound together, whose primary force, by which it functions, was located in that very notion of fellowship. It is certainly remarkable that à Lasco also understood the innate character of the Christian church and perceived it with his heart and soul. He eventually realized that the Christian religion had been wrongly reduced to particular individuals only, as if the religion of conscience were transacted with God. But indeed in the Christian church, just as in all things, a thing must be performed according to the divine will, yet so that neither would the liberty of the individual be infringed upon, nor would the most intimate notion of the fellowship be damaged. In that most polished system of Calvin you will scarcely detect traces of this fellowship. According to him, each individual must gauge how an angered God may be pleased, and unity is more imposed upon them from without than freely arising from an innate power and springing forth from within. Finally, in the Christian church the action of divine love for us is shown by the gospel, by which, having compassion on our calamity, God has indubitably testified of his enormous love toward us. In these matters Johannes à Lasco, in harmony with the goal of the gospel, placed the salvation of the human race first, which God especially had in view. Conversely, Calvin, who opined that God in a singular way generally sought his own honor and does not do anything that does not redound to his greater glory, so that finally his supreme glory may be increased unimpaired, set forth the church to us as established by God for the restoration of his own honor, so that at last the elect embrace God's divine doctrine revealed from heaven by a blind faith.

ROOTED AND GROUNDED

TEXT INTRODUCTION

Abraham Kuyper preached "Rooted and Grounded," his inaugural sermon as pastor in Amsterdam, on August 10, 1870. Kuyper left the conservative Utrecht parish for the more contested one in Amsterdam. That he chose ecclesiology as his topic demonstrates the importance of the topic in the Netherlands. Here Kuyper offers one of the most compact statements of his dynamic organism-institutional ecclesiology and presents this as an alternative to the various competing ecclesiologies of his day. He was particularly concerned with the fate of the church as a Christian institution; Christianity as a mystical feeling or mood was less disputed at the time. On one side were the liberals who thought that the state would take the place of the church as chief moral authority for humanity; on the other side, the Roman Catholic Church enjoyed renewed vigor in the nineteenth century—as the conversion of prominent Protestants like John Henry Newman and the convening of the First Vatican Council indicated. For his part, Kuyper wanted to retain both the hidden spiritual life of the church and its institutional form.

Source: Kuyper, Abraham. *"Geworteld en gegrond." De Kerk als organisme en instituut. Intreêrede, uitgesproken in de Nieuwe Kerk te Amsterdam, 10 Augustus 1870.* Amsterdam: H. de Hoogh & Co., 1870. Translated by Nelson D. Kloosterman.

ROOTED AND GROUNDED

THE CHURCH AS ORGANISM AND INSTITUTION

The subjects I spoke about to the church on the occasion of my departing from Utrecht and coming to Amsterdam are dominating the ecclesiastical situation. Orthodoxy is defending itself, laying its hand on a good that the spirit of the age wants to destroy. This makes orthodoxy conservative. But this is the question: Is orthodoxy fighting for a life principle, or merely for a few incidental consequences deduced from this principle? If the former, then orthodoxy will live. If the latter, it will die. There are only two principles that carry within themselves a characteristic world, an entirely distinctive world: eternal election and humanism. As long as orthodoxy does not choose between them with self-conscious decisiveness, then through its own fault it is leaving David's sling lying unused—the very weapon it possesses with that tremendous principle of election, according to Scripture and Augustine and Calvin.

Against such conservatism that preserves only the incidental consequences while surrendering the principle, I have given warning in my
farewell address.[1] In this, my inaugural address, I sought to arouse my listeners to return to the church's distinctive principle. If the church has a
characteristic life principle, then—but only then—that life must manifest
its independence in terms of essence and form.

~~~~~~~~~~~~~~~~~~~~

Both the denial of the church's characteristic organism and the failure to
maintain the church's characteristic institution[2] betray a vacillation in the
choice placed before every heart, the choice that at its deepest point exists
between election and humanism. At the close of the forty-second chapter
of his oracles, Ezekiel describes the wall that had been erected "to make
a separation between the holy and the common" [Ezek 42:20]. That wall
does not merely consist in the acknowledgment of sin, not merely in the
acceptance of miracles, but first of all includes election. The church must
live from the confession of these facts; its form must be the expression of
those facts. All issues relating to the church question must be decided by
the acceptance or rejection of these principles.

Therefore I thought that I ought intentionally to examine the effort
of so many in our time who seek to escape the difficulty of the situation,
either by denying the principle of the church's characteristic life or by
destroying the necessary connection between organism and institution.
Everything depends here on making the proper distinction: the only
true principle lies in orthodoxy. But the conservatives in this country

---

1. *Note by the author*: Although the publisher preferred to issue this as a separate
   publication, I nonetheless wish that the mutual connection between these two
   addresses might not be overlooked. The farewell sermon has appeared simultaneously, also published by Messrs. H. de Hoogh & Co. [Ed. note: See the English translation of Kuyper's farewell sermon, given in Utrecht, 31 July 1870: "Conservatism
   and Orthodoxy: False and True Preservation," in *AKCR*, 65–85.]

2. The key Dutch word *instituut* can mean *institution, institute, agency, department,* or
   office, depending on its context (see *Van Dale Groot woordenboek Nederlands-Engels*,
   4th ed. [Utrecht, 2008], *s.v.* "instituut"). Despite the somewhat common usage
   of the phrase "the church as *institute*," in the interests of uniformity with other
   contemporary English translations of Dutch theological works, this translation
   uses the term *institution* in agreement with the prevalent rendering employed in
   Herman Bavinck, "The Church's Spiritual Government," in *Reformed Dogmatics*,
   vol. 4, *Holy Spirit, Church, and New Creation* (Grand Rapids: Baker Academic, 2008),
   326–88, esp. 329–32.

are impotent to the extent that they are not living from this principle, whereas through the activities of their lives, the non-conservatives are exercising an unmistakable influence—but one that ultimately dissipates because they are not consolidating the roots of that life in the true principle. It is the nature of the case that the limited space of an ecclesiastical address excludes any attempt at completeness. For that reason I nevertheless thought that what was spoken should not be kept private. Only by publishing these addresses will those whom I oppose have a chance to critique me.

Kuyper

Amsterdam

August 10, 1870

"Rooted and grounded"

EPHESIANS 3:17

I

Let my beginning among you, gentlemen, be "in the name of the Father and the Son and the Holy Spirit," and as is fitting with such a glorious confession, I do so with quiet apprehension and yet with unshakable confidence. Accept then my testimony that I come to you with my whole heart, even as I have already bound myself to you in this very house of prayer with the sobriety of uprightness. I ask only this: Do not require that I already now celebrate in a happy mood that bond with your congregation. At the moment such happiness is impossible for me, since the farewell to so many longtime friends has only just faded from my lips. Were I able to rejoice already now, then either my testimony of pain to them or my display of joy to you would have to be mere pretense, betraying a shallow heart in which pain and joy could displace each other so quickly. For that reason, no matter how warmly I thank you for the love with which you have already greeted me, no matter how much within your congregation appeals to me, let the requirement of the heart, I pray of you, run its course for the present; bear with me as I accept my ministry in your midst with sedate sobriety and quiet gravity.

With respect to only one thing I will not suppress my joy even now: namely, that having arrived in your midst, I may come after being called by you. It is good for me that the free choice of the congregation itself commissioned me with this ministry, so that the foundation of my endeavor rests not in any outside body, but in you yourselves. I know very well that in such a choice not everybody desired my perspective; and even if united in perspective, not everybody took delight in my person. But I also know that this has repeatedly been the case with every choice made by free people. In this regard the significance of that free vote is not at all being minimized in my estimation. Even in this way the election of the congregation is the license from which I derive the right to labor among you. Through it I am standing on firm ground and the way to trust has been paved. Precisely through that choice I enjoy an uncoerced relationship with the congregation, and because I have never made a secret of my ideas, I know through that election what the congregation expects from me.

Do not think, however, that I am therefore glossing over the risk that lies embedded in this new legal situation. I sense deeply that this new method of election bears within its bosom a new church, and here too the birth pangs are not coming without pain and danger. Every transition is already uncertain, so why not also a turn of events such as the one we have witnessed so suddenly, so completely, in our denomination? We have left the ancient paths, but everyone is asking: Where are we headed?

This explains the linguistic confusion that is so disastrous, the befuddlement so regrettable, the error so dangerous, all of which are currently disturbing us in every controversy in our ecclesiastical life. We know that from which we have partially escaped and will one day entirely escape—but who will focus our eyes on a firm, unshakeable goal? And who will pioneer the way, leading us with certainty through this morass of confusion to that goal? Moreover, in those surging billows of our ecclesiastical life, where does the fixed position lie from which moral power can be exercised without an arrogance that excludes compassion, without a passion that makes one unfair, and even more important, without that reckless rashness that corrupts everything because it will drive us past our goal?

This is what people are asking, and the cacophony of voices that arises when the question is asked is confusing. But still, if we listen carefully, then three distinct voices can be heard above the others in that swirl of sounds. Over here people want the church to flow out into society, while over there they want the church revamped in line with Rome, and over yonder they want to make the church expand into the free church of our time.

The one cries out: "Away with the church, as institution or organization! Christian living must continue only as an organism." The humble testimony thought fitting for the church to bring to society is "You must increase, I must decrease." The goal of Christianity must be to flow out into the state; and therefore if one day the state takes to its own bosom what initially the church alone provided, that church will inevitably cease.

"But no, we want nothing of that super-spirituality that evaporates everything!" cries another voice. "Jesus' church must become for us not an organism, but above all an organization, above all an institution." Therefore Rome's model is being explored once again, to revive not Rome's abuses but Rome's church. One of two things must be true: either let it become once again a church that does not rest in the human race but is laid firmly and immovably upon the human race; otherwise what you wanted to stamp with the name of church is unworthy of that sacred name.

A third group, finally, just as vigorously opposed to spiritual mingling as it is afraid of petrification, pleads with us that, without surrendering either the church as an organism or the church as an institution, we must unite them both in the free church. The free church! Free, because the stream of Christian living must be able to flow unhindered—but let it continue to be church, because the stream will dissipate across the flat plains if its banks are demolished. "A free church"—there you see what can solve the riddle for us. We must be free in order to escape Rome's paralysis, but we must no less be church in order to escape the draining away of our lifeblood as a result of spiritualism.

~~~~~~~~~~~~~~

If Scripture is to be our touchstone here, and is to guide us in evaluating these voices, then it appears to me indubitable that only the last opinion is endorsed by Scripture. The first two perspectives that I outlined maintain the church either exclusively as an organism or exclusively as an institution. If either is the case, then the passage from the letter to the Ephesians argues sufficiently against both pursuits, and argues for a free church that neither surrenders the organism of the church nor destroys the church as an institution. "Rooted and grounded," says the apostle, and thereby declares with equal brevity and succinctness that twofold requirement, that double character trait of the Christian life. Rooted—that is the description of organic life; but also grounded—that is the requirement of the institution.

Rooted is the metaphor describing the free life that arises not through human artistry but immediately from the hand of the Creator, bearing in its own core the power of life and in its own seed the law of its life. You will find that metaphor earlier, in terms of the tree with spreading branches that grew from a mustard seed. It captures the spirit of what is termed "growing together into one plant," describing the bond that unites people with Christ. He is the vine, we are the branches, withering if we are separated from him but bearing fruit if we abide in him—this describes everything that lives organically, and does so with metaphors drawn from growing plants. Similarly, the yeast in those measures of meal points us to a fermentation process that operates spontaneously. Surpassing every other figure, we have the metaphor of the body that Scripture prefers to use for the church: an image that requires organic life, a figure that binds the parts together by means of a power operating invisibly, one that refers to a natural growth occurring not through something added but through a force that comes to outward expression from the inside.

Rooted, to be sure, but also *grounded*, because alongside that theme of fermentation and vital growth, another series of entirely different metaphors runs through Scripture. These are drawn not from nature, but from the work of human hands. In that series, the metaphor of the church that we are given most frequently is not the growing body but the constructed house—a house consecrated by the Lord's Spirit to be his temple, and later expanding to the dimensions of an entire city, whose name will express its nature: "Jerusalem that brings peace." The church not only grows, but is also built. This explains that repeated emphasis on the single foundation, that repeated reference to the base on which the house must rest. Buttressed by its pillars, fastened together in its security, that house is held together by its outermost cornerstone. It rises upward, the builders rejoice, and the goal of everyone's effort is that the house may be established.

"Rooted and grounded" unites organism and institution, and Scripture itself refuses to allow any separation—it weaves them together. By means of the person who sows and plants, the metaphor of vital growth overflows into that of the institution; by means of the living stone, the metaphor of the building flows over into that of the organism. The church of the Lord is one loaf, dough that rises according to its nature but nevertheless is kneaded with human hands and baked like bread. The church is called a multitude of priests, legitimated through birth but consecrated only through anointing. A bride brought forth by the Father but accepted by choice. A people, finally, who indeed sprouted from the living trunk but nevertheless are organized with wisdom and guided with self-motivation. The fact that the text connects the two is not accidental but normative. Every viewpoint departs from Scripture if it either dissolves the connection between both foundational themes, or erases the other while closely adhering to the one. Every understanding of the church must be considered mistaken if it prevents the conjunction of these two or disparages one of these two.

Indeed, let me proceed, my friends! That law expressed by Paul's formulation applies not merely to the church but to every kind of life that comes into contact with human consciousness. Eden is planted, but humankind will cultivate it—that is the fundamental law of creation. Which is to say: creation was fashioned by God, fashioned with life that surges and glows in its bosom, fashioned with the powers that lie dormant in its womb. Yet lying there, it displayed only half its beauty. Now, however, God crowns it with humanity. They awaken its life, arouse its powers, and with human hands bring to light the glory that lay locked in its depths but had not yet shone on its countenance.

The inanimate creation displays this. You only need to glance at the terrain of our habitation and ask what it once was in its natural state and what it has become through the energetic activity of our ancestors. Similarly, witness the power that speeds our word along metal wires or our very persons along iron rails. This power already lay embedded in creation from the time of Eden, but only now has it been discovered, analyzed, and harnessed by the spirit of man. Crops grow by organic power, but the human hand prepares a fertile soil for that crop, tames the wild acreage, prunes the wild shoots, guides the branches according to the flow of their sap, and by means of hybrids produces new kinds of plants. The wild forest creature rushes and wriggles with organic life, but only when tamed by people, bridled by the human hand, and ennobled by human technique into thoroughbreds, does that wild natural power attain its goal. In short, compare the desolate place with the inhabited region. Lay the creation accompanied by humankind alongside the creation apart from them; everything bears witness both of a creation immediately fashioned and of a perfecting of that creation that the Lord now completes through humans.

But of course this is evident even more strongly in the world of humankind itself. One dimension of our humanity involves instinctive life; another involves our conscious life. Whatever operates instinctively in us comes automatically into being in and through us with an iron necessity. That is how the family comes about, as well as the life of society and the state, with the first stage of its development proceeding exclusively from natural impulse. For that reason it everywhere displays the same shape, follows the same law, is rooted in the same ground. But that is merely the first phase, the phase of bare organic life, showing the features of a child—until finally it awakens in self-consciousness and analyzes the relationships belonging to that family, reflects on that society, regulates that state by means of ideas, and ennobles organic life through the power of the institution.

Just as it was related in the creation story: "his work that God created, to perfect it,"[3] that is how it is, my friends! Not as though to make a division, saying: "This is what the Lord wrought," and "This is what humanity made." If you insist on that contrast, then people are absolutely nothing, and would then be capable of nothing. I know of only One who called this mighty system into being, and now directs and propels all its parts. That is the Lord! He is also the One who does this with the second creation, using us as instruments so that later, if we refuse to be converted to him, in his sovereignty he casts us out. Whatever we endeavor—the plan we follow, the strength we apply, the material we employ, the foundation upon which we build—all of it is his. We ourselves who do it, what are we other than flimsy creatures? For that reason, even with that distinction as well, he alone is the Cause, the Source, the Fountainhead, and the Worker of whatever is built or is grown, of whatever is grounded or rooted. Everything is from and through and unto him!

~~~~~~~~~~~~~~~~~~~~~~~

Had there been no sin, with these comments everything would have been said regarding the church (assuming that apart from sin there still would have been a church on earth, something we deny).

Meanwhile, the fact of sin lies in our path, sin with its regrettable aftermath of corrupting souls, disrupting joy, and causing this earth to be cursed. Sin turned this mighty system in its course by shifting it off its axis anchored in the Eternal; due to sin there is no longer any consummation of the powers for this creation.

Had sin not come, Eden would have been cultivated and creation would gradually have been perfected, until finally it would have joined together with the life of heaven and transitioned into eternal glory. But now that is no longer the case. The vital root has been severed, the foundation wrested from its moorings. Whatever may be growing from that cancerous root, whatever may be constructed on that shattered foundation, it continues to bear the mark of its origin, and thus never reaches to the height of heaven. Though developments leap forward with giant steps, though every age brings to light for us a new treasure of powers, that blossoming

---

3. Here Kuyper is loosely quoting part of Genesis 2:3 from the SV.

fruit can never swell to its full greatness. Instead it falls down from the branch, prematurely ripened and inwardly cancerous, having displayed only a false blossom. That is what is meant by "this heaven and this earth shall pass away" [see Matt 24:35]. The relationship is irreparably broken. This sinful life cannot overflow into eternal life.

And yet this creation will not be lost, but its shell will one day be cast aside and a new form will emerge from it, developed from a life seed that was laid within creation *after* the fall. The cosmic conflagration is coming, but from this cosmic conflagration the precious metal will be saved into which a higher power will transform a part of its life. So although this world, even in its boldest development, will never reach the heights of heaven, nevertheless a glorious life will germinate from this world—a life whose seed descended from heaven, a life that one day will be melded together with this heaven in immaculate radiance.

That life, which exists in Christ as human life—that is, as life that in the highest sense functioned for this creation—proceeds from grace and not from sin-affected nature. That life is a miracle. It does not arise from this earth, but instead breaks in upon the earth. This life penetrates into the world's joints, melts down whatever it finds, and transforms it into its own life. Though compatible with this earth as the earth existed before sin, it is exactly for that reason in fierce opposition against what this earth has become through sin. Not merely in degree, but in kind; not merely in form, but in principle. You need only behold the cross! Separated from sinful life, it can never grow alongside that life from the same root; it can never be constructed alongside that life on the same foundation.

A double stream flows today through the kingdom of spirits: the stream of the old life that propels its waves onward but silts up before it reaches the ocean; and within that, a different stream, one that has trickled down from God's holy mountain. This stream never loses its course though it appears to merge with those other waters, and, soon turning aside, it carves out its own bed as it proceeds toward the ocean. Neither the organism nor the institution of this old life is adequate for that new life. That new life flows from another source and before long forms its own boundaries. As unique life, it must be rooted in itself; because it is a unique life, it must create a unique form in an independent institution.

That organism and that institution is the church. For anyone who denies miracles, for anyone who acknowledges only the creation of nature, that church has no meaning and can offer no lodging. That demand must be pressed very sharply in all its rigor. It comes down to the difference of degree and of kind between sinful life and sacred life.

"Consecrated and unconsecrated" or "everything alike"—that is the choice that either inflames our love for the church or dampens it; that must determine its right of existence. But once that separation is a reality for us, and thus a church is required by our faith, then it is obvious that such a church must obey its law of life: namely, it needs both an organism and an institution.

The church is an organism because it bears a unique life within itself and self-consciously upholds the independence of that life over against the old life. The church is an organism because it lives according to its own rule and must follow its own vital law. The church is an organism, finally, because what will later unfold from its buds is fully supplied already within its seed. As our fathers so correctly put it, the church is rooted in eternal election, or as the apostle expresses it here, it is rooted in love. It is rooted in another soil, therefore, than what the field of this world offers. If selfishness dominates there, then love is the indestructible material with which the eternal is dispersed. And precisely in that eternal field the organism of the church sends forth its roots, from that eternal it draws its life-giving sap, and under the rays of that eternal it flourishes.

That organism is the heart of the church. From that heart its lifeblood flows, and where that pulse of its life ceases, the institution alone never constitutes the church. If you send missionaries out to remote places and they do not bring with them this vital seed, your church is never born in those far-off places. A church cannot be manufactured. A polity, no matter how tidy, and a confession, no matter how spotless, are powerless to form a church if the living organism is absent. Let those who intentionally deny the unique life of the church just try to imitate the church of Christ in their own locale! People will see once again what has been seen so often already: with the erosion of the soil, their building collapses.

~~~~~~~~~~~~~~~~~~~~~

An organism, yes. But here as well, the coming to life is followed by consciousness, and with that conscious life there is a second creation in the advancement, nurture, and unfolding of what the organism carries within itself. So in addition to the growth there is a building, a plant but also an organization, a root but also a basis beneath it—an organism but also an institution.

The church did not possess this when it first arose. At that point its life was more instinctive, since the fullness of that life was not yet analyzed, the demand of that life not yet articulated, and its appearance in the world not yet realized. And yet already at that point the apostles appear to inject that young plant with an organization. They arrange, they regulate, they include and exclude, and they seek to give a form to this life that would preserve it from dissipating. This demonstrates the need of an institution, even though to its own hurt, the church virtually neglected this building of the institution for a century—so much so that the scourge of Gnosticism had to overtake it first and the self-consumption of Donatism had to gnaw at its life before it understood the duty of returning to the apostolic trail.

The church cannot lack the institution, for the very reason that all life among human beings needs analysis and arrangement. This is how it is with the soul; this is how it is with the body, which lives organically, but languishes if no regulating consciousness guides it and no structuring hand provides for it. This is how it goes with justice, which does indeed grow among humanity, but still must be classified, described, and maintained, and does not exist in any nation apart from a judicial institution. It is the same with God's revelation that became organic and still could not dispense with the institution of Israel or the form of document and writing. Indeed, it is this way above all with Christ himself, whose life does not simply flow about aimlessly but is manifested in human particularity through the incarnation.

This applies to the church as well. Since Christianity does not bring to life just an individual, but binds many together, there necessarily comes into existence a legal relationship that degenerates into confusion if there are no judicial rules. Since it places a task not simply on the individual but also on all believers together, there must be an organization that regulates the mandate for everything that happens in the name of everyone. Finally, since its own life constantly threatens to dissipate into the life of the world, it must not merely allow a spiritual sorting to function deep down, but also allow a tangible authentication to function at the surface, which determines inclusion and exclusion.

But this is still merely the institution from its human side, my friends, which recedes entirely in the face of the much more serious significance that the institution of the church possesses as God's institution. In this sense it manifests not merely the organism; the institution is a means supplied by God for feeding and expanding that organism. For just as was the case after the initial creation, here too there is a further bringing to life through man as instrument. Behold, on Pentecost the Holy Spirit descended—I do not say without preparation, but still immediately—and he created the church among men who could never have brought it forth. But after that miraculous creation, things were different. From now on, it is the church itself through which the Holy Spirit, who dwells within it, expands and unfolds that church. From now on, there is mutual interpenetration, a reciprocal influence. From the organism the institution is born, but also through the institution the organism is fed.

"Go, teach all nations and baptize them." "Teach and baptize," says the founding document of that institution. "Word and sacrament"—behold the foundational parameters of the design according to which the institution is constructed. Neither the proclamation of that Word nor the administration of that sacrament is an organic operation. They presuppose human consciousness; they need human organization; they require a human act. They do not operate automatically, but through people as the instrument of the Lord. Their figurative representation is not that of something growing from a root, but of something being constructed on a foundation.

It is a mistake to view the church simply as an association of like-minded people, one that simply manifests what they share. The church is not the instrument of humanity, but humanity is born from her maternal womb as her instrument. The church exists before humanity, because the church gives birth to humanity. The church stands above humanity, because the church nurtures humanity. "She is a mother"—to use Calvin's beautiful expression—"whose womb not only carried us, whose breast not only nursed us, but whose tender care leads us to the goal of faith. ... Those to whom he is a Father, the church must also be Mother, and apart from her motherly care no one grows to maturity."[4] The church is our mother! Behold the beautiful image, my friends, that expresses so attractively both the organism and the institution. Her womb granted us life; her care nurtures us.

But it is precisely this "nurturing" that renders the institution absolutely indispensable. Where any child starts from scratch, makes his own way, and is left to himself, there we find no hint of nurture. To nurture means specifically to bring to the child the treasure that was acquired

---

4. See *Inst.* 4.1.1, 4.1.4. Kuyper seems to be quoting from memory.

thus far, leading everyone along the pathway already cleared. The essence of nurture is unleashing, feeding, and pruning fully organic life according to a fixed protocol chosen purposefully, and according to an unswerving principle that governs the entire context. So there is no nurture where there is no regularity, no nursery where there is no order. Every sphere of nurture involves organism and institution.

Certainly the Spirit of God is a fountain of water within the human heart, springing forth unto eternal life [see John 4:14]. But the water coming from that source within the heart empties into a stream that incorporates the advances made by every new generation. It offers its waters to each coming generation, propelling its ripples further and deeper in order that, as it irrigates every generation, it may connect them with each other. The organism of the church is the nourishing source for that stream, but the institution is the bed that carries its current, the banks that border its waters. Only in this way is there development; only in this way is the progress of the Christian life conceivable. It is the church that makes us stand upon the shoulders of those who went before us and that preserves our harvest for the generation coming after us.

Only through the institution can the church offer us that unique life sphere where the ground we tread, the air we breathe, the language we speak, and the nourishment of our spirit are not those of the world but of the Holy Spirit. That institution positions itself between us and the world, in order to protect the uniqueness of our life with the power supplied by that unanimity and that order. Through that institution—with all its procedures and groupings and rich ramifications—the fruit, the higher nature of the new life, must be displayed to us as a fixed form in reality. The consciousness of the life of the heart cannot be awakened anywhere but in such a sympathetic atmosphere. Only the institution offers us such a life sphere in more than a vague sense.

For that reason we have an institution that is itself thoroughly formed; it works formatively upon the individual, structurally upon the family, directively upon society, and chooses the Christian school as its antechamber. It is an institution that calls into being, from the root of its own life, a unique science and art; it strives in its confession for a more correct expression of the eternal truth and for an ever purer worship of the Holy One. It is an institution, finally, that preserves discipline and justice, but is nevertheless flexible, tender, and supple, adapting to the nature of each, accommodating itself to every nation, and in every age adopting the language of its time—behold what the church of Christ needs as desperately as it needs its rootedness in God!

Let people simply ensure that the root of the organism continues to be in harmony with the foundation, and let people never separate the building of the church from its growth and inception. Let people continually draw from the organism their motive power, their formative capacity, and beware of Rome's error that moves in precisely the opposite direction. Rome wishes to govern the growth according to the building. Contrary to the nature of every kind of life, it allows the rooted to follow only when the grounded has first been completed.

"*First* rooted, *then* grounded, but both bound together at their most inner core!" Let that be the slogan of the church living from God's Word. For those who are the Dutch Reformed Church, may the sovereign election of God's eternal counsel remain, according to the language of our fathers, the *cor ecclesiae*, the heart of the church, and thus the root from which it blossoms, but also the firm foundation upon which its building must be built. The organism is the essence, but the institution is the form. To say it once again with Calvin: "What God has joined together, you, O man, may not put asunder!"[5]

Finally, if someone asks whether the building known as the visible church would be the completion of the spiritual temple building, such that the visible church on earth should be identified with the kingdom of God, I would counter with this question: does the prolonged tragedy of the church on earth tolerate for a moment the fueling of this delusion?

No, my friends, it is an entirely different bond that binds together church and kingdom of God. I prefer to indicate this for you in terms of an analogy. You know that in our cities we often see a stack of wood on an open lot. Bricks are piled up, joists are brought in, people walk around with measuring tools and plumbs; on that lot a wooden frame is raised, tied together with poles and boards and crossbeams, looking more misshapen than elegant. That scaffolding, as people call it, appears to be constantly rising higher, its dimensions constantly corresponding to the outline of the building. But that wooden frame is not the actual enclosure; that scaffolding lashed together is not the wall of the house. Look: When

---

5. See *Inst.* 4.1.1; Mark 10:9.

after many days the cornice is brought in and the gables are anchored in place, then that scaffolding is torn down, that frame is dismantled, and the house that was skillfully constructed out of sight now sparkles in the grandeur of its lines and shimmers in the beauty of its form before the eyes of everyone.

By now you understand what I am saying, my friends! That scaffolding is the church on earth, as it appears at present to the eye, defective and misshapen. It must remain for a time, since who can build without scaffolding? But one day, when the cornice is brought in and the last stone is set, then that scaffolding will be removed, then that church on earth will fall away, and then that glorious temple will shimmer in its eternal beauty—a temple that until now had not existed, but that the builders had been building while supported by that church.

II

So then, my friends, in the apostolic word we have found a clearly delineated starting point, and together with me you sense that this decides the criticism about the currents in our ecclesiastical life and the judgment about the state of our church. Precisely through the separation of organism and institution, and the indispensability of both, that judgment arises automatically. In that connection, if my eye automatically focuses first on the Modernist current, then I am not asking that someone praise my courage because I oppose it. That courage is completely imaginary in a situation that tolerates no contradiction. If I speak this way, it is merely because clarity about the situation is indispensable, and silence merely fuels misunderstanding.

The church of Christ—this appeared clearly to us just now—lives as a unique organism and requires a unique institution on account of sin. Leave sin out of the picture, and the church becomes inconceivable, since the world itself would then be the church. When considering the question whether a church has a right to exist, everything depends on that other question: what do we think about sin? If we view it as absolute, then there has to be a church; if for us sin is merely relative, then there is no place for a church. If creational life has become genuinely impotent through sin and profaned in the deepest sense, then—but only then—purity of life is imaginable as something coming down into that creation, breaking in as by a miracle, and thus blossoming from its own root that differs in its life-law and life-principle from the root of the world.

By contrast, when people call it "deceiving each other with drivel" (as I read recently in the devotional publications from that camp) to emphasize the depravity of our nature and to argue on the basis of human impotence that one cannot accomplish even the smallest beginning of obedience—then, as everyone senses, it is merely through lack of consistency that such people keep using the name of church. If people think that the life of Christ does not differ absolutely from sinful life, and so baptize their spirit in the waters of sacrilege in order to erase the boundary line that separates the consecrated domain from the profane domain—if they refer to those as a *club* who, with Jesus, speak of "many who are called, but few who are chosen" [see Matt 22:14]—then it brooks no contradiction to claim that in that case a church as a unique organism is unthinkable and necessarily merges together with society. Or if you will, if people view miracles not as indispensable but as impossible, and if they reject every fracture that would disturb the grand process of things, then there can be no other life than life from the world itself, and a church that is from the world would be a self-contradictory notion.

Consequently, my conviction rests on this foundation: the Modernist current has no moral right to exist in our church, even though it can still maintain its judicial right on the basis of a church law code, such as we have, that eschews nothing so much as the proper administration of justice. The proposal is therefore not acceptable that despite contradictory principles, we should nevertheless live together in the same house. For people to be called brothers and sisters they must have come forth from the same womb, and the art is still awaiting discovery whereby one can make the same kind of plant grow from two kinds of roots.

Finally, if people are seeking to maintain the church as an association for spreading moral and religious life, a nursery of piety, even then that demand must be denied them, and I do not hesitate to adopt Luther's bold proverb: "The purpose of the church is not to make people pious but Christian. One can be pious and still not Christian. A true Christian knows nothing of his own piety."[6]

That unique organism, denied by the Modernists, as you know, is gloriously maintained by that other movement that I prefer to call by the name *Irenic*.[7] "Irenic, peace-loving"—not as though they would not love to fight for their own slogan. Everyone who has a principle fights for it unto death. But "irenic, peace-loving," because they still consider a solution possible that avoids the pain of irreparable break. Do not think, however, that such people lack a deep view of sin. On the contrary—for them the cleft is very deep that separates the holy and consecrated life from the unconsecrated. In fighting for a unique life that Christianity shares with none other, they have rather gone ahead of others and have acquired unfading laurels. For them the Christian life is rooted very firmly. Indeed, they do not merely affirm this initial term of the apostolic watchword, but rather they are precisely the ones who once again have raised from the dead that

---

6. Martin Luther, Sermon on Mt. 9:8-26 (1526), in *D. Martin Luthers Werke* (Weimar: Böhlaus, 1925), 10.1.2.430:30-33. Kuyper's Dutch is adapted from the original German.

7. The Irenics were moderates in the church conflict who held considerable power on the church boards. They shared much of Kuyper's theological conservatism, but did not share his strict confessionalism. See "Editor's Introduction" in *On the Church*, xxi; James D. Bratt, *Abraham Kuyper: Modern Calvinist, Christian Democrat* (Grand Rapids: Eerdmans, 2013), 153–55.

grand conception of a unique life, that rich principle of a unique organism, making it live again in the consciousness of the church.

But even as every struggle that must once again give voice to a forgotten word—even as every movement that comes to restore the disrupted balance—is automatically inclined to throw all its weight onto one side of the scale and thereby itself to lapse into imbalance, so too it has happened in this movement. Because the church has forgotten the component of being *rooted*, the Irenics are forgetting the component of being *grounded*. This explains why this side is weak in terms of the church question, and continues to lack a concept of the church with which it can implement its sharp contrast of sacred and profane. This is what happens with all who dare not build for themselves. Sadly, they must live in what others have built, and gradually that domicile wins their affection; in spite of themselves they protect it to the end, and the solemn duty to build for themselves gradually retreats into the depths of their consciousness.

If such a movement arises in a time like ours, when especially the church question dominates every other issue, then, naturally, the waste of energy entailed by such a tortured position cannot remain hidden. Either they must advance from being rooted to being grounded, or else, without knowing it themselves, they will retreat even from being rooted.

Their favorite position—that the Christian life, no matter how intermingled it may be with foreign life in Jesus' church, nevertheless through its own power will arrest, convert, and control that foreign element—seeks mistakenly to apply to the church what in the great battlefields of the world is contested by no one. Most assuredly, the God who is with us will show himself mightier in this battle than the spirit fighting against us, as long as we do not resist God's ordinance that he desires to display that spiritual power through and in his church. The marketplace of the world, not the church, is the arena where we wrestle for the prize, the course where we run the race for the wreath. Far from being that battlefield itself, the church is rather like the army tent of the Lord where soldiers strengthen themselves before that battle, where they treat their wounds after the battle, and where one who has become "prisoner by the sword of the Word" is fed at the table of the Lord [see Heb 4:12]. That unsustainable striving for wanting only to be rooted, to be only an organism—what else is that but a return to the embryonic life even before the senses of the church came into use and before its feet were firmly planted? No, my friends, what was valid for the early church cannot be valid for our time, because it fails to appreciate the church's growth.

At the same time, the other extreme of the apostolic word cannot exist alone either. Those people committed to externality, who seek a sound and well-built house at any price but show no sign of concern for the life lived inside the house—those people infatuated with the surface of things, who delight in looking into a clear mirror but never bother themselves about what is dying off in the hidden recesses—they can never build the church, because the church of Christ never permits her walls to be constructed with dead stones. O, go ahead and cut off all those in the church of the fathers who cannot boast of having blood "free of foreign stains."[8] Measure everything in your church down to the last mark on your flawless yardstick. Bring your confession once again to unchallenged domination in your church. Indeed, let the external shape of your church be raised along the purest lines so that the church of every nation may be aroused to jealousy, and display a church so unblemished and unwrinkled as has never been seen in the course of time. ... Even then, no matter how radiantly that house may glisten with its architecturally beautiful lines, your church cannot bear the name of Christ if you banish life from it out of fear that people might tarnish your sheen, and if you exclude God's Spirit out of fear that his mighty works might tear up your beautiful pavement. Such a church—O my, what else would it be other than a rich Lazarus, yet where both physician and medicine are absent? And who will carry his sick ones there? No, beloved! Being grounded, being founded, cannot benefit you if you do not also have a life that blossoms forth from the eternal root.

Finally, there is one last current, or let me rather say, above Jesus' church there hovers a misting cloud that, bursting forth, now here and then there, continually makes the sounds of little rivulets but whose characteristic feature is that they never merge into one stream. You recognize that effort. Where, I ask, do you not detect its busy hands, in which field do you not find its footprints? O, I do love it, that zeal to convert that spares no one but seizes everyone and surmounts every obstacle, to lead souls to Christ. And yet, I cannot deny that there is something in this restless drive that disturbs me: Conversion is pressed, but instruction of the converted

---

8.　See C. W. Opzoomer, *Aanspraak bij de Opening van de 85ste Algemeene Vergadering der Maatschappij* (Amsterdam: Spin, 1870), 15.

is postponed. How could it be otherwise? There is no time; eyes and hearts are already focused on making more new converts. People rejoice especially in the number of converts. So they think they can dispense with any test and they welcome with nebulous indeterminacy every person as an ally who, on whatever basis, along whatever path, from whatever motive, simply wants to march in our ranks and join us in talking about the Lord. It is as though prevenient grace has stopped working, covenant blessing has lost its power, the church's past is purposeless, and every conversion, beyond the influence of God's faithful covenant, is an isolated fact, an incidental work of the Lord's Spirit. Sometimes it appears as though God's elect are not generated through rebirth from the one Christ in shared parentage, but are plucked from the river like drowning victims by the arm of the Spirit.

That may not remain unchallenged, beloved! Spiritual revival is an extraordinary grace, I know, and sometimes the only saving means. But when it is made the rule, it subverts Jesus' church. Then it is nothing but cuttings planted together here and there in beds, there is no root, and the vine has no stem that binds the branches into a unity. "Together with all the saints," says the man from Tarsus in the verse following our text [see Eph 3:18]—and that connection is never neglected without very serious injury. The bitter fruit is already growing. We already see how each one wants to travel under his own flag, to privateer under his own ensign. Already the many-headed monster of that all-fracturing individualism is sticking out its horns. O, if people only realized: in this way bricks are indeed brought in and piled up, but that pile of bricks cannot stack itself up into a wall. Without design, cement, and builder, a house will never emerge from those stones.

~~~~~~~~~~~~~~~~~~~~

But even though I oppose those three previous movements, my friends, I hasten to add that each finds its cause and thus its incontestable right of existence in the untenable church situation in which we live. Our house is not stable; we must rebuild or relocate. Everyone is saying so. If any are not, you can be sure it is fear for the feverish tension of the crisis far more than calm tranquility, that makes them say so. If a deep sleep were to fall on everyone and in our dreams the crisis, as if by magic, were ended and the purge had come, each of us would want to hold on to that dream when waking up to reality. People fear not the end result of the crisis, but the pain. People sense that this way would lead to improvement, but they shrink back from what must happen first.

I dare to pronounce that judgment, my friends, because I see that it is so. Every conversation with leaders of the most divergent movements convinces me time and again that these same people who amid the clamor of voices want to ward off the crisis, nevertheless in private, in the inner recesses of their heart, are busy with new building plans. And it is only because they cannot have "the fruit of the crisis apart from the crisis" that they are held back from completing their design. How else could it be, my friends? Both from this side as well as from the other side, we know without a doubt—every beat of our heart tells us, we feel it in our gut—that we have become altogether different spirits. If that is so, then I pray you, what can living together yield other than concealment of principle or interminable conflict?

Therefore, I ask you, not in the name of Christ—since I do not know whether you would all understand that as I intend it—but appealing to your moral earnestness that clings to what you all call sacred for your own heart, indeed, with my hand reaching into your conscience, I ask you: is any more tragic spectacle imaginable than a church of Christ that either dooms people to lying or condemns them to fraternal war? Either silencing what is sacred to us, or devouring one another—can that be the choice for Jesus' church, which before all else is called to uproot the lie and allay bitterness? If you should reply: Then let the church be simply a nursery for piety and for moral living—then I would still ask: Can there be inner piety as long as on both sides, heads are so hot and hearts so disquieted, and as long as the fiercest partisanship sweeps everyone away with its current? Immorality is nourished by a church that leaves its sacrifice unconsecrated at the foot of the altar and tempts even its own priests to a breach of faith.

Even so, people say that the church question has merely been inflated by a few individuals. No, my friends. Rather, it lies there thrown in our path by God; it lies there as a stone of stumbling that will expose hearts. O, how much more free would our conscience be, how much more tender our praying, how much more persistent our fellowship with God, if we were finished once and for all with that dancing on a tightrope in order to preserve the balance, if once and for all we could steer clear of the Scylla of lies and the Charybdis of false peace. We call for peace but also for truth, for truth but also for peace. Therefore our watchword is: Purge the situation, because that purging alone will once again wed truth to peace.

To that end we demand nothing other than freedom. Freedom, because no organism flourishes unless it can spread its roots freely and unfurl its crown of leaves in the fresh air. Freedom, so that the organism of our church itself may show us its nature, spell out for us its law of living, and form the life sphere needed for its blossoming. Freedom, so that in that system every force may discover its course, every gear its axis, every part its proper limits. Freedom, finally, so that with petty obstructionism gone, the battle may once again become spiritual—a face-to-face encounter of opposing sides with no pedantic standard. Instead, the life-law itself may choose what element the church can still assimilate within its own life and what it must reject out of hand as toxic to its spirit and dangerous to its life.

For that, the requirement of liberation is threefold: Let the church be free from the state, free from the money purse, and free from the pressure of office.

Let the church be free from the state, and thereby correct the enormous mistake committed by Jesus' church fourteen centuries ago to curry the emperor's favor. Precisely because the church wanted to dominate, it did not dominate the nations, and only if it is willing once again to serve will it win back its dominion. As long as a crown adorned her brow, the church was the do-nothing queen, princess without influence, and the mighty state, no matter how much it appeared to be her servant, was in truth her master. But even though this is how the church lost its freedom, even though the state itself subsequently took the crown, the church's freedom is still its inalienable right. No sovereign prince can ever break the sovereign right of the church's anointed King. Here there is no obsolescence; here there is no acquiescence. Because the church is an organism, the church possesses its unique life and thus its unique principle of law. Therefore, whoever seeks to force the operation of our church law to conform to the requirements of civil law or the workings of public law is confusing what in principle is distinct. They are surrendering the freedom and independence of the church organism.

Next, let the church be free from money. It does not suit the church of Christ to let itself be bound by golden fetters or silver chains to what conflicts with its nature. The early church began with nothing else than the Holy Spirit, and still the church's treasure gradually grew into a gold mine.

People have since then plundered it, and the Lord tolerated that theft so that his church would demonstrate what it treasured as of greater value, namely, the faith that had landed the gold in its lap, or the gold that faith had obtained for it. "With me," says the Lord, "gold and silver consist of enduring good and righteousness." But the state in turn declares: "With me you find the millions, with me you find the money that is needed for your church!" It is true, the church needs money. Now then, two offers are being directed to you. Whose promise will you trust, O church? The promise of him who provides you the gold as the fruit of faith? Or the promise of the state, which binds you with its gold as with chains in order to cause the freedom of faith to stumble in its course? The choice is yours, but this I tell you: your faith treasury must become increasingly more depleted as long as you do not learn to hate the money that is not free. The adage applies here as well: whoever would be saved will lose. Only one who is able to be poor becomes rich. Only one who dares to disdain the gold has discovered the goldmine.

Finally, the church must become free from the pressure of the office, the pressing burden of one of the ministries. The beautiful words spoken by the one who installed me—"for the teacher-pastor, the church is not only the field white for harvest, but simultaneously an immeasurable multitude of fellow priests"—unleashed a hallelujah in the depths of my heart, and my soul prayed for a blessed "amen" that might arise from the powerful activity of the church in response to those eloquent words. The office of pastor-teacher, as it has developed during the course of the present century as a result of idle overseers and a lethargic church, would be well suited in a church that could be only an institution. But it is completely out of place in the church of the Lord that, as a living organism, is itself consecrated to the ministry of the altar. One who holds office must be rooted in the priesthood of the church. Apart from that intimate relationship, the office becomes domineering.

Perhaps you are asking: how then are we to achieve such liberation? My friends, the Lord is our General in this battle, and the victory beckons us if we are only willing to follow him. Not we, but he creates the opportunity; he paves the routes; the preparations are his. Whoever does not find rest in that is not fighting for the Lord.

Let us only press forward and further into every domain that he opens for us, into every fortress to which he grants us access. The pretentious bond of unreformed church government will ultimately snap if we simply adopt the watchword that comes with autonomy, that is to say: the "self-government and self-direction of the congregation." That is our form of church life. That alone is Reformed. Within Rome's organization, each congregation is merely an impassive member that is never energized by its own impulse but always by the now-infallible head.[9] In Lutheran countries the life bonds of the congregations are consolidated in the hands of the state. In both systems the church exists first, only thereafter to give birth to the congregations. But that is not how it went on Reformed soil. There the congregations existed first; there the great stream of the church was not brought forth until the flowing together of the congregations; there the strictly administrative church government rose up from the independent congregations.

But do not forget that a Reformed form of church life grows up only in a church that is Reformed in its heart. Ours cannot be a colorless Christianity, one that differs in degree but not in kind from a version of Christianity that transcends faith divisions. Each person's calling is not simply to be a human being but to have one's own character. So too here, to be not merely a congregation but a congregation with its own hallmark is an inexorable demand for the church in every place.

People are well aware of what has become of the Great Protestant movement.[10] How ignominiously it has melted away! How to its disgrace Rome's power has again burst forth—perhaps most sharply in the financial realm, where it had wanted to engage the battle with Rome.

O, I fully agree that anyone entering a house in ordinary times is not thinking about the foundation on which it rests; so also in Jesus' church there can be times when people dwell together and labor together while hardly bothering themselves about any principles. But in times like these that we are now experiencing, now when in every area the foundations are being undermined, now when everything is pressing down to the depths and people are proceeding restlessly to pry the deepest principles loose—now in these times it would be all too naïve, all too negligent for

---

9. Only a month earlier, on July 18, 1870, the First Vatican Council had declared the pope infallible in matters of faith and morals.
10. Kuyper is referring to the no-popery movement organized in April 1853.

people to sidestep the issue of principles any longer. No, in times of peace let the sword remain unsharpened, but when the order to advance sounds through the ranks, one must not blunt the sharpness of its edge. If people have without injury permitted the sharpness of our principles to become dull over time, now that the time for self-defense has arrived the sword must be wielded once again or we will stand powerless in battle.

Therefore our church must again become not merely Christian, not merely Protestant, but Reformed: God is her Sovereign, eternal election is the heart blood of her life, and God's Word the foundation that cannot be dislodged, upon which she stands with both her feet.

Lastly, by appreciating the Reformed contours of church life, we are not closing off any development of our ecclesiastical organization. The Reformed ecclesiastical principle contains the germ of a rich, multi-dimensional development of which until now only the first new growth has budded. Let that which has come about in the absence of a proper church now become joined with it. Let its school, which in former times was lost through its own fault, be recaptured in the spiritual vitality of faith with the devotion of every effort. The collection of associations that have come into existence in the voluntary sector must be brought into relationship with the church, in order to double every effort by means of unity and order. Development must occur in our confession, development in our worship, development in our ecclesiastical government, development in all of the activities of the congregation. Above all, let our church not ignore the great social issues of promiscuity, overpopulation, labor, and poverty. The church especially must battle against sin; especially the church has the calling to support the relative right of the lower class over against the spirit of the times. Let whatever is oppressed have the church's support: may the poor find the church to be a place of refuge, and may the church become an angel of peace, for rich and poor together once again— an angel that gently leads us from both the abuses and the utopias of our age back to the ordinance of God's Word.

My friends, let me summarize. If our church is currently presenting us with two entangled shrubs, fastened with triple bonds and thereby hindered in her growth, then those bonds must be burst—that is the liberation. From the very root, up the stem, those shrubs must be disentangled—that is the implementation of the principles. Once liberated, the real shrub must grow new blossoms—that is the development to which God himself is calling us.

Congregation of Amsterdam! Your calling in this regard needs no coaching. The importance of the very size of your congregation indicates your obligation. You have already done much; your struggle has already been glorious. O, what beautiful days await you! Of this I am certain: a congregation that a half-century ago defended her independent government with such boldness[11]—yes, even more, that once sat at Da Costa's feet—brooks no comparison and until the goal is achieved, will not lay down its sword.

"Not many noble, not many powerful" [see 1 Cor 1:26]—perhaps those royal words apply to you as well. O, may you be simply noble in heart, may you be simply influential in the kingdom of God; then hope beckons us with a laugh of joyous ecstasy. Those among you who have received the truth of God from the hands of your ancestors, may you reach for nothing but the Word. Let that Word hold sway with power in your own heart, let it hold sway with majesty around your hearth, let it govern life with its purifying influence in all of life, let each one contribute but a single drop of the water of life—and O, I think I already hear it cascading down, that irresistible mountain stream that will flow from such small droplets down Israel's hills.

People had placed the sedative to your lips and you had almost died, O church of our fathers! But God revived your spirit, your heart is beating once again, your blood is coursing through the veins again, your limbs are already moving. O, continue to awaken and rise from your dishonored bed. You have only to lift high your crowned head and the former inheritance is yours.

Permit me, congregation, to join your ranks in that contest, not in order to hasten foolhardily along paths that our eye has never surveyed— the person misses the target who with one shot seeks to achieve what requires years of effort—no, but in order to keep battling with calm patience, quiet confidence, and persistent energy while the prayer never vanishes from our lips: "Lord! Guide me onto that rock that is too high for my strength" [see Psa 61:2].

---

11. In 1815, Classis Amsterdam, at the urging of the pastors from the Amsterdam church, was the only body that lodged an official protest against the Dutch government's reorganization of the Reformed Church. The government's General Regulations, issued in January 1816, effectively placed the denomination under the control of the Ministry of Worship.

I offer you my heart and my hand. I pray only this: do not demand that I ever lend my hand to an external building that lacks the inner rootedness of the heart. As minister of the Word, I have to preach that Word to you, and my strength lies in that alone. What you recently sang to me: "Do not conceal from us what has been commanded to you, for the congregation is listening," I will in God's strength accomplish, even if I have to flog you in your conscience, even if people leave because of the harshness of my words.

Indeed, permit me to conclude, congregation, by declaring that what I am pursuing is not simply the restoration of the church; what I intend is not simply doing battle with whomever dislikes my efforts. No; what moves my soul, what I beseech from my God, is that he may grant me to shine before your eyes a single ray of light from that eternally rich, never exhaustively adored mercy that is in Christ Jesus. What arouses my zeal is simply this, that I may dip the tips of my fingers in that Fountain of eternal Love in order to lay a few drops of those cool waters of grace on the burning lips of your heart. And if I then also seek the restoration of the church, if I then also reach for the sword—it is only because, congregation, I am convinced that the minister of Christ may not sit idly by while the access to those waters of life is barricaded for the Lord's congregation.

~~~~~~~~~~~~~~~~~~~~

I will direct an additional word to those, congregation, who are clothed with honor in your midst. You are the first who honored me, gentlemen, who as guardians and caregivers have been entrusted with the government of our church. You have already heard what it was from your past that aroused my admiration, how I applaud your courage in standing up when a half-century ago the congregation's freedom was endangered by the government's whim. The congregation has thanked you for that brave posture when recently they extended their confidence to you and chose to be freely governed by you instead of submitting to outside interference. May that proud spirit continue to animate you, may that freedom bear its generous fruit through your administration, and may the congregation demonstrate, by supporting you energetically, that they appreciate their independence as well as your care!

Maintain that independence also in the domain assigned to you, you members of the consistory and leaders of the congregation, you who especially in these perilous days bear such precious responsibility. Experience has already taught me what it frequently costs to defend the right of the congregation against the power of the church. Nevertheless, I appeal to you, do not shrink back. Do not falter in this battle. You are from the congregation. From them you received your mandate. They are looking to you. Carry on with our ancient Reformed life, then, with good courage. Carry it on in new forms, and as overseers and caretakers of the poor, enjoy the same rights and the same rank with your pastors; but join them also in contributing in equal measure to the work of ministry, each in his own field of activity. Above all, let us not focus on externals. Building up the congregation spiritually, feeding them with the Word of the Lord, remains our first calling in every battle. May our passionate zeal make us faithful especially in that!

To you, my fellow office-bearers, let me extend my thanks for the friendly goodwill with which you have received me. O, how I would wish I could say to you all: "Brothers, accept this young man in your hallowed circle so that hand in hand with you I may serve the one Lord." If regrettably I cannot say this to everybody, may it then apply at the very least to those of you who still stand fast in the Word and with me cling firmly to the Christ of God in quiet faith. And you who think you must not do this, who out of deep conviction fight against what for me is more sacred than anything else—O, I know that you would despise me if from my position, playing with what is holy, I sought to cover over the chasm that yawns so widely between us. Therefore I ask only this from you: let our association be uncomplicated, our relationship genuine, and may gallant openness and candid speech characterize the battle that you have undertaken with the church and that the church has undertaken with you. Let us not conceal from each other, either here or in our daily interaction, the most serious division that, if things continue as they are, will turn out to be irreparable from both sides. And since faith separates us, accept from my side the sincere declaration that precisely because of that division, I sense my calling all the more to minister to you with all that is within me, in the quest for mutual service as we strive to be of help to one another.

Finally, a word of thanks to you, my brother, who introduced me to the congregation three days ago. Your warmth of language cheered my heart. What you said was what you yourself had experienced, and every heart sensed it: that fire that came through in your words was not artificially ignited. Although you once picked up the pen in order to contend against my efforts,[12] I feel the need to tell the congregation how much I appreciate your efforts. I wanted to be presented to the congregation particularly by you, so that it would be evident how little my heart is closed to being contradicted and how highly I value a fraternal judgment. Continue, brother, with the bonds of grace, to bring back what has drifted away, to seek the lost, according to the talents so richly bestowed upon you. And if not everyone can follow you with that creative power, with that ceaseless persistence, seeking the lost remains the endeavor of all of us—the one for that individual sheep and the other for the lost sheepfold.

~~~~~~~~~~~~~~~~~~~~~~~~~~~~~~~~

And now, congregation, I conclude with one more request for you. I left many people behind, but nevertheless I am coming to you with an open heart. Do not withhold from me the love that my heart needs and that provides such powerful support. Only let it be a love rooted in a decisive choice, grounded in love for God's Word. Do not forsake me, but serve me with your fraternal judgment, and may what binds us together not be cowardly cajoling on both sides, but instead the serious discipline of the spirit. Without a doubt, we stand united, but only when all who are united in principle unite together in solidarity. The future does not lie in our hands, and therefore I make no promises to you. What I can be for you must become manifest to you not in words but in my ministry. In this manner, then, I accept that ministry, and in this manner I conclude this ceremony with my petition to the Holy One of Israel: that he not turn back my hand wherever it seeks to build up Jerusalem's walls. Amen.

---

12. During Kuyper's previous pastorate at Utrecht, he had caused a national stir by pressing hard for precise liturgical forms and opposing Synod. The Amsterdam pastor and social reformer Rev. C. S. Adama van Scheltema had published an *Open Letter to Dr. Kuyper*, in which he deplored Kuyper's conduct in Utrecht because it showed that "this talented man, this noble spirit," was in danger of becoming "an ecclesiastical Bismarck."

TRACT ON THE REFORMATION OF THE CHURCHES

TEXT INTRODUCTION

Kuyper's 1883 *Tract on the Reformation of the Churches* provided an outline of the pure church and a manual for reforming the church. It was also a defense of ecclesiastical secession from the state church, should that become necessary—which it did several years later. The *Tract* describes more than just a reform of the church; it promotes a complete razing to the ground of the NHK (the Dutch national church). Over against a state regulated and subsidized church, Kuyper argues for a more thorough separation of church and state. Over against the national church, Kuyper argues that the church of the New Testament is a worldwide church. Over against the centralized synodical bureaucracy of the NHK, Kuyper argues for a church that originates at the local level. The *Tract* mainly deals with the institutional church, though Kuyper's understanding of the organic church provides a background for his account of the institution. The organism, as a visible gathering of believers, is always a local gathering. Any such local gathering manifests all the traits of the organism and essence of the church, and it precedes the formation of the institution. The local gathering is thus fully a church, though not the complete church. The church exhibits its global identity through the confederation of local churches.

Kuyper's original references (indicated by "Note by the author") have been updated to modern style conventions.

Source: Kuyper, Abraham. *Tractaat van de reformatie der kerken, aan de zonen der Reformatie hier te lande op Luthers vierde eeuwfeest aangeboden.* Amsterdam: Höveker & Zoon, 1884. Translated by Arjen Vreugdenhil and Nelson D. Kloosterman.

TRACT ON THE REFORMATION OF THE CHURCHES

PREFACE

Days of commemoration were always considered sacred, among all nations, throughout all ages, in all spheres of human life. And frequently they brought a blessing as well. These days of commemoration set before our mind and bring to life the mighty events of faith from the past whose effects have come to a standstill. And the heart of man and of nations, reliving such an event along the way of commemoration, is overtaken with a feeling of shame and self-reproach for their own spiritual degeneration. The hearts of people and of nations take new courage as they behold what the resilience of faith once accomplished; with warmer enthusiasm than before they give glory and honor to him who once was pleased to work these powers of faith in people, and who still remains the same faithful God who works them in us also.

It is therefore with good reason that the German-Protestant nations prepared this fall to celebrate Luther's fourth centenary in all the countries of Christendom, on the tenth of November. October 31, 1917, will be an even more solemn day of celebration, but Luther's birthday is more than worthy of such a commemoration. The first act of Reformation took place at the castle's chapel in Wittenberg. But those who confess with us that the Lord our God prepares the instruments for his church from their mother's womb, know that Luther's birth in the quiet town of Eisleben gave us the man through whose courage the light would be returned to the lampstand, and who would reopen the way to peace with God for all those "storm-tossed and not comforted" [Isa 54:11].

We Reformed people in the Netherlands also join this jubilee of our German brothers and sisters. Luther is not merely the hero of faith of the Lutheran churches, but just as much the man of our sympathies, and the confidant of our heart as well. To his word and work all churches of the Reformation—including the Reformed churches of western Europe—owe not only thanks, but more importantly, the inspiring principle of their reformation.

Those in Lutheran countries may consider the Reformation complete without Calvin, but the Reformed churches would never think of Calvin apart from the broad shoulders of Luther on which his slender figure stands. Calvin finished for us the picture of Christ's church with even more detail, elegance, and purity than the hero of Wittenberg, but it was Luther who cut the granite out of the rock and in powerful strokes chiseled out the shape.

In the Netherlands, too, the first impulse of Reformation did not come from Calvin, who flourished later, but from Luther. It soon became clear that the German-Lutheran Reformation could not grow firm roots in this country, while the Genevan-Calvinistic Reformation immediately created order in the chaos. Nevertheless, our genuinely Reformed leaders have never forgotten that Luther's activity set fire to the powder, and that Calvin merely followed him to complete what he had started.

As firmly as they insisted on the purity of the distinctive features of their doctrine and the characteristics of their church organization, the Reformed have never forgotten the bonds that connected them to Luther and his followers. The Reformed always read Luther, while Calvin was forgotten in Lutheran countries. In Lutheran countries Calvin was despised, but Luther has always been mentioned with honor in Calvinistic countries. The German Lutherans have often refused to acknowledge us as brothers and sisters, but the Reformed have always warmly desired brotherly bonds with the Lutheran churches in Germany. While the Lutheran relies on his mildness and broadness of mind, and professes annoyance with our Calvinistic narrow-mindedness, it remains an incontrovertible

testimony of history that the initiatives of fraternal relations always proceeded from the Calvinists. Their rejection was due mostly to the theological Lutheran school. (Just read Villmar's essays even in our time.)[1]

Our Reformed leaders never went as far as many of our "mediating
theologians" today in their enthusiasm to hail Luther as their bosom
friend, while passing by the cold marble statue of Calvin—as they perceive it—with no more than a polite greeting. The Reformed could not do
so, since anyone who has tasted the superior drink could not return to the
inferior draft. Every good Reformed believer does not hesitate to profess
that Calvin brought the Reformation of the churches further than Luther
ever did.

But even though Calvin has and holds their grateful praise, they continue to honor Martin Luther as the man whom God appointed to break
the shackles that kept his church bound. They celebrate him as the theologian who in his youth was as firmly Calvinist as Calvin ever was. They
remember him gratefully as the founder of numerous Protestant sister
churches. Although these churches were less purely Reformed, as genuine churches of Christ they still proclaimed the Word of God. They are
acknowledged in our circles with unfeigned brotherly love as "members
of the mystical body of our Lord."

May it therefore be granted to a Reformed person of our time to express
publicly his grateful allegiance to Luther's person and work at this commemoration of his fourth centenary.

I have had the privilege of making some humble contributions to the
revival of the historic Calvinistic traditions in the Netherlands—among
the people, theologians, and statesmen. Frequently this has raised suspicion among others that this love of the Reformed principle was equally
matched with a narrow-minded jealousy toward non-Calvinistic brothers
and sisters. Not infrequently there even was a whisper behind my back
suggesting that in my view and the view of my colleagues, no one but
Calvin appeared to be worthy of our gratitude.

Well then, in order that it may appear how incorrect this impression is,
and how unjustly the Reformed people today are accused of narrow-mindedness, I considered it desirable not to let Luther's fourth centenary pass

---

1. Kuyper is likely referring to A. F. C. Vilmar (1800–68), a staunch defender of tradi-
    tional Lutheranism.

without offering a public token, from the Reformed wing, of sincere homage to the memory of the great Reformer!

And since among all nations and in every group it was deemed most worthy of the memory of great men to bring to life the main events of their life and work—so that painters were honored by writing about the art of their brush, poets by writing about their songs, rulers by writing about the art of ruling—how could anyone fault me when I attempt to honor the great Reformer by writing an essay about the reformation of the very churches whose reformational life finds its origin in Luther's courageous life?

For our German neighbors, Luther was also the national hero; also the fighter for freedom of thought and conscience; and also the theologian with a subjective element in his theology. But above all and before all else, Luther stands in history as the Reformer of the church of our Lord Jesus Christ.

I do not deny the German nation the right to honor Luther as one of her great sons; I do not dispute the freethinkers when they thank Luther for releasing their bonds; and I sincerely grant our mediating theologians the pleasure to lean their theology toward Luther's subjective side. Yet I claim that Luther is fully commemorated only by one who appreciates the reformational aspect of his portrait and does not forget his breaking with the organized church of his time.

A German can rejoice in Luther's memory even if he is Jewish or Roman Catholic. A freethinker can honor Luther, even if he denies the sacred truth for which Luther fought and wrestled. And even a legitimate opponent of every break with the church organization can appreciate Luther as a theologian. But the genuine Luther at the core of his person, the Luther in his role as a Reformer—him these people do not honor.

Conversely, I would insist that one who fights for Germany's rebirth apart from Christ or freedom of conscience apart from alignment with the Word, or who pleads for the healing of the church apart from breaking with human ordinances—such a person is unfaithful to Luther's spirit. That person far more denies his courageous deeds than honors the principle he held sacred.

At his fourth centenary, Luther's name must also be honored among us as a witness of God. A witness of God for all those anxious of soul, that they should seek their perfect peace nowhere but in the Christ of God as their Surety and Mediator. A witness for the doubting person, that with the words *"Das Wort sollen sie stehen lassen"* [The Word they shall leave unmoved] one should oppose as error any opinion that compromises in any way the absolute infallibility of God's holy Word, morally or historically. A witness for the patriot, that he should never separate his politics from his faith, but should always seek renaissance through Christ, also for his country and nation. But then also a witness for those who wholeheartedly love the churches of God, so that if evil pervades the churches even more, they should not shrink back from breaking with their church organization, and should not rest until our Zion is revived.

This at least seems to me incontrovertible among experts: Anyone who shouts: "Breaking with our church organization would be revolution!" forfeits the right to join, as a true son of the Reformation, the festive celebration of that hero of the Lord who, precisely by breaking with the church organization of his time, became our beloved hero and the founder of our churches.

Kuyper

Amsterdam

October 1, 1883

INTRODUCTION

A brief word to introduce this essay: Luther's fourth centenary has all the more significance today because the reformation of the churches is once again under discussion. Just as today, people in Luther's day did not start thoughtlessly the demolition of what had decayed beyond repair. Luther's deeds were preceded by a long and serious study of church government, and numerous writings pleaded the cause of the Reformation before it took place. Without this preparation, Luther's actions would have caused only chaos. But almost everything fell in place after the break he initiated. It is truly admirable how in those days the most correct concepts of church and church government developed among preachers, elders, and church members.

Today, sadly, we have not yet reached that point. There is talk of reformation in our churches, but the views differ too widely. A shared opinion is absent. Many are unsure about the path to be taken. This has led to unpleasant friction and dividing into groups, which is impure because many base their allegiance merely on how things sound. Thus they often separate what should be unified.

Yet this may not hamper the weighty work of the reformation of our churches. It is up to the sovereignty of the Lord God whether he will prolong the judgment that currently oppresses our churches. But that does not release us from the duty of obedience to find a way of healing the break in his churches. The misery is too great that this sad ecclesiastical state of affairs has brought, and is still bringing, over our country and people. The key of knowledge is being lost. Unstable spirits float along on every wind of doctrine. The house of our God has become a mockery. And the finer virtues and piety are threatened in the best circles in this land.

～～～～～～～～～～～～～～

For this reason I consider it advisable that those men in our circles to whom the Lord God gave occasion to consider and study this important issue, should present their views about the reformation of the church in an orderly manner through the publication of books. Individual articles in weekly magazines always treat the matter piecemeal, and without preparation the oral debates cannot advance much.

First, all those who think they can point out the way forward should present their views in books, well-structured and integrated. Only then can there be an orderly discussion of the issue and the possibility of clear and conscious action. This is why I have spent my free hours this year doing what I admonish others to do—subjecting my own views, as good or bad as they may be, to the judgment of my brothers.

I have attempted to organize this work in such a way that it is thoroughly transparent. To accomplish that, I did not limit myself to a discussion of reformation, but inserted before the chapter on reformation another chapter on the deformation of the church. To make clear what I meant by *deformation*, I inserted yet another chapter before that one about the formation of the churches. And because one cannot agree about the formation of the churches without a prior exposition of the general principles that govern the life of the church, I thought it best to discuss these principles in a separate chapter. The division into sections has been designed to facilitate the location of a specific topic.

Even though this essay only presents a dim shadow of what a manual for Reformed church government should be, I considered the possibility that this essay might provide emergency assistance in that respect, until the time comes when one of our professors in church government will give us that indispensable manual. May this labor be commended to the good favor of our God, to the love of the brothers and sisters, and to the charitable judgment of the specialists! My reward will be abundant if this essay provides a useful contribution to the reformation of those Dutch churches, which have all the love of my heart.

Kuyper

Amsterdam

October 1, 1883

CHAPTER 1 – GENERAL PRINCIPLES

WHAT THE REFORMATION OF THE CHURCHES PRESUPPOSES   § 1
Reformation of the churches presupposes, first, that the churches of
Christ have a certain form, shape, or figure that is characteristic for them
as churches. Second, it presupposes that this form, shape, or figure can
become impure through deformation or disfiguring. Third, it requires
that through reformation these deformed or disfigured churches can
be returned to the original form, the right shape, the normal figure that
flows out of its being and is defined by its character.

HOW THE RIGHT FORM OF THE CHURCH CAN BE KNOWN   § 2
The right form, shape, or figure of the churches is known from Holy
Scripture. Not, as is often thought, as if Holy Scripture offers a set of regulations for church planting, or a church order for the government of the
churches, or even a systematically organized exposition of the principles from which these can be derived. Holy Scripture offers none of this.
Therefore people are mistaken when they turn every example in Scripture
into a rule for us or string together individual sayings using their own
inventiveness to make up what they did not find in Scripture. Rather,
Holy Scripture exerts authority—absolute authority—in this matter only
because it shows to us infallibly how the Triune God brought and brings
operations and powers into this world, a world fallen into wickedness and
still lying in corruption. These operations and powers in turn, according
to unchangeable laws and in certain ways, brought his church into existence and still preserve it.

The world, stooping beneath the curse, does not bring forth a church
from the womb of its own life. Rather, its life directly opposes the church.
It does not tolerate the church and reacts against it because it is a power
that aims to restrict and rein in the world's sinful nature. Thus the root
of the church does not lie in this world but outside of it, in the counsel of
God. In the counsel of God is the eternal good pleasure to have all things
culminate in the glory of the Triune God, despite sin, death, and the devil.
For this purpose it contains the design of a kingdom of glory in which the
throne will stand firm forever; the anointing of the Mediator as the King
in that kingdom, as the ruler to sit on that throne; the determination of
a people for that King, a people that stands as one body under him and is
connected to him as the Head; and finally, the election of individuals who,
as subjects of that King, are by right the members of that body.

The outworking of that counsel creates the church in this world in a way we cannot understand. Words, powers, operations, influences, and ordinances flow from God to this world. As a fruit of these various operations of God, the church comes into existence. In spite of the opposition of the world, the church continues, and in spite of the sin that invades it and sometimes afflicts the very root of its life as a cancer, the church continues to increase according to the growth ordained for it by God.

These words, powers, operations, influences, and ordinances, which flow from God to the world, have continued uninterrupted from the very beginning until now. They will continue as long as the bride is awaiting the Bridegroom. If they would cease for a single moment, the church would wither, die, and cease to exist. No one may therefore restrict these words or operations or appointments to the time between Adam in paradise and that of John on Patmos. Rather, they continue unlimited from John to our day, and they will continue until Jesus' return.

But we must make distinctions in these operations of God, both then and now, according to their varied nature and their different dispensations. Two distinctions are especially important.

First of all, every form of life raises a twofold question: How does this life come into existence? And how is this life subsequently fed, sustained, perpetuated? First God creates and fashions a child in its mother's womb; only then it is born, and from then on it must be fed, first by its mother and later by its own hand. When the mother's blood is pressed into the fetus before birth, that is not for feeding but for fashioning, which is radically different in its nature and operation from all later, proper food. The same contrast speaks just as strongly in the two sacraments: holy baptism as the sacrament of newly created life, and therefore received only once; and holy communion as the sacrament of life that must be fed, and therefore repeated continually. Likewise, there is a twofold operation from God to his church: first, an operation by which he engenders his church, carries it within a secret place, and forms it into its true shape; and then a second, entirely different operation, through which he feeds the church first with milk and then with solid food.

This naturally brings us from the first distinction to the second distinction mentioned above. The church is not the church of one nation, but of the entire world. Humankind, not merely one nation, despised God. God's triumph must therefore be revealed not over one nation, but over humankind. The counsel of the Lord Yahweh will appear in power not when a circle of pious believers in a single nation calls on his name, but only when he has gathered his church out of the entire world, so that hallelujahs are raised from all nations and in all languages. Repeatedly and with emphasis, the holy apostle calls this the great mystery, "which was hidden through all ages, but is now revealed."[2]

Although the Lord has always had his true, essential church on earth from the beginning of the world until now, there is nonetheless a noticeable difference between the church during and after the time of special revelation. For as long as that special revelation continues, the church is still being formed, carried within the secret place, and remains woven into the fabric of Israel's national existence. Only with the apostolate—or rather when the apostolate comes to an end—does the hour of its birth arrive, its entrance into the light of life. Only then do you see it appear among the nations, and its manifestation in the realm of the world and of all humankind is completed. This is therefore its period of becoming, the history of the beginning of its existence. Only afterward comes an entirely different era, which still continues, the all-encompassing life of that church among the nations, disconnected from Israel, as church of the human race.

Summarizing these two distinctions, we therefore find first, a series of operations of God by which the church in Israel is prepared for its birth into the world. And second, we find an entirely separate series of operations of God by which the church, after its birth, subsequently is sustained within that world.

Now one should note carefully that those operations of God in the church's first period of becoming are also normative and binding for the second period of its existence. After all, the potter is free to shape a lump of clay into a bowl or pitcher or vase as he pleases. But once the shape of, say, a bowl has been chosen and the clay has been shaped accordingly, all further preparation is also bound to that chosen shape. Likewise, the Lord God could give to his church during its formation whatever shape he chose—or rather, had chosen—in his eternal counsel. But once the church had been shaped and thus formed, and once it had been born, God himself

---

2. *Note by the author*: Rom 16:25; Eph 3:9; Col 1:26; 2 Tim 1:19; Eph 1:9; Titus 1:2; 1 Pet 1:20. It is therefore not contradictory when our Catechism confesses that God has gathered his church from the beginning of the world until now, and when Jesus declares in Matthew 16:18 that now for the first time he will build his church on this *petra*. Here, too, one must distinguish between conception and birth.

was bound to that first operation; therefore the entire subsequent development of his church is subject to the authority of that original formation. This authority is not arbitrary, but required by the law of created life.

Thus God's current operations in his church must be directed according to the operations through which he previously brought the church to its birth into the world. Every person who is confessing, preaching, or working in that church is bound to obedience to the law of life that God Almighty himself bestowed upon the church in its conception and formation.

Holy Scripture is nothing else than the pure and organic exposition of all operations, influences, words, powers, and ordinances that flow from God to the world to bring his church to its birth into the world. The church of Christ among the nations is therefore bound continually, perpetually, and irrevocably to what Holy Scripture shows us to be its unchanging form and law of life in terms of the church's conception, formation, and birth.

§ 3   THE FOUR WAYS IN WHICH CHRIST'S CHURCH MUST BE UNDERSTOOD
On the basis of the authority of Holy Scripture, the essence of the church must be viewed from four perspectives. By the term *church*, one could mean the church as it exists in God's counsel, the church as its life is hidden in Christ, the church as it is realized among human beings on earth, or finally, the church as it will one day in glory sing praises before the throne. Confusion of these four meanings will impede any clear insight. It is not as if there were four churches. The same church is ordained in God's counsel, has been given to Christ by the Father, is realized on earth, and will one day sing in glory. But this fourfold perspective must be distinguished because the relationships in which the church is involved are entirely different depending on whether you view it in God's counsel, in Christ, in the world, or in heavenly glory. And this will change the answer to all the questions that arise concerning the church.

In God's counsel lies the church of all ages, with the full number of elect, completed according to its perfect plan, from before the foundation of the world. In that counsel it is ordained, called, justified, and glorified before the face of the Triune God.

However, if I speak of the church in Christ, then that solemn, majestic unity is immediately broken, since the patriarchs and prophets under the old covenant had a different relationship to the Mediator than the New Testament believers have to Christ. There was a moment in time when he became flesh, a moment in time when he suffered and died, a moment when he rose again, and thus there was also a time in which these miracles of mercy had not yet happened. The forgiveness and justification, which are eternal in God's counsel, appear in time with the Christ. The benefit for the church comes only when he dies, and the church is justified only when he arose.

Likewise, the relationship to the Mediator is different for the church on earth and for the church in heaven. Here on earth the bride is still calling for the Bridegroom; there she has already entered into the holy marriage. The difference is so profound that here she needs atonement, but there no longer. Nevertheless, this distinction does not sever the church in any way for both the elect from of old and those now living on earth, as well as those who already entered into glory, and even the seed of the church that must yet sprout—they are all given to the Son from eternity. They are in him, one body with their Lord. When he died, all of the elect died with Christ. When he arose, all of the elect arose with him. Yes, now already all of the elect are seated in heaven, along with Christ. "You have died, and your life is hidden with Christ in God" (Col 3:3). The holy, inscrutable mystery!

Again the relationships are very different if we view the church not as it is contained in God's counsel or hidden in Christ, but as it manifests itself on earth during this dispensation. Then we lose the unity that the church has in God's counsel, as well as the holiness that the church possesses in Christ. And the church on earth transverses all those different states and moves in all these various relationships that result from its contact with the world, from its infection with sin, and from the transitions and developments that are inseparably connected with any life in time.

Finally, when speaking of the church already in heaven, all these earthly relationships fall away, to make room for a new relationship, again of a very different nature, governed predominantly by the distinction in glory between temporary glory, which the blessed ones enjoy now, and the more perfect glory after the resurrection, which must wait until Jesus' return.

People who speak of the church will be confused and will confuse others if they fail to ask in every discussion which of these four relationships of the church is meant. Addressing as it does the reformation of the church, this essay must also ask this question, and the answer can only be that in the reformation of the church we do not speak of the church in God's counsel, nor of the church in Christ, nor of the church in heaven. In these three senses of the word the church cannot become deformed and therefore cannot be reformed. We must speak only and exclusively about the church of Christ as it manifests itself on earth.

§ 4   WHY THE ONE CHURCH ON EARTH IS BOTH INVISIBLE AND VISIBLE

This church of Christ on earth is both visible and invisible. Every human being is in part observable and in part not observable, without being two persons. Likewise with the church of Christ this distinction between the visible and the invisible in no way nullifies the unity of the essence of the church. It is one and the same church, which according to its hidden essence is concealed in the spiritual, manifest only to the spiritual eye; at the same time in its external form it becomes visible, to be publicly manifest to the natural eye, to believers as well as the world.

Because of its spiritual, invisible aspect, the church exists across all the earth, and in turn that entire church on earth is one with the church already in heaven. Meanwhile the invisible church is also holy. This is not only because it is an artful creation of God, fully dependent on his divine influences and operations, but also because the spiritual pollution and the sin dwelling within believers does not belong to it, but wages war against it.

According to its visible aspect, on the other hand, the church appears only in parts and therefore always locally. The national churches arise only when mutual connections are made between these local churches, as required by the nature of the church and national relationships. Even broader connections among the churches can only be temporary or extremely loose and flexible. And just as the churches (as visible manifestations of the invisible church) are not one, likewise they are not holy, since they share in the imperfection of all earthly life and are polluted by the power of sin, which continually undermines the well-being of the church, both internally and externally.

Therefore with regard to the church of Christ on earth, and more specifically its visible manifestation, the duty of reformation comes into existence as soon as deformation appears to be present. In fact, this duty of reformation is therefore an ongoing duty, because in a strict sense the church is always deformed. It is never seen in its pure, uncorrupted form, and it always carries unholy elements within it. Yet in this essay we do not mean reformation in this absolute sense. There is a deviation from the spiritual essence of the church that lies in the nature of its presence in the world, and without which the church cannot be manifested among human beings. This deviation, therefore, is such that, although it diverges from the spiritual ideal, it is and remains normal as far as the visible manifestation of the church is concerned, at least insofar as the dominion of the holy over the unholy, and of the truth over falsehood, remains pure and uncompromised. This inevitable deviation from the ideal cannot be removed by any reformation. Whoever tries to do so loses the church and finds the sect. No duty of reformation exists in this respect. That would be Donatism![3] Perfectionism! The pursuit of a congregation of angel-saints on earth! A hunt that, sadly, will always yield the "prize" of brutal savagery!

The visible church has a duty of reformation only when the deviation sinks below this normal level, such that the church not merely carries the unholy element in it, but tolerates it silently and without punishment; or even worse, if in the end the church gives power and dominion over what is true and holy to the untrue and unholy.

On this basis, the reformation of the church can be described only as fulfilling the duty resting upon the church in its visible manifestation—that is, upon the local church of Christ, both individually and in its communal relations—so that as often as falsehood and sin in its midst cast off their yoke with impunity, it might, by returning to the original form commanded for the churches in God's Word, ensure that truth and holiness again have dominion over falsehood and sin.

HOW GOD'S WORD GOVERNS THE ENTIRE LIFE OF THE CHURCH §5

The normal form or shape or figure of the church on earth is determined by God's Word. The Lord gathers his elect through that Word, making it effective in a saving way in regeneration through the Holy Spirit. Having been brought to life through that Spirit, the elect confess that Word to Satan and the world, to each other and themselves. They desire to be kept under the discipline of this Word through the establishment of preaching. They seek the administration of the sacraments to affirm their faith in that Word. They attempt to germinate the seed of the church through that

---

3. Kuyper here uses the term "Donatism" as shorthand for any movement that seeks a pure church consisting only of true believers, which was a goal of the Donatist sect of the fourth and fifth centuries.

Word. And they endeavor, likewise through that Word, to incorporate into the church pagans, Jews, and apostates.

The ministry of atonement, prayers, and praise to the Lord our God is not added to that Word; after Golgotha it lies contained within the ministry of that Word. This used to be different before Christ died. That is why in the period of the church's gestation, when the definitive sacrifice had not yet been made, when the intercessor was not yet praying at the throne of grace, and when the Spirit had not yet been poured out on all (Joel 2:28), there was the ministry of the ceremonies, consisting in the daily sacrifices, the priestly intercession, and the Levitical singing. But this ceremonial ministry did not end in the church after its birth into the world. Between the fading away of the Israelite church and the rise of the worldwide church lies the coming of the Mediator in the fullness of time. In and for the entire church of all ages that Mediator brought the definitive and all-sufficient sacrifice; then he ascended into heaven to bring to God the prayer for his people, in and for his church; and he sent the Holy Spirit who looses every tongue to proclaim the great acts of God and to magnify the virtues of him who called his people out of darkness into his wonderful light [1 Pet 2:9].

Therefore one cannot say that whereas the church in Israel brought sacrifices and had priestly intercession and spiritual praises, the church of today is lacking these. Rather, we must confess that in times of old these three were only inferior shadows, whereas in the church today they were and are administered gloriously by Christ and the Holy Spirit. Christ is in the church, and even today, every day, he applies his only sacrifice, lifts up his prayer of intercession for us, and empowers the Spirit unto the glory of the Father. The error of Rome is not that they wish to maintain these three sacred realities within the church, but rather that in a time when the Mediator himself performs them, they try to imitate him or perform them in his place, and thus take them out of his hands.

In a practical sense, as far as the reformation of the churches is concerned—since the work of the Mediator cannot be subject to deformation—these three ministries in fact flow together into the one ministry of the Word. The disciples of Christ are now clean because of the Word that he spoke to them (see John 15:3). No one has any part in his sacrifice, his intercession, or his Spirit, except through faith, and only faith in the Word applies these sacred realities to the soul. In the ministry of the Word we receive, as its main content administered to us, the sacrifice of Christ, his intercession, and the operation of the Spirit in the soul. All sacrament and all prayer and all singing of praise in the church are therefore bound to that Word, must be based on that Word, and through that Word taken up in that ongoing mediating work of Christ our Lord.

There is therefore no other ministry in the visible church than the ministry of the Word, and all manifestations of the church's life flow from that one ministry of the Word. For as often as the elect confess this Word of God to themselves, they travel in the way of repentance, self-condemnation, and conversion, and the result is the confession of sins. By contrast, when they confess this Word of God to each other, the result is admonition and rebuke and all of the glorious work of love. When they confess this Word to the world, the work of mercy, for body and soul, comes to manifestation. When they confess this Word to Satan, the result is a glorying in hope and entrance to martyrdom. Finally, when they confess this Word of God to the Lord himself and his holy angels, prayer ascends and the song of praise rings forth. The confession of the Word is the full expression of the life of the church.

HOW THE MINISTRY OF THE WORD WAS DIFFERENT IN THE PAST THAN IT   §6
IS NOW

This ministry of the Word has been different depending on when the special revelation of God continued, was temporarily suspended, or had already come to an end. While this special revelation of God continued and was active, then this service flowed directly from God though his seers and prophets. Then there was no organized continuation of this ministry, but that ministry came when the Spirit of God took hold of the prophets, ceased when the vision of the prophets faded, and resumes when the Lord God spoke to his servants.

Therefore, when the prophecy of the old covenant ceased with Malachi and was not resumed until John the Baptist, the organized ministry of the Word in the synagogues arose for the four intervening centuries—a ministry that retained its high value only until the resumption of special revelation in the days of John the Baptist. This event forced the synagogue service into the background, replacing it with the ministry of the Word of our Chief Prophet, preceded by the "Repent!" of his herald and followed by the ministry of the apostolate.

The ministry through appointed pastors and teachers matured only when, with the end of this apostolate, special revelation reached its completion. In the past people were instructed in the Word by the priest and by the father of the family, but before the deportation to Babylon there was no separate office of pastors and teachers. This office existed in the synagogue only as a prefiguring, and it became normal only after the ascension to heaven of him who had appointed some to be apostles, then appointed some to be evangelists, and ever since, throughout all ages, appointed and still appoints some to be pastors and overseers.

The prefiguring in the rabbinate of the synagogue could arise only when the Scripture of the old covenant was completed. Likewise, the formation of this office after the end of the apostolate could come to full growth and bloom only when the entire Scriptural revelation of old and new covenant had reached its completion. As long as this written Word of God was not yet able to function, God himself worked by speaking his Word in the soul of the prophets, but that spoken Word had to cease when the written Word was completed. After this, the activity of the Holy Spirit with respect to the Word continued, but in a different manner. From now on, the Spirit illuminates, just as in the past he had revealed.

Any movement that disrupts this fixed relationship, that fails to see this distinction between the ministry of the Word before and after the completion of the Holy Scripture, and that even now speaks of a revelatory operation of the Spirit in the same sense as before, overthrows the ordinances of God in a Montanistic or Anabaptistic[4] manner. Or worse, they make the "revelation of God through his prophets and apostles" [see Eph 3:5] common when they, as some members of the Ethical party do, make only a distinction of degree between the revealing operation of the Spirit in the apostles and prophets, and his illuminating operation in the elect.[5]

---

4. Kuyper here uses the terms "Montanistic" and "Anabaptistic" as shorthand for any theological movement that overthrows the authority of Scripture by appeal to extrabiblical revelation. Such an appeal was a feature of the second-century Montanists and of some sects in the diverse Anabaptist movement of the Reformation era.

5. The Ethical party was a group of theologians who followed the mediating theology of Friedrich Schleiermacher (1763-1834). Schleiermacher maintained that New Testament revelation was both normative for the church but also homogeneous with subsequent expressions of the gospel in the history of the church.

Why the Church Did Not Need Its Own Organization in the Past §7
but Now Does Need It

Under the ministry of shadows there was an organized ministry of the priesthood, but not of the Word. Today, however, there is no organized ministry of priesthood; instead there has arisen an organization of the ministry of the Word. These two arrangements are not of the same nature. When the priestly ministry of the church was still hidden in the fabric of Israel, the priestly ministry used to have a strictly national character. It was entrusted to a single tribe, or stricter yet, to a few families, and it was not spiritual preference but natural kinship to this family or this tribe that gave one the right of ordination. By contrast, after the end of the apostolate, when the church had become a worldwide church, the church lays aside this national restriction, displays more purely than ever its spiritual aspect, and can therefore no longer bind its ministries to descent and kinship of blood.

This naturally and gradually pressured the church to organize itself. Under Israel there was no need for this, since the national organism served simultaneously as the organization of the church. Nation and church were one, just as the yet unborn infant is yet one with the womb where it finds nurture and rest. But with the fading of Israel and the terminating of its entirely unique significance for the church, all of this changed. Since the church of Christ is not destined to become a Greek or Egyptian or Roman church, but rather to grow up as the worldwide church, it cannot compensate for the loss of the organizational power of Israel's national existence by subjecting itself to the national bonds of Greece or Syria, Egypt or the Roman Empire. Rather, in order to fulfill its calling it must be watchful against being bound in such an unnatural straightjacket, and it must protect its autonomy.

It can do so only by being organized on its own foundation, independent of the organization of the nations. Israel was designed for the church and created for the church, and therefore it could produce a fitting structure for the life of the church in its preparatory state. But this situation in Israel was entirely exceptional. This does not work for other nations. No other nation has been designed for this church in this sense and no other nation was created for the church in that particular way. Any attempt to force upon the church any other national organism as though that organism were designed for it, would be unnatural, inappropriate, and contrary to the nature of things. The church has no choice but to organize itself—not in the way Israel was organized, nor as a copy of the model of national organisms, but according to its own nature, corresponding to the requirement of its own life. Only in this way can it do justice to the great mystery of which the holy apostle Paul speaks.

§ 8   With Whom Does the Church's Sovereign Authority Originate?

This separate organization of the church presupposes that there is authority within it and over it. How could an organization, institution, or assembly exist, if within its sphere there were no power to command, and no obligation to obey that command? Any organization without original, granted, or vested authority would be like a wall without cement or a joist placed in a wall without anchors. Such authority existed in the preparatory church: first in Moses' governorship from Yahweh, then in the judges, and then in Israel's kingship. God clothed David's house with divine authority. But that authority was not just temporary; it was ongoing, laid upon David's royal dynasty:

> I once for all have sworn by my own holiness.
> I will not break my word, but David I will bless;
> his throne will evermore from heir to heir be handed,
> for like the sun it will endure as I commanded.[6]

Both must be true: Israel's kingdom did fall away, *and* David's throne stands forever—an apparent contradiction that finds its solution in that David's house first brought forth kings who were only a shadow of the true King. Then it brought forth that true King who is called to be King of kings and to continue as King forever. Rome's attempt to imitate the Mosaic and Israelite situation in this respect through its governorship therefore ends up violating the honor of our King. The Christ of God, and he alone, sits as David's son, Lord and King over his church forever.

§ 9   How Jesus Became King of His Church

Christ does not possess this royal power from himself; the Father gave it to him as the reward for his self-humiliation unto death. Therefore, because he became "obedient to the point of death, even death on a cross," says the apostle Paul, "Therefore God has highly exalted him and bestowed on him the name that is above every name, so that at the name of Jesus every

---

6. *Book of Praise: Anglo-Genevan Psalter* (Winnipeg: Premier, 2014), Psa 89:12. Kuyper quotes the corresponding lines from the Dutch versification, without reference.

knee should bow, in heaven and on earth and under the earth, and every tongue confess that Jesus Christ is Lord, to the glory of God the Father" [Phil 2:8–11]. "All authority in heaven and on earth," Christ himself testifies, "has been given to me" [Matt 28:18]. Thus the authority over the church, like all other power, rests with the Triune God alone, with the Father, Son, and Holy Spirit. It flows from the source of divine sovereignty, and inasmuch as Christ is God's own Son and is himself God, he certainly shares in this original sovereign power over the church.

But—and this must be noted well—Jesus is the appointed King of the church, not as God's Son, but as our Mediator. It is only as the Mediator that he does not possess sovereign authority over the church from himself, but he is King by the grace of God, or rather, since grace always implies unmerited favor, he is King by God's high command.

Therefore the situation is as follows: All sovereign authority rests in the Triune God, to command in the state and among the nations as well as to command in the church. Meanwhile it pleases the Lord Yahweh not to exercise this authority over the nations or over the church directly. Therefore he appoints rulers and governors over the nations, and likewise he appoints over his church the Mediator, Christ. Just as the kings of the earth have authority over the nations derived from the sovereign God, so too Jesus our Mediator is vested with an authority over the church derived from God.

Now in order that the Son could be a genuine king over his church, he is simultaneously given authority over Satan, who assaults the church and tries to overwhelm it; over the angels, who are sent out for the sake of those who shall inherit salvation; and over the rulers and nations, under whose crowns and in whose midst the churches operate and flourish. But this does not add to or take away from the serious and undeniable fact that Jesus' kingship over his church is a reward for his unspeakable love. His reward is based on his self-sacrifice.

Because of this, his kingship is inseparable from his priesthood, as well as from his prophetic office. Golgotha is no dead fact, but the eternal ever-living event, which is actively applied by him to the souls of his elect from hour to hour. And since without authority his Word would no longer be God's Word, in his church there can be no prophetic testimony alongside his kingship. The Priest and Prophet are one in the King. Concerning the organization and formation of the church on earth we must therefore reject and oppose as condemned by the Word of God and violating the honor of Jesus, any attempt to establish a priesthood after or apart from Golgotha, to establish a sphere of authority alongside the throne of David's Son, or to establish an untruthful human word alongside the Word of the man Jesus Christ.

We write emphatically of the *man* Jesus, for only as the Son of Man is Jesus our highest Prophet, our only high Priest, and our eternal King. The Triune God is outside the church, since he is above it; but the man Jesus Christ is in the church, living in our flesh and blood. And just as it pleased God to rule the nations through rulers who are men and to whom he gives power, so too God was pleased to rule his church through a king who is a man and whom he has clothed with power. The only difference is that the rulers are sinners, while King Jesus is separated from sinners, and therefore the authority that is placed on the rulers with their crown, is laid in Jesus Christ, as a power resting in his divine person.

Thus one can never think of the church as if Jesus were outside it. Jesus lives in it, eternally administers his sacrifice within it, continually prays his high-priestly prayer of intercession, and rules it uninterruptedly though his Word and Spirit. It is the church only through this constant prophetic, priestly, and kingly action of Christ; and on earth the church of God is revealed only insofar as it is recognized to be the outward form radiating from that ongoing, active operation of Christ.

§ 10   How This Kingly Authority of Christ Works on Earth Through the Instrumental Use of Human Persons

In order to exercise this kingly authority over his church, Christ had to ascend into heaven. On earth he had the form of a servant; only in heaven was he clothed with royal majesty. And he manifests that majesty not by virtue of his human nature, but in that human nature through the power of his divinity, which enables him to be present "with his grace, majesty, and spirit" in his church in all places at once.[7] "Where two or three are gathered in my name"—that is, the church in its smallest imaginable size—"there I am among them" [Matt 18:20]. "Behold, I am with you always, to the end of the age" [Matt 28:20]. "It is to your advantage that I go away" [John 16:7].

Let no one say, therefore, that in a proper sense Christ rules as King only in the heavenly church, and in the earthly church only through delegation of authority to people; that would deny and contradict his divinity. Christ is definitely present in his church on earth, present in the most

---

7. See Heidelberg Catechism, Lord's Day 18, Q&A 47.

proper sense of the word. And where he is not personally present you may have a robed man speaking, but there is no ministry of the Word. There may be sprinkling of water and breaking of bread, but there is no sacrament. People may mutter with closed eyes and sing with open mouths, but there is neither prayer nor praise. Finally, there may be ecclesiastical rulers on plush seats, but there is no consistory, council, or synod with authority in his name.

Only the presence of Christ in his church makes the holy things real. Without that presence of the Christ they are empty shells, vain displays void of essence or benefit. This presence of Christ is "not an external appearance but within you" [see Luke 17:21]; it does not rest in the ordinances or solemnities but exclusively in the people. One should not understand this as though the presence of Christ were manifest only in converted people. There are many elect who have not yet been converted, yet the presence of the Lord is also within them. The breath of his lips blows even in the chaff that is still mixed with the grain, albeit with a fragrance of death unto death, not unto resurrection but unto ruin—or even, as should never be forgotten, it may pass over two or three generations to sprout his elect branches out of the apparently dead trunk.

This presence of Christ in his church, although vested in the people rather than the ordinances, is nonetheless truly bound to those ordinances. The church's awareness of community grows only under and through these ordinances, and that glorious awareness achieves greater clarity through deeds of obedience to the King. For this reason, when the Word and sacraments are truly administered, there is an uncommon awareness of the presence of the Lord, a knowledge that he, the Lord, is in our midst. This is an exhilarating awareness that is enjoyed only when and insofar as it is the presence of Christ himself who is speaking through the minister, who is himself baptizing, who is himself distributing bread and wine, who is leading us in prayer so that we may pray after him, who is giving to us so that we may give alms, and who is himself singing praises to the Father through the sound of our own voices. "I," said the Messiah, "I have told the glad news of deliverance in the great congregation; behold, I have not restrained my lips, as you know, O LORD" (Psa 40:9). "Yours will be my praise in the great assembly" (see Psa 22:25). "The will of the LORD shall prosper in my hand" (see Isa 53:10).

But this does not imply in any way that in the exercise of Jesus' royal authority there should be no use of human persons as instruments in these ordinances. There certainly is such a use, insofar as the church acts visibly on earth, outwardly shows itself, and is revealed in discernible form. The royal authority of Christ must extend to that visible, outward aspect, and this is impossible without the instrumental use of people. But one must keep in mind two unchangeable facts: First, this instrumental use of human persons does not and cannot occur unless it is permeated and accompanied by the activity of the present Christ. Second, this use is not and cannot be anything but instrumental. He is and remains in everything the only and irresistible Worker, and the human person can never be more than an instrument being employed by him, the King, who has royal majesty.

This instrumental use of people is further distinguished according to its purpose: to bring the church to a more full manifestation in the world, or to maintain the rule of King Jesus in the worldwide church itself. The former use, which lasted until the end of the apostolate, bore lasting fruit because the instrumental use of prophets and apostles, among many other things, also resulted in a lasting, written Word of God. This Word is the abiding Word of the King in his church, to which applies in absolute sense the saying of Ecclesiastes: "The word of the king is supreme" [Eccl 8:4]. Even if the Lord, in his wrath over the sin of his people or in testing their faith, is pleased to cause the public preaching of the Word to cease for a time and to burden his church with the cross of persecution—even then the King is never silent. He speaks and continues to speak, every morning and every evening in every church, in every family, to every heart among his elect nation, through his eternal Word, put into enduring written form.

For this reason, his use of the ministry of the prophets and apostles stands out among all instrumental uses of human persons. Today as well, just as in the preceding eighteen centuries, these prophets and apostles are the instruments, ministering throughout the years, through whom King Jesus addresses his church—and in his church, day and night, he addresses his elect.

But alongside this exceptional and instrumental use of prophets and apostles stands, irrevocably linked to the fruit of their labor, the normal instrumental use of persons in the established ordinary church office. The purpose and calling of this office is to realize the Word of the King, to implement it with irresistible power.

The emphasis here is on the phrase *with power*. The office holds the authority of the keys. There is no office without the institution of the King and the investiture of his royal authority. Without that authority it can be an occupation, a human activity, an appointment, but the office will be lacking. The office is an organ of, an implement for, the sovereign power. An earthly king should really do everything himself. But that is impossible. He is lacking the thousands of arms with which the Indians endow their gods. Therefore he institutes the offices and gives them to people who, as the arms of his power, finish the job by his authority, for him, for his glory. That official operation is either directed toward the king or away from the king. It is directed toward the king if knowledge must be acquired to inform the king, and away from the king when it requires obedience of his command. It is directed toward the king when taxes and tribute are brought to the king's treasury, and away from the king when the favor of the king turns toward his people. It is directed toward the king when the praise of his people for him ascends, and away from him when he gives his gifts to his subjects.

In the very same sense, our Lord and King, Christ our Messiah and Immanuel, instituted an office for the visible manifestation of his church on earth, to be the bearer of his royal authorities and manifestation of his royal majesty.

How the Office in Christ's Church Functions Under the New   § 11
Covenant

The office was originally instituted as a single office in the apostolate. "As the Father has sent me, even so I am sending you" [John 20:21]. And "whatever you shall bind on earth shall be bound in heaven" [Matt 18:18]. The offices of teaching, of ruling, and of the [serving of] tables were all contained in that one apostolic office. Ananias and Sapphira laid their offering at the feet of the apostles, and the apostle of the Lord immediately rejected that offering. That was not because the gift should not have been brought to him, but because it was lacking the aroma that was pleasant to the Lord [Acts 5:1–4]. Likewise, the holy apostle Paul on his journeys always collects monies for the impoverished church in Jerusalem.

Thus the apostles initially both administer the Word and serve tables. This shows that the three or four offices that later developed separately do not stand alongside each other as individual offices, but together they really form one single office that must be understood in its oneness. This oneness lies in the oneness of the King's majesty. In the Lord's activity on earth, preaching the gospel did not stand *alongside* healing the sick, or teaching his disciples *alongside* feeding the hungry, but this preaching and this teaching and this wondrous display of love were all expressions of the same anointing. Likewise there is in essence only one operation, which even today proceeds from the King to his church through the instrumental administration of one office, albeit divided into several branches. Even today's missionary displays the oneness of the office in his person wherever new churches are rising up in the pagan world, since he is simultaneously preacher, governor, and provider for the poor.

This office was first divided because of the expansion of the church, in connection with the limited power of those who held the office. Thus we read in Acts 6 that this, and nothing else, was the reason why the diaconate separated from the apostolate. It was because "the disciples were increasing in number" (v. 1), and since this expansion of the church prevented the apostles from giving the necessary attention to the affairs of all, there was murmuring. And this murmuring moved the apostles to acknowledge, not: "As apostles we should not busy ourselves with material things," but: "It is not right that we should give up preaching the word of God to serve tables" [v. 2]. As long as the ministry of tables was so small that the ministry of the Word did not suffer, the diaconate and the preaching were combined in one office. But as soon as the expansion of the church increased the ministry of the tables so much that the Word did suffer, the apostles created a separate office for that ministry, or rather, out of the root of their original office they grew the diaconate as a separate branch.

This circumstance is significant because it shows how much it is in line with God's Word when our Church Order, Article 25, and our liturgical form for the installation of elders and deacons, acknowledge the diaconate as an actual office; and our Confession professes that deacons "with the pastors and elders" of the congregation "form the council of the church."[8] It is also significant because this development of the diaconate from the apostolate gives us the key to solve readily the age-old battle about the preeminence of the teaching office over the office of elders.

As you know, this dispute was and still is concerned with the question whether the teacher is the true office-bearer and the elder is merely his helper, or whether both teaching elder and ruling elder stand on equal

---

8. See also Belgic Confession, Art. 30.

footing as instruments of King Jesus. Just as the diaconate developed from the apostolate, the offices of teaching elder and ruling elder developed gradually and for the same reasons. At first, the Jerusalem church had a splendid consistory of twelve apostles who were at once teaching, ruling, and serving instruments of King Jesus. As a consequence of the growth of the church, seven deacons were added. Without a doubt, these nineteen persons would have been able to exercise the royal power of Jesus in his church if there had been a congregation only in Jerusalem and the call of the apostolate had been limited to Jerusalem. But it was not like that. Churches were to be established everywhere, and since it was impossible for each of these churches to have only the twelve apostles, the official ministry of the local teachers naturally sprang forth out of the worldwide apostolate. And since the number of these teachers remained very small in most churches, it was natural for the local ruling office to split off as a local official ministry, entirely equal in rank as the offices of teacher and deacon.

After this threefold development, the office of professor remained hidden for a while within the office of teacher. This was quite natural, since as long as the opposition to heresy and the defense of the truth took place exclusively in the practical-ecclesiastical realm, this important task could be fulfilled entirely by the teacher in his regular preaching and missionary epistles. But when in later times the battle against heresy was transferred to the scholarly realm, the pastor or teacher would have had to give up the ministry of the Word to serve his church successfully in the realm of the sciences. Because this was neither acceptable nor possible, the professorial office gradually grew as a new branch from the official trunk, and the teacher of the church became simply a pastor. This term *pastor* must be understood not in the usual sense as though the preacher on the pulpit were the teacher and is pastor only during home visiting; rather, he is pastor in the sense that, first of all on the pulpit and with every other official act, the pastor pastures the flock with the Word of God.

Two consequences of this require our attention. First of all, there is the undeniable fact that the four offices—pastor, elder, deacon, and teacher—grow like four stalks from one root, and therefore may never be viewed as four plants that are separate from each other, each with its own root in its own soil. In Jesus' church the office of pastor is therefore also a ruling office, whereas the ruling elders, far from being excluded from the ministry of the Word, must guard the purity of the ministry of the Word.

And whereas the diaconate must abound in the consolation of the Word—and for that reason in most churches it forms part of the church council—the diaconate likewise belongs to the ministry of the Word, and ought also be interwoven with the ruling body of the churches. Finally, although the diaconate is more specifically the office called to display a Christendom that consists not only in word but also in power, nevertheless none of the three other offices stands apart from the ministry of mercy, and any office that does not shine its light before men would be forfeit.

The other remark we must make is that this separation of offices in the visible church is no more than a repetition of what we saw in the messianic office of the Christ himself. Just as the office of Messiah is one in its origin, nature, and extent, yet divides into the threefold office of prophet, priest, and king, likewise the office of the visible church, while one in root and stem, is divided in its operations. Through the offices of pastor and teacher, our highest Prophet and Teacher speaks more specifically; through the presbyterate, our eternal King rules more particularly; and the diaconate manifests especially the mercies of our eternal High Priest, the *Christus Consolator*. But just as it is equally correct to say that the ministry of the Word testifies prophetically, prays sacerdotally, and rules royally, so that each of the three offices of Christ is in turn shared by the other two, similarly on earth, in the visible church, three stalks are intertwined, and the true knowledge of each office would be lost if we would lose sight of the single root of these offices together.

And our conclusion can therefore be none other than that ecclesiastical office on earth is nothing more and nothing less than the instrument of the messianic office, in order that he who has received a name above all names may prophesy, rule, and show mercy on earth, throughout the ages, among the elect of the Father. Thus, flowing forth from moment to moment from the Mediator's office, it also is a unified office that is called to preach the one Word in the pastoral office; to advocate for it in the professorial office; to bring it to glory in contesting against sin through the presbyterate; and in the office of deacon, to battle against misery, the fruit of sin.

§ 12   HOW THE HOLY SPIRIT UNITES THE EARTHLY OFFICE WITH THE
HEAVENLY MESSIANIC OFFICE OF KING JESUS
Jesus' ascension into heaven is a real fact that should be acknowledged in its undiminished significance. One may therefore not present the

situation as if Jesus was still on earth, even after his ascension. No, he is now in heaven and remains there until the day of the renewal of all things. True, he is present in those who are his, in the operations of his grace, majesty, and spirit, but not personally.[9] In the holy sacrament of the Lord's Supper, Jesus does not himself descend to the elect, but he draws their souls up to him, to feed them, not on earth but in heaven, with his true body and with the drink of his blood. Especially over against the doctrine of our Lutheran brothers and sisters, the pure or Reformed teachers, following Calvin, maintained consistently and insistently the *in coelum subvecta* of the redeemed soul, that is, that in the holy sacrament the soul of the elect is taken up into heaven, and thus fed by Immanuel.

Once there was a sending of Jesus to this earth, but this sending is now over and has now been replaced by another, namely the sending of the Holy Spirit. And not now, but only in the last day there will be another sending of the Son, not to show mercy, but to judge the living and the dead.

In this intermediate period, the church must therefore always seek its Head above, and it must "seek the things that are above, where Christ is, seated at the right hand of God" [Col 3:1]. But because it still lives on earth and must manifest itself on earth, the question arises regarding the way that the connection is made between ecclesiastical office on earth and the messianic office of King Jesus. And the answer to this question is that this connection is made by the Holy Spirit. The person of the Holy Spirit is now the one who has been sent, who works on the earth, and who therefore dwells not only in Christ as our Head, but also in us as his members. He thus binds together the Head and the church. First the Son was sent as our Comforter, but now that he left, another Comforter has come, from whom we benefit more than the disciples benefited from Jesus. This is because the person of the Mediator stood outside their persons, but the person of the Holy Spirit enters our persons. "Or do you not know that your body is a temple of the Holy Spirit within you, whom you have from God?" [1 Cor 6:19]. "It is to your advantage that I go away, for if I do not go away, the Helper will not come to you" [John 16:7].

Now this operation of the Holy Spirit is twofold: an operation upon human beings and an operation by human beings. It is an operation upon human beings because the person of the Holy Spirit enters into the elect,

---

9. Dutch: *persoonlijk* ("personally"). In the context, Kuyper seems to be affirming Jesus' divine presence but denying Jesus' human presence. See Heidelberg Catechism, Lord's Day 18, Q&A 47.

calls them internally, convinces them, bends their wills, vindicates and justifies them before the court of conscience; and furthermore he gives them a new birth and holiness, prays within them with unspeakable groaning, illuminates and comforts them, redeems and liberates them. But it is also an operation by human beings, because it has pleased God to bind the person of the Holy Spirit, in all his work, to the Word inspired by himself; and it is precisely because of this that the person of the Holy Spirit is the true inspirer of ecclesiastical office. In and through that office he works, first of all, by sanctifying the persons for that office; second, by giving to them in due time the internal calling to that office; third, by equipping them for and in that office; and fourth, by granting fruitfulness to the official work in the execution of this office.

Thus these two operations of the person of the Holy Spirit actually coincide. For his internal operation upon human beings, he employs the official ministry of people, through whom he works. Conversely, in order to perform such an operation through the ministry of human beings, the Holy Spirit accompanies that official external operation with his personal operation in and upon the soul.

Still, this is not the end of the glorious activity of the Holy Spirit. The operation of the person of the Holy Spirit not only affects individual members, but certainly also the members of the entire body. Therefore he "apportions to each one individually as he wills" [1 Cor 12:11], and in the communion of saints he urges God's elect to share their gifts and be mindful of the welfare of the other members. The church does not exist for the sake of the office, but the office for the sake of the church. And just as Israel was originally called to send priests from all its tribes to the Lord's sanctuary, but later, because of Israel's sins, Levi's tribe alone was separated to the ministry, so it is with special office in the church. The work of Christ should really go out directly through and to all believers, and it is only because of sin and our sinful limitation that ecclesiastical office, which should rest upon all, is now transferred to a smaller circle, which is especially placed in office. The office of all believers always undergirds this special office as is its broader foundation, and the Holy Spirit is delighted to triumph continually over sin by allowing this office of all believers to manifest itself—to manifest itself, not just in families, but also in churches when in the face of the degeneration and corruption of special office, this general office powerfully comes to life. Special office is and remains necessary and absolutely indispensable, but only the office of all believers, as it will one day shine brightly in heaven, is the high, holy, and glorious ideal that radiates from the Messiah's office into the heart of those who are his.

But there is more. Just as the person of the Holy Spirit manifests himself not only in the individual believer but also in the communion of the saints through the office of all believers, likewise the person of the Holy Spirit works not only in the individual holder of special office, but equally in the organic assemblies of the officers of King Jesus. As often as the royal officers of King Jesus meet together in organic gatherings, there is more present than the sum of the individuals. A gathering of Jesus' royal officers, provided they gather organically, represents the power of Christ over his entire church—in a gathering of the officers of a local church, over that local church; or in a gathering of the officers of all churches from one country, over that country; or in a gathering from multiple countries, over the visible church on earth.

In all these gatherings or assemblies, whether they are called consistory, classis, synods, or councils, the totality increases the significance of the single office-bearer. And it is precisely in this organic connection of the many that the person of the Holy Spirit can reveal the majesty of his divine, infinite, irresistible activity better and more powerfully than within the limitations of the individual. Therefore, such an assembly of office-bearers, where the Word of the Lord alone has power and Christ presides in the president through his Holy Spirit, has much greater spiritual authority than any private conferences, gatherings, or groups of believers. The key of wisdom for these official assemblies lies in the inscription of the decree of the Jerusalem synod: "It has seemed good to the Holy Spirit and to us ..." [Acts 15:28]. However, after the end of the apostolate, one may never identify the pronouncement of such an assembly with a pronouncement of the Holy Spirit. By doing so, Rome went wrong.

There is always a gap between the infallible Word of the Spirit and the fallible word of man. But even through this deviation and error and failure, the person of the Holy Spirit continues to lead the church on earth further in all truth. It is the calling of the Holy Spirit to glorify the Father and the Son. Therefore the Holy Spirit is the Witness in the word of the prophets and the apostles, and he approaches us as witness in the written Word. But that Word must not only be read and recited; it must also be soaked up by the church, and it must continually be brought from more obscure to clearer awareness. And for the church of all ages, the Word must become its own proclamation of the virtues of him who called it out of darkness into his marvelous light [1 Pet 2:9]. This, the person of the Holy Spirit, realizes in the development of dogma—that is, in the confession, formulated as purely as possible for the clear awareness of the church—the truth that the Word brings us concerning God eternal.

Such dogma is deeply rooted in the heart of the church. The person of the Holy Spirit prepares it in the hearts of believers through the struggle that must take place in that heart between the truth and the lie, and more profoundly, between the truth and sin. Then he prepares heretics so that now the deception that is suppressed in the heart of believers charges in full armor from outside toward the church. This forces the church and its teachers to spiritual activity so that the church's bread of life may abound in the sweat of that spiritual labor. Then the assembled body of Jesus' royal officers, in which the Word of the Lord has authority and he himself presides through the Holy Spirit, gathers in the harvest of this spiritual toil and finds both the words and the forms to confess God's truth. And finally, when that confession has been expressed—though it remains fallible and subject to appeal to the Word—at that point the cycle of official activity returns to the congregation of believers, placing this newly found confession on their lips.

Thus, the church receives this confession not as the fruit of contemplation by scholarly thinkers, but as a precious gem prepared for it by the Holy Spirit in the spiritual wrestling of believers and in the anxious suffering of the church. In that confession it finds part of its own life. It guards that confession as the precious document acknowledging its triumph over heresy and error thanks to the operation of the Spirit. It relies on that confession as the only compass that can guide safely through the many interpretations of the Word, to the true meaning of that Word. It would like to see this confession become more accurate, more correct, more perfect, but it never tolerates the mutilation or severing of any part of its glorious organism. And without ever equating this confession with the wholly unique Word of God, the church maintains nonetheless, in the power of the Lord God, its conviction that as long as no purer confession is found, its confession is the simplest and for now the most perfect expression possible of the all-glorious truth that God has revealed to us.

CHAPTER 2 – THE RIGHT FORMATION OF THE CHURCH

How the Formation of a Church is Brought About   § 13

The *formation of the church* refers exclusively to its visible manifestation, and therefore not to its inner, mystical, and spiritual existence. To the question of who brings about the formation of this visible manifestation of the church, we must answer: God, or rather, Christ, does this work through believers, under the leadership of offices.

God does this (1) through his counsel, in which lies the plan of the mystical essence of the church; (2) through his miraculous deeds and revelations, through which the foundation is laid upon which the church will be built, according to that plan; (3) through his Word and Spirit, bringing about the calling and ingathering of his elect; (4) through the drive to establish churches, which he works in his elect through the communion of the saints; and (5) through the demand to confess the Word, which he issues to every believer.

Without the counsel of God there would be no seed of God and there would be no church to manifest itself. But this impulse for the communion of the saints and this demand to confess the Word become visible only if they manifest themselves as an attempt to join together in obedience to the Word. In this way, in the formation of his visible churches the Lord God has bound himself to the activity of believers.

A certain number of believers living in the same village or the same city but without the ministry of the Word and organized communion, do not yet constitute the visible church; that function of the life of believers that constitutes the church is then still idle. The church manifests itself in the visible world only when the impulse of the communion of saints begins to work in the group of believers, and when in obedience to the Word it produces results. This is the result of this function of the believers' faith: that they forge mutual relationships, join together, and form a visible church; and that, in order for their formation to be a church, they do so in personal and communal obedience to the Word of God. Whether this formative activity of the function of faith in this group of believers is real and pure—that is, whether it originates in an impulse from the Holy Spirit in a part of the mystical body of Christ—is known to God and Christ, but never, at least not absolutely, to human beings. The person who does not know the heart can be deceived by appearance and pious display, and though God's elect sometimes receive in great measure the gift of distinguishing the spirits, this gift still is always exceptional and never perfect. For that reason we must adhere to the rule that any *iudicium de intimis*, any judgment concerning the hidden life of the heart, is excluded. All ecclesiastical judgment must deal with one's confession of the mouth and one's walk in public life.

We therefore understand the believers, as the instrument of church formation, to be the people who by their pure confession of God's truth and their honorable walk of life manifest themselves publicly as believers. This rule naturally implies that only rarely have churches been established without the hypocrite slipping in along with the gathering of God's saints.

For such an establishment of the church through the instrument of believers, the following are required: (1) their freedom to assemble, deliberate, and decide; (2) their will and declaration to bind themselves in this formation; (3) agreement between their formative act and the demand of God's Word; and therefore (4) the duty and freedom to sever this bond personally as soon as such a bond would impede their obedience to God's Word. For this reason any ecclesiastical organization can always be dissolved; or rather, it automatically falls apart as soon as the church, which was once established as a church of Christ, degenerates into a church of the Antichrist.

Finally, this formation of churches, through the instrumental activity of believers, occurs only under the leadership of church office. A church is not a fellowship or society that organizes its affairs according to its own choice and insight or that represents itself through certain committees that it creates and populates according to its will. If the church in its visible manifestation were such a society, it would be disconnected from the true spiritual, mystical, and real church. It would thus forfeit the name of church. It would have been established not principally by God himself, but only instrumentally by believers, and would constitute a merely human creation, apart from God. In order to be God's formation and thus an essential and actual church, they must conform to the formation ordained by God. Not the will of believers but God's will, not human choice but God's Word, must exert the formative power that governs its beginning.

Therefore the church is already in its beginning and origin bound to office. This means that the gathered believers who intend to establish a church do not have even the least power over themselves and from themselves, nor over one another and from one another. Rather, they must kneel together before the only one who has power over all: the Lord their

God. Since they possess no power in themselves, and therefore cannot assign or transfer power, they can only, in obedience to God, appoint men who are vested with power, not by them but by God.

It is only through such a divine office that the church acquires members and thus manifests itself as an organism. And it is only under the leadership of these members that the group that has formed can become a church in the full sense, or at least manifest itself as a church. The office can come to them from without, or grow from within. It comes from outside if overseers of other churches help a group of believers in the formation of the church. It grows within if such a group, cut off from any fellowship with neighboring churches, chooses and appoints people through the office of believers, asking God that he install them in office.

Thus there is a threefold requirement for church formation: first, the activity of the Triune God in the communion of saints; second, an initiative by believers to join together in submission to God's Word; and third, the presence of offices to distinguish the church of God from all other societies.

What Constitutes the Essence of an Established Church   § 14

When dealing with a church after its formation, one must sharply distinguish between the form of that formation as such, and the essence of the church manifested in that formation. The essence of a visible church is and always remains the invisible church, provided that this includes the innate drive of this spiritual and mystical church to show itself to the outside world. The invisible church is the body of Christ—that is, the organic connection of all elect, through the Holy Spirit, under Christ as their head. Therefore, if there are among the population of any city or village a certain number of living members of this body of Christ, then the essence of the church *is* there. And this becomes a conscious presence as soon as the members, no matter how imperfectly, exercise the communion of saints and have the will and desire to bring their communion to fuller and purer ecclesiastical manifestation as soon as the opportunity arises. Conventicles, as they exist in some unchurched sects or antichristian groups, do not belong here. This is not because these circles cannot contain living members of Christ, and not as if members of these groups fail to attempt to exercise the communion of saints, but because they lack the desire and will, wherever possible, to manifest the ecclesiastical formation.

A newly planted grapevine, even though it does not yet show a leaf or cluster, still possesses the essence of a grapevine because without a doubt its leafs and blossoms will bud, followed by the formation of clusters and grapes; so too a gathering possesses the essence of a church, even though its organs do not yet work. It is certain that as it grows up and buds, it will acquire these organs, and these organs will function. On the other hand, ivy is not a grapevine and lacks its essence, even though it shoots up high and is covered with abundant foliage, simply because no matter how much it grows, it will never grow a single cluster of the noble grape.

Thus the essence of a church does not lie in the means of grace nor in the ordinances that may aid in the use of these means. To continue the imagery, no grapevine can live, and certainly cannot flourish, without moisture and light, without soil and heat. But who would ever look for the essence of the grapevine in the moisture or the heat? Well, in the same way no church can live without the means of grace, but the essence of the church may never be thought of as being part of any means of grace. The same holds true for the ordinances that administer these means of grace. To keep a peach tree alive it must be fed, watered, and covered with reeds during frost, but neither that feeding of its root, nor the watering pot, nor the reeds the gardener uses for its care, belong to its essence. Likewise, the means of grace cannot very well be administered without ecclesiastical regulation—without a church building, without a baptismal font, bread and wine—but this does not imply in any way that this regulation and whatever it entails belongs to the proper essence of the church. The essence of the church always lies exclusively in what is contained in the formative power of the church, and for the invisible church that power lies, as we saw, directly in God, and for the visible church, in the members of Christ's body.

This implies that a gathering that no longer has any members of the body of Christ has lost the essence of a church, and is left with nothing but a mockery of a church, no matter however symmetrically pure its ordinances may be. Conversely, every church retains the essence of a church as long as it carries in its bosom a group of living members of Christ, even though all its ordinances may have withered. Even a completely chopped down tree still retains the essence of a tree as long as there is still life in its root.

Of course we are not saying that every church, however dilapidated, will nonetheless remain a church as long as there are a few children of

God passively present in it, but rather that these children of God, this group of Christ's members, still have the ability to reform the church of God, or to form it anew. As long as you still have some acorns, the essence of the oak tree is not yet lost. No matter how concealed it may be, it can reappear. However, we will elaborate on this in chapter 4.

At this point we must mention that one should not be too hasty in one's judgment concerning the essence of the church. For the first manifestation of the essence of the church, one definitely needs a group of elect who are also mature and strong confessors. Young children or persons not yet professing faith, are not equipped for church formation, even though they belong to God's elect. On the other hand, in an existing church the seed of the church certainly counts, and the essence of the church is not at all lost if the last elect among the adults have died and none of the elect among the young people have yet come to conversion. David's house remained the house of the Messiah even though men like Ahaz and Manasseh and Amon engaged in horrible idolatry, since Ahaz would bring forth a Hezekiah, and Amon would bring forth Josiah.

However, if in a once flourishing church all living members die out and no more seed of the Lord is recorded, so that the means of grace fade away and the ordinances are corrupted, there can be a revival of the church of Christ in that same town. But this can happen only through a new church formation from without, and no longer through a sprout from the trunk, which is not only cut down, but also inwardly dead.

Therefore nothing needs to be subtracted from or added to the description our fathers gave of the church of Christ, namely, "that she is a holy congregation of true Christian believers, all expecting their salvation in Jesus Christ, being washed by His blood, sanctified and sealed by the Holy Spirit,"[10] a description that applies equally well to the invisible church as to the visible manifestation of the church; it is therefore valid for every local church as well as for the church in general.

One must simply keep in mind that the essence of a church can be viewed from two points of view, depending on whether one considers its essence according to its potential (*potentia*), or according to its actuality (*actu*). Dynamite is dynamite even if it has not yet exploded, since it still carries within itself the potential to explode. Likewise, a gathering truly

---

10. Belgic Confession, Art. 27.

possesses the essence of a church, even if it lacks all offices, provided that it carries within itself the potential to establish the office.

Considered in terms of its potential, the essence of the church requires no more than the assembly of believers in Christ because this assembly has the potential to establish and utilize ecclesiastical office and the means of grace. But considered in terms of its actuality, the essence of the church cannot be separated from ecclesiastical office or the means of grace. And since in the visible church its essence almost always functions in its actuality, our fathers were entirely correct when they located the essence of the church in "the gathering of the believers," while still identifying the following as marks of the true church: Word and sacrament, secured by church discipline.

§ 15   HOW THE CHURCHES ARE DIVIDED AND YET ONE

The mystical body of Christ is one, and all its parts belong together. Therefore the church of Christ will come to full manifestation only when, after having triumphed, it sits with Christ on the throne. By contrast, all preliminary manifestations can only be divided and flawed—divided by time, since the elect of this century can have as little communion of the saints with the elect in Augustine's time as they can with the elect three or more centuries in the future. But they are also divided according to place, because believers are naturally restricted to having fellowship only with those who live with them in the same place. This division of time is directly administered by the Lord God, as he determines the time of birth and death of every man, "having determined allotted periods" (Acts 17:26), but the division of place is merely mediate through believers. It is not as though believers could arbitrarily separate and join, except with the understanding that they are thereby bound to "the boundaries of their dwelling place" as God determined them (Acts 17:26), as well as to the desire for unity that is always present in the body of Christ.

God has determined the dwelling place of everyone, and through his provident rule the boundaries of countries, cities, and villages came into existence. It is therefore the very same God who on one hand governs the lives of lands and nations, cities and villages, and on the other hand builds and sustains his church. Both arenas of life, though not identical, are therefore related to each other, and the Mediator has been given kingship over the church as well as all power over lands and nations, cities and villages.

Thus in the formation of a church, the believer must definitely take into account the distinction between nation and nation, country and country, region and region, village and village. The one body of Christ manifests itself differently in different countries, provinces, and regions, and even in neighboring villages and cities. In church formation, believers may not lose sight of the characteristics of every local church, or the bond that connects it with churches in the same region, churches in the same province, and churches in the same country. The ordination of God's providential plan and decree divided the church into local, provincial, and national churches, but the unity of the body of Christ keeps these individual parts together in an organic connection. These parts are so much together, in fact, that the church in one land must always be aware of the fact that only together with churches in other lands is it the church of Christ; this was the reason why our fathers at the Synod of Dort invited the churches abroad.[11]

But this brief introduction does not suffice. The view presented here—that the local church is the primary manifestation of the church of Jesus Christ, and the classes and national churches arise only as secondary through the federating of these local churches—is not generally held. We are not speaking here of the Independents or Congregationalists, nor will we address the Roman Catholic idea of the church. To think, as the Independents do, that every group, every congregation is an organic unity, or in the Roman Catholic view, that organic church unity is manifested only in the worldwide church, are errors promoted by no one among us.

But we must test the sentiment of those who judge that our national church is an organic unity, and that the classes and local churches exist only as parts or cells within this organic unity.

As we stated above, we readily grant: (1) that the Independent view, that each congregation can act as an organic unity, must be rejected; (2) that ecclesiastical relationships within the same nation are not arbitrary, but ordained by the arrangement of dwellings and cities, in the unity of a common past, by the impulse of love and community, and especially based in the oneness of the body of Christ, of which all local

---

11. The Synod of Dort (1618–19) was occasioned by controversies in the Dutch Reformed church, but had an international character, and included delegations with representation from England, Scotland, Germany, and the Swiss cantons. Representatives from France were also invited, but were prevented from attending by the French government.

churches are manifestations; (3) and therefore that, even if the confederative church organization were disrupted for some time, nonetheless the local churches of one nation, even without visible connection, definitely belong together, and should reestablish their relationships, the sooner the better.

But we claim, on the other hand: (1) that every local church possesses in itself the essence of the church; (2) that the external, judicial relationship with other churches arises only through confederation; and (3) that the organic unity consists only of the invisible church, while in this invisible church the local churches are the organic constitutive parts, and the classes and national church are no more than organic groups.

To convince yourself of this, you need only ask yourself what constitutes the essence of a church. It consists, on the one hand, of the group of believers, and on the other hand, of the administration of the means of grace; and thus it is settled that one does not add to or subtract from the essence of a church if a local church is temporarily isolated or divided. No doubt this will affect the state of the church, but not its essence. As soon as a gathering becomes a manifestation of the body of Christ, its essence as church is assured.

Moreover, the word *organism* must be taken in the correct sense, and this sense can be manifold. The organism of the church is complete only in the wholly mystical body of Christ. The full organism of the church includes all its parts, both those that have already grown and those that still must sprout. But if you mean a partial organic manifestation of this complete organism, insofar as the nature of the entire organism is stamped upon every cell of life, then such a church organism is present in every place where the church is unmistakably visible according to its nature as a church; and that is in every local church. Finally, we can take the word *organism* in a third sense, expressing the natural relationship of life that these individual organic manifestations of life have in relationship to each another. But this gives us only a relative and flexible concept, which can expand or contract, and therefore can never take the place of the organic notion of ecclesiastical unity that is already given in the local church.

It is also incorrect to say that this was the case at the beginning of the Reformation, but has changed in the history of three centuries. When the Reformers arose in the Netherlands, the local churches had already existed for centuries, and likewise for centuries the local churches had

had their church organization. At that time this organization also coincided with the national borders. Nevertheless our fathers did not hesitate for one moment to return swiftly to the local church, and only from these local churches did they revive the church organization for country and nation.

But what is decisive is the testimony that the Holy Scripture gives in this respect, in a twofold manner: First, the holy apostles acknowledge all local formations as ἐκκλησία, and always speak of the ἐκκλησίαι or "churches." They never speak of an ἐκκλησία to express external organic ecclesiastical unity. They address the church of Rome and the church of Corinth, but they write ταῖς ἐκκλησίαις τῆς Γαλατίας, that is, "to the churches of Galatia." Even the church of this one province Paul does not view as an external organic unity, but as organic formations with their own autonomy. Second, nowhere in the Scriptures of the holy apostles is there a single indication that they view the aggregation of local churches into a certain national unity as a condition for the preservation and essence of a church.

An even stronger testimony is when the Lord Jesus himself, in Revelation 2 and 3, dictates seven epistles for the seven ἐκκλησίαι, that is, churches, in Asia Minor: the Lord depicts the organic unity of the seven in the unity of the seven candles on the lampstand, but the churches themselves are addressed individually. Their essence is never made dependent on their external mutual relationship, and on the contrary, each local church is explicitly acknowledged as ἐκκλησία τοῦ κυρίου, as "a church of the Lord."

On these grounds we conclude, therefore, that Scripture, history, and a correct distinction of concepts oppose the view that the local churches in themselves lack the essence of the church. And if that is the case, then it is also clear that the ecclesiastical unity that we must take as our starting point is given, not in the worldwide church, nor in the national church or classes, but exclusively in the local church.

Whether More Than One Church Can be Established in the Same Town §16

In the formation of churches, believers may not act arbitrarily; they are bound by the unity of the body as well as the boundaries of each person's dwelling as God has determined them. This raises the question whether all believers in one town can establish only one church together. This one question is divisible into two others, namely: may one establish separate churches in the distinct parts of larger cities; and may one establish two similar church formations alongside each other without subdividing the cities?

Both questions must be answered in the negative. The unity of municipalities naturally determines the individual areas for church formation. In places like London, where the so-called city is merely a conglomeration of thirty or more municipalities, each with its own civil government, a division is recommended rather than discouraged. But if the municipality remains single, then the formation of the church ought to be one, even if it would include a hundred thousand individuals or more. This does not at all deny that such a church could be subdivided into parishes, as long as all these parishes have as their head one consistory, representing the unity of the congregation.

Likewise, it follows from our principle that there should not be multiple church formations alongside each other in the same locality. A Lutheran or seceded Reformed church alongside an original Reformed church in the same city, with members living along the same streets, is not as it should be, even though it should sometimes be tolerated temporarily because of the imperfection of the situation. Only those who principally disagree in their confession of the truth may establish churches separately. But those who are one in confession belong together. To do justice to the strict demand of the principle in case of difference of confession on minor points, one should not rest until everyone had the same "sentiment" in these matters [see 1 Cor 1:10], and should subsequently deny the name of church to all who oppose this confession of the truth.

Meanwhile, Rome shows to what danger believers expose themselves if, in putting this principle into practice, they fail to reckon with flaws and imperfections. They require that in our conscience we must always respect a boundary that may never be crossed. Where the formation of churches is based on the voluntary joining of believers, the unity of church formation cannot and may not go farther than the oneness in conviction. Therefore we must tolerate church formation alongside our church, provided it occurs on the basis of a deviating confession. And even if there is perfect agreement of confession, but due to external causes there are nevertheless two church formations in the same city or village, then in abnormal situations the one may not deny the other the right of the honorable name of church, but there must be a mutual zeal and a loving desire to unite both churches.

Believers who establish a local church in the name of the Lord do not intend to establish a church for their own profit—something that, when they move or die, would be superfluous or fade away for lack of members. This would be the case if they made the church. But the church was there before they took the initiative, and their formation merely intended to make visible the spiritual church that was already present. Therefore their action is like that of someone who drills down to a spring that already existed before he drilled it, but after being drilled, the spring is destined to provide water continually for every future generation. Or, to use a more Dutch example, taken from our polders: the formation of such a church is similar to the draining of an inland lake, under which there had always been a floor, which now becomes visible through the draining process, a polder protected by dikes that is supposed to provide farmland to current and future inhabitants.

Thus the continuity of a church certainly contributes to the serious nature of its formation, and one must therefore ask how this continuity is obtained. Two directions are possible here, which are commonly designated as the Reformed and the Methodist approaches.

The Methodist believes that the most profitable way to provide a church with continuity consists in the conversion of the unconverted, who after their conversion will be incorporated into the church. Thus dying saints are continually replaced with other saints who first were lost. From this point of view, baptism after confession of faith is the only correct position, and there is no point in providing Christian education. All that needs to be done is a continual recruiting for King Jesus, among the children of believers and among the Jews and among the heathen. If this is successful, then the goal is achieved, and the church increases in numbers. But after being converted a person really has no reason to exist on earth any longer. He may die, and that would by far be best for him. Only the motivation that he in turn must convert others can give him peace with the idea of continuing his earthly life.

For those who think along these lines, the church is therefore of minor importance. It is a means of conversion. But one can convert people in many different ways. And because those other means, such as the Salvation Army, prayer vigils, meetings, and so on, are much more effective, they usually assign the church an inferior place in their thinking. The church empties out while the private gatherings are more than full. The church is maintained in name, but in reality it is fading away.

Very different is the approach of the Reformed believer. It is the Reformed believer's conviction that there is only one who can effectively convert souls, and that is the Lord our God. This is not meant as a figure of speech, but actually and truly, so that not a single soul has ever been converted powerfully and truly, except when God the Holy Spirit planted in the soul the ability to believe and activated that ability. Reformed people therefore never imagine that they must convert others, but rather confess that they are unable to do so; they merely take care not to leave unused any means that in God's hand might be used for the conversion of their neighbor. They do not presume to make a private judgment about these means, but consider that only God can ordain these means. They believe that they will fail as soon as they do more than employ the means ordained by God in quiet obedience, each in the way of his or her calling. And because God has placed the means of grace in his church, they expect the ingathering of God's elect not from outside of the church, but from life within the church.

Their care for the continuity of the church is therefore very different. With their starting point in the spiritual church and as they seek to manifest it, they know that that church was not established as a collection of individuals, but men and women, fathers and mothers, with all that belongs to them. They entered the church with their children, or if you will, even with the seed in their loins, and all that is born to them is therefore born in that church. The river that moves its water alongside your land, says the Reformed person, does not continue to flow because you occasionally pour into that river a few buckets of water from elsewhere, but only through the streams that flow down from God's mountains. Likewise, the living stream of the church is not sustained by mixing in a few converts, but rather and much more through that new life, in the children who are born, whose life comes from God. Therefore they acknowledge even at the birth of their children that, although these children are by nature conceived in sin and subject to condemnation, at the same time they are sanctified in Christ, and therefore belong to the church as members, albeit not full-grown members. Hence their insistence on infant baptism. Hence their preference for thorough child-rearing. Hence their emphasis on Christian education. Hence also their tranquil calm as they obediently use the means, even where no conversion is visible yet. For this they know, that they must be obedient; and the number of elect will never increase, but it will certainly be full.

However external their church formation may be, it is therefore not for a moment separated from the spiritual background of the invisible church. The life lies under the soil, and from that soil it springs up. Their church is a living organism, whose leaves may wither only to rejuvenate in new growth. For this reason, their full inclusion of young members who have matured is never a formality, but always has a spiritual character. Naturally every new member must help in continuing the original church formation through a public act. Whether someone helps to establish a new church formation or functions as a new member in an existing church does not make the slightest difference. A member of the church must declare at some time in his life: "I am a believer, and as a believer I seek the communion of the saints with the other believers." Where is this expressed? In a church membership directory? Oh, certainly, the Lord our God is not too spiritual to bind us also to the order of the written text. Yet that book is only a catalog of life, and the life to which that book witnesses is the confession of the member's own worthiness of condemnation and of Christ's holiness, sealed in the communion of the saints at the Lord's Supper.

The Reformed leave to the judgment of God the reality that many hypocrites slip in among these mature members who come to the Lord's Supper—as long as they take care not to fall short in the way of obedience and do not fail continually to prune this hypocrisy through the exercise of church discipline. If there were a different way, they would rather judge the heart, but they know that this is God's inviolable prerogative, such that the most staunch Methodist is just as unable as they are to know the inner man; disappointment awaits anyone who lowers his sounding line into these spiritual waters. Therefore they are content with what the Lord God ordained for them, and so establish this rule: they will judge others according to the confession, but themselves by the light of God, according to the heart.

Meanwhile, when the members of the church who have matured are accepted—or rather, given access to communion—the congregation of believers must then be at least as involved as they are with the new communicant member. The church remains a gathering whose spiritual root contains the bond with Christ, but in its manifestation it has no visible bond except in mutual concord. Let the one who desires communion come, but let the church as the gathering of believers retain the full right either to include him in their midst, or to exclude him.

This is even more relevant in connection with the arrival of people from elsewhere, who have already lived in a church community in their previous town. A church in general never should be required or forced to accept a member simply because he was a member of a church elsewhere. Every church must decide for itself to whom it wants to grant participation within its group. And while issuing an attestation greatly facilitates the transition from church to church, this tool may never infringe upon the right of the church to request a fresh profession. Nor can it ever release the believer from his or her duty to make a fresh profession. Every good Reformed church must know well and thoroughly whether it can trust the content of an attestation, and is duty bound, when doubts arise, to make a fresh, independent investigation of the person who applies for membership.

Even with this, the church has not yet reached the limit of providing for its continuity. In addition to the children born in her womb and those who come to her from without, she must also look around in her location, to see whether there are others who might be won for the church. She must reckon with the possibility that there are elect of God hidden among them, and apart from that she must be zealous for the honor of God's name, also among her fellow citizens. The church is bound to the commandment, "Preach the gospel to all creatures!" [Mark 16:15 KJV]—a commandment that is not made redundant by having missionaries work on our behalf thousands of miles away. It is rather a command that must be obeyed first of all by going out into the streets and alleys. It must be done not only among church members, but also among outsiders; and not only by way of church service, but also through mission activity.

§ 18   WHERE AUTHORITY RESIDES IN THE VISIBLE CHURCH

Not all authority is equal. A Reformed church can desire and yearn for political rights, in order to be acknowledged, supported, and protected by the government. In this sense authority belongs to the national government, even over the church. Likewise, a Reformed church may wish to exert civil rights through the acquisition of property, deeds, purchase or rental, or the making of contracts. In this respect it is subject to the authority of the civil judge. In the case of disagreement over contracts with other churches, if no compromise or mutually binding resolution has been negotiated, it is also bound to the pronouncement of that judge. Meanwhile, all such authority is not the authority of the church in its proper sphere. One could readily imagine churches—there have been many in times of tribulation—that had no political or civil rights, that lacked any formal confederation, and yet were churches. When speaking of authority in the church of Christ, we therefore refer exclusively to that unique authority exercised within its own bosom concerning matters related to its essence as a church. Once a church has been established, it is an institution in which the mandate to command and govern exists alongside the implied duty to obey and honor. The question is where this authority resides, not for the invisible church in a mystical sense, but for the visible church institution.

This is the answer to that question: such authority within and over the church resides in its King and Lord, to whom it was given by the Triune God. This one King and Lord exercises this glorious and sovereign authority directly through his Word, that is, through Holy Scripture; through his Spirit, who works in human hearts; and through those joyful and sorrowful events that he ordains for his church on earth. The right to command and govern sovereignly, therefore, does not reside with human beings. In the church there is no other government than its King and Lord, and it may not be said of anyone either metaphorically or figuratively that that person has the ultimate rule over any church of Christ. One could speak of ecclesiastical government in the sense in which our fathers honored members of the parliament as representatives of the people and the government officials as *magistratus inferiores*; but in our day this use of the name "magistrates" has faded, and any talk of an "ecclesiastical magistrate" in reference to any person has become inappropriate. To seek sovereign rule or ultimate rule in the church among people is to deny that Jesus is King, that he lives, and that he still directly exercises real authority on earth.

All authority exercised through human persons in the church is therefore always the opposite of ultimate power: it is ministerial. A government official certainly exercises authority, but only in the name of and on the authority of his king, and under responsibility to him. So too all authority that is exercised in the church is never more than official and ministerial authority, in which the official is nothing and his King is everything. The authority exercised in the church is therefore also holy, because it never arises through agreement or from earthly power—which is mixed with sin—but it flows directly from that separately established realm of the kingdom of heaven, over which the Son of God wields the scepter as the Mediator.

Now this official ministerial authority is being discussed here in connection with our situation under the new covenant; we are not discussing the former privileges of Israel's tribes, nor the authority of the priest or the prophet in ancient days, nor the authority of David's descendants on the throne in Jerusalem. David does not live on in our kings, but David lives on in the Christ. And as we proceed from this extraordinary and temporary state to the normal and now perpetual manifestation of the church, we must ask through which human persons this King currently exercises his authority. The answer to this question is twofold: inherently or essentially through the office of all believers; and as for its organization, organically through appointed ministers.

Without for one moment surrendering the bond of Christ, we must therefore establish that authority within the church resides in the church itself, but its exercise is connected largely with certain official instruments. Spiritually, the church is strictly monarchical, being a kingdom under the absolute kingship of the Christ. In its visible manifestation it is definitely democratic, but with respect to its organization it is bound to the aristocratic form. Meanwhile—this should be noted carefully—it is not the case that the assembly of the believers receives the mandate of the King, and in turn transfers this authority to the ministers. Rather, both believers and ministers receive their official calling directly from the King. Thus the office of believers and the office of ministers stand on the same level. The congregation does not stand above the ministers and the ministers do not stand over the congregation, but over both stands Christ, who determines the mutual relationship between both by binding the authority of both to his Word.

If the congregation has the audacity to exert pressure on the ministers outside or against the Word of God, then the authority of such a congregation is null and void, and it does not affect the servant. Likewise, if a minister were to exert authority over believers outside or against the Word, then this authority falls apart completely and is no longer authority but pure presumption. This makes the relationship of this authority variable. It is distributed purely only where both believers and ministers stay close to the Word and act in terms of that Word alone. But when the congregation departs from the Word, the divine authority of the ministers rises over it. Likewise, if ministers abandon the Word, then the divine authority of the congregation rises over them, until eventually a church gathering that completely abandons the Word loses *all* authority; and likewise, ministers who act completely apart from the Word cannot claim any right of authority. The difference between civil authority and ecclesiastical authority is therefore clear. The civil government retains its authority even when it goes against God, and therefore even someone like Nero had to be obeyed. But it is not so in the church. There, obedience becomes sin, and homage becomes guilt before God, as soon as the person who commands and demands homage acts apart from the Word.

Therefore, those who are strangers to the first principles of church government, who speak of revolution in this respect, are merely showing the error of their own heart on the issue of the obedience that we owe to Christ our King. Revolution is to resist the authority of the king. And such resistance is perpetrated not by one who rebukes the wayward office holder, but exactly the opposite, by any believer who respects and tries to please the unfaithful officer holder.

What Systems of Church Government Have Been Tried?   § 19

Five systems of church government have successively been invented for the churches of Christ in their visible manifestation, which for the sake of clarity we will designate as Roman, Lutheran, Reformed, Independent, and Collegial.

The Roman system has these four characteristics: (1) it creates one government for the entire visible church on earth; (2) it divides the church into the two tiers of clergy and laity, and proceeds to exclude the laity entirely from the church's government; (3) in principle it is strictly monarchial; and (4) it stipulates the supremacy of the church over the state. The Roman system wants a single government for the entire worldwide church. Therefore it separates itself from the national particularities, and replaces the vivid variety of the national languages by a single, dead language that shall be the same for all. It loses its spiritual character especially because it does not trust the organic unity of the church in Christ; it therefore tries to secure that unity instrumentally through an external bond.

Directly related to this is the second characteristic: *the separation of clergy and laity, in order to henceforth declare the laity a minor.* The inclusion of the laity would automatically reintroduce national variety into church

government. The clergy, not the laity, can be placed outside national relationships, especially through the introduction of celibacy. In this way, as
it is separated from the national aspect of society, the clergy becomes a
distinct order that lives exclusively for the church, and therefore can be
instrumental in the creation of a worldwide church.

For this reason, in the third place, the Roman church had to develop
in a strictly monarchical manner. This was not immediately clear, and
Rome's popes had fought a hard fight before they were able to suppress
the republican idea of the sovereign council, consisting of all bishops
throughout the world. But that principle's consequences fought on the
popes' behalf, and it was not the episcopal opposition but Hildebrand[12] and
his papal school that grasped the profound idea that motivates the Roman
ecclesiastical system. The system of councils is not able to express the
unity of the worldwide church; only the papal system can do that. For in
a council, national differences are always bound to manifest themselves.
Only the papacy overcomes any national differences. Finally, in the council one will never find any connection to Christ. That is only found in his
governor on earth.

Therefore, as a fourth characteristic, one could point to the supremacy
that the Roman system claims over the state. Viewing the church as equivalent to the kingdom of God, autonomously organized under the pope as
governor of Christ, Rome cannot allow any higher power, since this would
be an authority belonging to the national government that would infringe
upon its unity. Nor can Rome allow any national government to exercise
an independent authority alongside itself, as this would force it to retreat
to the purely spiritual realm. The theory of two swords is therefore no
one-sided exaggeration, but merely the logical development of what is
embedded in the false idea of one single visible church.

The Lutheran church tried to resolve the question of the best form of
church government in a very different way. Its system is essentially the
same as the system promoted by the Remonstrants in the Netherlands,
and in the name of Erastus[13] in England. Since Thomasius,[14] it is best
known by the name "territorial system." It entails the division of the one

---

12. Pope Gregory VII (r. 1073–85).
13. Thomas Erastus (1524–83) was a Swiss theologian after whom Erastianism was
    named. Erastianism held that the civil magistrate had authority over the church.
14. Christian Thomasius (1655–1728), Lutheran jurist at the Universities of Leipzig
    and Halle.

worldwide church into as many sections and entities as there are political territories with autonomous sovereignty. This system is diametrically opposed to that of Rome, insofar as it deliberately breaks and disrupts the unity of the worldwide church. National distinctions become dominant, and instead of placing the state under the church, as a matter of principle it places the church under the state. The ongoing battle in Germany between the Prussian court and the Roman Curia represents the absolute opposition between the Lutheran and Roman systems.[15]

According to the Lutheran system, Christ placed authority over his church into the hands of the national ruler. The king, duke, or earl is lord over the church as he is lord over the country. The church as such does not have its own authority; all authority over it is given to the national ruler. This fact was explained in different ways: some taught that the original authority of the bishops had been transferred to the ruler, while others more consistently insisted that the ruler, due to his own sovereignty as a ruler, was also sovereign over the church. But in effect both were professing that the ruler alone possesses authority over the national church, according to the fatal maxim: *cuius regio eius religio*—"the one who is lord in the land has its religion in his hand." Within this Lutheran system, no justice was done to the laity. Its proponents distinguish three classes: the governing class, the ministerial class, and the laity. All authority resides in the governing class; the ministerial class stipulates how that authority should operate; and nothing is left for the laity except what people termed, with all seriousness, the right to obey and submit. Therefore this system was also called consistorial. To prevent loss of their authority to the ministers, the rulers appointed some ministers to form a consistory in the capital city, whose task it was to rein in their colleagues. This control was increased through the appointment of superintendents and general superintendents.

This already shows how the Erastian or Remonstrant system, although coinciding with the Lutheran system in its territorial principle, alters this system in a significant way. Erastus and the Dutch Remonstrants taught, partially following Zwingli, that in the church of Christ on earth there is really *no* authority. They taught that the authority exerted by the civil government extends to the church just as it extends to the whole state and

---

15. Kuyper is probably referring to Otto von Bismarck's *Kulturkampf*, by which he sought to bring the Roman Catholic Church under control of the state.

society, without a special ecclesiastical character. Therefore, preachers have the duty only to admonish and advise, but without utilizing the keys of the heavenly kingdom. This explains the Remonstrant opposition to a general synod, and their promotion of a territorial or provincial synod. It explains their opposition to the introduction of church discipline, which they did not acknowledge as a rightful power of the church. Finally, it explains their demand to tolerate various teachings in the church, a toleration that flows directly from the purely admonishing and non-authoritative character they ascribe to the ministry of the Word.

Thus you see that the ecclesiastical ideas of the so-called Irenics and Legitimists mainly follow the Lutheran system, and more specifically its Remonstrant variant.[16] In 1816, the national ruler of the Netherlands decreed the church order: The church must be one in the entire territory. The ministerial class must set the tone. The laity may not have any influence. Provincial and classical church governments take the place of the general superintendents and superintendents. The General Synodical Committee replaces the Lutheran consistory. All activity of the church should be no more than admonition. And finally, all variations of confession must be tolerated, to prevent any revival of church authority with regard to doctrine.[17]

Through the law of opposition this naturally brings us to the third, Reformed system, generally known as the presbyterial or synodical system. The main features of this system are: (1) the internal unity of the worldwide church, which the Lutheran system divided into territories, is subdivided even further, so that the local church becomes the starting point for all church government; (2) these local churches are connected by way of confederation into classes and synodical national churches, and, albeit in a lesser degree, into worldwide councils; (3) for the first time, the laity plays a significant role, and any form of clericalism is suppressed by the appointment of elders and deacons; (4) ecclesiastical authority, without assuming any authority over the state, places itself as fully independent over against the civil government. These are the four great principles of Reformed church government, and they determine whether one takes the Reformed, Roman, Lutheran, or Congregationalist side.

---

16. On the Irenics, see "Editor's Introduction" in On the Church, xxi.
17. In 1816, William I imposed these and other rules on the Dutch churches in the Algemeen Reglement (General Regulations).

In the foreground, as the cornerstone of the entire system, stands the theory of the local church. It expresses the godly confession of the hidden, spiritual character of the one, holy, universal church of Christ, which is manifest wherever believers live together. The Lutheran view of a single large national church, subdivided into sections called congregations, is absolutely incompatible with this. The Reformed church, following the Word of God, finds the *cor ecclesiae*, the heart of the church, not in the means of grace, but in God's sovereign election. Therefore the church does not manifest itself through the institution of any ministry, but through the activity of the believers.

But so that this local starting point would not diminish the glorious idea of the unity of the church, the second characteristic is that these local churches must forge mutual relationships. And they must exercise discipline, and therefore authority, over one another. There is therefore no classical government, but the glorious organization of the classis and the synod, ideally to be expanded, as at Dort, to a worldwide synod. Meanwhile, this confederative authority of classis and synod may never annul the character of the church as a church of believers by virtue of election.

The third characteristic is therefore the activity of the presbyters or elders and of the deacons, as representatives of the believers, to cut off any supremacy of clericalism.

Finally, with respect to their government, our Reformed churches have always firmly maintained the separation of civil and ecclesiastical authority. This manifested itself in an absolute sense in countries where governors had remained Roman Catholic, as in France and Poland. In those countries the Reformed church—following Calvin's advice—was developed, organized, and established with full independence. This was done so strictly and thoroughly that in our day, now that we Dutchmen also have a *non*-Reformed civil government, anyone who for that reason rejects the separation of church and state is taking a position in direct opposition to Reformed principles. The fact that Calvin and his followers also in the Netherlands actually allowed government interference does not add or subtract from the strict requirement and correctness of the principle.

The challenge, however, is that one must make careful distinctions. First of all, in Geneva for instance, the representatives of the boards of citizens acted not as a government with authority in the church, but as representatives of the laity, similar to today's delegates. Second, the government was not given a certain *ius in sacra*, a rule in sacred affairs, because of its sovereign right. Rather, the government officials, as excellent church members, were granted an authority of ecclesiastical origin. Third, the regulation of the church's position in matters of political and civil rights was left to the civil government, as it still should be done today. And fourth, the government was rightfully pointed to its obligation, because of its calling as sovereign by the grace of God, to promote God's glory and righteousness in the land according to the requirements of both tables of the law. We are deeply convinced that these views still define the correct lines, and we merely ought to follow them to arrive at a pure and correct separation of church and state—provided that in the absence of a Reformed civil government, as is currently the case in the Netherlands, one should not follow the Genevan system, but rather the system of absolute separation, as Calvin recommended for France and Poland.

Thus, after the complete failure of the Roman system and the cruel disappointment resulting from the Lutheran system, Calvin finally discovered the system of church government that was purest and best and required by God's Word. And it was especially our fathers who defended it courageously and successfully in opposition to the plans of the Dutch Erastian Remonstrants. This already suggests that the remaining two systems, the Independent and Collegial systems, are not at all purer systems, but rather bring us deformations of the only good system.

Generally speaking, the Independents or Congregationalists, in the Netherlands originally called Brownists,[18] definitely move along the Reformed line, rather than the Roman Catholic or the Lutheran. They are pure in most aspects of doctrine. For them, too, election is the *cor ecclesiae*, the heart of the church. The *norma ecclesiae*, the norm of the church, is the Word of God alone, almost in the same way as for us. But in matters of church government they deviate from the Reformed line at the following points.

First, the starting point of their system is not in the local church, but in any group of believers that organizes locally. Such a group is called a *congregation*, hence their name of Congregationalists. In London, for instance, there are currently hundreds of congregations, and each of them individually claims to have the power and authority of a church of Christ. In

---

18. Thus named after Robert Browne (d. 1633), leader of the first secession from the Church of England. In 1581, Browne led a group to the Netherlands to set up an independent church in Middelburg.

opposition to this, the Reformed maintained that, while in greater cities numerous parishes could be established, in each city or village there can be only one church, and therefore only one church council consisting of the teaching and ruling elders of all parishes.

Second, the Independents judged that not only ecclesiastical power in general, but also governing authority resides with the believers, so that the church members were to participate in all deliberations and even in decision making. Over against this, the Reformed insisted that the governing authority over the church resided not with the members, but rather with the presbyters. (This distinction can usually be clarified through the clear example that the power of life is distributed through the body, yet our body can see only through the eye, and can be directed only by the head.)

Third, the Independents effectively removed the distinction between teaching and ruling elders, and wanted every elder to teach, and therefore be elder for life. Over against this theory the Reformed stated that the ministry of the Word is a unique ministry, which requires a special preparation and a special gift, while on the other hand the introduction of an eldership for life unduly alienates the church and the congregation.

Fourth, they believed that multiple churches could organize conferences, but that the deputation of multiple churches could never exercise classical or synodical authority over the individual churches, not even when they were joined in a federation. Over against this, the Reformed held firmly to the principle that Christ's authority is over his entire church, and therefore that the discipline of multiple churches is needed to keep the individual churches walking in the ways of the Word.

Fifth and finally, the Independents denied the church any right to defend the truth of Scripture against heretical views through confessions, catechisms, or liturgical forms. The Scripture, they believed, must be the only creed—an idealistic, untrue thesis, which we Reformed refuted through the correct observation that the Holy Spirit expounds the Word in the church of all ages, and this historical exposition ought to have power and authority in opposition to the often arbitrary exposition of an individual preacher. In fact, Independentism is also an attempt to reduce the visible manifestation of the church to a shadow, to retreat almost entirely into its spiritual character as the assembly of the elect, and therefore particularly to move the governance in the church of Christ back to the gathering of the believers.

Such a system, needless to say, can function well for some time, as long as the spiritual life is kept on a high level under the cross of persecution, but as soon as this spiritual life weakens and collapses it must necessarily run entirely outside the ecclesiastical realm. And just as some of the Quakers in England and America practically slid away into Modernism, likewise the system of the Independents already in the eighteenth century degenerated imperceptibly into the so-called Collegial system. Meanwhile, that system is not of English but of German origin. This Collegial system is nothing but the application of the ideas of the French Revolution to the church of Christ. The doctrine of popular sovereignty as the source of all authority, even in the church of Christ—there you have the main feature of the Collegial system. The name means "gathering." It is derived from the law of congregation that used to exist in ancient Rome, and according to this law the church was acknowledged for a time as *collegia licita*, that is, legitimate gatherings. Here the sovereign authority of Christ is dissolved; the Word ceases to have authority; and the only thing that has authority and can transfer authority is the individual member with the other members, deciding according to the principle of absolute majority. If that absolute majority decides for Jesus, well then, the church keeps its Christian character, but if it turns out differently, that same church may tomorrow be Jewish or Muslim.

Thus, while for the Independents the members were still "believers," here the believers have become simply members without distinct character, and the definite Christian character is sacrificed. This Collegial system, which determines the organization of a good part of the Dutch Reformed state churches [*Hervormde kerken*], is purely revolutionary and, like the French Revolution, allows for all kinds of regimentation. On the basis of the Collegial system I can establish a Roman church, through the fiction that the members have transferred their authority to the pope. But I can also use it to promote the caesaropapism of the Lutheran churches and of the Dutch Reformed state church, by assuming that the members have, *rebus ipsis et factis* [by acts themselves and deeds], in all actuality transferred their right to the king. If the custom of kneeling before the king is reinstated and the ministerial class desires to reintroduce clericalism, well, what would prevent them from accomplishing that ideal by means of the Collegial system? One can simply pretend that the members have transferred their original right to the oligarchical consistories, in which the ministers are everything! This Collegial system is truly chameleon-like;

you can use it to justify any system. But its foundation is unstable and it removes the divine foundation from under each of these other systems, in order to replace it with the principle of revolution. For this is its sin: it will tolerate God's authority in his Christ only if it is based on the authority of man's free will.

THE COMPONENTS OF THE AUTHORITY EXERCISED IN CHRIST'S CHURCH   § 20
To say that there is authority in the church is to acknowledge that the church not merely advises, admonishes, and tries to convince, but also receives power to bind. This is customarily expressed symbolically in the "keys of the kingdom of heaven": "I will give you the keys of the kingdom of heaven, and whatever you bind on earth shall be bound in heaven, and whatever you loose on earth shall be loosed in heaven" [Matt 16:19]. This solemn word of the Lord may not be diminished. It implies that a church loses its noble identity when it loses the boldness to connect the profession of its creed to salvation. And conversely, the children of God lose the church they need when they no longer trust and follow the word of their church as interpreting the will of the Lord. And the only good state of the church is that where the church's rulers—knowing themselves to be interpreters of the Word of the Lord—powerfully lay the truth upon the consciences and speak what is right; and where church members, for the Lord's sake, yield to the authority of the rulers as the authority placed over them by King Jesus. They should do so, not passively for the sake of peace, merely externally, but as bound in the soul, for the sake of their salvation.

Taking the authority of the church in this high, serious sense, one must also recall that such authority is not born out of agreement, in which the church members surrender some of their freedom; this authority is imposed by Christ and has its origin in God's sovereignty. The obligation to respect this authority does not originate from our becoming a member of a church, but we become a member of a church because we sense that we must submit to that authority. Likewise, in organizing a church, church planters do not create that authority, but merely give to that authority the instruments for its work. Just as a mother who delivers a child does not create light or air, but only delivers a creature equipped with organs to breathe in that air and capture that light, likewise the establishment of a church does not generate new authority; rather, it brings to life yet another organism equipped with organs designed to allow preexisting authority to do its work.

This authority, which must be upheld in the strongest sense of authoritative power, is exercised by Jesus Christ, who is the King of his whole church, and therefore also King of every local church—also King of, say, the church of Amsterdam. This King exercises this authority in part directly, and in part indirectly. Directly, first of all, because he provides his churches the means of grace, his Word and sacrament; second, because he works in the members of those churches with his Holy Spirit; and third, because through his providential governance he determines the fate of these churches and of their members. But this King also exercises that authority indirectly, through people, and only this indirect authority will be discussed here.

Now this King exercises this indirect authority in a twofold manner: either through his entire church, or through those who hold an office in it. This happens in such a way that the King actually gives his authority to the entire church, but through ecclesiastical office he also provides it with instruments to which it is bound for the operation and exercise of that authority. Just as a man's ear ceases to hear and his eye ceases to see if he loses consciousness, likewise the organs of the church can no longer perform any spiritual function as soon as the church itself becomes paralyzed or falls asleep. Conversely, just as a person who is awake and alive cannot see or hear if his eyes or ears are damaged or lacking, likewise the church cannot rightly exert the authority given to it unless the organs of ecclesiastical offices are developed within it.

One must therefore keep in mind the proper relationships. All authority is in Jesus. He gives it to the church in its entirety, but this authority is bound to the official organs for its proper functioning. The church does not create these official organs but receives them, just as the body does not make the ear but was by God equipped and enriched with eye and ear. For a proper understanding we must therefore distinguish which part of the authority the church itself exerts, without the organ of ecclesiastical office, and which other part of the authority is bound to the organic official activity. Apart from the special functions of eye, ear, nose, mouth, brain, and so on, there are in the human body also general functions, of heat production, sense, and so on. Likewise, in the church of Christ there are the general functions of the whole body of the church, and also the special functions by its various organs. Both these general and special applications of authority extend over three areas, namely, over the means of grace, over the order of the church, and over jurisdiction.

The church exercises authority in the area of the means of grace, first of all ordinarily, because it receives power to administer the Word and the sacrament and to bind the consciences by them. This is the ministry of the keys exercised through preaching and personal admonition, from which the sacrament as a seal of the Word may not be separated. But also extraordinarily, by opposing that which opposes the means of grace—that is, by condemning heresy and confessing the truth over against it. Without heresy there would be no confession. But now that heresy has existed, still exists, and always will exist until the end, confession is inseparable from the essence of the church.

Likewise, the church exercises authority over the order that must exist in its midst, and does so in a twofold manner: first, by composing a church order and issuing detailed ordinances; and second, by implementing this church order and these detailed ordinances.

Finally, the church exercises authority in terms of ecclesiastical jurisdiction, again in a twofold manner: first, by officially rebuking, punishing, and if necessary excommunicating those who err in confession or life; and second, by restoring to honor the repentant one and receiving him again into the circle where the means of grace are enjoyed fully.

Now, of this threefold authority we must first consider the general authority, which belongs to the entire church; and after that, the special function of this authority, which is lodged with the official organs. To the church in its entirety belongs, first, with respect to the means of grace, the duty and right to testify, to confess, to pray, and to rebuke individually, as well as the freedom of prophecy. With respect to the order of the church, believers have the right to establish a church when there is none, or when an existing church has fallen away. Moreover, in an already existing church, they have the right to participate in judging attestations and requests for access to holy communion, to appoint people to office, to be present as the audience of ecclesiastical assemblies, to delegate representatives to other churches, to have influence in the appointment of church custodians, and to supervise the guarding of the church's possessions. And finally, with respect to ecclesiastical jurisdiction, believers have the right to administer the first steps of discipline in private disputes, to free themselves from unfit fellow members and office-bearers, to participate in evaluating excommunications and reinstatements, to protest against ungodly ecclesiastical situations and demand reformation, and, in case this is unfruitful, to proceed with the organization of their own consistories when the church becomes a dissenting congregation. Finally, when the church turns out to be lost completely, they have the right to send a farewell letter to that false church and to manifest the true church elsewhere.

By contrast, the church is bound to the official organs for that special authority by which church government comes to expression. Thus, to the office-bearers belongs the right, first with regard to the means of grace, to administer the Word authoritatively in the gatherings of the church, to lift up supplications and prayers, to administer the sacraments, and also to make decisions concerning the church's confession in ecclesiastical assemblies. Second, with regard to the church order, the office-bearers organize matters and establish rules of order; they manage the church's affairs according to these rules and execute the decisions that have been made; they form the governing board in the gatherings of the congregation or its representatives; they represent the church in visits to other churches, or in assemblies of classis and synod; in lower or higher assemblies they investigate the issues at hand and make decisions about them; and they appoint and install newly elected persons into office. Finally, with respect to ecclesiastical jurisdiction, they have the right to call people before them and question them; to admonish and censure with authority; to rebuke, excommunicate, and reinstate, in collaboration with the congregation; when wolves enter the church, to protect believers from them; if necessary, to assemble believers separately as a dissenting church; and, if that fails as well, to gather them in order to establish a new church.

§ 21   HOW THIS ECCLESIASTICAL AUTHORITY RELATES TO THE AUTHORITY OF THE GOVERNMENT

The authority of the church and the authority of the government are completely different with respect to their origin, essence, nature, and purpose. With respect to origin, because government authority springs directly from the sovereignty of the Triune God; ecclesiastical authority comes from the Mediator as the Head of his church. With respect to essence, because government authority concerns the external life of body, right, and possession; ecclesiastical authority concerns the inner person, in one's spiritual existence. With respect to nature, because government authority is an authority of power, which compels by violence; ecclesiastical authority is never more than an official or ministerial authority, before Christ as well as believers. Finally, with respect to purpose, because government authority purports to maintain the righteousness and honor of God in this life; ecclesiastical authority aims to glorify God in bringing the elect to their heavenly blessedness.

This immediately implies two things. First, all ecclesiastical persons are, as citizens of the state, subject to the rule and authority of the government, independent of whether the magistrate confesses the truth or opposes it. And second, the government as government can never, in any respect or in any capacity, exercise any ecclesiastical authority in the church. The government's obligation to uphold God's honor in the civil state is not an ecclesiastical but a political obligation that continues to exist even if the church were to disappear. That applies as much to someone like William the Silent as to someone like Philip II and as much to someone like Nero as to someone like Constantine. Anyone who rules, under any title, by the grace of God, must be intent on the honor of God in all of his leadership. Also, the boundaries placed on this obligation—namely, that it may not overshoot its goal or oppress consciences—do not constitute a compromise between state and church, but are boundaries defined by God in granting sovereignty, because the magistrate receives this sovereignty only with respect to the external man, not the internal man.

Thus, just as the church may never exercise any civil authority, the civil government may never exercise any ecclesiastical authority. These two spheres are completely distinct. There is a mixed arena where both authorities meet, since the member of the church is also citizen of the state. This can cause conflict if the church appropriates what belongs to Caesar, or if Caesar demands for himself what belongs to the church. And this does not negate the fact that these two spheres are strictly distinct. It merely shows that church and state sometimes fail to see this distinction clearly. Sadly, there is no arbiter in such conflicts, and the resulting conflict can be resolved only through reconciliation and agreement.

However, this does not mean that the obligation of the political government does not include the obligation to protect the true church. Just as any sovereign ruler is called, by the grace of God, to uphold all that is true and godly, likewise the government must support the true church. That obligation remains on the government, even if it chooses for the false church, or even if it persecutes the true church of God. The question how it should meet this obligation is a matter of application. In the past it was resolved in the way of manifold intervention, but today, because of the grievous results of such intervention, it needs to be answered in the sense of virtually complete detachment. The true church of God never flourishes better than where it has the opportunity to develop freely and out of its own spiritual power. Moreover, the fulfillment of this obligation will assume a different character depending on whether nearly all, some, or only a few of the inhabitants of a country belong to the true church. The character of the fulfillment of this obligation also strongly depends on whether the government itself believes and confesses the truth publicly, or is indifferent to or openly rejects the truth. Although none of this makes an essential difference in the government's obligation to protect the true church, it has a significant impact on the performance of that duty. This difference is affected by the tendency of confessing government officials who are church members to have a position of influence in the church and to receive more respect because of the majesty of God vested in them. Still, even if the magistrate is not a confessor of the truth, the church must insist that its public legal position be acknowledged. It may not be content with a position equal to that of other associations, as if the authority within it is of a mere corporate nature. It is ordained by God Almighty within the state to prepare the eternal kingdom of glory; it is there *iure divino*, that is, by divine right. Any government that does not acknowledge the civil right of a church in this capacity, and does not give it the honor due the church of King Jesus, falls short in the fulfillment of its duties and thereby sins.

Meanwhile we must distinguish from this the influence of representative bodies that are not governments. For instance, in Geneva and elsewhere, the citizens were represented in civil councils, and since the same citizens were also church members, these councils had a twofold function: they represented civil interests in political matters, and spiritual interests in the ecclesiastical realm. They were, if you will, a conflation of an electoral college and a consistory. Even today it frequently happens in villages where nearly the entire population confesses the same truth, that the very same group of persons is elected, first as delegates to represent the church, and then as council members to represent the citizenry.

To support the church of God financially is certainly a course of action for government officials, if it can happen without violating consciences, and if it promotes the well-being of the church. However, if it becomes manifest that through this financial support, the government rather upholds the false elements in God's church, and in addition violates the consciences of the citizens, it should forgo this financial support—but it must pay off whatever it legally owes the church.[19]

The government may never function as an ecclesiastical authority in the assemblies of synod, classis, or presbytery. When the government appears in ecclesiastical assemblies, it never belongs to the body of the assembly but stands outside. Its influence may be no more than to ensure that no political issues are decided and that personal rights are not violated, and to honor by its presence the public character of the church.

Finally, concerning the approbation of ecclesiastical appointments [by the government]: it can never consist in participating in the appointment to or the granting of a particular office. The appointment of a church official is completely ecclesiastical in nature, and the government can grant no grain of ecclesiastical authority to a church office-bearer. But that approbation can serve to regulate the payment of government salaries to office-bearers. Furthermore, when foreigners, or people from outside a city or village, are called to an office, the national or city government can decide whether they acknowledge the public legal status of these persons as church officials.

By contrast, the governor's rights of appeal or appointment, which under names like *right of patronage* and *floreen system* have left such a grievous memory, must be repudiated as being in absolute conflict with the pure principle of the church.[20] Even if one were to pretend that the congregation supposedly transferred its right of appointment to a third party, the response must always be that this transfer cannot be legitimate because the ecclesiastical authority of appointment is inalienable by its very nature.

Finally, concerning the "removal and prevention of all idolatry and false worship, that the kingdom of Antichrist may be thus destroyed and the kingdom of Christ promoted,"[21] here too we must firmly hold on to

---

19. In Kuyper's time, the Dutch government supported the Reformed churches financially. In special cases, the government might pay off its obligation through a single severance payment, thus providing the church with the capital needed for its own support.

20. The floreen system was a form of patronage in which those who paid a particular level of taxes were granted the franchise in elections of ministers as well as other offices. On the abolition of the floreen system, see David J. Bos, *Servants of the Kingdom: Professionalization among Ministers of the Nineteenth-Century Netherlands Reformed Church* (Leiden: Brill, 2010), 343.

21. Belgic Confession, Art. 36.

the principle, but make sharp and strict distinctions in its application. Without a doubt the magistrate has the obligation to promote God's honor, not in the least by suppressing idolatry. But this does not imply that every means to this end should be considered legitimate or effective. Had history shown that a violent removal of idolatry and heresy is actually fruitful and upholds the glory of God, then certainly that removal should be considered mandatory. But human nature is such that violence against moral error is ineffective; the nature of idolatry and heresy rather causes people to gain impetus when opposed; and the government, according to the testimony of history, has almost always erred by viewing the truth as being heresy and condemning the truth as being idolatry. Therefore we have convincing proof that with respect to the violent removal of heresy, heresy itself is impervious, human nature is inadequate, and the government is both ineffective and incapable. For this reason the practice of the ancient church must be rejected, and the government should be admonished not to try to remove heresy in any other way than to leave the true church free, and thereby to equip it for fuller development of its spiritual power.

§ 22   WHAT IS REQUIRED OF THE MINISTERS OF THE WORD

Among the office-bearers of the church, the ministers of the Word occupy the first place. They do not derive this preeminence from the dignity of their persons, or from any higher degree that would give their office a position above that of an elder or deacon, but only from the worthiness of the Word of God that they administer. And any claim of honor or appreciation that should be based on anything other than the worthiness of the Word must, for the sake of the person as well as his ministry, be firmly opposed as self-centeredness and arrogance of heart. In fact, the dignity of the minister of the Word is dependent on how he himself esteems God's Word to such an extent that his official authority, even if he still bears the title, pales and fades to the degree that the influence of the Word diminishes in his person and preaching. The Reformed church knows no Roman Catholic office that would operate through a priestly influence *ex opere operato*. For the Reformed person, a minister of the Word is a normal man, with air in his lungs, and therefore must be esteemed like other people; only God is great, and a creature can never be great. And even the office vested in him could in no way increase the worthiness of his person as a person. With or without his office, he is and remains the same weak, fragile man and erring sinner, who can stand only through the grace of God. A mayor is vested with his duty along with certain majesty from God, independent of how he performs his duty, but the value of a preacher's activity is exclusively determined by the truth of the Word he preaches. Insofar as the Word is brought by his ministry, he speaks with the King's power and handles the keys of the kingdom. But also, where he abandons or violates that Word, he damages his own ministerial work and surrenders the glory of his office.

Now the calling of these ministers of the Word is to shepherd the flock of the Lord with that Word—to pasture in a twofold manner, namely, through doctrine and life. Through doctrine in the gatherings of the congregation, in the training of the youth, and in the homes of believers. And through life, in his own home, among his fellow citizens, and especially among the saints. He must shepherd the flock of the Lord in the gathering of believers by expounding and applying the Word. The Word of God has relevance for every congregation in all times, and for every person at all times. And the mystery of the preaching lies precisely in this, that through conscientious exposition and appropriate application, the Word of God is given the relevance intended by the Spirit. Any topical preaching must therefore be condemned as sin. One must not shepherd the flock with one's own ideas, to which one connects a text. Rather, the Word must be preached as it presents itself, by unfolding it and applying it to the hearers. Any person who fails to confess the infallibility of Holy Scripture can therefore not be admitted to the ministry of the Word. To oppose this infallibility and yet to come to the congregation with the claim "it is written," is to pretend to confess what one denies, and is therefore immoral.

The person who is to serve in this ministry must be educated for it, both by training in godliness and training in academics. A learned yet ungodly man is powerless on the pulpit and pushes people away. But a godly yet ignorant man is also unsuited for the ministry. Study combined with godliness is therefore an indispensable condition, provided that in these various studies the study, not *about*, but *of* and *in* the Word of God, stands unrelentingly in the foreground. If the opportunity for such an education is lacking, then the church must call it into existence. If it exists, then it suffices for the church to examine the candidates after they complete their study.

The right of examination of candidates to the ministry lies with the consistory because the consistory extends the call. However, since neighboring churches have a common interest in this matter, and many village churches are not equipped for an academic examination, it is expedient to have many churches in the classis administer such an examination together. Such an exam must address both academic studies and personal godliness. It must address personal godliness, not to judge the state of such a person before God, but to observe closely his confession and walk—his confession, by investigating whether he is orthodox in all respects, and his walk by interviewing those who know him. Furthermore, there must be an assessment of the gifts granted to such a person or withheld by King Jesus, by investigating carefully whether he truly has the gift of preaching, of prayer, of instruction, and of consolation.

Next, persons who thus have thoroughly been examined by the church enter their office through the calling of the churches and installation into their ministry. The church must call their ministers of the Word—not through individual votes, not through electoral colleges consisting of anyone who may be interested, but in such a way that believers express their preferences to the consistory by nomination. The consistory then selects one of the nominees, calls the chosen person, and then with his consent installs him into the office, either through other ministers of the Word or through the ruling elders. If a church has correspondence with other churches, as it should, then the classis must also approve the call, because the ministers of the Word also work in neighboring churches; the churches have a mutual responsibility to guard the quality and integrity of each other's church life.

Since the ministers of the Word devote themselves entirely to serving the church, they must also live from the church. Concerning the way in which the church must receive these means, we only remind the reader that the oldest Reformed churches under the cross found these means both through individual assessments and through voluntary gifts. But no matter how the churches receive these funds, the churches must pay them to its ministers, not as alms, but as their honoring in love rather than as a right. The responsibility for this belongs to the church leaders, as is currently our custom, but it could also be given to the diaconate, which is then viewed not merely as taking care of the poor, but as a more general ministry of the tables.

All ministers of the Word are of perfectly equal rank. The minister of the tiniest village stands on the very same level as the minister of the Word in the capital city. Episcopal hierarchy is unknown to the Reformed church. It loathes it and rejects it as an unspiritual invasion and an inappropriate usurpation of authority.

Finally, since not only the souls of believers but also the churches, as bodies, must be governed by God's Word, the ministers of the Word are also governors of the church, just as the ruling elders. And because of the worthiness of the Word, they are also to preside in all assemblies of ecclesiastical origin.

THE POSITION THAT ELDERS OUGHT TO HAVE IN THE CHURCH §23

Elders, in the narrower sense, are equal in rank to the minsters of the Word, who are referred to in Holy Scripture with the same name of *elders* or *overseers*. For this reason, the distinction between the ministers of the Word as teaching elders and the ordinary elders as ruling elders is therefore not entirely correct. After all, the ordinary elder also teaches. The difference is only that the public exposition and application of the Word in the gathering of the congregation belongs to the minister of the Word, while the elder in the narrower sense teaches only privately through his admonition in home visits, and must confess the Word by means of his life. In the absence of a minister of the Word, the elder can also edify the assembled congregation, but then he is performing the office of someone else, not his own office. However, in church government and in the exercise of church discipline, the elders have the same rank as the ministers of the Word. With respect to the ministry of the Word they are only helpers—an addition to the ministers—but not so in matters of government and discipline. Then they, together with the ministers, constitute one assembly, possessing equal authority, and according to Q&A 85 of the Heidelberg Catechism they must be viewed as "those ordained by the church,"[22] as our form for ordination expresses, "to prevent all tyranny and domination." In matters of church government, they sometimes appear to stand above a minister of the Word, insofar as a supervisor stands above the person whom he supervises, and to the ruling elders—to use that phrase once

---

22. Some English versions of Q&A 85 render this simply as "proper officers," but Dutch, Latin, and German versions typically read "those ordained to this by the church." The quotation here uses the text of the Catechism as approved by the Christian Reformed Church in North America.

more—is given the specific instruction to "supervise the doctrine and life of the ministers of the Word."[23]

As stated in Q&A 85 of the Heidelberg Catechism, they must be chosen by the congregation, but they must be installed into their office by their fellow officers, either ministers of the Word or ruling elders. Concerning the method of election, refer to what was said in the previous section about the election of the ministers of the Word.

They can serve for life, if necessary, but preferably for a few years, so that the church may also profit from the gifts of others, and to keep oligarchy out of God's church.

If one or more elders are given a ministry in the church that requires one to abandon his vocation, then he and his family should receive everything necessary for life, in the very same way and on the same conditions as indicated above for the ministers of the Word. In such a manner, the goal currently being pursued through the appointment of religion teachers and so-called evangelists could be achieved in a more proper, effective, and orderly fashion.[24]

§ 24   WHAT SHOULD BE MAINTAINED REGARDING THE DOCTORS OF THE CHURCH

The question whether there exists in the church of God a fourth office, that of doctor or teacher, alongside the offices of preacher, elder, and deacon, cannot be resolved by referring to Ephesians 4:11. There it clearly states that the Lord appointed *some* as apostles and *some* as evangelists, but then it continues: *some as pastors and teachers*. Had it been: "some as pastors and some as teachers," then the matter would be decided. Not now. Our Belgic Confession, in Articles 30 and 31, knows only three offices; and although the Dort Church Order, Article 2, mentions four offices, the Church Order must be explained according to the Confession, not the Confession according to the Church Order. Moreover, even after 1619 the church did not proceed to create an ecclesiastical office of doctor. We must therefore admit that until now, the office of doctor is in a state of developing, and can only

---

23. These quotations are based on the form for the ordination of elders and deacons (*formulier van de bevestiging der Ouderlingen en Diakenen*), which has its origins in Dutch synods of the Reformation and post-Reformation era.

24. Kuyper may be referring to parachurch organizations (see sections 48 and 55) such as the Higher Life revivals at Brighton, England, with which he had been involved, and the religion departments at national universities, which allowed a number of ecclesiastically appointed professors in addition to the secular faculty.

gradually come into its own through further ecclesiastical development. In that further development, the following must serve as the rule:

(1) The ecclesiastical office of doctor must be distinguished strictly from the academic titles given to persons who earned a doctorate.

(2) The ecclesiastical doctorate should never be a mere title but rather an office, with the purposes of training future ministers of the Word, of expounding the truth scientifically, and of defending the truth as confessed by the church over against heresy. It should consist either of those three together, or one of them.

(3) Such doctors must be placed in ecclesiastical seminaries, preferably with a part-time appointment of the ministry of the Word.

(4) Such ecclesiastical doctors must be part of the consistory of their town, and have an advisory role at classis and synod.

(5) They may be eligible for the doctorate only after they are thoroughly examined in academics and godliness.

(6) These ecclesiastical doctors are appointed to their office by the church, and installed either by the consistory, if they are called locally, or, if they are appointed for a vocational school of the church, by the classis or the synod that established this school.

Professors of theology at the universities, that is, not in the schools of the church but in an independent, non-ecclesiastical, scientific institution, may be appointed ecclesiastical doctors by the consistory of their town, but they do not have this status automatically. It is advisable for such universities to ask the church for its collaboration in connection with the appointment of their theology professors, in such a way that these professors are given the ecclesiastical office and the church is given the oversight over the men in this office.

THE TASK OF THE DEACONS IN THE CHURCH OF CHRIST   §25

The office of deacon was corrupted somewhat in the early Christian church and entirely in the Roman Catholic Church, and it was restored only partially during the Reformation. Only partially, since the Lutheran church left it out, but also partially because even in the Reformed church this office was never sufficiently developed. A deacon holds an office royally granted to him by Christ, just as much as the minister of the Word and the elder. To say that deacons labor in the material world and therefore rank below ministers and elders who labor in the spiritual world, is a false dichotomy that evaporates as soon as the office of deacon is understood in its higher significance. The diaconate is the office of Christian love. And just as the Lord Christ during his walk on earth did a twofold divine work—preaching the gospel to restrain sin, and easing the misery of the sick and hungry to break the consequences of sin—similarly the diaconate must stand alongside the presbyterate in the church of Christ, to manifest the ministry of divine mercy alongside the ministry of the divine Word.

Thus the diaconate may certainly not be reduced to taking and distributing collections for the needy, but it must gradually develop into the glorious organ of the church for Christian philanthropy. The care of widows and orphans, of the elderly and the sick, of the blind and the mentally handicapped, of the psychologically ill and the terminally ill, and even of prisoners, sojourners, and so on, all belongs to the task of the deacon. And while they must help, support, and comfort the Lord's afflicted, not only financially and materially but also through spiritual consolation, they must also work spiritually with the congregation by teaching it. Those who are self-centered and greedy must learn that giving money is a spiritual deed that is enabled only by grace, but that also brings grace; and the deacons would be remiss in their duty toward the congregation if they fail to teach it this kind of giving. Far from despising the diaconate as a mere material office, one must rather honor it as a high spiritual office, even though today there are almost no churches where it functions as it should.

Deaconesses do not have an office, and must be viewed as helpers of the deacons, but they must therefore be honored as such in every church, since the love of Christ toward the afflicted can be fully manifest only if feminine gentleness is one of the church's instruments.

As in the case of the preachers and elders, those who have the office of deacon must be elected by the church, but called and installed by their fellow officers. The requirements for their office are first of all spiritual, but in addition to satisfying the indispensable requirements of orthodoxy and godliness, they must also have a stable position in society, in order not to endanger their soul through financial responsibility, and in order to ascertain trust.

Whether they must be installed with the laying on of hands, according to Acts 6:6, remains uncertain. But the fact that the apostles laid their hands on the first deacons certainly shows that their office may not be considered inferior in any way to the other offices.

Therefore, if in a further development of the ecclesiastical diaconate some people were to devote all their energy to it, there would be no objection against providing for the needs of these deacons and their families, just as in the case of the ministers—provided that the funds to do this are not taken from the alms but are paid by the church.

There has been much debate whether deacons participate in the government of the church. The custom in our Reformed circles was that in over 1,000 of about 1,100 congregations, the deacons did participate in church government—namely, in all rural churches and very small towns—while on the other hand in some 100 congregations the deacons formed a separate body and only had a vote in the council concerning the calling of office-bearers or the material affairs of the church. This explains the apparent contradiction between the Belgic Confession, which in Article 30 unites the ministers, elders, and deacons into a single consistory, and our form of ordination, which distinguishes the body of deacons from the assembly of the ministers and elders. And yet there is no doubt how this conflict must be resolved. The certain fact that after difficulties early on, our Reformed churches have never admitted a deacon to the classis or the synod, shows that our churches do not grant them the actual governance of the churches. They have a position in the broader council, where all the offices meet together and represent the congregation, but if they participate in church government in small towns, it is because of the small number of elders, and they make up for the deficit. On the other hand, we do not agree with those who involve the deacons in their calling as office-bearers only as honorable church members. That cannot be. Office is office. And the deacons, too, have a place in the church council as officers.

Another question, which we only mention briefly, would be whether the deacons of multiple churches should not ultimately meet together to take care of matters that affect many needy people, just as the classis and synod are assemblies of multiple churches. For the organization of orphanages in smaller villages, for the care of the sick, mentally ill, blind, foreigners, and so on, such a collaboration in a classical diaconate seems more and more to be indispensable.

WHAT KIND OF OFFICE BELONGS TO ALL BELIEVERS IN THE CHURCH OF CHRIST? §26

In Article 28, the Belgic Confession professes, among other things, that there is also an office of all believers. This expresses clearly and accurately what the Holy Scripture means when it adorns the people of the Lord with the honorary titles of kings and priests. Although this honor belongs to all, it does not lose the character of an office. What you do by virtue of your office, you do not do from yourself but because of a dignity laid upon you; and conversely, what I do when out of office, I do as the result of my personal initiative, without the involvement of a commanding power. In the United States of America, as well as in France, there exists a general right of voting in the civil realm, but between these countries is this all-important difference: the French voter says, "I vote because this is my right, a right that I possess and for which I owe thanks to no one," while the American who understands his constitution will say, "I do not vote because of my right as a person, but by the grace of God, for God has granted me this office." Well, the very same difference exists between the views of the fanatics and the Reformed. Both groups acknowledge that believers in the church have power. But while the enthusiast cries, "I, I as a personal believer, must decide in Jesus' church," the Reformed person confesses, "As a believer I have only the duty eternally to thank God for his grace, and it is only because King Jesus has given me an office that I now have a responsibility in the church."

This office of believer consists first of all in this, that where the governing offices go astray, the office of believer enters into that place. In a church on a desolate island, where the plague has suddenly brought all the office-bearers to the grave, the believers themselves would have to act as officers instead of these official persons. They should immediately perform the duties of the office on their own behalf, and they should elect new office-bearers. When an office goes astray, its duties always shift to the next office. If the minister of the Word goes astray, the ruling elder takes his place; if the ruling elders go astray, the deacons take over their duties; and if the deacons go astray, then the office of believer takes its place. As we will see, this rule also applies when the office-bearers do not *fall away* because they die or move away, but *go astray* through unbelief and unfaithfulness, or fall short through laziness or arrogance. Alas, there are far too many examples, and today the Sunday school and so many other institutions, which in themselves are unnatural and therefore illegitimate, stand as an indictment of officers and elders, but they were an indispensable corrective and must be appreciated.

Yet this official observation of the duty of others is merely a consequence of the more general duty, namely, the obligation consistently and relentlessly to check the decisions and activities of the other office-bearers in matters of confession, church government, and worship. A believer may never accept something because the ministers of the church said so. That is Roman Catholic, not Reformed. In a Reformed church, every believer must possess spiritual judgment and put that judgment to work. The believer does this not to be a know-it-all or a busybody, but out of spiritual obedience, and therefore never does it on the basis of his or her own opinion but exclusively according to the spiritual understanding of God's Word. In this way, all that is confessed, decided, or administered in the church must always be supported by the spiritually enlightened conscience of believers. If discord arises between these enlightened consciences of believers and the decision or action of the overseers, then the office of those believers who form a judgment in this matter must communicate this judgment first privately, with respect for the office of the overseer, then file a complaint, and finally, if necessary, give a public testimony. From this very solemn duty flows another official obligation, in case all attempts to hold the church's government to the truth remain fruitless—namely, to separate themselves from such overseers, since they are showing themselves as no longer belonging to the church, and to join the true church, or else to manifest that church anew.

But also in normal times this office of believer has yet another very active and positive aspect. As we just mentioned, the office of believer is not designed merely to make up for a deficit in the knowledge of the youth, through Sunday schools and other institutions. Rather, it also includes the duty to proclaim the gospel where this is not occurring, or occurs only in appearance, as soon as the Lord God grants the gift to do so—provided (and this is all-important) that it is done officially, on the basis of one's office, and not, as is the case with the enthusiasts, because one feels like doing it or imagines oneself to be compelled by the Spirit.

The older Reformed followed the early Christian church by going even further in this respect: initially they organized so-called prophecies, that is, gatherings of the congregation in which common believers, led by the consistory, tried to edify the congregation from the Word of God, so that all Jesus' gifts to his church might be used for the benefit of the church.[25]

---

25. Kuyper may have in mind something like the *Prophezei* of Zurich, inaugurated under the reformer Huldrych Zwingli in 1525. The *Prophezei* involved formal study of the biblical languages and scriptural exegesis, as well as more popular exposition in preaching and teaching for the public. But more likely and in connection

Recently it was discovered that Comrie too encouraged this ministry in the Word based on the office of believer.[26] Related to this is the fact that men with "extraordinary gifts," who apparently were equipped for this by the Lord even apart from academic training, were admitted to the office of the ministry of the Word.

§ 27   CONCERNING THE MATERIAL POSSESSIONS OF THE CHURCHES

Property or possession of goods is not indispensable for the essence of a church. Even without its own church building, a church of God can assemble in the open air, a barn, or a warehouse, without truncating the essence of the church. However, as the church expands, and during more peaceful times, at least in our climate, the possession of one or more church buildings is indispensable. And equally indispensable is some location for smaller meetings of office-bearers or church members. In addition to these buildings, a church usually possesses some capital in real estate or other assets, and the donor or testator of these assets has earmarked the income generated by them for the maintenance of the buildings, the worship services, or the salaries of the ministers. If the revenue from these possessions is insufficient to provide for location and janitors, to maintain the worship services, and to pay the ministers appropriate salaries, then the church ought to make up for this deficit through the collection of free gifts or individual fees.

The supervision of these goods and revenues belongs to the church. It is *its* property, *its* funds, to be spent for *its* benefit, and for which *it* is responsible. It can exercise this supervision in various ways. In the past the church left much of it to the Reformed state government. When that disappeared, it appointed its own superintendents and supervisors, in part directly, in part through the consistory. In principle the following rules apply as guidelines:

(1) In very small churches this supervision can be delegated to the deacons, as responsible for the general ministry of the tables, that is, of all monies, not only those to be given to the poor.

---

with the following reference to Comrie, Kuyper may also have something in mind like the conventicles of Scotland, England, and elsewhere, which were meetings of laypersons outside regular corporate worship.

26. Scotsman Alexander Comrie (1706–74) was a Reformed pastor in Woubrugge, a village east of Leiden.

(2) In midsize and larger congregations this is neither practical nor wise. It is not practical because the deacons, for lack of organization, are already forced to leave two-thirds of their own tasks unfinished. It is not wise, because it damages the spiritual character of the diaconate.

(3) It is better not to assign this supervision to the consistory. As a body of officers, the consistory has its own calling, and the supervision of church property is not spiritual but belongs to a committee.

(4) It is therefore safest if all church members, under the leadership of the consistory, appoint a separate body of church superintendents, as well as a committee consisting of some church members to audit these superintendents and hold them accountable.

Individual fees are not based on the principle of love but on the obligation according to rights. Therefore they may never serve to replace the giving of alms and to provide for the poor, but they may certainly be used as joint payment of the costs incurred jointly as a church. A church that uses a building, employs janitors, hires organists, and commits itself to support a minister annually incurs shared expenses, and therefore has an annual debt. All that is spent for the church itself, expenses for its own enjoyment and debt for its own spending, never falls under the heading of alms, but it is and remains *tributum*, that is, legally owed. One can collect it on a voluntary basis, or if that does not work, by dividing the costs among the members. Yet even if these monies are collected voluntarily, they can never be alms, but they always remain payments for the church's own accoutrements. Whoever imagines, therefore, that in the church service his offering for the church's general fund and his offering for the poor are on the same level, ascribes to himself a good work that is not legitimately his. Even the person who pays more to the church's general fund than is required, proportionally speaking, is not thereby giving alms to the church, but is paying, on top of what is owed, part of the debt of less willing contributors. For a proper functioning of the church, for a normal church in normal times, one would have to pay according to the rule that ecclesiastical payment is proportional to financial ability, whereas all benefit equally.

BY WHICH ASSEMBLY IS THE CHURCH GOVERNED? §28

The government of the churches is exercised by the consistories, which in the broader sense consist of the ministers, elders, and deacons, and in the narrower sense, as far as the second key of the heavenly kingdom [that is, church discipline] is concerned, consists only of the ministers and elders. Likewise, the deacons in turn form a separate body for the ministry of the tables. The fact that in smaller churches the deacons also participate in the government in the narrow sense is due to necessity, but does not follow from the principle. However, in all cases that do not deal exclusively with the use of the keys or exclusively with the ministry of the tables, but involve general interests of the church, the decision lies in principle with the full council of the church, in which deacons as well as preachers and elders take part. Matters of a general nature are: the call of ministers, the appointment of elders and deacons, the representation of the church to the government, the care of church property, and so on. In the broader council as well as in the consistory assigned the use of the keys, the ministers preside, but otherwise the elders and deacons are completely equal in rank. The consistory must deal with the matters at hand in an orderly fashion, and may never deputize others except for the execution of a specific task. It must receive members of the church who wish to speak with them. It best maintains a vibrant communication with the church by allowing believers to attend the meetings, except of course in meetings requiring executive session, whenever the nature of the matter requires it.

The ministers of the Word may organize a meeting to discuss their activities, and likewise the ruling elders may organize their own meeting to discuss how to divide their work, but that so-called ministerium or presbytery has absolutely no power or authority, and neither type of meeting was originally known in our Reformed churches. The deacons do have a distinct ministry and therefore they constitute a distinct body. But teaching elders and ruling elders are members of the same class, joined in administering the keys of the kingdom, and therefore, in accordance with the form for ordination, they cannot form any other assembly with power and legitimate authority except the regular consistory, in which they act together with equal vote and equal authority.

§ 29   THE ADMINISTRATION OF THE MEANS OF GRACE
The means of grace of the church are the treasures laid up in Christ for the elect, treasures which are presented to us in the Word and sealed through the sacraments. Word and sacrament are therefore rightly called the church's two means of grace. Now these means of grace are administered by one person and received by another. Therefore the sacrament is linked

to the presbyterial ministry, since nobody can *receive* a sacrament unless there is an administration. It is different with the Word. It can also be received and enjoyed without administration, albeit less fully. Therefore the means of grace of the Word is linked to the office only for its exposition and application. Specifically, the office of believer administers this means of grace to anyone willing to hear admonition; the office of priest, which belongs to a father in his house, administers it in all family homes; and the office of the minister of the Word administers it publicly to the entire congregation. This administration of the Word has a twofold character, depending on whether what must be administered is milk or solid food. The administration of milk is the administration of milk through the catechism class; the administration of solid food is the administration of this means of grace through exposition and application of the Word. The distribution of this milk is officially assigned to the minister of the Word for public and private catechism classes; to the ruling elders for private instruction; to the father, or also the mother, in every home; and to every believer in the case of children who are not dutifully taught by their parents or their relatives. On the other hand, the administration of solid food occurs officially in the home only by the father as the priest, and in the congregation by the minister of the Word. In both cases this is the application of the first key of the kingdom, not as so-called evangelism, but as a speaking in the name of the Lord, with power. It can only transfer to the ruling elder vicariously, and it occurs only in a subsidiary manner in the so-called prophecies,[27] or by regular church members in the absence of office-bearers. However, the minsters of the Word are no less obligated to bring this means of grace into the homes of the church members, to everyone by means of home visits before every Lord's Supper, to the afflicted in their sickness and grief, and to the dying as they approach death. Only faith is powerful to save, and to generate faith and keep it alive, there is no other means of grace but the Word.

The sacrament seals the Word and thereby strengthens faith, both to the church as a whole and to the individual who received faith. Just as any seal, in order to be a seal, must be public, so it is with the ministry of the sacraments. According to their nature, they must be administered publicly, and as such they are linked to the public ministry of the church. Therefore they are administered by the church to the church, under the

---

27. See *Tract*, in *On the Church*, 149n25.

leadership of the consistory and using the ministry of the shepherds. The sacraments are sacramental seals only in the church, under leadership of the consistory, and administered by the shepherds. Being seals of the Word, they may also never be severed from the ministry of the Word, and it is best to administer them after the sermon has ended. There should be no separate baptism services or communion services.

Every member of the church has a right to the administration of the means of grace, both the Word and the sacraments, but to receive and use them is also the member's duty. Therefore, as a rule, people are baptized as children, not as adults, and no one who qualifies in any way as a member of the church may be kept from baptism. The Word and the sacrament of the Lord's Supper would also be appropriate for infants, if they were receptive to them. However, since this is naturally impossible, the child first acquires the right to the Word when he or she can hear, and the right to communion when he or she can confess. A person who is not a member of the church, or who comes from elsewhere from churches that are not recognized, may not be admitted to the sacraments. Likewise anyone who is placed under church discipline because of heresy or wickedness must be excluded from the sacraments.

Conversely, every church member has the duty to make use of the sacrament. Everyone is obligated to baptize his child, and likewise all believers have the obligation to attend whenever the Lord's Supper is administered. Not as if their salvation depended upon the sacrament. Any good Christian knows better than that. But no good Christian repays the mercy of the Lord God with a disdain of his holy sacrament on the ground that God is sovereign to save him also without the sacrament.

§ 30   THE EXERCISE OF CHURCH DISCIPLINE
The administration of the means of grace must be kept holy, and the church of God must be governed with spiritual discipline. This is the twofold purpose of the exercise of Christian discipline, which is linked to the authority of the offices. This discipline is exercised (1) by any and every believer in the way of rebuke when one sees a brother go astray; (2) by any and every believer in the early stages of discipline, in the case of personal insult; (3) by all believers together in the excommunication or reinstatement of one who misbehaved, by agreement with the decision of the consistory or by opposing that decision; and (4) most principally,

by the consistory over the members of the church, and by the classis over wayward churches.

This discipline is not a fraternal admonition of love, but a moral jurisprudence exercised with authority in the name of King Jesus. This jurisprudence does not judge the state or intention of the heart. *De intimis non iudicat ecclesia*—the church does not judge what is hidden. Nor is this jurisprudence inquisitorial; it does not seek out the transgression that occurs in the home. Rather, it is aimed exclusively at public transgression, that is, transgression committed publicly, or committed privately but publicly known. This discipline concerns faith and conduct, and does so without partiality, over ministers of the Word and government officials as well as over the marginalized citizen.

It follows an orderly procedure, which ought to prevent the condemnation of the innocent. It proceeds through predefined stages to final excommunication from the church, but always turns back as soon as repentance is shown, and does so without leaving any disgrace on the repentant person.

It arrests the working of the means of grace, since the means of grace are for the believers only, and the application of discipline makes it uncertain and casts ecclesiastical doubt about whether someone is a believer. Although those who are under church discipline can be worked on with the Word, that Word comes to them as it comes to any others who stand outside, namely, to condemn them and to urge them to repentance, not to comfort them with promises. And, strictly speaking, the sacrament is discontinued, because the church may no longer seal promises to those whose faith is officially called into question. This does not apply to holy baptism, since a newborn infant cannot err or transgress. As for the idea of punishing the child for the transgression of the parents, this may and does happen on God's part, but the church has no authority to execute such a punishment.

The discipline in the home must not be discussed here, because the father's authority is of a civil nature, not an ecclesiastical nature.

THE WORSHIP SERVICE §31

The worship service is strictly limited to the sacred rituals that take place in the public gatherings of the churches. Neither what happens in the homes nor what happens in special meetings may therefore be included in this term. The worship service is what the church does as church during the hour of spiritual fellowship and communal worship, while using the keys of the heavenly kingdom. This implies, first of all, that the leadership of the worship service must be entrusted to the ministers of the Word, and that its structure and content must be decided by the consistory. If multiple churches are united [in a federation], then they can decide on this structure together in the classis, or in the case of even more churches, by the synod. But even in this classical or synodical decision, it is really the consistory that determines its structure. The second implication is that the minister of the Word does not appear in the gathering of the church to express his individual spiritual life, but to declare to the assembled congregation, in the name of the Lord, their sin and God's infinite mercies; and also on behalf of the gathered multitude to go to the Lord God with supplication, praise, and thanksgiving.

A certain fixed order is indispensable for this. Whether the ministers rotate or, in larger churches, multiple ministers conduct various services, it must always remain one church, which finds unity and consistency in its manifold ministry. For this reason, forms for the administration of the sacraments, for installations, for public discipline, and so on, are mandatory; the general structure of the worship service must be prescribed in the larger churches; what songs will be sung should be decided in advance; and even an occasional standard prayer is not at all to be rejected. But one should always avoid formalism, and one may not limit through human institutions the free expression of the Spirit in the congregation. A final implication is that every city or larger village may use multiple church buildings for the service. Specific ministers and geographical parishes may be assigned to each church building, but all these services must always be governed by a single consistory, so that in each service, in whatever building it is held, the same confession is made and the same liturgy is used.

From this perspective, the so-called hymnal issue is of the greatest importance. For instance, as long as the church of Amsterdam remains federated with those other churches with which it has been united since 1775, then the order and content of the worship service, and therefore what may be sung, can be decided exclusively by the national synods. Now all synods in the past have determined that only the Psalms are to be sung, and therefore this perpetual decision can rightfully be repealed only by a national synod. But the synodical committee that introduced the hymnal in 1806 had not received from any national synod a mandate to do so. And according to Reformed church law, a committee cannot and may not do anything else than what a synod in accord with its limits explicitly instructs them to do. Since a provincial synod cannot and may not annul what a national synod had decided, the provincial synods in 1805 had no authority whatsoever to negate the stipulations of the national synod of 1619. Likewise, the provincial synods could not transfer to their committees a power they themselves did not possess. The introduction of the hymnal was therefore absolutely unlawful. And the 1816 synod has not been able to correct this unlawful deed, because according to its letter of instruction it acted only as an administrative body, which deliberately excluded from its authority any decision-making in spiritual matters. We are not addressing the issue whether it is good to sing hymns in the worship services in addition to the psalms. We only express our sentiment that the introduction of the so-called evangelical hymns was entirely unlawful from the point of view of church polity, and to this day has never been made legitimate.

The objection that we should then still be singing the psalms of Dathenus is invalid.[28] This is a matter of implementation, and does not affect the core principle whether the singing in church is limited to the Word of God. That great principle, "In God's house nothing but the Word of God, also in your song!" was confessed emphatically by our legitimate, spiritual synods, under the leadership of Dathenus and Marnix; also over against the Remonstrants, who were the first to demand hymns.[29] And if such a principle turns out to be in conflict with the Word of God, then it can, and certainly must, be changed at a later national synod, provided that this change occurs in a lawful manner, and not, as happened among us, by those unauthorized to do so.

How a Church Enters into Relationship with Other Churches   § 32
A church may not remain by itself, because it is not *the* church of Christ, but only a manifestation of the church of Christ in a single location. Congregations in other places, which are likewise manifestations of the

---

28. In the late 1500s Peter Datheen (c. 1531–88) had written the psalter that was used in the Reformed church. In the 1770s a new psalter was introduced, though many still preferred that of Datheen.
29. The principle quoted here is attributed to Philip of Marnix, lord of St. Aldegonde (1540–98), who was a Reformed theologian, scholar, Bible translator, poet, political activist during the Dutch Revolt, and diplomat in the service of William the Silent.

same body of Christ, therefore belong to that universal church, and that church belongs to them. From this follows the firm obligation of correspondence with other churches, as much as possible. That obligation begins when in other locations the church of Christ can be recognized. If this is not the case, then a church cannot have correspondence with it. If churches elsewhere lose that character, then it must break off that correspondence. Unity of confession is the essential foundation on which any ecclesiastical correspondence or federation must stand.

Now where this oneness of principle is manifest, and federative relations are to be pursued through correspondence, this federation must have the following goals: (1) to express the common confession of the churches and to deal with complaints against it; (2) to jointly structure the worship service and teaching service; (3) to maintain mutual supervision; (4) to jointly defend the rights of churches over against third parties; (5) to resolve mutual conflicts among churches; (6) to organize the ministry of the Word, if necessary, through the establishment of seminaries, the assessment of candidates, the approbation of called ministers, and the dismissal of ministers who leave, and so on; (7) to structure the transfer of members from one church to another—that is, the so-called attestation—for the administration of baptism or the Lord's Supper; and (8) to maintain fellowship by sending delegates to one another's meetings.

Caring for the confession, the teaching ministry, and the worship service takes priority here, because they manifest the spiritual character of the church. Therefore the first duty of any churches in the formation of a federation is to adopt forms of unity [that is, confessions] and to ensure that they are complied with. To be sure, these documents are nothing in comparison to the worthiness of the Word of God, but they allow anyone inside or outside the church to know what the church believes concerning the Word of God. Therefore these confessions never bind the conscience. Only Holy Scripture binds the conscience, and these confessions must always be examined in its light. However, nobody is at liberty in the church to teach anything that opposes these confessions, and anyone who has complaints must bring them to the church for examination. And every person is bound either to submit to the decision of the church in this matter; or else to separate oneself from a church that, in one's conviction, has chosen against the Word of God. Herein lies the difference between a Remonstrant and a Reformed revision.

This federation or correspondence with other churches stands under the government of a synod. But because not all churches in a federation can meet together at the synod, the neighboring churches have always been combined in smaller groups under the name of classis. At this classis, all churches of the region ought to meet together as freely confederated or united churches. But because it is impossible for the entire church, or even all its consistories, to gather together, only their ministers with the elders meet together. Not every person, but every church must have a vote, and they are led by a board, which is elected before each meeting, and which is disbanded when the meeting closes. When the classis is not meeting, there exists nothing more than neighboring churches, and any idea of an ongoing ruling body or board must be zealously avoided and rejected as an invasion of papal tyranny. A classis can appoint a committee, but only with a specific task. There may never be a committee to deliberate and decide, like some kind of board, but only a committee of individually appointed members that executes the classis' instruction, and nothing more.

From this classis and by this classis, delegates are chosen to go to synod. The intermediate link of a provincial governing body is entirely contrary to the principles of Reformed church polity, especially now that provincial synods have been discontinued. There ought to be a direct delegation from the classis to the synod—either to the provincial synod, which in turn appoints a national synod, or directly to a national synod. But whether you climb up to the national synod in one step or in two steps, in either case the same rules apply to the provincial synods and general synods as to the classis. They come and they go, without leaving behind any synodical committee or any synodical board, and they are convened by the church or classis appointed for this purpose. They appoint their board when they convene and dismiss it when they are finished. Committees are instructed to execute the assembly's decisions, but only for a specific task and with a specific mandate, and these committees report only when the synod convenes again.

It is the custom for the national synod, and rightly so, to maintain correspondence with the churches abroad, insofar as these have the same confession. This correspondence can consist in a simple greeting, or, as in Dort, serve a twofold purpose, to help out churches in difficult situations and to express the unity of the Reformed church worldwide over against those who think differently.

The [Reformed] churches do not have correspondence with churches of a different confession, although the closer kinship with the Lutheran church has always been a basis for treating these churches with brotherly affection, and for always aiming at reuniting those who belong together but who, for lack of unity in confession, cannot live together.

§ 33   SHOULD THE CHURCHES BE INVOLVED IN NON-ECCLESIASTICAL MATTERS? A church of Christ may not be restricted to its own concerns, to living for itself. It also has a calling in terms of what lies outside of it, in three ways. First, after the household of faith is well cared for, it must extend its alms and compassionate care to those outside its gate who are in distress. Second, it must seek to win for the profession of Christ those who live in the same city or village but do not share in its glorious confession. And third, it must send evangelists or missionaries to other countries and regions, to plant the church where it does not yet exist. In summary, the church is called to the work of philanthropy, of evangelism, and of mission.

Works of compassion to those who are outside must be performed not to obtain a good reputation among the people, but for the Lord's sake, and from the awareness of communal guilt as the source of communal misery.

The exclusive purpose of evangelism must be the expansion of the church in towns where it already exists, and it must reach out to Jews and pagans, to the agnostics and the superstitious, to the poor and the rich. The preaching of the gospel to baptized persons is not evangelizing but catechizing, and must originate with the ministry of the Word, or, if the minsters fail to do their duty, with the office of believer. Everyone in particular is called to this work of evangelism, insofar as the Lord God brings a person into contact with the unchurched, but the church is also called as church, and for this work it can appoint certain men as evangelists. Their activity must aim at bringing outsiders into the church, for a well-instructed person who wishes to profess his or her faith must be baptized, and the right of administering holy baptism belongs to the church alone.

The mission to other regions or countries can likewise pertain to the individual or to the church. Every believer who feels called to do so may travel to foreign lands or regions to proclaim the gospel, and one would wish that more felt this calling. But we cannot tolerate private mission organizations that claim the authority to establish the ministry of the Word, organize the administration of the sacraments, and plant a church of God. Private persons may collect money to provide for the travel and living of a believer who wishes to go abroad. But then that person is not a missionary, not a sent one, not a minister of the Word. That person has no right to administer the sacrament, and may function there only as a witness of Christ, to proclaim the gospel. But if such a private person succeeds in converting Jews, pagans, or Muslims, and they desire to be baptized, then such an individual must turn to his or her own church or the neighboring church, so that this church may send a missionary. This missionary must administer holy baptism to these converts, gather them into a church, and prepare for the proper ministry of the Word through the election of elders and deacons. But a church can also send directly, that is, send an evangelist or minister of the Word with the task of preaching the gospel, and with the authority, in case God grants converts, to baptize them on behalf of the church, to unite them in a church, and to introduce a ministry of the Word among them.

Only a mission conducted according to these basic principles may count on the continued sympathy of the Reformed churches, although it would be inappropriate for those who themselves are sitting on their hands to judge others who did what their hands found to do.

One thing must be firmly condemned. The organization of so-called mission societies by a number of preachers is an irresponsible practice. Preachers are not Roman Catholic priests who function *ex opere operato*, and even if a legion of preachers joined together, apart from an ecclesiastical connection these individuals have no power and no authority to grant an ordination. An ordination can derive only from the churches in relationship.

THE CALLING OF THE CHURCHES WITH RESPECT TO THE SCHOOLS   §34

Education constitutes its own circle of spiritual activity, just the same as the rearing of children at home. Therefore the church may not simply take charge of the schools. This would slow down civic development, just as Rome's strong interference with home life in many countries killed the life at home.

However, the church must be involved with the school in a threefold manner:

(1) The church must, as a substitute, establish, nurture, and maintain schools, insofar as they do not exist due to the neglect of others, or if schools exist but in the wrong way, due to wrong influences.

(2) The church must see to it that the children of its indigent members receive education, which for the sake of frugality naturally leads to the establishment of diaconal schools.

(3) When the schools function independently, the church must watch over the proper education in the purity of the truth, according to the Word of God.

The first and last of these rules apply to education in all the grades, including higher education. According to its nature and essence, the church ought not to educate scientifically, although it is perfectly free to establish seminaries to provide candidates needed for the sacred ministry. But if any opportunity is lacking to receive education in the higher sciences, or if the existing education is useless for Christian youth, then the church certainly would be obligated to make up this deficit, not on the basis of its office, but by way of substitution. Additionally, however, where colleges exist, established by private persons or by the government, that are useful for its baptized children, the church should always be watchful and ensure that the education being provided does not detract from the truth of God.

She, the church of Christ, is the pillar and foundation of the truth, and wherever, within her own circle or beyond, the truth that is according to the Word of God is threatened or endangered, there it is *her* right and *her* calling to raise her voice loudly, and with heroic courage to stand up for the rights of her King and Lord!

CHAPTER 3 - THE DEFORMATION OF THE CHURCHES

WHAT IS MEANT BY DEFORMATION OF THE CHURCHES? §35

Deformation happens when churches with a good formation lose the quality of this good formation. It does not include any deficiency that results from the fact that the formation of the church is still in process. In the apostolic church in Jerusalem, in Antioch, in Rome, and so on, during the life of the apostles, the formation was still far from complete. Many members of the ecclesiastical organism were not yet fully grown, not yet developed. Likewise, the churches that came to a new manifestation in the time of the Reformation were often in a rather incomplete state. Before 1563 there was not even a common confession. But neither in the first century nor in the sixteenth century was this deformation, because deformation, distortion, or degeneration, always implies that the form or character used to be good at first, and then it suffered and deteriorated.

Likewise, one should not interpret deformation to be the failure to attain the ideal. When dealing with the deformation of churches, one could imagine an ideal situation in two different ways. First, one might imagine the situation of the heavenly church as the ideal for the church here on earth, but one should not do so, since it opposes God's plan for this dispensation and rebels against his sovereignty. Or one might think of a specific situation on earth that could exist and did exist at a particular time, in a particular place, under very favorable circumstances, for a short time, and take this situation as the model for the formation of all churches and all places and all times. Measured by this standard and compared to that ideal, virtually all churches fall short and will be judged to be imperfect. A positive aspect of this critical attitude is the vivid awareness that the church may never be content with itself or rest in what it has accomplished, but must always hold high its glorious banner, and never acquiesce to what is wrong and lacking.

But this method of assessment is wrong in two ways. First, our ideal must never be drawn from what has been manifest in a single church for a brief time period; rather, it must come from God's Word. And second, this approach does no justice to the differences between places, times, and circumstances. Turning the exception into a rule leads to a discouraging, unreasonable attitude, and promotes Donatism. Our only legitimate ideal, therefore, is what Holy Scripture requires of us concerning the church of God, either directly or by good consequence, and taking into account its explanation by the Holy Spirit throughout history. Furthermore, this high ideal, precisely because it is an ideal, is never fully attained on earth with any consistency. And finally, for this reason one can only speak of deformation if the church to which one belongs descends from a higher position to a lower position. Certainly, a church that never occupied a high position is still obliged to strive for perfection, and one can rightly view that striving for perfection as reformation, but such circumstances do not constitute deformation—that is, degeneration.

In order to proceed systematically and clearly, one must therefore make a threefold distinction between: first, church formations that only recently have begun to take a definite shape; second, church formations that have taken a definite form, but must still strive for a more complete shape; and third, church formations that, having fallen away from a former purer shape, must now pull themselves up from this lower state. Only the latter churches are in a deformed state.

§ 36   INCOMPLETE CHURCH FORMATIONS

Churches that, without suffering deformation, nevertheless do not manifest the true shape of a church, not even one that can actually be attained, are in a state of imperfection, and for the sake of comprehensiveness we must discuss these imperfect churches here, at least insofar as it concerns the churches of our time.

Imperfect churches can be of four different kinds: mission churches, occasional churches, churches under the cross, and aggrieved churches. We must treat each of the four separately.

Mission churches are not churches like those in Doetinchem and the Vluchtheuvel [in Zetten], which call themselves by that name.[30] Contrary to every good principle of church polity, these towns, which already had a church, added a second kind of congregation. In Doetinchem there is, first of all, the Dutch Reformed Church[31] with its own consistory and officers,

---

30. Doetinchem is a medium-sized town in the eastern part of the Netherlands. Zetten is a small town in the center of the country, between the Rijn and Waal rivers. In 1848, O. G. Heldring was the first to organize a shelter for pregnant young women, as well as other troubled youth. Apparently, the mission church of which Kuyper speaks was organized specifically for the youth in this institution. The church's name, *Vluchtheuvel*, means "hill of refuge." The institution still exists in Zetten and is associated with the Otto Heldringstichting.

31. The Dutch Reformed Church was the established church denomination of which Kuyper was still a member at the time of this writing.

ministers as well as elders and deacons. But now there is in the same town of Doetinchem another church, also with its own officers and organization, which calls itself a mission church. Likewise, regarding the church in the Vluchtheuvel it was decided that it would exist independently of the present church in the same municipality of Zetten, with the understanding that those living on the property of the Heldring institutions have the right to leave the church of Zetten and to join the Vluchtheuvel congregation.

Now suppose there was enough money to buy up half the town of Zetten [that is, to incorporate it into the Vluchtheuvel institution]; then successively half of the congregation would be bought out from under the Zetten consistory. However good the intentions may have been for organizing these institutions, on the basis of the principles of our Reformed church polity they still must be condemned most stringently. This is not permissible. No, mission churches can come into existence only in places where the church does not yet exist—either in those countries inhabited by Jews, pagans, or Muslims, or in regions of our own country where faith in Jesus Christ has been destroyed, but only in those places.

Such mission churches can arise in two ways: either because an existing church elsewhere sends representatives to establish a church, or because private believers are the means in God's hand to turn unbelievers into confessors and because these confessors then unite themselves into a church.

A mission church of the first kind starts out being very deficient, and at first consists only of the family of the minister of the Word who has been sent there. It is a daughter church of the sending church, under the supervision of her consistory, under her confession, and connected to the original plant as a sprout that has not yet been removed to live on its own. If the Lord God grants conversion to some people in that location, then they are baptized not by virtue of the office of the minister but by virtue of the authority granted to that minister by the sending church. If the group of believers expands, the Lord's Supper will be administered on the same basis. Only after some time will it be possible to supplement the minister with a few elders and deacons. Thus the church organization gradually attains some completeness, and the day will arrive when she can begin her independent existence, like a sprout removed from the mother church. In this way, these mission churches are examples of churches that are as yet imperfect, temporarily without the proper arrangement for the sacraments and without church discipline. Yet one cannot deny them the character of a church.

It is somewhat different with churches originating through private initiative. To take the strongest example, one might imagine that a number of shipwrecked people on an unknown island manage to convert the population, yet for lack of communication are unable to get in touch with any existing church. In such a case, these believers must not live without an ecclesiastical bond, but are required to establish a church, elect overseers and deacons, and have them appoint a minister of the Word, who then must establish worship services, the administration of the sacraments, and the exercise of church discipline. This is the purest, extremely rare case, which shows the beginning of a church in the clearest light. In most situations, however, such a group of people is able to have contact with existing churches, and in that case it is best to ask these existing churches for help, so that a delegation of a minister of the Word with an elder can come to supervise the election of overseers, to recommend a minister of the Word from elsewhere, and to seal through holy baptism the confession of the new converts.

Occasional churches are imperfect churches that exist temporarily, that never attain a definite or complete form, and that disappear along with the reason for their existence. For instance, in times of war an occasional church is established among the troops on the battlefield. An occasional church is established on a fleet that is at sea for a long period of time. An occasional church is established in beach towns where some Christians reside for a time. In the past, such occasional churches were also established in the embassies, when Christian ambassadors with their Christian staff and family resided in Islamic or pagan palaces, or even Reformed ambassadors in Roman Catholic or Lutheran palaces. With only a few exceptions, these occasional churches never obtained a definite form. Often there was no ecclesiastical structure at all, not even the administration of the sacrament. The minister of the Word, if such an officer was present at all, was on his own without any consistory and therefore without any church government. This was not so problematic with respect to merchant ships, since they were considered to belong under the consistory nearest their home port. But for the army on the battlefield and the mariners at sea there was no such connection. Often the minister of the Word was not chosen ecclesiastically but by the military board.

Thus these are examples of barely recognizable churches, which lack almost all the characteristics of a church, and yet even in their temporary and very imperfect form they are not entirely devoid of the essence of a church. The justification for maintaining this very imperfect form was the impossibility to do otherwise. However, these imperfect church formations were immediately terminated as soon as possible, putting an end to the attempt to establish separate churches in colleges, in royal palaces and castles, in shelters for the elderly and the indigent, and so on. The churches permitted the preaching and the administration of the sacraments in these shelters, as a separate district of the congregation, provided—and this rule was strictly enforced—that such districts were placed under the consistory of that town, and remained subject to the discipline, so that the administration of the key of preaching and administration of the holy sacrament took place under the authority of the consistory, rather than under the authority of the vicar or minister. The current practice at Het Loo, where the king appoints preachers of the court who function apart from the consistory of Apeldoorn as preachers and administrators of the sacrament, is in conflict with the demands of Reformed church polity.[32] Such ministers should either be commissioned by the consistory of The Hague, or be sanctioned by the consistory of Apeldoorn.

Churches under the cross, the third kind of occasional churches, are either still-imperfect or truncated churches. They are in a deteriorated state not because of internal corruption, but rather because of an intense display of strong faith. A church under the cross is always a persecuted church. If the government of a country or town has an unfavorable attitude to it and abuses its governmental power by hindering the church's ministry, then such a church comes under the cross of persecution. Such a cross can be very light, very heavy, or of medium weight, and the church's imperfection is correspondingly minute or significant. Now when such a cross of persecution is laid upon God's churches before they are able to organize fully, such a situation does not amputate an existing organization but does hinder its development. This was the case in the days of the Reformation, when the newly sprouted churches immediately experienced the heat of persecution. And it was the case, albeit much less, with

---

32. Het Loo, a palace in the city of Apeldoorn, is one of the residences of the Dutch royal family. Their main residence is in The Hague. At the time of Kuyper's writing, the head of the Dutch kingdom was King William III.

the new church formation in 1834, which in its new beginning was hindered more or less in its free development.[33] If the cross of persecution is very heavy, as it was under the persecution of the Roman emperors and the Roman Catholic popes, then such a church under the cross can become thoroughly defective, lose all organizational structure, be robbed of ministers and overseers, come to be separated from the ministry of Word and sacraments, and finally exist only as a group of believers—but all of this without losing the essence of the church. Under a less heavy cross, that church usually loses only its place of assembly and the regular use of its ministers, so that it must exist in secret, assemble in various places, and make do with lay preachers. Moreover, often it is cut off from correspondence with neighboring churches. Under a very light cross, on the other hand, the church experiences the pressure of a monetary penalty, the loss of certain privileges, and the inability to maintain its public-legal character. Due to the wide range of severity, therefore, these churches under the cross exhibit the full spectrum, from nearly complete to nearly unrecognizable, but such a church always distinguishes itself from all other imperfect churches, not only because it *wants* to be complete, but also because it *would* be complete if only the cross of persecution were lifted.

Aggrieved churches, the last type of occasional churches in our list, are also imperfect churches that would and could be complete, but are prevented from being complete—not by the cross of persecution due to the state government, but exclusively by the pressure exerted on it by a false church government.[34] Here too there are various degrees and cases, but they have in common that the church itself is not seen as false or degenerated, for then one should leave it and proceed with the formation of a new church. But rather, although it is still a good church of Christ, such a church, by the unfaithfulness or even overt animosity of church leaders

---

33. Kuyper refers to the Secession (*Afscheiding*, called the Christian Reformed Church at the time of Kuyper), a group that had left the national church fifty years earlier under the leading of Hendrik de Cock (1801–42). Early on, at the hands of the government this group suffered persecutions including fines, imprisonment, and disruption of their meetings. Although Kuyper is still in the national church at the time of this writing, he is sympathetic to this group. Nine years after the publication of this text, Kuyper's own group of churches would merge with many of the Secessionists to form the Reformed Churches in the Netherlands.

34. Kuyper called his own secession several years later the *Doleantie*, "the Aggrieved." Thus this is the category under which he interpreted the present situation of the Dutch Reformed Church.

who have falsely intruded, is being hindered from manifesting itself as the church and from manifesting its life. Different powers can perpetuate such a group of intruders in church leadership. First, that power can lie within the church itself, if many hypocrites have intruded and overwhelm the believers, thus maintaining the unbelieving and opposing leadership through the majority of their votes. That power can also lie in the correspondence undertaken with other churches within the church federation, when in a church with only a few hypocrites this federation supports the unfaithful overseers and protects them from being removed. Or, finally, this power can come from outside the churches, when the civil government through direct or indirect influence keeps such unfaithful overseers in office. It is also possible that two or even three of these factors work together, in churches that suffer under a majority of hypocrites, are bound in a restrictive church federation, and are hindered in their rightful activities by the state, for instance, through the civil government's salary for the minister. But whatever form this plague in Christ's churches may take, this plague still is never the cross of persecution; it is always that of suffering under an imposed unfaithful church leadership, which the church might want to remove but is currently unable to remove.

Now in all such cases, as soon as the church performs its duty it becomes an aggrieved church—that is, a church pleading with God that its plague may be removed. With the awareness that it will recover, however fatally ill it may be at this moment, and not being deceived by paralyzing theories, it manifests the sincerity of its plea in the very fact that, albeit imperfectly, it immediately regulates itself according to God's Word. A church that complains without such self-regulation is certainly a lamenting church, but not an aggrieved church. For a church to have the right to be aggrieved before God and humanity, it must be a community of believers that separates itself from those who oppress the church; a community that appoints overseers who are faithful to God's Word; and one that, leaving the results in the hand of Almighty God, works toward a well-regulated arrangement of the ministry of the Word and sacraments. Meanwhile, these attempts may at first have only very imperfect results. Perhaps only very few overseers can be found who are willing to receive this office. Perhaps worship services can be held only very sporadically, and the administration of the sacraments can occur perhaps only once a year. But this does not affect the character of the aggrieved church. It remains a church. It possesses its essence, and strives for its well-being.

For the sake of completeness one could also include in the list of imperfect churches the very small churches, and as a rule those with vacancies, but because this phenomenon is not abnormal, it will not be discussed here.

§ 37   THE CAUSES THAT EXPLAIN THE DEFORMATION OF THE CHURCHES
Deformation of the church is always and in every circumstance a matter of culpability incurred from sin into which that church fell before her God. Here we must point out three separate causes: the sins of individuals, the sin of the community, and the instigator of all sin, that is, Satan.

That most remote cause, Satan, is the source of every attack and every evil assault against the church of Christ. In his church Immanuel celebrates his triumph, and Satan, who suffers more deeply from Christ's victory than from anything else, therefore aims his fierce and angry attack particularly at that church of Christ. That church of God is a thorn in his eye, and he incites the gates of hell from below to overwhelm that church of the Lord. Now one must not think too little of Satan's power. Anyone investigating history from the beginning of the world until now—or more specifically, the renewal of the church through the outpouring of the Holy Spirit, or even only its renewal since the days of the Reformation—is constantly amazed at the remarkable fact that throughout these sixty centuries, God's church has known no more than perhaps three centuries of reasonable flourishing and triumphant rest. Throughout the vast majority of these sixty centuries, God's church could barely be recognized; in other centuries, it was scattered, shattered, and hard to find; and in the few centuries that remain, you find her mostly struggling, her blood fiercely and feverishly rushing through her veins, having recently emerged from severe affliction, and behold, she is soon threatened again by new affliction. This oppression and tribulation inflicted by Satan on the church of Christ goes so deep that her most tender sons and daughters dubiously wonder whether they were perhaps the victims of a horrific mistake, and had misidentified as the church of God what had already become the synagogue of Satan! This explains the Donatists' attempt to escape that stream of heresy and unrighteousness, to flee to God's city of refuge, and to manifest a holier, purer church with only God's saints. This attempt has been repeated often, and has been judged equally often in terms of its outcome. Indeed, the invariably terrible judgments of God over this essentially arrogant plan were more severe than the evil they sought to avoid.

Now Satan implemented this bitter enmity against God's church in two ways: in part through external persecution, and in part through internal poisoning. Thus, the murderer from the beginning is also murderer of the church of the Lord. First he would drive the governments and secular powers to use brute violence to deny the church a foothold; to kill, to murder, and to exterminate the faithful witnesses who proclaimed the death of Christ as the powerful atoning sacrifice; and through ruthless persecution to frighten, to vex, and to scatter the little flock so much that it had to withdraw, to the point when, for a brief moment, there seemed no longer to be a church of God. But realizing afterward that this raging generally had the opposite effect, and that new seed sprouted for God's church from the blood of the martyrs, Satan would then relent. He would have the world make peace with the church, and prompt the civil authorities to shower her with treasures and favor and honor. And when the poor church, intoxicated with so much glamour and glory, had fallen asleep at her triumph, the wicked foe would come in the dead of night to inject deadly poison into her veins, and soon she would feel her spiritual strength fade, and would once again exchange her triumphant song for bitter, grievous lamentation over her deadly exhaustion and spiritual lethargy.

Yet, Satan could not bring this terrible evil over God's church except with the permission and toleration of Almighty God. If God had wanted his church on earth to celebrate the triumph of the cross in peace and quiet, that would have happened. But that was not his good pleasure. Gathering a church out of a godless people in the midst of a godless world, the Lord repeatedly gave it over into the hand of Satan, as he gave over Job. The Lord did this in order that through spiritual struggle the triumph of the truth might shine brightly, and that in the perseverance of the church in such fierce assaults the power of the Lord God might be revealed gloriously. Therefore, while he is not the author or performer of the evil that comes upon his church, this evil has to come upon that church according to his eternal and unchangeable decree: the evil of suffering, to manifest the power of the faith that he planted within the church, and likewise the evil of sin, to manifest the power of the corruption out of which he redeemed it.

We give the glory to the majesty of the Lord's counsel—without hesitation and with all determination—by regarding this raging of Satan toward and within the church of Christ as something he not merely permitted but also desired. This does not, however, diminish in any respect the deep, serious, and irresponsible guilt of God's children. We already heartily confessed that God's inscrutable plan to lead the history of our human race through sin and grace in no way removes the damnable guilt of Adam. How much less could one find in that counsel of God an escape from guilt for God's regenerate children—those who have tasted the powers of the world to come, who have confessed the love of Christ, who could lift up the shield of faith, and yet have not quenched the fiery darts of Satan, but in unholy lust absorbed them into their own bosom? And therefore we may never let suffice the remote cause of this deformation, but we also must descend to the more proximate causes, which lie in the sin of individuals and in the sin of the community.

We mention the sins of individuals first, because this touches the conscience more strongly. Those sins of individuals began already when Jesus was still on the earth, in those questions: "Lord, who will be the greatest?" "Lord, when will you restore the kingdom to Israel?" [see Luke 9:46; Acts 1:6]; in that utterance: "Lord, that shall never happen!" [see Matt 16:22]; in their flight when Jesus was arrested [Matt 26:56]; in Peter's denial of Jesus while he was interrogated [Matt 26:69–75]; in that statement: "If I do not see, I will certainly not believe" [see John 20:25]; in that hypocrisy of Peter in Antioch [Gal 2:11–13]; and so much more. And those were the holy apostles, who will sit with Jesus on twelve thrones, judging the twelve tribes of Israel. What then must happen to the church? Or rather, what did happen to it already when it had just come into existence and was still radiating with the newness of its early life? Is not the case of Ananias and Sapphira shameful [Acts 5:1–11]? Is not the word *shameful* even too mild for the abominations that occurred in Corinth? And what must we say about the abominations that existed in the church when Jude first had to write his general epistle, and Peter his second, and when the Lord himself came to Patmos to threaten his church? And did it not continue, in various forms, in various sins, even the most horrible and unspeakable iniquities, over and over again in God's church, creeping in among God's own people, provoking to anger the One who had called them and justified them for the very purpose that they would proclaim the virtues of him who had called them into his marvelous light? They were supposed to stand *against* the world, and behold, they carried the world into the church! They were supposed to serve not Mammon, but God, and behold, in so many hearts Mammon enjoyed an uncontested victory. They were supposed to bring the flesh under the control of the Spirit, and behold, they walked again in the flesh.

Yes, Satan's work should have been destroyed, but once again the soul entered into an accursed, unholy covenant with Satan. In this way, spiritual strength diminished. Faith faded. Love withered. Hope wilted. And prayer, which should be a power, lost its glow and soul and voice. Poor church of God! And most terribly, if those sins had come upon you outside the church, then they could have been isolated, but when they arise among the people of the Lord, they are invariably followed by yet another sin, that of Pharisaism. In the church one cannot sin openly, or declare: "I am wicked." Within the church, along with sin the practice of godliness is always still observed, and that is precisely what constitutes the double-heartedness and fosters the spiritual insincerity, that horrible evil that calls forth the words "Woe to you! Woe to you, you brood of vipers!" from the very same lips that keep on praying for God's elect [see Matt 23]. And Satan knows this; he is even focused on it: first inject the poison of sin, and then cover the sore of sin with pious bandages, all in an attempt fully to destroy a heart that the Lord God has chosen to be a temple for himself.

Finally, apart from those sins of individuals, there is the sin of the community. The members of a church do many things communally. Together they form a sphere of life, with its own style. They breathe an atmosphere in which they all live together. They form shared understandings. They create a moral judgment. They form a common opinion, which becomes a communal power. And this is how such communal responsibility arises, and as a result that communal guilt. That guilt in turn has a most corrupting effect upon individuals and thereby infects the whole body of Christ, until finally the most holy members surrender, and sin becomes universal in the church of God.

This can go so far that finally the word comes even to the church of the new covenant: "When you spread out your hands, I will hide my eyes from you; even though you make many prayers, I will not listen" [Isa 1:15]. But just as after the withering of its leaves there is still life in the oak tree, likewise the holy Seed will still support the life of the church of Christ. His mercies are infinite and his callings irrevocable. Only because of this mystery is the church of God still standing!

§ 38   How Deformation Usually Erupts in God's Church

All deformation of God's church tends to begin when faith loses its enthusiasm. The church depends on Christ. Branches that are partially broken off from the vine begin to wither. At first, as the result of terrible struggles and tribulations, Christ manifestly lives in his people. The movements of life are felt, the warmth of his divine love radiates throughout; there is enjoyment of his salvation and display of his power. The Holy Spirit works this by making God's children tender, by beautifying them with spiritual adornments, and by causing the Lord's redeemed to live closely and intimately with their God. But then, for virtually unknown reasons, imperceptibly they grow cold. They forsake their first love. The church becomes less tender, less close, less intimate, and the seers already see that the intimate communion of the Holy Spirit, and therefore the intimate association with the Bridegroom, is about to leave the heart of the bride. Already at this point the deformation of the church has really occurred, but it is not yet manifest.

But this will not last long; "if you do well, will you not be accepted? And if you do not do well, sin is crouching at the door" [Gen 4:6–7]. Thus no sooner has the working of the Holy Spirit ceased than the door opens and sin creeps in, and the ungodly heart, released from the holy bonds, begins once again to rage in its own devilish lust. It begins in the little details, mere trifles that are still considered acceptable. And sin erupts more strongly. Ultimately you find in God's church entire groups of people who begin to think of the mask of piety as a burden, and openly fornicate with the world.

At this stage, only a small part of the church has been affected by that poison. The vast majority zealously opposes it, but that zeal no longer has the energy and enthusiasm to banish this evil. They still condemn it, but no longer dare condemn it as publicly as they once did. There is no moral working of faith to rebuke this evil through church discipline. As a result, the sin and the service of the world become even bolder. The roles are almost reversed. Instead of being able to act with moral power against the servants of the world, the children of God themselves become oppressed by the world. They are almost ashamed to maintain their way of living. They begin to apologize instead of rebuking the world. No longer does church discipline proceed from them to the sinner, but through intimidation and mockery sinners begin to exercise discipline upon them. In this way, the level of public spiritual life descends and diminishes.

The outcome is that the Lord, in his just judgment punishing such serious unfaithfulness, gives his church over into the power of its suitors, so that it will again learn to acknowledge its guilt and find the way of prayer.

Sooner or later there comes a turning point in this development of sin. It is like a scale with balances. At first the scale of holiness rested firmly on the foundation of the Word, and high up in the air was the virtually empty scale of ecclesiastical iniquities. But this has changed. The scale of glories has become lighter, and the scale of iniquities has gained weight. Thus the one scale went up and the other went down. Ultimately, the original situation is completely turned around, and the power of iniquities robs the scale of holiness of all its stability. Then the church gets off-balance, and evil takes on more powerful proportions by creeping in among the shepherds. This is how one can always recognize the turning point in Christ's church. If the church as a church manages to maintain its holy character, even though sin has crept in, then the shepherds are still examples for the flock, praying with urgent priestly supplication for the salvation of that flock and sounding the trumpet to call the people to repentance. But when that trumpet sound stops, when the very group of shepherds is corrupted, and when they begin to serve the world instead of fighting alongside and for the sake of the flock, then the hour of spiritual degeneration has irrevocably come for the church, and that corruption begins to affect the organization as well, turning its public activity as a church into an unholy display.

In this way, the lie creeps from the diseased congregation into the shepherds. And now, in a third stage, it creeps from these corrupted shepherds into the doctrine and the worship of the churches, so that it abandons its confession and introduces self-directed worship into the Lord's house. Supported by this, heresy begins to wreak more havoc, in various ways. Faith is replaced by doubt, firm foundations are loosened, and everything presses and pushes in the direction of identifying the confession of the church with that of the world once again.

In this way, the lie moves on to affect the worship service. No longer content with its simple, spiritual character, it begins to employ sensual means to please the eye and the ear, and to grieve the Holy Spirit.

In this way, tension and opposition arise; the bonds of church government are felt to be too tight and unbearable. And so the infectious corruption finally dismantles the church's government, and it progresses until the regulations have been deformed to such an extent that everything rejected by Christ is now acceptable, and everything still adhering to Christ is caught in the net of regulations.

In this way, the terrible corruption completes its course. It begins with leaving the first love. It continues by serving the world. That worldliness spreads from the flock to the shepherds. Through them, it finds its way into the doctrine; from the doctrine into the worship; and finally it affects the entire system of ecclesiastical government, turning it into an instrument of Satan, in service against God's people, and through this people against the Lord.

§ 39   THREE DEVIATIONS FROM THIS RULE THAT SHOULD BE NOTED

The general rule is that the corruption of the church begins with love growing cold. Then, in the form of worldliness, this corruption infects its members first, and then its shepherds. And from there it moves successively to corrupt the confession, worship, and government of the church. But this general rule is not always valid. Three frequently occurring deviations must especially be noted here.

The first deviation is that, due to a misunderstanding of spirituality, in very many cases during those spiritually rich periods in the life of the church, too little attention is given to the importance of a pure church government. To mention only two examples, this happened in Germany after Luther's reforms, and in England after the breakthrough of Reformed religion under Edward VI. In this situation, the spiritual is considered all-important, and the external form is regarded as less crucial, even if it should continue in a deformed condition. As a result, the purity of worship is not pursued, the shepherds do not remain connected to the flock, and the confession recedes into the background. For in all such cases, friction and opposition will ultimately arise between that impure church manifestation and the pure Word. In this struggle, most shepherds then take the side of the impure manifestation and side against the Lord's people who stand up for his Word. The resulting deformation of the church functions like a disease that does not come from the lower parts of the body, but from the brain; soon it numbs the consciousness of the church and increases its helplessness.

The second deviation that we have in mind consists in the impure formation of the church with respect to its members. Only very seldom have our churches arisen from a gradual gathering of confessors. The vast majority have first been under the Roman Catholic hierarchy and came forth from it through the Reformation. As a result, from the very beginning the purified churches of many cities inherited large crowds of people whose confession and walk left much to be desired in many respects. When these churches later obtained civic privileges, this situation worsened because many people joined the churches in order to receive offices and positions of honor. And this evil grew to even greater proportions when the idea of a national church began to intoxicate their minds and, with national interests as the norm for the church's activity, the floodgates were opened wide for whatever water sought entrance. In fact, the situation in these churches was never pure. Alongside the true, confessing component, the church harbored a non-confessing, indifferent, and worldly component, which from the very beginning opposed the health of its vital life.

Different still is the third or last deviation we have in mind, which has occurred where the corruption has arisen not within the church itself but entered from the outside. This occurred in various ways. Sometimes it came from a neighboring or related church, as in the case of the German Reformed churches, now recently from the union and earlier from the Lutheran churches.[35] In other situations this corruption came from the theological schools, as was the case with the University of Leiden in the days of Arminius, and in the Huguenot churches through the damaging influence of the school of Saumur. In still other situations this corruption came from general scholarship, as in the days of the English deists. Or yet again, the corruption originated from a government that stood outside the church and attempted to break the spirit of the church. Or, finally, this seed of corruption was sown generously through revolutionary and mystic enthusiasts, who undermined the consciences of the people and thereby endangered the character of the church.

These three deviations are sufficient to warn us, then, when it comes to the deformation of the church, not to assess all situations according to a rigid norm, as if the matter were decided by listing some characteristics of the church. And they urge us to judge every church on its own merits, taking into account its historical background and the various influences that have affected it.

---

35. Kuyper is probably referring to the 1817 union of Lutheran and Reformed churches under Frederick William III of Prussia.

We must emphasize this especially because usually the diseases of our churches cannot be diagnosed so easily, but exhibit what the medical doctors call a very complicated etiology—that is, the progress of a disease in which two, three, or more causes play a role and affect each other, and it is impossible to analyze the damages due to the individual causes.

Those who are led by the Spirit will, in their most gentle moments, refrain from any analysis. They will confess that the sole cause of their church's distress is the unfaithfulness of the Lord's children, converging and reflected in the iniquities of their own hearts. But if some are called to evaluate the situation and therefore must analyze and judge, they must take care to avoid superficiality. They must avoid generalities and pass no judgment as long as the pluriform processes of the disease do not lie disentangled before their eyes.

§ 40   DEFORMATION IN THE MEMBERS

All deformation among the members of a church, which misshapes the church itself as such, begins with their confession and not, as is generally thought, with their walk of life. It is not as though their life were less important, but because their walk of life has ecclesiastical value only insofar as it is a confession. In the church of Christ, everything is measured according to Christ. Only one thing has value for the church as church: your faith. Only your faith is an instrument unto salvation, and only your faith connects you with the Lord. The virtues of unregenerate people may have value for public society, and they may bring honor to God to the extent that they constrain the intemperance of the wrongdoers or even prepare a foothold for the church, but they have no ecclesiastical value. A church without a single licentious member, consisting of members who head for head were adorned with civic virtues but were far from faith in the Lord Jesus, would not only fail to be a good church, but would be no church at all. Such a group of people might as well be Islamic or pagan. We must therefore firmly reject any attempt to evaluate members of the church by focusing on their life. Let us retain the order that has been kept throughout the ages: confession *and walk*, not walk *and confession*. Confession must be first, because it is the Christian's characteristic feature, and the person's walk can be judged only in that light.

Degeneration among church members with respect to their confession has several manifestations. The most common manifestation, sadly, is indifference, when many declare agreement with the confession but barely know it. They do not sense what conflicts with it, and they do not care to defend its honor. The shocking sin of so many men and women, who at their public profession of faith, at baptism, and at the Lord's Supper repeatedly profess to adhere to the doctrine of the church, is that they have never lifted a finger to find out what that doctrine of the church might be.

An apparently opposite phenomenon is externalization, that is, the sin of divorcing one's confession from one's heart. People are very busy with the confession and defend it with ardent zeal. They investigate it thoroughly, yet they view it as a dry summary that must be impressed on the memory, upheld through reasoning, and recited in a fixed formulation. This sin really removes the act of confessing from the confession. You thought you heard a lion roar, and what you find is merely the skeleton of this king of the jungle.

The third way in which the confession of the members manifests its disease is the disruption of the balance. In the confession of the church, as in every organism, there are individual members or parts or components, all of which have their own place and purpose in the well-organized whole. These parts are not identical but differ, each according to its nature. One is the eye, the other is the ear, a third part is the heart, a fourth is the head; in short, the whole confession fits together harmoniously like a body. Therefore the confession must be able to see with its eyes, walk with its feet, and lift up its head. But sin continually disrupts this erect position. It shifts the emphasis. It reduces the weight of what must be emphasized and puts the emphasis on something unable to bear that much weight. It compels the eye to hear, requires the ear to see, and forces the head to do what only the heart can accomplish. This results in those many forms of one-sidedness, those monstrous unnatural elements that weaken the confession of the congregation. They have this in common: they disturb the balance.

The fourth manifestation is superstition, when the members of the church seek to mix with the confession what does not belong to it. This sin arises when they have no eyes for the true mystery of the kingdom and think that the confession is lacking in mystery. They take pleasure in inserting into their confession various false mystical elements, through exaggeration.

The fifth or last manifestation, finally, is unbelief, arising when the confession has been dislodged enough to be opposed publicly, and the members of the church no longer hesitate loudly to proclaim their denial over against the confession of the church. The sin against the confession cannot go any further. At this point the confession crumbles and evaporates, and the profession of sinful, secular principles replaces the profession of the truthful, sacred principles.

These five manifestations of deformation of the confession are generally accompanied by corresponding deformations in conduct. Indifference, its first manifestation, causes every difference in conduct between the confessors of Jesus and the decent children of the world to disappear. They just live. Their walk is like the walk of others. Their walk improves or deteriorates morally along with that of others. But nothing of Christ is visible in their walk. They do nothing for Jesus, nor do they deny themselves anything for his name's sake.

Externalization, on the other hand, fosters Pharisaism. The sinful heart rages beneath the colorful appearance of a strict confession, but it remains concealed, and therefore carries within itself the fungus of corruption and the odor of death.

Disruption of the balance creates in one's walk—just as it does in one's confession—multiple forms of one-sidedness, paradoxes of the human heart, a fierce eruption of sin in one area alongside profound self-denial in another area. Perfectly honest, but extremely stingy. Sober and moderate, yet internally enslaved to the lie. Generously compassionate, yet a slave of sensuality. Two hearts within one bosom. A simultaneous worship of both Mammon and God.

Fourth, superstition falsifies life through exaggeration, in self-directed religion, so as not to spare the body, and through internal urges it finally turns into its opposite, so that what began in the spirit ends in the flesh.

Finally, unbelief, the last manifestation of deformation, erupts in decisive enmity against the Christian forms of life, and eagerly celebrates servitude to the world in all its glory under the shadow of the cross.

Now if for lack of discipline such evil continues unpunished and unobstructed, then it ultimately also deforms the church as a church, as soon as it has corrupted the majority of its members. "With respect to those who are members of the Church, they may be known by the marks of Christians; namely, by faith, and when, having received Jesus Christ the only Savior, they avoid sin, follow after righteousness, love the true God and their neighbor, neither turn aside to the right or left, and crucify the flesh with the works thereof." Great weaknesses remain in them, "but they fight against them through the Spirit all the days of their life, continually taking their refuge in the blood, death, passion, and obedience of our Lord Jesus Christ."[36] However, if these marks gradually disappear completely—so that there is not only weakness but also a failure to fight, and not only a failure to fight but also deliberate opposition to Christ, and the floods of unrighteousness rise higher and higher—then the church as a church is imperiled, however pure its preaching may be. Although there can be unholy things in the church of Christ, they must be in subjection to what is holy. But if this relationship is turned on its head, if the wheel turns around so that the unholy elements dominate and suppress what is holy, then you have a gathering of the ungodly instead of the godly, and the life of the church is in mortal danger.

DEFORMATION IN THE OFFICE-BEARERS   § 41

The corruption of the members of the church is usually followed by the corruption of the ministers. Both are connected. A godly church is generally adorned with godly teachers. Conversely, a church that has degenerated will see its shame displayed on the pulpit. Yet this rule does not always apply, for two reasons. First, it often pleases the Lord God, out of sheer compassion, nonetheless to give teachers of righteousness to an erring church, in order to lift up his church once again. But conversely, the Lord God sometimes leaves a good church and robs it of ministers, if the church were at risk of giving to the ministers the honor that only he deserves, or if it must be tested through the trial of abandonment.

And that is why the deformation of the church can certainly proceed from the ministers. That is, the church can be corrupted by a disease that originates not in the common life of the members, but specifically in the official life of the ministers. The ministers of the Word especially occupy a very influential position in the church of Christ. They are therefore exposed to a rather unique, official temptation. This temptation takes four different forms. The first form of the disease process is that the minister of the Word is not inspired with regard to sacred things. He prays ardently, but with a cold heart. He sprinkles water and breaks bread, but with an unaffected soul. Thus, depending on his nature, he ends up with false enthusiasm or withers through professionalism.

---

36. Belgic Confession, Art. 29.

When through this sin the lie has crept into his ministry, the disease proceeds to its second form, and becomes an abuse of authority. The minister must speak in the name of the Lord. He not only advises, but also handles a key of the kingdom. He may and can do this as long as he allows himself to be governed absolutely by the authority of his King and Lord. But if his ministry has become professionalized, he moves out from under the authority of the Lord, and begins to assert his own authority instead of the Word of the Lord. He no longer preaches the Word of the King, but his own opinion.

The third form is to take what does not belong to him, the so-called deification of the minister. His task was only to evoke love for Jesus, but behold, he himself becomes the center in his realm. This strokes him and excites him. This is what he likes to see. And he does not realize that Satan's darts have already pierced his heart. "My glory I give to no other," the Lord declared [Isa 42:8], but such a minister takes it anyway.

In this way the disease finally develops fully, and that spiritual ailment is born that is commonly called clericalism. It follows the sinful rule that instead of the shepherd existing for the flock, the flock exists for the shepherd. The shepherd no longer gives his life for the sheep, but he fends for his own rights. He does not stand up for the greatness of the Lord, but for his own honor and prestige. Instead of committing themselves by oath to the salvation of the church, the ministers plot together as those who hold a similar office. Then, with an *Ichabod* on her lips, God's church laments that her glory has departed [1 Sam 4:21].

And because this clericalism provokes the members to mutiny, thereby undermining of the authority of the Word from two sides simultaneously, this clericalism can very well become the cause of the church's complete disintegration, so that it enters a condition of deformation.

§ 42   THE DEFORMATION IN THE CONFESSION

The members and ministers confess, but what they confess is the confession of the church. Therefore the church also becomes deformed, in the third place, if, while its members have a godly walk and its ministers are generally pious, it nonetheless allows the sinew of its public confession to be severed. This disease also progresses through multiple stages and has multiple manifestations. First of all, that sinew of the confession is severed if the church becomes confessional in the false sense, that is, if it draws its life principle from its creeds rather than from the Word of God.

Only God's Word has authority over the conscience. If therefore a church binds the conscience directly to the creeds, as if they possessed such dignity inherently; if it attempts at its synodical assemblies to prove its case on the basis of these creeds instead of the Word of God; if it does not allow gravamina[37] to be brought to it on the basis of God's Word; and if it loses sight of its constant duty to submit to the judicial authority of the Word, both over its organization and over its creeds; then the result is unwholesome confessionalism, against which the Holy Spirit dwelling within the congregation protests.

The disease has a very different manifestation when the confession is honored as a slogan, but not acknowledged in terms of its rights. This is the sin of ecclesiastical dualism, a disintegration of that connection which, if all is well, must function between the body and the soul of the church. In this case, the creeds are viewed as useful identity markers for the sake of those outside the church, but they are excluded from any judicial deliberations. This too is a corruption. It gives the appearance to the outsider that the church *does* profess something that in its inner chamber it appears *not* to profess, or at least, not in such a way that it has authority at the highest level, which stands under the sovereign rule of justice.

This brings us automatically to the confessional disease in its most acute manifestation, known as lack of enforcement or freedom of doctrine. This evil operates in two ways: in the internal organization of the church, and in its relationship to other churches. Internally this evil manifests itself in the church as soon as members from elsewhere are admitted without sufficient proof that they agree with the church's confession, or if within its circle the church grants full rights to persons who either are indifferent to or militate against the confession. This evil takes on even worse proportions if deacons, elders, and finally even ministers of the Word are tolerated who deviate from the confession, whether a lot or a little. By contrast, this disease manifests itself in the church's relationship with other churches when the church remains in correspondence or federation with other churches that do not have our confession or fail to maintain it.

This confessional disease generally causes two other evils. First, in the absence of justice, everyone in the church makes himself a judge, and

---

37. Gravamina (sing. gravamen) are complaints or grievances brought to some judicial body, often a synod.

there will be no end to the judging and condemning. Second, when the real creeds are put out of commission, a new, conventional norm becomes the standard for orthodoxy. People then think that one should no longer maintain the *Reformed* life principle, but rather remain *orthodox*; and the term *orthodox* becomes an honorary title for a certain arbitrarily defined creed, or rather, a creed that in its vagueness lacks any definition, a creed that no one can grasp. In this way, people begin by violating justice, and end up by replacing it with pure arbitrariness. Nothing is more arbitrary in a church, whatever church it may be, than calling orthodox something that does not agree with the creeds of that church. In the Church of Rome, only the Roman Catholic is orthodox; in the synagogue, only the Jew who rejects the Christ is orthodox. Likewise, in the Reformed church only that person is orthodox who cheers when seeing the Reformed battle standard raised.

§ 43   DEFORMATION IN THE ADMINISTRATION OF THE MEANS OF GRACE
The church lives from grace, and this grace comes to it through the God-appointed means, the preaching of the Word and the administration of the holy sacraments. Therefore the church weakens, like a body weakens through anemia, if these means of grace are kept away from it, or worse, poisoned, or if instead of these means of grace it is given the wrong food. This deformation begins because the listeners and the preacher want to hear the person of the minister instead of Almighty God. The Word is a means of grace if the minister and the congregation bow down under it and truly gather together to be taught from that Word. Any topical preaching is therefore strongly to be rejected as a desecration of the Word. Also to be rejected is the preaching of a text in which the Word of God is heard in any way other than through exposition. The deformation of this means of grace, therefore, begins under as yet orthodox preachers, especially among those who put experience in the place of the Word. But once it has begun among them, it propagates through half-believing and unbelieving ministers, and ultimately it destroys any preaching of Scripture, turning the church building into a lecture hall where one can hear interesting, or boring, talks.

It works in the same way with the holy sacraments. Once the minister has the fearful notion that the sacrament is dead, and that it comes to life only through his emotive speeches, by being solemn and impressive, then in principle the sacrament is gone. The essence of the sacrament is that

Christ should work through his Holy Spirit. Therefore, emotionality plays no role at all; rather, it is wise to restrain emotion. If a worship leader still relies on that emotionality, he clearly demonstrates that he does not believe in the power of Christ. This is most obvious in the treatment of ecclesiastical liturgical forms. One who occupies his office properly will gladly speak correctly and purely through the word of the church, and will therefore read those liturgical forms with a calm voice, clearly and completely, without modification or omission; and any word that he adds himself will be brief. But conversely, one who no longer believes in the sacred power of the sacrament will either discard the entire form, or distort it and rush through it, in order to proceed solemnly only with what he thinks is real and thus can continue with his own treatise and his self-invented, often empty, talk.

THE DEFORMATION OF CHURCH DISCIPLINE   § 44

To remove the discipline from the church of Christ is not only a failure to maintain the confession or to keep the sacrament pure, but in its core it is to surrender authority. Just as outside the church one might advise or admonish someone, so it is believed that the church also has no greater power than to recommend the confession to its members and to admonish them to godliness. To remove discipline is therefore to lose the keys of the kingdom, to destroy the power that Christ has given to his church, and to cut off the authority of King Jesus. It is to hear Jesus as the prophet, to thank him as the high priest, but to deny him authority as the king. For this reason, this disease has a lethal effect on the church. This disease usually originates in the elders. Having been called alongside the ministers with the specific office of church government, they begin by reducing their office to a mere appendix to the office of the minister, instead of professing that they have been appointed to this office by King Jesus in the same royal manner as the minister. Soon, they no longer recognize that their eldership is an office, and leave that nobler title to the minister. As a result, their spiritual and moral awareness of duty and calling diminishes, and they no longer consider the glorious authority given to them by their King. Finally, having become impotent and unmotivated, and no longer disciplining themselves, they lack the courage to exercise discipline over others.

The deformation of the church that results from this degeneration of the eldership is therefore at least as objectionable as the deformation originating from the degeneration of the office of the minister. With the elders, it is the disease of anarchy. It begins with abandoning justice and authority and order in the consistory, and results in abandoning all justice, also in the synodical assemblies. In essence, it is a revolution, in which the shepherds allow themselves to be judged by the flock, and the flock no longer learns to bow under the judgment of the shepherds. For this disease is also the source of the intemperance of the congregation, the spiritual adultery of the minister, the distortion of the means of grace, and the like. Yet all of this is merely the consequence, not the proper characteristic of this disease. Its proper characteristic is the surrender of authority.

§ 45   DEFORMATION IN THE WORK OF LOVE AND MERCY

In the church of Christ, love springs up for the afflicted among the brothers and sisters, and compassion for the afflicted who are outside, just as automatically and irresistibly as water springs up from the cracks that a fountain has found in a rock. There is therefore something disturbing in any church that no longer has this natural expression of its life, when love of money, the root of all evil [1 Tim 6:10], causes this source of love and mercy to dry up within it, and when the afflicted who cries out to God is sent away empty by the church of Christ. This is a huge offense before the Lord—before him who someday, in the great day of judgment, will measure the love of his bride for him according to the warmth or coolness with which she fed his hungry ones and clothed his naked ones. In wrath he must therefore turn against a church that excludes *him* from the sanctuary in order to erect once again the statue of Mammon, and there can be no "light of his friendly face" in his church if cold, calculating selfishness and greed replace mercy. It is therefore very wrong that until now, this gruesome evil has not been mentioned in connection with the deformation of the church. Admittedly, this deformation does not relate to the essence of the church but to the expression of its life, just as the withering or wilting of blossom and fruit does not prove that a tree has died in its root; yet the blossom and fruit are seldom lacking if the life in the root is not diseased. Therefore it is important henceforth to pay more attention to this, in three respects.

First, as far the diaconal office of the believer is concerned, one must see to it that in the members of Christ's church there is sufficient motivation to sacrifice one's gold and silver. A believer must always be a generous giver. The believer's gift must not be a coerced one but a freewill offering. More profoundly yet, one must evaluate the intention of the heart, whether there is not merely a handing out of alms but deep compassion, whereby the believer identifies with the poorest and neediest as brothers and sisters in the Lord. There must be no Pharisaic display of almsgiving, but a giving of gifts in secret, so that the Father, who sees in secret, may reward it publicly [Matt 6:4].

In the second place, one must investigate whether the church maintains its high calling, not only in its members through the office of believer, but also in its central office of love—that is, through the ministry of the deacons. And especially, one must investigate whether the deacons sense their calling to develop the art of giving within the church of God; whether they realize, according to the lofty significance of their office, that they must leave the footprints of Christ on the path they walk in feeding the hungry and healing the sick; and finally, whether they, rather than coldly distributing the incoming funds, have a heartfelt desire not to rest until everyone whom God has impoverished has also been helped through the love of God, which the Holy Spirit pours out in the church.

In the third and final place, there must be strict supervision to ensure that in this work of love and mercy, the church does not follow mere intuition but seeks firm ground in the Word of God, and that it does not restrict its duty to the giving of alms to the beggar but also seeks out the distressed, whose need cries out to God in secret. And above all, this supervision must ensure that the church, when needs increase, will be able to expand the measure of its love by caring for those who are sick and needy, abandoned and disfigured; and thus will be able to show mercy, as a church, in the name of the Lord Jesus, to those who are deaf or blind, affected by mental disorder or disease, crippled or leprous, or visited by whatever other suffering.

If one observes, sadly, that this powerful work of love and of compassion diminishes; that the church instead leaves this duty of honor to others; and that miserable and needy people turn their faces away from the church of Christ, knowing that it will not listen to their complaint anyway; then one may and must certainly conclude from this withering of the fruit of love that this church is corrupted in its root. "As you did not do it to one of the least of these, you did not do it to me," is its imminent condemnation [Matt 25:45].

§ 46   DEFORMATION IN WORSHIP

"The hour is coming, and is now here, when the true worshipers will worship the Father in spirit and truth," declared the Lord our King [John 4:23]. Therefore, if all is well, then in our worship service the sacred form will become visible only to the degree needed to make worship in spirit visible for the communion of the saints. This is why our fathers set strict rules: that the style and furnishing of our church buildings should be sober; that the playing of the organ should preferably be avoided, but if it is allowed, it should never be more than accompaniment; that all pretentious singing should be given up, so that the congregational singing may be the quiet expression of the soul before God; that the congregation sits calmly, interrupted only by the men standing up during prayer, so that all movement in bowing down and turning is avoided; and likewise, that in the prayers, sacraments, funerals, and so on, the church should strive for solemn and meaningful symbolism, which expresses a sacred divine peace.

Now in these external matters, it is as illegitimate to exalt solemnity too highly as it is to indulge sensuality; there are also differences of climate and nationality. What is solemn for an Italian would in our situation be considered overstated and extravagant. There are no firm rules in this matter, and therefore deformation is not easily detected. But this is no reason to imagine that no deformation could infect worship. The sad example of the ritualists in the English sister church proves that the opposite is true.[38] A large part of that church is perishing precisely because of the unconstrained and wild outgrowths of its worship. And even though this evil may not rise to such a height as in Great Britain, a church in our country already tends to deformation in worship if the absence of spiritual tone in the singing tempts the church instead to produce from the organ pipes, through artful playing, what no longer springs up from the souls of believers. It also already tends to deformation if the church tries to make up for the lack of spirituality in prayer through physical movements; and also, if through continual standing up and sitting down, through various forms of responsive singing, or singing in parts or in choirs, or by means of solemn vestments and the wearing of crowns and the like, the church tries to show externally what it lacks internally. It should be noted

---

38. By "ritualists," Kuyper is likely referring to proponents of the Oxford Movement who reintroduced Roman Catholic rituals into the Church of England in the second half of the nineteenth century.

that in our country as well, worship remained pure and solemn as long as the cry "My Lord and my God!" came from the heart [John 20:28]; but it became embellished and adorned with various strange elements when the Groningers removed from it the divinity of the Lord, and delivered speeches to the congregation with the flatness and monotony of the practical Arian.[39]

DEFORMATION IN CHURCH GOVERNMENT   § 47

Deformation in church government can arise because individual church leaders are unspiritual, bureaucratic, formal people, lacking any spiritual gift for the government of Jesus' church. They will not administer justice, even when heresy or licentiousness violates it, and eventually they will tend to abuse their power as judges, calling just what is unjust and condemning the innocent. Yet this is not the deformation of church government as such. This deformation is present only when the governing structure itself deviates from what it should be according to God's Word. There can be a church with an excellent governing structure, which nonetheless functions poorly due to bad personnel. But conversely, there can also be a very bad governing structure, which, in spite of having excellent personnel, can never function well. It is like an engine room on a steamboat. You may have the most beautiful ship with the most excellent engine possible, yet your ship will run aground if your engineer does not know how to operate it, pays no attention, or is inebriated. But if you have a miserable ship with useless engines, even though you man it with the most excellent engineers, they will not be able to move you forward. It is the same way with a church government. You cannot save your church through good church government if the Spirit of God has left it; but if your church government is bad, you cannot keep your church from corruption, even though you fill every position with strictly orthodox people.

One must therefore watch very carefully for this deformation, because it violates justice and paralyzes the best workers; it dislodges the foundations and beams of the house; it puts the future of the church at risk. And no wonder, certainly, since every deformation relating to church government is directly related to the question whether in the church of Christ all power continues to belong to King Jesus and his Word. And

---

39. Kuyper is criticizing what was known as the Groningen theology, represented chiefly by Petrus Hofstede de Groot (1802–86). In Kuyper's view, the Groningen theology gave a humanistic account of the person of Christ and Christian doctrine.

no less important is the question whether in the church of Christ, in which all are brothers and sisters, there shall be a new domination of one brother or sister over another. Revolution through rebellion against the King, and clericalism by lording it over the brothers and sisters, are the two manifestations of the disease that corrupts the life of the church through this deformation of church government. "You have one master, and you are all brothers!" is the word of life that alone brings healing here [see Matt 23:8 KJV]. It is the age-old battle between the sacred ordinances of God and the false ordinances of human beings.

§ 48   DEFORMATION DUE TO PARASITES ON THE ECCLESIASTICAL TRUNK, OR THE SECTS

Sects almost always arise through the fault of the church, in a three-fold manner. It may be because the church allows part of the truth to be obscured, and now it seeks a way out in the sect. Or because the church fails to meet the desire for communion of the saints, and now it pursues satisfaction on its own grounds. Or finally, because the church lets the reins of discipline slip, thereby allowing heresy to gain power and grow roots for its own formation, often feeding on the sap of the church's own ecclesiastical life.

This, too, is a dangerous deformation of the church of Christ, which usually manifests itself in milder form in sectarian pathways without yet revealing itself as a sect. In fact, every group in the church of Christ already practices sectarianism if it forms a separate group with a different focus than the unique focus of the church. The focus of the church is the entire truth, living in him who said, "I am the truth" [see John 14:6]. A group created around that focus in the church, temporarily over against the church, remains ecclesiastical and may never be called sectarian. But a group of more closely connected people who extract a single element from the full truth and make that their focus, or find their spiritual unity in any human person, either living or dead, or seek their true communion of the saints outside the means of grace—such a group is sectarian in its nature and in its essence, and will naturally develop into an actual sect.

We hardly need to speak here of schismatic formations, since usually these formations arise only out of murmuring discontentment with ecclesiastical justice, or out of undue attachment to external matters. These formations generally turn out to have no root; they wither soon and die out. In the estimation of the church, a schismatic person has always been considered to be a malcontent who acted on the basis of the flesh and gave in to unholy wrath, while sectarian people and the sects that result from their activity are almost always misguided people, erring in good faith. They are serious and heavenly minded, but due in part to a fault of the church, due in part to their own carelessness and stubbornness, they have not been persuaded. For instance, at the moment, perfectionism and the Ethical movement are sectarian movements within the church, but Darbyism, Irvingianism,[40] and so on, are sects that have already tried to organize on their own, and now live like parasites on the ecclesiastical trunk.

HOW DEFORMATION EVENTUALLY TURNS THE CHURCH INTO A PSEUDO-CHURCH

§ 49

If we summarize all of these deformations—among the laity and the ministers, in the confession and in the means of grace, in church discipline and in the works of love, in worship and in church government, through sectarian groups and through sects—then anyone will sense how these various diseases can ultimately corrupt the life of the church to such an extent that deformation comes to an end because all life has left the church. At that point, there is nothing left in the church that can be deformed, since all its life is lost. This is how the pseudo-church comes into existence, that is, the absolutely deformed church, which is leprous from the crown of the head down to the soles of the feet. Her skin is entirely white; no color of life is left in her, no trace of healthy flesh that could still be affected by the poison of the disease. In such a pseudo-church there is peace, quiet, and silence—like that of the grave. It is like a burned-out hearth, displaying only white ashes and grey cinders. A dead body, but not yet decaying! Such a pseudo-church would be unimaginable if a church stood on its own, if it were not temporarily impeded by its federation with other churches, by relations with the state, or by civil and legal relations of property, possession, rights, or titles! Without these it would, after the removal of its lampstand, simply collapse, enter a state of decomposition, and fade away. But when the collapse and decay are prevented through such relations of church, state, and law, such a formation that is no longer a church in any

---

40. Kuyper presents the Plymouth Brethren ("Darbyism," after John Nelson Darby [1800–82]) and the followers of the preacher Edward Irving (1792–1834) ("Irvingianism") as representatives of the schismatic impulse. The Ethical movement was a form of mediating theology that appeared in the Netherlands.

respect can still retain the appearance of being church. You find a skeleton, but still dressed in solemn, albeit torn and soiled, ecclesiastical garb. Such pseudo-churches you find, for instance, in our Indonesian colonies, maintained by state authority and funds. You find them in North Brabant,[41] where it was planted artificially and was never able to grow roots, yet is still hanging from a stake through the bond of governmental salaries for ministers. Finally, you find them also in North Holland, Groningen, and Drenthe, and perhaps elsewhere, in towns where no persons are left who profess their faith and no ecclesiastical ministry that brings the means of grace; where the sun rises every morning and sets every evening, but not a single knee bends before the Lord Jesus and not a single tongue confesses him.

§ 50   HOW THE FALSE CHURCH ARISES

Finally, one must carefully distinguish from this pseudo-church the most horrible of all deformations, which results in the false church, or the church of the Antichrist. The doctrine of the Antichrist is still underdeveloped in the church, and most people think that Antichrist is synonymous with Satan. But this is certainly not true. Satan stands opposite of God, and in his desperate powerlessness he imitates all of God's activity, trying to demolish God's kingdom with his own instruments. On the other hand, the Antichrist is a person in whom Satan imitates what the Lord God did when he sent us the Mediator. There are many of these antichrists today, and many have arisen in every century, insofar as the apostles gave that name even to Satan's failing and weak attempts to create an antichrist. However, the real Antichrist is he in whom Satan will one day succeed in accomplishing his deceptive and criminal display for a period of time. Just as Christ has his church and King Jesus has his subjects, Satan also, always imitating God's work, tries to fashion a church for his Antichrist and subjects for his false king. Hence the perpetual attempts of Satan to manifest an anti-church, an anti-Christian and false church.

Now Satan cannot do this through a new formation of a church; he has no power to do that. For that reason, Satan always watches for the opportunity to slip into an existing church and through trickery to turn that church into its opposite—just as in a battle on the high seas, the enemy might try to board one of his opponent's mighty ships, imprison

---

41. North Brabant (or Brabant) is a southern province of the Netherlands that was predominantly Catholic.

its mariners and install his own personnel. Then, with the battering ram or cannons of his opponent's own ship, under a false and deceptive flag, he can sink his opponent's other ships. This too is Satan's plan. For that purpose, he does not break down the church, but rather makes it powerful. He does not take away its sacred things but abuses them. And although he brings ravenous wolves into the church, still these ravenous wolves have the outward appearance of lambs; they walk about in lamb's wool, appearing harmless. At that point, devils minister to this false church, but their diabolic nature is not evident because they manifest themselves as angels of light. To use the example of a sick person, it is not the sufferer who faints from exhaustion, but rather the possessed maniac. While you were looking to find a sufferer who needed care, the maniac assaults you, grabs your throat, and kills you, if God permits it.

Therefore one must distinguish carefully between genuine churches of Christ that are in a state of deformation, pseudo-churches that have ceased to be churches of Christ because their deformation is complete, and false churches, where deformation served simply to inaugurate a satanic counter-formation.

Of this false church our fathers professed: "It ascribes more power and authority to itself and its ordinances than to the Word of God, and will not submit itself to the yoke of Christ. Neither does it administer the sacraments as appointed by Christ in His Word, but adds to and takes from them, as it thinks proper; it relies more upon men than upon Christ; and persecutes those who live holily according to the Word of God and rebuke it for its errors, covetousness, and idolatry."[42]

Meanwhile, this false church exists in various degrees. Just as a man can be possessed by one, but also by a million demons, a church can be misled by greater or lesser deception of Satan. Likewise, just as there were possessed people whom Jesus delivered from their demons in answer to prayer, so too there may be churches that partially and temporarily become instruments of Satan, but the Lord delivers them from Satan's influence, in response to humble prayer. In this respect one must be careful not to judge too quickly. Without a doubt, the church of Christ in Luther's day lay completely bound in the bonds of Satan, and when Rome drank the blood of God's saints there was most certainly an anti-Christian power that possessed its church. It would be cowardly and unspiritual not to admit

---

42. Belgic Confession, Art. 29.

this. However, whether the Roman Catholic churches in themselves are wholly and permanently abandoned by the Holy Spirit, and whether the pope is the Antichrist—these questions were answered affirmatively in 1603 by the French churches at their synod, but the Reformed churches in the Netherlands and elsewhere, although they were aware of this, did not copy this answer into their confession at Dort.[43] Apparently our fathers did not dare to give their full support to this absolute statement, even though they were inclined to do so. On the contrary, they continued to acknowledge the baptism administered in the Roman Catholic churches as a valid sacrament. And since the sacrament is nothing apart from the operation of grace, they were therefore confessing that even in these fully degenerate churches the Lord's grace was still at work.

If we comply with this judgment of our fathers, then it follows that history has shown us partially falsified churches, which are false to a certain degree. But the absolutely false church, that is, the perfected manifestation of the church in which Satan will try to celebrate his final triumph over the Christ, is yet to appear.

May Almighty God preserve us, so that our churches may not serve as an instrument of Satan, and so that Satan may not animate our churches with his demonic influence; and so that you yourselves, O confessors of the Lord, may not be possessed by the evil one. Rather, may our heavenly Teacher and beloved Comforter, God the Holy Spirit, dwell, work, and pray within you, as in his lawful temple!

---

43. The French Reformed synod of Gap in 1603 addressed the status of the early reformers' ordination in the Roman Catholic Church and added an article to the French Confession of Faith (1559) identifying the pope with the Antichrist. See John Quick, ed., *Synodicon in Gallia Reformata*, 2 vols. (London: T. Parkhurst and J. Robinson, 1692), 1:227.

CHAPTER 4 - THE REFORMATION OF THE CHURCHES

WHAT SHOULD BE UNDERSTOOD BY THE REFORMATION OF THE CHURCHES §51

The term *reformation* can be taken in a broader and in a narrower sense; for the sake of clarity these very different meanings, though we have pointed them out earlier, must be differentiated further, correctly and sharply. The most general and most encompassing concept of reformation is the bringing of truth and holiness instead of error and sin. Reformation in that broadest sense also includes ongoing illumination, which the church receives from the Holy Spirit, as well as the ongoing growth in sanctification—both of these with reference to the body of the church as well as to its individual members. Everything that brings the church closer to the Fountain of all good—or conversely, causes that Fountain of all good to flow out more smoothly and purely along the riverbed of the church—has reformed that church.

Yet we seldom use the concept of reformation in that broad sense. In regard to our body we usually distinguish, on the one hand, between its regular growth and development, and on the other hand, the healing of diseases that have intruded or wounds that have been inflicted. Similarly, with regard to the churches of Christ, it is customary to require, on the one hand, the regular growth in illumination and sanctification; and on the other hand, the recovery from the diseased state into which they fell, whether through their own guilt and unbelief or through Satan's wickedness. That regular growth through illumination and sanctification is then called the continual edification of the church of God through the working of the means of grace, and only that recovery from its wounds is called reformation.

But in this narrower sense as well, the concept of reformation still allows for three interpretations, depending on what kind of healing is being sought for the patient: in restoring diminished strength, in expelling the germs that have invaded the body, or in a surgical operation. The first method, which merely intends to stimulate the dulled spirits to new life, is currently usually called revival. The second method, which intends to expel the germs of the disease without surgery, is usually called church renewal. Only the third method, which puts the knife in the wound and proceeds with surgery, bears the name of reformation in the narrowest sense.

Which of these three degrees of reformation must be employed depends entirely on the nature of the symptoms that are present. If the organic fiber of the church is still undamaged, so that the church organization remains uncorrupted and the administration of the means of grace is pure, then the only thing necessary is a spiritual revival of both teachers and members. A new awakening of the Holy Spirit, through a resealing of the faithful covenant of the Lord. Revival! If the disease has progressed to the extent that not only the spiritual life of the church has deteriorated, but its inscription is also marred [see Zech 3:9], so that the truth stumbles in the public squares [see Isa 59:14], then the spiritual awakening must certainly be the starting point; but after that it should proceed to gradual improvement of the church's organization and the removal of heresy. Therefore, both revival and church renewal. Finally, it may have reached a point where not only the life of grace withers and the truth stumbles in the public squares, but the leaders of the church also make it permanently impossible to eradicate the error and to restore the honor of God's Word. Then the spiritual awakening, once it sees the way of gradual renewal obstructed, may not shy away from the most painful solution: in order to save its life it must proceed with a surgical operation, that is, with public reformation, just like the work that Luther began and Calvin completed.

But even when the Spirit of the Lord urges and compels people to take this extreme measure, spiritual awakening should still be the starting point at all times. If you work from the outside inward you only create the appearance of life; only what proceeds from the Spirit will last.

§ 52 ALL GOOD REFORMATION HAS GOD AS ITS AUTHOR

All human attempts in Jesus' church are vain and less than vanity. The church of Christ has been borne into the world through God's wondrous grace, despite humanity's sinful raging; century after century she was supported in spite of the opposition and unfaithfulness of human beings; and she did not flourish for a single moment, except from grace, by grace, and in grace. The church is also soiled with mud that she dragged in from the world, but for the church as church the saying is always true, unchangeably and absolutely: "In him she lives, she moves, and has her being" [see Acts 17:28].

No endeavor is therefore more vain than if anyone, though being the most excellent person, or any ecclesiastical assembly, though it be the most influential of all, would have the audacity to say or think, "Indeed, with our strategy we will quickly reform this or that deteriorated church!" Saying such a thing would be unreformed arrogance, and it can only lead to further deformation. It is thinking upside down, as if we could deliver a pure church to God, rather than having him grace us in his mercies with a church in a purified condition.

This attitude reverses the order of the gospel, discards the covenant of grace, and once again tries to earn a reward for good works. This desire reveals the error that still dwells in our heart, as if the children of God could produce a single speck of holiness on their own. And we fully conquer this error only if our soul sincerely confesses before God that every speck of holiness that shines within us first descended within us from the holiness of Christ—so much that even the best remaining effects of our natural life are to be considered sin rather than holiness.

In this respect, a godly Christian may know neither compromise nor negotiation. A child of the kingdom who desires to proclaim the virtues of the One who called him out of darkness into his marvelous light, cannot be halfhearted about this. From the human being nothing results but sin; all holiness comes from God. All that springs from oneself is deceitful; only the Lord is truthful. If therefore, as we stated in the previous section, reformation is the bringing of truth and holiness instead of error and sin, then one must ask: from where can that truth and holiness come, if not from him who alone has both?

God, the author of all sound reformation, is therefore the principle that the faithful children of the church have never denied. That is why they pray; that is why they wait; that is why they obey the Lord. This principle applies to reformation in its three stages.

First, from God comes every awakening of the congregation out of its deadly sleep. Not all revivals come from him; alas, too often human tinkering is given this glorious name. Rather, what we mean is that never and nowhere has life awakened in petrified bones, never and nowhere has there been growth in sanctification after a long period of stagnation, never and nowhere has the urge to win others for the Lord found an open door, except at those times and in those churches in which the Lord God was pleased—in spite of the sin and the unbelief and the unfaithfulness of his people—to have compassion on that wayward people. To have compassion, either by sending a prophet, saying, "Prophesy over these bones" [Ezek 37:4], or without any preacher of repentance, by instilling in people's souls a conviction of sin and unbelief, so that this awareness of guilt may lead to prayer.

Involved here is the age-old battle between the Reformed and the Arminians, applied to spiritual awakening. How shall the sleeper awake, unless he is awakened? How could improvement come from a people that deteriorate every day spiritually? Therefore, just as the unregenerate can come out of darkness into the light only through an act of God, likewise a church that fell into darkness can return to the light only through a gracious act of God. This gracing again of his people with the light, which they had forfeited a thousand times over, and which finally had been withdrawn from them, is his divine and inviolable privilege.

Therefore the people of God can never be admonished enough to wake up from their sleep, to rekindle their first love, to perfect their holy works before God, and to awaken in zeal for the salvation of other souls. But woe to the person who wants to draw this glorious revival from anywhere else than the Fountain of every good! Only that One increases faith, pours that warmer love into the heart through his Holy Spirit, grants victory over temptation, and gives us a concern for the salvation of others.

You will see this more sharply if you realize that a spiritual revival must awaken multiple souls at the same time. Suppose that you had control over your own heart (which you do not); even then you could never enter the souls of others in a saving way, and you would be just as thoroughly dependent on the sovereign grace of your God.

But also that second stage of reformation, which we called gradual renewal of the church, has God as its only Author. Apart from God, people might perhaps be able to compose better regulations for the government of the church, and thus reform the church on paper. But this dead thing, brought forth from death, will turn out to be absolutely unable to give back to the body of the churches even the tiniest bit of its spiritual well-being. No, if there is to be church renewal, then the composer of the improved church order must write down only what God, through his Word and Spirit, has already been pleased to awaken in the heart and mind of the people. For church renewal to occur, there must be opportunities, and who else determines these but the Lord our God? For church renewal to occur, people are indispensable, and who else creates people but the Lord? For church renewal to occur, there must be agreement of insights, uniformity of intention, willingness to cooperate, and who else turns the hearts like streams of water but the Lord?

Moreover, in the assemblies where that gradual church renewal is accomplished, the decision does not depend simply on the majority of a certain number of votes. Rather, the only decisive power is the present royal power of Christ, and the truth can triumph only under the presiding of the Holy Spirit. Thus it was at Nicaea! Thus it was at Dort! And precisely that was lacking in our Synod of The Hague.[44] It decided—*o conclamate vos, ecclesiae!* [O, bewail yourselves, churches!]—to reduce its prayer to once a week.

And finally, concerning the third stage of reformation, reformation through a rupture of the existing organization, as Luther and Calvin did: unconditionally, this rupture is either profoundly sinful or it is the work of God. Profoundly sinful, because terrible is the arrogance of him who tears apart the body of the Lord, and abuses the church of God as though it were a corpse, devoid of dignity, on which the surgeon practices his anatomy skills. He who has the audacity to do so, to disrupt the unity of the church in which he was born, must be very certain that God appointed him to do so; otherwise he takes on a responsibility that would bring a curse upon him. Such a reckless deed can be committed only by a cavalier person, whose unspiritual heart or fanaticism are clearly visible to the children of God. Among God-fearing people reformation through surgical operation, through rupture, through the severing of bonds, may only come when the Lord himself visits his people and raises up the men who can guide his flock, while the Lord himself is their front and rear guard on their way through the wilderness.

Not only must we readily admit that all activity, including the reformation of the churches, can ultimately be traced back to God, but we must also confess that there has never been any reformation in the church of the Lord, in the form of revival, gradual renewal, or necessary split, without the special operation of divine grace to begin that glorious work, to carry it out, and to complete it.

---

44. Here Kuyper may have in mind the national synod in The Hague of 1816, which among other things replaced the old church order dating back to the Synod of Dort with more modern ecclesiastical regulations. These changes were significant for the *Afscheiding*, a separation from the national church in 1834, as well as for the later *Doleantie* split, which Kuyper led in 1886.

§ 53   REFORMATION THROUGH SPIRITUAL REVIVAL

Spiritual revival is a more recent term for what our fathers more appropriately called a "renewal of the covenant." God's churches possess the glorious example for the motivation to such a spiritual revival in the seven letters that Christ sent through his apostle John to the seven churches in Asia Minor, and which still speak to us in the book of Revelation, chapters 2 and 3.

These letters are not directed to pagans or to the unconverted. Except for the one sent to the church of Laodicea, on which we cannot elaborate here, these letters all assume that the churches to which they are sent are standing firm in their confession, and that the vast majority of their members excel in strong, passionate faith. False elements had crept in. Sinful doctrine sought and partially found entrance. Their works were not complete. The Lord had a few things against them. Perfection was lacking. However, the churches in themselves were neither apostate nor compromised, nor had they become worldly in the way we complain about in our churches. In any case, these were still confessing and believing churches. And behold, Christ nonetheless deals with these churches, because of these small imperfections (as we would call them today), in such a strong and pointed way that they are admonished to "repent," to "strengthen what remains and is about to die" [Rev 3:2, 3] to remember from where they had fallen, and to do their first works; and all of this came with the stern threat that "I will come to you and remove your lampstand from its place, unless you repent" [Rev 2:5].

Now the Lord would not have sent these letters to the churches of that time and preserved them for the churches of all ages, if this false complacency had not been a common problem, and if this cry of "Awake, O sleeper, and arise from the dead, and Christ will shine on you" [Eph 5:14], were not indispensable, especially for the elect church, and within it, for the people of God.

To call for repentance and conversion, to admonish unto confession of guilt and a holy walk, is therefore the calling of the minister of the Word in every church of God, a calling that may never be ignored, because the Word is the means ordained by God to crucify and bury the indwelling sin of believers. The sound of the trumpet of repentance must increase in urgency as often as the judgments of the Lord are heard from afar, or when they come near, or even if they erupt as a plague in the very places where the church of God dwells. This call to spiritual awakening ought to take on a special character if, by God's permission, unholy worldliness or any specific sin visibly rears its head, and painfully affects the tender consciences for the sake of God's honor. But these preachers of repentance and conversions manifest their real, fully expressed character, only when God is pleased to impress overwhelmingly upon the soul of some of his children, or even only one of his elect, that he must call and may not keep silent because he has, in the words of Amos, heard the roaring of the lion [see Amos 3:8].

Then has come the favorable time when God visits his people; with the manifestations, influences, and workings of his Holy Spirit more powerful than before, he reaches out to the souls of his people. First in a few hearts, and later in smaller or greater groups, he produces dissatisfaction with the spiritual state of affairs. Once again souls are crying out of the depths, what seemed hardened melts once again, tongues are loosened, people take delight in self-denial, and the Word and prayer and praise acquire an inner sweetness that appears heavenly compared to the dryness over which they had been complaining for such a long time.

Such a watering of the garden of the Lord through dew from above, such a pouring out of fresh oil over the downcast, such a radiance of the vestments of praise for an anxious spirit, is then contagious, like a fire that propagates from spark to spark. It jumps from soul to soul, from home to home, from church to church, under the continual blowing of the Spirit's wind. And the result is that once again in a broad group, and more profoundly than for a long time before, people understand the damnability of our nature, confess our inability without restraint, take hold of the cross more readily, enjoy the riches of Christ more blessedly, and in them the fruits of the Spirit grow more abundantly in humility and long-suffering.

This stream of life then flows along three riverbeds. First of all, in the enrichment of the hidden life of the heart before God, is the mystical working of the revival. The rediscovery of the lost Comforter in our heart. Entering into the secret counsel of the Lord, which according to the holy covenant of grace is revealed to his beloved ones.[45] Indeed, a fulsome enjoyment; a foretaste of the manna grown in higher places.

Distinct from this is the stream that aims at the sanctification of the walk of life; not (unless it becomes sectarian) as something peculiar, in order to attain something higher than others do, but simply as the renewal

---

45. Kuyper quotes Psalm 25:14, using the language of the traditional Dutch versification.

of one's conversion, and therefore characterized by a greater dying-away of the old self; hating and running away from sin more and more; and likewise characterized by a greater coming-to-life of the new self, in wholehearted joy and delight, not only to live according to some, but all of God's commandments.[46]

Moreover, we have a holy zeal to tell others about the greatness of the love of Christ, or if you will, the riverbed of mission. To the church at Philadelphia, the Lord Jesus writes: "Behold, I have set before you an open door ... I will make those of the synagogue of Satan who say that they are Jews and are not, but lie—behold, I will make them come and bow down before your feet" [Rev 3:8–9]. And in the same sense, the Lord still gives power to win people for his kingdom to every church that awakens spiritually from its sleep of death—winning people not just through mission activity among Africans or Eskimos, but even more gloriously through winning those who are close to home.

Now the secret of a pure advancement of such a spiritual awakening lies in the question whether these three streams continue in the proper proportions. If that is not the case, the danger arises of sectarian degeneration, in an affected display of holiness among people of strong character and in superficial activism among people with a more external focus. But if those three streams remain connected so that in the one church of God, the people of emotion, of will, and of action balance each other, then together they avoid the sectarian path; then they seek the discipline of the church. And the rich life of grace that then blossoms in such a church will be glorious.

All artificially driven revivals are therefore to be rejected. They bring forth nothing but wind. And while it sometimes pleases the Lord God to scatter the seed of life on the wings of this wind, this happens only in spite of such an inflated movement; that is never the movement's natural fruit. One should not forget, however, that the right to denounce such false revivals can never arise from one's own inactivity, but only when God-willed, genuine awakening proceeds from the church or its members.

In a situation where the church has not deteriorated too much, its members will receive the incentive for such covenant renewal from the shepherds, and not conversely, the shepherds from the members. The Lord does not easily leave a church to such an extent that he no longer

---

46. See Heidelberg Catechism, Lord's Day 33, Q&A 88–90; Lord's Day 44, Q&A 114.

equips at least some sensitive children of God with talents, placing them in ecclesiastical office to shine as bright stars among the darkness that has descended. These shepherds are called in a very special measure to have closer fellowship with their Sender, to shine their light in a holy walk, and to carry in their priestly heart the honor of God and the salvation of souls. More than others they are the appointed watchmen, the faithful dogs that must bark for their Master. They must see the wolf before the sheep catch sight of it—and woe to the shepherd who fails to attack the wolf and to risk his life for the sheep! Indeed, Joshua and Josiah, Ezra and Nehemiah are the radiant witnesses who admonish every shepherd sent by God to be faithful in this work entrusted to them. And the history of Jesus' church in the time of the new covenant is full of inspiring examples of this tender life of the shepherds, in the church, before the face of God. Their trumpet of repentance still rings in their writings.

Indeed, there is more. In our own country also, the testimony of history shows several classis assemblies in which the ministers of the Word jointly confessed their own guilt and unfaithfulness before God, and together in his presence made promises of awakening with respect to their own ministry and life. It is known how in 1660 the preachers of all the churches in Leiden together, in the face of great danger confronted the Christians in this great city with their sins, and admonished them to covenant renewal. Even in the churches of later times there is no lack of glorious examples of churches that, when they had incurred guilt before God, in response to the preaching and rebuke of their shepherds, sealed anew their covenant of faith with the Lord, publicly in the sanctuary, with fasting and prayer.

But one can imagine worse deterioration, where the Lord God either completely strips his church of faithful watchmen or withholds from the remaining faithful watchmen the grace to fight for his holiness. Of course, in such a lamentable situation, the lack of zeal on the part of the faithful, or the faithlessness of the other shepherds, does not at all remove the duty of God's church to awaken in godliness. The only difference is that the duty to take the initiative, which the members normally have left to the shepherds, now transfers to them. However, in this matter the ordinance of God must be honored, lest the members corrupt their zeal for God's honor by despising the office instituted by him. Therefore, whenever the children of God who are not in office are moved by the Holy Spirit (without whose activity all work is idle display) in a special way through conviction of common guilt, and a fire of jealousy burns within their chests to agitate against the sin of the people, their zeal must begin with a display of love toward the church's leaders.

They must be addressed first. There must be no desire to do the work without them, but rather a quiet urgency and prayer: "Oh, that *they* might awaken to do it!" Only when the urgency and prayer turn out to be in vain, and the shepherds harden themselves in their unfaithfulness or the faithful shepherds are hardened in their lukewarm lack of zeal—then the time has come for such church members themselves to call the church to repentance and conversion.

No one may think lightly of this manner of honoring God's ordinances, or pass it by in a self-satisfied manner. One should realize that all our calling to repentance and conversion can bring forth only death unless the Lord God affects the hearts; that the trumpet of repentance is merely an instrument, and the God of glory alone is the one who awakens the sleeping ones; and that the blessing received from our Father's hand through prayer is forfeited as soon as we behave arrogantly and fail to follow his way.

When one applies these key principles to what is happening around us, the following points must be mentioned.

(1) In the preaching of our day, the call for repentance and conversion, not of the masses outside the church but of the people of the Lord, is being sounded much too quietly.

(2) Among the ministers of the Word, both in their mutual fellowship and in their care for the church of God, one can observe a deplorable lack of the kind of spiritual awakening that does not rest until the shame of corruption is removed from the land of the Lord.

(3) The spiritual awakening that proceeded from the members of various groups had many defects. Of these defects, the four most prominent are: first, ecclesiastical office is passed over or even despised; second, people pursue holiness without having admitted their guilt; third, there is a one-sided pursuit of the mystical, or moral improvement, or an increase in works, which leads to sectarianism; fourth, there is a pursuit of something peculiar, instead of polishing the regular furniture.

(4) Of the work of Dwight L. Moody in particular, we must say that it has nothing to do with a spiritual awakening, since it aims only at

the preaching of the gospel to the masses.[47] Thus it aims not at awakening after sleeping, but first at conversion out of spiritual death. To what extent the defects and failures of the churches in England and America encouraged such behavior cannot be discussed here.

(5) The spiritual awakening promoted by Robert Pearsall Smith, was on the right track insofar as it did not address the masses but those who were in the church. However, it went off track when it avoided the ecclesiastical structure, introduced new elements into the doctrine, and sought strength in means designed for overexcitement.[48]

(6) The Salvation Army, like Moody's movement, does not aim at spiritual awakening, but at reaching the unconverted; but in doing so, it completely misses the mark insofar as it bypasses the riverbed of the church, casts pearls before swine, and in order to gain influence it employs means that oppose the spirit of the Word.

(7) Among the children of God in these lands it will come to this divinely required spiritual awakening and covenant renewal only when and because every person puts the axe to the root of his own self; progresses from the conversion of his heart to the improvement of his family; and without asking what others are doing, stoops before his own household and group with the humility that has the immutable promise of grace.

REFORMATION THROUGH GRADUAL CHURCH RENEWAL   §54

Regrettably, the corruption of the church is rarely limited to its teachers and members despising grace. Almost always, growing cold in love and godliness also brings with it the corruption of doctrine and the collapse of church government. We must therefore investigate in the second place how to assess the second kind of reformation, which we called gradual church renewal.

By this we do not at all mean letting the sickness run its course. In the church of Christ one may never simply wait for the illness to pass, and the medical approach that has been contrasted with the legal approach

---

47. D. L. Moody (1837–99) was a renowned American evangelist and revivalist, associated with the Holiness movement.

48. Robert Pearsall Smith (1827–98) was an American evangelist and leader of the Higher Life movement. Kuyper visited one of Smith's meetings in Brighton, England, in 1875 and came away so moved that he supported similar meetings in the Netherlands. Kuyper soon became disenchanted, however, after suffering a breakdown and after learning of Smith's improprieties.

actually stands in opposition to the surgical approach. If one would compare the corruption of the church to corruption in our body, then medical treatment leaves the organism untouched, whereas with the surgical treatment, the scalpel disturbs a part of it for the preservation of the whole organism.

Leaving a discussion of the surgical treatment for later, we limit ourselves to the medical treatment, but this medical treatment comes in many different kinds. It depends on the nature of the disease. That disease can have affected one of the organs of the body or it can be the weakening or poisoning of the general powers of life without having affected a single organ. In the latter case, medical science attempts to heal that weakening through nutrition, or that poisoning through purification. But if one of the organs is affected, it attempts to keep the other organs from becoming affected, and if possible, to restore the affected organ to its original purity by removing or dissolving the defective parts.

Applying this metaphor to the church of God, one can imagine a disease in that church, caused by despising grace, manifesting itself only in the individual people, leaving the organism of the church uncorrupted. Against this evil one can and may use only the pure preaching of the Word, both from the pulpit and within the families. However, if the nature of the corruption is such that not only the members are affected but also the organism of the church itself, then this method is inadequate, and good medicine aims at restoring the diseased organism to its original purity through expulsion, dissolution, or absorption of the bad elements.

How this is to be accomplished depends, of course, on the nature of the organism. A wise physician uses different methods for the lungs than for the liver, and treats the kidneys differently than the heart. With respect to the church one must therefore also ask, as soon as there is corruption in its organism, what are the channels, the pathways, the mechanisms that the organism allows for expelling, healing, or dissolving the harmful elements. And if the answer is that there are two kinds of such channels, namely, the exercise of church discipline and the improvement of the ecclesiastical ordinances, then it is abundantly clear that the restraint of evil through rebuking, dismissing, or deposing unfaithful ministers; or also through rebuking, censuring, and if necessary excommunicating unfaithful church members, however legal this measure may be—all of this still belongs to the medical method of church renewal, just as the strengthening of the church's life through the preaching of the Word.

To allow the disease to run its course is no method at all, but is either a failure to do one's duty or inactivity borne of helpless desperation. The physician who lets the disease run its course is effectively quitting his job as a physician. And once you decide that a medical treatment is in order, the answer to the question whether it suffices to preach repentance and conversion, or if instead it is necessary to exercise discipline and revise the church order, does not depend at all on your approval. It depends only on the nature of the corruption of the church. If the evil lies solely in despising grace, then only the trumpet of repentance is called for; but if it has progressed and affected the organism itself, then you may not stop there, but you must also deal with church discipline and the church order.

The ministers in Jesus' church are certainly not exclusively preachers of the Word who can consider themselves responsible before God if they only preach the Word on the pulpit and in some of the homes. By virtue of their office they are also church governors, and as such they are duty bound to exercise discipline and enforce good order in all ecclesiastical matters. To imagine that preaching the Word should be sufficient, and the task of church government could remain undone, is therefore nothing less than the minister preaching that Word to others while he himself, with no qualms of conscience, disobeys that Word in his own office.

Yet we must warn equally against another one-sidedness, namely the activity and attempt of those who, without an eye for despising grace and in apparent disregard for the power of the Word, imagine in Pharisaic arrogance and highly unspiritual superficiality that the seriously ill church could be healed as if by waving a magical wand, merely by cutting off the heretical elements and thoroughly revising the regulations. Anyone who imagines this knows neither his own heart nor the needs of the congregation, nor the powers of the kingdom. What is manifest in the organism is present as an even more profound corruption in the hearts and the homes. And church renewal will never be more than a vain display if the healing process does not start with rebuking sin and renewing the covenant. This rebuke should not begin with the world, or with those who waver, but with the very people of the Lord, and among that people, in every individual, with his or her own heart.

Without that spiritual background, every attempted church renewal remains futile. One may polish things up, but there will never be the true radiance of life. If church members do not personally rely on grace, there may be much tinkering and tweaking, but it never leads to the growth of the church. With cold indifference, bureaucratic lawyers who together fashion plans for removing the existing problems may be able to deliver well-crafted regulations without ever being approved by the Holy Spirit for building the Lord's spiritual house.

That is abundantly clear in the sad example of the Synod of The Hague![49] How these gentlemen toiled and twisted, through constantly new stipulations and more refined regulations and more suitable measures, to heal the break within the church and iron out its wrinkles. And yet, what fruit did they see from their diligent work and undeniable talents and immense effort, except growing discontent, increased loss of strength, and an ever-progressing decay from gnawing cancer? Now was this because of a lack of sincerity, ability, or wise deliberation on their part? If you think that, you are wrong. Most of those who tried their hand at this vain and futile work were men of good will; in ability they certainly exceeded most of us; and in deliberation they were very skilled masters. No, the only thing they lacked was the knowledge of the disease and its cures. They sought in the skin what was hidden deep down in the kidneys. They circumvented their own heart. They were not even aware of the guilt incurred before God, whose name was being dishonored in and by his church. The Word of the Lord had no value for them. Sometimes they spoke of grace, but they did not understand it experientially. Prayer had become a formal custom for them, and the Holy Spirit did not preside in their meetings. Naturally, they ended up plowing on rocks.

Church decay is a punishment from God, a plague that he brings upon it and lays upon his people because of their sins; and precisely because of that, he cannot remove that plague from us unless that guilt is first felt, confessed, and atoned for in the blood of the cross. Without that conviction of sin, there can be no genuine repentance and conversion. And if this renewal of the covenant is lacking, how can one hope for a better state of the church? But also conversely, if that conviction of guilt is alive among the Lord's people, and the Spirit of God moves the souls to awaken, so that the law and the testimony are taken up again, and the covenant with the Almighty is reestablished in heart and home and land, how could the obedience of the faithful ministers be absent? That is impossible, because God's truth is like scented oil that seeps through every pore. When the

---

49. See Tract, in *On the Church*, 199n44.

name of the Lord is resurrected in the heart of his people, then not only godliness but also truth returns, and all heresy begins to feel crowded out and threatened. Imperceptibly and without any deliberate action, the foundations are exposed for all to see and follow. And wherever the foundations of God's secret work in the soul provide new stability, the power of that truth naturally affects the thinking about the organization of the church. The office that was once despised regains its beauty. He who used to present his own views from the pulpit in well-structured sentences now begins to deny himself and his own word, and manifests once again the power of the Word of his God. Once he begins to devote his service to that Word, he brings that word with urgency, in season and out of season, to rebuke sin and promote godliness in the land. And where the power of that Word finally shines its light on his own office as well, he becomes increasingly aware of the duty of church government, and the minister of the Word will not find rest until the house of the Lord is rebuilt.

The question where this gradual church renewal should originate is not difficult to answer. It happens only if the Holy Spirit inspires the ecclesiastical governments, or rather, the ecclesiastical assemblies, to do so. One man alone or a few together can never bring about church renewal in a sufficient, gradual manner; and the members [that is, non-officers] of the church can provide even less help. Once you realize that gradual church renewal consists in the exercise of church discipline and in the improvement of the church order, and you know that only legitimate consistories, classes, and synods have the authority to do so—then you must also realize that gradual renewal can be brought about only through consistories, through classes, and through synods.

Whatever individual ministers or members of the church might want to do in this respect would actually take away from the gradual character of the renewal, and would introduce the surgical approach, which we will discuss later. All that the individual minister or the members of the church can do in this matter is this: they can pray that the Lord would grant them their desire; they can urgently argue for the duty of renewal; and as members of the church through a letter of request or protest, or as ministers through advice and vote in the ecclesiastical assembly, they can admonish them to perform this duty.

If the church, as is usually the case, has a federative correspondence with other churches, then gradual renewal is even more difficult. Then whether one can exercise discipline and improve the church order does not merely depend on the goodwill of the consistory, but the cooperation of other churches in the classes and synods is indispensable.

Understand this well: we are not saying that the members, ministers, or consistories must refrain from their duty of church renewal because of these obstacles. Rather, we mean that as soon as members, ministers, or consistories are forced to act on their own, the medical approach has been abandoned, and in effect the surgical approach has been adopted. In this section, which deals exclusively with the medical or gradual process, this extraordinary possibility must be ignored, and therefore we establish this rule: Gradual church renewal can originate with the consistories in independent churches, but for churches in federation it can come only from the consistory with the cooperation of the classis and the synod.

Concerning the approach that must be followed here, we can only give suggestions, for here more than anywhere, it is the case that *variis modis bene fit*, that is, one can reach the goal in more than one good way. We limit ourselves to the following five general suggestions:

(1) The exercise of church discipline must address both doctrine and life. Resuming the church's discipline of heretical, sectarian, and schismatic people without also resuming the discipline of the fornicator, drunkard, and blasphemer, would stand condemned before every conscience.

(2) When resuming church discipline the judgment of discernment must rule. A minister who teaches poorly or lives poorly is more guilty than a deviating or wandering church member. All discipline must therefore begin with discipline of the office-bearers. Only office-bearers who discipline each other have the right to judge others.

Likewise, when church discipline is resumed after a long period of neglect, there must be more abundant rebuke, in tender compassion, in a desire to win others through the power of love. Censure or excommunication should be used only where there is evident unwillingness to repent or evident hardening.

Especially with respect to doctrine, strictness toward the ministers must be combined with extreme long-suffering toward ordinary church members. In the case of ministers, one may not hesitate. He who teaches others *must* speak the Word of the church. He who is unable or unwilling to do so may not be spared. To spare him is to sacrifice the church, whereby a false display of love for a single person is coupled with lack of love for thousands.

However, and this must be noted well, the solution may not be such that, in a serious attempt at church renewal (as in our situation), the first step would be the ruthless deposing of all preachers, elders, and deacons who have refused to subscribe to the Three Forms of Unity, or also of those who, after subscribing to them, were persuaded to oppose these confessions.[50] This would be the approach of fanaticism that seeks to destroy, but not of the church of Christ that prays for its enemies and denies itself in seeking to save. Instead, the ecclesiastical assemblies in this case would have the daunting task of discerning spiritually between those who oppose the truth out of the wickedness of their heart and those who err in ignorance. Unending patience, much persuasive power, and a rich gift of wisdom would be needed to win those who can still be won before severing the bond. Of course, in the end this ultimate measure is necessary with all who persist in their plans, but hopefully this is not the case with many.

For ordinary church members, one may even go further: At first, discipline only those who have openly opposed the church's doctrine in word or in writing. Next, inform and educate the church, and in that way, gradually reach a separation between those who deliberately reject the truth and those whose souls are still floating along on the currents of truth.

(3) In the improvement of the church order, the focus should not be the polishing up of an artful mechanism, but the healthy flourishing of the organism of the church. It is not about rules of order, but about principles of church government. The goal must be to see the sovereign grace of God rule in his church. To this end, one must remove all that stands in the way of that sovereignty or its full functioning. Everything else is of minor importance or even irrelevant. With unrelenting strictness, every word of human beings must be made to yield to the Word of God, and all human authority must flow directly from King Jesus.

---

50. The traditional Three Forms of Unity of Reformed churches are the Belgic Confession (1561), the Heidelberg Catechism (1563), and the Canons of Dort (1619).

(4) In order to accomplish this, the makeup of the Reformed assemblies must be supervised closely. Decisions should really not be made based on majority votes. It is much better to convince each other in the spirit of prayer until there is unity of insight. But because a majority vote could ultimately adopt a decision that goes against us, the makeup of these assemblies may not be indifferent to us.

(5) In these assemblies one must not deny the principle for which one is fighting. This could happen in various ways, and these must be avoided with care. First, one must make sure that no assembly issues a decision without being willing to defend it. A strategy of overwhelming others will not work. A spiritual, conscious conviction must be fostered, albeit in different degrees for different people. Second, one should not assemble if that assembly contradicts the demand of God's Word or the sovereignty of King Jesus. Third, anyone helping to make a decision should not withdraw when it is to be implemented. No one who puts his hand to the plow and looks back is fit for the kingdom of God [Luke 9:62].

§ 55   REFORMATION THROUGH A BREAK WITH WHAT EXISTS

Generally the term *reformation* is used neither for covenant renewal through spiritual awakening nor for the gradual renewal of the church. In the narrow sense, *reformation* means nothing less than the historical Reformation of the sixteenth century, when under the leadership of Luther, Zwingli, and Calvin there came a break with the existing national churches at that time.

Meanwhile, to prevent misunderstanding, we must again distinguish sharply between two very different cases. Making changes in what already exists, with the goal to reform the old church in which one was born, is entirely different than completely leaving that old church to establish a new church both alongside and over against the former one. Both situations occurred in the Reformation of the sixteenth century. For instance, in Amsterdam and London, as well as in Wittenberg and Geneva, the Reformers did not separate from the church in which they were born to establish a new church, but detached their own former church from its correspondence with other churches, established a new and better federation of churches, and purged their churches of abuse. On the other hand, in Paris and Vienna, in Poland and Italy, they left the church in which they had been baptized and established a new church formation over against the former one.

Little attention is given to this significant distinction. This is due to the mistaken view that the one large, universal church, as it had been joined together under papal authority, was to be considered *the* church. And since our fathers both in Paris and in Amsterdam broke with the Roman Catholic hierarchy, the wrong impression was received that in our country and in London, new churches were being established. But this was definitely not the case. And as soon as the government salary for ministers is at stake, even the most uninformed among us will point out that the reformation created no new churches in our country, but was merely a continuation in purer form of the old Christian churches that were established here in the sixth and seventh centuries. The motivation that some of us had in 1834 for their act of reformation[51] is therefore definitely different from what happened in Amsterdam when it opposed the Roman Catholic rule in the sixteenth century. It would have been similar only if these fathers had succeeded in abolishing synodical domination in the churches themselves. As it is, the movement of 1834 can only be compared to the reformation in those countries where, as in Poland and Italy, the old church remained and the churches of the Reformation could only sprout up as new shoots beside the condemned old churches.

For the sake of clarity, we will therefore discuss separately both forms of "reformation through a break with what exists": we will speak first of the break that leads to the reformation of the old church, and then of the break that leads to the establishment of a new church alongside an existing church.

A mixed situation can occur when one succeeds in purging one's old church through reformation, but is unable to move other churches in the federation to the same reformation. This causes a collision that must result in the demolition of the old and the construction of a new church federation. This is a mixed case, because not a new church, but a new federation is being established. With regard to the church this case belongs to the first category, but with regard to the church federation, it belongs to the second.

This inclines us, for the sake of clarity, to discuss this mixed case separately, such that we wish to address three categories: (1) reformation

---

51. That is, the *Afscheiding*.

through a break with what exists, where one nonetheless manages to salvage the existing church and its federation; (2) reformation through a break with what exists, where a new church federation is formed; (3) reformation through a break with what exists, where one is compelled to erect a new church formation in opposition to the old. Only with this division into three categories is it possible to gain clear insight into the course that reforming work follows.

The phrase "a break with what exists" is the most general expression that denotes the character of every more or less surgical reformation, but in such a way that this break can occur, either with the existing church organization alone; or with the existing organization and the existing church federation; or finally, not only with these two but also with the existing church as a body.

Thus there is not only a sharp distinction between these three categories, but also an ascending order from lesser to greater in this break. The first break is temporary—a wound that will soon close. The second break is definitive, but in its definitiveness it does not affect the church, but only the church federation. The third break, finally, not only definitively affects the organization and the federation, but also the church itself.

The best known historical example of the first kind of break is the action of the Reformed against the Remonstrants. In The Hague, Haarlem, and many other towns, even in classes and synods, this resulted in a very definite break, but it was healed at the Synod of Dort and the scars have since faded. For the second kind of break, we have the reformations of Wittenberg, Zurich, and Geneva, of Amsterdam, London, and Copenhagen in the sixteenth century. Finally, an example of the third kind of break is the currently seceded group of churches in our own country.

Those who initiate a break with the existing church always view it as a break with a degenerated, false manifestation, or with a false imitation, of the church. Therefore the justification or condemnation of such a break depends exclusively on the question whether this qualification of degenerate or false church is correct, and that is why this discussion of these three kinds of breaks must be followed by a serious review of the characteristics that are decisive for this matter.

REFORMATION THROUGH A BREAK WITH THE EXISTING CHURCH   §56
ORGANIZATION

With all reformation by means of a break, even more so than in the case of spiritual revival and gradual renewal, the starting point must lie in the conviction of sin and guilt. Those who initiate a break with the existing organization without this awareness forsake their faith in God's providential plan. It seems to such people that the church's reformation occurs only on account of the opposition and wicked intentions of some, so that the Lord God would have given us a good church situation if only the stubbornness of those few were no obstacle. And the deepest thought of their hearts is that they, being the better ones, will eliminate those evil-minded people, and thus recreate a good church situation for the Lord. Here are three sins in one: first, a failure to see their own guilt; second, an elevation of self above others; third, the illusion that a good church situation is not a gift of God to us, but from us to the Lord.

On the other hand, if one confesses that a good church situation is an excellent gift of God's grace, which he sovereignly gives to us and which we receive from him without having any right to it, then one realizes immediately that if the Lord withholds this good from us, it is because of the sin of the church; and therefore the punishment consisting in a bad church situation is always a judgment on unrighteousness. One who acknowledges the judgment of God in the sad state of the church can therefore no longer think that the godliness of the true members is merely being victimized by the wickedness of the others; rather, he will confess that all guilt and sin is corporate; and that to the extent that they knew more truth and received more tender grace, it is really the genuine people who have sinned the more terribly. Love is most tender, and it is not the wild animal that tears you apart; rather, it is the children of the house who violate that love.

Anyone preparing for reformation of the church in the name of the Lord neither may nor will do so in arrogance, and even less in a scornful way that looks down on others. Rather he will lack courage within himself to put his hand to such a work, and wonder anxiously whether it is also the Lord's will that his guilt before the Lord be punished further, more bitterly, through this plague of continuing ecclesiastical degeneration. And the true messenger of repentance who is equipped for this work will adopt the posture of expecting nothing else than the prolonging of tribulation because of his sin; yet in pure obedience he himself acts and compels others to act according to the Word of God.

God himself alone is the author of "reformation through a break with the existing church organization." It is not as though this would release us from our task, or give us an excuse for spiritual inertia. If you were to claim that, then you would have the entire Word of God against you; it would be official antinominianism! But such a reformation cannot rightly occur unless the Holy Spirit compassionately instills conviction of sin in dull hearts, and causes them to view the corruption of the church as a judgment of God. This conviction cannot be produced artificially. People may parrot each other in saying that all church renewal must start in confession of guilt, but this accomplishes nothing other than an outward show. This confession of guilt acquires truth, reality, and spiritual essence only if the Holy Spirit himself persuades the guilty heart while he also comforts that guilty heart, ever so tenderly.

Even more must be added to this. Church reformation is not something that occurs through the act of a single person. When Luther acted, he took the lead, but his work would have been forgotten and would have died away if not for the many others who lent their support after a long time of preparation and maturing, only awaiting a sign. It is therefore not enough if the conviction of ecclesiastical guilt arises within a single heart. Such a conviction must arise simultaneously within many, and become a spiritual movement among the people of the Lord. Only in this way does the heat arise that can melt everything; the stimulus of life that can awaken everything; the power that can overcome all opposition. And behold, precisely this shows how only the Lord God can be the author of such a reformation. Obviously, even though a man might foster enthusiasm for his ideas among a small group of friends, in a wider circle no one but the Lord can accomplish a similar spiritual movement within the souls.

This is not to say that one who has this conviction may and must sit still until he notices that this conviction is alive in other hearts as well. That would be a rejection and despising of the demand of God's Word. And those who think to themselves and tell others that, although they are convinced of ecclesiastical guilt and sin against God, they must nonetheless wait passively until the Lord reveals a special sign that resolves the situation, or until he awakens the hearts of everyone unto church renewal, so that it roars like the voice of many streams—those people clearly fail to understand the first principle of obedience.

A Christian must do everything out of the obedience of faith, not because of prospective success. He must be guided neither by the question whether he will succeed nor the fear of ridicule, but only by the commandment of God. A Christian's calling is not to implement God's hidden counsel, but to walk in the law of the Lord. Independently of what others may do, or what the results will be, or even what may be determined in the Lord's counsel, he must do his duty and testify where he is commanded to testify. If God willed to afflict our dearest child with a worrisome sickness, so that our hearts break and death seems poised to take its spoil, what Christian father would not feel the horrible judgment of God over his own guilt and sin? But also, how would you judge a father who, cast down by that conviction of guilt, would leave his helpless child to that illness without lifting a hand to heal it?

A return to the wholesome, true, only good principle, must therefore guide us to this rule: No reformation except out of conviction of guilt among the people of the Lord; no sincere conviction of guilt except through the convicting operation of the Holy Spirit; no operation of the Holy Spirit except according to God's hidden counsel. But even if that counsel is different, even if that operation of the Spirit is delayed, and even if that conviction of guilt is still lacking among the Lord's people, nevertheless it remains the precious duty for all and everyone to keep what is unholy from the altar of the Lord. And if there were even one person who received that conviction of guilt from the Spirit, he cannot and may not hesitate to act according to the Word of the Lord, regardless of what suffering it might bring him, even though it would leave him broken on the street.

God's commandment is unconditional and reaches to the depths of the soul. Any violation of that commandment, however miniscule, brings eternal death. Only the infinite sacrifice of Christ, because he was God, can remove the guilt incurred from violating that commandment. And precisely because of the absolute character of the commandment, every excuse that one might derive from required sacrifices or special circumstances in order to escape the severity of that commandment, will weigh less than a cloud of dust in the balance of God's justice.

One must consider well that a deviation from and violation of the existing ordinances is something horrible for a tender conscience, and nobody can have the holy courage to proceed unless he knows that God wants it! Disobedience to human ordinances may and can happen only out of greater obedience to the ordinances of God. And the overly spiritual people who use many arguments to silence the voice of obedience, cut the nerve of the Christian life. No, it is not just that there are varying views concerning church reformation, and that everyone can either do much or nothing according to his own insight. This is not a matter of opinion or viewpoint. If it is not the duty of obedience to God that is compelling, driving, and forcing one to act, then all action is sin. But also, if that duty of obedience to God holds true for one, then it applies equally and simultaneously for all. The commandment is universal.

Therefore we characterize the reformation discussed in this section as the ecclesiastical return to obedience to God and his Word, after ecclesiastical disobedience to that God and that Word. If someone has introduced rules and customs into his own home, and later he realizes that they oppose God's Word, he must immediately change those rules and customs in order to be obedient to God again. No appeal to either the authority or the antiquity of those rules could excuse him or anyone for a moment if he continued being disobedient. A break with existing rules or customs, or if you will, with the existing organization, is permissible to us, but then also absolutely mandatory, only if this organization prevents one from being obedient to the Lord God even in one's own church.

This implies that every reformation through a break must be preceded not only by spiritual awakening through conviction of guilt, but also with attempts at gradual renewal. A child of God has a spirit of caution. He abhors the eagerness that seeks a break, and rather considers possible means to prevent that break. Only hard, painful necessity presses and forces and compels him to this action. He *wanted* something else, but he *cannot* do anything else. Thus, every other path must be walked before one causes or allows that break to occur. Gradual renewal must first be desired, sought, and prayed for. And only if the ecclesiastical assemblies—the only possible starting point of this gradual renewal—instead of seeking God's honor, rather refuse principally and stubbornly to bring the ecclesiastical organization out of its disobedience of God to obedience to his Word; or worse, if they oppose any attempted obedience to the Lord and punish it; only then, but certainly then, the time has come when that break can and may no longer be postponed.

Because the break with the existing church federation will be discussed in the next section, we need to speak here only of the reformation that leaves the federation unaffected, or does not involve a conflict with the federation. Our focus here is therefore the reformation of the local church, that is, of that church with which every member is first and foremost concerned. The church to which we belong is the body of Christ, but that body of Christ manifests itself locally. It is therefore in the local church where we are directly in touch with the body of Christ. Each of us has direct responsibility only for that local church, and it is in, through, and with it that we must demonstrate our ecclesiastical obedience toward God.

"Demonstrate ecclesiastical obedience" is an expression that hardly requires explanation. The Lord God deserves obedience from us in every area of life. We must obey the Lord our God in our personal, domestic, social, political life, and also in our ecclesiastical life. There are no limits to obedience toward God. If someone walks in obedience in his personal and social life, yet fails to obey in his home, then he is still guilty. Likewise, if someone serves God in his home and society, but participates in disobedience to God within his church then he commits a public violation of God's majesty.

As a rule, therefore, one may not be disobedient to God within his own church, nor may he through participation or idle observation become an accomplice to the disobedience of others. Thus, if the church to which someone belongs lives in a state of disobedience, then every child of God is required to oppose this disobedience through obedience. If the disobedient church allows this to happen, if the church makes room for it and facilitates it, then there will be no break. But if it hinders or prevents this exercise of obedience to God, then the child of God may not give up, but must continue at the risk of punishment, even punishment with death. This holds true in two ways. First, every child of God must refuse to do anything or to participate or cooperate in anything that would constitute disobedience to God. And conversely, every child of God must perform and fulfill whatever obedience to God may require, even though it may be something that people would forbid, prevent, or make impossible.

The cases in which this could happen are principally these:

(1) As for doing things that God forbids: refusal (a) to worship images, or to pray to Mary or the saints; (b) to participate in religious gatherings where the truth is not spoken or is distorted; (c) to sing songs that are not according to the Word of God; (d) to participate in sacramental rites that are not administered correctly; (e) to have one's children instructed in religion with or through teachers who fall

short of the truth; and (f) to be forced to honor ecclesiastical persons in ways that compromise the kingship of Jesus.

(2) As for obedience to God when this is being opposed, we point to (a) the duty to have the Word preached, and to seek this preaching from others outside the congregation, or to establish it; (b) the duty to have the sacraments of holy baptism and the Lord's Supper administered, for oneself as well as one's children; (c) the duty to testify against sin and error in the congregation.

In each of these cases, every member of the church is bound to act and to walk in the way of duty and calling, in simplicity of heart. If the consistory opposes this, then this member must nevertheless persist. If punishment follows, he must receive that punishment, without forsaking for a moment pursuing that which occasioned the punishment. And if the consistory hinders him in obtaining from the church what he should obtain according to God's Word, then he has the obligation to provide for this lack through association with like-minded fellow members.

For instance, if the church is remiss in the distribution of the means of grace, so that the Christian cannot receive the preaching of the Word or the administration of the sacrament in the God-ordained manner, then he has the obligation to supply this. He can do so most easily by moving to another church where there is still a proper distribution of the means of grace. But not all are able to do so. Many are limited to their locale of residence. In that case, it is not sufficient to rent a room to have so-called evangelists preach there occasionally, but one must send for an ordained teacher. And because this can be done legitimately only by a consistory, the group of those who are aggrieved must proceed to appoint elders and deacons in order for them to call a teacher. A teacher for the ministry, that is, not just someone who preaches occasionally, but a teacher who also administers both sacraments—not only the Lord's Supper, but also holy baptism. And therefore, a teacher who with his consistory also exercises discipline, so that the administration of the sacraments is done properly.

That this constitutes a break we do not deny at all. After all, we are speaking here of reformation through a break. Yet we want to mention that such a break does not have to be permanent at all. During the Arminian controversy, the faithful everywhere in this country followed this code of conduct, and in various congregations this resulted in a public break between the consistory and these Reformed believers—so much so, that at the 26th and 29th session of the Synod in 1618–19 the Remonstrants openly accused these church members of schism, and on these grounds called into question their right to be part of that ecclesiastical body. But this sentiment found so little support that in separate declarations, the theologians from England, Geneva, the Palatinate, and Bremen expressed clearly that such a separation from what is disobedient to God has nothing in common with schism. While we do not deny that such a step *can* lead to a permanent split, yet it is equally true that the way to close the break is still open. The example of 1619 illustrates this.

To the question in what manner such aggrieved church members should proceed in this situation, the following rules may be adopted: First, if among the aggrieved members there is a preacher of the congregation together with other consistory members, then they must be acknowledged as the council of the church, provided that they meet separately. Second, if the aggrieved members are without a preacher, it is good to invite a preacher of one of the neighboring churches to be a consultant and to give guidance. Third, if this guidance is unavailable, they should proceed to elect elders and deacons under the leadership of one of the older brothers. Or, if the number of aggrieved members is too small to do so, then they should try to be supervised by a neighboring consistory, which should care for this congregation as a temporary measure.

All this concerns the attitude of the ordinary church members. But even more precious duties rest on the office-bearers. If they have no doubt that the church they are serving is not walking in obedience, then they may not rest, but must act and consider carefully how to walk obediently and how to obediently lead the flock entrusted to them. They must untiringly instruct the members of the congregation from the pulpit, in catechism instruction, in the families, and if necessary, through open letters that are sent around. Second, in the consistory they must urge for improvement of ecclesiastical life. Third, without asking permission from the consistory, they must do what obedience to God's Word requires of them, and what is necessary for the congregation to walk in the way of God's Word. And fourth, even beyond their own churches they must provide help to churches facing spiritual hardship.

If, while acting in this manner, an office-bearer incurs the rebuke of his consistory, then he must bear with it and meanwhile continue in the same manner. If he is silenced through deposition, then he must nonetheless continue with the preaching of the Word and the administration of the sacraments, since this is his mission from the Lord. And if in spite of this continual admonition and this display of resilience, his consistory continues stubbornly on the way of disobedience, then he is bound finally to sever fellowship with such a consistory, and aid his church in the gathering of a faithful consistory.

What the outcome of such a conflict will be, is hard to say, but the minister of the Word may certainly not avoid the way of obedience for fear of financial loss. If his goal were to be famous, then it would be the flesh, not the spirit that is at work, and any proud and arrogant start would be soon followed with a humbling and a bowing down in shameful humiliation. But if in uprightness of heart he is driven by the desire to obey the Lord God, then the hero who is willing to testify for the Lord's name even with his blood will never abandon his duty because of temporary loss of money or possessions.

In this situation, however, the break has already gone beyond the organization of the local church, and touched the church federation itself, and therefore no longer belongs in this section. But we must still discuss the question regarding to what extent shared guilt in the disobedience of others can justify a break, even if we are not forced into disobedience nor hindered in the way of obedience. In this respect, out of fear of excessive zeal and arrogance, we would urgently exhort people to use extra caution.

There are so few, especially among the more sensitive children of God, who feel this shared responsibility so keenly that they bring it as guilt before the throne of grace. And if this sense of guilt is absent, the first condition for a legitimate break would be lacking. But if it is the Holy Spirit who brings the soul to this point, so that you do not merely oppose the disobedience of others in words, but in the communion of the body of Christ you experience the weight of corporate guilt in your heart, so strongly that you invoke the blood of Christ to cover it—oh, then surely you have both the right and the duty, even the perfect right and the inescapable duty, to sever the bond with such an organization. And this is not because you leave your church or condemn it as church, and certainly not because you expose it as a false church, but because as a silent and solemn testimony against it you cease all fellowship with its consistory.

This duty manifests itself first and most simply in the refusal to receive for home visiting the teachers or elders who are disobedient to the Word of the Lord. But this duty may not stop here; it must progress to a protest to the consistory, because the consistory may not passively tolerate this evil.

Thus the presence of a few unbelieving consistory members may be the occasion for believers to assemble separately. This implies as well that the consistory as a whole can be called on God's behalf to separate themselves. A consistory that is eager to be obedient to God's Word may not rest until unbelieving members have been removed from among that body; until the church members' right to vote is once again subject to the confession; and until the ministry of unbelieving teachers has been stopped. The chairman of a consistory who desires to be faithful in this matter would no longer invite such unbelieving consistory members to consistory meetings, would pass over their names in a roll call, and would refuse to let them speak. This would most likely become manifest as a confrontation or even a split within the consistory, or at least in the local church, but this cannot and will not be a reason to forsake one's duty, if first the Holy Spirit has worked a sincere conviction of guilt and fosters the desire to obedience. Even church wardens may be called of God to do this, if they realize that they may no longer make the church buildings available for unholy preaching, nor pay salaries to unfaithful teachers.

In short, obedience has no limits. It extends to the organist who refuses to play, to the song leader who refuses to lead in singing, to the custodian who refuses to lead the minister to the pulpit, to the usher who refuses to serve, to the one who refuses to collect the offerings. Wherever disobedience has gained power, obedience will resist her to her face. And we do not fear for a moment the confrontation that may result. We even wish to bless this confrontation, if only it is a work from the Lord and not the wild sport of fanatic arrogance. If the motivation comes from the outpouring of a soul that is cast down in conviction of guilt and that has struggled with one's God in dust and ashes, then even the withdrawal of salaries by the church wardens must be applauded. But also, if there is no sense of guilt and the zeal is mere self-elevating Pharisaism, then woe to the slightest attempt at restoring faithfulness, because then it is not pleasing to the Lord, but stands condemned before him.

REFORMATION THROUGH A BREAK WITH THE EXISTING CHURCH FEDERATION §57

Our fathers, who in the sixteenth century undertook the reformation of the churches of Amsterdam, Rotterdam, Utrecht, and so on, did not break with *their church*, that is, with the church of their city or even with their parish. They broke with the *organization* of their local church and also with the *federation* in which their church stood with other churches, but their church *as a church* remained intact. After the reformation it was the same as before, and no new church was established alongside or over against the existing church. All that happened was that the existing church purged itself of abuses in its confession, worship, and organization.

This shows that a new reformation today, in order to be similar to the reformation of the sixteenth century, should change the *organization*, and likewise would break with the *federation*, but the *body of the church* itself should remain untouched. "A different garment, but the same body!" was the motto of that time. This already demonstrates the great importance of the second category that we must discuss in this section: the reformation through a break *with the church federation*.

This kind of reformation has a sharply delineated character. As we pointed out more generally in the second part, regarding the formation of churches, the church of Jesus is one everywhere on earth and even in all places of the blessed empire. One is the head of us all, and thus we are one body under him who bought us with the price of his blood. But as the one light of the same sun shines into the various rooms of the house through different windows and is separated by walls, without ceasing for a moment to be the same light of the same sun—in basement and attic, in front and back, in the front room and the bedroom—so it is with the light rays of Jesus' life in his churches on earth. All those churches together form a house, but in that single house there are many individual rooms, separated by walls, and in those separate rooms shines the light, not from some light source hidden in the center of the house, but directly from the sun, through skylight and window. Thus it is a single organized life of Christ, just as the one light of the sun is the same around the whole earth and in the sky is a single light. On earth it is one house, one church, in which the individual churches are merely the rooms or chambers, which are naturally connected to one another through doors. But the light that shines into all of them comes from outside, and makes every room into a unique room, with its unique light and its unique life.

This is the compelling reason why a local church may never be viewed as a part, a section, or component of a national church. This robs it of its glory as a church. It is part, section, component, or rather, to speak organically, it is a member or cell of the one indivisible church of Christ; as such it receives its light, its love, its life directly from him. Therefore it would remain a church even if all other local churches to which it is connected were to fall away. It does not exist because the national church exists, but simply because the life of Christ is manifest in it. Therefore, one may say that it is part of the universal, catholic, holy church on earth, but never that it is a component or section of any church group on earth. After all, it did not come into existence because the group existed, but conversely, that group came into existence because the churches of Amsterdam, Rotterdam, Utrecht, and so on, first existed independently of each other, and then entered into a federation and covenant with each other. This is not to say that this federation and covenant is unnecessary; good churches, driven by life and love will naturally do this. But the existence of the church always precedes the existence of the church federation, and the federation is born out of the churches. The opposite happens only as a rare exception!

Meanwhile, after some time and because of changing circumstances, this church federation that was established by the churches and for the benefit of the churches can become an impediment or even an obstruction to the spiritual growth of the churches and to its increase in godliness and sanctification. If the entire federation, after the spiritual deterioration of nearly all of its churches, has gradually degenerated into a withered and dead assortment of churches that are merely formally connected, then any spiritual awakening and any attempt at renewal in one or more of these churches is bound to encounter the contrary spirit that has crept into the federation. Such a church federation *binds* its member churches. Churches living in such a federation are no longer free in their movements. They live under common rules, and are subject to the power of communally conditioned assemblies in classis and synod. Through these common rules the door of one church is opened for the members of the other churches. Because of the mutual influence they exert, their church government is regulated through one common church order, and changing that church order is not the right of an individual church, but of all the churches jointly.

This has three implications. First, in the spiritual deterioration of the churches that live in federation and covenant, it is inevitable that any unspiritual influence will gradually creep into their church order and regulations, so that eventually the church government will oppose the Word of the Lord instead of serving it. Second, in this spiritual deterioration the churches lose their natural unity of a common confession, and are therefore naturally compelled to regain this unity through a tightening of the regulatory bonds, so that as God's Word recedes into the background, the authority of human ordinances will receive more emphasis. Third, when through this spiritual deterioration of the churches the regulations of their federation have been brought into conflict with God's Word and the authority of human ordinances is considered sacred, any church that desires to return from that apostasy to God's Word will be obstructed by ordinances in the corrupted church order that oppose God's Word, and by the imagined superiority of the human authority that holds on to that church order.

Now this situation develops very gradually. If through God's good favor in any church there is a renewed awakening of desire and motivation to live according to God's Word, then this motivation will manifest itself first within a small group, but soon it will seek to spread from that small group to the body of the church in its organization. Thus reaching the group of spiritual office-bearers, this motivation will naturally manifest itself within the consistory, and there it will raise the all-decisive question whether the consistory is willing to reestablish the honor of God's holy name in the congregation entrusted to them, or else oppose the spiritual awakening of the church. Neutrality is impossible here. A consistory chooses either for those who sense this motivation, or against them. The escape route, that every preacher on his own should continue proclaiming the Word, is absolutely useless. The Lord did not install individual preachers but an office. This office causes all preachers to be in a mutual fellowship in which they are responsible for one another. On their part, therefore, they will either organize the entire church according to the Word of God, or participate in their church's stubborn rejection of God's Word. The choice may be painful, but one cannot escape it.

Now there are two possibilities. If the church chooses against such spiritual awakening and maintains, for the sake of the federation, the human ordinances contrary to the Word of God, then this will result in a battle of the church federation against the spiritually awakened part of the church, in which the unfaithful consistory serves as a minion and agent of unholy church government against those who are zealous for the Word of God. Or else the consistory chooses for the Word of the Lord and acknowledges its obligation to return to the obedience to that Word, but it will be in great danger of being called to account by the hostile federation of churches.

These two different situations must be distinguished carefully. There can be a conflict between a few individuals and the church federation, in which the consistory acts as the agent and minion of the federation. But one can also imagine a very different conflict, not involving a few individuals but the consistory itself, as soon as it leads its church in opposition against the church federation. We will discuss both of these separately.

The individuals who enter into a conflict with the federation may be either ordinary members of the church or individuals who have any office or any ministry in the church. Ordinary members can enter into such a conflict in two ways: either because they act contrary to any regulation imposed on the churches by that federation, or because upon appeal the federation has judged that they are wrong.

In the former situation, if a church member is now classified as "violating ecclesiastical ordinances," then the federation may either decide to overlook this "irregularity" and let it run its course, or require that the "violator" cease his illegitimate activity. If this person complies, then of course the matter is finished. But if, in obedience to God's Word, he deems that he may not surrender and continues on the path he has taken, then the church federation will impose disciplinary measures on him and try to force him into submission. The means available to the federation to this end are: (1) declaring him unavailable for election to ecclesiastical offices and jobs; (2) denying him the sacraments; (3) suspending him as a member; and finally, (4) excommunication.

The "violator," convinced that he may not comply, will quietly continue, endure one form of discipline after another, and if he is denied the sacraments, for example, he will partake of them anyway. The consistory is now compelled to choose either to help discipline the "violator," or else, shrinking from this, to refuse implementing the imposed punishment. If the latter happens, then the conflict shifts from the individuals to the consistory, as we will discuss below. But if the consistory chooses the former and helps in the discipline of the "violator" of ecclesiastical ordinances by denying him the means of grace, then the conflict reaches its climax between the wrongfully condemned individual and the church federation that tries to compel him.

Now in such a situation it would be irresponsible for this person to submit. That would be to forsake his prior faithfulness. There is nothing left for him but to participate in the sacraments anyway, and if they are kept from him by force, to establish his own administration of the means of grace together with likeminded people, or in case there are no such people, to find elsewhere in a different church what his own church is withholding from him.

If this results in his excommunication, this is by no means reason for him to consider himself to be cut off from the church, but he will be obligated to proceed to new organization within his church, and without external display, to do his work in the fear of God, so that he may obtain once again for himself and his family and those of like mind the pure administration of the means of grace.

In the second situation, where the individual is in conflict with the federation through a verdict against an appeal, there are two possibilities. Either the individual himself filed an appeal against a decision of his consistory, or his consistory agreed with him but someone else appealed against the decision of the consistory. These two are really the same, and the conflict will soon proceed along the same lines as the conflict discussed above. He will either submit to the decision, and there is no longer a conflict; or he will not be able to submit, and then the federation must let the matter run its course or ultimately excommunicate him, which results in the same obligation for this person as discussed above.

Thus, a conflict between ordinary church members and the federation will always raise the issue of breaking with the church as such; therefore we will postpone further discussion of this kind of conflict to the next section.

What remains, before we address the conflicts between consistory and federation, is the essentially different conflict with the federation when the opposition does not come from ordinary church members but from persons in ecclesiastical offices or positions. Usually this type of conflict takes a more serious course. After all, ordinary members are less dangerous, but also less receptive to ecclesiastical discipline. Excommunication of ordinary members is extremely rare. A sense of shame and helplessness generally restrains church leaders from enforcing spiritual punishment or executing a sentence of banishment against someone whose only accusation is that he is zealous for the honor of his God. But the matter is very different if the "violator" is an office-bearer or ecclesiastical employee. In that case, his influence is much more threatening, and much more powerful means are available to make an impression on him. He who has an office can be suspended or deposed from that office. The same holds true for church employees that are not office-bearers. A church leader who does not want to be involved with ungodliness can become a serious problem for the federation, but the federation is also able to take away the membership of that church leader. A custodian, song leader, or organist who is unwilling slavishly to cooperate can be punished through his employment. The same can be done with "stubborn" religion teachers. As for the offices, what is easier for the church's leadership than removing a deacon or elder who dares to test the ecclesiastical ordinances on the basis of God's Word?

But we must especially bring out the great importance of a conflict between the church federation and a teacher. This is where this series of conflicts naturally reaches its climax—on the one hand, because of a teacher's powerful influence, and since his activities are public; but on the other hand, also because the federation can directly affect him, and can depose him from his office and employment, and even rob him of his home and possessions and money. It is no wonder, then, that nearly every thorough reformation was born out of this type of conflict, and it is obvious why especially here the greatest moral strength manifested itself.

An ordinary church member can allow himself to be excommunicated without having wrestled with his God, and perhaps even out of wicked arrogance. After his excommunication he remains who he was before. Especially nowadays the misery that comes over him means almost nothing. For a church governor or a custodian, an elder or deacon, to be deposed is certainly highly unpleasant, but all in all it does not make him unhappy. A church leader loses some financial influence. A custodian loses a very small part of his income. An elder or deacon returns to his normal life without having lost anything that the world considers desirable. But the situation of a preacher is entirely different. For a minister of the Word, deposition is nothing less than cutting off his position in life, taking away his employment, taking away his entire existence; and that is combined with the dilemma either to be unfaithfully silent or to keep teaching, thereby continuing the conflict on a new road of suffering. Think, for instance, of Kohlbrugge, and what walking that entire road of suffering cost him![52]

---

52. Hermann F. Kohlbrugge (1803-75), a Lutheran theologian in Amsterdam, was deposed from ecclesiastical office when he accused another preacher of Modernist teaching. He eventually embraced Reformed doctrine and preached in Reformed churches in Germany.

Because of this, we say that far more grace is required for a minister to remain faithful in such a conflict than for an ordinary member or elder. In the teacher the moral triumph over flesh and sin must shine so much more powerfully; his willingness to serve his Lord, so much more invincibly; his desire to obey, so much more strongly; his readiness to sacrifice, so much more radiantly. Ordinary members and elders who so quickly complain about the unfaithfulness of our teachers should therefore ask themselves if they would be equally faithful if their entire position in life was at stake, including the food of their wives and children.

On the other hand, however, there must be zeal in prayer, that God may be pleased to pour out this abundant grace into the heart of many ministers of the Word, to break the temptation in them of many false arguments with which they constrain their souls, and thus to grant those natural leaders to the churches of Christ for their reformation. Without such leadership and cooperation, the reformation of a church has seldom succeeded. And if that prayer were to be answered, then this exceptional moral courage and strength of faith that developed in the ministers would endow their words with such fire, and their actions with such power, that the opposition within the church federation would have to yield. Only through the spiritual awakening of the ministers of the Word can a church be rescued; but just as truly, only through the passivity of its teachers can a hostile church federation remain powerful.

The consequences of a conflict between the teachers and their federation are always serious. It may be serious in a grievous way if the minister of the Word, after a moment of zeal, gives up and abandons the work of God that he had taken upon himself. Or it may be serious in its immediate consequences. A teacher who is suspended must, in such a case, continue to preach in the church, or if this is impossible, then outside the church; and if he is deposed, he should immediately gather the faithful around him and preach the Word, if necessary in a barn or warehouse, from the deck of a ship, or in the open field. When this stage has been reached, the conflict can easily lead to a break with the church itself. Just as in the case of the conflict between ordinary members and the church federation, we must postpone our discussion of this for the next section.

~~~~~~~~~~~~~~~~~~~~~~~~

We arrive, then, at the second category that we outlined for conflicts with the church federation: conflicts that are not initiated by individuals (either ordinary members or office-bearers) but by the attitude *of the consistory*. Obviously, these conflicts are of a very different nature insofar as they instigate a battle not between individuals and the church federation, but between the federation and a whole church as an organized body.

Such a conflict can arise in three different ways. First of all, it may be that an individual (a regular member or an office-bearer) has been condemned by the church federation, but the consistory does not feel at liberty before God to help in the execution of this verdict. Then the consistory stands up for the condemned individual and, if it persists in doing this, will share in his fate. Second, it may happen that the consistory feels unable to implement a regulation or change in the church order adopted by the federation. Third, it is possible that the consistory, seeing no benefit but rather spiritual damage for their church in maintaining fellowship, discontinues its correspondence and introduces a new church order, intent on the formation of a new federation.

But within a short distance from their point of origin, these three paths merge into two. Whether the consistory, while maintaining the church order and remaining in the federation, comes into conflict through the opposition of church members or through its own opposition, makes no real difference for the further development of the conflict. Without danger of confusion we may therefore conclude that the consistory can enter the conflict in two ways: either under the existing church order, or by setting aside the current church order. We uphold *both* cases.

We are well aware that important men have defended the theory that insists that as long as you remain under an existing church order, you are bound to comply with it, but we oppose this false theory with strong conviction. The rule that no obedience to people, under any circumstances, can or may go beyond that what is compatible with full obedience to God's Word, is one that holds true not only for state, society, school, and family, but also—and even more so—for the church. A child stands under a family order, but if the father or mother or nanny were to command anything that would lead to disobedience of God's Word, then the child may not obey. The same is true of domestic servants in relationship to their mistresses, of pupils to their teachers, of workers to their bosses, of soldiers to their commanders, of citizens to their king, and therefore also, more so in fact, of the consistory in relationship to the federation.

To pretend that the promise of faithfulness or oath that has been pledged would rob this rule of its power, is absurd. The Theban legion also swore an oath of allegiance to the emperor, yet it refused to participate in the idolatrous sacrificial rite. After retreating to Geneva, it allowed itself to be decimated twice and then to be slaughtered like sheep rather than obey the instruction of their commander.[53]

Even though the church order has not yet been changed, and even though the church still lives in the federation, the consistory still may never do anything in submission to that federation or in compliance with that church order if they know it is not good, not honest, and not responsible before the Lord God. The all-decisive reason is that any required obedience, promised allegiance, or submission to human commandments, is always and everywhere and in all circumstance limited by the all-surpassing condition that never needs to be specified because it always speaks for itself: *insofar as it does not injure obedience toward God.*

The consequences resulting from a conflict like this are many, depending on the constitution of the consistory, the attitude of the instruments of the church federation, the political and legal position of the church, the bond between the church leaders and the consistory, and also on whether the church in its entirety or majority supports or opposes the consistory. If the church's political and legal relationship is free from any partiality on the part of administrative bodies and judges; if the church's leadership faithfully supports the consistory; if the consistory has no reason to fear alliances between its own members or fellow church members and the opponents—then such a conflict results in little risk, and the federation usually ends up surrendering, especially if the lower bodies of the church federation (for example, the classes) refuse to execute its orders.

But it cannot be denied that the situation is seldom this favorable. In many consistories, only a minority, usually led by ministers, will choose the side of the federation against faithfulness to God's Word. In nearly all congregations, a fraction of the church members will allow themselves to be used to oppose the consistory. In the vast majority of cases, the classical leaders will consent to serving as policemen. In very many cases, the church's leaders will hand over the buildings, possessions and the like to the leaders of the federation. Depending on whether the government officials who serve the king favor the spirit of the church federation, they

---

53. Kuyper refers here to the account of the Theban Legion, or the Martyrs of Agaunum, a legion of Roman soldiers who converted to Christianity and refused to participate in sacrifices to the emperor Maximian. They were then massacred in AD 286 in Agaunum (modern-day Saint-Maurice, Switzerland).

either will let the situation run its course or they will act to prevent it. And finally, to the degree that historical research in the prominent juridical circles has resulted in better knowledge of ecclesiastical-legal issues, or the lack of such research still compels adherence to conventional insights, the decision of the highest judicial power will either sustain the original right of the churches, or violate that right, perhaps forever.

The matter will develop in a parallel manner if the conflict has arisen not under the existing church order, but because of setting aside that church order—and more so, because for consistories that entered the conflict while still under the church order it is advisable to immediately break with the church order as soon as this conflict threatens to escalate.

Now this setting aside of the church order can also occur without a specific occasion. As soon as within a church of God there grows a sincere awareness of guilt with respect to the unacceptable and God-condemned state of the church, and this awareness reaches the consciences of the office-bearers and is brought by them into the consistory, then such a consistory would have to consider whether the existing church order allows reformation according to God's Word. And if not, it must consider whether it is possible at least to change that church order in order to remove the obstacles that would prevent reformation. And if that also turns out to be impossible, it would have to consider whether one can expect that the churches that wish to proceed with reformation will not be opposed.

If one can have at least that expectation, it would still be quite unnecessary to change the church order. But if, on the contrary, the consistory is certain that the existing church federation would oppose the necessary reformation, that the federated churches are not ready or willing to alter that church order, and that the organs of the federation would not allow the reforming church to proceed—certainly in that case there is not the slightest doubt that this consistory is bound to temporarily sever the bonds with the churches of the federation and to introduce a better church order on the basis of the historic confession.

If such a consistory can do this together with other consistories, so that they immediately enter into a new federation, so much the better. But even if this is not possible, and the choice must be made between going it alone or abandoning the reformation, their clear duty is to act entirely on their own. The consistory has the right to do this on two grounds. First, there is an obligation resting on it to keep the church entrusted to it close to the Word of God. And second, there is the fact that every church that entered into the federation retained the right to relinquish that bond, because no church ever had, or could have, the power to sell herself as a slave. Even if a consistory had entered into a contract to bind its church forever, even though that bond would cause it to go whoring away from the living God, then such a contract would be null and void because any immoral contract is declared illegitimate even in civil law.

Meanwhile, when proceeding in this manner, a consistory should pay careful attention to four concerns.

(1) The motivation and compulsion to this step may not originate in Pharisaical arrogance, belligerent discontentment, or from superficial views of the church, but it must be rooted in the obligation of the soul to submit to God's Word. Any motivation that is not rooted in obedience to God's Word is revolutionary arrogance and must be opposed.

(2) The consistory must be careful to lay the foundation for the new domicile correctly: it should not break with history but retain the historic confession of the church as its basis, and also codify the new church order in such a way that it does justice to the principles of God's Word, that it introduces no new tyranny, and that the way to a new church federation is not only left open but even included within its structure.

(3) The consistory must proceed with prudence—innocent as doves, yet also as wise as the serpent, as Jesus commanded us [Matt 10:16]. Thus, if there are three or four ways in which to approach the matter, the consistory must avoid the accusation that through inconsiderate and unwise planning it had carelessly endangered the affairs of the church, and even its future existence.

To mention an example: if the relationship with the church leaders is less than optimal, and one is able first to improve this relationship, then it would be reckless to neglect this option. Especially in the case of such an important work, one may not omit any good, effective preparation. If a conflict arises in connection with a particular matter, then one cannot choose the timing. Rather, the One who has confronted us with that occasion has chosen the time for us. But if, as in the case of the introduction of a new church order, one is able to choose the time, then that choice of a suitable time must be considered seriously. A consistory that prepares for such a holy work may not act too hastily, or without clear awareness of what it is doing.

(4) The consistory should manifest that moral solemnity also in impressing upon the congregation that a holy work is being undertaken for the congregation's own salvation. The consistory will show this by *not* reaching such decisions if there is only a slight majority—thereby avoiding the risk that the decision, before its implementation, turns into its opposite.

Therefore the consistory should not merely react against the false and corrupted church federation, but at the same time apply censure within the congregation, sending forth the power of the love that saves as well as of the love that punishes, acting not only against false doctrine but also against the desecration that flows from a careless walk of life. And the sermons of the teachers must no less untiringly serve to inform the congregation in this matter, binding the reformation of heart and home upon the listeners' souls. Finally, the consistory must inform the congregation about what is happening, either in specific meetings or through letters, allowing it to follow along in the battle that is fought for the honor of God and his Word.

In short, just as you would not have a beloved room in your house renovated with loud shouting but rather with quiet prayers and holy earnestness, so it should be done in this renovation of your church. Let there be *prayer*. Let there be clear awareness of the *danger* that may threaten. Let there be the conviction that nonetheless it *must* be done. And in all that, in order that it be a true and upright work for Almighty God, let there be heavy hearts and contrite spirits.

Then if some traitors come forth out of the bosom of the consistory; if the consistory is denied by some of the straying church members; if the higher authorities fall upon them; if the church leaders oppose them, and the state government hinders them; and if finally the judge declares that they are wrong—then all of that must be borne, endured, and wrestled with in the name of the Lord. When the Roman emperor locked the entire church of Nicomedia inside its church building and burned it, that church's endurance and suffering were ever so much more terrible than in our case, and yet the church of God triumphed over that powerful emperor.[54]

§ 58   REFORMATION THROUGH A BREAK WITH THE EXISTING CHURCH

The calling of God's child to break with the existing organization of his church is serious enough. This calling becomes still more serious if it involves the federation in which the church was related to other churches. Yet incomparably more serious is the calling of the Christian when it comes to a break with the church itself.

One should realize that both in the break with the organization and in the break with the church federation, the believer has never faced the question whether the once true church might have quietly changed into the false church. He saw that the governing regulations of his church were not what was required by God's Word; that its lifestyle was not according to the standard of God's sanctuary; even that the federation with other churches had become unholy; yet the church itself still remained the church of Christ. He never thought of leaving it.

But in the third chapter, on the deformation of the church, we noted that the corruption in Jesus' church could proceed to the most extreme desecration. A church that once was a church of Jesus can degenerate into a church of the Antichrist, and therefore continue as a false church, under false pretenses. The possibility of this is clear from Jesus' own word, when he says that the synagogue of the Jews after his death on the cross has degenerated into the synagogue of Satan. This is what the Lord wrote to the church of Philadelphia: "*Behold, I will make those of the synagogue of Satan who say that they are Jews and are not, but lie ...*" [Rev 3:9].

At first, Jesus definitely acknowledged the synagogue of the Jews as a synagogue of Yahweh. Otherwise he would not have entered into its prayer rooms, and he certainly would not have led his disciples there. Especially since we know that Jesus himself participated in the service in these synagogues, it is certain that Jesus initially recognized these synagogues as the true church of God. But behold, through and after his crucifixion, this changed. The synagogues stood under the Sanhedrin, and did not oppose that Sanhedrin—not even when the Sanhedrin broke forever

---

54. Kuyper refers to an event during the persecution of the church under Emperor Diocletian in the early fourth century. The Diocletianic or Great Persecution, conducted under a number of emperors, would last for about ten years, from AD 303 to 313.

with the church of God by condemning to death the Son of God as a blasphemer of God. The synagogue either had to keep its hands off Christ or choke him, and it did the latter. When the Sanhedrin had condemned him, and the priests had incited the people, and the men among that people had cried, "Crucify, crucify him!" and the women had called, "His blood be on us!"—at that point the grieved Spirit of God abandoned the churches of these synagogues, and allowed the spirit of Satan to invade them. Thus the church of the Jews became a synagogue of Satan, or what we would call a false church.

This shows that a church in which we were born, where we at one point found salvation, and where we often received the seals of the covenant, can degenerate into a false church. And this terrible truth gives the children of God the obligation, when the churches have fallen deeply, to investigate prayerfully, incisively, and most accurately, whether the church in which they are living is still the true church of Christ, or perhaps has changed into the form of the synagogue of Satan. This task is extremely painful, because so much is at stake. If that true church still *does* exist, a Christian *must* not separate from it. But also, if it has become a synagogue *of Satan*, then he *must* no longer remain joined to it. Then he must leave.

Thus it is clear that the question whether to separate or to stay is not at all up for discussion, such that one could argue for or against it, or express one's approval or disapproval on a whim. On the contrary, in times of church decay every child of God has to face this most serious question in the depth of his soul, and must be careful that in his response to it, he would be found faithful before his God. For it would be terrible if we with our children continue to live in a church, of which the Lord Jesus testified to his apostle: "These are a church of Satan; they say they are Reformed and are not, but they lie!" But it would also be terrible if we would leave or separate ourselves from a church that was still a manifestation of Jesus' body, and thus condemn as a synagogue of Satan that which was still an instrument of the Holy Spirit. Both sins would be equally serious, and therefore one cannot impress too urgently upon the hearts of God's people that through prayer and supplication they must seek illumination from the Only Wise God, to be kept from this error and remain free from this false choice.

To us, at least, few things appear so questionable as the external, flippant, and thoughtless way in which many children of God rush past this sensitive and serious issue. Just as there are, sadly, many who still believe in three states of the soul, likewise many still believe in good faith that there are three possible states of the church. Concerning the soul they believe that the soul can be dead, or alive, or still seeking; and likewise, they imagine that a church is either true, or false, or something between true and false. Yet all educated believers know better concerning the soul. For them it is clear, on the basis of God's Word, that every soul that is not wholly dead is alive, and that every soul that is not yet alive is completely dead. And thus those apparently seeking are actually completely dead, but also, true seekers have already been transformed from death into life.

And the same is true for the churches of our Lord. That which is *not yet* false, still *is* the true church; and that which is *no longer* the true church, *is* entirely the false church. There is no intermediate state; for the churches on earth there is no purgatory. Every church is either still the true church, or already the false church. To imagine a mixture of true and false is absurd.

But at the same time this condemns the rash attitude of many who deem that they *could* leave, but instead stay a little longer; or who think that they *could* have stayed but left, and yet even after their departure continue to support the church they left as a "still halfway true" church. It is one or the other: either you see, sense, and know that your church *has* become a synagogue of Satan, and then you must immediately leave and shake the dust from your feet against her; or you see, sense, and know that she has *not yet* become a synagogue of Satan, and then you *may* not give her the bill of divorce, but on the contrary, it is your duty to stay.

This makes it very important for the children of God to be educated well concerning the marks by which they can discern what is still the true church and what has already become the synagogue of Satan. For this reason, in the next section we will attempt humbly to shed some light on this question for our brothers and sisters. But we postpone that question for now, and continue in this section with the scenario in which a child of God is a member of a church that has actually become a *false church*; we investigate further how he must proceed with his work of reformation.

We wrote deliberately: how he must proceed with his *work of reformation*, and not *how he must walk away from it*. The latter would be an unspiritual interpretation of the matter. Not because it would be impossible in *the end* simply to leave that false church on his own, but because he would incur great guilt if he began with this, and he would show great lack of love if he asked the question in this way. To say "I am walking away," is selfish and egotistic. Then one is caring only for himself, and expresses a lack of concern for his brothers as well as the church. Or worse, because of one's lack of love for the brothers and for the church, he is in danger of lacking the proper love for himself.

This is brought out best if we sketch the correct way for a child of God to act under such circumstances. If the focus of a godly person is the reformation of the church, and not the wish to possess for himself a desired church, then such a child of God will begin his activity in the church by feeling sadness toward God about the grievous state to which his church has descended. That grievous state of his church will weigh on his soul as a judgment of God. He will sorrow for it for the sake of the name of the Lord, yet he will not complain or murmur, but confess that the Lord God is righteous in his judgment; the people of the Lord deserved this judgment threefold because of their faithless deeds. He will not do this by means of logical reasoning, thinking that the people of God is guilty, he belongs to the people, and therefore that guilt also rests on him—no, but in the spiritual way of conviction of sin. His own person will hinder him, and his own unbelief, lack of love, and coldness toward heaven are pressing upon his soul so much that he deems the Lord's judgment to be just, even if in the entire nation there were found no other occasion *than his own sin.*

Here, too, the spiritual starting point must be his personal dismay of soul over his own sin, as well as grief over the guilt of God's people. This sadness of heart will naturally lead to an inflow of greater grace and result in spiritual awakening, since God "gives grace to the humble" [Jas 4:6]. And thus the reformation of the church will begin where it must always begin—that is, with the reformation of one's own heart and the reformation of one's own life, and with a renewed conversion to the living God. We thus receive for ourselves and others, through covenant renewal with the God of our faith, the proof that our thirst for church reformation does not originate in the sense that we are better than others. On the contrary, it originates from the deep conviction that especially our own guilt has also incurred God's judgment.

From there, such a reformation then proceeds to one's own church. "As for me and my house, we will serve the LORD!" [Josh 24:15]. And just as the ripples on the water's surface expand outward, that reforming movement will automatically spread out to the even wider circle of the communal church.

As far as that person is concerned, he will not rebuke that church in arrogance, but admonish and plead with fervent gravity, as if God were pleading through him: "Be reconciled to God!" [2 Cor 5:20]. If the Lord granted him the gift to do so, then he will personally present the items to his consistory in which the love for God's name must become known. He himself will refuse, not out of arrogance but in quiet submission to the Word of God, to do what is not good before God; he will do what must be done according to God's Word, even though they try to stop him. If this brings him shame, if this affords him suffering, then he will gladly bear that shame, rejoicing that he was counted worthy to suffer dishonor for the name [see Acts 5:41]. When it finally comes to the point where he can no longer find the ministry of the means of grace for him and his family in the public worship of his church, then he will consider whether the illness of the church is perhaps only a temporal faintness, and he will actively try to restore it back to health as an aggrieved church.

And only when all these means have been exhausted, and every attempt at gradual reformation simply seems to bring out more and clearer hatred against God's name and his Word, then he himself will answer the question (or the Lord God might perhaps give him the light to see with certainty) whether his church has perhaps already become a synagogue of Satan. Then, if along the way of repentance and personal conversion rather than that of rhetoric and reasoning, he must sadly answer that question with a terrible "yes," then—it goes without saying—he must immediately grant her a certificate of divorce; then the break has been decided.

But his own departure does not end his task of reformation. A person who himself has been rescued after a shipwreck, but who does not care about his fellow passengers, would be guilty of callousness. And not callousness but tender love with heartfelt compassion is the characteristic of the One in whose likeness we must be renewed. To leave a church, therefore, brings with it the duty of moving your brothers and sisters to leave as well. Through the flames a firefighter sometimes rescues a child or woman unknown to him. That, children of the Lord, is the convicting example that depicts your sacred calling.

But even this is not the end of the task of reformation. True enough, the church in which you were born and baptized has, in your firm opinion, indeed become a synagogue of Satan; but where is the true church? You may not remain on your own. Unless it becomes evident that no church of Christ can manifest itself in your town, you must seek that church; and if it is not there, you must try with God's help to bring it to manifestation.

This has three possible consequences. Either you find in your hometown another church, which does not merely simulate the marks of the true church but truly manifests them in its life; then it would be your calling to beg the brothers and sisters in that church to receive you and your house into their fellowship after public confession of your faith. Or you do not find such a church in your hometown, whereupon it would be your task, together with others of equally strong conviction, to establish the church of God in your hometown on the basis of your common confession. Or finally, if this turns out to be impossible, you must look for opportunities to move elsewhere, to a town where the church of Christ exists. And if all three of these fail, so that you must stay where you are and are forced to live without a church, then it would be your calling to manifest your own home church more powerfully, and humbly pray to God that eventually he may grant to you again the ministry of the means of grace.

Now compare this way of the godly with the crooked path of superficial people, and see how great the divide is between them. You hear these people complain in loud voices about the abuses in the erring church, but they fail to recognize a judgment of God, and do not try to appease God's smiting hand. Without any sadness of soul or awareness of their own guilt, this zeal rather takes the character of an arrogant meddling, and remains far from repentance and conversion. There is no spiritual discernment, but a spiritual judgmentalism. Moved not by the soul's urging nor with a bleeding heart, but in agitation, in brazenness and overreaction, they sever the bond with their former church almost without prayer or earnestness, with a cold citation from Scripture, and they transfer to a new church with incomprehensible ease. The clothes had become too soiled; well, then, they take it off and quickly change clothes.

We are not saying this to pass judgment on someone's transition. Only the Knower of hearts judges, and even the best should rather condemn himself for his own work of reformation than others. He who puts his hand in his own cloak has enough of his own leprosy. But what had to be pointed out here is the twofold motivation for departure; one of them is laudable and precious, while the other is to be rejected.

In this section we must yet discuss the special cases that can lead to the severance of the bond between our church and ourselves. Four cases must be mentioned.

(1) The case in which not an ordinary church member but a minister of the Word feels compelled to reject his church as a false church. In this instance, such conviction results into two special obligations: first, the obligation to warn the faithful from the pulpit and to take them along; and second, the obligation to seek the ministry of the Word elsewhere in a true church, or to bring into existence a new church in his own locale. He may not bury his talent; his ordination remains unaffected, even though the church that ordained him has changed into a false synagogue of Satan.

(2) The case in which not a brother but a *sister* deems that she must leave her church because it has become a synagogue of Satan. Then her special position as a woman implies that she may not act publicly, she must limit herself to private admonition, and she herself must leave the church.

(3) The case in which the church membership of a person is revoked. It is possible, for instance, that the synod of a Reformed church, today or in the future, makes the final decision to cut me off and revoke my church membership, but that would not at all imply that the church of Amsterdam, where I live and where I belong as a member, has become a synagogue of Satan. The fact that an instrument of the church federation casts me out does not imply that the church in which I live has become a synagogue of Satan.

It is very important to consider this well. Nothing incites one more easily to an incorrect judgment of the state of our churches than one's own excommunication. In that situation it is almost impossible not to imagine that the church that excommunicated me must be a synagogue of Satan. And yet, it does not become a synagogue of Satan because it casts *us* out, but only because it casts *Christ* out. Now it may be true that the rejection of a minister of the Lord or the excommunication of an elect believer *can* be a casting out of Christ, but this is not absolutely certain. This is especially so because the consistory of our church can remain outside the issue, so that only the church federation has active guilt.

Therefore it seems to us that this member who is excommunicated by a higher governing body must (1) wait to see if his own consistory willingly implements that sentence; if not, if they permit him the enjoyment of the ministry of the means of grace, not removing his name from the membership roll or publicly denouncing him, he can continue quietly as if there had been no excommunication; (2) if his consistory implements his sentence, then he must gather likeminded people to establish an aggrieved church together with them; (3) and only when that is opposed, he may reject his church and begin a new church formation. The case of direct excommunication by the consistory is included in this.

(4) It may happen that the ecclesiastical government deposes the minister of the Word from his office and membership not because of misconduct, but because he is maintaining the Word of God. In that situation, too, it does not immediately follow that the church to which this minister of the Word belongs has become a synagogue of Satan. It is possible, after all, that a hostile church leadership passed this sentence without the consent of his own church. And even if his own church, caught in a misunderstanding of legitimacy or perhaps also fear, abandoned him, then this does not imply that his own church would have cast him out. It is possible that it has turned into a synagogue of Satan, but this is does not necessarily follow from his deposition.

Therefore, we believe that such a deposed preacher still must lead in the preaching of the Word, if possible in the church, but if not, then outside of it. And if the consistory would stay away from this service, he should establish an aggrieved church. And if that too is rendered impossible, he should find a ministry of the Word elsewhere, or lead the faithful out of the church to form a new church.

THE DISTINCTION BETWEEN THE TRUE AND FALSE CHURCH   § 59

But in order for the believer to have a firm criterion to decide when his church ceases to be a true church and when it becomes a false church, we must elaborate on the marks of the true and false church.

In the theological and ecclesiastical battle that our fathers fought with Rome in the sixteenth century, Rome listed fifteen marks of the true church, which our Reformed teachers dismissed for several reasons. On their part they made an attempt to define more correct marks instead. If we summarize the debates of that time, then it must be said that all Reformed theologians defined as a necessary mark the preaching of God's Word; most of them added as a second mark the administration of the sacraments; some also added the exercise of church discipline; and very few either replaced or augmented the latter with the features of Christian love, holy morals, and so on.

As you know, our Belgic Confession in Article 29 first states the three marks: (1) the preaching of the Word; (2) the administration of the sacraments; (3) the exercise of church discipline; and then summarizes these three in the general rule that one must join oneself to "the pure Word of God, rejecting all things contrary to it, acknowledging Jesus Christ as the only Head."

We must further remark that both our earliest theologians as well as this article of our Confession add to each of these three marks the requirement of purity. The preaching of the Word is not sufficient; it must be pure preaching of the gospel. Likewise, they require the pure administration of the sacraments. And the exercise of Christian discipline must be such that not only some, but all sins are punished.

Reading this, some brothers have decided that therefore every church must be viewed as fallen away from the true church if *anything* is lacking in their preaching, if *anything* is wrong with their administration of the sacraments, or if their church discipline had *softened*. This was the occasion for these brothers quickly to cancel their membership in this church and to establish a purer church, until that church also revealed her faults and sin, and they wrote her a certificate of divorce as well.

But it will not do to deal so superficially with such a profound issue. The generally known fact that someone like Johannes à Marck, followed by Bernhard de Moor, stated two other marks, namely, "purity in the foundations of doctrine and the holiness of life," should already be sufficient to keep us from such a rash judgment.[55] Wiser men, such as De Moor, [Francis] Turretin, and others, have always pointed out that not all of these three marks are equally indispensable, and that in the enforcement of these three marks some room must be left for gradual differences.[56]

On this basis we are taking the liberty of exploring this very important matter in somewhat greater detail than is commonly done. First of all, one must note that in establishing the marks of the true church, three directions can be taken. These directions could be designated as personal,

---

55. Johannes à Marck, *Compendium theologiae christianae didactico-elencticum* (Amsterdam: Wetstenios, 1722), 634. À Marck (1656–1731) and Bernard de Moor (1709–80) were Reformed theologians at Leiden University. One of de Moor's major works was a multi-volume commentary on à Marck's *Compendium theologiae*.
56. Francis Turretin (1623–87) was a leading Reformed pastor and professor in Geneva.

biblical, and ecclesiastical. We can be brief about the third, since that was represented by Rome, and the controversy with Rome plays no role in this essay. But we must briefly indicate the contrast between the biblical and the personal direction, which could also be distinguished as objective and subjective.

Throughout the centuries, part of Christianity has always emphasized that the mark of the true church should be sought in the subjective personal holiness of its members. Confessing very correctly that the church is the congregation of the elect, these brothers posited the understandable yet extremely dangerous requirement that these elect must therefore behave like children of God. This was the basis for their spurious opinion that the church must be judged in terms of the holiness of its members—holiness, that is, not in the external sense but in the spiritual sense.

Meanwhile, over against this subjective sentiment, the church of Christ has always maintained the view that the external church must not be judged according to the spiritual existence of its members, but only according to the external activity of the church as such. This insight naturally led to the following thesis: The identity of the church resides not in the holiness of its members, but in the character that it manifests as a church.

One should not condemn the first sentiment too harshly. A desire for holiness is created within God's child along with his new birth. To those who know God's secret fellowship, the worldliness into which the church continually sinks must be hurtful and cause them to look forward to the separation of the clean and the unclean, and to the end of evil. If these brothers had understood more profoundly the incredibly powerful essence of sin; if they had learned for themselves, in deep anguish of soul, how every snow-white flake of grace that lands in our soul becomes soiled through the corruption of our souls; then they would not have responded with the fanaticism of illusory purity, but with the gravity of urgent rebuke against these abominations. But living with a frame of mind that was too fanatical and too intense, the Donatists, the Catharists,[57] the Brownists, the Labadists,[58] and many others kept trying to sort out the contents of the fishing net before its time [Matt 13:47–50]. Invariably the

---

57. Catharism was a late medieval pure church movement. It was condemned for diverging from Christian orthodoxy.

58. Labadism was a French Protestant pietist movement founded by Jean de Labadie (1610–74). The group founded a separatist community in 1669.

sweet hope of their holy intention turned into bitter disappointment and took away from the freshness of their own faith.

And this was inevitable, because they erred in four respects. They forgot (1) that the reality of God's work in the soul cannot be judged externally; (2) that the dispensation in which we live until our death, in God's inscrutable sufferance, still includes the continual infiltration of sin into holy things; (3) that the elect can be in the church for a while before they are spiritually transformed from death to life; and (4) that people pass away and die, but the church remains.

For this reason, all of the Reformers, especially Calvin, have always opposed this Donatistic movement with full conviction. "In bearing with imperfections of life," says Calvin, "we ought to be far more considerate. For here the descent is very slippery and Satan ambushes us with no ordinary devices."[59]—"But, they cry out, it is intolerable that a plague of vices rages far and wide. Suppose the apostle's opinion here again answers them. Among the Corinthians no slight number had gone astray; in fact, almost the whole body was infected. There was not one kind of sin only, but very many; and they were no light errors but frightful misdeeds; there was corruption not only of morals but of doctrine. What does the holy apostle—the instrument of the Heavenly Spirit, by whose testimony the church stands or falls—do about this? Does he seek to separate himself from such? Does he cast them out of Christ's Kingdom? Does he fell them with the ultimate thunderbolt of anathema? He not only does nothing of the sort; he even recognizes and proclaims them to be the church of Christ and the communion of saints."[60]—"Christ himself, the apostles, and almost all the prophets have furnished us examples of this. Fearful are those descriptions with which Isaiah, Jeremiah, Joel, Habakkuk, and others bewail the afflictions of the Jerusalem church. In people, in magistracy, and in priesthood all things had been so far corrupted that Isaiah does not hesitate to liken Jerusalem to Sodom and Gomorrah."[61]—"Now what was the world like in the time of Christ and the apostles? Even then the desperate impiety of the Pharisees and the dissolute life which commonly prevailed could not prevent them from practicing the same rites along with the people, and from assembling in one temple with the rest for

---

59. *Note by the author: Inst.* 4.1.13.
60. *Note by the author: Inst.* 4.1.14.
61. *Note by the author: Inst.* 4.1.18.

public exercises of religion."[62]—"What about David? When he was chief administrator of justice, how wickedly did he open the way for his blind lust by the shedding of innocent blood! He had already been reborn, and among the reborn was adorned with the Lord's excellent praises. Still, he committed that crime (horrible even among the Gentiles) and yet received pardon."[63]

This has always been the judgment of our entire church. And because, as far as we know, no one in authority defends this Donatist sentiment today, we will move on from our discussion of this emphasis on the subjective or personal marks of the church. We direct the reader's attention to the second, the biblical or objective direction, which does not seek the marks of the true church in the personal condition of the members, but in the condition of the church itself.

This direction, defended by all our Reformers, by all Reformed confessions, and legitimately by virtually all of our good theologians, requires that there be in the church of Christ the purity of confession and purity of walk. Thus the heart is not judged; the state of the individuals is not involved. These individuals are considered only insofar as the work of the church is manifested in the appearance and activity of these individuals. Thus, the question is not whether each individual member makes a pure confession, but whether the church makes the good confession, and whether in its walk as a church, respect for God's Word is visible. But since this can be manifest only in its public actions, this automatically leads us to investigate first and foremost whether the preaching is truly the administration of the Word, whether the sacramental rituals can indeed be vehicles of the sacramental grace, and whether the church through exercise of discipline guards that preaching and that sacrament.

Many already let go of the discipline in this respect—not that they deny that the exercise of discipline belongs to the *essence*, but in the sense that it does not necessarily belong to the *well-being* of a church.[64]

---

62. *Note by the author*: Inst. 4.1.19.

63. *Note by the author*: Inst. 4.1.24.

64. *Note by the author*: Herman Witsius and Johannes van der Waeyen, *Ernstige betuiginge der Gereformeerde Kercke aen hare afdwalende kinderen, meest voorgestelt met de woorden van de outste en voornaemste leeraers, dienende tot wederlegginge van de gronden van sr. Jean de Labadie en de sijne* (Amsterdam: J. van Someren, 1679), 159–74; compare Bernhard de Moor, *Commentarius perpetuus in Johannis Marckii Compendium theologiae christianae didactico-elencticum*, 7 vols. (Leiden: J. Hasebroek & J. H. van Damme, 1771), 5:42.

They have to make this concession; otherwise the strict enforcement of this mark would undoubtedly have led the church back into the Donatist movement. Indeed, Calvin admits that the church is present only where the Word of God and the sacraments are visible.[65] And when we consult the experience of history, where throughout the eighteen centuries of the existence of Jesus' church under the new covenant, church discipline was enforced seriously only in the first two and in the sixteenth century at best, we naturally face the dilemma of either declaring that discipline is not indispensable for the essence of the church, or confessing that the true church of Christ was not found on the earth during fifteen of these eighteen centuries.

Let no one conclude that we consider the discipline of Jesus' church unnecessary. On the contrary, without discipline a church will be desecrated and perish. But if one believes and confesses that the church on earth has the purpose of being the instrument of the Holy Spirit, through which he regenerates the elect through the Word, then it follows directly that the essence of the church is already present, however imperfectly, wherever the Holy Spirit finds this instrument serviceable to the regeneration of the elect. And if it is established that the church can fulfill this ministry as long as the preaching of the Word is still found in it, and the sacrament still seals this Word, then it has been demonstrated from the root of the Reformed confession concerning the church, that the exercise of discipline cannot be an indispensable mark of the essence of the church. Just as a human organism stays alive even without arms and legs, but dies immediately without heart or head, so it is with the church of Jesus. No one considers it a matter of indifference if a person loses his arms and legs, and in the remaining torso one might barely recognize a person; likewise no one may think that a church can walk or work well if its discipline has been cut off. Similarly, just as the life, the essence, leaves a person only if the more vulnerable parts are fatally damaged, so too the essence of the church is lost only if the proclamation of the Word ceases, or the administration of the sacraments falls away.

Therefore our confession does not mean to say that every church that lacks one of the three marks in its full purity, has immediately become the false church, but merely this: that a church in which the three marks shine forth must certainly be acknowledged as the true church. There was

---

65. *Note by the author: Inst. 4.1.9.*

opposition in those days. On one side stood the Roman Catholic Church; next to it, the Anabaptist sect; and the churches of the Reformation took a position over against both. The latter churches at that time exhibited the three marks fully, and on that basis our churches asserted in their confession that they themselves were definitely and undoubtedly the true church of Christ.

That this is the intention of our Confession is convincingly shown at the end of Article 29. If the intention had been to say that a church is false if any of these three marks is lacking, then the false church would simply have been characterized as follows: *every church is false that lacks one of these marks*. But far from dealing with this matter so superficially, our fathers instead felt the obligation to describe the essence of the false church, not negatively but positively, as one that: ascribes more authority to its ordinances than to the Word of God; adds to and takes away from the sacraments; and ... *fails to discipline*? No, not that, but the false church "relies more upon men than upon Christ; and persecutes those who live holily."

Thus, if one does not look at the well-being but at the essence of the church, then the church may be called a false church only if it sets aside the Word, perverts the sacraments, and persecutes God's saints. Yet this too, according to the spirit and intention of Holy Scripture as our fathers understood it, may never be interpreted as if the preaching of the Word should be *perfectly* pure and the administration of the sacraments *perfectly* untainted, so that when these *perfect* qualities are lacking, the character of the church of Christ should be lost. In this respect, Turretin expresses the sentiment of our church most clearly when he says:

> Further we must observe about these marks: (1) That there are different degrees of necessity and some are more necessary than others. In the first degree of necessity is the pure preaching and profession of the word, since without it the church cannot exist. But the administration of the sacraments does not have an equal degree of necessity which so depends upon the former that it may nevertheless be wanting for a time (as was the case with the Israelite church in the desert, which was without circumcision). The same is the case with discipline, which pertains to the defense of the church, but which, being removed or corrupted, the church is not immediately taken away. (2) There is a certain latitude of these marks as they admit various degrees of purity—now more

perfect, then more imperfect, as they more or less approach to the rule of Scripture (hence they argue a church either purer or impurer). But not on this account is this latitude to be extended so far as that fundamental errors should be tolerated, but only faults and lighter errors. As therefore that society cannot retain the name of a true church which cherishes capital errors overturning the foundation of salvation, so it does not straightway lose the name of a true church which impinges anywhere upon doctrine. [...] (3) The church can be [...] in an impure and partly corrupt state. [...] (4) The opinion of the church is not to be estimated from the private opinions of rulers and bishops [...] Rather the opinion of the church is to be estimated from the doctrine and practice publicly received and retained.[66]

Calvin had the same sentiment. His statements are sometimes even more pointed. He recognizes a church of God wherever there still is preaching and the administration of the sacraments.

"However it may be, where the preaching of the gospel is reverently heard and the sacraments are not neglected, there for the time being no deceitful or ambiguous form of the church is seen."[67] Therefore Calvin sternly admonishes that one should not separate from a church in which these marks are found to some extent. "From this it follows that separation from the church is the denial of God and Christ. [...] Nor can any more atrocious crime be conceived than for us by sacrilegious disloyalty to violate the marriage that the only-begotten Son of God deigned to contract with us."[68]

In the next chapter, he says: "For who has dared to take the name of church away from those among whom God entrusted the preaching of his Word and the observance of his sacraments? [...] I say that in falling away [of Old Testament Israel] there were certain degrees."[69] And then he points out that in Israel at times nearly all preaching of the Word had vanished

---

66. *Note by the author*: Francis Turretin, *Institutio Theologiae Elencticae*, vol. 3 (Geneva: S. de Tournes, 1690), 98. [Ed. note: ET: Francis Turretin, *Institutes of Elenctic Theology*, ed. James T. Dennison Jr., trans. George Musgrave Giger, vol. 3 (Phillipsburg, NJ: P&R Publishing, 1992–1997), 87–88.]

67. *Note by the author*: Inst. 4.1.10.

68. *Note by the author*: Inst. 4.1.10.

69. *Note by the author*: Inst. 4.2.7–8.

and all the sacraments were desecrated, but even the idolatry that crept into the church did not remove its essence as a church.[70] The prophets and their faithful sometimes moved away temporarily, but the essence of the church continued, even under these storms of unrighteousness.[71] Calvin goes so far as to declare concerning the Roman Catholic Church: "However, when we categorically deny to the papists the title of *the* church, we do not for this reason impugn the existence of churches among them." He simply maintains that, with regard to the marks, each of these Roman Catholic congregations and the entire body of the Roman Catholic Church lack the legitimate ecclesiastical form.[72]

Add to this the following practical proof. The Lutheran church never exercised discipline in the sense of our Confession; yet there was never a doubt that the church of the Lutherans was genuinely a true church of Christ.

One may therefore never press the adjectives of *pure* preaching and *pure* administration of the sacraments to the extent that the marks must be considered lacking whenever the preaching or the administration of the sacraments leaves something to be desired, or when discipline is lacking. Here, too, the distinction must be made between the church's essence and well-being. There are components of preaching that adorn it, but one cannot say that the lack of them prevents it from being preaching. There are also components in the sacraments that increase their glory, but their absence does not annul the sacrament.

Yet let Calvin also inform us in this respect:

> The pure ministry of the Word and pure mode of celebrating the sacraments are, as we say, sufficient pledge and guarantee that we may safely embrace as church any society in which both these marks exist. The principle extends to the point that we must not reject it so long as it retains them, even if it otherwise swarms with many faults. What is more, some fault may creep into the administration of either doctrine or sacraments, but this ought not to estrange us from communion

---

70. *Note by the author: Inst.* 4.2.8–9.
71. *Note by the author: Inst.* 4.2.10.
72. *Note by the author: Inst.* 4.2.12.

with the church. For not all the articles of true doctrine are of the same sort.[73]

Our conclusion is therefore that for a good state of the church and the well-being of the church of God—that is, for churches in a healthy, normal state—both the pure preaching of the Word and the pure administration of the sacraments, as well as the strict exercise of discipline, are necessary and indispensable. But we also conclude that the churches of Christ, without losing their essence as a church, can be either disfigured or impure, and even, as Calvin says, partially corrupted. This disfiguring is usually seen first in the absence of discipline; this impurity, in blemishes that affect the doctrine or the administration of the sacraments; this corruption, in the rise of false doctrine alongside faithful preaching. Furthermore, where this disease and disfiguring continues, the church gradually loses its essence as a church and fades away into a spiritless association. And finally, where the toxic gases are produced in this corpse, this faded church can become a false church as soon as, under Satan's influence, it begins persecuting the truth and those who profess it.

In the footsteps of Calvin we would therefore admonish everyone to consider whether the church he would leave is indeed forsaken by God to such an extent that it has lost not only the well-being but also the essence of a church. That your church is diseased or disfigured does not mean that you may deny her your love. Rather, precisely because of that illness she may appeal for greater care on your part. Only when she dies does she cease to be your church, and only where the toxic gases of the false church puts you in lethal danger you may flee from her touch and withhold your love from her.

Note especially that the question is never whether you should leave a particular church federation, but only whether you should leave *your church*. A church federation consists of churches, and those churches consist of members.[74] Thus you are a member of your church, and your church is a member of a federation. Your church can leave the federation, but you can leave only your church. Now we know that some churches allow people to hold membership in the "federation" without being a member of a church, but that absurdity does not stop us. For you, for me, for anyone

---

73. *Note by the author: Inst.* 4.1.12.
74. *Note by the author:* The use of the term *kerkgenootschap* ["federation; community"] here is unhistorical. Originally the term referred to the local church.

the question is only this: Must I, may I, leave the church of Amsterdam, of Rotterdam, of Utrecht?

I must therefore not pay attention to what happens elsewhere, but should consider only my own church. The joint responsibility for what happens elsewhere rests on the consistory, not the individual members, and it may lead to a severing of the bond between my church and other churches, but it can never take from my church the essence of church. In the seven letters to the churches in Asia Minor, the Lord never pointed out a responsibility of the members for the church federation.

Therefore, just as our fathers did not leave the church of Amsterdam because it was in federation with the churches of Rome, and deemed that it still had the essence of a church, so too we may not give up on our church, even though it belongs to an untenable church federation, because this does not remove its essence as a church. Furthermore, as far as the churches themselves are concerned, I need only to ask: Does the church in which I live, my church, still provide me with the preaching of the Word and the administration of the sacraments, with such a degree of purity that the essence of both means of grace is still present in them? The fact that idolatry exists alongside this tolerably pure administration of the means of grace does not remove the essence of the church. While it does present the consistory with the obligation to cut off this abomination, it does not require a member of the church to leave it. The organization of my church may have become diseased, disfigured, and partially corrupted, but not so badly that it fails to give me the means of grace with tolerable purity, and therefore it has not yet lost its essence or its life.

Thus the prophets stayed in Jerusalem, even though idolatry had crept in; and our fathers lived for years under the Roman Catholic Church organization before they initiated the Reformation.

This last remark must lead to an equally serious warning. Some behave as if it were the duty and calling of God's children to sever the bond with their church immediately, on the very same day. But this also appears to be against Scripture and against history. In human illness there can be unconsciousness or even apparent death; the church can have similar symptoms. In Israel it too often appeared as if the entire church had been lost, and behold, the imperishable church always blossomed again. In the dark night of the Middle Ages, one would have thought constantly that the church had died, and behold, it raised its head again. So too in the days of the Reformation, it was certainly not the case that all churches were immediately restored, but it took from 1517 to 1570 before the work of church reformation had progressed more universally.

In our day this should motivate us to exercise caution. One who views the doctrine of the church externally and legalistically, without piety or exalted love, will immediately grab his suitcase and prepare to depart at any time. But one who with gentle seriousness and conscientious fear asks: "Do I also walk away into condemnation, do I also reject that which is still alive, do I also bury one who is only dead in appearance?"—he hesitates and waits. For he still hopes, he still attempts new ways to stimulate the spirits of life, and when others ridicule him, asking, "How long will you bother with that dead body?!" he reverently brings his finger to his lips and whispers, "She is my mother!"

§ 60   ZECHARIAH'S CALL: "NOT BY MIGHT, NOR BY POWER, BUT BY MY SPIRIT!"— REFORMATION AND LEGITIMACY

The point of the previous section was to prevent, as much as possible, a break with one's church as a church, and to impress firmly and tenderly upon the heart of every child of God that such a break with his church is permissible only when his church has either died or degenerated into a false church. Not for any other reason. Never any sooner. And that for the all-sufficient reason that our church, as long it has not died or become the false church, is still a manifestation of the body of Christ. Yet no one should imagine that we intend to promote false passivity or an unholy legitimacy. For that reason we must say a few words in this section and the next, about legitimacy and about revolution.

Anyone who takes his works seriously and desires to derive the reformation of his church from God as its Worker can never stretch forth his hand to this glorious work with an eye on a previously calculated result. He would be able to do this if he could unseal the book of God's counsel. But now that this book is and remains closed, he sees this outcome-based manner of directing his activities as irrevocably cut off for him, and only one way remains open to him: the way of obedience. All reformation of the church, whether through spiritual awakening, through gradual church renewal, or through a break with the organization, with the church federation or the church itself, cannot and may not be undertaken in any way except that of quiet, unconditional obedience. Although it appears that everything is going down with it, reformation must be done, because reformation is God's exalted commandment to his church and its servants and members. Nothing, in whatever form it may appear, can ever release the church, or its servants and members, from that obligation of obedience.

But in order for that obedience not to be an excuse for self-directed agitation, every child of God must first very seriously probe the thoughts of his heart to see whether the motivation that drives him is indeed the desire to be obedient. It is safest to decide this on the basis of the following two questions: (1) Is there experience of guilt regarding earlier disobedience? (2) Are means being chosen in such a way that they do not damage the honor of God?

Therefore we emphasized that grief under the judgment of the Lord must be the starting point of all good reformation, as well as reverence for the body of the Lord in every church that has not completely died away or been possessed by Satan. Especially significant is the consideration that Calvin gave, even concerning the Roman Catholic churches: "when we categorically deny to the papists the title of the church, we do not for this reason impugn the existence of churches among them,"[75] alongside the clear fact that in Israel the church flourished again even though idolatry had crept in as far as the temple itself.

Now if one would conclude from this that the tone of this essay is along the lines of: "Not by might, nor by power, but by my Spirit!" [Zech 4:6] then our response is that we thoroughly loathe this motto in the false sense, as it usually rests on passive lips, but we lift it up high and agree wholeheartedly with the meaning of this call as the Holy Spirit revealed it to the prophet Zechariah. We cannot impress too earnestly onto the hearts of our brothers that they must cease the unholy habit of abusing this precious passage of Scripture by distorting its sense and meaning, ultimately causing it to say the opposite of what it intended to say. Usually these words are quoted without paying attention to the context, and the conclusion is drawn that the Holy Spirit in these words means to tell us: "You, ministers and members of my church, please cease all attempts at reformation. It will not succeed anyway. All of it consists of might and power, and it is vain. You should do nothing but simply preach, and everything else must come from my Spirit."

But nothing of this kind is being said in the fourth chapter of Zechariah's oracles. There it is speaking about Zerubbabel, the leader who, at the head

---

75. *Note by the author: Inst.* 4.2.12.

of the returned captives, had undertaken the reformation of the fallen church in Jerusalem. He had done so, not merely through preaching, but as concretely as possible, through the use of a trowel and a pickax. Might and power in the most literal sense! According to the way many brothers interpret our words, on the basis of their sound alone, Zerubbabel should have been ordered to stop that work of reformation, that use of trowel and pickax, all that display of might and power, and to wait quietly for the Spirit of the Lord.

But the meaning of the oracle is precisely the opposite of this. Zerubbabel wants to stop, and the Holy Spirit orders him not to stop, but to persevere boldly. Zerubbabel is afraid. Now that the enemies from around Jerusalem are approaching him with their military power, Zerubbabel's courage is failing, and he thinks: "I have no army to send out against that military power. Therefore I am lost! I give up the reformation! Lord, please do it yourself!" But the Holy Spirit does not allow this, and gives him this revelation: "Zerubbabel, do not stop your reformation in Jerusalem's church for a moment. You are mistaken if you think that you can pursue reformation only if you can respond to the enemy's power through your own power. They will not be able to overwhelm you. The outcome does not depend on setting might against might, power against power, but exclusively on the secret and invisible operation of the Spirit of the Lord!"

Far from recommending passivity, this word of Scripture therefore condemns all passivity, and rather commands us to continue reformation calmly, in the way of the obedience of faith, even if we appear to hit our heads against a brick wall. Or to say it even more clearly, according to the very words of the passage, the call "Not by might, nor by power, but by my Spirit!" is an explanation of the immediately preceding vision.

And what was this vision? It was this: There was a golden lampstand, an image of the church of Christ. A lampstand with seven lamps. From each of these lamps, a pipe ran upward through which the oil, that is the inflow of the Holy Spirit, must be supplied to the churches. For this reason these seven pipes led to a bowl, and into this bowl also dripped the oil from two olive trees, placed to the left and to the right of this bowl of oil [Zech 4:1-3].

Without further investigation of the significance of those two olive trees—an investigation connected to the explanation of the two witnesses in Revelation 11:4—all interpreters agree that these two olive trees represent people, individuals in an office, namely, priests and prophets. The point of this prophecy can therefore never be to say: "The operation of the Holy Spirit comes without human effort," but on the contrary: "The Holy Spirit flows to the congregation through the intermediary of human individuals, in whose heart I work grace."

This naturally shows how to lay bare the fundamental error of this misplaced passivity. This error lies in an incorrect view of the work of the Holy Spirit. People think of this work of the Holy Spirit as something happening apart from the normal instruments and the normal operations of the ministry—something dualistic. But that is not the case; it cannot be. This would place us entirely on Anabaptist fanatic paths. It is the enthusiasts of all stripes, not the Reformed, who continually insist on such a dualistic operation of the Holy Spirit. And according the pure doctrine concerning the Holy Spirit, all official obedience in the ministry is either dead formality and cursed with fruitlessness, or it is the fruit borne of influences of the Holy Spirit.

One may not go down the Roman Catholic path by viewing the official obedience in the ministry as the minister's work that earns him merit. That would be a full departure from Reformed territory. And if one does not honor this official obedience as man's own work, then tell us, whose work could it be except that of the Holy Spirit?

Therefore, far from a person in office shunning his duty of reformation with an appeal to Zechariah 4:6, he must do it precisely because of this word. Any shunning of the duty of obedience in him must be halted and fought through the power of the Word, and this must fill his soul instead: that he must be incorporated into one of these two olive trees, through whose branches and twigs, that is, through whose obedience in the work of reformation, the anointing oil of the Holy Spirit must be applied to the seven churches of the living God.

REFORMATION CONTRASTED WITH REVOLUTION   §61
To those who thoughtfully yet boldly present the work of reformation in such a way that one may ultimately not shun a break with the existing church organization, nor with the existing federation, nor even with the existing church, their opponents usually object that this reformation is not permissible because any break of this nature is a disruption of the legitimate order and the legitimate course of events, and therefore must

be rejected as revolution. They are repeatedly badgered with many variations of this complaint.

Since it is our goal to inform, with fear and trembling, the children of God in these lands concerning the work of reformation, we consider it necessary to investigate this objection seriously. As for revolution in the bad sense, we pray that the Lord God keeps his people from it in holiness; our guilt would be great if, in arrogance or malice, we were to lure the Lord's people to such a sinful path.

Therefore we wish, through calm analysis, to demonstrate to our opponents why they have no right to make such a serious accusation, and why they would do well from now on to cease making this accusation, lest they burden their soul with sin against their brothers and sisters. To this end we point out, first of all, that there is revolution in the good sense and revolution in the bad sense, and that one may certainly not paint all revolution with the same brush.

In order to see this distinction clearly, it should be emphasized that no man ever has such a high position that he could of his own accord impose on his fellow man an obligation to obey him. Every man is sinful and has therefore forfeited any claim to respect for his person. The father has as little value as the child, and the father as a person does not inherently possess a single reason why the child should obey him. Every king is as sinful as the least of his subjects, and accordingly there is in his person no reason why his subjects should submit to him. Likewise in the church of Christ, every person who acts as bishop, member of synod, classical leader, or in whatever function, is as sinful and unworthy as any member of the church, and there is no reason in their persons why the members of the church should render to them reverence or obedience.

If I look at man as mere man, viewed apart from God, then the child is precisely the equal of his father, and there is no trace of sin if an obstinate child refuses to obey his father. By nature a king is worth no more than a beggar, and it is therefore neither wicked nor sinful if the beggar refuses to obey that king. And likewise, a member of a consistory or synod is by nature no better than an ordinary church member, and there is no trace or hint of sin if an ordinary church member simply lets him talk and takes no notice of him. This starting point must be kept in mind. Anyone disagreeing with this either is a Pelagian or does not know the deep corruption of sin.

But what then is the source of the obligation of obedience? Answer: Only and solely the fact that the Lord God entrusts some of his majesty to these individuals. The principle is and remains: You owe God absolute obedience, because he is your Creator, your Sustainer, your Owner, your Redeemer. But you never owe absolute obedience to human beings. There can be obedience to human beings only if, and only as long as and to the extent that, the Lord God indeed and in truth orders and commands me to render to certain people, in his name, the obedience that is due to him.

And what is the essence of revolution, its sin, its abomination? Does it lie in the fact that it constitutes opposition to human beings, and that it refuses to obey human beings, and that it treats king and beggar as equals among human beings? Absolutely not! No, the sin, the crime, the abomination of revolution consists exclusively in two very different things: first, that a person refuses to render to people who occupy an office the toll of obedience that he owes to God; and second, that he dares to say, "the authority is given to the office-bearer, not by God but by me and my fellow citizens." Now this is a terrible sin, for that person mocks God's majesty and steals that majesty for himself. Two sins in one: to un-deify the living God, and to deify oneself.

~~~~~~~~~~~~~~~~~~~~

If our critics believe that they can point out this kind of revolution in our presentation of reformation and apply it to the break with the church, then let them be faithful in this in brotherly love. We are grateful in advance for their brotherly faithfulness. But if they are not able to do so, and they cannot substantiate their serious accusation of revolution any further than that we recommend breaking with the existing legal situation if necessary, then allow us to cast this accusation far from us. After all, David also broke with the existing legal situation when he gathered troops and went up against Saul. Christ broke with the existing legal situation when he took ropes and made a whip and drove the money changers out of the temple. The Waldensians broke with the existing legal situation when they established their free churches over against the Roman Catholic hierarchy. Luther, Zwingli, and Calvin broke with the existing legal situation when they sent their letter of separation to their ecclesiastical leadership. Our fathers broke with the existing legal situation when they sent the Sea Beggars to Brielle and fought to liberate those lands from Spain.[76] Our churches broke with the existing legal situation when in the sixteenth century in Amsterdam and elsewhere they left the church federation with Rome. William III broke with the existing legal situation when he ascended to the throne of the Stuarts in England, just as William the Silent did when as a governor he opposed Philip II, his king. In 1813 our heroes also broke with the existing legal situation when they liberated us and later fought at Waterloo—since in terms of legitimacy, Napoleon was their lawful sovereign.

Since every child of God agrees with our judgment that neither David, nor Christ, nor the apostles, nor the Waldensians, nor our Reformers, nor our fathers, nor our monarchs sinned in this matter, but rather that through a break with the existing situation they fulfilled their duty of obedience to God, then it is evident that a break with the existing situation, in itself and as such, need not be sin, and instead may even be doing one's duty.

On what does it depend? Only on the question whether such a break with the existing situation happens in obedience to God, or not. Had David not received a revelation from Samuel, he should not have attacked Saul. Had Jesus not acted in fellowship with the Father, he would have had no right to exercise authority in the temple. Had the apostles not known that they were acting in obedience to God's Word, they should not have opposed the Sanhedrin. Likewise, if our Reformers and Sea Beggars had not known that their violation of Rome's and Spain's legally established authority originated in the motivation to obey God more than human beings, then their break would have made them terribly guilty.

This is precisely what the legitimist claims, and in England and Germany voices are arising to condemn our reformation as a revolution. And take note, our own legitimists will eventually have to take this position as well. Condemning us because of what they call revolutionary activity, they will have to pass the same judgment upon our Reformers and our fathers. Or—may God grant them this—if they back away from this, then they will be forced to reconsider their rash and thoughtless judgment, and say: Nobody is revolutionary because of the mere fact that he breaks with the existing situation; but one is revolutionary only if he

---

76. Kuyper refers here to the attack upon Brielle by the *Watergeuzen* ("Sea Beggars") in 1572. The victory began a more widespread revolt that would lead to Dutch independence.

makes this break for any reason other than to be more obedient to God than to human beings.

REFORMATION AND THE GOVERNMENT§ 62

Another important question has been raised: Should the government take part in the work of the reformation of the churches; and especially this: Is the government called, entitled, and required "to remove and prevent all idolatry and false worship"?[77] In this respect our conviction does *not* agree with that of our fathers. We make no secret of this difference. Only God's Word, not the word of the fathers, is ultimately authoritative for us. And on the basis of God's Word we have the conviction of conscience that we may *not* follow our fathers in this element of their confession. The reason is that the quoted words indicate and imply that the government has the obligation, ultimately, not only to admonish heretics or bar them from public worship, but certainly also to arrest them, imprison them, sentence them, and execute them publicly. This is indeed implied in these words.

The proof is Calvin's treatise in which he argues "that heretics must be put to death by the sword," Beza's essay "on the responsibility of the civil government to punish heretics," and also the sentiment of Maresius in his exposition of the confession of faith;[78] compared to the sentiment of our theologians: Voetius in his *Disput. Theol.* III.802–809 and II.122;[79] Henr. Alting in his *Script Heidelb.* Tom. 2. p. 2. probl. XX. p. 335 s. 9;[80] Spanheim, *Vind. Euang.* l. II. loc. 20;[81] Corn. van Velzen, *Theol. pract.* II, l. I. p. 632;[82]

---

77. Belgic Confession, Art. 36.

78. John Calvin, *Defensio orthodoxae fidei de sacra Trinitate, contra prodigiosos errores Michaelis Serueti Hispani: vbi ostenditur haereticos iure Gladii coercendos esse* ... (Geneva: R. Estienne, 1554); Theodore Beza, *De haereticis a civili magistratu puniendis libellus* (Geneva: R. Estienne, 1554); Samuel Maresius, *Foederatum Belgium orthodoxum; sive Confessionis ecclesiarum Belgicarum exegesis* (Groningen: J. Nicolaus, 1652), 542–61.

79. Gisbertus Voetius, *Selectarum disputationum theologicarum*, 4 vols. (Utrecht: J. à Waesberge, 1648–67), 3:802–9; 2:122–23.

80. Heinrich Alting, *Scriptorum theologicorum*, 2 vols. (Amsterdam: J. Janssonius, 1646), vol. 2, pt. 2, pp. 335–40.

81. Frédéric Spanheim Jr., *Vindiciarum biblicarum*, 2 parts (Frankfurt: A. Wyngaerden, 1663), 2:177–95.

82. Kuyper may have in mind the following passage from Cornelius van Velzen (or a similar passage in another edition of Van Velzen's work): *Institutiones theologiae practicae*, 2 vols. (Groningen: J. Bolt & J. a Velzen, 1748), 2:517–19.

Gerdesius, *Bibl. menstr. Belg.* m. Jan. 1742, p. 30;[83] J. à Marck, *Med. Theol.* c. [X]XXIII, §32;[84] De Moor, *Comm. à Marck*, VI. p. 490 vlg.;[85] and Turretin, *Theol. Hand.* T.1. XVIII. p. 84. §30.[86]

All of these theologians express the sentiment that Article 36 of our Belgic Confession indeed gives the government the obligation ultimately to put a heretic to death by execution. They differ from Rome in the sense that they let the government judge for themselves. Rome believed that the government must pass sentence on the basis of the ecclesiastical judgment. But these theologians say: Let the government see with its own eyes. They also admit that the government should not take this most terrible step as a general rule, but only in the extreme case, and only with the worst heretics. From à Marck onward it became customary to add that the government may execute a heretic only if he was also a threat to the republic. But in spite of the tuning down and dressing up, eventually their sentiment always implied that, if nothing else works, the removal of idolatry must happen by fire and by the sword.

We stand with full conviction against that confession, ready to bear the consequences of our conviction, even if some might condemn us as un-Reformed because of that. We would rather be regarded as non-Reformed and insist that heretics should not be put to death, than that we keep the name of Reformed at the cost of contributing to the shedding of the heretics' blood. Our conviction is as follows:

(1) The examples under the old covenant do not apply to us, because the infallible determination of what is heretical and not, as it could be made at that time, is now lacking.

(2) The Lord and the apostles never invoked the help of the government to punish with the sword those who deviated from the truth. Paul

---

83. Kuyper may be referring to a text related to the States of Friesland's suspension of the Mennonite pastor Johannes Stinstra in January 1742. Daniel Gerdes (or Gerdesius) (1698–1765), a professor at the University of Groningen, was a major opponent of Stinstra's views, which were seen as Socinian and as undermining the religious orthodoxy of the Dutch Republic.

84. Johannes à Marck, *Christianae theologiae medulla didactico-elenctica, ex majori opere, secundum ejus, capita, et paragraphos, expressa* (Amsterdam: G. Borstius, 1696), 299; compare à Marck, *Compendium theologiae*, 685–90.

85. De Moor, *Commentarius perpetuus*, 6:490–99.

86. Kuyper may be referring to the compendium of Francis Turretin's *Institutes* by Leonhard Ryssen: *Summa theologiae didactico-elencticae*, 2 parts (Bern: D. Tschiffelius, 1703), 2:84–85.

mentions nothing of this, even when abominable heretics corrupted the congregation, as in Corinth. There is not a single indication in the New Testament that in the days when special revelation would cease, the expulsion of heresy by the sword should be the duty of the government.

(3) Our fathers did not derive this monstrous position from their principles, but copied it from Roman Catholic practice.

(4) Victims of the adoption and execution of this principle were almost always non-heretics, and it was not the truth but the heresy that came to hold a position of honor.

(5) This position contradicts the spirit and the grounding of the Christian faith.

(6) This view presupposes that the government is able to judge between truth and heresy; but the history of eighteen centuries shows that the Holy Spirit did not grant the government this official grace, but has withheld it from it.

Thus we do not at all hide the fact that in this respect we disagree with Calvin, with the Belgic Confession, and with our Reformed theologians. We prefer to say that we feel the need to highlight this difference only out of necessity and through strong conviction. We readily admit that those who fully agree with this phrase in Article 36 have an easier position in this regard. We confess that those who publicly depict us as having deviated from the Confession give a perfectly truthful testimony.

But notwithstanding these serious objections, which we certainly do not take lightly, we still insist unwaveringly: *In the name of the Lord we do not ask for the gallows for the heretic.* Indeed, let the congregation of our Lord Jesus know and understand this well, and may it be clearly impressed upon the souls of the children of God who know love: Those teachers who insist even today on maintaining Article 36 in this regard, demand that the people of the Lord approve the execution of the heretics—even more, that the people confess that it is God's will, and take on the responsibility of once again shedding the blood of the heretics. If the children of God in these lands consider this to be legitimate, then naturally they must condemn us in this regard. But if a better testimony within them speaks: "I may not erect the gallows for the heretic!"—then let them have the courage publicly to support our view, so that the proponents and opponents of the burning or hanging of heretics take clear positions over against each other.

As the reader knows, we do not deny the implications of Christ's kingship and the two tables of the law for the government. But this has been dealt with in earlier sections and must not be repeated here. Let us merely add this. Although our opponents must insist that Nero also was ultimately obliged to burn the heretics (that is, those people whom he considered heretics) according to his own judgment, yet they basically admit that this duty can be fulfilled well only by a government that professes the Reformed religion. And since there is not and will not be such a government in our country, we would like to ask if it is good to separate the brothers over such a painful issue as sending the stubborn heretic to the gallows.

We, for our part, continue to foster the hope that those teachers who currently zealously promote keeping this "gallows clause" in Article 36 would themselves be the first to shun the consequences of their position if the mayor of their town were actually to bring a heretic to the gallows or the pyre. At that time, we imagine, rather than cheering at the blood of the heretic, they would bring water to extinguish the burning wood, or in loving zeal cut the rope that lay as a noose around the neck of their fellow citizen.

§ 63   THE REFORMATIONS THAT HAVE OCCURRED AND THEIR VARIOUS CHARACTERS

Because people are accustomed to view the reformation of the sixteenth century as *the* Reformation, many are under the impression that there have not been other reformations in the Holy Scripture or in history. This view is incorrect. There have continually been reformations, albeit on a smaller scale, less thorough, or with lesser consequences than the reformation associated with the names of Luther and Calvin. One must take note of this fact.

If we develop the habit of viewing Luther's reformation as the only essential reformation, then as a consequence we will think of reformation as something that has happened once and for all, and which has no relevance for us. But if we become aware of the fact that reformation has been a constant factor in the history of Jesus' church, so that whenever abuse or degeneration crept into the churches there have always been attempts, often successful, to restore it through reformation, then the idea of reformation comes to life for us and speaks to us, and naturally the question arises: "Could my church, too, be lifted out of its deep corruption through reformation?"

This compels us to survey briefly the various reformations of which the Holy Spirit and history give us an account, and also to indicate the nature, to point out the significance, and to bring out the characteristics of each of these reformations. To this end we speak first of the reformations that are recorded in Holy Scripture, and then of the reformations that are recorded in church history. This distinction may not be neglected, especially because in our estimation even our best canonists, by overlooking this distinction, have actually caused no little confusion in the views on reformation.

Who would deny how tempting it is to take what Holy Scripture tells us about the reformations and apply it as the norm for our church reformation? And precisely this will fail. In regard to keeping the Mosaic political and social, ceremonial and familial laws, everyone points out that it would be wrong to declare that this entire set of laws (even though they are recorded in Scripture) is still literally binding on us. And everyone insists that in all these laws a distinction must be made between their central idea and specific implementation, and likewise between their moral and ceremonial significance.[87] In the same way, sacred consideration requires that, in regard to the reformations of Holy Scripture, we must ask which aspects of these reformations are related to Israel's unique situation as people of special revelation, and which other aspects possessed a general character—and then apply only the latter to ourselves as a norm for our conduct.

Four particular elements in the reformations of Holy Scripture must be pointed out here.

(1) During the time when special revelation continued to be given, some men of God received a direct communication, instruction, and calling from heaven, in a way *no one* today receives such an instruction or calling.

(2) The legislation in the Israelite nation was of direct divine origin, so that transgression of the law, even in the smallest matters, was

---

87. *Note by the author*: See Franciscus Junius, *De Politiae Mosis Observatione*, in *Opuscula Theologia Selecta*, ed. Abraham Kuyper (Amsterdam: Muller, 1882), 336–92. [Ed. note: Kuyper is referring to nearly the entirety of Junius' treatise, originally published in 1593; ET: *The Mosaic Polity*, trans. Todd M. Rester, ed. Andrew M. McGinnis (Grand Rapids: CLP Academic, 2015).]

considered sin in the absolute sense. Today, ecclesiastical regulations originate in human insights and therefore lack that absolute character.

(3) In Israel the king was not merely a civil magistrate, but equally an ecclesiastical figure, who as the bearer of the messianic image held an office in the church just as the priest and the prophet. This is no longer the case, because Jesus himself is now King in his church. Any conclusions one might derive for our government from the deeds of David and Solomon, Josiah, Joash, and Hezekiah, are therefore invalid.

(4) In Israel it was possible to shed streams of blood of idolatrous heretics, as Elijah did, and apply the death penalty to false teachers as often as the Lord God gave a direct command to do so, as he did to Elijah and Moses. The theocratic character of the laws required these absolute punishments and justified them. But today, now that both this direct legislation and this direct command are lacking, it would be an abomination of unrighteousness to imitate Elijah's actions against the priests of Baal.

Those among our brothers who in the future wish to invoke the Old Testament as a norm for church reformation, must therefore reckon with this fourfold difference. They should consider well that, as Franciscus Junius says, "to hold on to a shadowy image, after the real thing itself has come, is not only unwise and pointless, but even sinful."[88] To continue sacrificing bulls and rams after Calvary would be a dishonor to Jesus' unique sacrifice. Likewise, it would also be a violation of the sovereign kingship of Jesus over his church if, after his ascension to the throne and during his divine rule from heaven, one would continue to give to an earthly government power over the church, which David and his successors possessed only as those foreshadowing Christ.

After these preliminary remarks, our enumeration of the reformations in the Bible can be brief. Already before Israel was a nation, we hear of four events in which the church of God was rebuilt after backsliding, or through separation was kept from complete degeneration. The first of these reformations happened through the separation of the Sethites and

---

88. Kuyper appears to be summarizing Junius' conclusions rather than directly quoting from Junius' treatise. See Junius, *The Mosaic Polity*, chs. 7–8.

the Cainites. In the days of Enosh, we read, they began once again to call upon the name of the Lord [Gen 4:26].

The second awe-inspiring reformation, worked by God himself, took place through the flood, when all of corrupted humankind perished in the water; only the ark with its precious treasure carried the church of the Lord and, after a short period of waiting, returned the church to the earth.

The third all-important reformation took place through Abram when he, on God's command, carried the church of God out of Terah's idolatrous family, and brought it to the land that God would show him.

Finally, the fourth reformation happened through the separation of Jacob and Esau. Esau too had been born in the church of God and had received the sacrament of the covenant in his body. But evil crept in, and the church of God would have degenerated completely had not the Lord countered the Edomites in their sin by separating Jacob and Esau, in order to keep his church free in and with Jacob.

The nature of these four reformations is that they did not come about through human intentions but rather through God's own activity. Therefore these reformations cannot be an example for us, because the human race no longer coincides with the church and God's governing rule follows other paths than it did at that time.

After these four pre-Israelite reformations come the reformations that took place in the nation of Israel. We divide them into two categories, in terms of whether they occurred before or during the period of the kings.

There are four reformations that happened before the period of the kings. First of all, God's church was rescued from the demise with which Egyptian politics threatened them, through transfer of the entire church from the land of Goshen to the wilderness. Second, there was the reformation accomplished by Moses after Aaron had established the worship of the golden calf. Third, there was the various reformations accomplished by Gideon, Jephthah, Samson, and other judges in national revolt. And fourth, there was the reformation to which Samuel called the people, and which he accomplished in part.

The nature of these last three reformations was the removal of evil, spiritual awakening of the people, and a powerful triumph over unrighteousness, yet always through men of God who had received special instruction to this end.

There are seven reformations that were accomplished by the kings: under Asa, Jehoshaphat, Joash, Hezekiah, and Manasseh in Judah, and under Jehu and under Ahab through Elijah in Israel.

These reformations were always occasioned by the terrible explosion of idolatry and ungodliness among the people. What Scripture tells us about this defies all description. Sometimes the sacraments had not been administered for years. The observance of the law disappeared. All kinds of idolatrous rituals were held publicly in villages and towns, even in Jerusalem. There was no limit to the corruption of morals. All that was sacred was mocked. God's faithful servants were murdered. And the corruption recklessly expanded even into the temple and among the priests.

Now in Judah the kings themselves took action against these abominations five times, in particular Jehoshaphat, Hezekiah, and Manasseh, while Asa and Joash are mentioned with gratitude and honor. In Israel, Jehu was the only king who stood up against the corruption in the church with the zeal of a Hezekiah, while the reformation under Ahab did not come from the king, but from Elijah in opposition to the king.

In connection with these seven reformations, which are of a fairly similar nature, one should notice that they did *not* lead to a break with the existing church, but came about through the legitimate, God-ordained instruments of the church. They did *not* result in a renewed form of the church or a change in worship practice, but only served to remove idolatry, put an end to immorality, and give new impetus to the neglected worship of the church.

For the period after the fall of the kings until Jesus' ministry, Holy Scripture records three additional reformations. The first took place when Zerubbabel led the exiled church back to Palestine and, together with Joshua, began rebuilding Jerusalem's walls. The second reformation was when Ezra and Nehemiah acted with great courage to stop the new corruption that was once again creeping in. And the third happened four centuries later, when John the Baptist appeared at the shores of the Jordan to urge Israel to repentance and conversion.

The first of these reformations completely changed the church's situation and split it definitively into two parts: the church that remained in Babylon, and the church that gathered again in Jerusalem. The second was a gradual renewal of the church to fend off corrupting elements. And the third was a reformation through spiritual awakening, a genuine revival, in which the form of the church as such remained unaffected.

As this brings us to the history of the church outside Scripture, we must carefully distinguish between (1) the reformations through the great councils, (2) the reformations through small groups, (3) the reformations that led to a split in the church, and (4) the reformations that served to preserve the purity of the split churches.

The great councils, which began in 325 with the Council of Nicaea, were reforming councils, and if the churches in 1517 had been able to bring about the reformation of the churches through a similar council, then the grievous split and separation of churches would never have torn our churches apart. Each of these great councils was occasioned by the sad fact that serious heresy had crept into the churches of Jesus, gained sympathy on a large scale even among the teachers, threatened the entire existence of the church with schism and perdition, and caused godliness to be shipwrecked in a grievous manner. And every time it was these ecumenical councils that, assembled in the Spirit of the Lord, maintained the truth, condemned the heresy, restored the church's unity, and put an end to immorality.

Of a very different nature were the reformations through small groups, of which the best known (but certainly not the only ones) were those by the Waldensians in Savoy, the Hussites in Bohemia, and the followers of Wycliff in England. These reformations did not originate in influential circles, but were rather directed against those in power, and served only to return to apostolic purity, either with or without suffering a break with the church.

The great Reformation that finally erupted in the sixteenth century was united and characterized by the fact that it led to a final break with the Roman Catholic church federation. But apart from this, it was of very different nature in various countries. One must specially note this three-fold difference. The German Reformation, followed by those in Denmark, Norway, and so on, originated mainly with the rulers. It came from above, and served to transform the entire national church without dividing it. The Swiss Reformation, on the other hand, and following in its tracks the Reformations in Scotland and the Netherlands, originated with the people, came from below, and served first to liberate the local churches and then to join them in a new federation. Finally, the Slavic and French Reformations are different again: in Germany and Switzerland there was a break with the federation but not with the churches, but in Poland and Bohemia, as well as France and Italy, the existing church was not reformed, but new, Protestant churches were established alongside and over against the existing Roman Catholic churches.

This difference does not for a moment remove their common character—that they all came about through severance of the legitimistic line and through a break with what existed.

~~~~~~~~~~~~~~~~~~~~~~~~~~~~~~~

Finally, a few words must be said about the post-Reformation reformations, though we limit ourselves to our own country, and point out three more notable reformations, without meaning to downplay the many lesser reformations.

The first of these was the reformation that took place at the Synod of Dort. At that time, too, corruption had crept into the doctrine and life of the church, and had even affected some of the teachers and consistories. At that time, too, people throughout the country broke with the existing situation by establishing aggrieved churches but without leaving the church. At that time, too, there arose counter-consistories and counter-classes. At that time, too, a split was imminent. But through gradual church renewal this evil was subdued at the Synod of Dort in 1619.

The second was the reformation through spiritual awakening that in the previous century led to the rising of many from spiritual death, in Zeeland, in rural Holland, and on the Veluwe.

The third reformation, finally, was attempted around 1830 through 1840 in various parts of our country by Budding, Ledeboer, De Cock, and Scholte.[89] In Zeeland it led to the formation of small groups, under the Ledeboerians it produced a kind of aggrieved churches, and under De Cock and Scholte, Van Velzen, and Brummelkamp it resulted in the well-known Secession.[90]

Of these three, only the last had effects on a somewhat larger scale, because independent activity and employing the power to organize actually resulted in the establishment of new churches. The Ledeboerians

---

89. Huibert Jacobus Budding (1810–70), Lambertus Gerardus Cornelis Ledeboer (1808–63), Hendrik de Cock (1801–42), and Hendrik Scholte (1805–68) were leaders of reform and secession movements from the Dutch Reformed Church.

90. That is, the *Afscheiding* of 1834, of which Simon van Velzen (1809–96) and Anthony Brummelkamp (1811–88) were also leaders.

wanted reformation through a break with the existing organization and, if necessary, with the existing church federation, but they judged that the churches in these lands should not yet be condemned as churches of Baal. The brothers who seceded later, on the other hand, considered it right to point out the marks of the false church in the Dutch churches, and on this basis to break with this corrupt synagogue of Satan through the formation of new churches.

Meanwhile, one must distinguish between those who were deposed and those who, without deposition, left the national churches of their own accord. There is so much to say in favor of the decision of the former, that we would not willingly have removed ourselves from their fellowship. But the actions of the latter are, in our opinion, subject to certain mild objections. After all, one may not leave one's church unless one is very certain that it has become a synagogue of Satan. Calvin especially warned against this. And we may and must raise serious doubt whether the churches of these lands, from which they departed, always and in every case, in every city and in every village, manifested the marks of the false church so clearly that departure was the duty of a wounded heart.

As you will see in the next section, we believe that, sadly, the conclusion to depart could indeed no longer be avoided in numerous cases. But on the other hand, there were also many at the time who left churches that certainly had not been deformed to such an extent, and who did so only because these churches refused to discontinue their federation with other, more corrupted churches.

Now we do not believe that, either on the basis of Scripture or on the basis of history, one can ever maintain that any church may be rejected as a false church—that is, as a synagogue of Satan, merely because of the unrighteous federation of which it is part.

If you consider how terrible the corruption and degeneration of the church had been under Israel, and also how many decades, or even centuries, our fathers waited before they thought the corruption of Rome's church serious enough to justify a break, then you get the feeling that the brothers who departed recently may have given up on the sick church too soon. And it is hard to escape the impression that they made arrangements for the funeral of many a church that, through the goodness of the Lord, has revived and is still alive.

§ 64   THE REFORMATION THAT MUST CURRENTLY BE UNDERTAKEN IN THE
REFORMED CHURCHES OF THE NETHERLANDS

The Reformed churches in these lands are also awaiting another thorough reformation, in order that they, restored to a better state of the church, may once again offer to God his honor, to his elect the enjoyment of his salvation, and to our people and fatherland the support against backsliding into deeper moral corruption.

That this reformation is necessary is apparent from sad facts that, alas, nobody can deny: The godliness among the Lord's people has sunk below its normal level. The key of knowledge is gone, except in some very small groups. Worldliness has reached not only the members of the churches, but it holds the masses in its grip. The most blatant immoralities and the most extreme heresies, to the point of denying God, are tolerated in the churches, publicly and without penalty. False doctrine has crept in among the teachers. In many churches the sacraments are desecrated. Love among brothers has given way to strife and division. The churches are split because many smaller groups are acting as separate churches. And finally, most of these churches live in a federation that manifests an increasingly unholy character and resembles more and more the papist hierarchy.

We do not want to exaggerate this matter, and must be careful of claiming inaccurately that the state of our churches is comparable to the church in Jerusalem under the later kings, for instance, or similar to the state of the churches in our fatherland in the late 1400s. Anyone who says that does not know history. Rather, it must be maintained that the Reformed churches of these countries are still different from both of the churches mentioned, in these respects:

(1) The ministry of the Word and sacraments still persists in many of these churches, in a purity wholly unknown at those times.

(2) The heresy and immorality that crept in are still a far cry from the idolatrous and satanic character they had at that time.

(3) Those who desire improvement can move about much more freely and are certainly not mistreated as they were then.

(4) The immorality among the teachers, although occurring occasionally, cannot be compared with what was found in Jerusalem and under fifteenth-century Rome.

If you ask, therefore, if the Reformed churches here should already be regarded as false churches or synagogues of Satan, then we wish to answer by making a distinction between three types of churches.

In the first category of churches we place those churches in which there is still a reasonably pure ministry of the Word and a reasonably pure administration of the sacraments, as is the case in the churches of Amsterdam, Rotterdam, Utrecht, and so on. We would guess that there are about five to six hundred of these churches. Concerning these churches we do not doubt for a moment that they are still actually churches of our Lord Jesus Christ. Nonetheless, we readily and generously admit that these churches suffer of the following wrongs:

(1) alongside the proper administration of the means of grace they also tolerate their desecration;

(2) they no longer exercise church discipline;

(3) they allow unbelievers to have a vote;

(4) they are in a false church federation.

We certainly do not take these imperfections lightly, but they cannot compel us to reject these churches as false churches. One should realize, after all, that our fathers, in spite of the continuing presence of false preaching, never considered giving up on their local church as a false church; they gave up only on Rome.

In the second category we place the churches where the proper administration of the means of grace may currently be lacking, but where there are still people in prayer, and where there is still hope that in the Lord's time, the worship of Baal will yield to the service of the Lord. Numerous examples could be named of churches in which for twenty or thirty years the teachers have only taught the lie, yet in response to the prayers of the believers they are once again graced with the proper administration of the means of grace. Oh, that they may thank God for it!

Now we consider the situation of these churches to be extremely dangerous, and we admit that they have almost lost the name of church, or at least "the lawful form," as Calvin says.[91] Nonetheless, if we consider what happened in Israel, or if we consider the preservation of the churches under the Roman Catholic hierarchy, and we also look at the signs that our own eyes have seen in many other churches, then we cannot yet justify before the Lord God to declare these churches dead, or to equate their consistory with a synagogue of Satan.

Sadly, we believe this is justified concerning the third category of churches, of which not a few are found in our provinces, and of which we

---

91. *Inst.* 4.2.12.

must say: (1) that their administration of the means of grace is not merely weak, but also without any promise or hope of return; (2) that the ministry of unbelief and idolatry has publicly occupied the holy place without offending consciences any longer; and (3) that enmity against the truth and the absence of godliness has progressed so far, that moral decay can be observed in all social relationships.

Of such churches, we believe, one must say: They have died. The lampstand has been removed from its place. And while the Lord God is able to build up a new church in that place, nothing will come out of that old, withered trunk. We do not think it impossible that, for instance, through the rotation of preachers during a vacancy, the grace of God may be preached again, that this preaching may move a few souls, and that from the group of those affected souls new life for the church may grow. But we strongly doubt that this could be called a fresh revival of the old church. In the very same way the Word may happen to come into a false church, but that does not move anyone to rehabilitate that false church just because of this incidental fact.

One may ask why we do not add a fourth member to these three categories of Reformed churches—a category for the churches of those who have seceded, consisting of their three or four groups that currently exist under various names. The reason for this is that in all of these seceded churches we cannot and may not see anything but aggrieved churches, which have temporarily organized themselves, perhaps a little too independently. We are convinced that if tomorrow the churches of Amsterdam, Rotterdam, Utrecht, and so on, were to be restored to their pure state, all these currently seceded churches would come together. Meanwhile, one can certainly not blame them for refusing to do so as long as that reformation is lacking and the churches continue in an illegitimate federation.

We know, of course, that these seceded churches themselves will not admit that they are aggrieved churches. But that does not matter to us. If they were not aggrieved churches, then they would insist that all of our churches are false churches, or synagogues of Satan. We are so bold as to believe that at least the godly members among them no longer do this. And if we assume that the dominant conviction among them is that certainly not all churches other than the seceded churches have died off, then it follows automatically that either these seceded churches would be schismatic, or—and this is our belief—we must honor them as aggrieved churches whose organization is somewhat too independent.

In the past there was an obstacle to holding this position, because from the Modernists and Groningen theologians they copied the incorrect view that there is in this country only one large church with local segments. From that perspective their reasoning was naturally as follows: "As the church does in its segment in Ulrum, so does the entire church all the time!"[92] This then implied that the entire church had to be rejected, in all its segments. But if we successfully replace this false collegial view by more Reformed views, then we may foster the hope that these seceded churches will agree with the distinction we made, by regarding the church federation as secondary and locating the essence of the church not in the federation but in the local churches.

This will also invite a reaction among those seceded people who have been recognized by the government under the name of Christian Reformed,[93] so that they might turn against the more or less collegial view that currently causes some of them to think of the seceded federation as the main idea, and the local churches as segments of that federation. This is un-Reformed, and the Reformed principle will gradually drive this idea out of these churches as well.

As for the question of how to go about the reformation of the Reformed churches in this country, since we subdivided them into three categories, we will respond by making distinctions both with respect to these three categories and with respect to the persons or bodies that are called to take action.

[First, our view concerning the ordinary church members:][94]

(1) All God's children in these churches will do well to bring this grievous state of the church to the portal of their hearts in a spiritual manner. The judgment of God in this grievous state of the church must be acknowledged more than has been done until now. Not only in the churches that are halfway destroyed but also in churches like that of Amsterdam, the lamentable state of the church must urge them to prayer and supplication. It must be desired of the Lord that for his holy name's sake, he be merciful to his Zion again.

---

92. Ulrum was the town in which Hendrik de Cock was a minister. In 1834 he and his consistory were the first to secede from the Dutch state church.

93. *Christelijke Gereformeerden*; in 1905 this became the name of what is known in America as the Free Reformed Churches.

94. This sentence is missing in Kuyper's text but clearly implied.

(2) This spiritual engagement with the misery of God's churches must lead to personal confession of guilt and personal repentance, also among the godly. God's child knows his own guilt to be the deepest. Let everyone be the chief of sinners in his own eyes. And let him rise up from that death. Let there be remorse, let there be repentance, let there be renewal of the covenant with the Most High!

(3) From the personal life this reformation must extend into our families and fellowship groups. The first impulses of the better life must be directed that way. Once again, let it be hope against hope. Away from the world, toward the Lord of hosts. From the tents of vanity to the tent of our Lord. Find a hiding place in *his* shelter.

(4) Reformation must spread outward from this group in the form of opposition against sin and heresy, and in the display of mercy, and through the publication of the gospel of salvation. The still slumbering office of believer must manifest itself in its glorious ministry.

(5) In the churches of our third category, those that have died completely, we would furthermore admonish believers either to establish a church of Christ, or to join another church that might exist in their town as a seceded church, provided that this church can be persuaded at least to leave open the possibility of a new federation with other Reformed churches.

(6) In the churches of our second category, where the pure administration of the means of grace is temporarily lacking but where there is still hope for renewal, we would request believers to immediately establish an aggrieved church, that is, bring to life an administration of the means of grace under the leadership of a believing consistory, chosen specifically for this purpose.

(7) And in the churches of our first category, where there is still a reasonably pure administration of the means of grace, believers will do well to use these means faithfully, to thank the Lord God for his grace shown in these means, and to pray that he may continue to grant to them these means. Furthermore, believers are obligated not to have fellowship in any way, be it through education, home visiting, baptism, or preaching, with those teachers or office-bearers in their church who resist the counsel of God.

Second, concerning persons in office this is our opinion:

(1) Ministers who live near churches of the second or third category have the obligation, in the way of mission, to lead people in these

dead churches to the knowledge of the gospel, and to offer to the aggrieved churches, as a consultant, any support they might desire.

(2) Ministers who work in churches alongside unbelieving teachers must break off all official fellowship with them, while continuing to show some interest in their personal lives, in order not to give offense.

(3) From the pulpit, in catechism, and during home visiting, ministers are to remind the congregation continually of the judgment of God resting on the church. They must admonish them to repentance and conversion, and they themselves must lead by example in their holy walk and the improvement of their lives.

(4) In the meetings of the consistory, the minister must urge church reformation according to the Word of God, and ultimately, if that has no effect, he ought to meet separately with the confessing consistory members.

(5) In their classis, the ministers must urge that special attention should be given to churches that deviate from the confession, or in which the administration of the means of grace is corrupted.

(6) In their classis, the ministers must be diligent to move the churches together to humility before the Lord and a return to his law and testimony.

(7) The elders, insofar as their office is involved, must follow the same path as the ministers of the Word. Moreover, in churches where there is no minister of the Word who feeds the congregation with the Word, they must strengthen it through substitute ministry, and must help it in the formation of aggrieved churches.

(8) The deacons, like the elders, insofar as it pertains to their office, must assist the ministers of the Word in the reformation of the churches, and must powerfully awaken people to the works of mercy through the reformation of love that has grown cold.

In the third place, with regard to the ecclesiastical assemblies, we believe:

(1) The consistories must be of the mind to help the churches of the second category, and to work through mission in the dead churches of the third category.

(2) The consistories must strive to remove non-confessing elements from among them, and to discontinue any fellowship with unbelieving teachers.

(3) The consistories ought to urge their churches to confession of guilt, to repentance and conversion and improvement of life. And to this end they must reinstate church discipline.

(4) The consistories must utilize their federation with other churches to try to move those other churches to reformation along with them. And if that turns out to be unattainable, they ought to discontinue membership in that federation by organizing their own church affairs properly through the introduction of their own church order, and by entering into federation with all aggrieved or non-aggrieved churches that are one with them in their confession.

(5) The classis must no longer hold elections for illegitimate governing bodies, so that these bodies automatically disappear, and they must enter into federation with other classes in order from these classes to call a legitimate, spiritual, national synod.

(6) The classical and provincial church governments, which are not based on the Word of God and therefore lack all divine right of existence, must be dissolved.

(7) The synod of these churches ought to relinquish its presumptuous sovereign authority; it must cease its attempts to reach for the crown of the Christ; and it should invite the classes to assemble on the basis of the Forms of Unity in a better synod, through delegates, in order to perform the task of reforming the church federation.

Fourth, concerning the government:

(1) The government ought to retract the royal decrees of 1815 and 1852 and to put an end to the fiction that in 1852 the churches were free to determine their own future. It is not correct to say that they were free to determine their own future, because the regulations adopted in 1852 were entirely dominated by influences that had entered the church by virtue of the decree of 1815.[95]

(2) The government must take the necessary steps to remove Article 168 from the constitution, insofar as it regulates the financial

---

95. Kuyper is referring to the new church-state relationship established by William I in 1815 and the General Regulations (*Algemeen Reglement*) of January 1816, which were revised in 1852. The 1816 regulations made the Dutch Reformed Church an administration of the state and imposed compulsory uniformity on the church. In Kuyper's view, the loosening of the regulations in 1852 did not go far enough. See "Editor's Introduction" in *On the Church*, xiii–xiv.

obligations, possibly after returning to the churches, either at once or in installments, the monies and the rights to which they are entitled.[96]

(3) To the churches that left the federation completely, the government ought to grant recognition according to the 1853 law on church denominations and, as long as Article 168 of the constitution remains valid, it ought to grant the enjoyment of the emoluments codified in that article.[97]

Finally, in the fifth place, concerning the seceded churches:

(1) With increasing clarity they must emphasize their independence as local churches in order to remove all remaining leaven of the collegial system.

(2) They must maintain fellowship with other aggrieved churches if they desire this.

(3) As soon as the original churches, through spiritual reformation, purging of false elements, and separation from any wrong federation, regain their freedom to act, the aggrieved churches ought to combine with them into a single local church, albeit in distinct parishes.

In this entire church polity aspect of reformation, our churches must stand on the basis of God's Word, according to the confession of it in our Three Forms of Unity. This is not because those forms could ever be of equal value, or even of comparable value, to that Word, but because neither an individual person nor any office-bearer, but only the churches assembled in a legitimate synod have the right to judge the gravamina brought against any form on the basis of God's Word, and to decide on this matter in the name of the Lord.

---

96. Article 168 of the 1848 Dutch Constitution ensured the continued payment of ministers' pensions and salaries by the state from assets that state had confiscated at the end of the eighteenth century. See Kuyper's discussion in *Our Program: A Christian Political Manifesto*, ed. and trans. Harry Van Dyke (Bellingham, WA: Lexham Press, 2015), §§305–6.

97. The Law on Church Denominations (*De Wet op de Kerkgenootschappen*) of September 1853 required churches and denominations to register with the government. See M. J. Aalders, "De Wet op de Kerkgenootschappen van 10 september 1853," in *Om de toekomst van het Protestantse Nederland: de gevolgen van de grondwetsherziening van 1848 voor kerk, staat en maatschappij*, ed. G. J. Schutte and J. Vree (Zoetermeer: Meinema, 1998), 91–127.

§ 65   TAKING POSSESSION OF THE HIGHER CHURCH BOARDS

I continue to discourage the manner of taking possession of the classical and provincial governing bodies of the church, which others prefer. In itself such an opportunistic strategy, whereby the principles lose their luster, seems less desirable. But more importantly, to sit on such a board, under the current church order, is to exercise an authority that does not belong to us but to Jesus our King. Furthermore, even if one would succeed with the help of dissenting brothers—and therefore without the firm foundation of a confession—to take over the church boards, then at the end of the path you would divide after all, and the old struggle would start over from the very beginning. Finally, and this is no less important for our brothers, it will make the renewal of the church rather unspiritual, and calculation takes the place of the power of repentance before God and of the nobility of prayer. But if many of our brothers think they *may* follow this path, we do not wish to judge them, and we leave the outcome of the battle to the One without whose superior inspiration all reformation must fail in the end.

But whatever other or better way one might outline for the reformation of our churches different than the one we have presented, let this one thing be the prayer of all brothers and sisters in the faith, with quiet devotion and holy insistence: May the spiritual stream, which begins with the confession of guilt and manifests itself in the conversion of life, not for a moment flow out from under the icy crust of preoccupation with matters of church polity. May the impulse toward reformation never be resisted, either within church members or office-bearers, on account of an antinomian theory of letting the disease run its course; nor may it come to rest before everything in God's church is once again organized according to his Word. And finally, in all our zeal for the name of the Lord, even when one brother or sister must testify against another, may the higher love not wither in any of us, but may it blossom abundantly within every heart upon the grave of our own ego.

TWOFOLD
FATHERLAND

TEXT INTRODUCTION

Kuyper delivered his speech "Twofold Fatherland" at the seventh annual meeting of the Free University of Amsterdam on June 15, 1887, in the Schuttershof in Middelburg. He presented it just months after the ecclesiastical secession (the *Doleantie*) from the Dutch Reformed Church. The Free University, which represented a historic effort to establish a private university, was still small, and its future was uncertain—all the more so because the church it served was equally humble. In his speech Kuyper presents a Christian social ethic for a church attuned to these circumstances. He describes three societies: the sinful world, contrasted with the believers' earthly fatherland and their heavenly one. Although the believer's ultimate loyalty is to the heavenly fatherland, Christians should not despise their earthly one as sects tend to do. The earthly fatherland is the field of God's common grace, contrasted with the heavenly fatherland of particular, saving grace. The significance of this thesis is evident against the background of Augustine's two cities. Between the city of God and the city of the earth, Kuyper inserts a third society, the earthly fatherland (that is, the nation), justifying his work in Dutch public life. Kuyper's treatment of the earthly fatherland shows the national affection characteristic of the nineteenth century and makes Augustine safe in the era of nations and nationalism.

Source: Kuyper, Abraham. *Tweeërlei vaderland, ter inleiding van de zevende jaarvergadering der Vrije Universiteit*. Amsterdam: J. A. Wormser, 1887. Translated by Nelson D. Kloosterman.

TWOFOLD
FATHERLAND

Our help is in the name of the LORD, who made heaven and earth. Amen.

Gentlemen, since I do not appear before you in a service of worship but to introduce our seventh annual meeting, I do not consider myself called to explain or apply a passage of Holy Scripture on this occasion. Permit me, however, to borrow a passage from that Word as inspiration for my address, and read again with me what the holy apostle wrote to the Hebrews in the eleventh chapter. Here he sang his paean regarding the cloud of witnesses and spoke of Noah, Abraham, Isaac, and Jacob, and how these holy patriarchs did not value their earthly fatherland—and much less the world—but as pilgrims bound for a better fatherland, had put their hope in their God. We read in that captivating chapter, beginning in verse 7, as follows:

> By faith Noah, being warned by God concerning events as yet unseen, in reverent fear constructed an ark for the saving of his household. By this he condemned the world and became an heir of the righteousness that comes by faith.
>
> By faith Abraham obeyed when he was called to go out to a place that he was to receive as an inheritance. And he went out, not knowing where he was going. By faith he went to live

in the land of promise, as in a foreign land, living in tents with Isaac and Jacob, heirs with him of the same promise. For he was looking forward to the city that has foundations, whose designer and builder is God. By faith Sarah herself received power to conceive, even when she was past the age, since she considered him faithful who had promised. Therefore from one man, and him as good as dead, were born descendants as many as the stars of heaven and as many as the innumerable grains of sand by the seashore.

These all died in faith, not having received the things promised, but having seen them and greeted them from afar, and having acknowledged that they were strangers and exiles on the earth. For people who speak thus make it clear that they are seeking a fatherland. If they had been thinking of that land from which they had gone out, they would have had opportunity to return. But as it is, they desire a better country, that is, a heavenly one. Therefore God is not ashamed to be called their God, for he has prepared for them a city. [Heb 11:7–16]

And now, gentlemen, before I begin my address, raise your voices and sing in the tone of the patriarchs the pilgrim song found in Psalm 89, stanzas 6 and 7:

6. Blest are the people who acclaim you as their King,
who know the festal shout and of your mercy sing.
They walk in radiant light, before your face rejoicing;
the praises of your name they all day long keep voicing.
Your wondrous deeds they laud, your righteousness recalling;
they go their way with joy, your steadfast love extolling.

7. You are our strength and glory, you exalt our horn,
and by your favour, Lord, our enemies we scorn.
To you belongs our shield, our king so great and glorious;
you, Lord, came to his aid and you made him victorious.
To you our praise we sing, to you we homage render,
O Israel's Holy One, our powerful Defender.[1]

---

1. *Book of Praise: Anglo-Genevan Psalter* (Winnipeg: Premier, 2014), Psa 89:6–7.

~~~~~~~~~~~~~~~~~~~~~~~~~

Gentlemen, no flower exudes a fragrance other than that of its own kind, whether it is a rose, a daisy, or a lily; and no precious stone sparkles except in accordance with the special name it bears, whether a diamond, a ruby, or a jasper. So also no human beings live under the sun without belonging to their own country and their own people, be it Russian, Spanish, Belgian, or whatever other nation you might name. It is no different with us. We too are not just human beings, but come from the province of Zeeland, Friesland, or North or South Holland. But together we are people of the Netherlands, and as such, we are proud of our country and thank our God that the love of our native soil dwells innately in our lives. We also love the House of Orange-Nassau, and we continue to grow in our national history. No blow would destroy our national conscience more than if our existence as a people were destroyed and the Netherlands were to disappear from the ensemble of free European states.

Yet although we may be together in the name of the Lord in the Schuttershof,[2] a higher honor draws us—namely, to be not just children of the Netherlands but also children of the kingdom, and to be counted not just among the people of the Netherlands but also viewed as belonging to the people of God. Thus, we have a twofold fatherland and live as a twofold people under a twofold King. Our fatherland here below was wrested from the waves, drenched with the blood of martyrs, and made great by the wondrous hand of God. But there is also our fatherland above, which Christ won for us by the labor of his soul, which was sanctified for us by the blood of the Lamb, and which the Lord has made ready for us by wonders of grace. There is our national people on these western shores, with their beautiful language and illustrious past, their immensely rich possessions, and even more important, their high calling. But there is also our spiritual people, part of whom has already entered in through the veil. The rest of them are spread out across the entire globe as a called and holy people, God's own people, meant to declare the virtues of their God. We have a princely House of Orange in our city of residence, and there on the throne the king ordained for us by God, and beside him his royal child on whom the hope of the Netherlands rests. But we also have the House of David in the Jerusalem above and there, at God's right hand, our eternal

---

2. Kuyper gave the lecture in Middelburg in the Schuttershof, a historic venue that had formerly been the Guild Hall of the Archers of St. Sebastian.

King. One day every tongue will confess him, and before him every knee will bow.

Yes, to come to the root of the matter, here below we have an earthly father, given to us by God. From his blood ours sprang forth—whether we still rejoice in his presence or whether we have already carried him out to the place of rest for the dead. But above, we have our Father in heaven, who will remain our Father eternally. Here below, there is a place where our cradle once stood after our first birth; but also above there is the counsel of peace from which our second birth sprang. Here below there is an inheritance that, whether large or small, becomes ours when our father dies; but also above there is an eternal inheritance in heaven which that better Father is bringing to us. And, if you wish, here we have our own house in which we live together with our nearest and dearest; but also above, in the city that has foundations, we have the Father's house with its many rooms, in which the Lord also prepares a place for us and in which the communion of saints thrives eternally.

Now, gentlemen, what a burden and cross would fall from our hearts and shoulders if the calling of that twofold fatherland, in the midst of that twofold nation and for that twofold king, never collided and never fought with each other. Then paradise would be back on earth, since that is how it was when God first created us and everything around us. In paradise, earth and heaven were one, and precisely for that reason we had to leave paradise. God's cherubim prevented our return as soon as the cleft of hell had split our heart and had torn apart that dual fatherland by our fall. Thus all these have come upon us, not by chance, but by God's just judgment: the burning division of the heart, that sharp discord in life that pulls one way and then the other; the striving of Satan in us to forget the fatherland above for the fatherland below; and finally—sinful as we are even in our godly intentions—we have the tension of hyper-spirituality that fanatically dreams of a higher fatherland already here and rejects, devalues, and neglects the duty that our earthly fatherland demands of us.

The establishment of our Free University also came out of no other discord than this one, finds its privileges and reason for existence in no other struggle, and the rule that governs it derives from no other antithesis. Therefore it did not seem to me inappropriate as an introduction to our seventh annual meeting to draw your attention to the fact that both of these two fatherlands are given to us by God's grace; brought into conflict by our guilt; and also, in that conflict, to be valued only in accordance with God's Word.

I

When I say that the heavenly fatherland is given to us out of mere grace, I am simply echoing the inspiration of your own souls, gentlemen! But if I say that the possession of our earthly fatherland is also a gift of pure grace, do you perhaps find that strange? Do you not know and confess that there is also a common grace—a grace that lies completely outside the root of the covenant of grace and that works its miracles in our natural and civil life? Do you suppose that if God did not restrain our sinful heart, did not cast a ray of light into our darkness, and did not come to our aid with restraining compassion, there would still be any fidelity and integrity, any virtue and dedication, any art or learning, or any human organization or sense of justice on earth? No, I tell you, if the Lord Almighty had left us to our own devices, all virtue would have turned into brutishness, all order into chaos, and all humanity would have descended in the dense smoke of hell. The fact that a human society, a civil organization, a natural flourishing of peoples is still possible, is owed not to nature—which was totally corrupted—nor to your nostalgia for what was. It is solely and exclusively due to that common grace by which it pleases God to restrain for a time the human descent into the deep. The division of peoples and, consequently, the institution of the fatherland, belong to this common grace.

You did not want that by nature. At Babel it was from your sinful human heart that the cry of thousands arose: "Come, let us build ourselves a city, with a tower that reaches to the heavens, so that there will be no division of people from people, but in which all are citizens of the world." And then it was the Lord who, in his anger, came between them, and his thunderous voice cried out: "Not so, but you will wander divided, split into nations and peoples!" And so he split that one language into a multitude of languages. It was in his anger, but in that anger was also his compassion. And so, in the ruins of Babel's destroyed tower, there sprouted the germ of all nationalities, including ours.[3]

This act of God broke the curse of uniformity and endowed our sunken race with that treasure of moral powers that was poured out into the heart of those nations: a nobler spirit for the fatherland, heroism to resist the conqueror, mutual devotion to the sovereign, a commonly experienced history, and an endless differentiation of callings. All the Lord's acts are majestic, and here too the wealth of the spiritual gain that became ours

---

3. See CG 1.41–42.

from this one division of the nations is immeasurable. Being conscious of this origin, every nation has always counted the love of fatherland among the holy things. Treason is branded as a hellish abomination; to live and die for our God-given fatherland has always been the honor that beckoned in every age and in every region. And the Kenau Hasselaars shared that honor with us, as was necessary.[4]

No, the fire that also glows in your breast for the people and the fatherland did not come to life from the smoldering ashes of your depraved nature. It was kindled in that broken nature by God's grace. It is his divine inspiration in the heart of the nations—a divine gift to our lost race! Indeed, it was impossible that our heart itself could cause such a precious inspiration to come to life; rather, human beings in their blindness sought to corrupt that gift of grace. If new grace had not prevented it, the enthusiasm for the fatherland in the human heart would long since have been quenched.

What else are the empires that Daniel saw in the animal forms of the lion, the bear, the leopard, and the gruesome monster that he saw rising from the deep, but terrible disruptions of the life of free nations and a thirst for power to try yet again what once failed at Babel? That which Cyrus, Alexander, Caesar, and Napoleon stirred to life—what was all this at its core if not Satan's urge to reestablish dominion over the graves of the nations and the ruins of all peoples, to reestablish that heartless kingdom, the realm of violence, and the realm of the inhuman portrayed thus in animal imagery?

And do not suppose that those world conquerors are the only ones who want to rob us of our sacred fatherland. Did you not hear the wild song of the French Revolution that elevated the world citizen above the nation's citizen, that wanted to suffocate all love for fatherland with tones of empty love for humanity, and supposed that the golden age would arrive when the boundaries of the nations ceased to exist? And what the Communist now intends, and the Nihilist, and the Social Democrat, and whoever else bent on anarchy hides under the "red hood with the dagger," what is it but the intent to cause all nationality to blend into one international jumble? These are altogether ungodly pursuits, the poisonous seed of which lurks

---

4. Kenau Hasselaar, a woman of the city of Haarlem, became a folk hero after commanding a group of women to defend the city's walls against the Spanish army in 1572.

in every sinful heart. You often observe this sinful germination among our upper-crust youth when you hear them mock the fatherland in a cynical and base way and when you hear how in their frolicsome company they boisterously ridicule all warm expression of passion for one's fatherland.

Thus it appears that it was the Lord Almighty who gave us our fatherland, and also the Lord's Spirit who ignited the love for the fatherland in our breast and kept it burning. This is the reason why the more humane among the pagans early on intertwined service to fatherland unchangeably with service to idols. And according to the singular witness of history, never has a noble dedication to the dear fatherland shone more than when piety was mingled with love for the fatherland—when Gustavus Adolphus, with his praying Swedes, or the Prince of Orange, with his brave *Geuzen*, fought for hearth and altar.[5]

<hr />

Despite the treasure of human nobility that the Lord God gave us in our earthly fatherland, his hand contains even more grace. He has prepared for us a still better fatherland. Our society in our fatherland here below, even considering its most beautiful features in its most glorious eras, is still far from approaching that of paradise. God has destined us for more than a paradise in our creation. In due course we shall die and our fatherland will take us to its bosom and our dust will be mingled with its soil. We still exist then, and we enter the gate of eternity, continuing to call with serious longing for another fatherland when this fatherland falls away.

Once through the gate of eternity, your destination will be one of two routes, according to whether in your death God or Satan reigned in your soul as father. If there are those of whom Christ says, "You are of your father the devil, and your will is to do your father's desires!" [John 8:44], then alas they fall into the realm of their ungodly father and experience eternal woe in their hearts. Satan is a father without compassion, a father without a fatherland, who had prepared for them an eternal inheritance of loathsome existence in the darkness of doom instead of a fatherland. If there are those who are immediately heard uttering—by wondrous

---

5. King Gustavus Adolphus of Sweden (r. 1611–32) was famous for his military intervention in the Thirty Years War on the side of the Protestants. The *Geuzen*, or Sea Beggars, were Dutch patriots who fought against Spanish rule during the Eighty Years War of the sixteenth century.

mercy—the "Abba, dear Father!" toward our God, then they will discover a Father richer than they could have ever known or guessed from their experience of even the best father on earth. And they will receive from that Father a certain inheritance, a home in which they will rejoice eternally, and a heavenly fatherland in and around the new Jerusalem. All the glory and all the sanctity of their earthly fatherland pales in comparison to that heavenly one. In that fatherland *common* grace no longer shines, but there *particular* grace shines. The glories of the covenant of grace form the ornament of this "holy temple" [see Psa 65:4]. That is where the throne is, where the altar of incense of the prayers of the saints is, where the seraphim spread their wings to form the canopy for the throne, where the cherubim give voice to their power, where the Lamb that was slain dwells, where the martyrs are who washed their clothes in the blood of the Lamb, and where the multitude that no one can count—a multitude from all nations, and peoples, and tongues—will sing the *Hallelujah* in heavenly choruses for him who is and who was and who is to come.

Those who are justified and perfected will first enter that better fatherland only in their souls, but later, after the day of judgment, also in their bodies, which will then be glorified. There the seeds that were already hidden in the hearts of God's children, but could not germinate in the harsh atmosphere here on earth, will bud and flourish. They will be handed palm fronds to wave, diadems to wear on their heads, and golden cymbals with which to make a joyful noise. And no one will weep anymore; everyone will laugh in holy joy, and every soul will be satisfied with the knowledge of God.

And so God's children will receive more than paradise, because all division and separation of the peoples will come to an end in that better fatherland. What existed before the flood, what the sinners intended by building the tower of Babel, and what, even today, Cosmopolitanism and the Internationalists pursue with their false ideals, will be realized there. There "all kingdoms have become the Lord's" [see Rev 11:15]. There will be one fatherland common to all, and the prophetic image of Pentecost—Parthians and Elamites, Cretans and Arabians with one voice bringing praise to the Eternal One—will be an abiding reality there.

Although the earthly fatherland will then be finished, gentlemen, it will not simply have passed on as a pointless form of life, but like all things on earth, it will then become apparent that the ordinance of the earthly fatherland has served God's counsel. When the angels of God will one day gather the full sheaves, they will also carry into heaven's barns the fruit of fidelity, of heroism, of dedication—in short, the fruit of all social excellence—and also the fruit of the patience of the meek saints, by which the Lord God, principally by the institution of the earthly fatherland, taught his children about a better fatherland.

I I

So it became apparent to us, gentlemen, that both the earthly and the heavenly fatherland are gifts of grace from our God. The one is connected to the other. The earthly, according to the great Article 36 of our beautiful Belgic Confession, is called to serve the glory of the heavenly, and both are destined to give honor to God the Father, the Almighty, who called both this earth and this heaven into being solely for his own sake.

Alas, (and now I come to the second part of my address) we have disrupted this beautiful order. By our guilt the earthly fatherland is no longer oriented toward the heavenly but stands constantly in opposition to it. And according to the rule of the *optimi corruptio pessima*[6] (that is, that the holy, by forsaking its calling, falls the more deeply into sin), human willfulness has time and again forged weapons from the precious ore of our earthly fatherland to fight against the heavenly. And if it were possible, it would erase the memory of [the heavenly fatherland] from the minds of the peoples.

The connection here lies in the word *world* that Holy Scripture uses so negatively—not the fatherland with its division and the particularization of the nations but "the whole world," the world taken in its entirety, "lies in the power of the evil one" (1 John 5:19). Satan does not want to be ruler of our fatherland or of another fatherland but ruler of the world. He showed the Son of God the enticing prize not just of the kingdom of Israel but of all the kingdoms of the world. Setting the world as one power over against God is exactly what failed with the building of the tower of Babel. That is why the world as such is opposed to God. With its spirit and intention it is against God, and it follows that "whoever wishes to be a friend of the world makes himself an enemy of God" (Jas 4:4). Those who walk in the ways of this world—that is, according to its lifeview (Eph 2:2)—systematically extinguish their higher life. And those who possess their portion (or inheritance) in this world forfeit their inheritance with our God. As a person conceived and born in sin, there is a dual principle, a dual beginning possible for you. You received your first principle from the world, and you must receive the second principle from the Holy Spirit. And therefore, those who do not die to this their first principle—that is, the elemental principles of this world—but continue to live according to it, cannot even see the kingdom of God (Gal 4:3; Col 2:8, 20). All that is in the world and

---

6. "The corruption of the best is the worst of all."

the world itself with its allurement—its striving, its intention, and its false ideal—will irrevocably pass away, and only those who grow according to the will of God abide forever! (1 John 2:16, 17).

Therefore, when the invisible commencement of the better fatherland was brought into the world and did not come with a physical countenance, but established itself within human beings, the Lord's preacher of penitence cried out: "Repent, for the kingdom of heaven is at hand" [Matt 3:2]. And the kingdom of heaven did not stand principally over against the kingdom of Israel (that is, against the earthly fatherland), but against the world (that is, the kingdom of Satan). The beginning of that better kingdom did not exclude the root of the institution of the fatherland, but the principles of the world. Before Pilate's judgment seat it was declared: "My kingdom is not of this world" [John 18:36]. And when the King of this kingdom of God died on the cross of Golgotha, the sign of shame did not state "Emperor of the whole world," as Caesar called himself, but "King of the Jews" in a divine and national sense. The goal of the work of redemption is thus not to take us out of our fatherland, but to "deliver us from the present evil age, according to the will of our God and Father" (Gal 1:4). Those who follow Jesus have not broken with their fatherland in the core of their heart, but with the world. To love the world again means deserting the Son of God (2 Tim 4:10). Being "conformed to this world" for those who know a better fatherland means that they forfeit their future (Rom 12:2). The petition in the high priestly prayer is for all those who are called: "Father ... the world has hated them because they are not of the world, just as I am not of the world. I do not ask that you take them out of the world, but that you keep them from the evil one"! (John 17:1,14-15).

Not the earthly fatherland, but the world in its principle, its spirit, and its striving stand directly and flatly opposed to the kingdom of heaven and therefore opposed to the better fatherland. And all the sin in our evil heart regarding this point consists of this: that we, in culpable audacity, loosen our fatherland from its connection to heaven and identify with that world. Our earthly fatherland was instituted by God not to strengthen the irreligious spirit of the world, but on the contrary, to raise it as a bulwark against that world and to serve the cause of the Lord. But our worldly heart and evil intentions have constantly turned this ordinance of our God around, and on almost every page of history you will find the ignominious story of how the earthly fatherland drifted away in the stream of the world. And as an instrument of that world, it resisted the dominion of Christ.

To see this more clearly, compare the service to which God called the visible fatherland with the service he demands of your visible form, that is, of your body. An angel who falls away lacks that body and is thus irrevocably gone. A fallen angel, being without a body, turns immediately into a devil. But God left Adam his body when he was driven out of paradise, and on that body he placed the calling of the sweat of his face and her pain in childbearing [Gen 3:19, 16]. And he added the curses of thirst, hunger, and all distress and pestilence. That is how the body and the limbs of the body were destined by God to be weapons and instruments of righteousness for righteousness. It is not the case that the seat of sin is to be found in that body. The foul spring of our bodily sins lies not in the body, but in our spirit. Indeed, your body as body is not destined for corruption, since your body is expected in heaven, where Immanuel will one day cause it to shine like his glorified body. Notice that while evil does not take refuge in the fatherland, but in the world, so also the deadly danger for you does not lie in the body, but in the flesh that God has cursed, that is, in the ungodly power that corrupts both body and soul, cuts off your entire person from your heavenly calling, and alienates you from God. "For I know," the holy apostle laments, "that nothing good dwells in me, that is, in my flesh" (Rom 7:18). And he declares even more strongly not that setting one's mind on the *body*, but setting the mind on the *flesh* is death (Rom 8:6). Therefore with the instrument of your body you must crucify the flesh and combat all its temptation. And the best place to conquer the goad of the flesh is not a cloistered cell where the body rusts and is taken out of service, but especially at the plow and the carpenter's bench where the body displays its powers. *With the body, against the flesh* is therefore God's holy ordinance. From it all the blessing of labor, all the glory of self-control, and all the mystery of suffering emerges. But what did we, sinners that we are, do instead? Only this: our evil heart has turned that God-given blessing into a curse by making flesh and body identical.

The sin in us commits the same robbery when it transgresses against the fatherland to accommodate the world. Just as the body must be a weapon against the flesh and stand in the Lord's service, so also the fatherland must be a weapon against the world and be used in the service of our God. But just as the body can systematically be misused to place the flesh in opposition to the Spirit, so also human evil misuses the institution of the fatherland century after century to allow the spirit of the world to triumph over the cause of our God. This was especially evident when Israel's national leaders cried out about the King of that better fatherland, "O mighty governor, we have a law of our fatherland and according to that law he must die!" [see John 19:7]. But also after Golgotha this misuse of the fatherland's power to allow the kingdom of the world to triumph over the kingdom of God was signified in streams of precious blood: when Stephen succumbed under the stones cast by the mob, the lions devoured Ignatius in the arena, Blandina was torn to pieces, and Laurentius was scorched on a red-hot gridiron in the name of the law of the fatherland. After these early martyrs, it was often the case that the more fulsome sheaves of Christ's martyrs were gathered in the name of fatherland interests. And when Savoy's prince raged against the Waldensians, France's king against the Huguenots, or Alva and Vargassen against our own people, it was always in the name of fatherland interests that they grabbed "the poor sheep of Christ" (as our fathers called them) by the throat and murdered them.[7]

Even when this ultimate penalty was not exacted, the sin that I am speaking about nonetheless occurred. Included in the institution of the fatherland are the government and the power of the law and the courts, the riches of taxes and tribute, the resilience of society, the superior strength of public opinion, the influence of art, the formative power of the school, and the power of learning. And now, too, with each of these precious gifts of your God you are given a choice: Will you let them flourish to his honor, by God's grace and bound to him by oath of fidelity; or will you, by trivializing that divine grace and freed from that oath, align them as powers against him?

This can be done openly, insolently, and audaciously. That is how the Commune of Paris wanted to do it, and the Nihilist in Russia wants to do the same. But there is also a more covert form of this evil. This happens when you still appear to maintain the established doctrine, do not seem to scorn piety, and especially when you still have Christ's name graven on your shield; but meanwhile, behind that shield, you extol the power of the state as highest and most sacred, and you refuse to respect any higher

---

7. The Spanish Duke of Alva (or Alba) waged Phillip II of Spain's war on the Netherlands during the sixteenth century and established the bloody "Council of Troubles" to summarily try Dutch Protestant iconoclasts. The Waldensians and Huguenots were Protestants persecuted by Roman Catholic officials in the sixteenth and seventeenth centuries.

criterion than the demand of the common good. Why not? Because then, as a private person, you can still keep the illusion of a heaven hereafter and behind closed doors enjoy the pursuits of fanatics. But the state then no longer reckons with God's Word, nor with his honor, nor with your better fatherland. Your piety will then still serve the fatherland here below in a passive sense and only as a factor in the development of your people, or, to use Locke's expression, "for economizing on behalf of the overly expensive state police."[8]

Then the entire institution of the fatherland on earth refuses to make itself subservient to the better fatherland above. It refuses to take its inspiration from that better fatherland. Neither pillar of fire at night nor pillar of cloud by day then hovers above its tent. It closes itself off; wants to be self-sufficient; and, rejecting all greater power over it, establishes itself as the highest power and standard—if necessary, even over the consciences of human beings.

This system can be called the apotheosis or deification of the state. Rome's Caesar adopted the title *divus* for himself—that is, called himself god. And as an altar burned before the image of Caesar and all citizens were required to bring divine honor to Caesar on that altar, it was the Symphorosas and the Saphyras, humble disciples of the Lord, who pleaded against these violent rulers of the earthly fatherland for a better fatherland in their martyrdom and at the cost of their lives. Today as well, audacity is gaining ground in order to subject our entire human existence to the insight of the state, to hand over our entire human development to the education of the state, and to sacrifice all human independence to the interest of the state. Just as formerly in Rome in superstitious forms, so also today in philosophical forms the idolization of the state's omnipotence threatens to cut off the institution of the fatherland from its calling on behalf of the higher fatherland. It presents citizens again and again with that painful choice regarding which law and which king they must obey as citizens: that of the better fatherland that is above or that of the fatherland they love on earth.

---

8. Kuyper presumably refers here to the political philosopher John Locke (1632–1704), who in his *Letter Concerning Toleration* (1689) contended that the purpose of civil government was to secure "the Temporal Good and outward Prosperity of the Society." See John Locke, *A Letter Concerning Toleration and Other Writings*, ed. Mark Goldie (Indianapolis: Liberty Fund, 2010), 47.

~~~~~~~~~~~~~~~~~~~~~~~~~~~~~~~~~~~~~~~

With that choice you see sons of the fatherland separated into three groups. On the left are those people who, having lost the faith of the fathers, search for support in reason or in naturalism or in the primitive ideal. They derive all their inspiration from the French Revolution and cause the old pagan idea of the state to come alive again in modern form. Caesar Augustus against the Holy Child of Bethlehem! Pilate on the judgment seat against the Anointed of the Lord! By the power of the state they break all who do not submit to the will of the state. For all of these there is no longer a better and higher fatherland. The state has become their all in all.

But you also see a flocking together of a quiet brotherhood of men and women who have seen the cloud of witnesses around them and learned to gaze with steadfast wonder at the ancient heroes of the faith—those who suffered mocking, flogging, chains, and imprisonment; who were stoned, sawn in two, and killed with the sword; who, forsaken and oppressed, went about in the skins of sheep and goats; who wandered about in deserts and mountains and in dens and caves of the earth; and who, with a burning love for their earthly fatherland in their hearts, nonetheless steadfastly refused to deny their better and higher fatherland (see Heb 11:36–38). It is a brotherhood mostly of the ordinary people in the land but who, rich in the glory of their national history, would regard themselves contemptible if they should ever close their ears to the voice that calls out from the blood of the martyrs. It is those who, having heard the cry, "I have set my King on Zion, my holy hill" (Psa 2:6), would consider it a cowardly corruption of character and an ignoble neglect of duty if they should not dare to bear witness to that kingdom that is not of this world, before governments and rulers—if necessary with their property and their blood. These are the ones whom the earthly fatherland excommunicates and damns as a danger to the state!

And between these two equally vibrant groups a third group of people takes its place on the ivory seats of honor and the soft satin pillow. Their worst example is a Gallio,[9] a better one is a Gamaliel,[10] while the finest character can reach the stature of an Erasmus.[11] These are people who drift along with the stream but who were never able to chart a course or set the tempo. They are those who, lacking the will to choose and having a passion inadequate for robust deeds, swing between two poles for their whole lives. Never having understood what heroic courage is nor what a higher passion means, they regard coastal navigation as very pleasant but never sail off to the deep seas. Half for the earthly fatherland and half for the better fatherland! Mediocrity is their perpetual slogan and moderation their shibboleth. They are heroes on the paved sidewalks, but they collapse with dizziness or tremble with fear along the high, wild mountain path.

As the separation occurs at the start of this three-forked road, the ideas are shared, the principles exercise their divisive action, and a triple stream becomes clearly noticeable in national life. And those three streams toss and turn, and then push and pull against each other. First the water seethes and foams, then it churns and roils, until finally in this strife, according to divine counsel, the group that has remained immovable in its adherence to principle and was equipped for rendering the greatest sacrifices takes the spoils and receives the palm of honor.

~~~~~~~~~~~~~~~~~~~~

But meanwhile it is a difficult time for our fatherland and for the citizen, gentlemen! It is a time when the demons are being released, hatred is rampant, slander spews out its poison, and the pool of human passion causes its most vile slime to bubble up. And therefore it is also a time in which extra vigilance and manifold grace are necessary, so that the coarseness of the battlefield does not reduce us to our own base nature.

---

9. In Acts 18 Paul is brought by his Jewish opponents before Gallio, the proconsul of Achaia. In what is sometimes interpreted for indifference, Gallio refused to hear anything of the case, preferring not to interfere in Jewish religious matters.
10. Gamaliel was an esteemed Jewish rabbi and Paul's teacher. In Acts 5 Gamaliel subdued the Jews who wanted to kill Peter and the apostles. He prophetically warned that if the nascent Christian movement was from God, then it would succeed, and otherwise it would not.
11. Dutch humanist scholar Erasmus of Rotterdam (1466–1536) sought to maintain a mediating position in the Reformation disputes between Roman Catholics and Protestants.

Oh, the Holy Spirit is so often bitterly and humiliatingly grieved in such a tenacious struggle!

Therefore, brothers and sisters, in this unavoidable upheaval in this painful struggle, let it be deeply imprinted in our soul that he who provoked it is the tempter and accuser, but that Satan would never have succeeded in this way had not the people of the Lord broken trust, also in our nation. I tell you this: you must not cast the blame on a few persons, such as your philosophers, your statesmen, or the leaders of public opinion. What are all of these but children of a misguided spirit that gained power over our people in an evil hour? That such a spirit could become powerful among us, gentlemen, did not depend on an evil plan, a sly conspiracy. No, the reason for it lies in us and in them because all of our hearts are so deeply corrupt. Actually, even more clearly (we may not deny it) more so in us than in them, because we, having shouted with joy about that better fatherland, were nonetheless enticed by the attraction of conformity to the world. Oh, when the salt lost its taste, who resisted such a disastrous corruption of our fatherland?

III

Gentlemen, I now come to the last part of my inquiry. Our better and our earthly fatherland are both together a gift of God united in a higher goal, but the two were torn apart and brought into conflict with each other by our sin. Consequently, there arose for your Christian conscience this very serious question: What rule, in accordance with God's Word, should govern our conduct in this struggle?

I immediately make a distinction that can never be disputed among Christians who have not wholly fallen away. I mean this: if pushed to the limit, we must, without a hint of hesitation, forsake our earthly fatherland so as not to give up our heavenly. The absolute rule that was imposed on children and their earthly father is also the measurement for citizens and their fatherland, and that rule remains irrevocably this: "Whoever loves father or mother more than me is not worthy of me" [Matt 10:37]. Applied to our issue, this means for every Christian citizen: "Those who love their fatherland more than Christ are not worthy of Christ." Among the godly there has always been agreement on this point. Abraham, the father of all believers, having been called by God, left Ur of the Chaldeans when the service of the idolatrous fatherland was beginning to usurp the service of God. When in a later age the tyranny of Philip of Spain in our country forbade the service of God, our people became exiles and went across the sea, to the Palatinate, and to Emden to find refuge for God's children. Our Prince of Orange once spoke this word: "If necessary, cut through the dikes and sail to a safer haven." When in the once free England a fierce new hierarchy exercised its evil in support of the state, the Pilgrim fathers fled to the still free open spaces of America. Of course you know how, even in this century, the shining exodus of our Transvaal brothers has demonstrated what passion exists in Dutch blood to create, if necessary, a new fatherland.[12] If the authorities prevent you from leaving or, even worse, force you to stay in your fatherland so that you might disavow the service to your God, then the mother with her seven sons from the days of Antiochus Ephiphanes will ever call out what Christ later so sharply expressed: "Fear him who, after he has killed, has authority to cast into hell. Yes, I tell you, fear him!" [Luke 12:5; compare 2 Maccabees 7].

---

12. In the first half of the nineteenth century, waves of Boer migration northward across the Vaal River led to the formation of the South African Republic in 1857. The Transvaal region was subsequently annexed by Great Britain in 1877, but after a revolt against the British a new independent republic was formed in 1881.

And so, if the antithesis should arise again, God's people should immediately apply the fixed rule: those who can, flee far across the border, and for those whose flight is prevented, the honor of the martyr's crown beckons.

But, with deeply felt thanks to the God of our fathers, we do not face such a choice today. The authorities grant us—and this is already a treasure that can never be appreciated enough—freedom of our person, of our speech, and of our confession. It has not yet come to direct persecution. And even if you compare 1886 with 1834, we have won huge gains in freedom![13] Back then, mounted soldiers with raised swords were sent into the praying throng; now those who dissent are left undisturbed in their places of worship that are filled to capacity. Oh brothers, our timid spirit so often raises a complaint, but let us not forget the good things of our God. Our fathers suffered a thousand times more than us!

Yet, no matter how strongly I urge on you the acknowledgment of that generous blessing, we may not hide the fact that the choice that our more gentle age gives us heightens the danger rather than reduces it. When the muzzle of a rifle is directed at your chest and you are told, "Deny your Lord," grace comes to you immediately, and you bare your breast and kneel in order to die with Christ in your heart. Then in that exigent situation there is a goad. That goad motivates your fortitude, and there is no place for cowardice within you, with its emasculating effect. But when substantially the same choice is presented to you, dressed in flannel and proceeding from flattering lips, and you are given the choice of three ways out instead of one, the danger of infidelity threatens much more alarmingly. Then it is so much easier to calculate than to pray, to glance backwards to the three ways out instead of looking Satan in the face defiantly and bravely. Then incense clouds your heroism and hesitation weakens the driving power of your more sacred inspirations. And because the poison of denial is offered to you silver plated, it slides into your soul before you can recoil from your misdeed. Oh, to be obedient in small things is often ten times more difficult than to be faithful before God in big things!

---

13. In 1834 a group of orthodox Reformed Protestants led by Henrick de Cock (1801–42) left the *Nederlandse Hervormde Kerk* (the national church), prompting a larger exodus of congregations, the *Afscheiding* ("separation"). These churches experienced persecution by the state. Their meetings were broken up, they were fined, and some were even jailed. Kuyper's own secession from the NHK, the *Doleantie*, occurred in 1886. It was not beset by persecution thanks to a more liberal constitution.

Our Anabaptists of old have sensed this, our Moderates have pondered it, and our Calvinists have grasped it, and so each has followed their own path in this wilderness according to their own rule. The Anabaptists were the first to occupy the terrain and initially almost all who were religious in Holland, Zeeland, Friesland, and Flanders adopted their position. What did the Anabaptists propose, gentlemen? Oh, there was much in their point of view that was attractive! "In a little corner with a little book" was their sweet thought. That is, live in the earthly fatherland, but as though not living in it, and be engaged only with the heavenly fatherland—have no involvement with the task of governing, with politico-phobia and all its consequences, refuse to serve as soldiers in the army, refuse to swear an oath in court, shun the society of the world by "avoidances," look straight ahead of you, and wear distinctive dress. In addition, do not concern yourself with studying, distance yourself from learning, and reject all higher education! After all [they thought], the Lord was about to return, so with the heavenly fatherland before your eyes, why bother yourself about the earthly?

So it began innocently. They were fanatically prepared for sacrifice, yet no sheep were ever killed more passively than these oldest of our Anabaptists. But alas, their history itself became their judgment. They had tried to apply to the entire fatherland the poignant concept of the monastic cell, but expanding that idea wreaked havoc on them. When the nudists agitated Amsterdam and when John of Leiden broke loose in wild passion in Münster, everyone asked, "Are these the same people?"[14] All of Europe, the whole of Christendom, realized that this path of avoidances did not lead one to the heavenly fatherland but, rather, led one to horrors of hell.

The problem was that these Anabaptists did not regard the earthly fatherland as a gift of God but, rather, as a creation of the Evil One. For them, fatherland and world were the same thing. And when, connected with this, they extracted baptism out of the covenant of grace and thus rejected the baptism of infants and spurned the rule of Paul that the natural comes first and then the spiritual [see 1 Cor 15:46]; they severed the bond between the first creation and re-creation, between the first birth and the second birth, and thereby between the earthly and the heavenly

---

14. In the 1530s Anabaptist leader John of Leiden led a revolt against the magistrates establishing the Anabaptist Kingdom of Münster. Another group of Anabaptists ran naked through Amsterdam proclaiming the judgment of God on the city.

fatherland. Oh, I know the heart of God's pious ones aches with nostalgia for the fatherland above. Whom else should they love, whom better to love, than the One in whom is all the delight of their soul? They are strangers on earth. If things are well with them, God's commandments are as songs in the land of their pilgrimage. Oh, the real pilgrims know but one refrain for the holiest of their sons, namely, "Come, Lord Jesus, come quickly!" [see Rev 22:20]. Nonetheless, Abraham fought to free Lot, Joseph ruled the land of the Pharaohs, Moses was instructed in all the wisdom of the Egyptians, and David and all the prophets loved their earthly fatherland with the blood of their soul. We may summarize this by saying that the Anabaptists have been judged by Jesus himself. Never have Anabaptists wept for their fatherland as Jesus did for his, with his "O Jerusalem, Jerusalem" [Matt 23:37] on his lips.

What then, gentlemen? Shall we avoid the slippery path of the Anabaptists and enter the smooth highway of our Moderates? Certainly, their ideals also contain something that is attractive! Wary of division, averse to strife, they call from the depth of principle back to the placid mirroring surface of the water: "There is your fatherland; there your people live and thrive; see, there flows the stream of national life. Sail together with us in that stream. It will carry you along with your religion, with your hope of a better life. The state wants to marry the church of Christ, and never was a more beautiful sound raised from human throats than when the honor of the high God was swallowed up in singing praise for the fatherland! Certainly, after the grave there follows a heaven, and in that heaven it will be even better than in our sacred fatherland, but we are not yet in that heaven. Now this good earthly country is our inheritance and that country is governed by a king given to us by God; and in the broad channel of that fatherland there is room for the development of all human endeavor: of your trade and your shipping, your industry and agriculture, but also your art and learning; and there is also room for your religious and moral life. So why would you then not resign yourself with your religion in the national church and not recognize the right of your earthly king to regulate that national church?

True enough, not all that glitters is gold. Thrashing about in the stream of the fatherland are malevolence, lies, evil heresies, and diabolical sins. But is it any different with your own body? In it too, sometimes poison or bacteria war against you, but then God sends you a fever and makes medical doctors available, and you wait until the illness has run its course.

And soon, fully recovered, you feel even stronger than before. Think about the struggle for religion the same way. People and church are not to be separated. What ferments among the people must ferment subsequently in the life of the church. And although it may seem that this will be at the expense of the truth, put aside your fears. In the end the truth will overcome the lie. Just as you need to allow an illness to take its normal course, so too your church and your religion and your sacred principles will later arise that much stronger from the struggle!"

That, gentlemen, is how the Moderates of all ages sang their siren song. It does not matter whether you hear this song from Erasmus, Oldenbarnevelt, Coornheert, or the later tolerationists; in the Santhorst Confession; or in the latest synodical encyclical—the theme is always the same.[15] The church of Christ must be made subservient to the unity of the fatherland in this life. That unity of the one fatherland's stream, along with both the public school and the national church (which are necessary in this system), is propelled forward under the guidance of the national monarch. That is how you remain a "Christian" nation and your youth are taught "Christian" virtues in addition to social ones at the public school, and the Rabbi of Nazareth will still be honored in the national church, even above Buddha and Muhammad!

But why should I detain you any more with this moderate and irenic twaddle of the tolerationists of all ages? Stroke for stroke, each point of departure is spurious, and the entire alluring representation has been proved wrong by the outcome of history. For it is not true that the medical doctor can do without the surgeon, nor that fever and illness always lead to recovery. The grave that is never satisfied can tell you of more sorrowful things. The thousands upon thousands who plod along until their end in a broken body and in poor health cry out in protest against an unpardonable illusion that mocks their creeping suffering. It is not true, regardless of how long you let the truth struggle with the lie, that Christ's church

---

15. During the early seventeenth century, the time of the Remonstrant-Arminian debates, and the Synod of Dort, a group of Arminian supporters, including statesman Johan van Oldenbarnevelt (1547–1619), advocated renewed trade relations with Spain, former oppressor of the Netherlands. Dirck Coornheert (1522–90) was a Dutch humanist and Protestant pastor in the late sixteenth century, and it was in studying his writings that Jacob Arminius (1560–1609), formerly a Calvinist and student of Beza, came to his modified views of predestination. Generations later Elisabeth Wolff-Bekker (1738–1804) wrote the Santhorst Confession (1772) in support of the Remonstrant (Arminian) position of greater religious tolerance.

will in the end always triumph on earth. Were the ten thousand churches in Asia and the north coast of Africa that once flourished so purely and gloriously under men such as Athanasius and Augustine not destroyed without a trace? Did Rome not win the struggle against the Huguenots in France, and even worse, against the pious confessors in Spain and Italy? Was the gospel not smothered in Flanders and Hainaut, from which came our Guido de Brès, Datheen, and with them our most illustrious martyrs?[16]

Nor is it true that the church of Christ occupies a position whose nature and rights are simply equal to those of the arts, industry, and learning in the single life of the fatherland. Those who say this are drawing Christ from nature instead of from heaven. They bridge or fill the deep chasm that sin has brought through our life. They deny miracles. They negate regeneration. And in true rationalistic fashion they do not derive the truth of God from Scripture but, even when that Scripture still apparently continues to be honored, they do so with misguided conscience or darkened reason. Even though one may plead against this with an "it is written" (as the Tempter did), in terms of the leaven in measures of flour, the weeds in the field, or the two kinds of fish in the net, it is all stamped as misuse of Scripture by this single cry of the Lord: "Do not think that I have come to bring peace to the earth. I have not come to bring peace, but a sword" (Matt 10:34); or even more strongly, "I came to cast fire on the earth, and would that it were already kindled!" (Luke 12:49).

Our Calvinists, gentlemen, are therefore motivated by different considerations. They are just as much opposed to the Anabaptist "avoidances" as they are to the "blending" of the Moderates. From the beginning they adopted the watchword that for both the earthly and the higher fatherland a distinct law and rule exists, so that consequently for each of them a distinct honor for the king must apply. Their system was not that of the Old Testament, but of the New Testament theocracy—that is, God's rule. The Lord Almighty is entitled to preeminence over both the earthly and the heavenly fatherland. Under him the governance of his nations on

---

16. Guido de Brès (1522–67), author of the Belgic Confession, was martyred by the Spanish Inquisition. Peter Datheen (1531–90), known for his metrical psalter in Dutch, was an early sixteenth-century Dutch Calvinist who was forced to flee religious persecution on various occasions, from the Low Countries to England and from England to Emden.

earth must be exercised by magistrates and governments; and likewise under him the governance of his people that he has obtained on earth and in heaven must be exercised by the King, whom he himself had anointed over Zion and had made to sit down at the right hand of his power [see Luke 22:69].

The guideline was and remained, therefore, according to the beautiful intention of Article 36 of our Belgic Confession, that the earthly fatherland is called to serve the heavenly. The ideal is a state of the people that exists for the sake of the kingdom of heaven. The ideal is not a national church but, rather, a churched nation whose realization beckoned enthusiastically. Thus, "church, the House of Orange, and the Netherlands" was also the threefold unbreakable cord for the Dutch Calvinists.

A theocracy, certainly (how could we possibly have abandoned that only true concept?). But note carefully, not a theocracy as existed in Israel. In Israel the law of the land and the laws that governed the people's lives were not imposed by their earthly king but were received from heaven. There was no lawgiving power in Israel. "The Lord is our lawgiver," the people confessed for their national existence as well. But the Calvinists did not want that for their earthly fatherland. They knew very well that neither Geneva, nor France, nor the Netherlands could be equated with God's old covenant people, so they duly acknowledged the power of the earthly government to make laws for the people. No Calvinist has ever had the absurd notion of proclaiming Israel's laws of punishment for our own land. No sentence of stoning has ever been executed here, no cities of refuge were ever named, and the avenger of blood would never have been tolerated. So we are not at all guilty of imitating Israel's theocracy, gentlemen, nor of any attempt to establish that other hierarchical theocracy in which the government is demoted to being a servant of the ecclesiastical regiment and, blindfolded and without its own input, simply carries out the bulls and decrees of the church.

Yet they also were too aware of the extra-ecclesiastical origin of the power of government and the related concepts of the government's own independent calling and its own sphere of life and task of governing. They had too much regard for the high view of Christ's church that may never involve itself either in a political cabal or in imperious ways. And they confessed clearly and resolutely that the Holy Spirit not only distributes spiritual grace to the regenerate but also gives the nation's magistracy, lawgiver, and judge their own talents, competence, and ability to plumb the depths of God's Word.

Consequently, there was no vacillation or hesitation in reaching the point of view they adopted. The Lord Almighty, and he alone, was entitled to glory both in the earthly fatherland and the church—which as a colony of the heavenly fatherland still exists on our soil for the Lord. God, not human beings, has authority over both terrains. But also, the sovereign God gave each terrain its own institutions and persons, each with their own strengths and talents and their own task and calling. Each terrain has its own responsibility. Yet this was all so connected that God's church should nurture virtue and subjection in the earthly fatherland, while the earthly fatherland, by giving free rein to the course of the gospel, should serve the heavenly.

~~~~~~~~~~~~~~~~~~~~

However, this high ideal allowed for two very different possibilities. If both government and church walked the clearly demarcated path that God had shown them, this beautiful harmony would lead to the birth of a rare and handsome aggregate of people, just as when persons may carry a soul inspired by God in a perfect and healthy body and who are therefore almost to be envied for their happy state. Indeed, a few times it pleased God to grant such a desired state of affairs to a single people, at least for a time. England under Edward VI, Sweden under Gustav Vasa, the Palatinate under Frederick, more than one of the American states under the leadership of the Pilgrim Fathers, Geneva under Calvin, and our fatherland under the first princes of Orange have experienced this. There was then in our fatherland certainly not a national church—an ungodly concept that would have horrified our fathers—but there was a people that devoted itself with all its strength and talents, even at the cost of its most noble Nassau blood, to the cause of God's church. The theocracy, as it can flourish on earth, not like Israel's but most closely approximating Israel, was established for the duration of a precious century in the Netherlands.

Nevertheless—and this was also embedded in Calvinism—no nation could demand such a wonderful state from the Lord. Whenever it occurred, it happened by undeserved grace, and in extending that grace, the King of kings did not oblige himself. Therefore, without ever giving up this enthralling, rich, and ideal prize, one could take account of imperfect relationships. In God's counsel it could also happen that the government chose its course and direction outside God's Word, something that mattered not to the entire nation, but only to a group in the "gathering of believers." And in consequence the national institutions and the powers of art and learning that were rooted in national life would be used in opposition to God's church instead of for its honor. The Calvinists of old did indeed experience this in France and Italy, under the Guelphs in Bavaria, under the Habsburgs in Austria, in Poland, and in Zevenbergen.

Just as the Lord is sovereign in allowing the best of his children to live in ill health—and he does so—he does the opposite still more. Thus, it is improper for a child of God to grumble against his sovereign rule if it pleases him to cause Christ's pure church to live and operate in a fatherland that is no longer Christian, or at least no longer purely Christian. Of course then an entirely different rule applies, which applied also in Israel according to God's Word and which is irrevocably fixed for every people in every age in this call of Isaiah: "Bind up the testimony; seal the teaching among my disciples" (Isa 8:16). That is, when a nation as a whole can no longer be the instrument for expressing your confession and life, create your own instrument for your Christian life, or as Groen van Prinsterer recently called it, a separately created terrain.[17] This is the law that speaks from Noah's ark; Abraham's rule when he stands in isolation in Canaan; Jacob's petition when he pleads with Pharaoh for his people's own domain in Goshen; the holy isolation of Christ in Israel; his apostolate in the apostolic church; and, until Constantine, from all the churches in Christendom. The Waldensians understood this. Calvin gave this advice to the believers in Poland, Bohemia, and Zevenbergen. And our fathers followed it in Flanders and in the Netherlands with their churches under the cross. The Calvinists in England also understood it. And this must also apply to us today as the law appointed for us by God.

There can be no difference of opinion about the actual circumstances in which we find ourselves. It is public knowledge that our government, in the cities and in the countryside, no longer confesses the Reformed religion and no longer honors the church of Christ for Christ's sake. It is public knowledge that the confession of the purified religion is practiced consciously only among a portion of the people—and without consciousness, there is no confession. It is public knowledge that the manifold branches of national life—the greater part of what makes our society

---

17. Guillaume Groen van Prinsterer (1801–76) was a conservative critic of the French Revolution, follower of the *Réveil*, and Kuyper's mentor. For this phrase, see *Nederlandsche Gedachten* 33–34 (June 7, 1870), 264.

function—and the absorbing influence of the groups that set the tone in society are no longer focused on the service of the heavenly fatherland. Nor are they directed to their ultimate end—the honor of God. It is also public knowledge that learning and art have created their own temple, but the altar to the creator and giver of all genius and scientific curiosity, of all talent and artistic acumen, is missing from that dechristianized temple. Public life is being identified more and more with the stamp of secularization. And secularization, derived from *saeculum*, that is, "century," or "age," means precisely that one wants to withdraw the entire institution of the fatherland from service "to the coming age" in order to make it totally part of "this current age." I shall not evaluate this situation now, nor am I going to trace its deeply sinful cause, which is also in our own circles and our own hearts. I am simply observing this situation, and then I say only what is obvious to all: namely, that what is called faith, what is meant by religion and a heavenly purpose, no longer determines the direction of the public life in the nation as it did in times past.

~~~~~~~~~~~~~~~~

With that, gentlemen, the call came to the people of the Lord in these lands to act reformationally—or as I prefer to put it, prophetically—again, just as in the sixteenth century. According to the Lord's own dictum, "No prophet is acceptable in his hometown" (Luke 4:24). This is the case because he refuses to swing with the wind and to cry with the wolves and also refuses to sacrifice his fatherland. He instead rows against the stream of that fatherland out of a burning love for it. It is not in the priest, but rather in the prophet that there is power in a conscious isolation. And the idiosyncrasy, the character, the distinctiveness of each prophetic action lies in this, that you hear a call for the higher fatherland. That call comes from a person, a school, a group that does not hide itself away like an Anabaptist; instead, as a group they throw themselves into the life of the nation, take part in the debate of the people, and make themselves heard in the public square. You find such a prophetic group wrestling in the stream of national life, not outside it. Such a group prays; they suffer for the distress of their fatherland; they sigh and weep for their heavenly Jerusalem; their hope is for hope against hope; *Luctor et emergo*[18] is their life's motto. Knowing that their people and nation cannot have a future

---

18. "I struggle and I emerge."

unless they turn back to the Lord's Word, they dare, despite the evidence, to prophesy a better future for their dear fatherland and, enraptured by that prospect, they call king and people back to the law and the testimony.

So, gentlemen, we also have not pursued an Anabaptist division but a Calvinistic and a real prophetic isolation, not in order to place ourselves outside national life but precisely in order to save the pledge entrusted to us for that fatherland. In the same way, men and sons leave their households in time of danger not to give up those households but, rather, at or over the borders to put their lives at risk for their homes and dear ones. And that is why we also, pursuant to Da Costa's[19] prophetic wake-up call, set ourselves against the spirit of this age, and have organized ourselves, in response to Groen van Prinsterer's cry, into our own organization!

Hence first Heldring's actions, and later those of 't Lindenhout and Pierson, started again the work of mercy that languished when it had to depend on the notion of "common human affection." They did this by bringing the compassion of Christ again into isolated institutions.[20] Hence in various ways there has been an ecclesiastical endeavor, as in Ulrum's secession, by Kohlbrugge's and Ledeboer's isolation, and now in the current secession, to separate the gathering of believers again from those who are, both in root and branch, nothing but those who reject the confession.[21] Hence also our political expression as Anti-Revolutionary Party, *parti du Dieu vivant*—not floating like a drop of oil on the water like the Labadists,[22] but instead striving against and with all other political parties for such a regulation of law and justice that the freedom of everyone can run its free course unhindered, but still according to God's Word. Hence our young people's societies, which were formed to nurture young people with the societal concern when the common association in society threatened

---

19. Isaac da Costa (1798-1860) was a Jewish convert to Protestantism, poet, leader of the evangelical *Réveil*, and critic of liberal progressivism.

20. O. G. Heldring (1804-76) and later Jan van 't Lindenhout (1836-1918) and Hendrik Pierson (1834-1923) were ministers who came from Dutch *Réveil* circles and are remembered for their dedication to addressing social causes including poverty, prostitution, alcoholism, and Christian education.

21. Herman Kohlbrugge (1803-75) and Lambertus Ledeboer (1808-63) both left or were ejected from their churches for their opposition to theological modernism (Kohlbrugge from the Lutheran church and Ledeboer from the Reformed church).

22. The Labadists, led by Jean de Labadie (1610-74), were a well-known seventeenth-century sect in the Netherlands who withdrew from the mainstream church to form a community of true believers.

to secularize the spirit of our young people. Hence our Christian press, which was formed first to protest and then, by our own formulations, to provide access to better ideas than the principially false concepts that, day by day, drop by drop, threatened to erode the stone. Hence also our school of the Bible, which was formed because our Christian people must not be allowed to take second place to their fellow citizens in the development of society. Lastly, hence our Free University, gentlemen, which was formed so that the fear of God that is the beginning of all wisdom may not be allowed to die out in our national learning.

If we had been concerned only with providing aid to our church, and had we focused solely on our heavenly fatherland, a theological training college would have sufficed; and if that is all we could have managed, it would have been something—indeed, it would have been much. But the Lord God gave us greater courage and caused us to cast our hopes further. No, we did not give up hope for our national life, the hope for a better future also for our people and nation. Article 36 was not written in our glorious confession without a purpose; rather, it is written in our hearts. And knowing that learning also belongs to God and his Christ, knowing also that our people and nation cannot forgo the service of higher learning, and knowing also what terrible destruction an unbelieving science has caused more than once in our national life, we have, with God's help, undertaken to give back, if it were possible, a Christian development of science to our own children and our own fellow citizens.

Had we, like our brothers in Belgium, Italy, and Spain, almost disappeared, such a high ideal never would have entered our hearts. But our people were extended a greater grace. We had our historic past. We had the covenant that Prince William of Orange entered into with the Lord of Lords. We still had the aftereffects of the Reformed tradition in higher and lower spheres. Ours was yet the favor of God in the *Réveil* of 1830, the ecclesiastical heroics of 1834,[23] and the actions of Kohlbrugge and Ledeboer. And, what is no less important, there is the regeneration to life that remained in thousands and thousands of people throughout the cities and towns. He who said, "The silver is mine, and the gold is mine" (Hag 2:8), also allowed us to give generously to meet many needs.

---

23. In 1834 Henrick de Cock initiated the *Afscheiding* (Secession) from the Reformed church by leading his congregation at Ulrum to form a separate church over matters of confessional integrity.

When we saw, both by the driving power of history and the favor of God in the recent past, that our state universities had almost completely severed the bond with the heavenly fatherland, we asked our God: "Merciful God, God of our fathers, do not punish us according to our guilt and according to what we deserve, but give back to our people—give back to our inheritance, a school of the sciences that can imbibe its inspiration from the higher fatherland, in order to benefit also our earthly fatherland with that higher inspiration." Those three measures of flour, which included scholarship, could not remain without leaven, and therefore we asked the Lord for a university in which that leaven could be preserved also for the thinking and for the higher consciousness of the nation.

We know that our endeavors have been ridiculed and scorned. What did those pretentious people want? Of course, gentlemen, those who see only our little institution, our small number, and our insignificant power will probably smirk as they say, "Do you call that a university?" They will be vexed by the disproportionality between the plan and the result. But let them laugh. If we are no further fifty years from now when our sons will inherit our work, we shall speak together again. Sturdy wood grows slowly. It is not the willow or the elderberry, but the oak and the cedar that last.

Thus, the initial insignificance, the laugh of the mocker, and the vial of bitterness of the envious will not prevent us from flourishing and prospering. No, the only way our school can be destroyed is by our sins and by losing the favor of our God. If we were to cry *corban* [see Mark 7:11] against our fatherland and exalt ourselves above others in spiritual pride; if we were no longer to appreciate the talents and gifts that it has pleased God to give also to unbelievers in our fatherland; if our love were to cool and our willingness to make sacrifices for the fatherland were to slacken; if we in our own circles were to pay high regard to people of note instead of to the Eternal One; if any should say, "This is the Babel that we built!"; if, in accordance with God's righteous judgment, Satan gained entrance into our lives and divided the brotherhood, so that some no longer regarded others but, rather, themselves as more excellent; if scholarship were to replace humility and much knowledge were to replace the quiet spirit before God; and if among us we were again to rely on our own strength and to praise our own work; O that then fear for our souls would steal over us, since the hour might be near that the Lord Almighty would take away our breath and also cause our institution to die.

O men and brothers, if Satan, who wants to disrupt all who seek the honor of Christ, could only attack us from the heart of the scoffer or the envious, I would not fear with faint heart for our future. The field of our nation is ready, the seed has been sown in the plowed furrows, the heavens drip with rain, and soon the nourishing sun will shine on us. But alas, this is not so. Satan has his devious ways by which he can also attack us on the inside. That is where the deadly danger threatens. None of us is pure, and the poison of false learning and the deadly spirit of enmity that roils against God are common to us and to all our fellow citizens. We are not any better at all but are open to such terrible spiritual sin, especially because of the grace given to us. Judgment has always proceeded from the house of God, and our God is a jealous God who is doubly jealous of his honor when his name is engraved on our banner.

~~~~~~~~~~~~~~~~

He does not reject us because of that, not even if there might already be a beginning of this evil. On the contrary, the little worm of Jacob always finds complete consolation in him who is merciful. The fountain that was established in Israel against sin and iniquity flows also for us, but on the condition that there then is also confession of transgression, that atonement be sought, and that we appear before our God—not with our own conceit—but in our shame and with a contrite heart.

Thanks be to God that so far we have felt the need to do that. Therefore we have never yet come together on our anniversary without first seeking the place where we may find the holiness of God. Every time there was so much to be thankful for. After every year of courses there was so much to confess, and every year there was so much to ask and desire of our God, to ask on behalf of our earthly fatherland, to call out on behalf of our heavenly fatherland. We stood, year after year, before the river of waters and cast ourselves down to seek the face of our God.

Come, men and brothers, let our gathering find its conclusion also now in that. O that our prayer and thanks may be given and that our souls may be made prayerful. The Lord wants us to call upon him, and he alone causes us to call upon him in truth. Let us therefore also now call upon our God and do so first by raising our voices in the words of Psalm 27:5.[24]

---

24. "For he will hide me in his shelter / in the day of trouble; / he will conceal me under the cover of his tent; / he will lift me high upon a rock."

LORD'S DAY 21

TEXT INTRODUCTION

Kuyper's use of the traditional confessional standards of the Dutch church was key to his efforts at mobilizing and reforming the church. From 1886 to 1894 he wrote a commentary on the Heidelberg Catechism, which was published in weekly installments in his religious newspaper, *The Herald*. The three catechism questions of Lord's Day 21 deal with the church, the communion of the saints, and the forgiveness of sins. In his explanation of these questions and answers, Kuyper seeks to avoid two errors—the institutionalism of the Roman Catholic Church, which invests too much power in the institution of the church, and the individualism of evangelical revival movements. Kuyper's proposal is the organic church. Here, not in the institution and not individually, is the forgiveness of sins. Outside of the organic church, there is no salvation. The institution is a mere scaffold that is bound to fall away when the building is complete. Kuyper's social ethic of the church is included within his doctrine of the organic church. The church as organism is a provisional gathering of the saints that looks forward to a final future establishment of the kingdom of God; for the time being it stands over against the world. The organic church has a sub-eschatological and antithetical existence.

Source: Kuyper, Abraham. "Zondagsafdeeling XXI." In *E Voto Dordraceno.*
    Toelichting op den Heidelbergschen Catechismus, vol. 2, 108–58.
    Amsterdam: Höveker & Wormser, 1905. Translated by Arjen
    Vreugdenhil and Nelson D. Kloosterman.

LORD'S DAY 21

Question 54: What do you believe concerning the "Holy Catholic Church"?

Answer: That out of the whole human race, from the beginning to the end of the world, the Son of God, by His Spirit and Word, gathers, defends, and preserves for himself unto everlasting life a chosen communion in the unity of the true faith; and that I am and forever shall remain a living member of this communion.

Question 55: What do you understand by the "communion of saints"?

Answer: First, that believers, one and all, as members of the Lord Jesus Christ, are partakers with him in all his treasures and gifts; second, that each one must feel himself bound to use his gifts readily and cheerfully for the advantage and welfare of other members.

Question 56: What do you believe concerning the "forgiveness of sins"?

Answer: That God, for the sake of Christ's satisfaction, will no more remember my sins, nor the sinful nature with which I have to struggle all my life long, but graciously imputes to me the righteousness of Christ, that I may nevermore come into condemnation.

FIRST CHAPTER

And I tell you, you are Peter, and on this rock I will build my church, and the gates of hell shall not prevail against it.

MATTHEW 16:18

Lord's Day 21 of the Catechism deals with the church, and we notice immediately that the Heidelberg combines three articles of the Apostles' Creed here. It speaks not only about the church but also about the communion of saints and the forgiveness of sins. Yet these articles are not mindlessly strung together simply because it worked out better for the organization of the Lord's Days. The combination is deliberate and indicates that the forgiveness of sins can be experienced only in the fellowship of the church. Anyone outside the church of Christ is separated from the body of Christ and lacks the benefits of salvation, which can be enjoyed only through incorporation into this body. This, of course, is not about the incidental fellowship with any church denomination. That has no bearing on the spiritual benefits of salvation. It is about belonging to that true church of Christ, which he as the Mediator purchased at the price of his blood. A sinner is not justified separately as a single person on his or her own. One's solitariness, independence, and separation are actually consequences of one's sin. Sin separates, severs, and splits apart. When grace comes, this grace must, therefore, immediately remove this solitariness, discontinue this separation, and put an end to this independence. Grace can come to us only by pulling us out of our self-centeredness and placing us once again in organic connection, now with our fellow recipients of grace. This is, on the one hand, the mystery of the body of Christ, and on the other hand, the high commandment of that marvelous Christian love. Enjoying the benefits of salvation, here summarized as the "forgiveness of sins," is conceivable for us only after our transition from our solitariness into the body of Christ, and from our self-centeredness into the "communion of saints." Whoever pulls away from it (if that were possible) ceases any longer to experience what one used to enjoy in that fellowship and would lack the sweetness of the atonement. Such a person is no longer at peace with his God.

This is enough on the necessary connection between these three articles concerning the body of Christ, or "the church" of the "communion of saints" and the "forgiveness of sins." We will now discuss the first of these: our belief that there is a holy, catholic, Christian church.

During the revival of Christian life in the early 1800s, this article of the Apostles' Creed was generally ignored. The so-called *Réveil* was intent on saving souls, was therefore methodistic in its principles, and its error was bound to develop into Darbyism.[1] The main characteristic of Darbyism is the fundamental denial of the existence of such a church. Darby, who was otherwise a pious and meek man, denied its existence on the basis of Romans 11:22, where the holy apostle declares to the church of the new covenant: "Note then the kindness and the severity of God: severity toward those who have fallen, but God's kindness to you, provided you continue in his kindness. Otherwise you too will be cut off." On the basis of this apostolic statement, Darby reasons as follows. First, there was the church of the old covenant, and this church of Israel was ultimately rejected and cut off because it rejected its Savior. Next came the church of the new covenant, which received even richer benefits of salvation. But this church was also told that it would be cut off and rejected, because it followed Israel in its unbelief and apostasy. According to Darby, that church of the new covenant also became apostate. According to this apostolic declaration we must, therefore, assume that it has now been cut off and rejected, and that according to his counsel, the Lord God still redeems individual people and saves individual souls, but we can no longer speak of an organic church.

Undoubtedly Darby should be honored for being more profound in his thinking and more advanced in his views than the leaders of the *Réveil*. They essentially valued the church as little as did Darby, but they gave no explanation of their view; they were not thinkers and did not look beneath the surface. Darby was different. As a child of the *Réveil*, he needed to understand clearly how it could be possible both that the Holy Scripture speaks so decidedly and elaborately about the church, and yet that he and his fellow Christians had so little affection for the church and were, in fact, hostile toward it. This inevitable consequence of his thinking led him to the conviction that there used to be a church of the new covenant, which since faded away and apostatized, and that what still calls

---

1. In the early nineteenth century the Netherlands experienced the revival movement spreading throughout Europe and the United States which rejected rationalism in religion for feeling. In the Netherlands the *Réveil* (*Het Réveil*) took place largely within the Dutch Reformed Church, and it stressed individual piety and concern for the poor. Darbyism is named after John Nelson Darby (1800–82), a revivalist and leader of the Plymouth Brethren.

itself the church today is nothing but a sinful caricature of the real church that used to exist.

The same phenomenon occurred in the days of the Reformation. Then too the church was initially opposed to the revival of the spiritual and tried to suppress it. The Anabaptist movement arose, which basically denied the church, just as even today the Mennonites essentially want to know nothing of the church.[2] But alongside and over against them stood the Reformers, who saw the profound apostasy of the church as clearly as the Anabaptists did and even admitted that what pretended to be the church had become a false church. Nonetheless, instead of giving up on the church, they prepared to reform it. But that motivation was absent in the *Réveil*. The *Réveil* gave up on the church, without principally opposing it; and it organized its manifold activities alongside and outside the church, to call sinners to Jesus and to do works of mercy in his name. The first among us who saw the inconsistency of this view were the Secessionists of 1834, who tentatively brought the struggle back to the arena of the church, although they did not immediately consciously apply the principle of the sixteenth-century Reformation. Thanks to their resilience, ecclesiastical life revived, even within the circles that opposed them. Thus, the movements of the *Réveil* and the Reformation came to stand opposed to each other, and under the Lord's marvelous guidance that church, once so despised, about which God's most pious children in their overly spiritual focus hardly cared at all, once again became an object of interest.

In the course of all this, it was inevitable that the confession concerning the church gradually was corrupted. Even today, God's people still do not feel quite at home in the doctrine of the church. They are just starting to become more comfortable with it. Thus, one brother stands opposed to another. There are still many prayers to be prayed, many struggles to be waged, before the Lord's people in these lands see a straight path cleared for the doctrine of the church and before they travel that path as a unified people.

Precisely because of this it is important to investigate this doctrine of the church somewhat more carefully, guided by the Catechism; and you should notice first how the Catechism does not permit the church to be established by people, but first states and emphasizes that the one who

---

2. Mennonites are an Anabaptist group with roots in the teachings of Menno Simons (1496–1561).

does this is Christ himself. That is how it begins: "The Son of God ... gathers, defends, and preserves ... a chosen communion [*gemeente*]."[3] This one thought already elevates the church, which will be an object of our faith, above all that is earthly; thus, it elevates the essence of the church above its earthly form in which this essence manifests itself.

Mighty empires have been established on earth: Alexander the Great was considered ruler of the entire East together with a part of Greece. Caesar Augustus wielded his scepter over the entire known world of his time. Napoleon's crown once shone radiantly. Yet all these empires were established by man. Their origin lay in this world. They were part of the life of the world. Therefore, they shared in the fate of all things of this world. So all these empires disappeared as well.

It is different with the kingdom that we call church. He who established this empire was no man, but the Son of God. Therefore, its origin was not of this world but from heaven, not from below but from above. It was established not in cooperation with the world, but after breaking the world's fierce and fundamental opposition. Thus, this church descended into the life of this world as a heavenly power. Of a different origin than the world itself, the church stood its ground in the midst of the world as a foreign power, bound continually to clash with the world. And when one day the world will no longer be, and all glory that came out of it will have faded away, the church will remain eternally and rise in glory, simply because it was not of the world. Anyone who does not see this clearly does not grasp the beauty of the church and can never reach the point of being enraptured by its glory.

If you were to measure the appearance of the church in this earthly life according to earthly standards, then either you must become Roman Catholic—seeking your enjoyment in the external radiance, with which the papal church in the Vatican operates in its dioceses and cathedrals—or you must admit that the activity of the church is pitifully small and unimpressive, and far inferior to the glory of the worldly kingdoms. And if you do look no deeper, if you do not peek through the curtain, and if you lack the sense to view the church of Christ in light of its spiritual mystery, then

---

3. The Dutch term *gemeente* has a concrete sense that is not fully captured in the term "community." It might also be translated "parish" or "congregation" and is similar to the German *gemeinde*.

you are bound ultimately to treat it with contempt, to turn away from it, and to retreat into the spiritual experience of your own soul or circle.

If, on the other hand, you understand once and for all that majesty of the confession concerning the church, which is expressed in the fact that God's Son and not a mere human being founds, establishes, or gathers it, and that it is this Son of God—and he alone—who still continually protects and maintains it, oh, then suddenly all relationships are turned upside down. Then you can and will no longer value any denomination—that is, the scaffolding built for that church of Christ by some ecclesiastical people in cooperation with the worldly government—but, through that scaffolding, you will behold the spiritual building itself. With much greater beauty than the world can ever give, and hidden from the world's view, it rises ever higher throughout the ages and extends its peak into the heavens.

Your church is then a colony of heaven living on the earth. It has its own autonomous existence, resting on its own foundation; it is constructed in its own unique style; it is built of very different stone than those offered by the mines of the world; and in its state and organization it depends not on the laws of nature, nor on the legislation of earthly lawmakers, but only on the law of life of its divine founder.

Its battle with the world no longer appears strange to you, since you know that it is opposed in principle to that world's principle. You are not amazed that the battle is occasionally fierce but, rather, that the battle often ceases for so long. And, taught by the lessons of history and of the present, you suddenly understand why it is that, as soon as the church wakes up spiritually, the battle resumes so fiercely; but also that, when the church declines spiritually, it is granted peace by the world.

In fact, when you hear of that battle and the hardships and sufferings of Jesus' church, you no longer think: "I will stay out of it. I will retreat into spiritual enjoyment of my soul." Instead you will be driven by the high and holy honor to draw the sword of the Spirit in that never-ending struggle in which the Son of God continues to gather his church. And you will bring your sacrifice for what has become for you "the sake of God's Son,"[4] the continuation of the triumph that he gained once over that world, on Golgotha.

---

4. See Belgic Confession, Art. 37.

Although they are closely related, the church and the kingdom of God are not the same. Scripture speaks of both of them separately, and if you confuse them you open yourself up to all kinds of misunderstanding. A kingdom is established; the church is gathered. When Alexander the Great was going to establish his empire, he first gathered his army, and with that army he established his kingdom. Just as it is easy in the case of Alexander the Great to distinguish between his army and his kingdom, so it should not be difficult to distinguish between the kingdom of heaven and the church of Christ.

The church of Christ consists of people, as is clear from the expression that it is gathered. In the church these people are joined together into a solid structure, into an inseparable body. At the head of this body stands Christ as the Commander. And under this Commander, this army—that is, the church—is to fight the battle of the Lord, so that the kingdom of God may be born as the fruit of that battle.

Rather than being the same, church and kingdom of God are therefore, to some extent, opposites. A kingdom presupposes lordship. Therefore, God's kingdom will fully arrive only when all that is in heaven and on earth is subjected to God as the King of kings. A kingdom presupposes that all available powers and forces are organically connected and cooperating. Therefore, God's kingdom will shine in its full glory only when all the powers and forces that the Creator embedded in his creation work together in mutual harmony and in correct proportion according to his plan and design. Finally, a kingdom presupposes a constitution that is obeyed, and the violators of which are punished and sentenced. Likewise, God's kingdom can radiate in its full majesty only when the law of our God shall be obeyed by all of his creation, and the violators of his holy law will have perished in his judgment. Thus, God's kingdom can break through in its full glory only when the end of days will have come, the last judgment passed, all opposition broken, and when God will be all in all [see Psalm 110]. What will radiate then—and only that will radiate—is the kingdom of God, the kingdom of heaven.

Meanwhile, that kingdom of God also has a starting point. It will be completed only after the judgment day, but its establishment began much earlier. Holy Scripture leaves no uncertainty about the time of its inception but says very clearly that its coming began with the coming of Christ. At that time, John the Baptist cried: "The kingdom of heaven is at hand" [Matt 3:2]. At that time, Immanuel himself made a similar announcement, sent his disciples throughout Israel, and testified to Pilate that he had come into the world to establish that kingdom.

In paradise that kingdom of God had *potential* existence. It was damaged through the rebellion of Satan and of humankind. Under Israel a visible picture of it was shown in the splendid kingdom of Solomon and in all of Israel's national existence. But in reality it came first with the manger and the cross. From paradise onward, after the fall there was a church of Christ, but the kingdom of God arrived for the first time forty centuries later. This is immediately clear if one simply considers the distinction we just outlined between the church as the sacred army of the Commander who will establish the kingdom and the establishment of that kingdom by this army.

The Son of God began gathering his hosts in paradise, in Noah's ark, in Ur of the Chaldeans, in Egypt, under Moses, later under the judges, and even more powerfully under David and his royal family. But this church of the old covenant was and remained constrained within narrow boundaries, and it was not yet time for the church of God to become active in the world as a power to conquer it for Christ.

In Israel you see the formation of the sacred army, the training of the troops, the preparation of this host for the moment when it must enter the world, but it does not yet set out for the great battle. Israel was created separate. Through the miraculous birth of Isaac, Israel is God's unique creation, and Israel remains strictly constrained within its national boundaries. Indeed, Israel is the foreshadowing and type of God's kingdom over which the battle will one day be fought, and Israel shows that in its national life. But far from being God's kingdom itself, Israel is not even allowed to begin the battle for this kingdom until Immanuel arises as its leader.

This continues until the incarnation and the horrible tragedy of Golgotha. Now the Commander stands at the head of his troops. Now the national boundaries are removed. The church of Christ enters the world, and now in that church functioning as a sacred army for the Lord, those who are his elect and his called accept the enormous challenge to fight the battle, under him as their Head, for the establishment of God's kingdom.

In every battle won by this church of Christ one can see something of that kingdom of God. Its establishment has begun. These beginnings increase. The region where the banner of the Lord of lords shall be planted grows ever wider. Thus, the battle continues, through defeat and triumph, until it reaches to the end of the world on the last day. Then the last enemy will be destroyed. The last adversary will be bound. At that time Christ will function as the Commander of God's kingdom to plant the banner of Yahweh on the mountaintops as a sign that the universe is once again subject to God. Thus, God shall be all and in all.

So you see how absolutely correct our Catechism is when it states that Christ gathers his church as a holy army of the living God. He gathers his church in order to establish the kingdom of God through it as his army. That is why this army is called church, that is, *ecclesia* or called-out, select troops. The church of Christ is his glorious bodyguard, the unit of his personal bodyguards, incorporated under him as the Head of all.

To this we must add one brief note to prevent an incorrect view. Christ does not fight with and through his church alone. He also has another unit of bodyguards, his angels. Both of these armies, the select troop of his elect and the host of angels, fight under him the battle that one day will result in the subjection of all power in heaven and on earth to the majesty of the Lord of lords.

SECOND CHAPTER

*This applies to the Levites: from twenty-five years old and upward they shall
come to do duty in the service of the tent of meeting.*

NUMBERS 8:24

We described the difference between the church and God's kingdom (with
an appeal to Psalm 110) in this way: the church is the army, and God's kingdom (or the kingdom of heaven) is the kingdom that is being established
by means of this army. We must now give further proof of the validity of
this distinction.

In ancient times, when the difference between Christ and the world
was still felt every step of the way, every child of God knew the honorific
militant church, which everyone was convinced belonged to the church
of Christ, and the perspective and hope of all was one day to make the
transition from militant to *triumphant* church. This was the only way the
church was viewed. People could not think of it otherwise. At that time,
any church of Christ that would not have stood up as a holy army and
battled for Christ's cause and name would have looked like anything but
a church. This elevated awareness subsided only later, when in the state
churches and national churches a compromise was made with the world,
and when finally in the Middle Ages all distinction between Christ and the
world fell away. Then the name and honorific "militant church" was no
longer understood. The ancient expression was still used, being repeated
out of custom, but it no longer carried its true meaning and significance.

Eventually this reached the point where the expression "militant
church" was used merely for the struggle that every person of noble
intent is called to wage while upon earth. Militant church now referred to
a number of people who still have inner struggles, who still wrestle with
circumstance and inclination, and who each in their own way still wage
the battle with besetting sins. In contrast to this, the *triumphant* church
was viewed as those who had passed away, who had been removed from
this struggle against suffering and cross, and who no longer had to fight
with inner sins. They did not realize that this put an end to the entire concept of a militant church. After all, even the Chinese and the Muslim, even
the Jew and the unbeliever, struggle against adversity and sin. Therefore,
this view does one of two things: either it makes Jew, Chinese, Turk, and
atheist members of your militant church, or it eliminates the whole idea
of militant church, leaving nothing but the ordinary struggle of all human

living. This is something to be aware of in preaching as well. In order to speak rightfully of a militant church, the distinction must be clear between that daily struggle, which is inseparably connected to our human existence and is common to all humanity, and that other battle that must be fought against the world, not by individuals but by the church of Christ viewed as a whole.

In the Old Testament you find that in Israel's ceremonial dispensation, the sacred ministry in the narrower sense was taken from the eleven tribes and assigned to the one tribe of Levi. Levi functions as a representative of all of Israel, and his ministry occurs in the sanctuary of the Lord. And how does Scripture present to us this Levite ministry in the sanctuary? Just read in Numbers 8:23–26: "And the LORD spoke to Moses, saying, 'This applies to the Levites: from twenty-five years old and upward they shall come to fight the battle [ESV: "do duty"] in the service of the tent of meeting. And from the age of fifty years they shall withdraw from the battle [ESV: "duty"] of the service and serve no more. They minister to their brothers in the tent of meeting by keeping guard, but they shall do no service. Thus shall you do to the Levites in assigning their duties.'" And so the service of the Levites is presented in a military manner, not just in this passage but also in the entire law. They are an army in which everyone from twenty-five to fifty years old is obligated to serve and go up for the battle. Once he passes fifty, the Levite is added to the reserves, who no longer go to war but stay on duty to keep guard.

"Keep the watch of the Lord," "keep watch in the tabernacle," "keep the watch of the children of Israel," "keep the watch of the tent of meeting," are all recurring expressions in the Levitical law. Now what does this mean? Israel was the people of foreshadowing. Its people prefigured the church; its national existence prefigured the kingdom of God. Israel had two armies, one with military power to battle against Edom and Syria and Egypt; the other was the army of Levites who waged the Lord's battle in the tabernacle. We are, therefore, not dealing with a merely figurative or metaphoric use of language. Far from being just a metaphor, this expression is of the greatest significance. That significance is that in the tribe of Levi and in its duty are prefigured and foreshadowed another battle and another watch, which one day, when the church would become a worldwide church, would be observed by the church of Christ in the battle between Christ and the world.

In full agreement with this, the New Testament consistently presents the calling of the church as a battle, which will end only with the return of the Lord on the clouds. It is a battle in which the church will certainly be the conqueror, and which will be followed one day by a glorious triumph when Christ, the Head of the heavenly host and the one under whom the battle was fought, will give the crown to those who remained faithful to him unto death. Paul himself testifies to this at the end of his life: "I have fought the good fight, I have finished the race, I have kept the faith. Henceforth there is laid up for me the crown of righteousness, which the Lord, the righteous judge, will award to me on that Day" [2 Tim 4:7-8]. This declaration is connected to the picture of a wrestling match, but only to emphasize the idea of the struggle. In the same way, he admonishes Timothy to "fight the good fight" [1 Tim 6:12]. To the church of Philippi he expresses the wish that they may stand firm in one spirit, "with one mind striving side by side for the faith of the gospel" [Phil 1:27]. Of Euodia and Syntyche he declares that they "struggled side by side" with him in the gospel [Phil 4:3]. He himself labors "struggling" with all Christ's "energy that he powerfully works" within him [Col 1:29]. To Timothy he exclaims, "Fight the good fight of the faith." And according to Jude (Jude 3), it is the duty of God's church to "contend for the faith." Paul even calls the confessor of the Lord a soldier: "Share in suffering as a good soldier of Christ Jesus" (2 Tim 2:3).

The entire life of the church, therefore, lies in the war it must wage with the world. "Though we walk in the flesh," says Paul, "we are not waging war according to the flesh" [2 Cor 10:3]. He continues speaking about the weapons used in that war: "For the weapons of our warfare are not of the flesh" but spiritual, and precisely because of that they are powerful "to destroy strongholds" [2 Cor 10:4]. So it is our calling to present ourselves "with weapons of righteousness" [2 Cor 6:7] and to put on "the armor of light" [Rom 13:12]. Even the full armor of a soldier of the Lord is described to us. "Put on the whole armor of God, that you may be able to stand against the schemes of the devil. For we do not wrestle against flesh and blood, but against the rulers, against the authorities, against the cosmic powers over this present darkness, against the spiritual forces of evil in the heavenly places. Therefore take up the whole armor of God. ... Stand therefore, having fastened on the belt of truth, and having put on the breastplate of righteousness, and, as shoes for your feet, having put on the readiness given by the gospel of peace. In all circumstances take up the shield of faith, ... and take the helmet of salvation, and the sword of the Spirit, which is the word of God" [Eph 6:11–17].

This battle, this war that the church of Christ must wage, continues until the end, and only the one who perseveres until the end will receive the crown. The one who conquers will share in the spoils and will receive honor and praise in the finished kingdom of God. The triumphing Christ will give to his entire army—to his bodyguard, to his courageous and faithful soldiers—the gifts of sitting with him on the throne [Rev 20:4], of eating of the tree of life [Rev 22:2], of carrying a white stone [Rev 2:17], of being clothed in white garments [Rev 19:14], of bearing the name of their God [Rev 21:7]. In short, they will share in all of the glory of Christ, their triumphant King.

This character of the church as a militant power, that is, as army and host of the Lord, flows from the martial character of Christ's own activity. He is the Head of the Lord's army. In his mouth is a sharp sword. He wages war in righteousness. He rides successfully on the pure word of truth to conquer his foes. He has come not to bring peace but to cast the sword upon the earth [see Rev 19:11–16]. In principle he already "conquered the world" on Golgotha. His enemies stand opposed to him. Those enemies must be subdued and made a footstool for his feet. Only when the last enemy is destroyed and all opposition is broken will the kingdom of glory fully begin.

Christ is Captain, Chief Commander, just as he appeared to Joshua as a soldier [Josh 5:13–15]. Satan, sin, and the world have waged and still wage the war against God. In that battle, the angels of God stand against the angels of Satan, and Christ is the highest Commander in this dreadful war. He leads all God's armies to victory and all resulting triumphs are from him.

At first there was only God's kingdom. Sin broke that kingdom and established a kingdom of darkness opposed to it. That is why every unconverted sinner, consciously or subconsciously, serves as a soldier of Satan opposing the kingdom of the Lord. Yet that kingdom of the Lord must return. It will certainly be restored. Christ is the one restoring it. And for that restoration of God's kingdom he employs soldiers who were initially in Satan's service. He sets them free from Satan's service and draws them to himself, equips them with the armor of God, and as soldiers so armed he makes them participate in his army.

So Jesus is a mighty warrior, a King who wages war and will not rest until God's enemies have been fully subdued and destroyed. But, although the victory over his enemies has already in principle been won on the cross of Golgotha, that war still continues and will come to an end only when this Commander of God returns on the clouds; then in actuality he will subject all of creation to himself. Until then, the war is raging. The battle continues. How could it be conceivable that while our Jesus is constantly engaged in battle, that his church, his people on earth, would be indifferent, letting him fight alone and abstaining from the battle?

No, if the church is one with Jesus, if he is its Head and it is his body, then it is inconceivable that it would watch from afar without participating in the battle. Wherever the King wages war, all his people fight alongside him, and anyone who does not fight along with the people is a coward who will be cast out. So we see that because we have a militant Messiah, his people can have no other calling but to be a militant church on the earth.

This leads us to the nomenclature "the people of the Lord," which is used so frequently in Scripture, but which many no longer wish to use today. For a good understanding of the relationship between the phrase "people of the Lord" and "church," one must note that in Israel the army was the entire nation, and the entire nation was the army. It is the same as in today's Prussia, where every man is a soldier; but it was then even more strongly so, since every adult male in Israel was to participate in the battle. There was no army of professional soldiers, no army of recruited soldiers. In Israel there was a universal and personal obligation of military service. Army and nation were the same, and one could call the troops of Israel an army as well as a people.

This is especially clear in times of war. If you go to Prussia in times of peace, people are more visible, and the army appears to be something altogether separate. But once war breaks out, the entire people becomes the army, and these are no longer distinct. So it was in Israel as well. And so it is still with the people of the Lord. This people is always at war. With Satan no truce is made, not even a cease-fire. This people is always not just at the *brink* of war, but in *actual* war. And whenever it seems to be otherwise, that is only because part of the people have become unfaithful, have deserted the cause of their Lord, and have gone over to the enemy.

Therefore, the people of the Lord can never be thought of as anything but a nation at arms, always involved in battle and waging war under its Lord and King. Yet there is a difference between the names "church" and "people." "Church," or *ecclesia*, derives its name from "called out." The church is the multitude of those called out, of those called to war. It means the same as "select troops." They are the faithful, given to him by the Father, whom he now calls out of the world, calls to himself, and gathers around him.

By contrast, the term "people" emphasizes the organic relationship of king and subject. When one day the last battle has been fought and God's kingdom completed, this kingdom also will have citizens, inhabitants. And those citizens of God's kingdom will not be a collection of individuals but an organic whole, a nation, a people. Thus, the Lord's called are all connected to each other. They are connected by mutual bonds, and together they stand in subjection and obedience to their Sovereign Ruler and King, to share in his peace and his salvation.

Now this people is not merely brought under one King, but was, as it were, brought forth by the King. It has a vital connection to its King. Their King originates from them, and they originate from their King. King and people together are one. He is their Head, and they are members of his body. Precisely in this lies the guarantee of the unity of this people, the guarantee of its unity through all ages and generations. Because of its organic connectedness it carries its seed within itself, so that it keeps bringing forth new subjects for the King.

Over against the multitude of peoples and nations, therefore, stands this one people of the Lord as his own, purchased people. Thus, there can never be a national church. The very notion of a national church is already a complete subversion of what the sacred Scripture teaches us about both the church and the Lord's people. There was a national church in Israel— certainly, because the Lord created this one people deliberately, not from the peoples and nations, but as a separate people. But beyond Israel there is nothing other than the worldwide church, nothing but the one people of the Lord, from all families and nations and languages. Anyone still clinging to the false concept of a national church is still standing at the tower of Babel and is failing to go back to that higher unity that began in paradise and has been restored in the Savior of the world.

If you wish to distinguish carefully, then Jesus is King of this his people and Head of his church, just as our last king in the royal family[5] was king

---

5. King William III of Orange (1650–1702).

of the people of the Netherlands and highest commander or head of his army. However, in this state of perpetual battle, "the people of the Lord" and the church, or his select troops, completely coincide and are one and the same. The people is the entire army, and the army is the entire people. Therefore, this contrived distinction is irrelevant. The beautiful nomenclature of head of the body serves simply to express concisely and powerfully the organic connection between this King and his people, between this Commander and his army. Because he is not an appointed head of a hired army but the Head of the heavenly host, he may call his faithful ones *flesh of my flesh* and *those obtained by my own blood.*

The distinction between people and church becomes significant only when a group of people presents itself as "church," in which only some are of genuine origin while others are not. In the army of Jesus every soldier must belong to his people. If there are foreigners mixed in with the troops, people who do not belong to his people but are interlopers, then it goes without saying that we must distinguish between those in the army who do belong to the Lord's people and those who do not. Therefore, it was sound instinct that compelled God's children to have high regard for the nomenclature of *the Lord's people* and to resist any attempt to eliminate the use of this nomenclature. The only ones interested in discontinuing the use of this name are those who want to mix the church with the world and discontinue the battle between the church and the world. By contrast, those who are convinced that only those who are born from above and incorporated into the Lord's people are able to fight the Lord's battle must hold fast to this honorific. After all, the heart of our sacred confession is that Jesus is a king who has his own subjects and, therefore, a people over which he rules.

The great importance of maintaining this scriptural view of a people of the Lord as militant church, and, therefore, as an army of Christ, is manifest especially in our days when the so-called Salvation Army presents itself as a caricature of what the Lord's army should be. The error of this Salvation Army is not that it employs the idea of battle and has astutely perceived that those who would enter battle together constitute an army. Its mistake consisted simply in this, that instead of allowing the church itself to function once again as militant church, it formed a kind of new "army" alongside the church, with a man as "commander" instead of Christ as the Commander-in-chief.

All the outward activism of the Salvation Army is connected to this fundamental error. For our part, we may, therefore, not oppose this phenomenon with scorn and mockery. After all, this "Salvation Army" constitutes a valid indictment of the church of Christ. And this anemic phenomenon will automatically disappear only when the church of Christ conducts itself once again as militant church. It will disappear if, instead of either sinfully uniting with the world as a national church or retreating into pious little groups for mutual spiritual enjoyment, the church once again becomes aware of its high and holy calling to wage war with the powers of darkness, as an army of the Lord, one in mind and one in purpose, standing in its spiritual armor, under its King, Head, and Commander.

THIRD CHAPTER

For we do not wrestle against flesh and blood, but against the rulers, against the authorities, against the cosmic powers over this present darkness, against the spiritual forces of evil in the heavenly places.

EPHESIANS 6:12

We have indicated the distinction between the concept of church, the concept of the kingdom of God, and the concept of the people of the Lord. We can do without none of these, because each of these three determines the character of our battle. We are a people born from God, which must battle as the church or elite troop, and, therefore, as an army under Christ, its Commander, until one day the kingdom of God—which was already established in the beginning—rules in the entire creation.

The idea of the battle or the war that we are to wage must, therefore, play a central role in every discussion of the doctrine of the church. If you omit this principle of our battle from the concept of church, then you will miss your active, driving force, and your resilience as a church will be less. In that case, there is no good reason for once godless but now regenerated sinners to remain on the earth. They are ready for heaven. They can depart immediately. None of their struggles on earth, none of their good works, will make the slightest contribution to their salvation or to their sanctification. They have been cleansed, they have been washed, and they have been sanctified in the Mediator. There lies a finished work in Christ, for every child of God. Nothing can be, and nothing may be, added to it. Our Savior is a perfect Savior.

If you still fail to see that the church is a militant church, an army of the Lord, and troops of the living God, then you have no clue why such people, ready and assured of their salvation, would remain on the earth. They become mere pilgrims—in itself a beautiful thought, but one that has been terribly abused in preaching and in literature. Pilgrims are travelers in a foreign land, a country in which they are uninterested, a land through which they travel merely to get through it, on a long journey whose next mile always seems too long. Pilgrims leave nothing behind in the land through which they travel; they do nothing for it, know nothing about it, and all their attention is focused on that high mountain range appearing on the horizon—the destination of their journey. Because that is what a pilgrim is, this image naturally came to be applied to Christians as well. After all, they too are a stranger on earth. They too have no lasting city here but reach ahead for the city yet to come. They too are not attached to this earth but long to be released and to be with Christ. They too are on a journey, and the destination is not a city on earth but the New Jerusalem.

Therefore, if I wish to describe the wide chasm between the disciples of the Lord and the world, if I intend to oppose worldliness, if I desire to encourage the people of the Lord on their way to eternity and to comfort them by its glorious anticipation—then indeed there is no greater picture than that of the pilgrim, the person who travels through foreign and dry deserts to the city of his refuge. But be careful not to abuse this glorious image. Sentimentality has overtaken this image. It is especially poignant for women to foster a fanatic indifference concerning the Lord's creation. The monastic movement especially arose from this misconception of the metaphor of the pilgrim, and all false mysticism finds its origin in that same abuse.

In God's sacred Word this image of the pilgrim is presented initially for us, but not this image alone. In Scripture the Holy Spirit uses a multitude of images in various ways to illustrate for God's children their earthly existence. One of these images is certainly that of the stranger on earth who, as the father of all believers, traveled from place to place to see the promised land. And all of Israel in the wilderness is one pilgrim people, journeying to the land of promise, a land of milk and honey, through a drab desert and past uninhabitable cliffs. But alongside this metaphor, Holy Scripture presents the image of the faithful steward, of the courageous soldier, of the maiden holding a lamp, of fishermen casting their nets, of the merchant seeking beautiful pearls, of the farmer sowing seed in his field, of children singing at a wedding, of musicians singing praise— and many more. The calling of preaching is, therefore, to bind all these features, one by one, upon the hearts of God's people, according to the sin that must be opposed or the comfort that must be imparted. If, instead of unfolding this biblical wealth of images, the preaching restricts itself to the notion of pilgrimage, then the inevitable, fatal consequence of such incomplete preaching will be that the resilience of God's people is broken; the active principle in Christ's church is killed; and the glorious, living, militant church of the Lord gradually transforms into a half-sleeping, half-dreaming circle of disillusioned people who really should be in heaven already but, without knowing why, have not yet been rescued or taken away by God's angels.

That loss of the resilient and inspiring idea of the militant church is due to Emperor Constantine the Great, a powerful ruler and serious Christian, but someone who brought serious harm to Christ's church. The thought entered his soul that already here on earth, the church of Christ must be a *ruling* church. It seemed to him that if only the rulers and kings of the earth keep extending the cross of Christ, through political power or, if necessary, through violence, the battle would soon be over and the church would already be triumphant on earth. He acted according to this idea, and the church, tired of the long and anxious battle, eagerly took hold of that powerful idea. From that moment on, it handed its own leadership to the imperial palace. Indeed, the world was soon conquered; nation after nation was added to the church; paganism was eradicated through violence. With the help of the state's money, power, and military, the church was planted in all of Europe and, until the rise of Islam, also in Asia and Africa. Then there was nothing left to fight for. The goal of the battle had been achieved. The kingdom that had to be established had now been established. In this manner, the kingdom of God was confused with and identified with the church. People had fought, but no longer. Now people ruled. Whereas Jesus had said, "My kingdom is not of this world; otherwise my servants would have fought for me" [see John 18:36], the church now turned this gospel of the kingdom on its head by seeking its security and salvation in a state-church or a church-state.

Yet in this bad situation a principle of *battle* still remained in the church as it awaited the Reformation. At this peak of power and dominion the effort and struggle to maintain this worldwide dominion continued. Under the medieval popes you find the Christian church struggling and battling—not in the sense intended by the gospel, but still driven to ceaseless effort. Even at the beginning of the Reformation the church retained this character, because the Protestant governments needed all their strength to remain in power during the long and varied religious wars. But again it is a battle using weapons. The church's battle became antipapism. Sadly, it was a battle in an unspiritual sense. It was unspiritual to such an extent that the Netherlands collected funds and commissioned armies and fleets to quell the influence of Rome in the European balance of power, meanwhile allowing the Roman Catholic population to live unconverted in their midst. When these religious wars finally came to an end and different struggles entered the political scene, this martial character of the church was lost entirely. Even in the Netherlands the church had become the ruling church. To the degree that people gradually lost their understanding of the church's spiritual character and made their peace with a mere semblance of dominion, it became increasingly easier for the church to fantasize that its salvation was found in this illusion of being a ruling church. People continued pressing demands against papists and kept pressing for special political privileges, but eventually no trace remained of any battle against Satan and against the spiritually wicked powers of the air.

Deceived by this error of the church, pious children of God then retreated into pietistic circles. In undeniable spiritual selfishness, they were almost exclusively focused on their own salvation. And throughout our country that spirit of indifference and passivity possessed the people of the Lord, who were at peace with anything provided that they retained their liberty to assemble with their conventicles and could count on orthodox preaching in their own village or a neighboring town. That is why it was so easy for the revolutionary rulers in the late eighteenth century to abolish the ruling church in the Netherlands and why there was so little resistance when in 1816 King William I incorporated the entire church into a state organization. And even though battles developed within the church subsequently, the church still did not reach the point where the war could be waged by the church against the world. It was still too much a battle to regain lost power. Many believers still held on to the false idea of Emperor Constantine, and there is still too little spiritual enthusiasm to fight the battle, as the people of the Lord, for the cause of God's kingdom.

The cause of all this misery was that the church of Christ had lost sight of the battle that it was to fight. It was mistaken concerning the nature and purpose of that battle and, therefore, erred in its choice of weapons and allies. Its armor should be spiritual only; but behold, it sought political patronage in state funding and in the support of the state protection. Its allies should be the angels of God and the saints on earth; but behold, it sought help from the mighty and prominent of the earth, also in the realm of science. Its battle should be a battle against Satan and the evil spirits in the air; but behold, they treated the most faithful part of God's people as its enemy.

It is, therefore, of the utmost importance, when defining what the church should be, to give a clear account of the enemy that it must fight. Now the holy apostle describes this enemy as being not "flesh and blood" but "the rulers, the authorities, the cosmic powers over this present darkness, the spiritual forces of evil in the heavenly places" [Eph 6:12].

How should we understand this? Certainly not as though it referred only to sin, as many preachers misinterpret it and water it down. Not that the battle against sin can be put on hold for a moment, but sin is only one of the effects of the real power against which the struggle must be waged. Anyone who says "the battle of the church is against sin" does not understand the depth of the problem and directly contradicts Paul's statement. What such superficial preachers mean by "sin" is exactly what Paul here calls "flesh and blood." "Flesh and blood" are the temptations of sensuality and lust, of temper and anger, of various sins and sinful thoughts and desires to which flesh and blood tempt us. And Paul does not say that the main battle of the church should be aimed at this, but on the contrary, that this is not the main battle, and that the church's actual battle is being fought against a much more powerful enemy who hides behind all these and many other sins and merely exerts his power in these sins.

The battle is between Christ and Satan. Satan fell first; only after him and through him did Adam fall. The root of evil is, therefore, not in this world and not in our human heart. If that were the case, no human being could receive redemption. Rather, the source and spring, the ultimate cause and root of evil lie outside this world in Satan. The history of paradise shows that. You see this in Jesus, whom Satan sought out in the wilderness before Jesus went into the world. It is obvious from the book of Revelation, which presents to us the end of the battle in the casting down of Satan and his minions.

Now Satan is—if we may say this for the sake of clarity—not a solitary person or an individual spirit; rather, Satan is a prince. He is a commander. He is the head of a kingdom. Thousands upon thousands of spirits are subject to him as his minions. And precisely that appalling authority makes Satan such a great power. That is why Paul describes to us his kingdom and dominion as a kingdom of "rulers, authorities, cosmic powers, darkness, and spiritual forces of evil." This power now pervades the earth. It invaded this world and dominated this world. It is important to have a clear view of this.

Our world on earth is not an autonomous world and does not have a life of its own. You can compare this somewhat to the many dead regions in the heart of Africa and Asia, which are unable to wake up to a life of their own.[6] It is possible that from powerful Europe either the English or the Germans could come to these lands and establish their influence, their banner, their language, their power; develop the natural resources of such a land; get out of it what is in it; and thus establish their dominion there. It is somewhat similar to our world on earth, and the powers that come to this world to establish their dominion there must come from either heaven or hell.

Two princes send to this world their missionaries, their troops, and their powers, to establish their dominion in this dead world. On the one hand, this is done by King Jesus, Prince of the heavenly host; on the other hand, it is done by Satan, the prince of the host of hell. First the heavenly dominion entered this world. That was paradise on earth. And this world was oriented to the arrival of that heavenly dominion. We had been created for that. But the prince of the host of hell could not allow this to happen. He too dispatched his powers. Humanity listened to these powers. Thus, our world was breached. Satan's armies invaded, and soon Satan's dominion was established in actuality on this earth. Jesus himself admits this when he calls Satan the "sovereign" or "ruler" of this world [John 12:31].

This is also evident from the character of Jesus' temptation. If Jesus would only worship Satan, that is, acknowledge Satan's sovereignty over this world, then Satan was willing to appoint Jesus as his steward or governor-general and to give him all these kingdoms and all their glory [Matt 4:8–9]. The declaration of war lay precisely in the fact that Jesus rejects this and claims the entire earth for his God. That is where the battle really begins, but the opposition between Satan and Christ is much more extensive.

When the Germans or English want to expand their colonial power, they not only send a fleet and troops, but they also try to make their way into the heart of the land. They try to take over the institutions of the nation, to become the legislators and judges, and gradually to rule over the spirit and customs of the nation, and in this way to turn all the power and influence and energy of that nation to their own advantage. Satan did exactly this.

---

6. These kinds of culturally-bound stereotypes are fairly common in Kuyper's writing. On his treatment of three main people groups (European, African, and Asian), see CG 1.41.1. See also the volume editors' introduction to CG, as well as CG 1.12.10n4 and 1.41.1n3.

He was not content to draw the *hearts* of people away from God, but he invaded the organic system of our human life. He breathed his spirit into all the institutions and customs and habits of life. He invaded all those influences and powers and energies that rule our human life. He subjected to himself and made subservient to his rule all connections and relations, all rules and patterns of our human life. Only in this way did he succeed in establishing his dominion through various "rulers and authorities," through all kinds of "darkness and spiritual forces of evil."

The individual human being is overwhelmed by the influences from all these powers and energies, from all these forces and authorities. We are dominated by all kinds of influence from our legislation, jurisprudence, and customs; from public opinion and dominant fashion; from the powers that determine the course of events in finance, trade, and industry; from the powers of false philosophy, of slanderous speech, of mockery and scoffing, of untruthful literature, and of mighty personalities. And because Satan grabs hold of all these channels and wires and vehicles—or if you will, all these cylinders, springs, and gears of our human life—to subject us to his dominion, therefore the church has been given the enormous task of breaking Satan's influence in our human heart in all these activities, functions, and expressions of our human life, and to replace it with the godly influence of Christ.

This would be in vain without the miracle of regeneration, worked by God in the hearts of his elect. No matter what better influences you apply to the human soul, as long as the sinner is anchored to Satan with the fibers of his heart you will essentially accomplish nothing. At best, you may be able to gild him on the outside, but you can never make gold shine within his soul. That is why the church always continues to honor the *cor ecclesiae* [heart of the church] in election and always takes its starting point in the wondrous work of the Lord that is wrought in the return of the prodigal, in the justification of the ungodly, in the enlivening of one who was dead.

Assuming this work of God and the church's origin in this work of God, it is and remains the task and high calling of that church, in a world whose entire structure is full of Satan's dominion, to stand up courageously against that dominion, to strap on the sword against that dominion; and without retreat or cease-fire, restlessly and ceaselessly, now and forever until the Lord's return, to continue the struggle, the fight, the war involving life and death waged against this Satanic dominion. Therefore, one can never be pious in the church without making the Christian confession or waging the Christian battle in the world.

Peace will never come and cannot ever come upon earth for the simple reason that there may never be any pact or pacification with Satan, so there cannot be peace until Satan is completely driven back, felled, and crushed. And since you know from God's Word that the church itself is not able to do this and that Christ has claimed for himself the honor of striking the final blow to Satan in the final cataclysmic struggle, therefore it is obvious that the church of Jesus must remain a militant church, in open war every day and every night with the enemy of God and humanity—that is, with Satan and his kingdom and dominion and ubiquitous power and influence.

FOURTH CHAPTER

How then will they call on him in whom they have not believed? And how are they to believe in him of whom they have never heard? And how are they to hear without someone preaching? And how are they to preach unless they are sent?

Romans 10:14–15

So we see that God had possession of this world before paradise. When humanity surrendered to temptation, Satan wrested this world from God and incorporated it into his kingdom. Subsequently the Lord began to demand that world back and, therefore, provided in Immanuel a ruler of the hosts and in his church an army. This army came into existence as "the people of the Lord" through the supernatural act of regeneration, and under its Head and King is destined to reclaim God's kingdom in the entire sphere of this creation from Satan, who is God's enemy.

Now we must investigate in what manner this army, this host, these select troops, this war machine of the living God came into existence and continues until today. The Catechism says that the church is a congregation—that is, an elect multitude, chosen for eternal life. The Son of God gathers, protects, and preserves them for himself, through his Spirit and Word, from the beginning of the world to its end. Let us first consider this last part.

The Lord God had entrusted the Garden of Eden to Adam—not only to cultivate it, as Genesis 2:15 states, but also to guard it. This means, of course, guarding it against Satan. But Adam failed to do so. Cowardly and shamefully he committed treason and handed this fortress of God to Satan without a fight. Precisely for that reason it was necessary for God to take measures to occupy this world. Satan could not possess the world unchallenged, not for a moment. Thus, in the very beginning already, we see in Abel a soldier of the Lord, a hero of faith, as Hebrews 11 teaches us, who gave his blood for God's cause. (We will not speak of Adam and Eve, as we are told nothing more about their spiritual life.)

From that moment on Holy Scripture continually parades before us a cloud of witnesses that continues uninterrupted to Abraham, the father of believers. With Noah suddenly a mighty change takes place in the relationship between the church and this world. Up to this point a nearly untraceable church had stood over against the innumerable world population; now suddenly that entire world drowns, and only the small church of the Lord finds shelter in the ark and floats on the waters. This put an end to the supremacy of the world. The church was rescued from being overpowered, and after the flood a new life begins under more favorable circumstances. It was not as if Satan's dominion had ended; sin came along into the ark, and immediately after the flood Noah lies drunk and Ham commits a shameful act. Soon evil invades and infects the world. Idolatry arises again. With Babel the mutiny against God reaches its peak. The good stream dissipates so quickly that Abraham in Ur and Melchizedek in Canaan are practically the only ones faithful to the service of their God. Again the church would have perished, which either would have necessitated another flood or something different to save the church. Now God had promised not to bring another flood of water on the earth, so that did not happen; the Lord had ordained a different way. He segregated his church from the world and enclosed it within a national existence, which he created for that specific purpose. And in that wonderful way he prepared a mighty army that later, in the fullness of time, when the Messiah would come, would break out of that narrow national existence to plant his divine banner among all the nations and would reinstate the worldwide character of God's church with the motto, "Preach the gospel to all creatures" [see Mark 16:15].

Thus, there is a church of God on earth from the very beginning, first in individuals and families but belonging to all parts of the human race. Then it was segregated as the national church of Israel, created especially for that purpose. And now, since the coming of Christ eighteen centuries ago, it has emerged from the Jewish national church and through Pentecost has become the worldwide church. It brings the battle of the Lord into new parts of the world, until the Commander himself shall appear with his heavenly hosts to finish decisively the battle with Satan and to manifest the kingdom of God in all its glory.

Now how is this church, this army of the living God, formed and sustained on the earth? Here we address the distinction between the visible and the invisible church. The Catechism says that the Son of God has done this. As we proved in connection with Lord's Day 19, this presupposes that Christ did not become Head of his church only after his ascension but was Head of his church from the beginning. Already in the days of the old covenant it is said of the Messiah: "In all their affliction he was afflicted, and the angel of his presence saved them" [Isa 63:9].

Although the Son of God gathers the soldiers of his select troops, he does not elect them; he recruits them but does not select them. Therefore, the Catechism adds that God's Son gathers only those who are chosen for eternal life. Before the gathering of the army comes the selection of individuals of whom it will consist. And thus, the beginning of the church points back to that eternal act of the Triune God, by which he elected from the entire human race; and throughout all the ages he elected his own, whom he destined to be incorporated into his elect troops. They would fight the battle with him and ultimately share eternally in the glory of God's kingdom.

In due time these elect, chosen by the Triune God, are gathered by God's Son. This happens through his Spirit and Word. Note that it does not say "through his Word and Spirit" but "through his Spirit and Word." The Spirit comes first, then the Word follows. The recruiting of this holy host happens differently than that of earthly armies. Earthly generals take their soldiers as they are and put a different uniform on them. Not so this Commander of God's hosts; his people do not wear an external uniform. Any attempt to introduce an external uniform—whether the monk's habit, the Quaker's suit, or the uniform of the Salvation Army—has resulted in nothing but damage to the Lord's cause. He requires no external uniform because he transforms, changes, and regenerates his people internally. This transformation, renewal, and regeneration begins with an operation of the Holy Spirit, which consists in this: the germ of new life, the power of faith, and the motivation for God's kingdom are planted as a possibility into the heart of people who were first Satan's minions.

But you must understand that there are no neutral people in this battle. Whoever is not against Jesus is for him [Mark 9:40]; whoever is not for him is against him [Matt 12:30]. In reality, every person who does not fight for the cause of Jesus is, therefore, intentionally or unintentionally supporting Satan's cause. Jesus gathers those given to him by the Father, but he gathers them out of Satan's army. Every individual who is incorporated into Jesus' church was first a member of the militia of God's enemy. They are transferred from the kingdom of darkness (that is, from under the sovereignty of the prince of darkness) into the kingdom (that is, under the sovereignty of the Son of his love).

But this is not enough. Through this act of the Holy Spirit these individuals have been transformed with respect to their soul's ability. But without something more, it has no effect. If someone whose eye is blind has been anesthetized and operated on, and his eye is restored, then he has indeed recovered his ability to see, but that does not mean that he is actually seeing or observing anything. That happens only when he also wakes up from that deep sleep and his eye adjusts to the light. The same applies here. By nature we are blind. In Satan's kingdom there is no light. It is a kingdom of darkness. If people are to enter Jesus' service, they must be given the ability to see, because in Jesus' kingdom everything is light. In him is no darkness [1 John 1:5]. That is the purpose of the first act that flows from election—that is, regeneration, which happens supernaturally through the Holy Spirit in a manner that we cannot understand. But more must happen. This person who is now able to see but is not actually seeing yet must be called to awake, so that he or she may stand up and walk. "Awake, O sleeper, and arise from the dead, and Christ will shine on you" [Eph 5:14].

This wake-up call happens through the Word—not in the sense that the Word should be considered separate from the Spirit. On the contrary, without the Spirit every word is powerless. Rather, the Spirit first implants the ability to believe supernaturally, apart from the Word; then that same Spirit activates this ability through the Word. How this happens psychologically belongs to the doctrine of salvation, not to the doctrine of the church, so we will not elaborate on it here. At this point we ask only in what way the Son of God published this Word. And then Romans 10 gives us the answer, loosely translated: "How will they call upon a Christ in whom they do not believe? How will they believe in a Christ of whom they have not heard? How will they hear of Christ if Christ is not preached to them? And how will Christ be preached to them if no preachers are sent?" [see Rom 10:14–15]. In these words lies the visible church.

If the church, the select troops of Christ, is to be gathered, fed, sustained, armed, trained, and propagated throughout the generations, it needs an institution or organization through which the ministry of the Word can take place. The visible church is no more than that. It is simply an institution for the ministry of the Word. It is certainly not the entirety of the church, not the essential church, not the church itself, but an institution established by the church and for the church, so that the ministry of the Word may take place in its midst. Take away that ministry of the Word and there is no visible church left. Only in the ministry of the Word does the institution of the visible church find its cause and origin. It exists only because of that, and any reasoning about the visible church goes wrong unless you go back, always and invariably and unconditionally, to this principle of the ministry of the Word.

The actual battle against Satan is not fought by this visible institution—far from it. That awful battle fought against Satan by the army under its Commander, to establish God's kingdom, extends throughout the entire arena of our human life on earth. That battle is fought in hearts, in households, in families, in conversations, in public opinion, in trade and work, in industry and profession, in science and art, at the cradle, and at the grave. In short, the battle extends as far as your entire human life. That battle is never fought by anyone but Jesus himself. As the living Lord, he is the one who places motivation and insight in the hearts of his elect, his faithful soldiers. He is the one who stimulates enthusiasm, operations, powers, and gifts; who creates in his soldiers devotion and love and even brings words to their lips. This arena of the battle that the spiritual church wages under its Commander is, therefore, incomparably larger than that of the institution of the visible church. The elect, the spiritual individuals, are exclusively of help to Jesus in this battle—never the hypocrites. And in this colossal battle no fight is fought unless Jesus himself leads and governs it, and unless he supplies the power and motivation for it. This spiritual church of which the Catechism speaks is his spiritual body, which is animated and moved by him as the Head, and which does not tolerate the inclusion of foreign elements. This spiritual church has no hypocrites. A hypocrite is not a solider of Jesus but a spy of Satan.

We may not for a moment lose sight of the profound distinction between this spiritual or *invisible church*—which is an object of faith and whose existence is confessed in the articles of our faith and explained by the Catechism in Lord's Day 21—and that very different phenomenon that we are calling the institution of the *visible church*. Here is an analogy for the sake of clarification: a commander can have a military camp in which he gathers his army, feeds, arms, and trains them, but that army in the camp must still be distinguished from the army on the battlefield. Similarly, the institution of the visible church is our camp, in which the Commander gathers us and continually feeds, arms, and trains us. But the real fight begins only when we leave that camp and approach the enemy on the battlefield.

If you do not keep this distinction in mind, you will end up either on the cliff of *churchism* or on the reef of *churchlessness*. Churchism treats the visible institution of the church as the real, essential church itself, and, therefore, wants to churchify the world. Everything must be incorporated into the church and be initiated by the church. To the church belong scholarship, science, and art. Preferably society must be fully incorporated in and governed by the church, as has been tried in Paraguay. Rome took this route, although it stopped halfway. The Reformation in particular put an end to this churchist movement and vehemently opposed Anabaptism because of this. Originally the visible institution of the church came into existence under the leadership of the apostles only as an institution for the ministry of the Word. The Reformation restored this character of the church. And even today the success of the new Reformation depends only on whether it will be able to recover this clearly delineated character of institution for the ministry of the Word.

The opposite danger lies in churchlessness, the elimination of the church, which was the error of the *Réveil*. In opposition to churchism, this movement defends the kingdom of God. People sense that there is more than just going to church to hear preaching; they sense that a battle must be fought for the honor of God in every arena of our entire human life. They reach a point of despising the visible institution of the ministry of the Word; they regard the "church" as superfluous and focus all their energy on what is called the extension and expansion of the kingdom of God.

With the correct distinction, by contrast, both this perilous churchism and this lethal churchlessness are avoided. Then you realize that the body of Christ—supported, animated, and honored by him as the Head—is part of the organism of this human world; you join the battle that seeks in various ways to expel Satan and to establish God's kingdom. Then you acknowledge as well that this church, this body of Christ, also has an institution in which it manifests itself, an institution whose only purpose is the ministry of the Word, and you realize that the church cannot exist without this institution of the ministry of the Word, not even for a moment. Confusion is thereby eliminated. People come to understand that, as the visible church, this institution has no other business except what flows from the ministry of the Word. It should leave everything else to the church as a spiritual body in its organic connection to the life of humanity. But people also come to understand that, in order to fight this battle in the organism of our human life with any hope of success, this spiritual body needs this visible institution of the ministry of the Word. The battle is not fought in the camp; nevertheless, in order to be able to fight, the army must be gathered, organized, fed, armed, and trained in the camp. This will naturally make preaching vivid and passionate. The ministry of the Word serves simply to equip for battle against Satan and for the kingdom of God.

The ministry of the Word includes not only the preaching of the Word but also the administration of the seal of the Word in the sacraments and likewise in the answer to that Word in the prayers and in praise. Indeed, there is more. Ministry of the Word is much more than mere proclamation of the Word. The Word is our King's proclamation. It is a word that comes with authority and power. Those who are sent to proclaim it are, therefore, vested with spiritual authority to acquit or convict according to this Word. That is why it is a single ministry of the keys of the kingdom, exercising the power of this Word both in the public worship service and in the church's discipline. Moreover, this ministry is missional. There is always more area to claim. The composition of the army must be expanded. Thus, the church may not be content with those who came near but must seek those who have remained far off. Therefore, there must be mission in one's own city and town as well as in distant lands. Finally, because the ministry of the Word brings believers together and stimulates them as an assembly for the work of giving and love, the ingathering of offerings is also inseparable from the ministry of the Word. These offerings are not gathered to provide for every need—by no means should the works of charity only go forth from the institution of the visible church—but rather are meant to bring an offering to the Lord, and out of that offering to spread through the Lord's community the fragrance of love that unites rich and poor in one divine love.

FIFTH CHAPTER

And I tell you, you are Peter, and on this rock I will build my church, and the gates of hell shall not prevail against it.

MATTHEW 16:18

We have seen that the visible church is nothing but an institution for the ministry of the Word and what belongs to it: the sacraments, prayers, songs of praise, and offerings. However, one must take care not to confuse the ministry of the Word with the reading of the Bible or an edifying address. "Ministry of the Word" is official duty.[7] It takes place at the command of our King and Commander and, therefore, has divine authority. This is why such ministry cannot be performed by just anybody on his own initiative and authority, but ought to take place officially and in connection with the consistory.

Many fail to understand this principle, and yet it is so clear. Three analogies should serve to remove any remaining confusion. When a judge at home, in his study, reads a verdict to someone in order to frighten him, then that may well result in such a person acknowledging his crime, but it certainly lacks the power of a verdict. If the same judge reads that same verdict concerning the same person ten days later in open court, then it is an actual verdict that is binding and has serious consequences for the guilty defendant. Likewise, a captain accompanied by his lieutenants on the patio of a social hall may speak with them to give them advice and warning, and this may have a good result, but it is not spoken while on duty and therefore carries no authority; it is merely advisory. When the next day that same captain gives orders in front of his troops, then every lieutenant is bound by them, and woe to the one who fails to obey! As a third and final example, if a shipmaster encounters three of his sailors in the street and gently points out that they are behaving drunkenly, this may have a positive effect, but if the sailor does not change his behavior, he still cannot be punished. However, if ten days later that same shipmaster is on board with the same sailors and he orders them in a severe storm to climb aloft, yet they fail to obey him, then they will be put in the brig.

The difference between what happens while on duty and off duty always plays a role in the church as well. In the context of the church we can also distinguish between what occurs within the ministry of the Word

---

7. The Dutch word *dienst* means both "ministry" and "official duty."

and outside the ministry of the Word. Therefore, what is spoken outside the ministry of the Word, in evangelism or small group, may have very profitable results, but it is not ministry. When the same preacher speaks at an evangelism event in the morning and in a public assembly of believers at night, and he delivers the same speech, then the former is unofficial, outside the ministry, and only the latter is ministry of the Word. Ministry of the Word does not necessarily take place when a preacher speaks, but only when an ordained person proclaims the Word as an ambassador of Christ, in the assembly of believers, within the framework defined by the consistory, in the name of King Jesus, and vested with Jesus' authority.

This is also why home visiting and catechesis are different within and outside the ministry. There is no objection to someone visiting his neighbor to speak with him about his faith confession and way of life, and there is nothing wrong with someone teaching a child a few things from the Bible. We should wish that this happened more. Even though all of this activity outside the ministry may bear good fruit, nevertheless it may never be confused with the catechesis and home visiting that proceeds from the church within the ministry. If the office-bearer, by the mandate and in the name of the consistory, and thereby in the name of and commissioned by King Jesus, teaches you in catechism class and admonishes you in your home, then these two have a very different character and have binding power for you.

So this ministry of the Word is absolutely not limited to preaching in the narrow sense. Within the ministry of the Word the Catechism can be explained to the assembly of believers, and within the ministry of the Word discipline must be maintained. All of these: first, ministry in the ordinary assembly of believers with the proclamation of the Word, exposition of the Catechism, administration of the sacraments, prayers, songs of praise, and alms; second, instruction in catechism classes; third, home visiting for admonition, rebuke, and consolation; fourth, the exercise of ecclesiastical discipline—all of these together constitute the one encompassing ministry of the Word, for whose purpose Christ desires that the institution of his visible church be maintained.

If our transfer from the realm of darkness into the kingdom of Jesus were a complete and suddenly perfect conversion, then the establishment and maintenance of the institution of the visible church would not present any objection or difficulty. In that case, first, the institution of the visible church would belong only to those who were given by the Father to the Son, without a single hypocrite. Second, these perfectly converted people would fully, exclusively, and consistently fight for Jesus' cause and never collaborate with Satan. Third, the administration of the offices in this visible church would always be pure and impeccable. But that is not the case. Even the most holy saints have in this life only the beginning of this perfect obedience. A converted man cries out, with Paul, that when he wishes to do what is good, evil is with him [see Rom 7:21]. The terrible example of Peter shows how far temporary denial can go.

This points to the following sad facts: there is no certain and unfailing test to distinguish the children of God from the children of the devil without error in terms of our human evaluation. And even the genuine children of God have all kinds of spots and blemishes. Because of these realities, it is sadly and painfully inevitable that the institution of the visible church can manifest itself only in an imperfect condition.

This results in a fourfold difficulty: First, in the visible church there will always be children of the devil mixed in with the children of God. Second, the children of God in the visible church will always be guilty of various acts of faithlessness. Third, the office-bearers in the visible church can commit acts of denial, even in the ministry, by which they oppose Jesus' kingdom and lend support to the kingdom of Satan. This threefold evil is made even worse by the fact that, fourth, the army or troops of Jesus together constitute one people, cultivated continually throughout the generations from age to age, so that there are many children who are unconverted, although they may belong to the elect. This compels the institution of the visible church to be involved with the children and to proceed to cutting them off from the church only in the extreme case of evident stubbornness in unbelief and ungodly behavior.

As a result of these various circumstances, therefore, a very significant distinction exists between, on the one hand, the actual army of Jesus, his real select troops, his spiritual body or his real church, and on the other hand, the institution of the visible church, instituted for the sake of the ministry of the Word and all that belongs to it. While the real church of Christ is pure, perfect, and unmixed, this institution of the visible church is impure, very imperfect, and mixed with various unholy parts. Not only is this so, but it *must* be so as well. Any attempt by Montanists, Donatists,

Novatians, Cathars, Anabaptists, and Labadists[8] to establish a different institution of the visible church that is nothing but pure, unmixed, and holy, was opposed in principle to the ordinances of the Lord and was therefore bound to fail. Indeed, this Labadistic thirst for a pure institution on earth cannot be satisfied; on the contrary, sometimes the institution can degenerate so much that it must be partially torn down and renovated or even completely razed and rebuilt from the ground up.

Precisely because of this, one may not think of this institution of the visible church apart from the sacred duty of continual reformation. Since the nature of the institution of the visible church implies that it continually tends toward deformation, there must be a continuous opposing activity designed to press it back into its proper form. This takes place effectively and gradually as long as evil has not invaded the offices too strongly. If the officers are faithful to our Commander—if the officer corps, if we may put it this way, continues to adhere loyally to the Commander-in-chief—then the reformation of the troops continues smoothly. This is the exercise of ecclesiastical discipline.

If evil has invaded the governing body, if the organization itself has been infected, if the officer corps has become unfaithful, then of course any reformation of the army cannot take place without severe upheaval. Then discipline must be exercised not by the officers upon the troops, but by the faithful troops upon the officers. And even if some officers remain faithful and support the troops in their zeal for their Commander, then the unfaithful group of officers will nevertheless endeavor to suppress this movement and crush the allegiance to our Head and our Commander. However, this opposition does not relieve the faithful officers and soldiers of their duty, so that the reformation of the military institution must go forward; thus, there must be a separation. The old, degenerated, and apostate institution does not give up and perhaps even succeeds in subduing or forcibly restraining part of the army. The faithful soldiers thus are compelled to act in their own power to fill the vacancies for officers and thereby to remain faithful to Jesus as their Commander.

This would be less of a problem if the select troops of the Lord's soldiers were an army of hirelings, rather than an army of the people. But that is

---

8. The Labadists, led by Jean de Labadie (1610–74), were a well-known seventeenth-century sect in the Netherlands who withdrew from the mainstream church to form a community of "true believers."

not the case. The kingdom of God that is being established and is being reclaimed from Satan must certainly manifest itself in spiritual powers and marvelous glories—but still, it consists first of all of people. A kingdom of God without a people of God is impossible. Therefore, the battle against Satan consists not only in reclaiming from Satan the spiritual treasures of human life, but first of all in retrieving human beings from Satan—both in body and soul. This gives the church a twofold character. It is a select troop, an army of the Lord, a host of the living God, to wage the battle of the Lord against Satan under Jesus as their Head. But at the same time it is a people destined to enjoy life under Jesus as its King. This shows how shallow the opinion is of those who deny that Jesus is both Head and King of the church. Under Jesus as the Head we fight, but under Jesus as our King we live.

This implies that the church must take care of two things: on the one hand, the church must prepare the army for war and fight the war; and on the other hand, already from the start the church must ensure that these people live under their King, ready for the glory of the kingdom of God. Therefore, the institution of the visible church requires a threefold destination. It serves, first, to reclaim people from Satan; second, to repel Satan in the organism of our entire human life; and third, to have the people of the Lord living under their King and maturing for the kingdom of his glory.

All of this happens through the ministry of the Word with everything that belongs to it. This ministry of the Word has the purpose, first, to issue the call, in order that those whose ears have been opened by the Holy Spirit may hear the voice of Christ, leave Satan, and come to Jesus; second, to nourish, arm, and train those who have joined the service of Jesus; and third, to give the people of the Lord a foretaste here already of Christ's salvation, thereby to comfort them and to mature them for eternity.

None of these three may be omitted, or else the ministry of the Word fails. A ministry of the Word that does not lead to the conversion of people, who until that time had walked with Satan (albeit as hypocrites in the visible church), is lacking fruit. A ministry of the Word that does not nurture, arm, and train for battle against the evil one lacks fervor and resilience. And a ministry of the Word that does not comfort, give enjoyment, and sanctify is cut off from our eternal destination. The ministry of the Word cannot suffice with one of these three, nor with two of them; justice must be done to each of these three. The fact that so many preachers are at a loss for something to say or fall into repetition, and by their empty preaching empty out the churches, is simply due to lack of clarity about this threefold purpose of the ministry of the Word.

One who simply preaches in a fawning or pious fashion neither persuades nor arms. One who tries to function simply in a methodistic fashion neither arms nor comforts, and one who only sounds the battle clarion and blows the horn of repentance neither persuades nor comforts.[9] To *persuade*, to *arm*, and to *comfort*—in these three lies the unity of preaching, and in this unity of proper proportion lies the power of preaching. Naturally, one preacher has received more talent to persuade, another to arm, a third to comfort; and depending on the occasion, the focus lies on an attempt to persuade, or to arm, or to comfort. However, not one of these ingredients may ever be missing. The ministry of the Word depends on these three: to persuade through faith, to arm through hope, and to comfort through love.

This has an important implication for the visible institution of the church and its continual reformation: the ministry of the Word, together with the administration of the sacraments and discipline, are sufficient for deciding what impurity may or may not be tolerated in the visible church. What matters here is not the Confession. The Confession is not the ministry of the Word but only a manifesto, a declaration of war to Satan, which is dead as soon as it is denied in the ministry of the Word. Our fathers were absolutely correct, therefore, in continually insisting that the tolerability of impurity in the visible churches should be measured only according to the ministry of the Word.

In this regard we must note two things. The ministry of the Word has two aspects: first, the content that is presented and, second, the authority with which it is presented. In order to know whether the content is pure, you need only to ask whether it corresponds with the Word in terms

---

9. Kuyper's criticism of Methodism (understood as a practice or tradition rather than as a particular denomination) lies in part in his observation that it focuses on bringing "a sinner to conversion by a fixed method. This is based on the notion that all sinners must come to life in the same manner; that the awakening from death to life is tied to a certain method; and that when we apply this method in the work of conversion, it will succeed, and when we do not apply this method, we plow on rocks; and thus also that those who walk the path of conversion in this way are truly included among the sheaves of the living, whereas the state of grace of those who have not trod this fixed path of conversion must always be in doubt." See CG 1.43.4, p. 379, and see also *CG* 1.34.1n1.

of the three purposes listed above. Whatever is not ministry of *the Word* must be mercilessly rejected. But this work must also be *ministry* of the Word. As we discussed before, evangelism is very different from the ministry of the Word, and likewise it will not do to say: "I preach the pure gospel and preach it in the name of Jesus." After all, an evangelist does that too. Rather, the ministry of the Word arises, as far as your authority is concerned, from the commission of your consistory, and that consistory has the right to give you that commission only in connection with the organization of the entire institution of the visible church. Therefore, if you live in a church denomination that is unfaithful to Jesus, that has denied its Head, become unfaithful to the Commander, and replaced his authority with a human authority—then your consistory has no power in the name of Jesus, and then your consistory cannot give you power in the name of Jesus. And while you may be able to evangelize, you cannot fulfill the ministry of the Word.

For this reason it is not enough for believers to have a preacher in their local church who preaches no falsehood. They must establish a ministry of the Word, if one is lacking. The ministry of the Word takes place, first, only if the content of the preaching, according to the three aforementioned requirements, persuades, arms, and comforts; second, only if this authority with which you bring the Word comes from Jesus; and third, only if this authority is not vested in your person but comes to you from the consistory. Because of this it is clear that the ministry of the Word fails not only if the content is impure but also if the consistory is on slippery footing and actually, through a false church denomination, in its very organization is denying the authority of King Jesus.

SIXTH CHAPTER

But you are a chosen race, a royal priesthood, a holy nation, a people for his own possession, that you may proclaim the excellencies of him who called you out of darkness into his marvelous light.

1 PETER 2:9

So the kingdom of God in its consummation is the kingdom of glory. The church is the army or host that surrenders itself to Jesus as its Head and Commander for the establishment and propagation of that kingdom. Meanwhile this army is a people, from all nations, tongues, and tribes, which one day will flourish in this kingdom but now fights as an army for its King. The ministry of the Word and everything that belongs to it is an institution ordained by this King for his church—to gather, protect, and sustain this church, this host, this army fighting for him, as an instrument in his hand.

We must be on guard against a gross misunderstanding: blinded by the false outward appearance of our deteriorated churches, a less careful reader might get the impression that this institution of the ministry of Word is identical to the visible church—that in the spiritual realm there would be an invisible church, and in the visible and observable realm there would be nothing but this institution. If, therefore, one would remove this institution of the ministry of the Word, then, according to the uninformed opinion of these superficial people, nothing would be left but the mysterious, hidden, invisible body of the Lord; and this would not be able to manifest itself or become visible. Then of course—and this would be even more ridiculous—one would be compelled to believe the error and heresy, which we have already opposed so often, that the visible church would be something different, an altogether different kind of church, than the invisible church.

As for this latter heresy, our *Tract on the Reformation of the Churches* and repeated articles in *De Heraut*[10] have stated clearly enough that this cannot and may not be the case, because it is one and the same church of Christ that—not to elaborate further—is spiritually invisible and becomes externally visible. Unless this has been firmly established, so that no Reformed believer would ever doubt that the church that becomes visible is that very same church that remains spiritually invisible, we will constantly

---

10. *De Heraut* (*The Herald*), the weekly church newspaper edited by Kuyper.

be exposed to the misconception that in the visible realm the church of Christ is identical to the institution of the ministry of the Word. This is a gross error. This would imply that if the ministry of the Word has not yet been established or is temporarily hidden or absent, then the church would cease to be visible. This misunderstanding must be eradicated from among our people. It must become clear again to everyone that, on the contrary, in order to be able to establish an institution for the ministry of the Word, the church itself must first have become visible and that, even if the ministry of the Word were compromised temporarily or even ceased for a time, this does not at all imply that the church of Christ would necessarily remain unobservable or invisible.

Let us be lucid and simple in our views. The invisible side of the church never becomes visible, since a spiritual being or spiritual function will never be visible as such. Just as your soul can never become visible, likewise the spiritual side of Jesus' church can never be observed by our senses. True, just like the church, you have a visible aspect observable in your appearance and form, which reveals characteristics and expressions of your soul, but the essence of your soul is not, and never will be, accessible to the senses. In order to know whether the church of Christ is visible in any land or locale, only one question needs answering: Do you and others observe that it is there? If so, then it is visible in that place. If not, then it would remain invisible. This is crystal clear.

Now if one can determine whether the church of Christ is present in any place only in terms of the ministry of the Word and its accoutrements, then naturally the visible church and the institution for the ministry of the Word would be one and the same thing. That is absolutely not the case. As soon as there are any individuals who openly confess the Lord Jesus, and who show this among themselves and to others, anyone who pays attention can observe that the church of Jesus is also present in this place. The church is the body of Christ, and as soon as there are as few as two or three people in a certain locale who belong to this body, then this body exists not only elsewhere but also in that place; and as soon as these two or three persons gather in his name, he is among them, and in their confession the body of the Lord becomes manifest or visible.

Note carefully that the entire ministry of the Word and everything that belongs to it do not even belong to the body of Christ in its essence. After all, when everything on earth comes to its end, this ministry of the Word ceases forever, but the body of Christ continues. In fact, only then shall it be manifested in its true glory. By contrast, persons do belong to the essence of the invisible church, because they are members of the body and therefore belong to it forever.

The situation is, therefore, this: First, there exists a body of Christ, which is the church in its invisible aspect, consisting of elect individuals under its Head. This body has been foreknown from before the foundation of the world and continues forever. Second, in various locales the presence of this body becomes manifest, noticeable, observable, and visible when there are as few as two or three people who openly confess the name of the Lord Jesus. Third, these persons in whose confession and walk the invisible church becomes visible are required, by Christ's command, to establish immediately an institution for the ministry of the Word and everything that goes with it. It must as much as possible be in connection and communion with other manifestations of this same body of the Lord in other locales.

Our later Reformed authors from the end of the seventeenth century, and especially in the eighteenth century, were no longer very clear about this. Specialists and insightful Reformed theologians, such as the truly unique Voetius, knew this very well and expressed it clearly.[11] According to them the external institution belongs to the well-being, not to the being or essence of the visible church. Likewise, the church does not become visible for the first time with and through the institution but is already visible by the time it begins establishing the ministry of the Word.

This distinction between the visible church, on the one hand, and the institution of the Word that must be established and sustained by it is very simple. If in a town, village, or city where the church of Christ had not yet been observed, there is a man or woman who openly confesses the Lord Jesus, along with a second and a third, and they know this about each other, then the church of Christ has become manifest there. But this is very different than their admission to the Lord's Supper and their registration in a membership book. Those things become possible only when the church not only becomes visible but also acquires an institutional form.

If the church has become visible in any place and, following the Lord's instruction, begins establishing the ministry of the Word with its accoutrements, then something must be done by all of them together. This is

---

11. Gisbertus Voetius (1589–1676) was an important Reformed theologian at the University of Utrecht.

possible only when it is has been decided who will take action and in what way they will act together. Together they must find a connection to what is done elsewhere. There must be an election and appointment of people to the offices and an installation of these people in these offices. In order that the office-bearers do not exercise partiality or lordship, a regulation or church order must be drawn up, and this church order defines the unique character of the institution.

Whether this involves seeking a relationship with the government is an entirely different issue, which we will leave here. But even if one has nothing to do with the government, every local church that became visible through its confessions must nonetheless endeavor to seek the government's well-being. To that end it must establish, in connection and collaboration with other churches, an institution for the ministry of the Word and everything that belongs to it.

Now if this institution consisted only of the offices, then the people themselves would have no dealings with this institution except in a passive sense. But this is not the case. The persons themselves must function in this institution. They too have a public calling and, in that sense, an office. Therefore, it must also be determined for this institution who are to be considered as its participants and its leaders. This leads to composing a document that stipulates the features of joining a denomination as far as that affects the institution. If all goes well, then a Christian person must belong to the church of Christ—first, because he is elected by God and has been incorporated by the Savior into his body; second, because he publicly confesses the Lord, and thus on his part makes this church manifest and visible, in association with other persons in the same locale who confess the Lord Jesus; and third, because he joins an institution for the ministry of the Word, which already exists or which he helps to organize.

Our ancestors said that the church was *invisibilis, visibilis,* and *formata*—that is, invisible, visible, and formed (organized as an institution). One can, therefore, belong to the invisible church without yet having lived in a visible church. Likewise, the church can have become visible without yet having been organized. If all goes well, then all three must occur. One must be of the invisible church, belong to the visible church, and join an organized church institution or established institution. This implies that the organization can fall into disarray without the church ceasing for one moment to be visible, but it also implies that such an organization must immediately be repaired and therefore deformation or defect in such an organization must lead to the repair of that organization.

Now if we consult our Catechism, we find that in Lord's Day 21 it discusses the invisible church in Question 54, the visible church in Question 55, and the institution of the ministry of the Word of the Reformed church in a very different Lord's Day: namely, Lord's Day 25, Questions 65–68, dealing with the ministry of the Word and the sacraments. Postponing the issue of the organized church until we arrive at our discussion of Lord's Day 25, we, therefore, limit ourselves to two remaining points in Lord's Day 21 related to the invisible and visible church: first, the confession concerning the invisible church, that "I am and forever shall remain a living member of this communion";[12] and second, the confession concerning the visible church, that there must be communion of saints.

Our entire Christian religion is based on faith, and our Christian faith is not only an assent to the truth but also a possession of assurance. Concerning this, Question 21 confessed that our Christian faith is also a firm assurance that "not only to others, but to me also" the benefits of the covenant of grace have been given. This assurance is inseparable from faith, and without this assurance, faith is not faith. As we discussed before, it is not as though the operation of this faith must be clear, conscious, and unclouded, or else one faces the punishment of woe; but rather, it must operate in such a way that the faith planted in us decisively contains in its germ, root, and bud both this assent to the truth and this assurance. This occurs with the understanding that as soon as this planted ability to believe begins its powerful work in us through the grace of the Holy Spirit, both of these [assent and assurance] always manifest themselves, naturally and inseparably.

Now this is what the Catechism here applies more specifically to the body of Christ. Two elements always lie at the root of our ability to believe: first, the discovery and acknowledgment that there is a body of the Lord, and second, the awareness of assurance of our personal belonging to that body. It is not that every Christian at every moment of his life would have a clear, spiritual view of the body of Christ or would experience his belonging to it. Far from it. But as soon as this ability to believe begins to sprout in us and to become active through the grace of the Holy Spirit, it will always naturally and spontaneously grow upward—both to the acknowledgment

---

12. Heidelberg Catechism, Lord's Day 21, A 54.

that there is such a body of the Lord and to the blessed experience that the believing person is an inseparable and essential member of this body. A believer may feel disconnected from an organized church for various reasons. Faith may even temporarily lack a connection to the visible church. But it immediately, automatically, and without hesitation directs itself to the invisible church. Faith in Christ that at the same time is not faith toward his body is unthinkable and does not exist.

The situation with the communion of saints is somewhat different. The regrettable and grievous error of all hierarchists and clericalists— namely, supposing that the institution of the Word or the Reformed church would be the visible church itself, rather than having been established through the visible church—has thoroughly obscured the matter. It has resulted in the evil that many are content to be joined to an organized church without having any appreciation for the communion of saints. People then fall into a narrow ecclesiastical attitude—one that bans and bars others and breaks off from them without ever realizing what the communion of saints requires of every brother and every sister.

Nevertheless, in this respect as well it is not difficult to return to a purer path, if only one takes a moment to think about our beautiful Confession. The communion of saints is the link between the invisible church and its visible side. According to our Catechism, this includes two things: first, that every believer shares in Christ and in all his treasures and gifts, and second, that they are obligated to hold the gifts given to them, not individually, but communally. The former—sharing in Christ and his treasures—touches upon the invisible church; the communal possession of the donated gifts touches upon the church as something visible.

This is clear from the nature of the matter. Sharing in Christ and his treasures is a spiritual matter, which is hidden. It is the hidden grace of the mystery of salvation and of God's covenant of peace. It is turned inward and comes from above; it is what Paul means when he says that our life with Christ is hidden in God [see Col 3:3]. This refers to our walk in the heavens, not to our conduct here below on earth. But it is very different with the second element that our Catechism identifies: our duty to employ communally the gifts of grace given to us.

These freely given gifts have come down from heaven to us from the Father of lights. These gifts of the Holy Spirit, therefore, function in people on earth. And concerning these gifts, which have come down and were placed in us on earth by the Holy Spirit, the Catechism tells us that all should feel the duty to utilize their gifts willingly and joyfully for the benefit and the salvation of the other members. This involves not the invisible church but the visible church, which must be distinguished clearly from the organized church or institution. If I use the gifts of the Holy Spirit that have been given me for the benefit of other members of the body of the Lord, then this implies that I know people by name and that I believe and assume that they are members of this body. How else could I act for the benefit and salvation of someone unless I know who that person is? This shows that with this second component of the communion of saints we are standing in the middle of the visible church.

This automatically entails a limitation. None can employ their gifts for the benefit of all the members of Christ's body who are on earth, but only for the benefit of those whom they either know personally or know about. From this it follows that all Christian people are called to investigate which gifts of the Holy Spirit have been given to them: gifts of a general nature, such as faith and hope and love—expanded further in terms of humility, meekness, patience, and humble compassion; but also gifts of a special nature, such as gifts of prayer, praise and thanksgiving, prophecy, of discerning spirits, and of the soul-piercing word—manifested in counseling, admonition, and consolation. It also follows that as someone who is subject to the commandment not to bury these gifts in the ground but to multiply them [see Matt 25:14-30], you may not keep them for yourself but are called to employ them in your context, to the extent that you find opportunity, for the benefit and salvation of the other members of the same body of the Lord.

Finally, it follows that you must seek out those others, that you must make yourself known to others, that you must foster fellowship with others, not only to be a blessing to them, but also to receive a blessing from them. In this way, through the confession of personal faith and through the manifestation of personal gifts, the members of the body of Christ become known and visible to each other, and the church becomes visible to them.

SEVENTH CHAPTER

To the praise of his glorious grace, with which he has blessed us in the Beloved.
In him we have redemption through his blood, the forgiveness of our trespasses.

EPHESIANS 1:6–7A

In the Apostles' Creed, following the confession about the Holy Spirit, the church, and the communion of saints, before moving on to the resurrection of the body, an additional matter is indicated with the words "the forgiveness of sins."

The treatment of this weighty article of faith in our Heidelberg Catechism is not felicitous, and in Ursinus' *Commentary* it enjoys only a brief discussion.[13] The reason for this is that the Heidelberg Catechism intentionally presents this matter in depth in Lord's Day 23, under the doctrine of justification, to which Ursinus then refers at this point. In order not to repeat the same material, this article of faith is given somewhat short shrift, and Ursinus and Olevianus discussed it as an appendix to the confession about the church.[14] The result is that when this part of our Catechism is explained on the pulpit, even less attention is usually paid to it. If explaining the material about the church and the communion of saints has already required several sermons, then there is simply no time left for this tenth article of faith. This is all the more so since the Heidelberg has inserted the matter of election into Question 54, and so this *cor ecclesiae* needs only brief discussion then in connection with the consideration of Question 54.

We must pause for a moment with respect to this apparently insignificant and purely formal question, and it needs to be shown how this article about the forgiveness of sins came to appear precisely at this point in the Apostles' Creed. We need to explain as well why our Catechism writers nevertheless shifted its content to a separate Lord's Day dealing with justification.

When the Christian church arose and emerged out of Israel to enter the world, it came out of the ministry of shadows. In this ministry of shadows, everything that was intended as *spiritual* and invisible was presented *tangibly* and outwardly. Deliverance from Satan meant being delivered from

---

13. Zacharius Ursinus (1534–83) was a principal author of the Heidelberg Catechism and his lectures were later published as an exposition or commentary.
14. Caspar Olevian (1536–87) was also traditionally understood to be involved in composing the Catechism.

Egypt's house of bondage. The land of promise was not heaven, but the visible land of Canaan, flowing with milk and honey. Purification was essentially a bathing with water. Atonement was sought in an animal, whose blood was shed. In short, every spiritual reality was depicted in the ministry of shadows by something that one could perceive with the senses and came to expression in externalities.

The same was the case under this ministry of shadows with respect to sin. Spiritual sin was symbolized by the material reality of Levitical uncleanness. Every stain connected with Levitical uncleanness rendered someone or something unholy and alienated them from fellowship with the holy God. In order to enter into communion with this holy God, this Levitical uncleanness had to be removed beforehand. This is what the priestly ministry accomplished. This led to the existence of two spheres. By means of his priests, God separated between the clean and the unclean, the holy and the unholy spheres. Every impulse of an Israelite who feared God was to avoid all communion or contact with what was unclean or unholy and to be part of what was holy and clean. This is why a high priest was not permitted to bury his father's body—because it was dead and thus unclean.

To a certain extent, the memory of something similar existed in the pagan world as well. There too various consecrations and purifications occurred that all proceeded from the suppositions that (1) a distinction existed between a holy and an unholy sphere; (2) by nature people belonged to the unholy sphere; and (3) people had to be transferred from one to the other sphere by means of priestly service at a sacred location.

When, therefore, the cup of the new covenant was received in Jesus' blood, and with that the "ministry of shadows" came to an end—becoming the ministry of fulfillment—the question arose as to where, in terms of the holy, this distinction between the holy and the unholy was to be sought now in the new dispensation.

The Lord himself had prompted this question by telling his disciples, "Already you are clean because of the word that I have spoken to you" [John 15:3], which went back to the statement made in connection with the holy Supper. This question was prompted no less by his assurance in connection with the foot-washing: "The one who has bathed does not need to wash, except for his feet, but is completely clean" [John 13:10]. The holy apostles also repeatedly moved this deep, fundamental idea to the foreground in their preaching, whenever they addressed the congregation of believers as saints or appealed to them by saying, "But you were washed, you were sanctified, you were justified in the name of the Lord Jesus Christ and by the Spirit of our God" (1 Cor 6:11). This "being sanctified" evidently does not refer to sanctification, since sanctification follows justification, and here in 1 Corinthians 6:11 it precedes justification.

In this way, then, the picture of a holy church was formed. Among Israel, one could move from being unclean to being clean as long as one sought to share in the priestly cleansing that saved from Levitical uncleanness. From their own past as well, Gentile Christians were familiar with priestly sprinkling and purification rituals that transferred them from the unconsecrated to the consecrated sphere. This explains the very natural question that arose among the early Christians about what sphere was for them consecrated and holy. They answered that question very correctly by teaching that the ministry of shadows was past and was taken up into the ministry of fulfillment. They answered that external holiness was no longer the benchmark, but only the spiritual cleansing in Christ, such that therefore the consecrated arena and the sacred sphere for them was to be sought only where the powers of the atonement sacrifice of the Lord were operative—that is, in his church.

Holy baptism strengthened this insight. Through a *holy* baptism as a water bath, cleansing from guilt and defilement is portrayed. Because this baptism is the sacrament of incorporation into the church of the Lord, by means of that sacrament the conviction is confirmed that the world outside the church is indeed the unconsecrated sphere, and the sacred sphere is entered only in the church of Christ.

As long as this was intended and understood spiritually, everything proceeded well. People confessed and acknowledged that the body of the Lord was holy and clean in its sacred Head; that everything belonging to this body of the Lord was thereby freed from sin—could no longer sin—because the seed of God remained in them; and that the body possessed complete forgiveness both from sins that had been committed and from the sinful nature that clung to each person. This was what Paul had confessed: "So now it is no longer I who do it, but sin that dwells within me" [Rom 7:17].

Quickly, however, people took this glorious confession in a wrong direction. When hypocrites in the church began to outnumber genuine believers, this highly spiritual position could no longer be maintained. The persistent outbreak of sin was too obvious and manifest for that to happen. This led in turn to two abuses: first, that of the holy orders, and second, the confessional. Both abuses involve the intermediation of the priestly service administered to real believers or nominal believers.

By falling back into the ceremonies of the ministry of shadows, people thereby once again distinguished between holy places and unholy places, and this provided entrance for the view that sprinkling with consecrated water could remove uncleanness. This came to expression in baptism by means of exorcism or the casting out of the devil. It came to expression in consecrating churches, chapels, and monasteries. And it came to expression in connection with entering the sanctuary, by means of the consecrated water with which those entering were sprinkled. In this manner, the glorious thought of a holy arena that was purified spiritually by Christ was reduced to the banal notion of an external stain that was removed by means of outward sprinkling.

But that was not all. People also had to deal with the sin that repeatedly erupted so crudely and terribly, and thus a means needed to be invented for removing these repeatedly erupting sins that disrupted holiness, one that would restore holiness. That means was found in the confessional, which assumed that the members of the church who had fallen out of holiness were now supposed to come to the priest to ask for the restoration of their holiness; in this way, they would obtain absolution from all confessed sins.

In this manner, the notion was preserved of the church as the sphere of the holy. Every stain of uncleanness was removed through consecration, and every stain of sin was removed through confession. The outcome was that the spiritual church was externalized, while the church nevertheless continued to be the arena where the forgiveness of sins exercised royal dominion.

The church is holy because it is the body of the Lord, and it is that in the absolute sense of 1 John 3:9 that believers cannot sin because they are born of God. But of course this is a potentiality—that is, not something automatic but in Christ; not by means of the church's own confession but by means of the Word that he has spoken to it [see John 15:3]. This agrees entirely with our liturgical formulary for the Lord's Supper: "Considering that we seek our life out of ourselves in Jesus Christ, we acknowledge that we lie in the midst of death."[15]

At this point, however, people lost sight of this spiritual vantage point and went looking for this sacred character, in part in priestly consecrations, and in part in the subjective sanctification of the persons themselves. The practice of indulgences emerged from this. By means of this false standpoint, the entire doctrines of sin, of humanity, and of salvation were taken down the wrong path, and the outcome was that when the Reformation of the sixteenth century arose, the entire concept of the forgiveness of sins had been incorporated within an ecclesiastical enterprise. It occurred outside of Christ and ultimately outside the soul as well. This gripped Luther so powerfully in his distraught conscience, which explains why he rejected this entire approach to the forgiveness of sins as the church lay claim to it and offered it. He did this in order to go behind the church's back to seek the basis of the forgiveness of sins in justification by faith.

This was viewed correctly to the extent that it pressed for a going back from the visible church into the invisible church. The forgiveness of sins is a spiritual benefit that belongs in the invisible church as the body of the Lord. One who belongs to it shares that benefit; one who roams outside it misses that benefit. Only to the extent that you are conscious of your affiliation with the body of the Lord do you taste the full comfort of that forgiveness of sins.

Luther did not maintain this connection, however, and later Lutherans in particular made the forgiveness of sins far too much a personal matter between God and one's heart, apart from affiliation with the body of Christ. In so doing, it became a transaction between individual A and his God, and individual B and her God. Thus, there was now scarcely any sense of possessing this treasure of salvation together as the church of the living God. The reaction against the error of Rome had led in turn to an opposite imbalance.

All the churches of the Reformation suffered from this imbalance, but the Reformed suffered the least, because among these churches, regeneration and conversion featured more prominently than justification. Among us who are Reformed, people did indeed sense that one shares in the

---

15. See "The Liturgy of the Reformed Dutch Church," in *The Constitution of the Reformed Dutch Church of North America* (Philadelphia: G. W. Mentz & Son, 1840), 101.

saving benefit of the forgiveness of sins only when one is engrafted into Christ, becomes a child of God, and is incorporated as a member into his glorious body. Among us, people knew and understood that sinners must be changed and converted if they are to enter the kingdom of God and find the forgiveness of sins in that kingdom. Apart from an intervening act of God in the soul, this comfort would not be tasted by we who were Reformed. This resulted in the doctrine of justification being held very highly among us, and apart from this glorious confession no soul can be quieted. Nonetheless, belief in justification among us who were Reformed was far more a fruit of implanted faith and regeneration than a desire that this doctrine in itself would be the sum and substance of our spiritual life. One can see this best in the resistance of our people against neo-Kohlbruggianism, which in this respect is more Lutheran than Reformed, and here as in other doctrines, betrays its German and non-Dutch origin.[16]

This is not to deny, however, that our Heidelberg Catechism, having reached this point, refrained from discussing the actual doctrine of the forgiveness of sin and skipped over it here, setting it forth partially in Question and Answer 21 dealing with faith, partially in Question and Answer 61 dealing with justification, and partially in the doctrine of the sacraments.

As long as the historical process of this matter is clear to everyone, we have no reason or cause to deviate in this from the method of treatment provided by the Heidelberg, even though we would prefer the method of consideration followed by Calvin and our Belgic Confession. Especially the discussion of the doctrine of election, considered incidentally in connection with the doctrine of the church, constitutes a difficulty in our Heidelberg Catechism. Nevertheless, let us never forget that a document like our Catechism originated under particular historical challenges, and at that time the hope had not yet been abandoned that by being more circumspect in their expressions, people would probably be able to achieve the amalgamation of the Lutheran and Reformed churches.

This yielded less objection, however, because our Catechism, albeit briefly, discusses the forgiveness of sins at this point in Question and Answer 56, thereby seeing to it that the beautiful harmony and sequence of the Apostles' Creed was not broken.

---

16. Hermann Friedrich Kohlbrugge (1803–75) was a Dutch minister. His German father and Lutheran upbringing may be the occasion for Kuyper's speculations about the foreign influence on his theology.

In what does this harmony consist? In order to sense this, pay attention to how, following immediately after the forgiveness of sins, we have the confession of *the resurrection of the body* and of *the life everlasting*. Between living in the church on earth and transitioning into the church above stands the article of faith involving the forgiveness of sins, placed where otherwise the confession of the last judgment would belong.

For the unbeliever the sequence is: (1) living in terms of the world; (2) fellowship with the works of darkness; (3) the last judgment; and (4) eternal perdition. By contrast, the Apostles' Creed sets forth for believers this fourfold sequence: (1) living not in terms of the world but in terms of *the church* or *the body of Christ*; (2) fellowship not with the evil works of darkness but *the communion of saints*; (3) not facing judgment but possessing the *forgiveness of sins*; and (4) a transition not to eternal perdition but to *eternal life*.

The forgiveness of sins is the salvation treasure that the body of Christ possesses. It is the rich gift of grace that is enjoyed in the communion of saints. And it is the link that binds the church on earth to the church above in eternal life. This link cannot be missed, and far from being superfluous or incidental, this forgiveness of sins is the gracious gift and promise of God that causes the church here below to live already in eternity.

The forgiveness of sins begins in the church, and it is sealed already with the sacrament of baptism to the little children of believers. The existence of the forgiveness of sins constitutes the basis upon which the entire church lives and labors. To possess the forgiveness of sins is what distinguishes it from those who are not of the church. The forgiveness of sins is the glorious preaching with which the church goes into the world to entice sinners and the wicked into heaven. It is the summary expression of the divine fact that there is a gospel and that there is grace with God. Cain opposes it. Esau does not find it. For the person who is upright, it is the most tremendous doctrine to believe and to accept. But precisely for that reason, it is the summary of our entire Christian confession. You do not chase after this forgiveness of sins; you do nothing for this forgiveness of sins; you do not think of it as the goal reached at the end, but this is a forgiveness of sins with which everything begins.

First comes John the Baptist, and his baptism is a baptism unto repentance and the forgiveness of sins. Then comes the Christ, and the cup of thanksgiving that he raises is the New Testament in his blood that was shed for many unto the forgiveness of sins. When he ascends, his apostles go out into the world, calling and testifying to this Christ, "in whom we have redemption, the forgiveness of sins" [Col 1:14; compare Eph 1:7].

This is why the church of Christ throughout all ages, whether walking faithfully or in error, has always been tethered to the forgiveness of sins as its midpoint. This is why when his soul lay in the bonds of death, Luther reached out for the true forgiveness of sins in opposition to the hypocritical and imitation version. And this is why to this day, in every church in every part of the world, the chief question, decisive for the flourishing or the floundering of ecclesiastical life, always is and remains this: Does this church have power and authority to offer distraught souls assurance that there is with God forgiveness for their sins?

This could not and cannot be otherwise, precisely because sin is falling away from God. For your soul there cannot be any fellowship with the Eternal Being, and thus, neither rest nor comfort nor delight in salvation, until you know, and know for certain, that also your sins and your entire sinful nature are personally forgiven.

STATE AND CHURCH

TEXT INTRODUCTION

This chapter on the separation of church and state is from Kuyper's *Antirevolutionary Politics*, which was written from 1915 to 1916 and published in 1916–17, in the middle of World War I. Kuyper's corrections, written while he was on vacation in Dresden, were carried by a special courier of the German ambassador back to the Netherlands. This work summarizes the main points of Kuyper's antirevolutionary political philosophy. His account of church and state follows lines common to his thought. Perhaps sobered by the experience of war, he begins with a realistic account of the antagonistic relationship of church and state in Europe but soon returns to a more idealistic account of the proper integration of church and state. He rejects three options: theocracy, the application of Old Testament norms to the state, and the approach of the early magisterial Protestants. An overly close relationship of church and state is, according to Kuyper, the cause of secularization rather than its remedy. The American arrangement is ideal, and Kuyper interprets American civil religion as an exposition of common grace. The dominant features of his proposal are the separation of church and state, the state's recognition of God as creator (if not as Trinitarian redeemer), and the democratic influence of Christians in the state and civil society.

Kuyper's original references (indicated by "Note by the author") have been updated to modern style conventions.

Source: Kuyper, Abraham. "Staat en Kerk." In *Antirevolutionaire Staatkunde met nadere toelichting op Ons program*, vol. 1, 417–86. Kampen: J. H. Kok, 1916. Translated by Arjen Vreugdenhil and Nelson D. Kloosterman.

STATE AND CHURCH

Two Different Starting Points

The equally important issue of state and church is directly related to the conclusion we drew in chapter 10.[1] You cannot understand it if you view the church merely as a spiritually intended outward expression of faith in Jesus Christ as the captain of our soul. In that case the church stands entirely alongside practical life, since that requires regulation and attention in society and state. This implies two distinct and easily distinguished realms, one for the state and one for the church. The church then exists only for the mysticism of the human soul, and everything else in life that requires order and regulation falls under the scepter of the state. According to this view, the church, insofar as it functions in practical social life, must therefore submit to the state. A Masonic lodge, an association of spiritists, or an artist group can pursue a purpose that has a subjective character, and can therefore thrive only in freedom. As soon as they acquire outward expression in the life of society, however, they are subject to the law of the state. In the same way the church, as simply the embodiment of whatever mysticism moves the soul, may claim

---

1. In chapter 10, Kuyper concluded that the state must be understood as an instrument of God and that international law also must be grounded in God's rule. Kuyper defended the legitimacy of the civil authority as divinely instituted to do what only God, and no individual, may do, that is, deprive someone of property, liberty, and life. This contrasts with various theories of social contract that allow the deprivation of liberty for the good of the community or by consent of the governed.

full freedom in its own sphere, but as soon as it expresses or manifests itself in the civil realm through parades, tolling bells, church buildings, collections, wedding ceremonies, or otherwise, then it too must abide by the general rule of society and is obligated to obey the government in an equally unrestricted sense.

Principally opposed to this position is anyone who honors the church as an organization not of people but of Christ himself—anyone who confesses Christ as the King of God's kingdom, and who views this kingdom not merely as a concentration of spiritual elements but sincerely believes, on the basis of the Holy Scripture, that the kingdom of God that awaits us shall encompass both soul and body, both the invisible and the visible; that it shall raise both heaven and earth to renewed and exalted manifestation; that it shall manifest a character just as physical as it is spiritual, and therefore will include not only spiritual life but also social life, as well as what we call political life. The church, in its current earthly existence, is a foreshadowing of that coming worldwide kingdom; it is thus directly related to it.

That is why there is an undeniable correlation between the church, as the foreshadowing of the future kingdom, and the state, as the organization of man's external social life today. The church does not function in a human society that is by nature governed by the state, but she carries within herself the germ of the all-encompassing worldwide kingdom, which will one day replace every state and assume its function. It is therefore decidedly incorrect to honor the state as the palace in which the church is assigned no more than a side wing. Rather, the state is little more than the scaffolding erected on the building site where the church is busy laying the foundation for the palace in which Christ will one day establish his royal throne. The state is a surgical implement to come to the aid of human society in its situation of bondage; the church supplies the strength needed for the restoration of life as it existed originally, life that was lost but one day will return. This is why, when the consummation arrives, the state as we know it today will be discarded completely, just as an invalid discards his crutches as soon as his broken legs are fully healed. Conversely, when that final hour arrives the church will appear more glorious than ever in its everlasting governance. When the battle is over, the state will disappear forever. The dawn of the eternal existence of the nations will rise out of the church, not the state.

Because many statesmen failed to understand this revelation of Holy Scripture, but instead saw in this scriptural view little more than a dream of fanatics, it was inevitable that they completely corrupted the relationship between church and state. The state is the cloak wrapped around the body; in the church lies the seed of new life growing in the womb of the body. Naturally, if you think that the cloak is the body, you cannot do justice to that seed of new life. That is why the debate about the significance of the church that is occurring between these statesmen and believers can only be a debate about principles. Even if you hold this view and succeed in finding a way to enable both the state and the church to live together, you allow for an incorrect view of the state, in which the church is reduced to a private organization for satisfying a certain mystical need. This organization can be allowed some freedom, but is always subject to certain rules determined by the state. Conversely, the politician who views the realization of Christ's kingship as the final goal, cannot and may not do less than esteem the church to be much higher than the state—even when it comes to that part of human society that is currently entrusted to the care of the state.

THE RESURRECTION   § 2
The resurrection gives essential support for this conclusion. If our personal death would forever separate us from living amid the visible and tangible, so that only the soul continues to exist after our body and everything related to it has ceased to exist, then there would be no resurrection from the dead. Then the great day of Easter would be irrelevant not only for Christ but for every human being. Those who have died would have nothing more to do with life on this earth. Their existence on this earth would be finished for good. As a result, their continued existence would have no significance for this visible world, and this earth would have no significance for them any longer. Those who die would leave us and never return to this world. More than this, just as *they* died off, so too this very world would eventually die away as well. However many centuries it may take, one day the end will come when this earth itself will perish in a cosmic fire. Nothing will be left except—and this many do not deny, but neither do they dare affirm—the souls of those who died, assuming that those souls continued their existence as spirits in the spiritual realm. Many do not accept even this. But if it is assumed that our spiritual existence will continue, it would certainly be a mystery in the invisible realm. We would

know nothing about it, and it would have absolutely nothing to do with our existence as it is now. The state, which orders human existence on earth, could therefore not be involved in this at all.

Thus, if there is an eternal spiritual realm, it lies entirely outside the jurisdiction of the state. The state has nothing to do with it. The state cannot have anything to do with it, because it lies altogether outside its reach. The state can assist believers on earth, insofar as they join a church for their spiritual needs, by allowing the church to be active and by coming to her aid, but the state still has the governance, the authority to make rules and to enforce the law for everyone. The church is no exception to this. Rather, there is good reason for the state to be more watchful and careful when it comes to the church. This explains why many statesmen or government officials take a vague position in reckoning with the church's realm, since they cannot at the same time acknowledge its eternal and its cosmic character. But then—as we noted before—Easter has been destroyed and one has chosen the denial of the resurrection as one's starting point.

The separation between the spiritual and the material, between the physical and the psychological, between the temporal and the eternal, is taken to be *absolute*. The church may concern herself with the future of the spiritual, the psychological, and the eternal, but the state does not and cannot do so, because there is no resurrection from the dead, and as a result no new earth that will thrive under the new heaven. All these things are merely fantasies. Much of it is very charming and poetic, but it is the kind of poetry to which the practical politician has no connection. After all, both believers and unbelievers die. Their fantasies die with them in their graves or are cremated into ashes along with their bodies. One can therefore not count on something after death. Only what we can observe here and now is real. The practical politician does not busy himself with poetic imagery. If sooner or later the earth dies away and is destroyed with water or with fire, so be it, but that will be the end of it.

In all this, the church will be as powerless as the state. Any pretense on the part of the church, as though it could have a rich existence in a concrete future or could already in this dispensation on earth lift itself up to a higher form of existence, is the imagination of spiritual self-deception. One may imagine such a future as a kind of cinematic fiction, but its realization is in fact a complete absurdity. The dead do not rise, at least not in bodily form. No one who dies receives a new body. There is no renewal of the earth, either. In the entire existence of the church there is not a single element that could have anything in common with such fantasy. If the church approves of dealing in such fantasies, one can let it be. The state cannot forbid a poet his enjoyment of poetry and dreams. But if any church has the audacity not only to express the great idea of the resurrection in words, but also to want to apply it in reality, then a higher sense of duty requires that the state in its unalterable superiority resist such excesses. The dead do not rise. Death is the end of it. There will be no new earth. How then could the church carry within itself a seed out of which would rise, sooner or later, a new order of the visible realm? The fact that the government tolerates the celebration of Easter, and even gives its officials the next day off, has a very different explanation. It means simply that a person can *reckon with* a certain immortality of the soul; that even after death, a purely spiritual, continued existence of something called the *soul* is considered not entirely inconceivable; and that there is not yet a deliberate denial of Kant's trio, "God, virtue, and immortality."[2] But certainty no longer exists. Even the agnostic can join the chorus, if only in hope. But—and this we strongly emphasize—the public celebration of Easter by the state does not at all mean that people believe in Christ's resurrection on the third day, and even less does it mean that they believe in our future resurrection from the dead in a new physical appearance. One should realize the following: the modern theory of the relationship of state and church arose from the persistent denial of the future resurrection from the dead, this denial of our resurrection entails simultaneously a denial of Jesus' resurrection. Therefore the divine Person and divine mission of Christ are violated here—all for the sake and the glory of the state. The same earth, the same human race on this earth, and the same life of our race, are now being placed under the authority of state and government, and will one day manifest in perfect form the kingdom of glory, the spiritual seed of which is now already concealed by God himself in the church on earth.

ANTICLERICALISM   §3

The perpetual battle between state and church provides the decisive proof that this entire theory, which denies that the church has any significance

---

2. The German philosopher Immanuel Kant (1724-1804) identified the existence of God, freedom as necessary for moral virtue, and the immortal soul as three basic postulates of practical reason.

for social life in the state, is incompatible with reality. Is it not the case that especially the proponents of the modern theory of the state feel compelled repeatedly to involve themselves in the political struggle with what they call clericalism? The term *clericalism* is certainly not correct. Derived from *clerus*, it refers to the class of people who took upon themselves the leadership of the Roman Catholic Church and, to some extent, of the Greek Orthodox Church. Such a *clerus* is completely excluded from the churches of the Reformation—especially the Reformed churches, which originated with Calvin. As a matter of principle these churches oppose the function of a *clerus*. Yet in the past few decades it has become more common in our country to peg statesmen and voters of Calvinistic origin as *clericals*. This shows how the battle is being fought not merely against a *clerus* as such, but against any attempt to allow the church to have any position that grants it a legitimate influence on the life of the state. This anticlericalism dominates the political struggle in the Netherlands, as well as in neighboring Belgium and Germany.

If this crass expression of anticlericalism concerned only the rejection of a specific demand of the church, for instance, concerning the pension of ministers or the subsidy for widows, it could be maintained that anticlericalism means simply that one dismisses this demand as absurd or extravagant. But our history shows quite a different picture. The struggle between the so-called clericals and anticlericals is dominating all of politics more and more. The voters group themselves into two factions, which have taken diametrically opposed positions in all political affairs. Even in matters with no direct connection to the rights or claims of the church, the clericals and anticlericals always oppose each other in the political arena. In political science, entire schools have arisen to defend or oppose these two contradictory views with every legitimate weapon, not only at the voting booth but also in scientific debate. That which presents itself among us as clerical or anticlerical politics not only endeavors to realize or reject ecclesiastical interests, but covers the entire range of politics, both the principles and the conclusions derived from them. And the proponents of Liberalism realize full well that this is not about special rights or material interests of the church but rather a comprehensive opposition between two systems. And so they continue pursuing their main purpose of neutralizing the voters, politicians, and scientists who operate from a Christian point of view. They do so by taking the leadership out of their hands.

While we therefore may not place church and state over against each other as two heterogeneous powers, history shows how very difficult it is to define the correct relationship between the two. Both of them are to blame for this. It is certainly not only the heroes of the state that restricted the rightful position of the church; there were just as many attempts on the part of the church to extend its power beyond legitimate boundaries. The old battle between pope and emperor continued after the Reformation, albeit in a different form. The idea of a worldwide empire continued as the dominant view from the Roman Empire far into the Middle Ages. Currently, the pacifist movement revives this view in a different form, but this movement has gradually fallen into discredit from the sixteenth century onward. Of course, the Holy Roman Empire continued to exist, but only in appearance, since it had hardly any influence. Otto Gierke did not exaggerate when he wrote: "It was as but a lifeless phantom that the 'imperium mundi' was dragged along by the imperialistic publicists."[3] Indeed, in the nineteenth century the idea of a worldwide empire had lost all of its former charm. People reckoned with autonomous states, but the political vision was no longer driven by the unity of our human race. Today for the first time, the study of the pacifist movement has shown once again how important it is always to keep an eye on that worldwide kingdom that one day will encompass our entire race. The natural-law movement gave new impetus to the idea of a worldwide kingdom to the extent that international law came to be understood as a right that would function in the *societas gentium*, the community of nations. It left the sovereignty of the individual nations untouched, while placing the unity of our race under a weak yet grandiose authority. When you consider the last period of ancient history, you sense how at that time state and church stood in a very different relationship than they do for us today, namely, they stood over against each other. In the political arena, the predominant idea at that time was of a government administration encompassing the whole world and therefore our entire human race. Certainly a very large part of the world existed outside of the Roman Empire, both in Asia and in Africa, but that did not count. These undomesticated fragments

---

3. *Note by the author*: Otto von Gierke, *Johannes Althusius und die Entwicklung der naturrechtlichen Staatstheorien*, 2nd ed. (Breslau: Marcus, 1902), 235. [Ed. note: ET: Otto von Gierke, *The Development of Political Theory*, trans. Bernard Freyd (New York: Howard Fertig, 1966), 262.]

did not have any significant influence. Even when the migration brought large communities of these nations to Europe, they fit naturally into the existing unity and were not yet of a mind to introduce a patchwork of states. The picture of a worldwide empire, which is so often presented in the Holy Scripture in connection with the future and is even dominant in the apocalyptic visions, appears in our time to belong to the imaginative world of fantasy. At that time, however, this was the leading thought, not only in poetic imagery but also in actual politics. The idea of a worldwide empire was the starting point and was thought to be the only way in which the nations could be united.

§ 5   THE UNIVERSAL CHURCH

That was the situation in the political realm when a fully universal model of the church of Christ was also presented to the world, and it was said in various ways that even the contrast between Abrahamic and pagan peoples had become obsolete, so that there could no longer be Greek and Jew, Scythian and Barbarian, but all must be and really had become one in Christ. This seemed to trump even the idea of a worldwide empire. The idea of a universal empire at least acknowledged boundaries among the Barbarians, and especially in the east between the Parthians and Scythians, but the church of Christ crossed even those farthest boundaries, and encompassed the entire cosmos. It is indeed remarkable how broadly the idea of "the world" functions in sacred revelation. The Psalms and Prophets constantly call "all the inhabitants of the world" to serve Yahweh. "Mine, says Yahweh, is the world and its fullness" [see Psa 24:1]. He shall not merely judge a single nation but rather "the entire world in equity" [see Psa 9:8]. Christ himself testified that his gospel would be preached to the entire world. He called himself the light of the world, and commanded his disciples to preach his gospel in the entire world. Dying on the cross, he gave his life for the entire world. Satan is described as the ruler of the world, in his battle with Christ. The mediator brings his sacrifice for the sin of the entire world. In Christ, God reconciled to himself not only some nations, but the world. In 1 John 4:14 it is even said that Christ was sent as "the Savior of the world." And in Revelation 11:15 we hear the triumphant language of victory, that "the kingdom of the world has become the kingdom of our Lord." This is consistent with the same universal idea presented to us in John 3:16, namely, that God "so loved the world, that he gave his only Son, that whoever believes in him should not perish but have eternal life." We therefore find a worldwide focus, both historically and in the hope of the nations, as well as within revelation, and particularly in the mission of Christ. And though it may be true that for years now the movements of mysticism and pacifism have adopted that worldwide focus, it cannot be denied that among Protestant nations it was considered of little value.

With Napoleon, the last world-conqueror seems to have been defeated. Since 1814 we deal exclusively with nations. The idea of an empire no longer plays a role. As for the church, the *Réveil* and the Irenical party prompted our minds to peek over the fence of our small ecclesiastical yard, but virtually no people considered themselves members of a *universal church*. At the Synod in Dort (1618–19), the concept of a universal church was still honored through the inclusion of delegates from churches abroad, but subsequently this rich idea became gradually impoverished. The so-called national church—the church of one particular country—became dominant at the expense of the high ideal that earlier had been such a powerful motivator. This resulted in an even more cumbersome opposition between life (both political and ecclesiastical) and our Christian confession. Our Christian confession demanded a return to paradise, and thereby to the unity of the human race. Even the sacrifice of Christ on Golgotha would lose its significance if we would not maintain the unity of our race, its unity in the origin of sin, and therefore also the worldwide unity in the work of redemption. In sacrificing this unity, our entire Christian confession fell. But even though we sang in the words of Te Deum, "You, eternal Father, all creation together exults you!"—within the political realm the idea of unity in fact had been swallowed up by the idea of the nation. And in the ecclesiastical realm the national church—unintentionally and unwillingly of course—readied itself to put the axe to the very root of our faith. The national idea pushed away that of the one human race. Likewise, the national church pushed away the idea of the one, universal, Christian worldwide church.

Article 27 of our Belgic Confession so clearly confesses: "We believe and profess one catholic or universal church, which is a holy congregation of true Christian believers," and at the end: "Furthermore, this holy Church is not confined, bound, or limited to a certain place or to certain persons, but is spread and dispersed over the whole world." Answer 54 of the Heidelberg Catechism is no different: "the Son of God, by His Spirit and Word, gathers, defends, and preserves for Himself unto everlasting life a chosen communion in the unity of the true faith." But due to the circumstances, none of this prevented the idea of the worldwide church from being gradually swallowed up by that of the national church. Even today, otherwise very capable theologians hold on to this false idea without realizing how much they are going against the core of our Christian confession. Therefore we must still leave this distorted pattern of thinking and return in a twofold way to the former pattern, which used to be dominant: first, in the universal idea embodied by the Roman Empire; and second, in the accommodation of the entire pattern of our lives and of all history to the cosmological idea. The national idea was powerful and victorious in Israel. When Israel perished, it did so precisely because it failed to understand the sacred skill of gradually transforming its original national thinking into universal thinking. The church, especially under Paul's leadership, consciously corrected Israel's error, so that the idea of the universal church, in the context of the idea of a worldwide Roman empire, triumphed over the national church.

§ 6   ROMAN CATHOLIC

It cannot be adequately lamented that today the idea of the catholic church has almost entirely been incorporated into that of the Roman Church. *Catholic* simply means *universal*. In the catholic church lies a principal protest against the national church. Both our Belgic Confession and our Catechism acknowledge without hesitation that the catholic idea is to be confessed by all Christian churches. A church that is unwilling to be catholic is not a church, because Christ is the savior not of a nation, but of the world. The Synod of Dort in 1618 intended to be as catholic as the Council of Trent. We cannot therefore, without being untrue to our own principle, abandon the honorable title of "catholic" as though it were the special possession of the Roman Church. The entire revelation of the Holy Scripture forbids us to do so. Therefore we may never promote the view that the papist hierarchy was the first to develop the catholic idea. The catholic idea is dominant in the Gospels, is the focus in the apostolic epistles, and is ubiquitous in Revelation. The papist hierarchy adopted this idea, as did the Reformers. The difference is merely that the hierarchy understood how to maintain this catholic idea, in spite of the split, while the churches of the Reformation gradually let it go, in a most careless manner.

The name "Rome" played a highly significant role in this. When the spiritual purity of Christ's church began to fade away, the (still powerful)

Roman Empire fell apart into an eastern half and a western half, in such a way that for a while Byzantium outshone Rome in glory and significance. This historical fact has had enormous influence on the historical development of Christ's church. It had two consequences. First, the separation of what we usually call the Greek Orthodox Church from the Western church; and at the same time, in the West, the rise of the all-dominating power of the hierarchy. Whatever fame Byzantium might have boasted for a time, it remained inferior to the glorious imperial identity it had stolen from ancient Rome. Among all the places on earth, Rome remained in the foreground. When the imperial power of Rome faded, then the ecclesiastical influence of the Bishop of Rome increased. It was inevitable that the ecclesiastical power, which continued to develop under this hierarchical presidency of the pope, became the competitor of the decaying political unity. Once so powerful, the Roman Empire not only split, but also gradually crumbled altogether. Suffering one defeat after another at the hands of the invading Germanic nations, its prestige fell apart. And since the significance of the political unity of power continually diminished, it was inevitable that the ecclesiastical power—which even more strongly possessed a universal character—eventually overshadowed the political power. This could change only when the Roman Empire was transferred to the Germanic nations as the "Holy Roman Empire," but this happened by making an ever-stronger opposition between emperor and pope. The doctrine of the two swords entered the world. It was not long before four or so men in Peter's chair, of rare genius and activity, expressed the idea that by divine ordination and inspiration, the pope was to be honored as the representative of the Christ, and therefore all worldly power should be subject to Rome's tribunal.[4]

---

4. Kuyper may have in mind the famous papal bull *Unam Sanctam*, promulgated in 1302 by Pope Boniface VIII, which discusses the doctrine of the two swords and concludes "that it is absolutely necessary for salvation that every human creature be subject to the Roman Pontiff." *Unam Sanctam* drew on a number of medieval sources, including Pope St. Leo IX (d. 1054), Pope Nicholas II (d. 1061), and Pope Innocent III (d. 1216).

The Reformation

The events at Canossa manifested the unnatural incarnation of this system.[5] A principled reaction was inevitable, and it must be acknowledged that in this reaction lay all too many of the initial causes of the Reformation. If the Reformation had remained a purely spiritual action, it would have triumphed on a much larger scale, and boasted a much more exalted character. Yet the facts of history cannot not be ignored. The spiritual struggle that broke out in the Reformation was preceded by a struggle of earthly power in the political realm, and because of this the Reformation was infected from the start with a nonspiritual, purely political motif, whose negative effects are still operative today. This error could have been avoided if the church of Christ had not already made similar mistakes in the events leading up to the Reformation. But that mistake contributed to it. Over and over, the spiritual office fostered megalomania in those who held it. This had been avoided in the early rise of the church of Christ, and was absent as long as the church of Christ struggled through a period of scorn and tribulation. But once the victory was won in the spiritual battle with the help of the worldly powers, and the power of the church was established, the human heart repeatedly showed itself unable to resist the temptation of domination, and the thirst for power that followed. This happened in our Reformed circles after the Synod of Dort. Irrefutable proof of this is found in a comparison between the tone of what was said in the days of Dathenus and à Lasco,[6] and of what could occasionally be heard from preachers' lips after Dort. And that very same evil afflicted the office-bearers from the fifth century onward. Eager for influence, power, and dominion, they constantly sought to expand their own supremacy, and ultimately they could not help but seek to establish this supremacy either in the pope or in the emperor.

Given the sinful nature that manifested itself also in the office-bearers of Christ's church, this process was inevitable, and the situation in Europe at the time drifted in the very same direction. After the fall of Rome, the power of the magistrate had not yet acquired a firm foundation, and especially the central imperial power suffered loss on account of the

---

5. In 1077, at Canossa Castle in southern Italy, the recently excommunicated Holy Roman Emperor Henry IV did penance before Pope Gregory VII and was restored to communion.

6. Petrus Dathenus (1531–88) and Johannes à Lasco (1499–1560) were early Reformed theologians.

increasingly powerful magisterial power in the vassal states. The general culture was not yet refined, and at least in the Germanic regions it was far below what it once had been in ancient Rome. The military glory of the Roman Empire had faded away completely. The Huns and Mongolians had been defeated long ago. The Crusades at first renewed the fame of warfare, but here too the excellence of certain heroes among the knights gained fame, rather than the central power of the emperor. In the broader circles of the population, at least, the imperial refinement and the empire itself lost almost all its influence. In contrast to this, the nations newly converted from paganism became zealous for their new faith, so that soon the spiritual influence of the clergy on the people became far more significant than respect for the magistrate. This became even more so as the armies became more ruthless, the Condottieri[7] brought terror, and the extravagant taxing for the state's treasury grew more oppressive. The distinction between the pressure of imperial power and that of ecclesiastical power naturally led to an increasing influence of the clergy and a decreasing influence of the magistrate. In nearly all of Europe this resulted in a situation where the word of the pope of Rome was deemed law. Ultimately the magisterial power yielded and collapsed. This changed through the revival of Italy, the Renaissance, and the rise of universities, and especially the lack of self-control that weakened the clergy spiritually and occasionally cost the clergy its prestige through arrogance or even immorality. But this process dragged on until the sixteenth century, when the magisterial power consolidated against this spiritual decay of the clergy. The need for more civil law and order also encouraged an appeal to the magistrate, who with the development of the cities could now offer help in a very different way. Finally, there was an increasingly louder protest of conscience against the clergy's abuse of their power in sacrament and indulgences. More and more people realized that the church had principally distorted and defiled its true relation to the state by demanding that the government's power should derive in part from that of the Bishop of Rome. The conviction grew that Holy Scripture demands an entirely different relationship between the two. It could not remain the way it was. Nor could people slide into the anarchism of the Anabaptist sects. Thus arose a desire for the spiritual cleansing of the ecclesiastical structure, as well as an urgent need to ensure more autonomy for the magistrate apart

---

7. Italian mercenaries of the late Middle Ages and Renaissance.

from the power of the church. If at this time the verdict of the church had been more yielding, the split might have been less definitive. But when the church's attempts to correct the growing evil turned out to be a mere formality, and the church limited itself only to banning excesses, the separation grew. And this explains why finally, through the Reformation, the church itself split in two, the papist power lost its universal significance, and the church, after its attempt to lord it over the state, now in turn became subject to the power of the state.

§ 8   LUTHER

It is telling, after all, that since the time of Gregory VII, the church changed its relationship with the state, making the church absolutely useless for the life of the state; and that there developed, from 1517 onward and especially under Luther's leadership, an entirely new relationship with the opposite tendency to subject the church more fully to the state. There was a desire on both sides to break the hierarchical power of Rome, both on the side of the German rulers and on the side of the ecclesiastical and academic leaders. England came close to a breach between Rome and the civil power. In their separation from Rome, the German rulers celebrated the conquest of the Ghibellines over the Guelphs.[8] Scandinavia longed for the abolition of the hierarchical power. And since Luther and his followers needed support to achieve their goals for the ecclesiastical realm, it was quite natural that Luther also made a pact with the German rulers, the more so because anarchism was rampant, especially in Saxony. Moreover, such a coalition of civil and ecclesiastical power to ensure a safer position over against the hierarchy, appeared even more attractive because the same road had been taken in Greek Orthodox countries. There, too, the government had assumed supremacy over the church, without having been prompted by any reformation. As a result, it was believed to be the natural thing to do, when, under Luther's influence, support was sought from the state in Germany and Scandinavia. This is especially significant because both in the caesaropapist countries of Greek Orthodox confession and in the German Lutheran domains, the princes not only received power over the church, but even claimed spiritual influence within the church. After all, the Byzantine rulers, like the Russian czars, claimed

---

8. Kuyper refers here to names associated with partisan support for imperial (Ghibellines) and papal (Guelphs) power, a conflict arising out of Italy in the medieval period.

episcopal jurisdiction. Entirely in line with this, Luther agreed that the rulers of Germany and Scandinavia should receive episcopal rank to function as leaders in the church as well. In each case, both in the liberation of the Greek Church and in the Lutheran Reformation, the separation from the hierarchy of Rome happened only because the ancient rule that the church was supreme over the state was turned on its head, so that now the church became subjected to the state.

THE CALVINISTS. EARLY POSITION.   §9

Only in the Reformed churches did an entirely altered relationship between church and state gradually develop. This different point of view, however, was not initially supported by Calvin himself or his first followers. Even in our Belgic Confession the endpoint of this development was not yet reached. Article 36 of the Confession of the Reformed Churches of the Netherlands still stated explicitly that the government must act in the name of the Lord, not only in civil but also in ecclesiastical affairs. Their office, it says, "is not only to have regard unto and watch for the welfare of the civil state, but also that they protect the sacred ministry, and thus may remove and prevent all idolatry and false worship, that the kingdom of antichrist may be thus destroyed and the kingdom of Christ promoted. They must, therefore, countenance the preaching of the Word of the gospel everywhere, that God may be honored and worshipped by every one, as He commands in His Word." As late as 1690, professor Johannes à Marck stated that, properly viewed, the civil government does not stand alongside or over against the church, but acts *within the church*. In chapter 33 he deals with the *Regimen Ecclesiae* [rule of the church]. After discussing the ecclesiastical part of this rule in twenty-seven sections, in §28 he introduces the second part of chapter 33 with these words: "Now we move on to the rule of the church that is common to other people."[9] This means that if all citizens and inhabitants of a country were members of the Reformed Church, then there would really be no separate civil government, because those who are not particular members of the church also belong to the nation and are in the church. It says: "Now we move on to the rule," not of *the nation*, but "to the rule of *the church*" insofar as this affects unbelievers also. À Marck sees a twofold order within the one church: a particular order for the service of Word and sacraments, and a general order applying to

---

9. *Note by the author*: Johannes à Marck, *Compendium theologiae christianae didacti-co-elencticum* (Amsterdam: G. Borstius, 1690), 590.

all citizens; but concerning the citizens, he asserts emphatically that they really are in the church, just as the particular members are. He writes that all of history "always places the political rule within the church."[10] In §32 he repeats: "It cannot be denied that the Christian magistrate has some general power in ecclesiastical matters."[11] Bernardinus de Moor cites this view without any reservation in 1771.[12] The very same position is taken by Voetius,[13] Walaeus,[14] and likewise Rivet.[15] Calvin himself had written more soberly about this complex matter, and limits himself in his *Institutes* to the statement that the task of the government extends to both tables of the law of the Ten Commandments. He claims that this has been the case among all nations. If we had not known it from Scripture, "we could learn this from secular writers: for no one has discussed the office of magistrates, the making of laws, and public welfare, without beginning at religion and divine worship."[16] This, he says, was the judgment of all secular statesmen and philosophers, and we as Christians must take the same point of view. He urges us to do so with an appeal to the theocracy in Israel, and to the ordinances given by God for that theocracy.

§ 10   MIDDLE POSITION

In this way, a middle position is taken between the Roman view that the church stands above the government, and the Lutheran view that the state is ruler of the church. Only two things are acknowledged: first, that maintaining God's honor is a duty that rests on the magistrate in the civil government as well, and second, that the magistrate is called to support and protect the church. Article 36 of our Confession actually went much further. Although the statement that the government must "protect the sacred ministry" is very flexible, the removal and prevention not only of all idolatry, but also of all false worship, and the promotion of the

---

10. À Marck, *Compendium*, 590.

11. À Marck, *Compendium*, 593.

12. *Note by the author*: Bernhardinus de Moor, *Commentarius perpetuus in Johannis Marckii Compendium theologiae christianae didactico-elencticum*, vol. 6 (Leiden: J. Hasebroek & J. H. van Damme, 1771), 470–87.

13. *Note by the author*: Gisbertus Voetius, *Politicae ecclesiasticae*, part 1 (Amsterdam: Waesberge, 1663), 124–49.

14. *Note by the author*: Antonius Walaeus, *De munere ministrorum ecclesiae: et inspectione magistratus circa illud*, in *Opera omnia*, vol. 2 (Leiden: F. Hackius, 1663), 1–62.

15. *Note by the author*: André Rivet, *Praelectiones in cap. xx Exodi. In quibus ita explicatur Decalogus*, in *Operum theologicorum*, vol. 1 (Rotterdam: A. Leers, 1651), 1371–76.

16. *Note by the author*: *Inst.* 4.20.9.

preaching of the kingdom of Jesus, and doing that *everywhere*—all of this points to a much stronger involvement of the magistrate, and presupposes that the government must determine, even in the smallest details, what must be confessed on the basis of God's Word, and which church is to be supported by the government as the keeper of this confession. This view developed naturally, because the ecclesiastical issues of these days increasingly became major political issues. When people started to be persecuted because of their faith, when rulers took up arms for religious reasons, and when the believers could not establish or develop an independent church life except with the support of an armed political power, everyone felt that they could not declare themselves to be independent of the magistrate, as this would be equal to the destruction of their own church life. In the Netherlands, too, it would have been unthinkable to overturn the Spanish confession, if the rulers of Orange had not provided a civil power to withstand the Roman hierarchy on the battlefield. As long as there was no power to defend the Reformed, they were forced to flee to London, Emden, Frankfurt, Wesel, and everywhere. In those fearful days it was impossible to obtain a supportable, stable position without civil support. The hierarchy did not limit itself to spiritual weapons to defend its authority, but moved the Roman Catholic rulers to suppress the Reformation with violence, if necessary. At first, one could seek safety by fleeing, or else by receiving the honor of martyrdom, but it was impossible to attain a peaceful position in the Netherlands without protection from the magistrate. However powerful exile and martyrdom might have been, once people got the chance to return to their land and to confess freely in that country, the churches were powerless to organize the new situation on the old foundation. The Anabaptists, as individual believers, had pulled back entirely from civil life to usher in the future of Christ, but that position, too, turned out to be untenable when the Spaniards were forced to leave the Dutch to themselves. A new state of affairs had to be established, and the churches were unable to do this, so the civil leaders automatically took the lead. Two things were needed now. First, there had to be a magistrate who, by virtue of common grace, would promote and maintain a society with honor and virtue. Second, order had to be established regarding the use of the church buildings, the salaries of the teachers, and the attitude toward heretics, Jews, and unbelievers. In all this, the churches were not able to maintain their autonomy, so that even the great National Synod in 1618 could only convene under the patronage of the government, and afterward every attempt to convene a new National Synod was simply obstructed by the government of the Republic.[17] Sooner than expected, the magistrate was inclined to restrain the power of the churches.

§ 11   TURNING POINT: MAURICE'S DEATH[18]

Already in 1625 one could say that the balance tipped, and the state finalized its supremacy over the churches. Had the old energy of faith remained awake among the ministers of the Word, at least some level of ecclesiastical freedom could have been salvaged. But the opposite was true. Most preachers felt honored by the magisterial involvement, considered it a boost for their own position, and tended to grant the government almost anything it appropriated. Only a very few continued to fight the battle against the illegitimate supremacy of the government, but more and more they became the "scattered swimmers in the vast waste."[19] Lutheran influences had highly negative effects on national life, which explains why, when King William I in 1815 completely overthrew the Dutch ecclesiastical organization and replaced it by a nearly German, Lutheran, and caesaropapist model, only very few resisted, and the monumental building once erected by our fathers was almost flattened. We have been spared an episcopal hierarchy. The Dutch government did not claim for itself a spiritual character, as usually happened with caesaropapism, so both extremes were avoided. But the view that our ancestors initially took could not develop fully because of the course of history, because of the need to fight violence with violence, and because of the weakening of faith. The churches here in the Netherlands remained more free from the power of the state than in Germany, Scandinavia, and the Church of England, but there was no room to continue the fight for principles. Contacts with the church worldwide diminished. Unwillingly, the church became a national church. And when in 1789 the entire relation of church and state in our country was turned on its head, not a single baseline of our own system could be found in the surviving ruins.[20] The

---

17. The Synod of Dort was convened by the States General of the Netherlands.
18. Maurice of Nassau, Prince of Orange, a leader in the Dutch Revolt against Spain, died in 1625.
19. Lat., "rari na[ta]ntes in gurgite vasto," Virgil, *Aeneid*, I, 118.
20. Kuyper is referring not only to the French Revolution, which began in 1789, but also the related Batavian Revolution in the Netherlands and the resulting Batavian Republic (1795–1806), when the Netherlands was a client state of the French Empire ruled by French and Dutch revolutionaries.

Dutch were no longer Roman hierarchical, but had not become Lutheran caesaropapist either, and of the Calvinistic trunk, out of which the proper relation between state and church was supposed to spring up, nothing was to be seen but the hewn stump. The churches did not yet understand their calling to become independent by taking care of their own worship and preachers. Church property and salary continued to be the pottage for which they sold their freedom. There was no longer room for church discipline except in a moral sense. The churches lost all their influence on the theological faculties.

Thus the autonomous character of the churches gradually diminished. One could even call this the defeat of Calvinism, except that later another development arose among the Reformed churches here in the Netherlands and in Germany. The Reformed churches had gradually lost any influence on the life of the state in both countries. Under the rule of regents in the Netherlands and the vexing domination of the local rulers in Germany, the open artery that once had transported the national life from Geneva was now almost entirely blocked; this explains why ultimately, in otherwise solid Reformed circles, people confused the spirit of Paris with that of Geneva[21] and danced around the Liberty Pole. This opened the way for the rise of modern thinking, which refused to ascribe to the church any other character than one of collegiality as an association among other associations. This was equal to a principal denial of the kingship of Christ.

VISIBLE AND INVISIBLE CHURCH   § 12

Once the straight path was left, the distinction between the *visible* and the *invisible* church, however correct, undoubtedly made matters worse. Zwingli pointed out that the visible church is made up of "all throughout the whole world who have enrolled themselves under Christ [through baptism]." But he added: "Among these are all who are called Christians, even though falsely, seeing that they have no faith within."[22] The true church is called invisible, not because true believers do not act visibly, but because it is not evident to the human eye who do not believe. Likewise, Calvin

---

21. That is, the spirit of the French Revolution with the spirit of Calvin's Geneva.
22. *Note by the author:* Ulrich Zwingli, *Christianae fidei a Huldrico Zuinglio praedicatae brevis et clara expositio*, in M. Schuler and I. Schulthess, eds., *Huldrici Zuingli Opera*, vol. 4 (Zurich: F. Schulthess, 1841), 58. [Ed. note: ET: "Fidei Expositio (1531)," in *Reformed Confessions of the 16th and 17th Centuries in English Translation: 1523–1693*, ed. James T. Dennison Jr., vol. 1 (Grand Rapids: Reformation Heritage Books, 2008–2014), 197.]

says: "Holy Scripture speaks of the church in two ways. Sometimes by the term 'church' it means that which is actually in God's presence, into which no persons are received but those who are children of God by grace of adoption and true members of Christ by sanctification of the Holy Spirit.... Often, however, the name 'church' designates the whole multitude of men spread over the earth who profess to worship one God and Christ."[23] This does not refer to two churches, then, but always the same church, yet, as Maresius says, "vario respectu," in different respects.[24] It even used to be emphasized that the visible church does not include the triumphant church in heaven. The distinction concerns only the church of Christ and its appearance on earth, insofar it can be seen, in part as it really is, that is, as a product of the Holy Spirit, and in part as it carries within itself the real church, with which a false element is mixed. Peter Martyr wrote: "Only those who are holy and truly in God's presence [coram Deo] are of the church," but in the church there are also others, and the church contains several people mixed in who are alienated from God, and these belong to it only in appearance, not in essence.[25]

Now this doctrine effectively made church discipline more lax. Once it was established that there was such a large mass of hypocrites in the church as one saw it, it did not seem to matter much whether a few more or less would slip through. Likewise, if this doctrine were emphasized too much, it could give occasion to worry less about the state of the visible church, and to be less annoyed when the government intervened in ecclesiastical affairs somewhat more than it should do in principle. In this connection it is remarkable that in the Statenvertaling the word church [kerk] has been avoided, seemingly deliberately. The word ἐκκλησία [ekklesia], used in the original, is consistently rendered as gemeente [congregation], and this word gemeente is used in various instances where we would speak of church, both of the local church and the worldwide church, and both of the church in its pure form and of the church as it manifests itself in this sinful life on earth. In his testimony to Peter, that his church shall be built on him, Christ says (Matt 16:18): "You are Peter, and on this Petra I will build my ἐκκλησία," by which he means, of course, the worldwide

---

23. *Note by the author:* Inst. 4.1.7.

24. *Note by the author:* Samuel Maresius, *Collegium theologicum: sive systema breve universae theologiae* (Groningen: Nicolaus, 1649), 446.

25. *Note by the author:* Peter Martyr Vermigli, *Loci communes* (Zurich: C. Froschouerus, 1580), 390.

church of all ages. Yet our *Statenvertaling* translates the term here also with *gemeente* in the singular. On the other hand, the Lord says in Matthew 18:17: "And if he refuses to listen even to the *gemeente*, let him be to you as a Gentile and a tax collector," in which the term of course speaks of the *local* congregation. Likewise, the word refers to the local church when it speaks of *gemeenten* in the plural (2 Cor 8:18; Rev 1:4; and so on). And while these passages speak of the worldwide church or the local church in its observable form, our *Statenvertaling* uses the word *gemeente* also when it means the church in a *spiritual* sense, apart from its earthly appearance. Just consider Ephesians 5:25 and following: "As Christ loved the *gemeente* and gave himself up for her, that he might sanctify her, ... so that he might present the *gemeente* to himself in splendor, without spot or wrinkle or any such thing, that she might be holy and without blemish." Or also Ephesians 1:22-23: "And gave him as head over all things to the *gemeente*, which is his body, the fullness of him who fills all in all."

If this word *gemeente* had been used to refer only to the local assembly of confessors, it would have made sense, because the word *gemeente* implies the idea of a collective. But this is not the case. Everywhere and in all places, in reference to the old as well as the new covenant, the word *kerk* was avoided and the word *gemeente* preferred. It cannot be denied that this reveals antipathy against the Roman Catholic use of the word *church*, probably in connection with the higher meaning that the local congregation had had in the *civil* sense, through the rise of the cities—especially in Germany, the Netherlands, and in Flanders. This must be pointed out because the English translation chose *church*, and the French translation, *église*, the former corresponding to the Dutch *kerk* and the latter directly derived from the Greek *ecclesia*. Luther, however, chose *gemeinde* [related to *gemeente*, "congregation"]. And what is even more remarkable, the word *church* [*kerk*] occurs one time in the *Statenvertaling*, but then it is used for a pagan temple. This is the case in Acts 19:35, where it is said of Ephesus that it is the *kerkbewaarster* [church keeper] of the great goddess Artemis. Luther's translation cannot have been the occasion for this strange wording, since he speaks of *Pflegerin* [nurse], and only the Berleburger Bible editions of Bengel gave a correction of this.[26] In later

---

26. The Berleburg Bible, which appeared from 1726-42, was one of the earliest original German translations from Greek and Hebrew after Luther's initial work. Johann Albrecht Bengel (1687-1752) produced a Greek edition of the New Testament (1734).

editions of the *Statenvertaling*, the word *kerkbewaarster* [church keeper] has been changed into *tempelbewaarster* [temple keeper], which was legitimate because the Greek word νεωχόρος apparently derives from ναός, that is, "temple." The translator likely had in mind a Roman Catholic church with all its splendor and wealth, and therefore deliberately spoke of *church* keeper, especially because many Reformed people in France called their own church building a *temple*, as it is still commonly done today.

§ 13   LOCAL SITUATION

The local circumstances in which the Reformation took place generally had a strong influence on the concepts that were developed. We must distinguish especially between two situations. There were towns where the entire confessing congregation left Rome and joined the Reformation, but there were also many towns, especially in France and the Netherlands, where the Reformation gained only a relatively small following among the population. A significant factor in this was the attitude of the government. If the government and those in high places joined the Reformation, the entire city usually followed; those who could not agree would leave for other places. This happened especially in Geneva, where Calvin encountered opposition from the Libertines, but otherwise the entire city broke its ties with Rome. As a result the entire congregation, led by the magistrate, became a Reformed church. But it happened quite differently in towns where the government chose for Rome, the Reformation was obstructed, and people ultimately went as far as persecuting and executing the apostates. This was the case in France, in parts of England, in modern-day Belgium, and initially also in the Netherlands. As a result, the population of villages and cities remained connected to Rome, and the Calvinists, operating in small numbers, were barely able to survive, causing many to flee to England or Germany. This resulted in the profound difference that in Geneva and elsewhere, the entire civil community suddenly changed allegiance; the Dutch population remained mostly Roman Catholic, as it had been, while the Calvinists worked alone and had to flee. Thus, on one side there is the picture of a church incorporating everyone, to which virtually all citizens belonged, and on the other side there is the picture of a small group of enthusiastic believers standing over against the majority.

The former situation often resulted in insincere situations, as was the case in Ghent, for example. Before the persecution started, Calvinist preachers were preaching in all the church buildings and the entire city appeared to be Reformed, but after 1576, when the Spanish occupied Ghent, the truly Reformed were forced to escape to England and Holland, and the city once again was Roman Catholic. The exact same thing happened north of the border, in the Netherlands. As long as Spain dominated the area, the Calvinists throughout the country were isolated groups who lived in oppression and fear, or fled. But as soon as the Spanish were expelled in 1572, one village after another and one city after another chose as one for the Reformation, which usually meant that the entire local church turned Calvinist, with few exceptions. Now wherever the majority remained Roman Catholic, the Calvinists operated in a fairly pure church association, since only sincere and enthusiastic believers chose for the Reformation. But in towns where under the leadership of the government almost the entire population remained Roman Catholic, people encountered local churches that evidenced a very weak organization and allowed virtually no church discipline. This can be explained from the ubiquitous third group at that time, which had no enthusiasm for the Reformation but did not wish to remain under Rome: the secular circles, supported by proponents of Humanism and by the Civilists, a movement already present in the early seventeenth century; they also altered public opinion in the Netherlands through the Remonstrant movement. Now take into account that both our [Belgic] Confession of Faith and our [Heidelberg] Catechism were written in the first period, when the Calvinistic group was still small yet pure, and that only after the death of Prince Maurice did great changes take place in our country. This explains directly why the concepts you find in the confession of the Calvinists bear fully scriptural characteristics, but why the later situation, when the church became a national church, was no longer compatible with these original views.

The ideal for which the martyrs had shed their blood and for which the survivors had toiled with zeal and full conviction, was buried after the Synod of Dort in 1618. Ecclesiastical issues arose that, as a mockery of this high ideal, were no more than the product of unprincipled practice. Just consider this one fact, that the Reformed Churches in the Netherlands from 1619 to 1798—that is, for a century and a half—were not able to gather as a general synod because the government did not allow it; and even at the general synod in Dort, the governmental authority controlled the ecclesiastical authority. Then you see that it was precisely the so-called Reformed government of our country that obstructed and hindered the development of Calvinism. And soon, the vast majority of the ministers of the Word sadly lacked the courage to stand up to the government for the sake of the Reformed principles. People could not do without their church buildings, salaries, and various grants for ministers. Only with the government's favor could one be assured of the availability of these earthly means. It was especially attractive for the ecclesiastical leaders that through the support of secular powers, they could gain influence over the citizenry, especially in rural areas. In many villages, the minister of the Word thus became the local authority, and thirst for power naturally crept into the life of the church as soon as the fire of holy zeal had died out.

The eighteenth century had barely dawned before those who still had spiritual zeal retreated not only from civil life, but also from church life, into what we call the conventicles. Hereby the church became even more impoverished. Even the universities, which were under the control of the higher group, grew suspect. And so, shortly before 1800, we see the shameful situation where not even the faintest aftereffect of the zeal of the ancestors survived in our churches. The "seven thousand" of Ahab's day [1 Kgs 19:18] certainly have never been lacking, but in the universities and in the consistories not a single spark of the higher life continued to flicker—the life that once had animated De Brès and Dathenus. The church lay lifeless in its shame. No wonder that the church suddenly collapsed from distress when the rulers appointed by the Sansculottes put an end to the salaries of ministers![27] And when King William I in 1816 placed the *entire* Dutch church life under the control of the state, the occasional protest was entirely bereft of heroism. The state, born out of the church, had overtaken the church, and had cut off her national significance.

This deplorable result would never have happened if the Calvinistic view concerning the relationship of church and state had been maintained consistently. This is exemplified by America, where the circumstances did allow this to happen. Calvinism sought the realization of its ideal and the creation of a new state of affairs, in which its principle could be worked out free from false admixtures. In Europe, this had turned out to be impossible. All of Europe had been Christianized in the past. Baptism was a common good. People did not genuinely *confess* among the masses, but went along with the creed being muttered by the cleric, without any

---

27. Kuyper refers here to the French Revolutionaries and the period of the Batavian Republic (1795–1806).

opposition. Even though more than one individual plotted to escape the control of the clergy to be free to live a worldly life, no one among the general population thought any longer about defending a more gentle, more pure religious principle. Every region had its band of fighters for this principle, but they were small minorities. If the people, led by their government, chose against Rome (as was the case in northern Germany and in Scandinavia), then the masses praised that liberation but remained Christian in appearance only, as they had always been, without inner conviction. They went along in complacency. They had a desire for something different and a desire to be free from the dominion of the clergy, but spiritually they remained as poor as ever—equally worldly-minded, equally indifferent concerning the heavenly things, equally lacking in initiative. However excellent the Reformation was in the circle of their spiritual leaders, no zeal could awaken the inert masses. They remained unaffected and used the spiritual weakening only to ensure their own position, just as in the Boer War. Nevertheless, after going over to the Reformation, the churches were stuck with these unmotivated masses. They could not be sent away. This was the heritage of the Roman Catholic past, which could not be dismissed. Meanwhile, the churches now lacked means that Rome at least formerly had—such as the distinction between clergy and laity, as well as the sacrament of confession—to moderate excessive lust and the intrusion of corruption among the ministers of the Word and in the universities.

CALVINISM IN AMERICA   § 14

This explains why Calvinism was unable to move forward consistently in the European countries. It had to put up with the existing ecclesiastical situation or was forced by the government to accept it, even though it might have wanted to make changes. This was also the reason why that which blossomed so beautifully in the sixteenth century was ill-suited and already faded toward the end of the seventeenth century. Only in America was Calvinism able to escape these aftereffects of the past, especially in what later became the United States. Think of the Presbyterians in England, and their struggles from every side; over against this, the Pilgrim Fathers are a church of tranquility. And although numerous Baptists and other sectarian groups could move about freely, America's unique advantage and the source of its strength was and remained the absence of ecclesiastical circumstances formed by Roman Catholic influence and its inescapable aftereffects. Here there was no past that one had to connect with, but an open territory where people could build from scratch. Here one was not bound to lines drawn wrongly in the past and now unchangeable, but everything could be planned and drawn according to the designer's wishes and according to the demands of the ideal that was being pursued.

Moreover, in America one did not run into that European stumbling block that always existed, of not knowing how to deal with church property, church buildings, and church income provided by the government. The same thing happened throughout all centuries and in all lands: those that wanted to break with a degenerate church life were free to leave, but often faced the harsh obligation to build according to their own design, to pay all costs and salaries, and in addition to contribute to the finances from which salaries were paid in the church they left. This had excellent results, insofar as it required spiritual superiority, and therefore fostered much energy in the church community. But there was always the drawback that those who complacently stayed behind retained all the buildings, finances, and income, so that they were able to continue their sickly compromise. People in America immediately escaped this very serious danger because all churches had yet to be built, all finances had yet to be provided, and all salaries had yet to be collected. So people could work according to their heart's desire and conscience. One could, it might also be said, create something new according to the requirements of one's own principle. That is what people did, and the happy result was that a relationship between state and church grew up naturally in the United States of America, one that was entirely new, not formerly known (or at least not implemented), and one that is in full agreement with the requirement of the Calvinistic principle. This relationship between state and church, first created in America, essentially means that the churches in the United States enjoy the most complete freedom by not being hindered at all by the state in their activities, and have an influence unknown in Europe.

Now, this freedom is the result of the unique fact that the churches in America are entirely self-supported, and receive not a single dollar from the state. Does this mean that the churches in America are poor, that they live in extreme poverty, that they can barely feed themselves? Not at all. In no other country in the world is the church better supplied, in every respect, with what a church needs. Nothing pertaining to the church is skimpy or minimal. All that is church-related grows and flourishes there.

And if you compare the salaries of the preachers and pastors in Chicago and New York to the annual salaries of those in Amsterdam or Berlin, you would rather fear that those in America might live too luxuriously. This is not to deny that there are disadvantages. Too often the poor are left to Methodism, and individual churches too often end up in the hands of a few wealthy families. What is especially lacking is the awareness and experience of participating in a common ecclesiastical life. Class differences never belong in the church. But apart from this, the result of this new creation is that American church life is free, grows in freedom, and is treated with respect and sympathy by everyone. The condescending attitude of looking down one's nose at the church, so common in Europe, is absolutely unknown in America. Public opinion honors and loves the church. In no European land does the life of the church flourish with such tranquility and abundance as in the United States. This phenomenon is something all the more noteworthy, because even children and young people participate in this church life.

EUROPEAN EMIGRANTS   § 15

Here we see an important phenomenon, namely, that once the emigrants from Europe's very small church groups have established themselves in America for good, they soon join this kind of life. This may not apply to the gigantic crowds entering Chicago and New York, but in the smaller towns and in the country it is customary for the arriving immigrants to become "churched." The remarkable phenomenon, which can be observed everywhere, is that they soon compete with the original Americans in bearing the costs of the church body. It was understandable, of course, that in the seventeenth and eighteenth centuries the Presbyterians and Independents, who had fled from England, sacrificed readily and generously for their church life. You can see that in all times and places with groups of people that, in order to be free, separate from a national church. This also happened in the Netherlands. But for the immigrants to join in the customs of the Pilgrim Fathers is highly remarkable. After all, the vast majority of these immigrants came from Ireland, Germany, Russia, and Italy, where the individual pays almost nothing for his church life, and the activities of the church tend to be fully covered from state finances and . contributions. One might fear that this newly arriving unchurched stream of immigrants, who never used to contribute to their church, would stubbornly refuse to join the customs of the Pilgrim Fathers. This would not be so bad if the total inflow of immigrants had been no more than 5 percent of the total population. However, the immigrants soon became more numerous than the original Presbyterian population, so that one might fear that the old European customs would take over, and that even the descendants of the Pilgrim Fathers would no longer be willing to sacrifice generously for their church. But the opposite happened. As though a self-sustaining yet vibrant church life were the most natural thing in the world, one generation after another of immigrants, who used to contribute hardly anything to their church, once they arrived in America, they not only became accustomed to contribute to their own church, but also took pride in doing as much as the Americans.

If you visit the Dutch immigrant cities in Michigan, Iowa, Illinois, New Jersey, and elsewhere, you will notice how it is taken for granted that all people pay for their own church, that everything pertaining to the church comes from its members, and that, while the government spends not one penny on the churches, the church is burdened less with deficits than in the Netherlands. Does this not show that the idea of the "free church," which flourishes in perfect financial independence, should hardly be viewed as a peculiarly English notion that could be adopted among the church members of other nationalities only in rare cases? The population of the United States has grown to its current size by receiving people directly from all nations of Europe, and yet the idea of the free, wholly financially independent church has been embraced by almost everyone. People give readily and are happy doing so. And while in most other areas of life financial challenges prohibit them from following their most cherished dreams, in this respect the generosity of the voluntary offerings has ensured victory for the system of the free church in a free state. This is the more remarkable because the vast majority of immigrants are business-people or needy persons; emigration for spiritual reasons was no longer common after the eighteenth century. As for the Dutch colonies, while most of the first migrants were Secessionists, this is no longer the case for the later waves of Dutch emigrants; and for other regions of Europe it is impossible to point to a single religious motive for emigration. Moreover, a similar phenomenon was seen among Roman Catholic emigrants. They also felt compelled to seek shelter in their own ark. They, too, went to work. At this moment, their church organization is entirely free, just like the Presbyterian, Independent, and Baptist churches.

PROSPERITY

If there were reason to complain about shabbiness in American church life, then this might be given as an argument against the system, but this is not the case. Rather, everything pertaining to the church has a certain level of luxury, albeit a different kind of luxury than what you find in Europe. Especially in the south of Europe, church life radiates in its abundance of monumental buildings, first-class paintings, and high quality sculptures, with which America cannot compete at all. Although a few cathedrals were built, the building of churches in America had, and still has, a very different character. The church in Europe endeavors to bring out the clergy in their great importance while the common people are left to fend for themselves, and hardly ever visit the church. In America this is not at all the case. The church buildings are designed to be practical. You will not be cold in church, and you will enjoy good lighting. The seating is arranged well, easily accessible, and nicely finished. From almost any seat you can easily listen to what the minister has to say. Every member of the church has seats personally assigned to himself and his family. Sunday is held in honor. It is customary to go to the house of prayer not only in the morning but also at night. The churches provide for good quality singing; too often there are even soloists. Often, the church building is a place for education, for sport and even food, for the sake of those who come from afar and wish to stay for the evening service. We already pointed to the negative aspect that the social classes separate themselves too much among the churches, and that evil must certainly be addressed. But apart from this it must be said that, while in Europe the church in its monumental glory often isolates itself from and elevates itself above the congregation, in America the congregation lives in its temple. Its church building is for it the focal point of all communal life. Among Christians in Europe, the custom that everything is paid from special finances or by the government has fostered indifference, and has encouraged people to keep their purses shut. Conversely, in America the habit of paying for your own church led to an appreciation of church life, so that the church is loved by all and can count on the cooperation of all. The sad phenomenon that little more than 25 percent of the European population is involved in the church, did not repeat itself in the free churches of America. Of course, there are things to complain about in America, but generally one may boast that the majority of people are under the influence of the church and, more importantly, appreciate the influence.

§ 17   PEACE IN THE CHURCH

There is another, no less attractive characteristic of the American church: it has been affected less by ecclesiastical strife. Wherever churches live alongside each other in Europe, the mutual relationship is generally poor. There is so little contact between the churches that the members pass by each other with indifference, and thus there is no bond of faith. In other cases, there is such bitter opposition that Christian love is often forsaken, or worse, replaced by enmity. The anti-papist attitude in northern and central Europe is a disease that cuts off all fellowship. Certainly this can be explained from the past. The papal power has always cursed the principle of the free church, resisted the confession of this principle as a most offensive heresy, and considered it her calling, at least until the eighteenth century, to fight this view through the secular powers, with violence if necessary. This was the origin of the mutual relationships between the European states and empires in the sixteenth and seventeenth centuries, when international politics was closely and rigidly connected to the religious principle. As a result, the national governments in the predominantly Protestant countries almost had to assume that their Roman Catholic subjects were in league with the enemy; likewise, in Roman Catholic countries the impression arose inevitably that the Protestants living there were traitors. Thus there was, from the Roman Catholic side, the St. Bartholomew massacre;[28] and along the same lines, albeit less gruesome, the Republic of the Netherlands felt compelled to vilify the Generality Lands[29] as well as the Roman Catholic population in the seven united provinces, and even limited their religious liberty.

This had to have consequences. And while it may be said that the mutual friction diminished, the events in 1853 show how easily the evil fire of religious passion can flare up in the Netherlands,[30] especially since liberal politics systematically feeds and abuses the anti-papist sentiment. No less sad is the fact that the division did not limit itself to historical disagreement. Alongside this anti-papism arose enmity against the so-called Precisionists. With this name, the segment of the population that had a

---

28. Thousands of French Protestants (Huguenots) were killed in the St. Bartholomew's Day massacre in Paris in 1572.
29. Territories in the Dutch Republic that were governed directly by the States General and that consisted of large numbers of Roman Catholics.
30. In 1853, the restoration of the Roman Catholic dioceses in the Netherlands was answered by Protestant protests known as the April Movement (*Aprilbeweging*).

more flexible attitude toward the faith expressed its hatred of those who had a more "precise" religious faith. This anger was directed against the mystics, against the members of the conventicles, against the strong dogmaticians and against the "night school."[31] But in whatever form it came, it brought bitterness and alienation. The Secessionists were met with arrogant scorn, and the government even punished them with billeting. And when in 1886 the *Doleantie* occurred, journalists of all kinds and even street beggars competed—through cartoons, name-calling, and unholy slander—in vilifying those who fought for freedom in the church. In Belgium and France and other Roman Catholic countries, a similar struggle has been fought for more than a century under the name of anti-clericalism. This struggle was less unholy in its character only in England and Scandinavia, but otherwise it is undeniable that almost everywhere in Europe, a thoroughly unhealthy spirit of fierceness reigns, between the church and the world as well as among churches, which often ruins the peace of families.

In view of this, it is extremely interesting that such a demonic passion is virtually unknown in America's church life. People definitely have opposing views. They express their views boldly and strongly. They do not shy away from firm polemic. Blandishments are found only in a few irenic circles. But what they avoid is the hatred and slander of one another. They do not live in one house, but in separate houses next to each other. Yet they respect their neighbors, even though the front of the house looks different, and even though the language spoken may differ from house to house. A significant contribution to this is the fact that those who love the free church, unlike people in the Netherlands or Germany, are not required to pay national taxes for the sake of the other church that is not their own. No more odious situation is imaginable than this: when you must pay everything for your own organization, and the government comes to take away yet another part of the available money to give it to a church that in principle opposes yours. That, of course, does not happen in America. All people contribute to their own church, but they do not contribute a single penny to another. All this led to a good mutual relationship among the churches in America. If you come from the European situation of strife and you get to know these churches, it will warm your

---

31. The "night school" (*nachtschool*) was a derogatory term for those who held to traditional Reformed doctrines and refused to be "enlightened."

heart and give the impression that they have attained the ideal situation—though not perfection (we hardly need to add that). And if in America an actively participating church member pours out heartfelt concerns about all that needs to be improved even in the church there, you might be discouraged. But if you limit yourself to a comparison between the old European and the new American situations, you can rightfully boast that the situation in America is peaceful, and that the system of free churches, which has much to recommend itself in many respects, has indeed proven to be excellent in comparison.

§ 18   MUTUAL RELATIONSHIP

You find this especially confirmed when you ask what relationship of church and state results from this. This is our main purpose in this discussion. I pointed to this already in my publication *Varia Americana*, published in 1899, when in December 1898 I returned from New York with the strong conviction that my 1874 lecture[32] had been proven true in practice. In particular, Dr. Herman von Weingarten, drew a conclusion that strongly influenced me when I first formed my thinking about this important subject.[33] I will discuss this later. At this point we must note more generally, concerning this complete separation of state and church and this perfectly equal freedom of all church life, what consequences it has had for the life of the state in America. Note especially what Von Weingarten writes: "This gives our period a significance in the general development of the Reformation ... which is only trumped by the first decades of the German Reformation. For the factor in all these struggles and developments ... from the first beginnings of Puritanism to its last offspring, *is exclusively the Christian congregation*."[34] He continues: "The history of the English churches of this time is *not*, like that of the Lutherans ... of the seventeenth century and nearly the entire sixteenth century, a history of theological development in which the Christian congregation participates only as recipient. All religious battles and results of this period have their origin in the Christian people, and therefore were of a *communal* nature."[35]

---

32. See "Calvinism: Source and Stronghold of Our Constitutional Liberties," in AKCR, 279–317.

33. *Note by the author*: Hermann Weingarten, *Die Revolutionskirchen Englands: Ein Beitrag zur inneren Geschichte der englischen Kirche und der Reformation* (Leipzig: Breitkopf & Härtel, 1868), 430–451.

34. *Note by the author*: Weingarten, *Die Revolutionskirchen Englands*, 441–42.

35. *Note by the author*: Weingarten, *Die Revolutionskirchen Englands*, 442.

Precisely this factor also defined the changed relationship between state and church, which soon would dominate public life in the great American republic. Once again, the state became purely state, and the church was free to spread its wings.

This immediately raised the very important question whether the state, in order not to be a power apart from God and against God, should unite itself in any way with a specific church as the state church. That had always been the understanding. In fact, we do not know of any developed country in Asia or Europe, among pagans as well as Muslims, where the government is not officially connected to a certain religion. And when Christianity entered the world, it soon, under Byzantine influence, followed this pattern, and the state church became the rule in Christendom. Even the Reformation did not really put an end to this system, though it did so in France, Belgium, the Netherlands, and somewhat in England, in the early years of the Reformation. But everywhere else, and soon in the Netherlands as well, it was the rule of law, even more strongly than before the Reformation, to acknowledge a state church. The people knew no different, wanted nothing different, and tolerated nothing different. Without an officially acknowledged state church, they could not imagine any well-organized political life. This is still the case for almost all of Europe, with the exception of the Netherlands, Belgium, and Switzerland. Even Italy, with its perpetual battle with the papal seat, confesses in article 1 of its constitution: "The Catholic, apostolic, Roman religion is the only religion of the state. By law the other worshipers are the tolerated ones." In Sweden, article 1 of the constitution stipulates that the Swedish state shall be governed by a king, and in article 2, "that the king must always confess the pure evangelical confession, as adopted and explained by the unchanged Augsburg Confession and the Synod of Uppsala in 1593." In Denmark, article 3 of the *Grundlov* stipulates that the Lutheran-Evangelical Church is the national Danish Church and as such is maintained by the state, while article 5 adds "that the king of Denmark must belong to the Evangelical-Lutheran Church." It must be mentioned that the previous constitution spoke of the *Statskirke*, and only in 1866 was this changed into *Danske Folke Kirke* [Danish National Church], to express that the choice of the people is decisive here, rather than a decision by the government.

But apart from such small modifications and distinctions one still finds the consequences of the ancient rule among pagan nations, which later became the rule of Islam and which was the rule in Israel from the beginning: that the government, and with it the country, was bound to one specific religion and acted on its behalf. The connection of state and government to one specific religion, cult, or church, was the fixed custom and rule in the political realm in Europe, especially in the period when in America a more definite situation was developing. In the Netherlands, too, people knew no better than that it had to be this way. Precisely for this reason it is highly significant that this connection was severed in the United States; this allowed for an entirely new view to be adopted, in which church and state—each operating in its own sphere—live out their own organic life, without forging any constitutional or perfunctory bonds between them.

§ 19   STILL A RELIGIOUS FOUNDATION

Does this imply that, in this newly acquired view, religion is locked up in the church, and that there can no longer be a religious foundation underneath the edifice of the state? Not at all. This is not even the case in various European states that followed the line of the French Revolution. The Swiss Constitution of May 29, 1874, begins with the following introduction: *Im Name Gottes des Almachtigen* [In the Name of Almighty God]! In his collection *Constitutions Modernes*, Dareste left this formula out,[36] but it is definitely found in Posener's edition.[37] References to a higher order have not completely disappeared from the Dutch constitution, either. Every legislative proposal submitted by the crown to the States-General has the introductory formula: "And hereby we commend you to God's holy care" and virtually every state of the nation speech used to conclude with the commendation of the States-General and the country to the blessing of God. Sunday and the Christian holidays are still officially observed. And while the constitution does not require it, the crown introduces its legislation with the confession that the king or queen rules *by the grace of God*. Yet both in Switzerland and in the Netherlands, most statesmen consider these remnants of an antiquated worldview to be meaningless.

In contrast to this, it is significant to note the position of the government of the United States of America in this respect. This shows itself in

---

36. *Note by the author*: F. R. Dareste, *Les constitutions modernes*, 3rd ed., 2 vols. (Paris: A. Challamel, 1910), 1:536.
37. *Note by the author*: Paul Posener, *Die Staatsverfassungen des Erdballs* (Charlottenburg: Fichtner, 1909), 838.

three ways. First, in the official days of prayer, which are still announced annually by the president of the republic. Second, in the religious character of the American public elementary education. Third, in the fact that Congress, when it convenes, is officially opened with prayer, offered by a clergyman in the full assembly. The prayer day has been observed from the very beginning. A president who would fail to call for such a day would violate the honor of the country. Of course, although America has its share of people who are indifferent or scornful about prayer, the public opinion still clings to that day of prayer, which generates and feeds the mystical aspects of the nation's well-being. Maintaining a religious character in the public school has certainly been a challenge because of the continuing attempt to uphold its character as a school of the Bible. The Roman Catholics in particular protested against this. There is a growing private school movement, and it is doubtful that this specific character of the public schools can be maintained. But even if this religious character of the national public school might diminish, it remains a fact that America never wanted a school without religion. And while opening Congress with a prayer may have degenerated into a dead formula, a mere imitation of English custom, it is and remains a public acknowledgment of God's superior rule over the country and its people, and is therefore valuable. This is especially the case because history shows that the United States of America always deliberately aimed to allow God's sovereignty to speak in the sovereignty of the people.

HAMILTON AND JEFFERSON[38] §20

There were attempts already under Jefferson, to root the independence of the English colonies in America in the principles of the French Revolution, but both Washington and Hamilton opposed this consistently. People felt that the liberation of the colonies in America was along the same line as the liberation of England from the Stuarts. What was accomplished in England by Cromwell and later by William of Orange has nothing to do with Danton and Robespierre. As Burke said, "Our revolution ... and that of France are just the reverse of each other in almost every particular

---

38. See Abraham Kuyper, *Lectures on Calvinism* (Grand Rapids: Eerdmans, 1931), 84-87.

and in the whole spirit of the transaction."[39] John Hancock[40] said in the Declaration of Independence that America acted according to "the laws of nature and nature's God," that they acted as "endowed by their Creator with certain unalienable rights," that they invoked "the supreme Judge of the world for the rectitude of our intentions," and that the Declaration of Independence was issued "with a firm reliance on the protection of Divine Providence."[41] Likewise, the introduction of the Articles of Confederation confesses "it hath pleased the great Governor of the World to incline the hearts of the legislatures."[42] In the preambles to various state constitutions one can still read: "grateful to Almighty God for the civil, political and religious liberty, which He has so long permitted us to enjoy, and looking to Him for a blessing upon our endeavors." God is honored as "the Sovereign Ruler" and "great Legislator of the Universe," and therefore it is confessed explicitly that God gave the people "the right to choose our own form of government."[43] The leaders of the revolution were so serious about this that in a crisis situation Franklin invited his fellow members of the Council to kneel down together with him and seek the light from above. Those who sympathized with the French opposed this, which resulted in 1793 in a fierce struggle between Hamilton and Jefferson, but this struggle was so essential that Von Holst does not hesitate to acknowledge: "It were folly to say that Rousseau's writings exercised any influence on the development of things in America."[44] Hamilton himself went even further and clearly expressed his conviction that the principles of the American and

---

39. *Note by the author*: Edmund Burke, "Substance of Mr. Burke's Speech in the Debate on the Army Estimates . . . Comprehending a Discussion of the Present Situation of Affairs in France," in *The Works of the Right Honourable Edmund Burke: With a portrait, and life of the author*, vol. 5 (London: T. McLean, 1823), 19.

40. In fact Hancock was not among the writers of the Declaration, which were Benjamin Franklin, Thomas Jefferson, John Adams, Roger Sherman, and Robert Livingston.

41. *Note by the author*: See Franklin B. Hough, *American Constitutions*, 2 vols. (Albany: Weed, Parsons & Company, 1872), 1:5, 7–8.

42. *Note by the author*: Hough, *American Constitutions*, 1:19.

43. *Note by the author*: Hough, *American Constitutions*, 2:549, 550. [Ed note: Kuyper quotes from the preambles to constitutions of various states including Illinois, New Jersey, Rhode Island, and Massachusetts.]

44. *Note by the author*: H. Von Holst, *Verfassung und Demokratie der Vereinigten Staaten von Amerika*, vol. 1 (Düsseldorf: Julius Buddeus, 1873), 96. [Ed. note: ET: *The Constitutional and Political History of the United States*, 8 vols. (Chicago: Callaghan, 1881–92), 1:30.]

French Revolutions were just as similar as the quiet Puritan housewife and the adulterous woman in a scandalous French novel.[45]

That all of this echoes the keynote of Calvinism, I have proven in more detail in my Stone Lectures, published under the title *Calvinism* in London and New York in 1899, with for instance a reference to Calvin's commentary on 1 Samuel 2:27, where he wrote: "And this is the most desirable kind of liberty, that we should not be compelled to obey every person who may be tyrannically put over our heads; but which allows of election, so that no one should rule except he be approved of by us."[46] Calvin also says that "God's people must be grateful if he gives a nation the right and power to choose its own governors."[47] The people, or its delegates, never do more than select the person who will have authority, but that authority comes down from God and can never be given to him by the nation. The authority for people to make laws, to respond with violence to opposition, and if necessary to punish them even with death, can come only from God, no matter whether God gave this power to a ruler or to an entire nation. I worked this out in more detail in *Common Grace*.[48] This truth has applied to all nations in all times, and it alone can guarantee the freedom of Christ's church.

Caesaropapism assumes power over the church, and then the church turns to stone. If the modern state denies the autonomous character and higher right of Christ's church, then the church degenerates into the status of a society or an entirely ordinary association. The opposite is also true, that the state will become either fully atheistic or subjected to the church. Therefore the only good way out is what was realized in America: a wholly free church that is not connected to the state or dependent on it. The context for this free church life is an equally freely developing civil society, which stands outside of particular grace, but which as a state is

---

45. *Note by the author*: See John T. Morse, *Thomas Jefferson* (Boston: Houghton, Mifflin and Company, 1883), 146–47.

46. This quote is actually from Calvin's discussion of Deuteronomy 1:13. Kuyper's next quote, however, is from Calvin's sermon on 1 Samuel 2:27. See Calvin, *Commentaries on the Four Last Books of Moses*, trans. C. W. Bingham, 4 vols. (Grand Rapids: Eerdmans, 1950), 1:310. Kuyper quotes the Latin edition of Calvin's *Opera omnia*, 9 vols. (Amsterdam: J. J. Schipper, 1671–67), 1:321.

47. *Note by the author*: See *Lectures on Calvinism*, 81–85. [Ed. note: See also Calvin's sermon on 1 Samuel 2:27–30, in *Opera omnia*, 2:45. Here Kuyper renders the quote in Dutch.]

48. *Note by the author*: See *CG* 1.2.3–1.38.6.

bound to common grace, and therefore to the acknowledgment of the Almighty God. Country and nation depend on the favor of God and are therefore bound to respect his ultimate authority and power; this has been the actual situation in every continent, in every century: in polytheism, by binding the country and nation to a national god; in Israel, by binding the country to Yahweh; in Christian nations, by binding the life of the state to the Creator of heaven and earth; in Islam, by binding the civil state to Allah and his Qur'an. Never did the magistrate embrace atheism, let alone materialism. The rule of absolute right is not the same as arbitrary self-governance in and by the nation. We are subjects of a majesty ruling over us. As a nation, too, we have our calling and duty. And regardless of who functions in this respect as the figure of authority or as the minister of the Almighty, it is and remains the fact that we are not free people but God's creatures, and that only by acknowledging and respecting this universal governing authority can we ourselves attain freedom and the development of our own power.

§ 21   THE POWER OF GOD

When the state and government are bound to God by a bond of their own, even before the church of Christ was there and also without her involvement, then the result is the natural, simplest, and, in comparison with other systems, the most desirable relation of church and state. It is not the church that hands the scepter to the government. In every pagan nation the government possessed that scepter apart from the church. In the days when Christ was on earth, before his apostles established his churches, Christ himself testified to Pontius Pilate that the power wielded by the Roman emperor and his governor was power given to them by God [John 19:11]. Later, Romans 13:1–7 presented the view that the entire pagan power of that time was power given by God to the government. In Christ the Reconciler and Healer and Savior of souls appears, but this sphere of particular grace stands by itself, and entirely distinct from it is the sphere of governmental authority. Whether the nation over which the government received power is a pagan, Muslim, or Christian country, does not change anything pertaining to the magistrate. The same kind of authority was wielded by the government in Babylon and Persia, in Baghdad and Cairo. In all these situations it possesses all the instruments needed to perform its actions. It is complete in itself. When governing a Christian nation it can count on more submission, and may be able to bring about and maintain a happier national situation; but just as a kitchen or a laboratory remains the same when its managers are in Christ or outside of Christ, the same is true here. Even under pagan rulers there were excellent governors, and many Christian princes fell short in the performance of their calling. The government builds and sustains the state in its own terrain, and common grace provides it with everything it needs for ruling rightly. All that can be demanded of the government in this respect is that it make clear to all people, openly and officially, also in the governing of the state, that it is not ruling over the nation for its own profit, but as a God-ordained power to guard the interests of the nation and to honor God in the nation.

If at this point one asks whether the Christian religion should not also influence public life, the answer is: without a doubt, just as always was the case in America—but that influence must come to expression along the constitutional route. If the nation to be ruled is a baptized Christian people, then one must ask in what way this people can influence the government legally. That would be the appointed way for the church of Christ to exert its influence on law and justice. The nation to be governed might be a people of low standing. In that case they would have a less desirable influence on the government. In extreme cases, an increase of the influence of the people on the government would lead the entire nation to perdition. In that case the only solution is to cut off the people's influence and to turn the mind of the nation through the rule of a monarch or an aristocrat. But if the people are of a high quality, as indeed was and still is the case in the Netherlands, Switzerland, Scotland, and the United States, then they will have a wholesome influence on the government, and it would be desirable if that influence increases. This was the case for a while in Athens. The same could be said of the Roman state for more than two centuries. And after the Christianizing of Europe, the church of Christ succeeded in introducing better morals, improving the national character, and exerting a positive influence on the government. Under such circumstances it is, of course, desirable that the people themselves are heard, as much as possible, and that the government draw support from the larger portion of the population. Where the situation is good, you will always see both of these go together. If the people advance in the rich development of their religious, ethical, intellectual, and technical strength, then they will usually acquire more influence on the government. There can be an unnatural relationship, as was the case in the Netherlands over against Alva,[49] but this does not endure. Tension grows, and that tension leads to a break. As a rule, the fortunate historical result has been that the tyrant was subdued and the nation liberated. In the Revolutionary War of the United States, the favorable circumstance was that this action of the colonists against England arose from a very serious religious movement of the seventeenth century. History proves that the Christian element among them was of very high standing, and in general one can boast of the valuable influence exerted on the first thirteen states by the Christian church in its various denominations. As a natural consequence, the Christian influence continued its expansion in these states as the constitutional system assigned more importance to the representation of the people.

Since in any newly Christianized land the visible church consists of many who still crave the meat-pots of Egypt, the leadership of such a church will do all it can to increase its power as church over such a multitude and be the guardian over such a people, in collaboration with the government. That was the actual situation at the beginning of the Middle Ages, when one single church covered the entire country, the clergy tried hard to lead the populace away from its sins and abuses, and the government supported the church in doing so.

§ 22   CHRISTIAN INFLUENCE BY THE PEOPLE

But the situation in America was very different. There was not one church, but several churches with different creeds and systems of church government that had organized themselves alongside each other, and the membership of these churches was generally of high religious and moral standing. For this reason there could not be an alliance between government and church, since the churches were not of one mind. But conversely, such a collaboration of state and church to be guardian of the people had never been so unnecessary, because the churched population had outgrown such supervision. Thus arose the highly desirable situation that as the people were allowed more influence on the government, the Spirit of Christ gained influence over the entire nation though it. Just think about the war against slavery. A church would never have been able to abolish slavery through rebuke directed toward the government. The objections to this abolition were so manifold and profound that no statesman would

---

49. Fernando Álvarez de Toledo (1507–82), Duke of Alva, was the Spanish governor of the Netherlands from 1567 to 1573 during the intensification of the Dutch Revolt.

have dared to take such bold action merely on the basis of the church's admonition. On the contrary, in this case the Christian popular spirit gradually inspired almost the whole nation. And as a stream of higher purpose began flowing, carrying along more and more people, ultimately there was such strong pressure from the Christian nation itself on the president and the Congress that they no longer shunned this war with the South and went to battle. Admittedly, not all excesses were avoided. But throughout America everyone now acknowledges that in the war on slavery, the requirement of Christian compassion triumphed over greed and tyranny; no one would suggest for a moment that the nation should return to the situation before 1863. Lincoln's proclamation that declared all slaves free as of January 1, 1863, was the triumph of the Christian religion in the United States.

There is no country where the representatives of the people have more power than in America, but there is also no church life that dominates the representative groups more than in America. Not a single country can be found in Europe where the relation of state and church is more blessed than in the United States. The national government honors God, does not meddle in ecclesiastical disputes, and is free to set its own course. Conversely, the church of Christ, far from being an obstacle, instead satisfies life's needs with the richest variety, has a place of honor throughout the entire land, is financially independent, and influences public opinion (and through it the president and Congress); it does so to such a degree that no European national church can even begin to be compared with the powerful influence of America's churches on the life of the nation.

IDEAL SITUATION   § 23

The churches do not hinder the state in any way, and the state does not place any obstacle in the way of the church's life. Both have complete autonomy and independence. The growth and flourishing of both corresponds to the most fervent desires of pious Americans. No constraints are placed on their reciprocal influences. In short, there is literally no link in the chain that one might wish to remove. The churches in America do not complain about the state and the state does not complain about the churches. Christ's Spirit can freely rule in the churches, and through the churches over the people, and through the representation of the people over the state. State and church do not obstruct each other at any point. You do not hear about strife and conflict. Even the Roman Catholic Church, which originally followed a very different line, found plenty of opportunity to develop here. One hears nothing of a plan to redesign this relationship.

Of course there are complaints about this arrangement. Because of sin's operation, a perfect situation can never be attained. Defects can be seen on all sides. But all of this concerns the particulars, has to do with the implementation and application of the system, and relates to personal affairs. The American state, too, saw the rise of political parties. In the Republican party and the Democratic party the aftereffects of past traditions live on, and new evils have surfaced. Even among the Republicans, who used to stand so high and pure in politics, there is now an economical bias, which recently led to their defeat. But all of this applies to life's ebb and flow, not to the system itself. In religious life as well, people have too often slipped in the direction of modern heresies. Evolution in particular has dislocated much that used to be established. But these, too, are merely diseases that disturb the normal situation for a moment, and in all this there remains the highest commitment to the confession of the Lord God.

Thus, if one also applies here the always valid principle that a sharp distinction must be made between what a rule requires in the normal sense and what occurs abnormally, then one may confess the following without hesitation: no better relationship between church and state can be imagined that answers to the ideal that addresses us from the Gospels than what we observe in America. Almost everywhere else, and especially in Europe, one senses so vividly the great wrath with which Christ would condemn the shameful state of his churches if he appeared among us. And if one wonders where Christ, when he returns, would find the realm in which his Spirit can move freely and without obstruction, then we have not the slightest doubt that there is no country on earth where the relationship between church and state would obstruct Christ less than in the United States. This is especially because the irreconcilable bitterness, which still continues to disfigure the church life of the Netherlands, is almost unknown in America. If in every Christian country the relationship of church and state could become what it is now in America, virtually no desire would remain unfulfilled, and the churches would have full control in their attempts to influence the life of the state for a blessing of the people. From this we may readily conclude that in regard to the state, the picture of the church presented to us in the New Testament has almost been realized.

As for the national church of Israel, we will soon deal with this subject, but we skip over it for now. If we ask ourselves how the emerging Christian church presented itself in the New Testament, then all we find are local churches, most of them governed by elders, to whom were added the deacons, and ruled to some extent by the apostles. There is hardly any trace of an organization that connects the individual local churches into one entity and allows for corporate action. The only evidence one could cite is the assembly reported to us in Acts 15, commonly known as the Synod of Jerusalem. Yet it is not the case that the delegates of all the churches that had been established at that time were called to the assembly. Only the church of Antioch sent Paul and Barnabas to Jerusalem to gain the approval of the other apostles. Upon arrival in Jerusalem, these two delegates approached the congregation, the apostles, and the elders. We read that especially James and Peter acted officially. The request made by Paul and Barnabas served merely to elicit a decision as to whether it was legitimate to baptize converts from among the Gentiles without prior circumcision, and to incorporate them into the congregation. That is what the assembly addressed, not in a gathering of delegates, but in a meeting of the Jerusalem church. In that meeting were (1) the apostles, (2) the elders, and (3) the whole congregation (see Acts 15:22). In this meeting the principal issue was discussed and decided in agreement with Paul, not through a majority vote but unanimously. Then Judas and Silas personally communicated this decision to the church in Antioch, in a letter with this opening: "The brothers, both the apostles and the elders, to the brothers who are of the Gentiles in Antioch and Syria and Cilicia, greetings." And the letter testified: "It has seemed good to the Holy Spirit and to us to lay on you no greater burden" [Acts 15:23, 28].

So this was a broader ecclesiastical assembly under the leadership of the apostles, but not in the same spirit as what in America and Scotland is called the *general assembly* of all churches together. Nor did Paul with his authority as church planter and apostle cut through the knot of Judaism, but only the church of Jerusalem endeavored to render a decision, and the church of Antioch submitted to it. As an apostle, Paul continues to exert some authority as church planter in the local churches, but otherwise every church acts as an independent organization. In every church, offices are independently instituted and held. There is preaching. Two sacraments are administered. There is church discipline. A collection is organized for impoverished churches. But these churches sought so little financial aid from the government that even the apostle Paul could write: "no church entered into partnership with me in giving and receiving" (Phil 4:15). Voluntary love gifts were given or sent to him, but otherwise the apostle provided for himself, sometimes by working late into the night as a tentmaker. In particular, even as an apostle, he did not ascribe to himself any authority except over churches that he himself had founded, and not at all, for instance, over the churches in Jerusalem or in Judea. In general the newly founded churches live in local independence and without external compulsory authority, and only in fraternal fellowship with other churches. The government has no authority over it. It honors the government as being a servant of God in civil and political life, but in the churches no mention is made of the government except in prayers, prayers lifted up for pagan governments as well.

It is therefore safe to say that if you try to find an example of church life in our time that is most similar to the picture of the church sketched in the New Testament—where apostolic authority, which according to Acts and Paul's epistles used to be personal, is now represented in the writings of the New Testament, or if you will, in the whole Bible—you will not find it in Europe but almost exclusively in America. Without a doubt, in the New Testament all the local churches together constitute the single congregation of the saints, which exists in organic unity before God as the body of Christ. Christ is the Head, not of a few local churches, but of the church viewed as a whole. In Christ this is the church "without spot or wrinkle" (Eph 5:27). The distinction between local churches (to which the hypocrites belong as well) and the "church of the living God" [1 Tim 3:15] (to which only God's regenerate children must be reckoned) holds good, and it is this distinction that especially Calvin tried to clarify by disentangling the *visible* and *invisible* church.

Meanwhile, what lives and operates in the spiritual background cannot be judged in connection with the life of the state. We will not discuss that here. But if we restrict ourselves to the churches in their *external* appearance—as they manifest themselves in the state—then in no country can a better reflection of the New Testament picture of the church be perceived than in the ecclesiastical system in America. Indeed, Calvin carefully followed this New Testament portrait of the church when he drew the architectonic plan for the new church construction he undertook. When he had to deal with the practicalities, he failed to realize this picture in its pure characteristics. The ecclesiastical situation that he found did not allow him to do so. History obstructed his ideal. Still, the outcome shows that when an entirely new situation arose in America, one that was unmarked by the highly suspicious inheritance of history, "the free church in the free state"[50] developed on its own from the fundamental concept theoretically mapped out by Calvin, which could assume a purer form only in this new world. As a result, the picture presented to us in the New Testament and the situation found among the Presbyterians in America manifest a surprising harmony, both in terms of the mutual relationship between the churches and with respect to the relation of church and state.

ACTUAL OPPOSITION   § 24

If one should seek to explain the fact that almost all European Reformed churches have largely strayed from this original line, one will discover clearly that this must be explained from two facts that fit together remarkably well and that occurred simultaneously, almost fortuitously. The first is the condition of the churches when they went over to the Reformation, and the second is the Old Testament character of the view of the church that many people held. The people were not neutral toward the government. The conviction that the government should support the church was deep-rooted. That is why the Roman Catholics continually required the government to uphold the Roman Catholic organization over against the emerging Reformation, with force if necessary. The result was that great questions either had to be decided on the battlefield or be compelled by means of the gallows. On the side of the Reformation one could take the position only of victim or martyr. The Anabaptists initially believed it to be their calling to accept this entirely passive position.

But the Calvinists did not think this way. While they also took part in the passive opposition, they soon realized that they could not maintain this attitude of idleness. And thus, in Switzerland, France, and the Netherlands, no less than in Scotland, people reached the conviction that they should

---

50. This formula, coined in reference to movements against established churches in Europe and particularly with the Italian statesman Count Cavour (1810–61), became a watchword for independents and Baptists in America. Philip Schaff, comparing Europe to the American experience, identified the "distinctive character of American Christianity in its organized social aspect and its relation to the national life" as "a free church in a free state, or a self-supporting and self-governing Christianity in independent but friendly relation to the civil government." See Philip Schaff, *Church and State in the United States; or, The American Idea of Religious Liberty and Its Practical Effects* (New York: Charles Scribner's Sons, 1888), 9.

set, if possible, the power of the Reformed government against the power of the Roman Catholic governments. Therefore, as soon as there was an opening and an opportunity to turn the government itself away from the Roman Catholic position toward Calvinism, they made this transition. They were convinced that without the activity of a Reformed government on their behalf, the Roman Catholic authorities would soon completely suppress the Reformation and put an end to their liberty of confession before God. If the Protestant rulers in the Netherlands, England, and Germany had not displayed their power on the battlefield, then Austria, France, and Spain would have completed their cruel destruction and annihilation of Protestantism. The choice was, therefore, to be executed on the gallows like the Anabaptists, or to erect another government in opposition to the ruling government; the Calvinists chose the latter.

§ 25   ISRAEL's EXAMPLE

Meanwhile this widely held position had to be justified theoretically as well, and people thought they could derive that justification from the Old Testament, proceeding from the basic principle that both tables of the law were placed under the oversight of the power that bears the sword. And this could be defended only by generalizing and transferring the wholly unique and special position of Israel as covenant people to the church of Christ. Two lines of reasoning could lead to this view.

First of all, one had to oppose the idea that the salvation of the elect began for the first time at Golgotha. It would not do to assume that the finished sacrifice of Christ would have created the possibility for people to be saved for the first time. Enoch, Noah, Abraham, David, Hosea, Isaiah, Zerubbabel, and Daniel could not be excluded from the inheritance of the saints. Whatever mistaken view people held in those days about the Old Testament eschatology, the Old Testament must have had its elect, and these Old Testament elect could not have been lost forever. It had to have been clear, as we read in Hebrews 11:40, that the fathers of the old covenant could not be perfected without us, so that the blessedness of the Father's house began first with the ascension of Christ; but the elect of the old covenant could not be excluded from that blessedness. For this reason, the dispensation of the old covenant was included as part of the history of Christ's church. And in connection with this, Scripture's teaching about the Israel of the old covenant was also applied to the Israel of the new covenant, that is, to the Christian church. Thus, the dispensation of the law and the dispensation of the gospel, incorporated into the national ecclesiastical constitution of Israel, were carried over into the national church, and the calling of the government in Israel was identified with the calling of the Christian government.

Second, this mistaken view was fed by the prophecy given in the old covenant concerning the coming, position, and work of the Messiah. Naturally everything prophesied about the church of Christ took as starting point the *qahal* [assembly] as it existed in Israel, and such prophecy always hinted that, at that time already, Israel could enjoy spiritually what would be revealed for the first time in the Messiah. On the part of the world there was a distinction and even some opposition. Under the old covenant the entire activity of grace was limited to one single people. All that was to be realized in the future was depicted symbolically for this one people in sacrificial rite and worship. A glorious kingdom was presented—a kingdom to be expected on earth, in which the Messiah would rule, but which would appear at the end, in the hour of the consummation. It appeared as if the spiritual had receded into the background, and as if the future glory was being presented to us in the flourishing form of an earthly kingdom. This explains the antedating of Christ's appearance and work as early as in paradise, shortly after the fall. Theologians imagined they could find among the patriarchs the fully developed confession of the Calvinists. There was and remained a difference in dispensation. But the content of that dispensation functioned from the time of the paradise promise. The material dimension of Old Testament goals easily became spiritualized. And the church unwittingly arrived at the conclusion that the distinction between old and new covenant was, in the final analysis, only imaginary.

The cross of Golgotha cast its shadow not only forward but also backward. The church of Christ was one, from the time of paradise, and now, and until the consummation. With this understanding it was inevitable that the government of Christendom believed it had the same calling as the government under the old covenant. The king of Israel was the prototype for the Christian king. And thus the view developed and gained popularity, which we also find in Article 36 of our [Belgic] Confession, that the government must function not only in the civil realm "to have regard unto and watch for the welfare of the civil state"; but it has an equally clear calling to "protect the sacred ministry, and thus may remove and prevent all idolatry and false worship, that the kingdom of antichrist may be thus destroyed and the kingdom of Christ promoted. They must, therefore, countenance the preaching of the Word of the gospel everywhere, that God may be honored and worshipped by every one, as He commands in His Word."

Notice that the government did not concoct this view, but merely allowed its inclusion in our Confession. No, this requirement, this postulate was set before the government by the theologians and by the churches. After having suffered under the Roman Catholic government all the bitterness of government intervention concerning religion, the theologians and churches decided that it was now the turn for those who had been persecuted to enjoy equally powerful support and protection from the government and to avenge former abuse on their persecutors. This position is difficult for us to fathom, and hardly anyone would seriously defend it today, but at the time it was pursued ruthlessly and embraced as the only satisfactory solution. This can be explained only from the fact that our ancestors did not want to become Anabaptists and had to pursue the struggle against the Roman Catholic government as far as the battlefield, but they could not do so without the support of the Reformed government. Therefore, to secure a peaceful future, they had to apply to the Christianized nations the position held by Israel under the royal shield of David. Now it was truly remarkable that, in all this, they did little more than imitate Roman Catholic practice. In the Thirty Years' War, the two religious powers opposed each other, both supported by political power.[51] There was, of course, a profound difference at a deeper level. In Rome, the ecclesiastical organization was opposed to the government. Rome was a church that, as an independent power, used the government in its service. The Protestant government dealt only with compliant, obedient churches that had to submit to it. Moreover, no less significant is the distinction that the Roman Catholic Church had incorporated the priestly element from Israel into its own priestly organization, and in doing so was less liable to fall back too much into Old Testament structures and relationships. As a result, both parties—the Roman Catholic Church and the Protestant churches—continued to hold the Old Testament portrait high and forged a close connection between the church and the government, but with this difference: the powerful Roman Catholic Church continued

---

51. From 1618 to 1648 war raged across Europe between Protestant and Roman Catholic nations.

to resist the supremacy of the magistrate, while the Protestant church gradually changed into a national church. And precisely in this form of a national church, it lost all of its independence and was forced to bow to the powerful arm of the government. Rome's church held up its head proudly, but the Dutch churches debased themselves and threw away their honor. And sadly, we must add that they themselves are to blame for this self-debasement (at least partially), because of the issue of clergy salaries. When after 1619 no permission could be obtained for convening a national or international synod, from that moment on, it was the government that tyrannized the churches.

WEAK APPEAL TO THE OLD TESTAMENT   § 26

In defense of the view that the government has the power and duty to prevent all false worship, an appeal was made to the Old Testament, but this appeal is extremely weak. Just consider Deuteronomy 17:18-20. There it says only that the king of Israel must obtain a copy of the law and read from it daily. It says this: "He shall read in it all the days of his life, that he may learn to fear the LORD his God by keeping all the words of this law and these statutes, and doing them" [Deut 17:19]. What could this imply for our government? Israel's law also included the ceremonial law. Would anybody claim that these apply to us today? Nobody who thinks about it would make that claim. Only what follows, "that his heart may not be lifted up above his brothers" [Deut 17:20] would certainly apply to our situation, but this is nothing more than an admonition against immoral abuse of the government's power. Still, even if one would interpret these words as saying that Israel's king is required to protect the maintenance of the priestly service, with the sword if necessary, what could this imply for our government today, when no such ministry exists any longer among us at all?

It is no different with the reference to Joshua 1:7, which says: "Only be strong and very courageous, being careful to do according to all the law that Moses my servant commanded you. Do not turn from it to the right hand or to the left." This was a special commandment given to Joshua because he now held the office that Moses had formerly held among the people, to be both the spiritual and political leader of the multitude. But how could this ever imply that this commandment, given to Joshua, should now be applicable to all rulers and governments? The unique character of this commandment to Joshua, given in such specific circumstances, simply cuts off any possibility of transferring this requirement to all rulers and governments. The particular may never be generalized like this.

Even less effective is the appeal to 2 Kings 11:11-12. This account of the crowning of Joash mentions that the high priest not only placed the crown on Joash's head as a symbol of his kingship, but also gave him the testimony. Assume that this was the entire Torah. Even so, this implies nothing but that a king of Israel was of course bound to the law that was valid for Israel. Now, if it had said that he was to be given a copy of the Ten Commandments, then one could make the argument that the law of the Ten Commandments still applied today, and that therefore the government is still required to maintain this law, not only in terms of its second table but also its first table. But it only says that when the king was crowned, the high priest gave him at his crowning what at that time was the equivalent of our Bible. What could that imply for our government, especially because it does not say that God commanded the high priest to hand it to Joash, but only informs us that he did so in his function as high priest?

And one can proceed similarly with Psalm 2:10-12 and Psalm 72:10-11. Each time the result is the same: In part we find special stipulations concerning the government in a specific country—which is not in the least on the same line as ours, so that nothing whatsoever can be derived from it for our government; and in part we find statements that are so general that they never imply a concrete conclusion for our governments. It would therefore not be profitable to comment on each of these texts successively. Israel's kings occupied a position that our governments do not occupy, and the nation of Israel, over which they ruled, was distinguished from all peoples and nations of the earth in order to fulfill an entirely separate function in the historical progress of God's kingdom. Thus, even if one were to assume that the king of Israel was bound to ensure that every stipulation of the Torah was implemented—which was not the case—it would still not imply any firm conclusion for the governments of the nations, nor therefore for the Dutch government. Our national state does not share the theocratic character of Israel's national state.

Nor can anything be concluded from other evidence that people have appealed to, such as the honorary titles given in the Old Testament to the governments. For instance, when it is said to Israel (and, as people thought, in this nation of Israel to the church of Christ), "Kings shall be your foster fathers" [Isa 49:23], the conclusion was drawn that the modern government must still give financial support to the church of Christ. To this people add a reference to Isaiah 60:10: "kings shall minister to you." Even less can be derived from what we read in Psalm 82:6, which says to the judges: "You are gods, sons of the Most High"; from what Isaiah 44:28 testifies of Cyrus: "...who says of Cyrus, 'He is my shepherd, and he shall fulfill all my purpose'"; or from what, according to 1 Samuel 24:11, the young man David says to Saul: "my father," from which the conclusion is drawn that every government must provide for all the needs of God's church with fatherly care. All these statements are gathered together with the sole purpose of deriving from Scripture the claim that the government has the duty to honor the church and her ministers in every way, to support them and to aid them, but every time these words are clearly made to say what they do not. And above all, we are always dealing with special and very unique relationships, from which no general rule can be drawn concerning God's universal intention for the relationship between government and church.

HISTORICAL PROGRESS §27

Yet this flow of thought could not be avoided after Constantine's conversion to Christianity. The Christianizing of the emperor's crown in Byzantium was in itself too surprising an event not to give joy to all that was Christian. The persecution was now over. Instead of persecution came elevation and honor. And as usual with such a turn of events, thousands and ten thousands of pagans joined the Christian church, as is characteristic for that indifferent crowd that naturally joins every movement that arises. But on the other hand, there is no doubt that the baptism of Emperor Constantine became the starting point of an internal decay in the church and in its relationship with the government, and its consequences negatively affect the well-being of the churches still today. Constantine's conversion not only arrested the persecution but brought in its place power and wealth for the leaders and the heads of the churches. The poverty in which the church had struggled was now replaced by abundance, and thus the bishop's word gained unchallenged authority, even in matters of the state. With very few exceptions, the clergy of that time could not resist this inherent temptation, and they gladly granted the emperor superior influence in all ecclesiastical affairs as long as it remained clear that pagan philosophy and pagan religion were to be restricted and that the church should no longer suffer at their hands. There was little opposition when

Emperor Constantine in his famous speech[52] established the rule that the bishops would hold all authority as far as the *internal* affairs of the church were concerned, but that he, Constantine, was appointed by God as the bishop for *external* affairs.

It is therefore safe to say that from 324 AD the authority in the entire Eastern church was actually in the hands of the emperor. As the seat of imperial power was shifted more and more completely from the West to Byzantium, the position of so-called Byzantinism became more firmly established in the East. Even today, the so-called Orthodox or Greek Church is still built on this foundation of governmental authority. In Russia today, the czar still has the same power in ecclesiastical matters as Constantine claimed for himself in the fourth century. In Serbia, Bulgaria, and so on, the king has similar power. Once this view of caesaropapism had taken root in the East, it could not be destroyed. And now that, especially in the second half of the ninteenth century, the political power of the East is increasing so visibly and the population in the East is growing more rapidly than in the Western countries, it will no longer do in Europe today merely to point to Roman Catholicism and Protestantism. Byzantinism or caesaropapism must be added as the third, very significant factor for the Christian life. It must be openly admitted that the bishops of Rome are the ones who prevented the church from being swallowed up in the state, as was the threat back then. And in this struggle of the church of Christ to withdraw from the tyranny of the government, the Calvinist still sides invariably with Rome.

In all this, one must never forget that Rome fell into an equally suspicious one-sidedness, and tried not only to subject the government to the church, but also to make all churches of the world dependent on its bishops. This imbalance is precisely what the Reformation protested. But when it came to upholding the liberty and independence of Christ's church over against the magistrate, the Roman Catholic and the Calvinist always stood on the same principle. And what now has been realized in America, as a fruit of the Calvinistic principle, in the perfect liberty of the churches of Christ, crowns the principle of ecclesiastical independence. Since the days of Constantine, the bishop of Rome used the fact that the

---

52. *Note by the author*: See Eusebius, *De vita Constantini*, book 4, chapter 24. [Ed. note: ET: Eusebius, *Life of Constantine*, ed. Averil Cameron and Stuart G. Hall (New York: Oxford University Press, 1999), 161.]

imperial throne moved from Rome to Byzantium to inflate the ecclesiastical power of the West at the expense of the secular power. The absence of the emperor in the ancient capital city promoted this, and material prosperity aided the church in this matter. And when shortly thereafter, large-scale migration blanketed Europe with younger nations who were ready to receive baptism, it was perfectly understandable that the bishop's influence soon encompassed all of life and could develop so much power as to endanger the civil authority. Almost all dynasties of that time, including that of England under Henry VIII, experienced this pressure by the church on the government. Rome stood up for the liberty and independence of the church, but at the expense of the liberty within the church. The unity of the church worldwide was sought in the external organization, instead of spiritual harmony. Ultimately, the relationship between church and emperor became so tense that one had to yield to the other. As a consequence of this tension, the unifying bond of the church broke during the Reformation, and the churches fell apart; and the government was able to introduce a type of caesaropapism in the West as well, in the middle of Europe. In Germany the old battle between the Guelphs and the Ghibellines ended, at least in northwest Germany, in a complete defeat of papism. In England, the Church of England came into existence as a separate church, and the ruler was given the honorary title of *Defensor fidei* [defender of the faith]. In the three Scandinavian states, caesaropapism triumphed. And in the Netherlands the Remonstrant politicians pushed in the same direction with their *pietas ordinum*.[53]

The Current Situation §28

It must be noted that in the early eighteenth century, caesaropapism gradually encompassed all of Protestantism, and the necessary change did not come. The Roman Catholic ecclesiastical power has been pushed back almost everywhere. Even in Spain, Bavaria, and Austria, nearly half of the population tends to take a stance against the church and for the civil power. In the rest of Europe, both in regions that are Greek Orthodox and those that are Protestant, it is largely the case that the church is bound hand and foot, feeling unable to maintain her confession, and that the

---

53. In Kuyper's usage, *pietas ordinum* (piety of the states) is shorthand for a form of Erastianism, in which the state is the guardian of the church. The phrase comes from a work advancing this position by the Remonstrant Hugo Grotius (1583–1645), *Ordinum Hollandiae ac Westfrisiae pietas* (1613).

material factors of church buildings and salaries are the strongest factors that keep her together.

If those material factors would diminish, the Protestant church would split apart nearly everywhere. In a country as small as the Netherlands, the number of individuals opposing the church is already as high as three hundred thousand. In Germany, it may be more than three million. The Greek Orthodox churches have not been able to escape this fate, either. In Germany they combined with the Lutheran magisterial churches into one Evangelical Church. In France the collegial system has been accepted on the basis of revolutionary principles. The Church of England tends more and more toward Puseyism.[54] In France, England, Scotland, and the Netherlands, free churches exist alongside the state churches, but the original free churches, which were established in the sixteenth century, have almost all developed into a sponsored state church, for the love of money. The Erastians, with their collegial system, perfected this supremacy of the state over the church even more than in Russia or Berlin. The Lutheran system began with allowing the ruler to participate in the church as a *confessor*, and on the basis of that confession, in connection with his high position in the state, he was honored as *summus episcopus* [highest bishop]. The proponents of the *pietas ordinum*, on the other hand, viewed the state as the true kingdom. In that kingdom of the state, the church functioned as one association among many other associations and organizations. The state or government had the divine mandate and calling to protect the well-being of the church, just as it had to protect the well-being of other constituent parts of the life of the state.

Even the Dutch Reformed theologians were not clear about this. As à Marck and many others presented the situation, there was a Christian society in the Netherlands; that Christian society was led by the church of Christ; and in this realm that stands under the church's authority, the government appeared—the civil power—to protect external, civil affairs. But the Remonstrant nobles, essentially one with the Socinians in this respect, granted supremacy to the state. In that state the church appeared, and therefore, just as with all other phenomena in society, that church was entrusted to the leadership of the government. The collegial system

---

54. Puseyism, named after Edward Pusey (1800–82), is also commonly known as the Oxford Movement, a movement centered around the University of Oxford that advocated for High Church principles and ancient liturgy and practice.

exacerbated the situation, as it misunderstood the church in terms of its exalted character. In the purely caesaropapist systems the church is and still remains something sacred, and it can expect the government, for the sake of Christ, to treat it with respect and to sustain it with care and love. But in the collegial system as it originated with the Socinians and Erastians, which is now also the rule in the Netherlands, this entire higher view of the church of Christ falls away. There is no difference between a Christian church or a Jewish synagogue or a Buddhist monastery. They are all *collegia*—that is, societies—and the government's responsibility is to ensure that these societies will not dishonor it and will not limit the freedom of individuals.

CONCLUSION   § 29

Thus, this entire development comes down to this: In the New Testament, the churches act as entirely free, local churches, linked only through the apostolic bond—churches without finances and buildings, churches that even allow the apostle to work for wages to provide for himself. All of this changes with Constantine the Great. The church must now be one, become rich, and wield power, and to achieve all of that she binds herself to the magisterial government. Rome opposes this and fights for liberty, only to limit that liberty later in an even more constrictive manner. Thus, first the East and later the Reformation falls away from Rome's church, and even in a country that remains entirely Roman Catholic nearly half of the population often becomes disloyal. This breach of Rome's power would have been impossible if the government had not supported the Reformation groups with the force of arms. But the churches of the Reformation paid a high price for this support, in an almost complete loss of freedom. Thus we now have the virtually universal situation throughout Europe where, except for some smaller free churches, the government has gained power over the churches everywhere, placed the churches under its control, and kept the churches in its power through financial dependency, thus making it impossible to maintain the confession and seriously endangering the Christian character of the churches.

RESULTS IN AMERICA   § 30

Over against this European misery the situation of the churches in the United States stands as an eloquent contrast. This is not the case in all of America, since South and Central America are still dominated by Rome. But the United States has achieved the unique situation that there is no national church at all, that the government is involved in no respect with the organization or governance of the church, and that churches of various kinds are established and operate in perfect liberty. These churches receive not a single dollar from the government but are self-sufficient. Finally, through the constitutional system, thanks to the electing of the government by their members, these churches exert an influence on public life and even the life of the state, an influence unconstrained by law. The United States really has Calvinism to thank for this entirely unique state of affairs, and Calvinism owes the honor it receives for its principle exclusively to the fact that in America Calvinism did not have to deal with situations that arose in the past, but was itself able to create both an ecclesiastical life and a political life that corresponded entirely to the impulse of its principle. Both government and church are entirely free in their own realms. The church exerts its influence only on its members, through its members on the press and the public opinion, and then in the nation's elected officials. This is Calvinism's ideal, where it can operate freely. In the Netherlands this was impossible because Hugo Grotius and his followers put it in shackles. This explains why the full flowering of Calvinism's bloom became possible for the first time in the United States.

§ 31   ANABAPTISM

Meanwhile, on the sidelines, entirely separate from the Reformation movement, stood the Anabaptists, from whom the so-called Mennonites later emerged. These Anabaptists were idealists who refused to reckon with reality. They made a principal distinction, which they thought was entirely in line with Holy Scripture, whereby even in politics, the inhabitants of a country who counted as regenerate children of God were distinguished from the others, who still lived exclusively according to their old, sinful nature. For the Anabaptist this latter group was all the same: all these people lived under the influence of diabolical powers and had nothing to do with Christ, and therefore nothing to do with the work of salvation. Their sinful lives made it necessary to have a government to restrain them, but the police, army, and so on were—just as the oath, and ultimately even marriage—nothing but unholy helps for maintaining at least some order in this demonic situation. In contrast, the regenerate, the saints, had nothing to do with the government. They were not touched or harmed by it. They had no dealings with it. All of it had to do with the poison and the antidote of the unholy world, which remained far from the sacred position of the Anabaptist multitude. This is why in Amsterdam some went about naked in public. The custom of clothing was necessary in the sinful world but did not exist in paradise, and since these saints were now spiritually in the state of paradise once again, clothing was useless to them.

Münster[55] experienced the public scenes featuring these benighted folk who had been instigated by John of Leiden. There the bond of marriage was discontinued, which led to a revival of harems. Thus the situation went from one extreme to the other. Ultimately the government had to subdue and remove them with armed force. This was all the more tragic because Anabaptism really arose in a group of very pious and holy people. The blood of the martyrs testifies to the respectable courage of faith with which numerous Anabaptists faced their martyr's death, and even after the suppression of Anabaptism it is apparent, in the much smaller group of Mennonites or Baptists, what interesting elements were unleashed in these Anabaptist groups. Most of them are currently alienated from the faith of their fathers, and Modernism is rampant among them, but even as late as the middle of the eighteenth century they often excelled in piety. Their thinking centered on baptism, as is clear from their name of *Anabaptist*. They took baptism as the external sign of a person's incorporation into the body of Christ, and thus as fruit of regeneration and conversion. According to them, since a child or minor cannot be converted and therefore cannot be regenerated, they taught that no one should receive baptism unless that person first confessed to be a child of God, an elect, a regenerate, a convert, a believer. Their pure Christian component had to be removed from the world, separated from it, and every baptized person was to form a separate group with the other regenerate. This was not to be a church; there was no point in that. For three centuries they had seen the consequences of the so-called church of Rome, and now also that of Calvin. So they did not call themselves *church*, but always *society*: the Mennonites in the Netherlands still call themselves the Anabaptist Society.

Now you can imagine the serious difficulty these "faithful" had to face. They felt offended that the sacraments, both baptism and communion, were commonly administered to thousands and ten thousands who were not living a holy life, confessed no faith, let alone experienced any

---

55. In 1534–35, the city of Münster, Germany, was controlled by radical Anabaptists led by John of Leiden (1509–36).

powerful regeneration. All of this evil arose from infant baptism. Children, who knew nothing, who could not yet stammer a single word, had been recognized through baptism as belonging to the body of the Lord. When the children grew up it sadly became clear how people had been deceiving themselves. The result was an ecclesiastical situation in which believers and hypocrites, intermingled in a large mass of people, lived together in the so-called church of Christ. The Anabaptist wanted no part of this. This could not be acceptable before God. The problem was not just the sacraments, but rather the all-important question whether a baptized person, before his or her baptism with water, had been baptized with the Holy Spirit. This position seemed to be on much firmer ground. This would put an end to the intermingling of people. Only genuine believers would have fellowship together and realize the body of Christ. The rest would fall back into the world. The Anabaptists had no further dealings with the unholiness of that world. They held no office in the government, they swore no oath, they carried no sword. All this belonged to the unholy life of the world, and the child of God most decisively withdrew from it, across the entire range of life.

But soon it became clear that whereas this idea seemed to be beautiful and holy, there was no certainty that there would be a corresponding result. If only it were possible to determine whether regeneration had truly taken place; if only it could be proven and determined whether your confession that God had made you his child was indeed a spiritual reality; surely, then one had achieved the best that could be attained on earth. The boundary between believers and unbelievers would then be visible for everybody. Mistakes could no longer be made. Baptism would be administered only to God's true children. No Judas would be able to infiltrate the sacred societies. But this turned out to be impossible. First the Anabaptists imagined they could accomplish this, and they took it very seriously. They had a very strict selection procedure, and without a doubt they succeeded at first to unite only regenerate believers in their groups. But soon it became clear that self-deception was possible, and through self-deception came the spiritual deception of others. There was a growing realization that spiritual selection among people can always be mistaken. And when ultimately the sacred principle developed into carnal abominations, they finally realized their dream to be a meaningless fantasy, and the entire foundation on which the Anabaptist building was resting collapsed.

But the very same events also provided the justification for the model the Calvinists had developed for the organization of the church. There was the so-called worldwide church of Rome, commending itself with the claim that it has consistently maintained the universal bond with the other churches, and rejected any government authority over the church. But it went wrong in its separation of clergy and laity, in its destruction of the local freedom of churches, and in its pretense of political authority. Second, there were the churches under caesaropapism, without any freedom, in the Greek Orthodox Church and Lutheran groups. Then there was the collegial system, which denaturalized the church of Christ and reduced it to a pious society. There was the Anabaptist system of those who withdrew from the world and who thought they had the right to decide who are the saints. Alongside and over against these five systems Calvinism erected its system, based not on a regeneration that cannot possibly be determined externally, but on holy baptism, and maintaining its holy character through admonition and discipline among these baptized members. The Anabaptists wanted the *pure* church, but the Calvinists realized that it was impossible to make an infallible spiritual selection.

CALVINIST DISCIPLINE §32

But the Calvinist refused with equal determination to accept a church that was not purged through discipline. With only nominal discipline you get, once again, a blending of church and world, and this is bound to result in the demise of the true church. The church in America maintains itself only with the unrelenting demand that it implement its own discipline, and only in this way can the church begin to revive in the Netherlands. However, among the members of the Reformed Church[56] people continue to bump up against what has been handed down to us from the past, and the question arises repeatedly regarding what position should be taken concerning the buildings, finances, and salaries. The free churches consistently give this answer: If the choice is between faithfulness to Christ and to Mammon, do not hesitate for a moment. You will be provided for. Many times this has proven true, and in Scotland, England, as well as in the Netherlands and Germany, various free churches have been able to survive. But it would be incorrect to assume that the majority of the people can easily be convinced to accept this system. This is dependent on the

---

56. The Dutch Reformed Church, also called the *volkskerk*, the dominant Protestant church in the Netherlands in the nineteenth century, from which Kuyper seceded.

degree of their faith and their temperament. It is equally dependent on the offense presented by unbelief. If one's faith is too weak, one's temperament is too melancholic, and the offenses one faces are not severe enough, then one may get used to it all, withdraw into mysticism, and adapt. So then let no one place too quickly upon others the requirement under which one weakens oneself.

We must keep in mind, of course, that with very few exceptions the followers of Erasmus in the sixteenth century returned to Rome; conversely, if we are zealous for the purity of the church, we must learn the holy art of waiting patiently. Even in times of indifference there is always a hidden force for changing the circumstances, which in retrospect is often surprising. The most important thing for us is to sharpen our own insight concerning the relationship of state and church, and that we bring clarity to the insight of those who are confused. If the choice is between a church leadership forced on us by the government and the clear demand of God's Word, then every believer must learn that he may not acquiesce before the word of a secularized church, but must be obedient to God. If he sees clearly that it is precisely the finances and salaries that cause spiritual decay, then he may not be content that, because of the country's constitution, this unholy yoke remains on the church of Christ. He must seek solutions to remove the connection between the spiritual church and this material support. You should never be offended if not everyone follows your example exactly.

There are no fixed rules here that could be applied with great precision while keeping an eye open for all the various circumstances. The circumstances are vastly different, and the consequences of these circumstances often even more so. Do not be the judge of one another in this matter, but let our King be the judge of each in his own conscience. Let your zeal be unrelenting against one evil only: the evil of passive complicity when God's word is being violated. In short, to acquiesce to something your conscience has earlier condemned—to fall asleep on the pillow of indifference—is from the Evil One. State and church must not merely lie alongside each other, but must live together in the right relationship. Yet your motivation must come from two sides simultaneously: on the one hand, the motivation to keep your church free from the state; and on the other hand, as members of Christ's church to influence the state and its government. Calvinism is both a postulate for the church and a postulate for the life of the state. Calvinism is Christian, so that it might remain faithful to Christ, and democratic, so that Christianity might influence the life of the state. No system can compete with Calvinism in terms of its effective functioning for both church and state.

ADDRESS ON MISSIONS

TEXT INTRODUCTION

The nineteenth century saw intense interest in missional activity. Kuyper presented his address on missions in Amsterdam at a missions conference held January 28–30, 1890. The conference was a meeting of the recently formed Nether-German Reformed churches, which had seceded from the Dutch Reformed Church under Kuyper's leadership. Talks had begun about the possible union with the Christian Reformed Church of the 1834 secession. It is remarkable that missions would receive so much interest at a time of ecclesiastical upheaval.

From the broader perspective of nineteenth-century Protestant missions, at least two things are striking about Kuyper's address. First, Protestant missions activity in the nineteenth century was carried out mainly by voluntary societies. Kuyper, however, insists that missions is the work of God through the church. Second, the civilizing imperative was very strong among missionaries, and one might expect just that from a culture warrior like Kuyper. Yet for Kuyper, civil and social reform are the least important aims of missions. Kuyper addresses two main subjects with regard to mission: the work of God in missions, and the work of the church. Missions is foremost a work of God in his Trinitarian life. It is the sending of the Son by the Father, and the Spirit by the Father and the Son, to reconcile alienated humanity; the missionary is God's instrument in this work.

Although we do not have the very words of Kuyper himself, the proceedings were recorded in extensive minutes, which were published in a synodical report. Kuyper's theses are presented here with minor omissions, and his commentary and responses have been abridged. The text of Kuyper's address was reissued in 1940 with an introduction by J. H. Bavinck (1895-1964), who was a nephew of Herman Bavinck and had been a missionary in the Dutch East Indies. In his introduction Bavinck stated his disagreement with Kuyper's segregation of law and gospel (Theses 14 and 15) and his rather optimistic view of Islam (Thesis 16), but he praised him for emphasizing, as early as 1890, that churches must be "planted" and that missions was the task of the Christian church, not missionary societies.

Source: *Historisch Document. Referaat van wijlen Professor Dr. A. Kuyper over Zending, uitgesproken op het Zendingscongres te Amsterdam, op 28, 29 en 30 Januari 1890*. Utrecht: J. Bootsma, 1940. Translated and annotated by Harry Van Dyke.

ADDRESS ON MISSIONS

THESES 1-8

The first group of eight theses dealt with doctrinal propositions that focused on determining the relationship between missions and the eternal Being.

1. All missional activity proceeds from the sovereignty of God; is based on the creation of human beings in the image of God; is necessitated by sin; and is grounded on the confession that the Holy Spirit proceeds not only from the Father but also from the Son.

2. All missional activity by human beings is just a shadow, a reflection, or an instrument in the service of the one fundamental mission—that of the Son by the Father.

3. The mission of the angels, whose very name is that of messengers or missionaries, is the main purpose of their existence as far as our human race is concerned.

4. The mission of Moses and the prophets was the substitutionary means employed by the Son before his incarnation to carry out his own missional task during the dispensation of shadows.

5. The incarnation was the coming of the Son into the world in order to carry out in person the first phase of his mission.

6. The mission of the Gospel writers and the apostles, unlike that of the prophets, was not substitutionary but rather instrumental in the hands of Christ. It was different from all later mission activity in that it concerned the church of all times and places.

7. Holy Scripture is the enduring revelation of the mission of Christ and his charge or command to the world.

8. Throughout the ages Christ exercises his mission in local churches through his ministers of the Word. This mission is directed to all who are baptized and are thus members of the covenant of grace.

COMMENTARY

Following the presentation of these eight theses Kuyper gave a commentary.

Regarding Thesis 1, Kuyper stressed that mission does not flow from God's love or mercy, but higher—from his sovereignty. Foundationally, mission activity is obedience to God's command; its message is not an invitation, but a command. The Lord does not recommend or exhort, but commands: "Repent and believe!" This is shown formally in Jeremiah 14:14, where it is written that God did not send the false prophets and did not "command them or speak to them." It is shown materially in that he punishes those who will not "obey his voice." The New Testament speaks repeatedly of obedience of faith (Rom 1:5; 16:26; see also Acts 6:7), of obedience to the truth (1 Pet 1:22; see also Rom 6:17), and of obedience to the gospel (2 Thess 1:8). The comprehensive standpoint for missions is indicated in Psalm 119: "Your commandment is exceedingly broad" (Psa 119:96). The whole will of God for his creatures is contained in a series of testimonies that consist of commandments and ordinances of an obligatory nature.

Missions assumes sin—alienation. God pursues sinners who have alienated themselves from him. He does not pursue plants and animals; in nature he gives effect to his ordinances without mediation. But human beings are his offspring. They bear his image, and God pursues people's consciousness and wills. Thus, missions is based on the creation of humanity after God's image.

Missions is grounded in the confession that the Holy Spirit proceeds not only from the Father but also from the Son. The work of the Holy Spirit is not only bound to the counsel of the Father but also to the mediation of the Son and thus to the Word. Because the Father works through the Spirit of the Son, there is room for missions through the church. The *filioque* clause is rejected by many mystics. Accordingly, they have no eye or heart for missions: the Greek Orthodox Church does very little in missions; it suffers from fanaticism and fosters nihilism.

In summary, missions delivers a command, is directed to the fallen image-bearer of God, and is based on the confession that the work of the Spirit is bound to the Word.

Regarding Thesis 2: missions is related not only to the divine Being but also to the Mediator. Christ emphasizes that he is sent by—that he is the missionary of—the Father. Many people place Christ next to the prophets and apostles. However, the latter are subordinate to the One sent by the Father. Cocceius taught that the Old Testament did not have Christ, the gospel was not proclaimed until Matthew, and the Son did not become Mediator until he took on our flesh.[1] We believe instead that the Mediator became active right after the fall and that this was part of God's eternal plan. However, before his incarnation Christ used prophets and shadows. Pagans seek to know God through witchcraft and sorcery, but God tells the church to listen to Moses (Deut 18:10-15). God himself echoed this at Jesus' baptism and on the mount of transfiguration. An ambassador must be able to represent his Sender, and for us that can be only the Son of the Father.

Regarding Thesis 3: angels too are sent out. They are ministering spirits for the sake of those who stand to inherit salvation. In the book of Revelation, ministers of the Word are likewise called angels of the churches.

Regarding Thesis 4: the Son carried out his mission during the Old Testament by means of shadows. Abraham saw his day and was glad (John 8:56). "In all their affliction he was afflicted" (Isa 63:9). From time to time Christ appeared in the form of a human being or an angel. The contrast between Melchizedek and Aaron marks the difference between the shadowy and provisional priesthood and the priesthood that was real and permanent. All missionary activity in the Old Testament was a shadow and representation of Christ's mission as prophet, priest, and king.

Regarding Thesis 5: when he personally assumed our flesh, Christ put aside his representatives and carried out his office directly. This first stage of the Son's official work ended with his ascension. The second stage will commence with his return.

---

1. Johannes Cocceius (1603–69) taught theology in Leiden and became well-known for his views concerning the progressive dispensations of the covenant of grace, known as federal theology.

Regarding Thesis 6: between his ascension and his return, Christ works by means of instruments. Office-bearers in the church do not possess the substitutionary nature of the Old Testament prophets and priests. The church has no vicars of Christ, *pace* Rome! Christ himself ascended to heaven in our flesh, and it is from there that he executes his office. Apostles, evangelists, and pastors are only instruments in his hands. The four Gospel writers and the twelve apostles are distinguished from all other office-bearers in that they even now are also our evangelists and apostles. Their ministry applies to the church of all times and places. They could say to all generations: we declare to you what we have heard and seen with our own eyes, "so that you too may have fellowship with us; and indeed our fellowship is with the Father and with his Son Jesus Christ" (1 John 1:3).

Regarding Thesis 7: Holy Scripture has a unique role in the work of missions. It is the Word of God in time-honored language of the people. Everything around Scripture changes; the Word abides. All proclamation of Christ's charge to the world is administration of the Word.

Regarding Thesis 8: Those who administer the Word in the churches of the Son are likewise missionaries. They work among the baptized. Pastors share with them membership in the household of faith. Their preaching should not distinguish between believers, seekers, and unbelievers. In church the minister preaches to the baptized. No matter how far they may have strayed, they must never be put on a par with unbelievers. Missional work inside the church is premised on baptism, whereas missions among Jews, Muslims, and pagans is done with baptism in view.

RESPONSE

No one asked for the floor during the scheduled discussion period.

THESES 9–17

Kuyper proceeded after a brief intermission to present his second group of theses, which focused on missions among the unbaptized.

9. Christ carries out his mission among Jews, Muslims, and pagans through his churches. He seeks out those whom the Father has given him through election and incorporates them into the covenant of grace through baptism.

10. Every attempt by churches to promote missions among the Jews, Muslims, and pagans is Pharisaical if it serves only as a cloak for hiding their neglect to conduct missions among the baptized.

11. Christ's mission entails a charge or command to which every person who is reached must submit. It consists in bringing the Word of the King, by his ambassador, who represents Christ himself.

12. Whenever Christ uses human beings in his missionary effort, he empowers them with his own authority, so that whoever rejects the missionary also rejects Christ, and whoever receives the missionary receives Christ.

13. Missions among the Jews, Muslims, and pagans has to be carried out through the churches, just as missionary work among the baptized is to be performed by the ministers of the Word. Any other form of proclaiming the gospel among Jews, Muslims, and pagans is not missions but is similar to the efforts of a non-ordained evangelist who addresses his fellow human being on his own initiative.

14. All missions among Jews, Muslims, or pagans starts with the law and then with the message of the gospel.

15. Missions among Jews should not aim at making a convert of an individual person (in which case there would be no need for a separate mission to Israel) but rather should strike at the core of the rabbinical system. Armed with sound knowledge, one has to enter this difficult terrain and seek to rebuke the pride of the Jews with the law; once this pride is broken, one may heal the wounds with the gospel.

16. Similarly, missions among Muslims should not be confined to individuals but rather should deal with Islam itself. It has to connect with Islam's anti-pagan efforts as well as with the true elements that still remain in Islam's confession of Moses and the Christ. It has to attack the teachings of Muhammad and the Qur'an that have overgrown these good elements like choking weeds. It should rebuke the Muslim's sensuality draped in piety, and restore the law and gospel in its fullness and purity, thus replacing the essence of Islam with the Christian religion.

17. Missions among pagans has four objectives. First, to reject their idols. Then, to bring the idolaters to the sacrament of baptism, so that they can be a manifestation of the church of Christ among their people. Next, to link this manifestation of the church with the mother church. And finally, to replace the pagan way of life with a Christian lifestyle.

COMMENTARY

Kuyper's commentary ran approximately as follows.

Regarding Thesis 9: missions should never be severed from the ministry of the Word. Rome thinks that all spiritual treasures are found within the Church; therefore Rome conducts missions only to those outside the Church. Our forefathers always spoke not just of missions but of expanding and planting the church. That is correct. The church needs to be brought to the people. The way missions is conducted at the present time is not correct. It betrays the time of its birth: the French Revolution. People were fascinated in those days with "man in the state of nature," who was believed to be innocent, happy, and unspoiled. Christian people had pity on these ignorant people. As a counterweight to the coffee houses and clubs of those days that were organized for popular enlightenment, Christians set up "societies" to spread the gospel among unbelievers and bring them the message of peace. But this way of conducting missions by the various missionary societies was not scriptural and actually quite revolutionary. That these societies were nevertheless effective was due to the fact that they included many outstanding Christian leaders whose devotion and sacrifice flowed into those available channels. But when the church revived, the question arose: How shall we correct the practice of conducting missions?[2]

First, it has to be clearly kept in mind that Christ is the Missionary. He is carrying out his mission. The missionary societies place the emphasis on the person of the missionary. Let's take care not to idolize missionaries and missionary families. It should never be that humanity comes first, and in its train, God the Lord. Unless God comes first, with his electing love, no missionary efforts can be blessed. Every notion of a missionary as a hunter who catches souls for Christ must be banned. The missionary is sent by Christ and follows him, seeking his elect. Let's stop talking about "leading people to Christ" and "saving souls for Jesus." We cannot save people, not even our own children. Only Christ is able to draw people to the faith. Away with the leaven of Pelagianism! The work of Christ alone should remain.

The goal of missions should be holy baptism, and thereby incorporate the convert into the covenant of grace (in the external sense).

---

2. Kuyper is referring to the general restoration and revival of European Christianity in the early part of the nineteenth century.

Regarding Thesis 10: the main motivating force behind missions must be obedience—obedience without dissembling. To ignore the baptized in our own churches who live ignorantly like unbelievers among us, and then to compensate for this neglect by mission activity among the unbelievers abroad is the rankest Pharisaism that Christ will denounce.

Regarding Thesis 11: missions carries with it a burden, a command of the Lord—a burden for the unbeliever as a human being. As a creation of God, the unbeliever too is to honor God and come to repentance. In the person of his ambassador the Lord himself comes and claims the unbeliver as his inheritance.

Regarding Thesis 12: missionaries have authority. They are not salesmen whose wares can be turned down. They come with the authority of Christ. "As the Father has sent me, even so I am sending you" [John 20:21]!

Regarding Thesis 13: it seems necessary from time to time to recall what the Heidelberg Catechism says about the keys of the kingdom.[3] They have been given to the ministers of the Word, who have authority in the house of God—the burden of commanding repentance. An *oefenaar* tells what the Lord has done to his soul, and as a brother among the brothers he can speak words of exhortation and encouragement.[4] The relationship between such an *oefenaar* and an ordained minister of the Word is comparable to that between the society missionary and the ordained missionary. The brothers of the Secession have come to see this too. And it is a healthy sign that the brothers of the Dutch Reformed Missionary Society stand ready to disband their organization.

Regarding Thesis 14: the gospel has to be brought to the Jew, the Muslim, and the pagan. But the natural heart lacks a channel for receiving the gospel; it has to be carved out by the law. The missionary must first get unbelievers to repent, feel crushed, fall to their knees. The missionary must start with God's justice before bringing the unbeliever to the gospel.

Regarding Thesis 15: missionary activity has to be attuned to its audience. Missions among the Jews bears a special character and can be undertaken only in large cities, such as here in Amsterdam. A Jewish butcher here or there in the country can be approached by the local church; there is no need for a special missionary to be brought down from Amsterdam.

---

3. See Heidelberg Catechism, Lord's Day 31.

4. An *oefenaar* was a non-ordained person with special spiritual gifts who was authorized to preach lay sermons, teach catechism classes, visit the sick, conduct prayer meetings, and so on.

As Christians we have no room for hatred toward Jews, but neither do we nurse favoritism toward them. The antithesis stands: Christ versus the Jews.

The sin of the Jews is their pride, their self-exaltation. Jews have to be told that they destroyed the law; they falsified the original revelation in the law and cut off its spiritual roots by supplanting it with their own precepts. Hence they could not understand the nature of the law as a type, and Christ became for them foolishness and an abomination. This is pride!

The sabbatarianism among us is a Jewish byproduct.

Most people who proselytized among the Jews did not really know their audience. We can distinguish three groups of Jews: modern Jews (virtual pagans); orthodox Jews; and a small group of rabbinic Jews. This last group is the most dangerous. We must show them the falsehood of their presuppositions and the untenability of their basic premise. We must bring them the law again, in its spiritual, vital essence, which Christ delivered on Mount Sinai and explained during his sojourn on earth. That will break their pride and carve a channel for the gospel. Again, first and foremost should be the glory of God!

Regarding Thesis 16: the sin of Islam is its sensuality. We have to acknowledge and honor the line by which Muslims are linked to Abraham. Ishmael was born of Abraham and circumcised by him. Christ saved Ishmael's life by showing his mother the well. The world-historical mission of Islam is to be a bulwark against paganism. Their main error is to posit a revelation that is higher than Scripture (a hallmark of the Mormons as well). A Muslim from Sumatra assured a colonial official: "I don't reject your Jesus," and then went on to praise Jesus and the Christ in finer words than the official had expected. What then is it about Islam that dishonors God? Christ preaches a spiritual life as being against a sensual life. Islam emphasizes a life of pleasures and delights, under the delusion that this can be combined with the glory of Christ's return. This also helps explain why Islam believes it has a calling to convert all nations—with the sword! Christian missions is to counter this sensuality with the law of the spiritual life.

Regarding Thesis 17: idol worship is the cardinal sin of the pagan. The idols are a provocation of the Almighty. In medieval times our missionaries destroyed the images and cut down the sacred oaks. Those were great deeds, with great consequences! Today's missionaries are not to use force, yet they know that the point is to topple the idols. Furthermore, the church has to come to manifestation and pagan society has to be transformed through better views of marriage and family.

RESPONSE

Several brothers participated in the discussion that followed.

One brother objected to the rather favorable view and diagnosis of Islam. Experience shows that Islam is the most difficult enemy of the Christian missionary.

Another objected to the view that the missionary movement in England and Scotland was based on unscriptural and revolutionary ideas. Carey, Fuller, Ryland, and others from the very beginning based their activity on Holy Scripture and the Lord's command to preach the gospel to every creature. These men, as well as the great Church Missionary Society and the pioneer missionaries of the Scottish churches, were church people. They desired to bring the gospel to the pagans and Muslims not out of some sort of altruism or to improve their culture and general well-being, but rather in obedience to the command of the Lord to plant his church. In their work, the Bible was the foundation and rule. This was also the opinion of Hardcastle, Bogue, Eyre Love, and the other founders of the London Missionary Society, even though they did not adopt church-sponsored missions. These men had nothing to do with revolutionary ideas. And regarding the Dutch Missionary Society, if it were abolished and the work taken over by the church, it would constitute a fruitful evolution and a real fulfillment of the Society's original objective.

The question was raised whether the word "represents" in Thesis 11 did not contradict what was stated in Thesis 6.

Another respondent pointed out that the *oefenaar* and the society missionary also have authority because they come with God's Word and the call to believe.

Still another wondered whether baptism by society missionaries should be acknowledged even though they are not ordained.

To give the lecturer some rest,[5] Professor Rutgers responded to some of the questions and comments.[6] He began by saying that Dr. Kuyper did not call Islam a bridge to Christianity but a retaining wall against paganism. Rutgers believed that opposition to the Christian faith was stronger among

---

5. Kuyper was still recuperating from a bout with the flu.
6. F. L. Rutgers (1836–1917) taught church law and church polity at the Free University of Amsterdam.

Muslims than among pagans, and stronger again among Jews. The rule seemed to be that an error is more difficult to overcome if it contains some elements of truth. On the issue of baptism by private persons rather than by ordained ministers, Rutgers argued at length that while sometimes things are done that are not wise and should not be recommended, it nevertheless should not be ruled out as invalid. In the Christian church baptism is not declared invalid when it is administered by a person who has no official qualifications.

After thanking Professor Rutgers for his willingness to answer questions, Kuyper resumed his role. He said he wished to distinguish two types of authority: sovereign and moral—that is, authority of the speaker and authority of the Word. An *oefenaar* speaks with moral authority. As regards a possible contradiction between Thesis 6 and Thesis 11, Kuyper admitted that he had not felt completely happy about the wording. He had used the word "represents" in Thesis 11 in a broader sense, and suggested it should be read as follows: missions is "bringing the Word of the King through his ambassador, in whom the King himself comes." As for the British missionary societies, Kuyper acknowledged the participation in them of ardent Christians; yet in structure and language the societies were more or less revolutionary, such as in their infatuation with man in the state of nature, the noble savage.

The morning session was concluded with prayer.

THESES 18–22

In the afternoon Dr. Kuyper presented his next group of five theses.

18. Missions among pagans and Muslims, when preaching law and gospel, must be attuned to the distinctive character of the people, particularly the special nature of their idol worship. Complete freedom should be allowed as to the manner in which faith in Christ is confessed, so that when these people are ready to form their own churches their distinctiveness will be preserved.

19. Churches must not select their areas of missional activities randomly but should focus on those peoples with whom historical circumstances have brought them into contact. When selecting a mission field they must avoid all clashes with other churches and preferably cooperate with other churches in allocating the mission fields.

20. The right and duty to engage in missions rest with the local church. Because of the limited strength of individual churches, it is advisable that several churches cooperate for the purpose, using the existing ecclesiastical bodies rather than a separate organization.

21. Missionaries must be trained in a way that is not inferior to that of other ministers of the Word. Their course of study should provide them with full knowledge of the idol worship, the social situation, and the language of the people to whom they will be sent.

22. It is desirable that missionaries are sent out two by two.

COMMENTARY

Kuyper's commentary was approximately as follows.

Regarding Thesis 18: What should be the aim of missions? To establish a daughter church? Or simply to bring the Lord's command and leave it to his leading to discover suitable forms? The fathers of Dort wanted to Christianize the unbelieving nations by having children on the mission field memorize the Heidelberg Catechism, the Lord's Prayer, the Ten Commandments, and the Apostles' Creed, and then baptizing them. After this a church could be organized, strictly according to the model of the sending church. Rome even goes one step further: it establishes Catholic churches among the unbelievers, complete with services in Latin. But we plead for variation in how people confess their faith and conduct their worship. The Bible does not lay down specific guidelines for many of these things. While upholding certain principles, therefore, it is desirable to maintain as much variety as possible in terms of a people's cultural level, social conditions, and ethnic character.

Regarding Thesis 19: much effort and money has been wasted because of dissension among churches. I do not belong to those who underestimate the net results of missions, but I fear the numbers would be disappointing. I have observed this during visits to Protestant missions in Belgium and France. Seven different Catholic orders run mission organizations, and it has happened that some rascals, for monetary gain, became converts under each of these organizations and so also entered the statistics seven times. Not enough has been done to allocate the fields of labor profitably.

Regarding Thesis 20: in contrast to the Congregationalists, we send the missionaries out from the local church. From this cell as the local church, the worldwide church might expand again. Common issues can be dealt with by a group of local churches. No separate organization needs to be set up and then attached to the church.

Regarding Thesis 21: we have to send our best equipped people to the mission field. As the priests in medieval times looked up to a Boniface, so we should esteem our missionaries. Training as a catechism teacher, along with a smattering of a foreign language and some ethnography, is not enough. A genuine missionary, as understood at this Conference, needs much more. Instead of giving him a modest education of lesser quality, he should receive a superior education.

Regarding Thesis 22: the Lord sent out his messengers in pairs. There is much to be said for this.

RESPONSE

The above explanatory commentary was again followed by a time of discussion.

One brother asked: How are we to divide the mission field with Rome? Or must we regard the work of Rome not as Christian missions in accordance with God's Word?

Another brother agreed with the speaker's claim that out of the local church the worldwide church could once again see growth. Yet he would urge that congregations carry out their mission efforts through the broader assemblies of the denomination. These bodies are better suited to recruit the best candidates for missions. He moved that Thesis 20 be rewritten, as follows: "The right and duty to engage in missions rest with each local church. Because it concerns a common interest, and because of a local church's small size and limited resources, cooperation with other churches should be a goal, if not a requirement." This amendment was duly seconded.

Another brother warmly affirmed Thesis 21. Missionaries need the best education possible. For example, doctors in theology of the Free University who have received their degree with the highest honors and who also receive two years of additional specialized education should be the kind selected for the mission field. But should it be limited to them? Is there room for people with singular gifts who feel called to mission work at a more advanced age, or for people who for whatever reason were not able to receive an appropriate university education? The answer should be yes. Therefore he proposed to add to the wording of Thesis 21: "*As a rule*, missionaries should ... and so on." Finally, this brother related that at the great London Conference many authorities complained strongly about the waste of money and effort on the mission fields and urged that mission fields be properly divided.

Kuyper replied by suggesting that the question about Catholic missions be treated at a future conference; it would require another set of theses to deal with this issue. The amendment to Thesis 20 he accepted, provided it incorporated as a friendly amendment the words: "common calling" instead of "common interest."

THESES 23–27
At this point the lecturer developed his last group of five theses.

23. A missionary among Jews or pagans holds an office not unlike that of an evangelist and can as such administer the sacrament of holy baptism, though not that of holy communion. The latter can be administered only after a church has been instituted and arrangements have been made in this church for preaching the Word and administering the sacraments.

24. Once a missionary has baptized a number of converts and organized a church, he has become the minister of the Word in that church and is no longer a missionary. His preaching of law and gospel and his administration of baptism among the unconverted are done by him not as a missionary sent by the mother church but as a minister of the new local church.

25. If these newly established churches are not yet able to support themselves completely, the mother churches can support them on a temporary basis, but the former missionary should not be paid by the mother church.

26. Missionaries in the proper sense of the word continue to be the responsibility of the sending church.

27. Since missionaries may soon have to function as ministers of the Word in a new church if their labors are successful, they ought to be examined and declared eligible for call prior to being sent out. This invests them with the authority to preach among a designated people, to incorporate any converts into the covenant of grace by baptism, and to gather the baptized into churches.

Commentary

Kuyper commented somewhat as follows.

Regarding Thesis 23: a missionary who speaks with authority must hold an office. But which office? It is the office of minister. Apart from Mark and Luke, Scripture mentions evangelists who were called to preach the gospel from place to place. Although our missionaries are not on a par with the evangelists who worked alongside the apostles, nevertheless I would prefer to call them evangelists because to call them missionaries would create the mistaken impression that regular ministers of the Word are not missionaries. The task of the evangelist ceases with baptism, and his place of work is not tied to a certain location.

Regarding Thesis 24: when a church has been formed in, say, the East Indies, and that church still stays under its missionary, it denies its character as church. Once a church has been established, that church carries the missionary, not the other way around.

Regarding Thesis 25: needy churches, like those in the East Indies, may be supported by the churches in Europe, but there should be no other tie that might influence the way the needy churches operate. That would be hierarchy.[7]

Regarding Thesis 26: it is desirable that less attention be paid to the financial arrangements and fewer inquiries be made whether salaries are secure. The missionary should say: I do not ask; and the sending church should say: we will take care and pay!

Regarding Thesis 27: it is very important that the authority of the missionary is clearly spelled out in the letter of call.

Response

In the discussion of these last theses, opinions were divided whether a missionary lacks authority to administer holy communion. The "servants who gather churches" mentioned in Article 7c of the Church Order of Dort (1619) were not missionaries sent to unbaptized people but ministers who gathered the baptized that were scattered abroad. Thus ministers and evangelists hold distinct offices.

Professor Rutgers also took issue with the preference for calling a missionary an evangelist. In the New Testament evangelists had a different task than today's missionaries. Christ himself called the evangelists, while

---

7. The *Doleantie* or "aggrieved" churches, of which Kuyper was a leader, were sworn enemies of a hierarchical church structure.

today the churches call the missionaries. It is not advisable to differenti-
ate too strongly the various duties or authorities between ministers and
missionaries, also because newly created churches should not be left to
fend for themselves too soon.

Another brother agreed with the speaker that churches have to take
care of their missionaries. It is wrong to expect them to be tentmakers.
The sending church should make sure that its missionary does not have
to worry about his daily bread and any other financial needs connected
with his work. It has happened too often that missionaries went hungry!
A missionary should not be paid a salary or an honorarium but sufficient
subsidy to cover his needs. Missionaries who think otherwise should not
be sent out, or if they are already en route, should be recalled.

At the conclusion, the chairman thanked the speaker for his important
work. Since it was already late afternoon, it was decided to postpone the
next scheduled lecture until the following morning. The meeting was concluded with a prayer of thanksgiving.

BIBLIOGRAPHY

À Marck, Johannes. *Christianae theologiae medulla didactico-elenctica, ex majori opere, secundum ejus, capita, et paragraphos, expressa.* Amsterdam: G. Borstius, 1696.

———. *Compendium theologiae christianae didactico-elencticum.* Amsterdam: Wetstenios, 1722.

Aalders, M. J. "De Wet op de Kerkgenootschappen van 10 september 1853." In *Om de toekomst van het Protestantse Nederland: de gevolgen van de grondwetsherziening van 1848 voor kerk, staat en maatschappij.* Edited by G. J. Schutte and J. Vree. Zoetermeer: Meinema, 1998.

Algemeen Reglement voor de Hervormde Kerk van het Koningrijk der Nederlanden. The Hague: H.C. Susan, C.Hz., 1852.

Alting, Heinrich. *Scriptorum theologicorum.* 2 vols. Amsterdam: J. Janssonius, 1646.

Bass, Diana Butler. *Christianity after Religion: The End of the Church and the Birth of a New Spiritual Awakening.* New York: HarperOne, 2012.

Bavinck, Herman. *Holy Spirit, Church, and New Creation.* Vol. 4 of *Reformed Dogmatics.* Translated by John Vriend. Edited by John Bolt. Grand Rapids: Baker Academic, 2008.

Berg, C. H. W. van den. "De ontstaangeschiedenis van de Doleantie te Amsterdam." In *De Doleantie van 1886 en haar geschiedenis.* Edited by W. Bakker, et al. Kampen: Kok, 1986.

———. "Kuyper en de kerk." In *Abraham Kuyper: zijn volksdeel, zijn invloed.* Edited by Cornelius Augustijn, J. H. Prins, and H. E. S. Woldring. Delft: Meinema, 1987.

Berger, Peter. "Secularization Falsified." *First Things*, February 2008. http://www.firstthings.com/article/2008/02/002-secularization-falsified.

———. *The Heretical Imperative: Contemporary Possibilities of Religious Affirmation.* Garden City, NY: Anchor, 1979.

Beza, Theodore. *De haereticis a civili magistratu puniendis libellus*. Geneva: R. Estienne, 1554.

Bolger, Ryan K., ed. *The Gospel after Christendom: New Voices, New Cultures, New Expressions*. Grand Rapids: Baker Academic, 2012.

Book of Praise: Anglo-Genevan Psalter. Winnipeg: Premier, 2014.

Bos, David J. *In dienst van het koninkrijk: beroepsontwikkeling van hervormde predikanten in negentiende-eeuws Nederland*. Amsterdam: Bakker, 1999.

———. *Servants of the Kingdom: Professionalization among Ministers of the Nineteenth-Century Netherlands Reformed Church*. Leiden: Brill, 2010.

Burke, Edmund. "Substance of Mr. Burke's Speech in the Debate on the Army Estimates . . . Comprehending a Discussion of the Present Situation of Affairs in France." In *The Works of the Right Honourable Edmund Burke: With a portrait, and life of the author*, vol. 5. London: T. McLean, 1823.

Calvin, John. *Commentaries on the Four Last Books of Moses*. Translated by C. W. Bingham. 4 vols. Grand Rapids: Eerdmans, 1950.

———. *Defensio orthodoxae fidei de sacra Trinitate, contra prodigiosos errores Michaelis Serueti Hispani: vbi ostenditur haereticos iure Gladii coercendos esse*. Geneva: R. Estienne, 1554.

———. *Institutes of the Christian Religion* (1559). Edited by John T. McNeill. Translated by Ford Lewis Battles. 2 vols. Philadelphia: Westminster, 1960.

———. *Opera omnia*. 9 vols. Amsterdam: J. J. Schipper, 1671–67.

Cole, Neil. *Organic Church: Growing Faith where Life Happens*. San Francisco: Jossey-Bass, 2005

Cox, Harvey. *The Future of Faith*. New York: HarperOne, 2009

Dareste, F. R. *Les constitutions modernes*. 3rd ed. 2 vols. Paris: A. Challamel, 1910.

Dennison, James T., Jr., ed. *Reformed Confessions of the 16th and 17th Centuries in English Translation: 1523–1693*. 4 vols. Grand Rapids: Reformation Heritage Books, 2008–2014.

Diemont, Abrahamus. *Disquisitionem de Ecclesia Christiana e Christi Mente*. Groningen: J. B. Wolters, 1844.

Douthat, Ross. *Bad Religion: How We Became a Nation of Heretics*. New York: Free Press, 2012.

Eijnatten, Joris van, and Fred van Lieburg, *Nederlandse Religiegeschiedenis*. Hilversum: Verloren, 2005.

Eusebius. *Life of Constantine*. Edited by Averil Cameron and Stuart G. Hall. New York: Oxford University Press, 1999.

Gibbs, Eddy, and Ryan K. Bolger. *Emerging Churches: Creating Christian Community in Postmodern Cultures*. Grand Rapids: Baker Academic, 2005.

Giddens, Anthony. *The Constitution of Society: Outline of the Theory of Structuration*. Cambridge: Polity Press, 1984.

Gierke, Otto von. *The Development of Political Theory*. Translated by Bernard Freyd. New York: Howard Fertig, 1966.

———. *Johannes Althusius und die Entwicklung der naturrechtlichen Staatstheorien*. 2nd ed. Breslau: Marcus, 1902.

Haight, Roger. *Christian Community in History: Historical Ecclesiology*. 3 vols. New York: Continuum, 2004.

Harinck, George, and Lodewijk Winkeler. "De Negentiende Eeuw." In *Handboek Nederlandse Kerkgeschiedenis*. Edited by Herman J. Selderhuis. Kampen: Kok, 2006.

———. "The Nineteenth Century." In *Handbook of Dutch Church History*. Edited by Herman J. Selderhuis. Gottingen: Vandenhoeck & Ruprecht, 2015.

Hauerwas, Stanley. *After Christendom? How the Church Is to Behave if Freedom, Justice, and a Christian Nation Are Bad Ideas*. Nashville: Abingdon, 1991.

Historisch Document. Referaat van wijlen Professor Dr. A. Kuyper over Zending, uitgesproken op het Zendingscongres te Amsterdam, op 28, 29 en 30 Januari 1890. Utrecht: J. Bootsma, 1940.

Hofstede de Groot, Petrus. *Pauli conversio, praecipuus theologiae Paulinae fons*. Groningen, 1855.

Hough, Franklin B. *American Constitutions*. 2 vols. Albany: Weed, Parsons & Company, 1872.

Hunter, James Davison. *To Change the World: The Irony, Tragedy, and Possibility of Christianity in the Late Modern World*. New York: Oxford University Press, 2010.

Junius, Franciscus. *De Politiae Mosis Observatione*. In *Opuscula Theologia Selecta*, edited by Abraham Kuyper, 329–392. Amsterdam: Muller, 1882.

———. *The Mosaic Polity*. Translated by Todd M. Rester. Edited by Andrew M. McGinnis. Grand Rapids: CLP Academic, 2015.

Kuyper, Abraham. *Bekeert U, want het Koninkrijk Gods is nabij!: leerrede op den laatsten dag van 1871 gehouden*. Amsterdam: De Hoogh, 1872.

———. "Calvinism: Source and Stronghold of Our Constitutional Liberties." In *Abraham Kuyper: A Centennial Reader*, edited by James D. Bratt, 279–322. Grand Rapids: Eerdmans, 1998.

———. *Common Grace*. Translated by Nelson D. Kloosterman and Ed M. van der Maas. Edited by Jordan J. Ballor and Stephen J. Grabill. 3 vols. Bellingham, WA: Lexham Press, 2016–.

———. "Confidentially." In *Abraham Kuyper: A Centennial Reader*, edited by James D. Bratt, 45–61. Grand Rapids: Eerdmans, 1998.

———. *Confidentie: schrijven aan den weled. Heer J. H. van der Linden*. Amsterdam: Höveker & Zoon, 1873.

———. "Conservatism and Orthodoxy: False and True Preservation." In *Abraham Kuyper: A Centennial Reader*, edited by James D. Bratt, 65-85. Grand Rapids: Eerdmans, 1998.

———. "De Doopskwestie." *De Heraut*, October 7, 1870.

———. "De menschwording Gods: het levensbeginsel der kerk (1867)." In *Predicatiën, in de jaren 1867 tot 1873, tijdens zijn predikantschap in het Nederlandsch Hervormde Kerkgenootschap, gehouden te Beesd, te Utrecht, en te Amsterdam*. Kampen: Kok, 1913.

———. *De overheid: Locus de Magistratu*. Kampen: Kok, 1901.

———. "De Sleutelen." In *Uit het Woord. stichtelijke Bijbelstudiën*. Amsterdam: J. A. Wormser, 1896.

———. *"Geworteld en gegrond." De Kerk als organisme en instituut. Intreêrede, uitgesproken in de Nieuwe Kerk te Amsterdam, 10 Augustus 1870*. Amsterdam: H. de Hoogh & Co., 1870.

———. "It Shall Not Be So among You." In *Abraham Kuyper: A Centennial Reader*, edited by James D. Bratt, 125-42. Grand Rapids: Eerdmans, 1998.

———. *Lectures on Calvinism: Six Lectures Delivered at Princeton University Under Auspices of the L. P. Stone Foundation*. Grand Rapids: Eerdmans, 1931.

———. *Our Program: A Christian Political Manifesto*. Edited and translated by Harry Van Dyke. Bellingham, WA: Lexham Press, 2015.

———. *Pro Rege: Living under Christ's Kingship*. Edited by John Kok with Nelson D. Kloosterman. Translated by Albert Gootjes. 3 vols. Bellingham, WA: Lexham Press, 2016-.

———. "Staat en Kerk." In *Antirevolutionaire Staatkunde met nadere toelichting op Ons program*, vol. 1, 417-86. Kampen: J. H. Kok, 1916.

———. *Tractaat van de reformatie der kerken, aan de zonen der Reformatie hier te lande op Luthers vierde eeuwfeest aangeboden*. Amsterdam: Höveker & Zoon, 1884.

———. *Tweeërlei vaderland, ter inleiding van de zevende jaarvergadering der Vrije Universiteit*. Amsterdam: J. A. Wormser, 1887.

———. "Uniformity: The Curse of Modern Life." In *Abraham Kuyper: A Centennial Reader*, edited by James D. Bratt, 19-44. Grand Rapids: Eerdmans, 1998.

———. "Zondagsafdeeling XXI." In *E Voto Dordraceno. Toelichting op den Heidelbergschen Catechismus*, vol. 2, 108-58. Amsterdam: Höveker & Wormser, 1905.

Leithart, Peter J. *Defending Constantine: The Twilight of an Empire and the Dawn of Christendom*. Downers Grove, IL: IVP Academic, 2010.

Lightfoot, J. B., and J. R. Harmer, eds. *The Apostolic Fathers: English Translations*. Revised by Michael W. Holmes. 2nd ed. Grand Rapids: Baker, 1999.

"The Liturgy of the Reformed Dutch Church." In *The Constitution of the Reformed Dutch Church of North America*. Philadelphia: G. W. Mentz & Son, 1840.

Locke, John. *A Letter Concerning Toleration and Other Writings*. Edited by Mark Goldie. Indianapolis: Liberty Fund, 2010.

Lovelace, Richard F. *Dynamics of Spiritual Life: An Evangelical Theology of Renewal*. Downers Grove, IL: InterVarsity Press, 1979.

Luther, Martin. "Sermon on Mt. 9:8-26 (1526)." In *D. Martin Luthers Werke*. Weimar: Böhlaus, 1925.

Maresius, Samuel. *Collegium theologicum: sive systema breve universae theologiae*. Groningen: Nicolaus, 1649.

———. *Foederatum Belgium orthodoxum; sive Confessionis ecclesiarum Belgicarum exegesis*. Groningen: J. Nicolaus, 1652.

McLeod, Hugh. *Secularization in Western Europe, 1848-1914*. New York: St. Martin's, 2000.

Moor, Bernhardinus de. *Commentarius perpetuus in Johannis Marckii Compendium theologiae christianae didactico-elencticum*. 7 vols. Leiden: J. Hasebroek & J. H. van Damme, 1771.

Morse, John T. *Thomas Jefferson*. Boston: Houghton Mifflin, 1883.

Mosse, George L. *The Culture of Western Europe: The Nineteenth and Twentieth Centuries*. 3rd ed. Boulder: Westview Press, 1988.

Mouw, Richard J. *Abraham Kuyper: A Short and Personal Introduction*. Grand Rapids: Eerdmans, 2011.

Murray, Stuart. *The Naked Anabaptist: The Bare Essentials of a Radical Faith*. Scottdale, PA: Herald Press, 2010.

———. *Post-Christendom*. Carlisle: Paternoster, 2004.

Opzoomer, C. W. *Aanspraak bij de Opening van de 85ste Algemeene Vergadering der Maatschappij*. Amsterdam: Spin, 1870.

Posener, Paul. *Die Staatsverfassungen des Erdballs*. Charlottenburg: Fichtner, 1909.

Quick, John, ed. *Synodicon in Gallia Reformata*. 2 vols. London: T. Parkhurst and J. Robinson, 1692.

Rivet, André. *Praelectiones in cap. xx Exodi. In quibus ita explicatur Decalogus*. In *Operum theologicorum*, vol. 1. Rotterdam: A. Leers, 1651.

Roth, John D., ed. *Constantine Revisited: Leithart, Yoder, and the Constantinian Debate*. Eugene, OR: Pickwick, 2013.

Schaff, Philip. *Church and State in the United States; or, The American Idea of Religious Liberty and Its Practical Effects*. New York: Charles Scribner's Sons, 1888.

Schans, A. A. van der. *Kuyper en Kersten: ijveraars voor herkerstening van onze samenleving*. Leiden: J. J. Groen, 1992.

Schilder, Klass. *De Kerk*. 2 vols. Goes: Oosterbaan & Le Cointre, 1960-1962.

Schutte, G. J. *Het Calvinistisch Nederland: Mythe en Werkelijkheid*. Hilversum: Verloren, 2000.

Segers, Mary C., and Ted G. Jelen. *A Wall of Separation? Debating the Public Role of Religion.* Lanham, MD: Rowman & Littlefield, 1998.

Skillen, James W. Introduction to *The Problem of Poverty*, by Abraham Kuyper. Sioux Center, IA: Dordt College Press, 2011.

Skillen, James W., and Rockne M. McCarthy. *Political Order and the Plural Structure of Society.* Atlanta: Scholars Press, 1991.

Smith, James K. A. *Desiring the Kingdom: Worship, Worldview, and Cultural Formation.* Grand Rapids: Baker Academic, 2009.

Spanheim, Frédéric, Jr. *Vindiciarum biblicarum.* 2 parts. Frankfurt: A. Wyngaerden, 1663.

Trapman, J. "Allard Pierson en zijn afscheid van de kerk." *Documentatieblad voor de Nederlandse Kerkgeschiedenis na 1800* 19 (1996): 15-27.

Trimp, C. "De kerk bij A. Kuyper en K. Schilder." In *De Kerk: Wezen, weg en werk van de kerk naar reformatorische opvatting.* Edited by W. van 't Spijker, et al. Kampen: De Groot Goudriaan, 1990.

Troeltsch, Ernst. *The Social Teaching of the Christian Churches.* Translated by Olive Wyon. 2 vols. Louisville: Westminster John Knox, 1992.

Turretin, Francis. *Institutes of Elenctic Theology.* Edited by James T. Dennison Jr. Translated by George Musgrave Giger. Phillipsburg, NJ: P&R Publishing, 1992-1997.

—————. *Institutio Theologiae Elencticae.* Geneva: S. de Tournes, 1690.

Velzen, Cornelius van. *Institutiones theologiae practicae.* 2 vols. Groningen: J. Bolt & J. a Velzen, 1748.

Vermigli, Peter Martyr. *Loci communes.* Zurich: C. Froschouerus, 1580.

Voetius, Gisbertus. *Politicae ecclesiasticae.* Amsterdam: Waesberge, 1663.

—————. *Selectarum disputationum theologicarum.* 4 vols. Utrecht: J. à Waesberge, 1648-67.

Von Volst, H. *The Constitutional and Political History of the United States.* 8 vols. Chicago: Callaghan, 1881-92.

—————. *Verfassung und Demokratie der Vereinigten Staaten von Amerika.* 8 vols. Düsseldorf: Julius Buddeus, 1873.

Vree, Jasper. *Kuyper in de kiem: de precalvinistische periode van Abraham Kuyper, 1848-1874.* Hilversum: Verloren, 2006.

—————. "More Pierson and Mesmer, and Less Pietje Baltus: Kuyper's Ideas on Church, State, and Culture During the First Years of His Ministry (1863-1866)." In *Kuyper Reconsidered: Aspects of His Life and Work.* Edited by Cornelis van der Kooi and Jan de Bruijn. Amsterdam: VU Uitgeverij, 1999.

Vree, Jasper, and Johan Zwaan, eds. *Abraham Kuyper's* Commentatio *(1860): The Young Kuyper about Calvin, a Lasco, and the Church.* 2 vols. Leiden: Brill, 2005.

Walaeus, Antonius. *De munere ministrorum ecclesiae: et inspectione magistratus circa illud.* In *Opera omnia*, vol. 2. Leiden: F. Hackius, 1663.

Weingarten, Hermann. *Die Revolutionskirchen Englands: Ein Beitrag zur inneren Geschichte der englischen Kirche und der Reformation.* Leipzig: Breitkopf & Härtel, 1868.

Welch, Claude. *Protestant Thought in the Nineteenth Century.* 2 vols. New Haven: Yale University Press, 1972–85.

White, Philip L. "Globalization and the Mythology of the 'Nation State.'" In *Global History: Interactions Between the Universal and the Local*, edited by A. G. Hopkins, 257–84. New York: Palgrave Macmillan, 2006.

Wilson, Jonathan R. *Living Faithfully in a Fragmented World: From* After Virtue *to a New Monasticism.* Eugene, OR: Cascade, 2010.

Witsius, Herman, and Johannes van der Waeyen. *Ernstige betuiginge der Gereformeerde Kercke aen hare afdwalende kinderen, meest voorgestelt met de woorden van de outste en voornaemste leeraers, dienende tot wederlegginge van de gronden van sr. Jean de Labadie en de sijne.* Amsterdam: J. van Someren, 1679.

Wood, John Halsey, Jr. *Going Dutch in the Modern Age: Abraham Kuyper's Struggle for a Free Church in the Nineteenth-Century Netherlands.* New York: Oxford University Press, 2013.

Yoder, John Howard. *The Politics of Jesus: Vicit Agnus Noster.* 2nd ed. Grand Rapids: Eerdmans, 1994.

Zwaan, Johan. "Sociale bewogenheid in een jeugdwerk van Abraham Kuyper." In *Een vrije universiteitsbibliotheek: studies over verleden, bezit en heden van de Bibliotheek der Vrije Universiteit.* Edited by Johannes Stellingwerf. Assen: Van Gorcum, 1980.

Zwingli, Ulrich. *Christianae fidei a Huldrico Zuinglio praedicatae brevis et clara exposition.* In *Huldrici Zuingli Opera*, vol. 4. Edited by M. Schuler and I. Schulthess. Zurich: F. Schulthess, 1841.

APPENDIX

DETAILED TABLE
OF CONTENTS

GENERAL EDITORS' INTRODUCTION vii

EDITOR'S INTRODUCTION xi

TWO ECCLESIOLOGICAL QUESTIONS   HISTORICAL CONTEXT   KUYPER'S
ECCLESIOLOGY   CONCLUSION

VOLUME INTRODUCTION xxv

OVERVIEW   A TWOFOLD FATHERLAND   KUYPER IN NEW CONTEXTS
KUYPER'S UNIQUE ECCLESIOLOGY   KUYPER AND CONTEMPORARY
ECCLESIOLOGY

ABBREVIATIONS xxxviii

COMMENTATIO 1

Text Introduction

OVERVIEW   § 1 Introduction   § 2 The Plan of the Argument

THE VIEWS OF JOHN CALVIN AND JOHANNES À LASCO JUDGED ACCORDING TO
THE NORM OF THE GOSPEL

§ 164 Introduction   § 166 On the Notion of the Church According to the Mind of
the Gospel, or, on the Basis for Judgment   § 167 The Path Through the Course of
Ages that the Dogma Concerning the Church has Traveled

PART I – WHICH IS PREPARATORY. ON THE DOGMAS RELATING TO THE
CHURCH, AND ON THE ORIGIN OF THE CHURCH

CHAPTER 1 – DOGMAS CONCERNING THE CHURCH   § 169 The Dogma
Concerning the Invisible and Visible Church

PART II – THE CHURCH CONSIDERED IN ITSELF

SECTION 1 – ON THE NOTION OF THE CHURCH   § 172 *The Character of the Church*   § 173 *The Bond of the Church*

SECTION 2 – ON THE MEANS OF THE CHURCH   CHAPTER 1 – ON THOSE MEANS THAT THE CHURCH USES   § 182 *Ecclesiastical Property*

SECTION 3 – THE ORGANISM OF THE CHURCH   CHAPTER 1 – THE BELIEVERS OR MEMBERS OF THE CHURCH THEMSELVES   § 188 *Who and What Sort They Are*   CHAPTER 2 – ECCLESIASTICAL RULE § 196 *The Duties of Those Who Lead the Church*

PART III – THE CHURCH'S RELATIONSHIP TO OTHER THINGS

SECTION 2 – THE CHURCH'S RELATIONSHIP TO WORLDLY THINGS § 205 *The Church's Relationship to the State*   § 206 *The Church's Relationship to Those Who are Alongside It*   § 207 *Conclusion of the Third Part*

ROOTED AND GROUNDED 41

Text Introduction

PART I   PART II

TRACT ON THE REFORMATION OF THE CHURCHES 75

Text Introduction

PREFACE

INTRODUCTION

CHAPTER 1 – GENERAL PRINCIPLES   § 1 *What the Reformation of the Churches Presupposes*   § 2 *How the Right Form of the Church Can be Known* § 3 *The Four Ways in Which Christ's Church Must be Understood*   § 4 *Why the One Church on Earth is Both Invisible and Visible*   § 5 *How God's Word Governs the Entire Life of the Church*   § 6 *How the Ministry of the Word was Different in the Past Than It is Now*   § 7 *Why the Church Did Not Need Its Own Organization in the Past but Now Does Need It*   § 8 *With Whom Does the Church's Sovereign Authority Originate?*   § 9 *How Jesus Became King of His Church*   § 10 *How This Kingly Authority of Christ Works on Earth Through the Instrumental Use of Human Persons*   § 11 *How the Office in Christ's Church Functions Under the New Covenant*   § 12 *How the Holy Spirit Unites the Earthly Office with the Heavenly Messianic Office of King Jesus*

CHAPTER 2 – THE RIGHT FORMATION OF THE CHURCH   § 13 *How the Formation of a Church is Brought About*   § 14 *What Constitutes the Essence of an Established Church*   § 15 *How the Churches are Divided and Yet One* § 16 *Whether More Than One Church Can be Established in the Same Town* § 17 *How an Established Church Acquires Continuity*   § 18 *Where Authority Resides in the Visible Church*   § 19 *What Systems of Church Government Have Been Tried?*   § 20 *The Components of the Authority Exercised in Christ's*

Church   § 21 *How This Ecclesiastical Authority Relates to the Authority of the Government*   § 22 *What is Required of the Ministers of the Word* § 23 *The Position That Elders Ought to Have in the Church*   § 24 *What Should be Maintained Regarding the Doctors of the Church*   § 25 *The Task of the Deacons in the Church of Christ*   § 26 *What Kind of Office Belongs to All Believers in the Church of Christ?*   § 27 *Concerning the Material Possessions of the Churches* § 28 *By Which Assembly is the Church Governed?*   § 29 *The Administration of the Means of Grace*   § 30 *The Exercise of Church Discipline*   § 31 *The Worship Service*   § 32 *How a Church Enters into Relationship with Other Churches* § 33 *Should the Churches be Involved in Non-Ecclesiastical Matters?* § 34 *The Calling of the Churches with Respect to the Schools*

Chapter 3 – The Deformation of the Churches   § 35 *What is Meant by Deformation of the Churches?*   § 36 *Incomplete Church Formations*   § 37 *The Causes That Explain the Deformation of the Churches*   § 38 *How Deformation Usually Erupts in God's Church*   § 39 *Three Deviations from This Rule that Should be Noted*   § 40 *Deformation in the Members*   § 41 *Deformation in the Office-Bearers*   § 42 *The Deformation in the Confession*   § 43 *Deformation in the Administration of the Means of Grace* § 44 *The Deformation of Church Discipline*   § 45 *Deformation in the Work of Love and Mercy*   § 46 *Deformation in Worship*   § 47 *Deformation in Church Government*   § 48 *Deformation Due to Parasites on the Ecclesiastical Trunk, or the Sects*   § 49 *How Deformation Eventually Turns the Church into a Pseudo-Church*   § 50 *How the False Church Arises*

Chapter 4 – The Reformation of the Churches   § 51 *What Should be Understood by the Reformation of the Churches*   § 52 *All Good Reformation Has God as its Author*   § 53 *Reformation Through Spiritual Revival* § 54 *Reformation Through Gradual Church Renewal*   § 55 *Reformation Through a Break with What Exists*   § 56 *Reformation Through a Break with the Existing Church Organization*   § 57 *Reformation Through a Break with the Existing Church Federation*   § 58 *Reformation Through a Break with the Existing Church*   § 59 *The Distinction Between the True and False Church*   § 60 *Zechariah's Call: "Not by Might, Nor by Power, but by My Spirit!"—Reformation and Legitimacy*   § 61 *Reformation Contrasted with Revolution*   § 62 *Reformation and the Government*   § 63 *The Reformations that have Occurred and Their Various Characters*   § 64 *The Reformation that Must Currently be Undertaken in the Reformed Churches of the Netherlands* § 65 *Taking Possession of the Higher Church Boards*

TWOFOLD FATHERLAND 281
    Text Introduction
    Part I   Part II   Part III

LORD'S DAY 21 315

> Text Introduction

> FIRST CHAPTER   SECOND CHAPTER   THIRD CHAPTER   FOURTH CHAPTER
> FIFTH CHAPTER   SIXTH CHAPTER   SEVENTH CHAPTER

STATE AND CHURCH 373

> Text Introduction

> § 1 Two Different Starting Points   § 2 The Resurrection   § 3 Anticlericalism
> § 4 Blame on Both Sides. The Worldwide Kingdom   § 5 The Universal Church
> § 6 Roman Catholic   § 7 The Reformation   § 8 Luther   § 9 The Calvinists.
> Early Position.   § 10 Middle Position   § 11 Turning Point: Maurice's Death
> § 12 Visible and Invisible Church   § 13 Local Situation   § 14 Calvinism in America
> § 15 European Emigrants   § 16 Prosperity   § 17 Peace in the Church   § 18 Mutual
> Relationship   § 19 Still a Religious Foundation   § 20 Hamilton and Jefferson
> § 21 The Power of God   § 22 Christian Influence by the People   § 23 Ideal Situation
> § 24 Actual Opposition   § 25 Israel's Example   § 26 Weak Appeal to the Old
> Testament   § 27 Historical Progress   § 28 The Current Situation   § 29 Conclusion
> § 30 Results in America   § 31 Anabaptism   § 32 Calvinist Discipline

ADDRESS ON MISSIONS 439

> Text Introduction

> THESES 1–8   Commentary   Response
> THESES 9–17   Commentary   Response
> THESES 18–22   Commentary   Response
> THESES 23–27   Commentary   Response

BIBLIOGRAPHY 458

APPENDIX: DETAILED TABLE OF CONTENTS 465

ABOUT ABRAHAM KUYPER 469

ABOUT THE CONTRIBUTORS 471

SUBJECT/AUTHOR INDEX 472

SCRIPTURE INDEX... 490

ABOUT ABRAHAM KUYPER (1837–1920)

Abraham Kuyper's life began in the small Dutch village of Maassluis on October 29, 1837. During his first pastorate, he developed a deep devotion to Jesus Christ and a strong commitment to Reformed theology that profoundly influenced his later careers. He labored tirelessly, publishing two newspapers, leading a reform movement out of the state church, founding the Free University of Amsterdam, and serving as prime minister of the Netherlands. He died on November 8, 1920, after relentlessly endeavoring to integrate his faith and life. Kuyper's emphasis on worldview formation has had a transforming influence upon evangelicalism, both through the diaspora of the Dutch Reformed churches, and those they have inspired.

In the mid-nineteenth-century Dutch political arena, the increasing sympathy for the "No God, no master!" dictum of the French Revolution greatly concerned Kuyper. To desire freedom from an oppressive government or heretical religion was one thing, but to eradicate religion from politics as spheres of mutual influence was, for Kuyper, unthinkable. Because man is sinful, he reasoned, a state that derives its power from men cannot avoid the vices of fallen human impulses. True limited government flourishes best when people recognize their sinful condition and acknowledge God's divine authority. In Kuyper's words, "The sovereignty of the state as the power that protects the individual and that defines the mutual relationships among the visible spheres, rises high above them by its right to command and compel. But within these spheres ... another authority rules, an authority that descends directly from God apart from the state. This authority the state does not confer but acknowledges."

ABOUT THE CONTRIBUTORS

Ad de Bruijne (Ph.D., Leiden University) is full professor of Christian ethics and spirituality at the Theological University Kampen, the Netherlands. His main field of research concerns public theology, where he tries to bring the neo-Calvinist tradition into dialogue with contemporary debates and proposals concerning the public calling of church and Christians in a post-Christendom context.

Andrew M. McGinnis (Ph.D., Calvin Theological Seminary) is a research fellow at the Junius Institute. He is the author of *The Son of God Beyond the Flesh: A Historical and Theological Study of the* extra Calvinisticum (Bloomsbury T&T Clark, 2014) and the editor of Franciscus Junius' *The Mosaic Polity* (CLP Academic, 2015). He has written various articles and reviews and has assisted in the compilation of several academic bibliographies.

John Halsey Wood Jr. (Ph.D., Saint Louis University) is an independent scholar from Birmingham, Alabama. His book *Going Dutch in the Modern Age: Abraham Kuyper's Struggle for a Free Church in the Nineteenth-Century Netherlands* (Oxford, 2013) examines the development of Abraham Kuyper's free church ecclesiology.

SUBJECT/AUTHOR INDEX

Abraham, 284-85, 301, 304, 309, 344, 450

Adam, 172, 295, 339, 343

Adolphus, Gustavus, 209

aggrieved churches, 168-69
    secession, 169, 240, 243, 270, 274-75,
        276

Alexander the Great, 289, 322, 324

alms, 32, 142, 151, 160, 187

Alting, Heinrich, 261

American Calvinism, xxx-xxxii, 400,
    401-03, 421, 432. *See also* United States
    of America.

Amsterdam, 212-13, 214, 260, 303, 433
    church of, xix, 43, 156, 223-25, 253,
        273-74, 275
    classis of, 70-73
    Free University, xxi, xxvii, xii, xxix-
        xxx, 283, 287, 454

Anabaptists, xxxv, 94, 353
    baptism, 433-35
    earthly fatherland and, 203-04, 310-11
    government and, 389, 393, 432-33
    Kuyper and, xxix-xxxi, xxxii
    Mennonites, 321, 432, 433
    Reformation and, 249, 321, 348, 421-22

angels, 97, 193, 291-92, 295, 326, 330
    mission, 443, 445

Antichrist, 192, 194, 236

anticlericalism, 381-82, 407

antinominianism, 216, 280

Antiochus Ephiphanes, 301

Anti-Revolutionary Party, 311-12

Antirevolutionary Politics, 375

apostasy, 320-21

Apostles' Creed, 319, 320, 364, 369-70

apostolic church, 31, 55, 172, 260, 420, 443
    bond of church, 23-26
    definition of church, 14-15
    heretics, execution of, 262-63
    local churches, 117, 419-20, 431
    poor and needy, care for, 32-33
    Synod of Jerusalem, 107, 419
    See also early church.

appointments, ecclesiastical, 139, 169

Arminius, Jacobus / Arminianism, 177,
    198, 220-21, 305

army of God, 331
    church metaphor, 62, 324-26, 347-49,
        353-54
    of God, 343-46
    Jesus Christ as Commander, 330-31,
        345, 347
    See also militant church; Salvation
        Army.

Athanasius, 306
Augustine, xvii, 17, 44, 283, 306
authority, 96, 97, 452
   in church, 96, 97–98, 122–25, 133–36
   of the church, 126–27, 133, 135–37,
      350–51
   church, government and, 136–37, 280
   of consistory, 350–51, 356
   discipline, church and, 154–55, 185–86
   of God, sovereign, 97–98, 123–24,
      413–15
   of King over church, 98–101, 123–24,
      134, 155, 185
   of office, 100–01, 133–34, 136
   popular sovereignty, 132
   of Scripture, 85, 91, 124–25
   state, separation of church and,
      137–38, 139

Babel, tower of, 288–89, 291, 293, 313,
   332, 344
balance, 62, 65, 175
   imbalance, 179, 180
baptism, xviii–ix, 14, 86, 154, 160–61
   forgiveness of sins, 366–67, 370–71
   infant, 120, 155, 303, 433–34
   membership, church, 29, 154, 400–01
   missions and, 446, 447, 448–49, 452
   Methodist, 119
   See also sacraments.
Baptists, 401, 404, 433
Bass, Diana Butler, xxiii–xxiv
Bavinck, J. H., 442
Belgic Confession, 211, 293, 307, 312, 369,
   399
   church, definition of, 113, 244, 362
   elders and deacons, 102, 147
   government and, 391, 392–93, 423–24
   heretics, execution of, 261–63, 264
   ministry of the Word, 144, 355
   office of all believers, 147–48
   on universal church, 385, 386
Belgium, 312, 382, 398, 407, 409
Berger, Peter, xiin5
Beza, Theodore, 261
body of Christ, 17–19, 106, 324, 348, 368,
   423
   Head of, 332–33, 344–45

Heidelberg Catechism, 361–62
   invisible church as, 111–12, 361–62
   local church as, 115–16
   mystical, 17, 109, 114, 116
   visible church and, 361–62
body, church as metaphor, xix, 134, 179
   reformation as medical treatment,
      195–96, 205–07, 280, 304–05
body, human, 295–96
Bohemia, Hussites, 269, 270
bond, of the church, 29
   Christ as, 23–26, 49–50
   in gospels, 23–26
   Reformers on, 26–27
breaking with existing church, 81–82,
   216–20
   confession of guilt and, 215–18, 220,
      222–23
   consistory and, 218, 221–23
   individuals, 252–53
   local church, 219–23
   membership revoked, 242–43
   ministers of the Word and, 221–22, 243
   obedience, disobedience and, 216–20,
      223, 240
   obedience, ecclesiastical, 219–22
   temporary, 220–21
breaking with false church, 236–38, 242
   finding true church, 240–41
   motivation for departure, 238–39, 241
breaking with a federation:
   consistory, 226–27, 231–35
   individuals, 227–28, 242–43
   local church, 224–27
   ministers of the Word, 229–30
   officers, 228–30
de Brès, Guido, 306, 400
Brownists, 245
building metaphor for church, 50, 58–59,
   62–63, 224, 235, 323
Burke, Edmund, 411–12
Byzantine Empire, 387, 390–91, 409,
   427–28, 409, 427–29. See also Constantine.

caesaropapism, 132, 394, 413, 428–29, 435
Caesars of Rome, 289, 294, 297, 322
calling ministers, 142

Calvinism / Calvinists, xxxi–xxxii, 306–09
  American, xxx–xxxii, 400, 401–03, 421, 432
  discipline, church, 435–36
  dispensations, 422–23
  Dutch, 307, 391–95, 399–00
  free churches, 435–36
  prophetic isolation, 310–12
  state, church and, 35, 391–92, 400–01, 421–22, 423–25, 436–37
  See also Reformed church.
Calvin, John, 26, 29–31, 33, 39, 37, 105, 273
  doctrine of, 30, 38–39
  Dutch Reformed Church, poisoning of, 8–10
  execution of heretics, 261, 263
  freedom, 41, 390–91, 428
  Geneva and, 129–30, 308, 398
  German Lutherans and, 79–80
  God, church and, 38–39
  gospels, church and, 11–12, 22
  institute, church as, xxxiv, 58
  invisible church, xvii, 17, 20, 395–96
  Kuyper and, xvii–xviii, 3
  Luther, Martin and, 79–80
  Netherlands and, 79–81
  poor and needy, care for, 32–33
  predestination / election, 3, 44, 99
  Reformed Christians and, 79–80
  as reformer, 259–60
  Roman Catholic Church and, 16, 251, 255
  state, church and, 35, 391–92, 420–21
  true church, marks of, 246, 248, 250–52
Catharists, 245, 353
catholic, 318–19, 386–87. See also Roman Catholic Church; universal church; world-wide church.
Christianity, xxix
  in Europe, 400–01, 402–05, 406–07, 418
  governments and, 409–10, 416–17, 429–31, 432
  mystical experience, xxiv, 43
  organizations, xxvi, xxxii–xxxiii, 57

Satan and, 171–72, 287, 302, 313–14, 330–31, 341–42
  See also education, Christian.
church, definition, 16, 88–90, 113–14, 338–39
  apostolic, 14–15
  Belgic Confession, 113, 244, 362
  Greek Orthodox, 15–16, 22
  Reformed, 16, 120
  Roman Catholic, 15–16, 115
churchism and churchlessness, 347–48
civil rights, 122–23, 130, 138
civil religion, xxix, 375
classis, 107, 129, 136, 155–56, 159
  reformation of churches, 277, 278
  renewal, 209–10
  officers, church, 142, 145, 147
clericalism, 182, 209, 381–82, 400–01
Cocceius, Johannes, 445
de Cock, Hendrik, 168n32, 270, 275n91, 302n14, 312n24
collegial government system, 130, 132–33, 279, 430–31, 435
colonialism, 340–41
colony of heaven on earth, xxvii–xxix, xxxv, 323–24, 325–26
Commentatio, xvii, xxxiv
common grace, xxvii–xxviii, 288–90, 375, 413–15
communal guilt, 160, 173
communion of saints, 109–10, 111, 318–19, 362
Communists, 289
Comrie, Alexander, 150
confessional, 367–68, 401
confessions, of the church, 93, 108, 118, 128, 385–86
  deformations of, 178–81, 182–83
  faith and, 29, 30, 309
  heresy and, 108, 135
  orthodoxy, 184, 247
  Santhorst, 305
  unity of, federations and, 158–59, 183, 225–26, 278–79
  Word of God and, 158, 182–83
  See also Apostles' Creed; Belgic Confession.
Confidentially, xx

Congregationalists, 115, 130–31, 453
congregations, 68, 72, 124–26, 397–98
consecrated water, 367–68
consistory, 71–72, 103, 107, 118, 127, 167
    authority, 350–51, 356
    breaking with existing church, 218,
        221–23
    discipline, church, 154, 209–10,
        227–28, 278
    federation reformation, 233–25, 278
    government, church, 151–52
    Lutheran, 128
    material property management,
        150–51
    ministry of the Word, 154, 156, 350–51,
        356
    officers, church, 142, 145, 147
    order, church, 209–10
    reformation of churches, 277–78
    renewal, 209–10
Constantine, xxx, 137, 337–38, 431
    separation of church and state,
        427–28
Constantinian model, xxvi, xxxii, xxxvi
context, xxix–xxxiii
continuity, 119–22
conventicles, 150n24, 338, 400, 407
conversion, 63–64, 119–21, 200–04,
    208–9. *See also* missions.
Coornheert, Dirck, 305
da Costa, Isaac, xii, 70, 311
covenant, 64
    new, 101–04, 124, 173, 320–21, 365–66
    old, 88, 93–94, 422–43
    renewal, 196, 200, 202–03, 205, 207,
        239, 276
Cox, Harvey, xxiii–xxiv
creeds, 182–84
    Apostles', 319, 320, 364, 369–70
    See also confessions, of the church.

Darby, John Nelson / Darbyism, 191,
    320–21
Dathenus, Petrus (Datheen, Peter), 157,
    388, 400
David, king, 96, 247, 259–60
    house of, 113, 266, 286–87, 425–26
deaconesses, 146

deacons / diaconate, 102–04, 128–29, 142,
    152, 162, 277
    apostolic church, 145–46
    elders and, 128–29, 145–46, 152
    material property management,
        150–51
    ministries, 146, 162, 186–87
    requirements, 145–47
deformation of churches, 6–7, 163–64,
    173
    in confession, 178–81, 182–84
    diagnosing, 177–78, 206
    in discipline, church, 174–75, 185–86,
        189, 190, 396
    doctrine and, 175–76
    elders and, 185–86
    false churches, 192–94, 214
    in government, church, 175–76,
        189–90
    grace, means of, 184–85
    heresy and, 175–76, 189, 190
    individual sin and, 172–73
    members and, 176–77, 178–81
    process of, 174–76
    pseudo-churches, 191–92
    punishment / judgement of God, 208,
        215–16, 239, 241, 255
    reformation and, 90–91, 272
    sacraments, 184–85
    Satan and, 170–73, 192–94
    by sects, 190–91
    shepherds / ministers of the Word
        and, 175–76, 181–82, 184–85, 186
    sin and, 172–73, 174–76
    in worship, 175, 188–89
Denmark, 269, 409
denominations, 20, 155, 323, 454
Diemont, Abrahamus, 14–15
discipline, church, 114, 121, 128, 135–36,
    273
    authority, 154–55, 185–86
    Calvinism, 435–36
    consistory and, 154, 209–10, 227–28,
        278
    deformation of churches and, 174–75,
        185–86, 396
    elders, 143–44, 185–86

excommunication, 154–55, 210, 228–29, 242–43
grace, means of, 154–55
individuals, 227–28
ministers of the Word, 207–09, 210–11
ministry of the Word, 351–52, 353
renewal and, 206–07, 209–11
sacraments and, 154, 155
synods, 209–10
true church, as mark of, 243–44, 247–48, 251
disestablishment, xii–xiv
dissension, dogmatic, 36, 72–73
divisions, of churches, 114–16, 117–18, 163
doctors of the church, 144–45
doctrine, 130, 183, 321–22
of Calvin, John, 30, 38–39
decline of, xx–xxi, 3–7
deformation of churches and, 175–76
of Kuyper, xxvi–xxvii, xxxii–xxxiii
of ministers of the Word, 141, 144
orthodox, 6, 26
Reformed, 79, 105
renewal and, 205, 210–11
Doetinchem, 164–65
Doleantie (secession church), xxii, 283, 302n14, 407, 456n7
Donatism, 55, 91, 163, 170, 352
true church and, 245–47, 248
Dort, Canons of, 211
Dort Church Order, 144, 453
Dort, Reformation and, 199
Dort, Synod of, xvii, 3, 8, 159, 194, 388, 399
Remonstrants, 214
world-wide, 115, 129, 385, 386
Douthat, Ross, xxiv
Dutch Reformed Church (NHK), xx–xxi, xix, 58, 77, 128, 271, 338
assemblies, 277–78, 280
collegial government system, 132, 278–79
false churches, 273–74, 276
false church federation, 273–74, 278
government, state and, 278–79, 393–95, 424–25
Kuyper and, xv, xviii–xix, 48
members, 275–76

officers, 276–77
pluralism, xviii–xix
poisoning of, 8–10
reformation, 272–73, 275–79
seceded churches, 274–75, 276–77, 279

early church, 55, 62–63, 66, 89, 163
deacons, 145–46
individual sin in, 172–73
poor, care for, 32–33
preaching, 149–50
visible and invisible, 90–91
See also apostolic church.
earth, church on, 89–90, 91–92
Christ as King over, 98–99
earthly fatherland, xxvii–xxx, xxxii, 283, 304–05
Anabaptists, 203–04, 310–11
heavenly and, 284–85, 301–02, 307
nations, 288–90, 291
prophetic isolation, Calvinistic, 310–12
sovereignty of God over, 306–07
world and, 295–97
Easter, 379, 381
education, 303, 305, 411
church and, 161–62
education, Christian, 119, 153, 120
catechism, 153, 160, 351
of ministers and missionaries, 141–42, 454
seminaries, 145, 158, 162, 177
Sunday school, 148–49
elders, ruling, 33, 143–44, 152, 277
deacons and, 128–29, 145–46, 152
deformation of churches, 185–86
ministry of Word, 103–04
teaching, 102–03, 131, 153
elders, teaching, 102–03, 143, 152–53
election, eternal, 120–21, 344–45, 369
church rooted in, 54, 130
God's sovereign, 129, 344–45
humanism and, 44–45
predestination and, 3, 44, 99
England, 176–77, 205, 260, 301, 340, 407
Calvinists / Presbyterians, 309, 401, 403–04
Church of, 390, 394, 408, 429
under Cromwell, Oliver, 411

under Edward VI, 176, 308
free churches, 435
under Henry VIII, 429
missionary movement, 451, 452
Oxford movement, xvii–xviii, 188, 430
equality, 14, 218, 258, 403
of church officers, 103–04, 107, 143–44, 152
Erasmus, 3, 8, 299, 305, 436
Erastus, Thomas / Erastians, 126–28, 130, 430–31
eschatology, xxxi–xxxii, 53, 324–26, 344, 380–81, 423
essence, of church, 111–14, 116, 248–49
authority, 123–24
false church, 249–50
local church, 116, 253–54
potential, 113–14
well-being and, 247–49, 251–52
eternal life, 379–80
Ethical
Irenical group, xxi
movement, 191
party, 94
theology, xvi
wing, Dutch Reformed Church (NHK), xix
Europe,
Christianity in, 400–01, 402–05, 406–07, 418
governments, Christianity and, 409–10, 429–31
religious conflict in, 337, 406–08
See also individual countries in Europe.
evangelism, 153, 160, 202, 204–05, 351, 356
evangelists, 144, 160, 447, 455–57
evil, unification of, xxviii, xxxv
excommunication, 154–55, 210, 228–29, 242–43

faith, 92–93, 178, 361
confession / profession of, 29, 30, 121–22, 154
confessions and, 29, 30, 309
obedience of, 217–19
fall, the, xxvii–xxviii, 325, 423, 445

false churches, 236–37, 271
breaking with, 237–39, 240–43
deformation and, 192–94, 214
discerning, 237–38, 253–54
Dutch Reformed Church and, 273–74, 276, 278
essence, 249–50
reformation, work of, 238–41, 253–54, 273–74, 321
Roman Catholic Church and, 193–94
true church and, 237–38
family, church as, xix, 13, 20–22
fanatics / enthusiasts, 148, 177, 199, 211
Father, God the, 22, 287, 291, 295
fatherlands, two-fold, 287, 291, 293
fatherland, two-fold, 286–87
conflict between, 287–88, 293–94, 296–97, 298–02
sovereignty of God and, 306–07
See also earthly fatherland; heavenly fatherland.
fathers, 153, 155, 287, 301
federations of churches, 252–53
confessions and, 158–59, 183, 225–26, 278–79
false church, 273–74, 278
order, church, 225–26, 232–33, 234
reformation and, 213–14, 233–25, 278
See also breaking with a federation.
fellowship, church as, 13, 20–22
finances, church, 151, 402–05
alms, 32, 142, 151, 160, 187
government support, 138–39, 278–79, 394–95, 400, 425, 427, 435–36
missions, 455–56, 457
in United States, 402–05, 407–08
forgiveness of sins, 318–19, 364–71
baptism and, 366–67, 370–71
Lutherans, 368, 369, 371
formation, of the church, 85–86, 118, 121
army of God, 343–46
communion of saints, 109–10, 111
continuity and, 119–22
differences by place, 115–16
God and, 109, 110–11
incomplete, 163–70
Israel, church gestation, 87–88, 92, 95–96

Mediator, relationship to, 88–90, 92, 97

ordinances, 99–100

organization, 95–96

Word of God, obedience to, 109–10

world-wide, 86–87, 95, 332, 344

France, 129, 130, 148, 309, 397–98

anticlericalism, 407

collegial system, 430

French Revolution, 132, 289, 298, 395, 410, 411–13, 448

Huguenots, 296, 306, 406

Paris, 212, 296, 395

Reformation, 269–70, 398, 421–22

synod, 194

Franklin, Benjamin, 412

free churches, xxi–xxii, 48–49, 278, 404, 430

Calvinism, 435–36

in United States, 404, 407–08, 408, 413–14, 421

freedom, 66–67, 110, 183

Calvin, John on, 41, 390–91, 428

state, church from, 66–67, 69, 302, 393–95, 403

Free University, xxi, xxvii, xii, xxix–xxx, 283, 287, 454

French Revolution, 132, 289, 298, 395, 410, 448

United States and, 411–13

Gamaliel, 299

Gallio of Achaia, 299

gemeente, kerk and, 396–98

Geneva, 129–30, 212, 214, 308, 395

Calvin, John, and, 129–30, 308, 398

civil councils, 138

Theban legion, 231–32

Gerdesius (Daniel Gerdes), 262

Germany, 7, 260, 340, 382, 403

collegial government system, 132–33

government, church and, 127, 435

idealism, xxxiii–xxxiv

Lutherans, 79–80, 176, 177, 269–70, 401, 429–30

Luther, Martin and, 81–82, 390–91

Münster, 433

Reformed churches, 177, 394–95

Ghent, 398–99

Gierke, Otto, 383

gifts, of the Spirit, 142, 149–50, 362–63

giving, 146, 420. See also deacons / diaconate.

Gnostics, xxiv, 55

God, 85

army of, 343–46

authority, sovereign, 97–98, 123–24, 413–15

deformation of churches and, 208, 215–16, 239, 241, 255

election, sovereignty over, 129, 344–45

formation of churches, 109, 110–11

honor of, 137, 140, 391, 392, 424

missions and, 441, 443–44

obedience to, 216–20, 223–24, 240, 254–56, 260–61

punishment / judgement of churches, 208, 215–16, 239, 241, 255

reformation of churches, 215–16, 239, 241, 255, 277

sovereignty, 114–15, 137, 211

See also Father, God the; kingdom of God; sovereignty of God; Trinity

gospel, 11–14, 17–19, 20–26, 38–39

gospels, church and, 11–12, 16, 22–23, 26–27

government, church, 124–28, 147, 149, 152, 205–07, 430–31

authority, 136–37, 280

Calvin, John, in Geneva, 129–30

collegial system, 130, 132–33, 279, 430–31, 435

Congregationalist system, 130–31

consistorial, 127, 151–52

deformation of churches and, 175–76, 189–90

false, 168–69

Independents system, 130–32

Lutheran system, 126–28, 29

national particularity and, 125–27

officers, 143–44, 147

Reformed system, 128–30, 131–32

Remonstrants, 126–28, 130

Roman Catholic system, 125–26, 127

governments of states, xxxv–xxxvi, xxxvii, 171

Anabaptists and, 389, 393, 432–33
authority, church and, 136–37
Belgic confession and, 391, 392–93,
    423–24
Christianity and, 409–10, 416–17,
    429–31, 432
church, independent from, 128, 135–36
church, relationship to, 34–35, 48,
    308–10, 378–81, 383–87, 388–95
church subservient to, 127–28, 266,
    304–05, 337–38, 377–78, 390–95,
    427–31
church supremacy over, 126, 307,
    386–87, 392
ecclesiastical appointments, 139, 169
financial support of churches, 138–39,
    278–79, 394–95, 400, 425, 427, 435–36
Greek Orthodox Church and, 390–91,
    428, 429–30
heresy, obligation to remove, 139–40,
    261–64
honor of God and, 137, 140, 391, 392,
    424
idolatry, obligation to remove, 139–40,
    261–62, 391–93, 423–42
national churches and, 127–28,
    304–05, 307–08
Old Testament on, 421–22, 423–27
pagans and, 383, 409–10, 414–15, 420
people, influence on, 415–17
Reformed Church and, 391–95, 399–01,
    421–22, 423–25
religion, connection to, 409–13, 414
sovereignty, 137, 309
true church, obligation to, 137–38,
    392–93
See also state, separation of church
    and.
grace, 288, 319
    common, xxvii–xxviii, 288–90, 375,
        413–15
    gifts of, 362–63
    particular, xxviii–xix, 53, 291, 413–14
grace, means of, 112, 120, 129, 152–54, 293
    authority and, 134–36
    deformation of churches, 184–85
    essence of church and, 114, 116

Greek Orthodox Church, 382, 387, 435,
    444
    definition of church, 15–16, 22
    government and, 390–91, 428, 429–30
Groen van Prinsterer, Guillaume, 309,
    311
Groningen theology, 189, 275
Groningen, University of, xvii, 3, 7–8,
    23n24

Hague, The, Synod of, 199, 208
Hamilton, Alexander, 411, 412–13
Hancock, John, 412
Hauerwas, Stanley, xxx
Head of body, Jesus as, 332–33, 344–45
heaven, church and, 89, 98, 163
    colony on earth, xxvii–xxix, xxxv,
        323–24, 325–26
heaven, kingdom of. See kingdom of
    heaven.
heavenly fatherland, xxviii–xxix, 283,
    288, 290–92
    earthly and, 284–85, 301–02, 307
Hebrews cloud of witnesses, 284–85,
    298, 343–44
Hegelian thought, xx, xxiii, xxxiv
Heidelberg Catechism, 211, 317–19, 399
    body of Christ, 361–62
    elders, 143–44
    forgiveness of sins, 364, 369–70
    gifts of grace, 362–63
    ministry of the Word, 351, 449
    organic church, 321–22, 326, 343,
        344–45
    universal church, 385–86
    visible church, 347, 361
The Heir of Redclyffe, xvii–xviii
Heldring, O. G., 311
heresy, 103, 131, 209, 269
    confessions, church and, 108, 135
    deformation of churches and, 175–76,
        189, 190
    governments and, 139–40, 261–64
heretics, execution of, 261–64, 266
Hervormde Church, 435
history, church 8–10, 14–16
Hofstede de Groot, Petrus, 23
holiness, 197, 365–66, 367–68

personal, 245-47
Holy Roman Empire, 383, 387-88
Holy Spirit, 29, 57, 307, 444
    church and, xix , xxiii, 56, 106, 107-08,
      248
    conviction of sin, 208-09, 216-17
    gifts, 142, 149-50, 362-63
    humans, actions upon, 105-06
    membership, church, 28-29
    officers, church, 105-06, 107
    reformation, 196-99, 255-57
    renewal / regeneration, 208-09,
      345-46
    revival, 201, 204
home visiting, 103, 143, 153, 222, 276-77,
    351
Huguenots, 177, 296, 306, 406
Humanism, 44-45, 399
hymnal issue, 156-57
hypocrites, 121, 169, 347, 366-67, 396, 434
    Pharisaism, 173, 179, 80, 223, 234

ideal, 91, 163-64
idealism, xxxiii-xxxiv
idolatry, 251, 268, 290, 344, 450-51, 452-53
    governments and, 139-40, 261-62,
      391-93, 423-42
    heresy and, 139-40
immorality, 65, 272
imperfect / incomplete church forma-
    tions, 164-69
Independents, 115, 130-32, 403, 404
indifference, 178-79, 180
individualism, 64, 317
Indonesia, 192
institution, church, xvii-xviii, xxi-xxii,
    48-49, 54-58, 63
    banks of river metaphor for, 50, 57,
      62-63
    Christian organizations and, xxxvi-
      xxxvii
instrumental use of people, 99-101, 110
invisible church, xxii, 17-20, 116, 358-59,
    368
    as body of Christ, 111-12, 361-62
    Calvin, John and, xvii, 17, 20
    visible and, 90-91, 344, 347
    world-wide, 90-91

Irenics, xxi, 61-62, 128, 305, 385
Irvingianism, 191
Islam, xxxii, 409-10, 414
    missions to Muslims, 446-47, 449-50,
      451-52
Israel, ancient, 96, 265, 331
    as church, 320, 332, 344, 422-23
    church gestation, 87-88, 92, 95-96
    heretics, execution of, 261, 266
    kingdom of God and, 325, 328, 386
    kings of, 113, 266, 286-87, 425-26
    Levite ministry, 328, 364-65
    Mosaic law, 265-66, 307, 425-26
    preaching of Word, 250-51
Italy, 321, 389, 403
    Reformation, 212-13, 270, 309, 388
    Roman Catholic Church and, 306, 409

James, brother of Jesus, 32
Jefferson, Thomas, 411, 412
Jesus Christ, 22, 28-29, 92-93, 104-05,
    117, 294
    army Commander, 330-31, 345, 347
    binding agent, church, 23-26, 49-50
    church and, 13-14, 99-100, 322-32,
      325-26
    Head of body, 332-33, 344-45
    heretics, execution of, 262-63
    Jews and, 236-37
    King of church, 96-98, 100-01, 104,
      190, 332-33, 354
    King of earth, 98-99
    mission of, 443-47, 448-49
    new life in, xxviii-xxix, 24
    poor and needy, care for, 27, 32, 102
    revolution, 259-60
    sacrifice of, 92, 96-97
    Satan, battle with, 339-40, 341-42,
      345, 347
    world-wide focus, 384-85, 396-97
Jews, 236-37
    missions to, 446-47, 449-50, 452, 455
John, apostle, 25-26
John the Baptist, 18, 93, 268, 370
    kingdom of heaven, 28, 324-25
Judaism, 10, 93-94
Junius, Franciscus, 256
jurisdiction, ecclesiastical, 135-36

justice, 55, 186, 189
    schismatic formations, 190-91, 221
justification, 364, 366, 369

Kant, Immanuel, 381
à Kempis, Thomas, 3, 8, 10
Kenau Hasselaars, 289
King over church, Jesus as, 96-98,
    100-01, 104, 190, 332-33, 354
    authority, 98-101, 123-24, 134, 155, 185
kingdom of God, xxvii-xxviii, 357-58
    church and, 58-59, 85-86, 126, 324-26,
        337
    citizens of, 332-33
    Israel and, 325, 328, 386
    restoration of, 330-31, 354
    world-wide, 293-94, 383-84, 384-85
kingdom of heaven, 28, 291-92, 324-25
    invisible church and, 17-19
    Jesus and, 28-29
    keys to, 133, 152, 153, 156, 449
    world and, 294, 380
    See also heavenly fatherland.
Kohlbrugge, Hermann F., 229, 311, 312,
    369

Labadists, 245, 311, 353
à Lasco, John, xvii, xxxiv, 3-6, 35, 37-39,
    388
    Dutch church and, 9-10
    gospels, church and, 11-12, 16, 22-23,
        26-27
    ministry, 32-33, 37
    preaching and worship, 30-31
    visible church, 17, 20, 29, 33
leadership, church, 29-33, 71-72, 168-69.
    See also classis; consistory; deacons;
    elders; government, church; minis-
    ters of the Word; synod.
Ledeboerians, 270-71
Ledeboer, Lambertus, 311, 312
Legitimists, 128
Leiden, John of, 303, 433
Leiden, University of, 177
Liberalism, 382
Libertines, 398
life, xxviii-xxix, 24, 247, 379-80
Lincoln, Abraham, 417

't Lindenhout, Jan van, 311
local church, 115-19, 224-25, 359-60,
    419-20
    apostolic, 117, 419-20, 431
    as body of Christ, 115-16, 117
    breaking with existing church, 219-23
    breaking with federation, 224-27
    essence, 116, 253-54, 275
    missions, 444, 449, 453-54, 456-57
    national church and, 115-16, 128,
        224-25
    number in one area, 117-18
    Reformation and, 116-17, 398-01
    in Reformed government system,
        128-29
    relations with others, 157-58, 183-84
London, 130, 212-13, 214
Lord's Supper / communion, 154, 365,
    367-68, 455, 456
    as life food, 86, 105
    Reformed Church, 121-22
love, 54, 71, 73
Lutheran church, 68, 79-80, 105, 251, 435
    forgiveness of sins, 368, 369, 371
    in Germany, 79-80, 176, 177, 269-70,
        401, 429-30
    government, church, 126-28, 29
    Luther, Martin and, 79-80, 390-91
    as national church, 409, 430
    Reformed Church and, 79-80, 160, 394
Luther, Martin, 61, 264, 390-91
    breaking with church, 81-82, 83, 216
    Calvin, John and, 79-80
    forgiveness of sins, 368, 371
    fourth centenary celebration, 78-82,
        83
    gemeente (congregation), 397-98
    German rulers and, 390-91
    Reformed Christians and, 79-80,
        81-82
    Reformer, role as, 81-82, 259-60

Mammon, worship of, 172, 180, 186
à Marck, Joannes, 244, 262, 391-92, 430
Maresius, Samuel, 261, 396
Marnix, Philip of, 157
Martyr, Peter, 396
martyrs, 93, 171, 286, 296-97, 298, 306

medical treatment, reformation as,
195-96, 205-07, 280, 304-05
membership, church, xii, 28-29, 111, 133
aggrieved, 221-22
baptism and, 29, 154, 400-01
deformation, church and, 176-77,
178-81
Reformed Church, 121-22, 275-76
revoked, 242-43
Mennonites, 321, 432, 433
metaphors for church, xx, 49-50, 336
army, 62, 324-26, 347-49, 353-54
body, xix, 134, 179
building, 50, 58-59, 62-63, 224, 235, 323
family, xix, 13, 20-22
grapevine, 112
medical, 195-96, 205-07, 280, 304-05
mother, xviii, xxxiii, 56-57
river, banks of, 50, 57, 62-63
rooted, 49-50, 62
yeast, 49-50
Methodists, 119-20, 121, 320, 355, 383, 403
Middle Ages / Medieval period, 253, 327,
337, 416
militant church, 327-32, 333-34, 335-37,
352-54
enemy of, 338-42
loss of view, 337-38
See also army.
ministers of the Word, 124-25, 142-43,
145, 153, 156, 182
breaking with existing churches,
221-22, 243
breaking with federation, 229-30
clericalism, 182, 209, 400-01
democratic election of, xxi, 47-48
discipline, church and, 207-09,
210-11, 226
doctrine and, 141, 144
education of, 141-42
missionaries and, 455-56
oefenaar, 449, 451, 452
professionalism, 181-82, 184-85
reformation of churches, 276-77
repentance and conversion, 200-04,
208-09
requirements for, 133, 140-42
revival of churches, 202-01, 202-04

as shepherds, 175-76, 181-82, 184-85,
186
See also pastor-teachers.
ministry of the Word, 92-94, 99, 104,
128, 346-47, 348-49
consistory and, 350-51
elders, 103-04
missions and, 448
preaching, 351, 355-56
visible church and, 93, 346-49, 354-55,
357-60
miracles, 60-61
missionaries, 54, 102, 122, 160, 161, 453,
454-57
ministers of the Word and, 455-56
mission churches, 164-67
missions, 35-37, 160-61, 202, 349, 446
baptism and, 446, 447, 448-49, 452
Christ, mission of, 443-47, 448-49
church and, 446-47, 452-53
conversion without instruction, 63-64
financial support, 455-46, 457
God, sovereignty of, 441, 443-44
to Jews, 446-47, 449-50, 452, 455
local churches and, 444, 449, 453-54,
456-57
minsters of the Word, 448, 449
to Muslims, 446-47, 449-50, 451-52
obedience, act of, 444-45, 449
to pagans, 160-61, 165, 446-47, 449-51,
452-53, 455-56
Reformed Church, 122, 448, 453, 454
Roman Catholic Church, 448, 453, 454
salvation and, 14, 37, 39
Trinity, work of, 444-45
mission societies, 160-61, 448, 449, 451,
452
Moderates, xxx-xxxi, xxxii, 304-05
Modernism, theological, xi-xii, xxi,
60-61, 132, 433
Dutch Reformed Church, xx-xxi, 275
individual focus, xvi, xxiii-xxiv
Möhler, Johann, xvi
Montanism, 94, 352
Moody, Dwight L., 204-05
de Moor, Bernhard, 244, 262, 392
Moses, 96, 266-67, 304, 325, 443, 445
law of, 425, 443

mother, church as, xviii, xxxiii, 56–57
Münster, 433
mystical, xxiv, 3, 43
   body of Christ, 17, 109, 114, 116

Napoleon Bonaparte, xii, 260, 289, 322, 385
national church, 128, 308, 338
   governments and, 127–28, 304–05, 307–08
   Israel as, 332, 344
   local churches and, 115–16, 128, 224–25
   Lutheran churches, 409, 430
   Reformation and, 269, 271
   Scripture and, 332, 334
   state churches, 327, 409–10
   universal church and, 385–86
   See also Dutch Reformed Church (NHK).
nationalities, 288–90
national particularity, church government and, 125–27
nations, earthly. *See* governments of states; states.
Nero, emperor, 125, 137, 264
Netherlands, xii, 289, 309, 410, 435
   Calvin, John and, 79–81
   free churches, 435–36
   pseudo-churches, 192
   Reformation in, 79–80, 177, 223–24, 393–95, 398–01, 421–22
   religious conflicts, 406–07
   Sea Beggars, 259–60, 290
   Spain and, 259–60, 290, 301, 399, 416
   Statenvertaling, 396–98
   William I, xiii, 9n6, 128n16, 278, 338, 394, 400
   See also Dutch Reformed Church (NHK); William III of Orange.
New Testament, 11–12, 329
Nicaea, 199
   Council of, 269
Nicolas I, Pope, xvii
Nihilists / nihilism, 289, 296, 444
Noah, 284, 309, 325, 343–44

obedience, 88, 301–02, 353

breaking with existing church and, 216–20, 223, 240
   ecclesiastical, 219–22
   faith and, 217–19
   to God, 216–20, 223–24, 240, 254–56, 260–61
   to humans, 285–86
   missions as, 444–45, 449
   to Word of God, 109–10, 216–20, 231–32, 234
occasional churches, 166–67
offerings, 32, 142, 151, 160, 187, 349
office, apostolic / ecclesiastical, 101–04, 124–25, 133, 446
   of all believers, 147–50, 203–04, 360
   formation, church and, 110–11
   Holy Spirit and, 105–06, 107
   See also deacons / diaconate; elders; ministers of the Word; pastor-teachers.
Oldenbarnevelt, Johan van, 305
Old Testament, 11, 304, 309
   elect, 422–23
   governments, churches and, 421–22, 423–27
   missions and, 445–46
   Mosaic law, 265–66, 307, 425–26
   reformation in, 265–68
Olevian, Caspar, 364
order, church, 135, 156, 360–61, 391–92
   Dort, 144, 453
   federations and, 225–26, 232–33, 234
   renewal and, 206–08, 209–10, 211–12
ordinances, 99–100, 135
ordination, 95, 143–44, 147, 152, 161
organic church, xix, 317–18, 320, 322–26
   Christ established, 322–23, 325–26
   Heidelberg Catechism on, 321–22, 326, 343, 344–45
organism, church as, xxxii–xxxiv, xxxvii, 54, 66–67, 77, 116
   only as, 48–49, 61–63
   rooted metaphor, 49–50, 62
   yeast metaphor, 49–50
organism and institution, connection, 45–46, 71
   creation as metaphor, 51–54
   humanity as metaphor, 51–52

sin and, 52–54, 60
organism and institution distinction, xvi–xviii, xx–xxiii, xxvi–ii, xxxii–xxxiv
  nurture of, 55–57
  metaphors for, xx, 49–50
  See also organism, church as; institution, church as.
orthodoxy, 44–46, 184, 247
Oxford high church movement, xvii–xviii, 188, 430

pacifist movement, 383
pagans, 166, 389, 427
  fatherland and, 290, 298
  government and, 383, 409–10, 414–15, 420
  missions to, 160–61, 165, 446–47, 449–51, 452–53, 455–56
  religion / paganism, 10, 178, 337, 365, 445
paradise, 287, 290–91, 325, 339–40
Paris, 212, 296, 395
particular grace, xxviii–xix, 53, 291, 413–14
pastor-teachers, 67, 141
  congregations and, 124–25, 125–26
  covenant renewal and, 202–03
  definition, 103–04
  deformation of churches and, 175–76, 181–82, 186
  as shepherds, 141, 154, 175–76, 181–82, 184–85, 186
Paul, apostle, 30, 32, 246, 352
  body of Christ, 17–19, 25
  on church, 18, 21–22, 49, 419–20
  on enemies of church, 329–30, 338–40
  heretics, execution of, 262–63
people of the Lord, 331–33, 353–54
persecution, 100, 132, 302, 398
  churches under, 167–68
  Roman Empire, 168, 235
  Satan and, 171–72
Peter, apostle, 22, 25, 352
Pharisaism, 173, 179, 180, 223, 234
Philip II of Spain, 137, 260, 296, 301
Pierson, Allard, xviii, xx, xxiii
Pierson, Hendrik, 311

pilgrims, 335–36
Pilgrims, American, 301, 308, 401, 403–04
pluralism, religious, xiv–xv, xxxiv–xxxvi
Poland, 129, 130, 212–13, 270, 309
political rights, 122–23, 130
poor and needy, care for, 27–28, 32–33, 69, 160
  deacons, 146, 186–87
possessions, material, of the church, 150–51
post-institutional church, xxvi, xxxvi–xxxvii
prayer, 188, 193, 411
preaching of the Word, 13–14, 30–31, 36, 100, 161, 336
  early church, 149–50
  in Israel, 250–51
  as mark of true church, 243–44, 247, 250–52, 253
  ministry of the Word, 349, 351, 355–56
  lay, 149–50
  renewal and, 206–07
  repentance, calls for, 204–05
  topical, 141, 184
Precisionists, 406–07
Presbyterians, 401, 403–04, 421
priesthood, 95, 98, 367–68
  Levite ministry, 328, 364–65
professors, 103, 145
property, church, 27–28, 31–33
Prussia, 331
Psalms, singing, 156–57
pseudo-churches, 191–92. *See also* false churches.

Quakers, 132, 345

reformation of the church, xxi–xxii, 9–10, 91, 213–14, 264–65, 353–54
  in church age, 269–71
  consistory and, 233–35, 277–78
  conviction of sin and, 208–09, 216–18, 239, 276
  definition, 195–96, 212
  deformation and, 90–91, 272

Dutch Reformed Church (NHK),
 272–73, 275–79
 of false church, 238–41, 253–54, 273–74,
  321
 government, heresy and, 261–64
 Holy Spirit as author, 196–99, 255–57
 human effort, 196–97, 199, 215, 254–57,
  280
 judgement of God, 215–16, 239, 241,
  255, 277
 medical treatment metaphor, 195–96,
  205–07, 280, 304–05
 in Netherlands, 270–71, 275–79
 obedience to God, 216–20, 223–24, 240,
  254–56
 officers and, 276–77
 in Old Testament, 265–68
 publishing books on, 83–84, 276
 Reformation and, 212–13, 321
 renewal, 67–70, 83–84, 195–96, 205–12
 revival, 195–96, 200–05, 230
 revolution and, 257–61
 See also breaking with existing
  church; breaking with false church;
  breaking with a federation; Dutch
  Reformed Church (NHK).
Reformation, Protestant, 68, 79–82,
 269–70, 393, 401
 Anabaptists, 249, 321, 348, 421–22
 as battle, 337–38
 church, 7–9, 163
 forgiveness of sins, 368–69
 local churches, 116–17, 398–01
 national churches and, 269, 271
 in Netherlands, 79–80, 177, 223–24,
  393–95, 398–01, 421–22
 persecution, 167–68, 393
 politics and, 388–90, 393–94
 reformation of churches and, 212–13,
  321
Reformed Church, 120–21, 131, 184
 Arminians and, 198, 220–21
 associations, 69, 160
 baptism, infant, 120, 155, 303, 433–34
 confession / profession of faith,
  121–22, 154
 congregations, 68, 149, 212
 continuity, 120–22

conversion, 120–21
crisis in, 64–66
deacons, 128–29, 142, 145–47
definition of church, 16, 120
elders, 128–29, 143–44
forgiveness of sins, 368–70
freedom from the state, 66–67, 69,
 393–95
German, 177, 394–95
government and, 391–95, 399–01,
 421–22, 423–25
Lord's Supper, 121–22
Lutherans and, 79–80, 160, 394
Luther, Martin and, 79–82
membership, 121–22, 275–76
ministers of the Word, 140–43
missions, 122, 448, 453, 454
principles / foundations, 68–69, 73
renewal / reformation of, 67–70,
 83–84
schools / education, 57, 69, 120
synod, classis and, 128–29
unity, three forms of, 211, 278, 279
See also Dutch Reformed Church
 (NHK).
Reformers, 26–27, 321. See also Calvin,
 John; à Lasco, John; Luther, Martin.
religion, 304–05, 306
 civil, xxix, 375
 conflicts, 337, 406–08
 governments of states and, 409–13,
  414
 paganism, 10, 178, 337, 365, 445
 pluralism, xiv–xv, xxxiv–xxxvi
Remonstrants, 126–28, 130, 157, 429
 Reformed and, 214, 220–21, 399
Renaissance, 389
renewal, church, 170, 268
 assemblies, 209–10, 212, 226–27
 covenant, 196, 200, 202–03, 205, 207,
  239, 276
 discipline, church and, 206–07,
  209–11, 226
 doctrine and, 205, 210–11
 Holy Spirit and, 208–09
 human effort, 198–99, 207–08
 medical treatment metaphor, 205–07

ministers of the Word and, 207,
208–09, 226
order, church and, 206–07, 209–10, 211
reformation and, 67–70, 83–84,
195–96, 205–12
repentance, 155, 449
conversion and, 200–04, 208–09
salvation and, 28, 93
resurrection, 379–81
Réveil, 312, 320–21, 348, 385
Revelation, book of, 256–57, 339
seven churches of, 117, 200–01, 202,
236, 253
revelation, special, 87, 265
revival of churches, 113, 197–98, 268
Holy Spirit and, 201, 204
human effort, 196–97, 202
ministers of the Word and, 202–01,
202–04
reformation and, 195–96, 200–05, 230
seven churches in Revelation, 200–01,
202
spiritual, 63–64, 200–05, 323
in United States, 204–05
revolution, 257–61
Rivet, André, 392
Roman Catholic Church, xv, 43, 92, 161,
213, 322, 404
Calvin, John and, 16, 251, 255
church, definition, 15–16, 115, 118
clerical power, 161, 388–90, 392–93
confessional, 367–68, 401
congregations, 68, 397–98
deacons, 145
definition of church, 15–16, 115, 397,
435
as false church, 193–94
government, church, 125–26, 127
governments and, 406–07, 421–22,
424–25, 428–29
governments, church supremacy
over, 126, 307, 386–87, 392, 424
heretics, execution of, 262–63, 306
hierarchy, 386–87, 390–91, 393
indulgences, 368, 389
institutionalism, xx, 48–49, 58, 107,
317, 386–87
Jesus Christ and, 92, 96

membership, church, 29
missions, 448, 453, 454
in Netherlands, 398–99, 401
priestly services, 257, 367–68
Protestants and, 168, 263, 337, 393,
406–07, 421–22, 424–25
Reformation, 213, 249, 251, 253, 255,
269–70, 393
true church, marks of the, 243, 249,
251
as universal church, 15–16, 213, 386–87,
390, 435
Roman Empire, 95, 383, 386–89, 415
Caesars, 289, 294, 297, 322
Holy Roman Empire, 383, 387–88
persecution in, 168, 235
Romanticism, xvi, 23n24
"Rooted and Grounded," xxxiii, 43
Rotterdam, church of, 223–25, 253,
273–74
ruling church, 337–38
Russia, 296, 390–91, 403, 428
Rutgers, F. L., 451–52, 456–57

sacraments, 14, 152–54, 184–85
discipline, church and, 154, 155
mark of true church, 243–44, 247–48,
250–52, 253
See also baptism; Lord's Supper /
communion.
sacrifice, 92–93, 96–97
salvation, 133, 319, 341, 370–71, 422
missions, 14, 37, 39
repentance and, 28, 93
Salvation Army, 119, 205, 333–34, 345
sanctification, 195, 201–02, 366, 368
Santhorst Confession, 305
Satan, 170, 192, 290
Christians, war against, 171–72, 287,
302, 313–14, 330–31, 341–42
Christ's battle with, 97, 339–40, 341–42,
345, 347
deformation of churches, 170–73,
192–94
nations and, 289, 300
persecution, 171–72
Word and, 91, 93
world ruler, 293–94, 339–42

Scandinavia, 390–91, 394, 401, 407, 429

Schilder, Klaas, xxvi–xxvii, xxxiii

schismatic formations, 190–91, 221, 274–75

Schleiermacher, Friedrich, xvii, xix, 16, 94

  Kuyper and, xvi, xxiii, xxxiv, 3

science, xiv, 312–13, 338, 382, 418

Scotland, 150n24, 415, 419, 451

  free churches, 430, 435

  Reformation, 269, 421–22

Scripture, Holy, 94, 131, 306, 332, 334

  authority, 85, 91, 124–25, 141

  formation, church, 85–86, 91–92

  revelation, special, 87–88, 93–94

  See also Word of God.

Sea Beggars, 259–60, 290

Secession (*Afscheiding*), Christian Reformed Church, xv, 167–68, 119n43, 213, 270, 275, 321

  Doleantie, xxii, 283, 302n14, 407, 456n7

secession, of churches, 135–36

  aggrieved churches, 169, 240, 243, 270, 274–75, 276

sectarianism, 204

sects, xii, 91, 190–91

secularization, 171, 180, 309–10, 312, 375

servant, church as, 66, 72

serving the world, 174–75, 180

sin, 106, 183, 285, 319

  church and, 52–54, 60, 85–86, 90

  clericalism, 182, 190

  communal guilt, 160, 173

  confession of, 93, 183

  conviction of, 208–09, 216–18, 239, 276

  deformation of churches and, 172–73, 174–76

  externalization / Pharisaism, 179, 180

  of flesh, 295–96, 339

  imbalance, 179, 180

  indifference, 178–79, 180

  individual, 172–73

  revolution, 259, 260

  superstition, 179, 180

  topical preaching, 141, 184

  unbelief, 179–80

  See also forgiveness of sins.

Smith, Robert Pearsall, 205

society, xii, xxxiv, 3, 69

soul, 238

sovereignty of God, 97–98, 114–15, 123–24, 137, 211, 413–15

  over earth, 306–07

  election, and, 129, 344–45

  missions, 441, 443–44

sovereignty, popular, 132

Spain, 305n16, 306, 393, 399

  Netherlands and, 259–60, 290, 301, 399, 416

  Philip II, 137, 260, 296, 301

Spanheim, Frédéric, Jr., 261

"State and Church," xxii–xxiii

Statenvertaling, 396–98

states, xxviii, 297–98. *See also* governments of states; state, separation of church and.

state, separation of church and, xii–xiv, xxii–xxiii, 375, 427–28

  authority and, 137–38, 139

  freedom, church from state, 66–67, 69, 302, 393–95, 403

  Reformed government system, 129–30, 307–09

  United States, 402–03, 408–11, 413–18, 431–32

Sweden, 290, 308, 409

Switzerland, 269–70, 409, 410, 421–22

synagogues of Satan. *See* false churches.

synods, xiv, 107, 128–29, 147, 145, 159

  discipline, church, 209–10

  doctors of the church, 145

  of Dutch Reformed Church (NHK), xxi, 77, 278, 393–94

  gravamina, 183, 279

  government and, 139

  Hague, The, 199, 208

  hymnals, 156–57

  of Jerusalem, 107, 419

  provincial / classical, 157, 159, 278, 280

  Reformed system, 128, 131

  renewal of churches, 209–10

  See also Dort, Synod of.

teachers, 67, 103, 146, 158

  elders, 102–03, 143, 152–53

  See also pastor-teachers.

theocracy, 307–08, 392

Thomasius, Christian, 126–27

topical preaching, 141, 184

Tract on the Reformation of the Churches, xxi–xxiii, xxxiii, 77, 83–84, 357

Trinity, 444–45. *See also* God; Holy Spirit; Jesus Christ.

triumphant church, 327, 396

true church, 240–41, 244, 395–96
    Donatism, 245–47, 248
    false and, 237–38
    governments and, 137–38, 392–93

true church, marks of, 245–47
    Calvin, John, 246, 248, 250–52
    discipline, church, 243–44, 247–48, 251
    Donatitsts and, 245–47, 248
    preaching and sacraments, 243–44, 247, 250–52, 253
    purity, 244, 247–52
    Reformed, 243–44
    Roman Catholic, 243, 249, 251

truth, 13–14, 305

Turretin, Francis, 244, 249–50, 262

"Twofold Fatherland," xxii, xxvii–xxix. *See also* fatherland, two-fold.

Ulrum, 275, 311

uniformity, curse of, xxviii

United States of America, 375, 405, 411–13, 421
    apostolic church and, 419–21
    Calvinism, xxx–xxxii, 400, 401–03, 421, 432
    Civil War / war against slavery, 416–17
    Christian influence on government, 416–17, 432
    financial support of churches, 402–05, 407–08
    free churches, 404, 407–08, 413–14, 421
    French Revolution and, 411–13
    government, 148, 410–13, 418
    immigrants, 403–05
    Pilgrims, 301, 308, 401, 403–04
    relations between churches, 407–08
    revival, 204–05
    separation of church and state, 402–03, 408–11, 413–18, 431–32

universal church, 15–16, 129, 173, 225, 384–86
    Roman Catholic Church as, 213, 386–87, 390, 435
    See also world-wide church.

universities, 400, 401

Ursinus, Zacharius, 364

Utrecht, church of, xviii–xi, 43–44, 47, 223–25, 253, 273–74
    liturgical reforms, 73n12

visible church, 18–20, 29, 33, 58, 104
    authority, 122–23
    body of Christ, 361–62
    churchism and churchlessness, 347–48
    essence of, 111–13, 150
    formation of, 109–10
    gifts of grace, 362–63
    Heidelberg Catechism, 347, 361
    imperfection, 351–53
    invisible church and, 357–59, 362, 395–98
    local, 90–91
    ministry of Word, 93, 346–49, 354–56, 357–60
    reformation of, 91, 353–54

Vluchtheuvel, 164–65

Voetius, Gisbertus, 261, 359, 392

Von Holst, H., 412

voting, 148, 273, 382

Walaeus, Antonius, 392

Waldensians, 259–60, 269, 296, 309

von Weingarten, Herman, 408

Wessel, Gansfort, 8

William I of Orange, xiii, 9n6, 128n16, 278, 338, 394, 400

William III of Orange, 167n31, 260, 332, 301, 312, 411
    house of, 286, 290, 308

William the Silent, 137, 260

Wittenberg, 212, 214

Word of God, 100, 153, 184
    administration of, 153–54
    authority of, 85, 91, 124–25
    obedience to, 109–10, 216–20, 231–32, 234

proclamation of, xxxvii, 70–71
   sacraments and, 135, 152–54
   Satan and, 91, 93
   See also ministry of the Word; preach-
     ing of the Word; Scripture, Holy.
world, 289, 295–97
   church and, 85–86, 322–23, 328, 333
   kingdom of heaven and, 293–94, 380
   Satan and, 293–94, 339–42
world-wide church, 90–91, 384–85,
   396–97
   formation of, 86–87, 95, 332, 344
   kingdom of God, 293–94, 383–84,
     384–85
   See also universal church.
worship, 30–31, 156, 185, 188
   celebration of, 31, 188–89
   deformation of churches and, 175,
     188–89
   liturgy, xxxvii, 102, 156, 185
   music and singing, 156–57, 188
   services, 155–57, 158
Wycliff, John, 269

Yoder John Howard, xxx

Zechariah, prophet, 255–57
Zerubbabel, 255–56
Zetten, 165
Zwingli, Ulrich, 127, 259, 395

SCRIPTURE INDEX

Old Testament

Genesis

2:3 .... 52n3
2:15 343
3:16 295
3:19 295
4:6–7 174
4:26 267

Numbers

8:23–26 328
8:24 327

Deuteronomy

1:13 .... 413n46
17:18–20 425
18:10–15 445

Joshua

1:7 425
5:13–15 330
24:15 239

1 Samuel

2:27 413
2:27–30 .... 413n47

4:21 182
24:11 427

1 Kings

19:18 400

2 Kings

11:11–12 426

Psalms

2:6 298
2:10–12 426
9:8 384
22:25 99
24:1 384
25:14 201
27:5 314
40:9 99
61:2 70
65:4 291
72:10–11 426
82:6 427
89:6–7 285
89:12 .... 96n6
110 .... 324, 327
119:96 444

Ecclesiastes

8:4 100

Isaiah

1:15 173
8:16 309
42:8 182
44:28 426
49:23 426
53:10 99
54:11 79
59:14 196
60:10 426
63:9 .... 344, 445

Jeremiah

14:14 444

Ezekiel

37:4 197
42:20 45

Joel

2:28 92

Amos

3:8 201

Haggai

2:8 312

Zechariah

3:9 196
4:1–3 256
4:6 ....255, 257

New Testament

Matthew

3:2 ....294, 324
3:12 18
4:8–9 340
5:3 28
5:14 37
5:20 28
5:22–24 22
5:25 34
5:37 36
5:47 22
5:48 13
6:4 187
7:3–5 22
7:21 28
8:5–13 36
9:15 21
10:10 27
10:16 234
10:18 24
10:21 22
10:22 24
10:34 306
10:37 301
10:39 24
10:40 24
11:28 29
11:29–30 24
12:29 21
12:30 ....24, 345
12:49 21
12:50 22
13:24–30 29
13:30 18
13:33 37
13:47 18
13:47–50 245
15:22–28 36
16:18 ....37, 87n2,
             319, 350, 396

16:19 133
16:22 172
16:25 24
17:25–27 34
18:5 24
18:12 21
18:15 22
18:17 397
18:18 101
18:20 ....24, 98
18:21 22
18:35 22
19:13–14 36
19:14 28
19:21 32
20:1–16 21
20:22 24
20:28 24
21:42 25
22:2–14 18
22:14 60
22:15–22 34
23 173
23:8 ....22, 190
23:9 21
23:13 36
23:37 304
24:5 24
24:14 36
24:35 53
25:1–13 18
25:14–30 363
25:31–46 18
25:34–36 32
25:40 ....22, 24
25:45 ....24, 187
26:56 172
26:69–75 172
28:10 22
28:18 97

28:20 98

Mark

3:35 22
7:11 313
8:35 24
9:37 24
9:39 24
9:40 345
10:9 ....58n5
10:15 .... 28, 36
10:21 32
10:29 24
10:38 24
12:17 34
13:6 24
13:9 24
13:12 22
13:13 24
16:15 .... 122, 344

Luke

4:24 310
6:41–42 22
7:21 22
9:24 24
9:28 24
9:46 172
9:48 24
9:62 212
10:16 24
10:18 37
10:20 .... 18, 19
10:25 36
10:37 36
12:5 301
12:32 21
12:33 32
12:49 306

15:2–7 18
15:4 21
15:27 22
15:35 22
16:19–31 32
17:3 22
17:20 18
17:20–21 20
17:21 99
18:17 36
18:22 32
20:25 34
21:8 24
21:12 24
21:15 24
21:17 24
21:27 24
22:32 22
22:69 307

John

3:3 29
3:4 36
3:5 29
3:16 384
3:19 37
4:1–19 36
4:14 ....24, 57
4:23 188
5:24 24
6:35 24
6:41 24
6:47 24
6:48 24
6:51 24
6:56 24
7:38 24
8:12 24
8:23 34
8:41 21
8:44 ....36, 290
8:56 445
6:51 24
6:54 24
10:1–16 18
10:2 21
10:7 24

10:9 24
10:10 24
10:11 ....21, 24
10:14 ....21, 24
10:16 21
10:27 24
11:25 24
12:6 27
12:31 340
12:44 24
12:46 24
12:48 24
12:50 24
13:10 365
13:15 24
13:29 27
13:34–35 24
14:1 21
14:3 21
14:6 ....24, 25, 190
14:12 24
14:13–15 24
14:19 24
14:20 24
14:21 24
14:23 24
14:27 25
14:28 24
15:1 24
15:1–6 17
15:3 ....92, 365, 367
15:4 24
15:5 ....24, 25
15:9 25
15:10 24
15:12 24
15:14 21
15:16 24
15:20 24
16:7 ....98, 105
16:8–11 36
16:27 24
16:33 ....21, 24, 36
17:1 294
17:6 21
17:9–10 21
17:12 21
17:14 21

17:14–15 294
17:15 34
17:21 36
17:22 21
17:23 ....24, 36
17:24 24
18:36 ....294, 337
18:37 24
19:7 296
19:11 414
20:21 ....101, 449
20:25 ....36, 172
20:28 189
21:15 24
21:15–17 21
20:17 22
21:23 22

Acts

1:6 172
1:14 26
1:16 ....22n22
2:15–41 26
2:29 ....22n22
2:37 ....22n22
2:45 32
3:17 ....22n22
4:3 ....35n29
4:19 ....35n29
4:32 21
4:35 32
5 ....299n10
5:1–4 101
5:1–11 172
5:18 ....35n29
5:29–41 ....35n29
5:41 240
6:1 ....31n28, 102
6:2 102
6:3 ....22n22
6:6 146
6:7 444
7:26 ....22n22
9:22 26
11:30 33
11:42 21
13:26 ....22n19

13:38 .... 22n19
14:15 21
15 419
15:2 33
15:7 .... 22n22
15:22 419
15:23 .... 31n28, 33,
    36, 419
15:28 .... 107, 419
17:26 114
17:28 196
18 .... 299n9
18:5 26
18:26 36
18:28 26
19:4 26
19:35 397
20:7 31
20:17 33
20:32 .... 22n19
20:35 32
21:17 .... 22n19
21:18 33
22:1 .... 22n19
28:17 .... 22n19

Romans

1:5 444
1:7 26
1:13 .... 22n19
1:23 21
2:16 26
5:17 21
6:3 25
6:17 444
7:1 .... 22n19
7:17 366
7:18 295
7:21 352
8:6 295
8:12 .... 22n19
8:17 25
8:29 25
9:3 .... 22n19
10:1 .... 22n19
10:14–15 .... 343, 346
11:22 320

11:25 .... 22n19
12:1 .... 22n19
12:2 294
12:4–8 21
12:5 25
12:10 22
12:13 32
13:1–7 414
13:3–7 35
13:4 34
13:6 34
13:12 329
14:10 .... 22n19
14:13 .... 22n19
14:15 .... 22n19
14:21 .... 22n19
15:6 22
15:14 .... 22n19
15:17 25
15:19 26
15:20 26
15:26 32
15:30 .... 22n19, 26
16:17 .... 22n19
16:25 .... 87n2
16:26 444

1 Corinthians

1:3 26
1:10 .... 26, 118
1:26 70
2:2 25
2:16 25
3:9 31
3:11 25
3:16 21
3:17 30
5:12 36
6:2 36
6:6 34
6:8 .... 22n19
6:11 366
6:17 21
6:19 105
8:4 21
9:14 .... 26, 27
9:23 25

10:16 26
10:17 21
11:17–34 31
12:4 21
12:5 21
12:6 21
12:9 21
12:11 .... 21, 25n25,
    106
12:12 21
12:13 21
12:26 21
12:27 25
14:1–5 31
14:13 31
14:15 31
14:33 31
14:40 .... 31n28
15:22 25
15:46 303
16 32
16:1 31

2 Corinthians

1:2 26
1:19 30
3:18 21
4:13 21
5:6 xxvii
5:14 21
5:20 240
6:7 329
6:15 25
8:18 397
9:13 21
10:3 329
10:4 329
10:14 26
12:18 21

Galatians

1:3 26
1:4 294
1:11 26
2:10 32
2:11–13 172
3:20 21

3:27 17
3:28 ....22, 25
4:3 293
5:1 30
5:13 30

Ephesians

1:2 26
1:6–7 364
1:7 371
1:9 ....87n2
1:12 19
1:22–23 397
1:23 21
2:2 293
2:5 25
2:18 21
2:19 .... 18, 21
2:20 25
2:20–22 18
2:21 .... 21, 25
2:22 18
3:5 94
3:6 25
3:9 ....87n2
3:17 ....xx, 47
3:18 64
4:1 18
4:3 25
4:4 .... 18, 21
4:4–6 18
4:5 .... 19, 21
4:11 144
4:12 ....30n27
4:16 25
5:7 25
5:14 .... 200, 346
5:19 31
5:25 397
5:25–27 .... 18, 19
5:27 420
6:11–17 330
6:12 .... 335, 339
6:19 26

Philippians

1:7 25

1:27 ....21, 26, 329
1:30 21
2:2 21
2:8–11 97
2:10 36
2:18 21
3:20 xxxvii
3:21 25
4:2 21
4:3 .... 18, 19, 25,
329
4:15 420

Colossians

1:14 371
1:15 19
1:26 ....87n2
1:29 329
2:8 293
2:13 25
2:20 293
3:1 .... 25, 105
3:3 .... 89, 362
3:14 25
3:16 31
4:16 31

1 Thessalonians

2:9 26
2:14 21
3:2 26
4:9 22
5:27 31

2 Thessalonians

1:8 444

1 Timothy

1:4 30
2:1 31
2:5 21
3:15 ....21, 420
4:13 31
5:9 21
6:3–4 30
6:10 186
6:12 329

6:18 32
6:20 30

2 Timothy

1:19 ....87n2
2:3 329
2:12 25
2:20 29
2:23 30
4:2 31
4:7–8 329
4:10 294

Titus

1:2 ....87n2
3:1 35
3:9 30

Hebrews

2:9 25
4:12 62
11 343
11:7–16 284–85
11:36–38 298
11:40 422
12:22 20
12:23 .... 18, 19
13:9 30
13:16 21

James

1:2 .... 22n20, 26
1:9 ....22n20
1:16 ....22n20
1:18 19
1:19 ....22n20
1:27 36
2:1 ....22n20
2:5 ....22n20
2:12 30
2:13 32
2:14 ....22n20
3:1 ....22n20
3:10 ....22n20
3:12 ....22n20
4:4 ....36, 293
4:6 239

4:11 ....22n20
5:7 ....22n20
5:9 ....22n20
5:10 ....22n20
5:12 ....22n20
5:14 33
5:17 21
5:19 ....22n20

1 Peter

2:4–5 18
2:5 19
2:9 357

1 John

1:3 ....21, 446
1:5 346
1:7 ....21, 26
2:6 26
2:7 ....22n21
2:9–11 ....22n21
2:16 294
2:17 294
2:27 26
3:9 367
3:10 ....22n21
3:12–17 ....22n21
3:13 26
3:17 32
3:23–24 26
4:14 384
4:20–21 ....22n21
5:4–5 37
5:16 ....22n21
5:19 293

3 John

3 22
5 22
10 22

Jude

3 329
12 31

Revelation

1:4 397

1:9 ....22n21
1:10 31
2 117
2:5 200
2:17 330
3 117
3:2 200
3:3 200
3:8–9 202
3:9 236
6:11 ....22n21
11:4 256
11:15 ....291, 384
12:10 ....22n21
13:8 19
19:11–16 330
19:14 330
20:4 330
20:15 19
21:7 330
22:2 330
22:20 304